BRUGES, CRADLE OF CAPITALISM, 1280–1390

Teeming with merchants from all over Europe, medieval Bruges provides an early model of a great capitalist city. Bruges established a sophisticated money market and an elaborate network of agents and brokers. Moreover, it promoted co-operation between merchants of various nations. In this work James Murray explores how Bruges became the commercial capital of Northern Europe in the late fourteenth century. He argues that a combination of fortuitous changes, such as the shift to sea-borne commerce and the extraordinary efforts of the city's population, served to shape a great commercial centre. Areas explored include the political history of Bruges, its position as a node and network, the wool, cloth and gold trade, and the role of women in the market. The work serves not only as a case-study in medieval economic history, but also as a social and cultural history of medieval Bruges.

JAMES M. MURRAY is Professor of History at the University of Cincinnati.

BRUGES, CRADLE OF CAPITALISM, 1280–1390

JAMES M. MURRAY

CAMBRIDGE
UNIVERSITY PRESS

CAMBRIDGE UNIVERSITY PRESS
Cambridge, New York, Melbourne, Madrid, Cape Town, Singapore, São Paulo, Delhi

Cambridge University Press
The Edinburgh Building, Cambridge CB2 8RU, UK

Published in the United States of America by Cambridge University Press, New York

www.cambridge.org
Information on this title: www.cambridge.org/9780521120531

First published 2005
Reprinted 2006
This digitally printed version 2009

A catalogue record for this publication is available from the British Library

Library of Congress Cataloguing in Publication data
Murray, James M., 1954–
Bruges, cradle of capitalism, 1280–1390 / James M. Murray.
p. cm.
Includes bibliographical references and index.
ISBN 0-521-81921-0
1. Bruges (Belgium) – Commerce – History. 2. Bruges (Belgium) – Economic conditions.
3. Bruges (Belgium) – Politics and government. I. Title.
HF3610.B78M87 2004
330.9493′12201 – dc22 2004045746

ISBN 978-0-521-81921-3 hardback
ISBN 978-0-521-12053-1 paperback

For Jimmy
And in memory of
Dries Vandeweghe and
Ann James Murray OSF

Contents

Illustrations, maps, and tables

FIGURES

MAPS

TABLES

Acknowledgments

This book's long, winding path to completion began with the chance discovery of a charter in the collection of the Episcopal Archives of Bruges. It concerned the distribution of property that once belonged to the bankrupt money changer Willem Ruweel, whose name I recognized from the work of the great economic historian Raymond de Roover. After a decade and a half, and many, many hours of research and writing, I have completed a work that gives context and background to that rather simple property transfer so long ago.

Of course my own research and writing have a background and context as well, one made possible by the generosity of friends, family, colleagues, and institutions without which I could not have succeeded. Friends who played multiple roles in the making of this book include David Nicholas, John Munro, and Walter Prevenier, who have been my teachers, mentors, and inspiration for many years. Friends and contemporaries of mine at the University of Ghent were also critical to my work, especially Marc Ryckaert, who provided both the maps and much helpful feedback; Marc Boone and Thérèse de Hemptinne; and younger Ghent colleagues such as Guy Dupont and a new friend from the University of Leuven, Mariann Naessens, who provided crucial statistical information. My thanks also go to André Vandewalle and Noël Geirnaert, friends and archivists of the City of Bruges, who made their important archive a fabulous place to work. I owe a special "thank you" to Anke Greve, my collaborator on a biographical dictionary of the fourteenth-century hostellers of Bruges, for her help; and to Sid Hunt, good friend and valued collaborator. For warm hospitality and friendship, I also wish to thank Dirk and Annemie Vandeweghe and Frank and Leen Surmont.

Chief among the institutions I must thank is the Medieval Institute of the University of Notre Dame, which granted me a research fellowship for a most valuable year of research, writing, and stimulating company spent in South Bend, Indiana. To the then director, Patrick Geary, as well as Michael

Lapidge, I want to express my gratitude for the valuable gift of time. Second only to the Medieval Institute is the Charles P. Taft Memorial Fund of the University of Cincinnati, which funded research trips and book and microfilm acquisition over many years. Thanks also to the Fulbright Commission, the American Philosophical Society, and the American Council of Learned Societies for fellowship help. Last but not least, my thanks to the University of Minnesota Press for permission to reproduce previously published material.

My son, Jimmy, was born midway through this project, and some of his earliest memories involve attending a Flemish school during one of his father's research trips. Both he and his mother, Susan, have put up with my absence and inattention with good humor and patience. To Sue's parents, Ron and Arleen Smith, I owe a very great deal for their support both moral and monetary. And to James and Carolyn Murray, I owe the inestimable debt a child owes to truly great parents.

At work's end I have come to adopt the dictum of St. Augustine, who wisely credited all the good in his work to others and claimed only the errors as his alone.

Abbreviations

ARA	Algemeen Rijksarchief (General Archives), Brussels
ASEB	Annales de la Société d'Emulation, Bruges
BAB	Bischoppelijk Archief, Bruges
BCRH	*Bulletin de la Commission Royale d'Histoire*
HMGOG	*Handelingen der Maatschappij voor Geschied- en Oudheidkunde te Gent*
OCMW	Openbaar Commissie voor Maatschapelijke Welzijn (Archives of the Office of Public Relief), Bruges
RAB	Rijksarchief, Bruges
RBPH	*Revue Belge de Philologie et d'Histoire*
RR	Rolrekeningen
SAB	Stadsarchief, Bruges
SR	Stadsrekeningen

CHAPTER I

Political background

> La boine ville de Bruges, une des milleurs villes marchandes qui soit en Chrestienté. *Le livre des mestiers*, c.1369[1]

Our story begins with fire and ends with civil war. In August 1280, fire struck the "Belfry," the seat of civic government and symbol of urban independence, which dominated the south end of the "Grote Markt" – the central market square of Bruges. The building was more than a symbol: in its function of both seat of government and market place for the sale of cloth, it neatly symbolized the economic, political, and social bases of the city. Those who controlled and profited from the buying and selling in the cloth hall were the very same men who dominated the political life of the city. The Belfry fire of 1280 neither completely destroyed the building nor ushered in an era of total social revolution, but it served as a portent of developing and impending change for a city torn between commerce and industry and divided in its social and political allegiances. Our period's outer boundary is marked by the war of 1379–1385, known to contemporaries and historians alike as the Ghent war, one of the most destructive and disruptive conflicts in Flemish history. It, too, is symbolic of the political and economic changes that had occurred in Bruges in the course of the fourteenth century, changes that turned the city away from its traditional role as a nest of rebels into a pragmatic supporter of the count. Politics and its underlying meaning are the subjects of this introductory chapter.[2]

[1] Jean Gessler, *Het Brugsche Livre des mestiers en zijn navolgingen*, 6 vols. (Bruges, 1931), vol. 1, p. 14.

[2] The Belfry (Dutch "Belfort") was the tower attached to the Old Cloth Hall, or Hallen. It was also known to contemporaries as the "Halletoren". The fire was often associated with the outbreak of the Moerlemaaie revolt, but there is no firm evidence of this. On the general history of Bruges, the recent *Brugge: De geschiedenis van een Europese stad* (Tielt, 1999) written by a team led by Marc Ryckaert and André Vandewalle, is excellent. So, too, is J. A. van Houtte, *De geschiedenis van Brugge* (Tielt, 1982). Both books also offer good bibliographies on the history of Bruges.

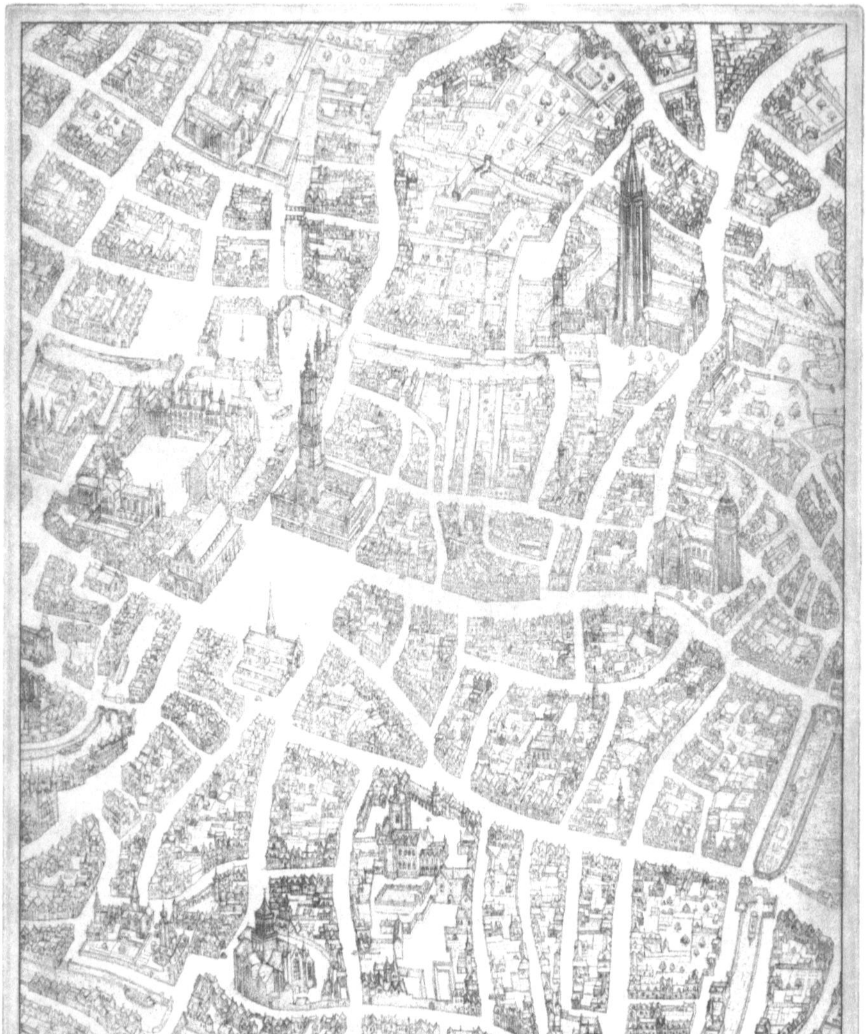

Figure 1: Detail of the map of Bruges by Marcus Gerards (1562). At center left is the "Great" market square (Grote Markt) and above it left is the Burg square. At the lower left is the Great Crane and the commercial district leading to the Bourse square at the extreme left.

The fact that arson connected with political agitation was suspected in the Belfry fire reveals the tense and violent atmosphere then dominating the city. Opposition to the long tradition of social and political oligarchy pitted a group of upstarts – the self-proclaimed "Many" (*Gemeente*) – against the elite membership of the so-called Flemish Hanse of London.[3] Political uncertainty was compounded by the recent coming to power of Count Guy of Dampierre (1278–1305), who promised to be the first ruler in generations of Flemish counts and countesses to contest the power of the great Flemish cities of Ghent, Bruges, and Ypres. And the Belfry fire, which destroyed the city archives, including the charter of urban privileges, gave Guy his first opportunity to make his influence felt in Bruges.[4]

The revolt of 1280 entered history under a single name – "Moerlemaaie" – yet in fact it occurred in two distinct phases. On 1 October 1280 a group of discontented citizens staged a coup against the incumbent city government, who were deposed, not without some justification, because of fiscal mismanagement and general dishonesty. With the coup came some rioting, plundering, and fires set in a number of houses.[5] The count seized the opportunity to side with the old urban regime in forcibly restoring order as well as imposing both a hefty fine and a new urban charter to replace the one destroyed in the Belfry fire. Comital "Keuren" (literally privileges) drawn up in a charter functioned as constitutional documents for the city, and the new redaction reduced the power of the aldermen, much to the displeasure of an even larger group of Bruges burghers than had supported the initial coup. In the summer of 1281 a new revolt broke out, now aimed directly at the count's attempts to limit urban autonomy.[6] The cycle of violence, reimposition of order, and punishment by the count was repeated,

[3] Ryckaert and Vandewalle, *Brugge*, p. 40. The "Gemeente" drew most of its strength from more recently enriched merchants and artisans and disaffected members of the traditional elite. In other words, it was an alternative oligarchy, not a party of democratic reform.

[4] J. A. van Houtte, *Bruges, Essai d'histoire urbaine* (Brussels, 1967), pp. 30–31.

[5] A good summary of the events leading up to the revolt is David Nicholas, *Medieval Flanders* (London and New York, 1992), pp. 180–185; earlier publications by Carlos Wyffels, "Nieuwe gegevens betreffende een XIIIde eeuwse 'democratische' stedelijke opstand: de Brugse 'Moerlemaaie' (1280–81)," *BCRH* 132 (1966), 37–142, and idem, "Kanttekening bij de Brugse 'Moerlemaye' 1280–1281," *Album Albert Schouteet* (Bruges, 1973), pp. 253–258. A revisionist look at the revolt in Bruges and Ypres is Marc Boone, "Social Conflicts in the Cloth Industry of Ypres (Late 13th-Early 14th Centuries): The Cockerulle Reconsidered," in *Ypres and the Medieval Cloth Industry in Flanders* (Ypres, 1999), pp. 147–155; another is Agatha Ann Bardoel, "The Urban Uprisings at Bruges, 1280–1. Some New Findings about the Rebels and the Partisans," *RBPH* 74 (1994), 761–791.

[6] The count's imposed changes were a £400 parisis fine for damages and a perpetual rent, a removal to the count's court of most cases involving violence, and abolition of customs; the making of new law was also reserved to the count alone. One change that survived was the requirement of an annual audit of the city's accounts by the count and representatives of the Bruges commons; for this see Nicholas, *Medieval Flanders*, p. 182.

this time with executions of some of the leaders of the October uprising.[7] A tense, armed truce ended the violence for the next decade.

Count Guy in turn faced more than the opposition and resistance of his three leading cities to a revival of comital power. Flanders had for centuries enjoyed semi-autonomy from its chief liege lords, the Capetian kings of France. Even the exception to this general Flemish freedom, the civil war that ensued after the murder of Count Charles the Good in 1127, tends to prove the rule, since the French king's candidate for count was ultimately defeated and killed by the candidate who gained the lasting support of Bruges, Ypres, and Ghent. Bruges in this case had been the first of the three cities to shift allegiance to Thierry of Alsace and against the king of France.[8] Guy, however, faced a French king and kingdom vastly strengthened by a century and a half of successful action against the autonomy of royal vassals. And within his own county, extremely close economic and political bonds had developed with England as ever larger quantities of English wool were woven into cloth on Flemish looms. Yet the growing dependency on this crucial English raw material came just as the epic feud between France and England was gathering force. The clash of shifting and conflicting allegiances and interests across political, social, and economic lines is a constant feature of the period from 1280 to 1390.

The preliminary sparring among the French, English, and Flemings turned to war through a complex series of diplomatic and dynastic actions that occurred between 1294 and 1297.[9] For Bruges this meant virtual conquest and occupation by a French force in the summer of 1297, as well as a deep polarization of the urban populace into pro- and anti-French camps, or Lilies and Claws (so called after their symbols – the fleur-de-lis and the Lion rampant).[10] Many of these social and political fissures were not new, but were reformulated around support for either the king or count with the additional factor of the newly organized urban guilds. These groups had taken form in the second half of the thirteenth century without receiving voice or vote in urban government, although some of their demands brought forward in the 1280 conflict were fulfilled.[11] Now

[7] Bardoel, "Urban Uprisings at Bruges," 765. The amount of physical damage to the city from the 1281 revolt was apparently much greater than in the earlier outbreak; see Ryckaert and Vandewalle, *Brugge*, p. 40; see also Maurice Vandermaesen, "Vlaanderen en Henegouwen onder het Huis van Dampierre, 1244–1384," in *Algemene geschiedenis der Nederlanden*, second edition, vol. II, pp. 403–404.

[8] Nicholas, *Medieval Flanders*, p. 65.

[9] Ibid., pp. 186–190.

[10] Ibid., p. 190.

[11] For the general history of guilds, see Carlos Wyffels, *De oorsprong der ambachten in Vlaanderen/Brabant* (Brussels, 1951) and the essays contained in Pascal Lambrechts and J. P. Sosson (eds.), *Les métiers au moyen âge* (Louvain-la-Neuve, 1994). For Bruges in particular see J.-P. Sosson, *Les travaux publics de la ville de Bruges, XIVe–XVe siècles* (Brussels, 1977).

they saw a chance to realize their ambitions of sharing power in the city by backing the count and his struggle against the French king and his faction in Flanders. Nonetheless, the count's party (Claws) was not uniformly drawn from the artisans, but contained disaffected elements from the urban patriciate as well as wealthy merchants of humble social backgrounds.[12] On the other hand, the Lily party of Francophiles was more uniformly drawn from the urban patriciate, a fact true across Flanders, although the urban elite of Bruges seems to have been more evenly divided between Claws and Lilies than was the case elsewhere.[13]

The French king, Philip IV, struck first. He outmaneuvered count Guy by goading him through a series of humiliating actions, including imprisonment, forfeiture, and a mock trial in Paris, into an alliance with the English by early 1297. Relying on Edward I of England's promise of armed support, Guy renounced his oath of fealty, thereby opening Flanders to attack. This came in an unopposed invasion by French forces in June, 1297, which Guy, deserted by the English, could not resist. Bruges, together with all western Flanders, was overrun and occupied, and a treaty divided Flanders, allotting Bruges and its surrounding territory to direct administration by French royal officials. This was replaced in 1300 by direct annexation to the crown lands of France.[14] For the city the most visible change was a new set of walls and defensive works that enclosed a vastly larger space than the old twelfth-century walls.[15] Though ordered built by the king, the city alone bore the cost. The fiscal burden resulted in increased tension between the Lily and Claw factions, with the ascendant Lily faction held responsible both for the construction costs and for the growing unpopularity of the French occupiers among Brugeois. Anti-French feelings only grew after the triumphal progression of Philip through pacified Flanders in May, 1301.

Discontent became action in the wake of a failure of French officials to lighten the tax burden for Bruges as they had for Ghent by lifting consumption taxes on drink and other commodities. Two charismatic leaders of the Claw party emerged to organize opposition, the weaver Pieter de Coninc and the butcher Jan Breydel, and the defection of at least five sons of prominent Lilies to their party was one sign of their success.[16] The growing threat posed by the Claws led to the incarceration of de Coninc and Breydel, from

[12] Walter Prevenier, "Motieven voor leliaardsgezindheid in Vlaanderen in de periode 1297–1305," *De Leiegouw* 19 (1977), 273–288; Nicholas, *Medieval Flanders*, p. 190.

[13] Nicholas, *Medieval Flanders*, p. 191.

[14] Ibid., p. 192 and F. Funck-Brentano, *Les origines de la guerre de cent ans. Philippe le Bel en Flandre* (Paris, 1897).

[15] See below chapter 2 and Ryckaert and Vandewalle, *Brugge*, p. 38.

[16] *Algemene geschiedenis*, vol. II, p. 409.

which they were quickly freed by a mob of their supporters. The two Claw leaders and their followers took over the city government, but were forced to yield upon the approach of a French army led by the count of Saint-Pol. De Coninc and many of his followers were banned from the city, and most humiliating of all, they were ordered to begin dismantling the recently completed city walls.[17] A mob inspired by the absent de Coninc was able to stop the demolition work prior to his return to the city in March 1302. His party succeeded in regaining control of city government, with guildsmen making up a majority of aldermen for the first time. They and the count's sons, John and Guy of Namur, who had managed to escape French captivity, began plotting a counteroffensive. This "Prague Spring" was brought to an abrupt end, however, as the Gentenars refused to follow Bruges's lead in organizing resistance to the French. This resulted in a second exile for de Coninc and his followers and the occupation of Bruges by the royal lieutenant, Jacques Châtillon, and his troops in May 1302. Pacification and restoration of the Lilies to power seemed all but certain.[18]

The Claws moved quickly to reverse the fortunes of their enemies. Exploiting the chaos in Bruges and the gaps in the partially dismantled city walls, de Coninc and his followers slipped back at dawn on Friday, 18 May, fanned out through the city and upon a prearranged cry ("Schild en Vriend!") burst into the houses of the French occupiers and Lily supporters.[19] What emerged from the slaughter was a renewal of the "popular" government and a reinvigoration of the pro-count, anti-French alliance. The Bruges countercoup was quickly dubbed the "Good Friday."[20] Throughout West Flanders villages and cities rallied to de Coninc's cause, with Ghent remaining as a lone holdout supporter of Philip IV. Likewise new urban governments came to replace the old oligarchies throughout Flanders, and these new *populares* moved to confiscate the property of their now exiled Lily opponents. The energy and ardor of the triumphant Claws failed to cool even with an invasion of the French and a new, almost nationalist ferocity that now entered the struggle.[21] A Flemish militia began to

[17] Nicholas, *Medieval Flanders*, p. 192.

[18] Henri Pirenne, *Histoire de Belgique*, 6 vols. (Brussels, 1909–1926), vol. I, pp. 418–419; *Algemene geschiedenis*, vol. II, p. 412.

[19] The war cry (meaning "Shield and Friend") was a shibboleth containing two consonant sounds proper to the Germanic Flemish spoken by most Brugeois, but very difficult for speakers of Romance languages.

[20] It only later became known as the Bruges Matins: F. Verbruggen, "De Goede Vrijdag van Brugge, 18 mei 1302," *Het Brugs Ommeland* 17 (1997), 115–131.

[21] Nicholas, *Medieval Flanders*, p. 193. The Ghent annalist reported terrorizing of citizens only when French troops entered Flemish speaking areas; see Hilda Johnstone (ed.), *Annales Gandenses: Annals of Ghent* (London, 1951), pp. 27–31.

gather with the Bruges levy at its core for the march south to lay siege to the castle of Kortrijk (Courtrai) recently captured by the French.[22]

The battle that ensued pitted Flemish foot soldiers (aided by only a few knights) against a large army composed mostly of mounted knights and had the (for the Flemish) miraculous outcome of a total victory. So staggering was the slaughter that five hundred pairs of golden spurs (symbolic of knighthood) were stripped from the French dead and given as near-holy relics to the church of Onze-Lieve-Vrouw in Kortrijk, conferring the name "Golden Spurs" on the battle, which entered into legend.[23] Contemporaries compared it to the greatest victories in history, worthy to be numbered with the taking of Troy, or King David and the Israelites' triumph at Gilboa, or Scipio Africanus' crushing of Carthage.[24] All hyperbole aside, the Flemish victory was the first major battle of the Middle Ages in which infantry defeated cavalry, and it ensured in the long term that "Germanic" Flanders would never be ruled directly from Paris. In the short term, however, there was a good deal of confusion and indecision among the Flemish rebels that enabled Philip IV to mitigate the decisiveness of the battle.

It is well at this point to reject the largely nineteenth-century image of Flemish nationalists led by Bruges capitalizing and pressing on their victory over the French in a surge of unity and brotherhood. The events prior to 1302 had shown that all sides in all cities were open to the blandishments of either count or king, and that many commoners joined the struggle to realize limited and largely intramural political goals. In Bruges the events of 1302 brought changes in privileges and government that went some way to realizing the hopes first expressed in the revolts of the 1280s. These were embodied in the count's new city privilege, issued on 4 November 1304, which granted the right to trade freely or to exercise a profession to all residents of Bruges and not just the members of the *poorterij*, as the corporation of the traditional elite was called. The count coupled this with an exemption from all comital tolls throughout Flanders. Moreover, guildsmen finally received political emancipation through the grant of seats on the city's benches of aldermen.[25] Last but not least, the count gave up

[22] Events of the battle are given up-to-date treatment in Kelly DeVries, *Infantry Warfare in the Early Fourteenth Century: Discipline, Tactics, and Technology* (Woodbridge, UK; Rochester, NY, 1996), pp. 9–22.

[23] J. F. Verbruggen, "De Historiografie van de Guldensporenslag," *De Leiegouw* 19 (1977), 245–272. The picturesque name – Golden Spurs – was not attached to the battle until the eighteenth century. To contemporaries it was the Battle of Kortrijk or Groeninge; see *Algemene geschiedenis*, vol. II, p. 412.

[24] DeVries, *Infantry Warfare*, pp. 10–11; Nicholas, *Medieval Flanders*, p. 193.

[25] The charter is edited by L. Gilliodts-Van Severen, *Coutumes des pays et comté de Flandre. Coutume de la ville de Bruges*, 3 vols. (Brussels, 1874–75), vol. I, pp. 308–332; Ryckaert and Vandewalle, *Brugge*, p. 41; van Houtte, *Bruges, Essaie*, pp. 36–37. Of thirteen aldermen and thirteen counselors chosen annually, nine in each body came from the guilds and four from the *poorterij*.

his right to make the final appointments to the city benches from among nominated candidates. Taken together these reforms pushed the city a considerable distance along the path to democracy. Yet power sharing within a small (if expanded) oligarchy was still not democracy, as ordinary laborers, women, and apprentices and journeymen were effectively excluded from participation. This was not the "democratic revolution" in the modern sense proclaimed by early twentieth-century historians.[26]

The violent expulsion of the French brought no return of peace, and the period after 1302 was also one of continual unrest and occasional uprising. Even the victory at Kortrijk led to a series of Flemish defeats and standoffs, which severely strained the unity of the three leading cities. At the battle of Mons-en-Pévèle in 1304, for example, the militias of Ghent, Ypres, and Kortrijk deserted the field at a crucial point. The disappointing outcome of victory for the Flemings was the treaty of Athis-sur-Orge, sealed in 1305.[27] The treaty's terms were humiliating: a huge war indemnity and a perpetual rent to be paid to the king, who would also be provided with an army contingent of 600 men. The fortifications of all Flemish cities were also to be destroyed. Bruges not only had to pay the largest share of the fine, it was also forced to send some 3000 citizens on expiatory pilgrimages for the "Good Friday" massacre.[28] More galling was the order to restore the confiscated property to the Lilies and pay them damages. Victory had come to resemble defeat, much to the bitter surprise of the townspeople, who refused to honor many of the treaty's conditions. A decade of intermittent war with the French resulted, ending in exhausted stalemate in 1320.[29] But the French kings' desire to bind Flanders and its count more closely to France ultimately prevailed, although Bruges remained the most staunchly anti-royal of Flemish cities.

Internal political struggles continued in Bruges, sharpened by the disruptions and disorder caused by war and famine. In 1315–1316, in the midst of the French wars, a famine broke out in West Flanders and throughout northern Europe, causing chaotic migrations of starving peasants to Bruges and other cities, who together with some of the urban poor literally starved to death in the streets and alleys of the city.[30] Despite the extraordinary

[26] Raymond van Uytven, "Plutokratie in de 'oude demokratieën' der Nederlanden," *Handelingen Koninklijke Zuidnederlandse Maatschappij voor Taal- Letterkunde en Geschiedenis* 16 (1962), 373–409.

[27] For the battle see DeVries, *Infantry Warfare*, pp. 32–48; Nicholas, *Medieval Flanders*, p. 193.

[28] Nicholas, *Medieval Flanders*, p. 195.

[29] Hans van Werveke, "Les charges financières issues du Traité d'Athis (1305)," *Revue du Nord* 32 (1950), 81–93; Nicholas, *Medieval Flanders*, pp. 195–197.

[30] Hans Van Werveke, "La famine de l'an 1316 en Flandre et dans les régions voisines," *Revue du Nord* 41 (1959), 5–14, esp. 6–7, reprinted in *Miscellanea Mediaevalia: Verspreide opstellen over economische*

measures taken by the city government to buy grain and distribute it to the city's bakers, thousands perished. While the effects of the mortality were still being felt in Bruges and elsewhere, a new crisis occurred with an interfamily squabble over succession within the comital house. This pitted the eldest son and heir of Count Robert of Béthune, Louis I of Nevers, against his younger brother Robert of Cassel, in a war of influence over their enfeebled and failing father.[31] Robert acted against the decision to grant the succession to his nephew, Louis II of Nevers, refused to be satisfied with a grant of an apanage, and organized his own power base. He and his party succeeded in gaining enough influence with Count Robert to enable the arrest of Louis I on "criminal" charges, with imprisonment and finally banishment to France as the result. Louis I died an exile shortly before his father in 1322.

Robert of Cassel, once the political stage was cleared, missed no opportunity to exercise the count's power in his father's name. He provoked a rebellion in Bruges by arresting a supporter of his brother's faction there, violating all the city's privileges. According to a memorandum of 1322, he was also guilty of corruption and attempts to profit from a monopoly he sought to impose on the sale of alum. Further, he was guilty of failing to advance the best interests of the county by opposing peace with France and ignoring urban privileges. Meanwhile bloody riots broke out in the city, and Robert was given a free hand to crush them. Instability within the comital house thus reinforced and redoubled political strife within Bruges. And when Robert moved to pay for his military operations by levying a tax on the use of the Ghent-owned Lieve canal, Ghent joined Bruges in violently opposing his actions. For whatever reason, by the time of his death in September 1322, Robert of Béthune had confirmed his grandson, Louis II, as his successor, buying off his son Robert with a large cash payment and a grant of some territories. After his father's death, Robert tried to renege on his promise and began organizing resistance to his nephew; but, weary of his megalomania, the Flemish cities supported Louis II's accession in return for grants of privileges and other favors.[32]

The honeymoon was brief between urban Flanders and its new teenaged count. In an astonishingly short time he managed to alienate his Flemish

en sociale geschiedenis van de Middeleeuwen (Ghent, 1968), pp. 326–338; for the edited sources, van Werveke, "Bronnenmateriaal uit de Brugse stadsrekeningen betreffende de hongersnood van 1316," *BCRH* 125 (1959), 431–510; for Flanders in general, Nicholas, *Medieval Flanders*, pp. 206–208; and for Europe as a whole, William C. Jordan, *The Great Famine: Northern Europe in the Early Fourteenth Century* (Princeton, 1996).

[31] *Algemene geschiedenis*, vol. II, p. 419; Nicholas, *Medieval Flanders*, pp. 209–210.

[32] *Algemene geschiedenis*, vol. II, p. 420; Nicholas, *Medieval Flanders*, p. 210.

subjects by meekly giving in to French demands that he observe the terms of all previous treaties, particularly the financial penalties from the hated peace of Athis-sur-Orge. More serious for Bruges's interests were the thoroughgoing pro-French and anti-English sentiments of Louis II, whose loyalty to the French crown transcended any consideration of the close economic interdependence of Flanders and England. Last but not least was his inability to control the actions and ambitions of his relatives, John of Namur and Robert of Cassel. John in particular secured from the count a grant of "lordship" over ships entering the Zwin, Bruges's access to the sea.[33] The intention was to benefit the growing towns along the Zwin's banks, especially Sluis, which John held in fief. This was a direct provocation, striking at Bruges's traditional monopoly over trade goods entering the Zwin and threatening the careful control Bruges exercised over its "outports."[34]

After John of Namur garrisoned Sluis with troops in order to enforce his claims, the Bruges militia took up arms. Nearing the walls of Sluis, the Brugeois attacked and destroyed the column of John's men that had marched out to meet them. Louis was forced to be a powerless witness to the two-day sack and destruction of Sluis at the hands of the Bruges militiamen (31 July to 1 August 1323). John of Namur was captured and imprisoned in the Steen, Bruges's unsavory prison, and avoided execution only through the entreaties of the count. His eventual escape from prison and departure from Flanders for a well-deserved exile cooled the tensions, as did Louis's uncharacteristic wisdom in imposing no penalties on the Brugeois for their actions.[35] But new reasons for revolt awaited.

Though a commercial city, and, as we shall see, one that catered to long-distance trade and traders, Bruges still maintained a close if somewhat troubled relationship with the castellany for which it served as governmental seat. This "Franc" or "free district" of Bruges consisted of the coastal areas wrested from the North Sea through three centuries of land reclamation as well as inland areas with numerous small towns and villages. This history had resulted in a populace famed for its independence and relative affluence whose political will could develop unblunted by a relatively weak and

[33] The count's "officer of the water," or waterbailiff, enforced the count's sovereign rights over shipping traffic in the Zwin. John's energetic exercise of these rights could obstruct free passage of ships to Damme and Bruges. On this see Jacques Sabbe, *Vlaanderen in opstand, 1323–1328* (Bruges, 1992), pp. 18, 96, n. 60.

[34] For the outports see chapter 2; Nicholas, *Medieval Flanders*, pp. 212–213; *Algemene geschiedenis*, vol. II, p. 421.

[35] Nonetheless, the count lost considerable face and authority as a result of the Sluis affair; see *Algemene Geschiedenis*, vol. II, p. 421; Sabbe, *Vlaanderen in opstand*, p. 20; Nicholas, *Medieval Flanders*, p. 213.

scattered aristocracy.[36] While many of these "free" peasants had joined in the war against the French in 1302, there remained tensions with Bruges over jurisdiction and taxes levied on goods brought to the city.[37] Included with the country dwellers of the Franc were the residents of several smaller towns and villages, such as the cloth town of Veurne and the fishing villages of Heist, Oostende and Blankenberge, to name but a few. Compared to most districts in Flanders, particularly that of Ghent (the Oudburg), the Franc of Bruges was populous, wealthy, and intensely jealous of its independence and privileges, with close if ambivalent ties to Bruges.[38]

Just as the Brugeois were successfully turning back John of Namur's challenge at Sluis, the residents of the Franc were preparing to confront another unpopular effect of their count's adherence to the terms of old treaties. The financial exactions demanded of the populace were collected by all-too-often corrupt comital officials, who took advantage of the opportunity to squeeze far more out of the peasants than was justified. This, coupled with decades of suspicion and the recent hard times and poor harvests, caused a revolt to break out, first in the castellanies in the far west of coastal Flanders, but joined by many from the Franc of Bruges by November 1323.[39] From the first, many disaffected burghers of Bruges, especially textile workers, found common ground with the peasantry in their complaints of the financial burdens imposed by new taxes, burdens they suspected were heavier for the poor than for the urban rich.[40] It would thus be a mistake to draw too fine a line between town and countryside in tracing the origins of the rebels.[41] The revolt was to last for five years, astonishing all Europe with its ferocity, its radical democratic and chiliastic propaganda, and its tragic denouement with the rout of the Flemish militia by a French army at the battle of Cassel in August 1328.[42]

36 Wiliam H. TeBrake, *Plague of Insurrection: Popular Politics and Peasant Revolt in Flanders, 1323–1328* (Philadelphia, 1993), pp. 15–44; Sabbe, *Vlaanderen in opstand*, p. 11; Peter Stabel, *Dwarfs among Giants: The Flemish Urban Network in the Late Middle Ages* (Leuven and Apeldoorn, 1997), pp. 26–32. Stabel cites fifteenth-century statistics that show the Franc to be the most densely populated area of Flanders.

37 Nicholas, *Medieval Flanders*, p. 212.

38 For more on the Franc, see Walter Prevenier, "Het Brugse Vrije en de leden van Vlaanderen," *ASEB* 96 (1959), 5–63 and Prevenier, "Réalité et histoire: le Quatrième Membre de Flandre," *Revue du Nord* 43 (1961), 5–14.

39 The events are recounted in Nicholas, *Medieval Flanders*, pp. 213–217 and in greater detail by Sabbe, *Vlaanderen in opstand*, pp. 22–29.

40 Sabbe, *Vlaanderen in opstand*, p. 22.

41 This is the major flaw of William TeBrake's *Plague of Insurrection*, pp. 132–138, as the author takes the distinction between peasant and urban dweller as almost an article of faith.

42 It is unnecessary here to retell the entire story, since it is done by TeBrake, *Plague of Insurrection*, pp. 51–98, and DeVries, *Infantry Warfare*, pp. 100–111.

The twists and turns of the revolt of maritime Flanders were mirrored in the internal politics of Bruges. While the action against Sluis and John of Namur had involved both patricians and commoners, the revolt that swept through the Franc in the late summer of 1324 attracted support mostly from the poorer, disaffected groups of Bruges. And as the revolt became increasingly a war of extermination of the aristocracy with the implicit threat of overturning the entire social order, many Bruges patricians found they had more in common with the aristocracy than with fellow Brugeois.[43] Yet the government of Bruges was largely in the hands of artisans (especially weavers and fullers) and *poorters* allied with them, so the rebels found support from a significant segment of Bruges burghers.[44] Bruges, alone of the great cities of Flanders, became the center and chief support of the revolt as it entered its most radical phase. Two of the best-known peasant leaders in fact became external burghers (*buitenpoorters*) of Bruges.[45]

By 1325 a commanding personality emerged in Bruges who attempted to manage the violent currents of the revolt to some advantage. This was the broker William de Deken, who became burgomaster and almost constant ambassador during the remaining three years of the conflict. As a man whose economic interests lay with Bruges's growing role as a destination for foreign merchants, he sought to repair relations with England as well as to restore some order to the region around Bruges. He was at least partially successful in both quests, gaining from Edward II a renewal of trading privileges and allying more closely the rebel leaders with Bruges.[46] Then through a spectacular error of judgment, Count Louis himself fell into the hands of the Brugeois and thus became a pawn in the hands of the rebels.[47] With Ypres and Kortrijk joining the side of the rebels in the wake of Louis's capture, together with the opportunistic reappearance of Robert of Cassel to lead the rebel cause, the revolt seemed close to toppling the established order within Flanders. Only Ghent, her close allies, and John of Namur remained as chief adversaries.[48]

The French king, Charles IV, was alarmed enough at events in Flanders to intervene on the side of Count Louis and his ally, Ghent, at a moment

43 Sabbe, *Vlaanderen in opstand*, 33–34.

44 Ibid., 34; Nicholas, *Medieval Flanders*, 214.

45 They were Jacob Peyt and Nikolaas Zannekin; for biographies of them see TeBrake, *Plague of Insurrection*, pp. 148–152. As a *buitenpoorter* an individual could claim urban privileges while residing elsewhere: see David Nicholas, *Town and Countryside: Social, Economic and Political Tensions in Fourteenth-Century Flanders* (Bruges, 1971), pp. 235–249.

46 Sabbe, *Vlaanderen in opstand*, p. 38; André Vandewalle, "Willem de Deken (1328), volksleider en makelaar," *ASEB* 115 (1978), 207–211.

47 The events leading up to the capture are narrated by Nicholas, *Medieval Flanders*, p. 214.

48 Ibid., pp. 214–215; TeBrake, *Plague of Insurrection*, p. 87, has a map showing the greatest territorial extent of the peasant revolt.

when all appeared lost for their cause. With the Pope having proclaimed an interdict in the rebel parts of Flanders, a trade boycott between France and Flanders and the stubborn and successful resistance of the Gentenars, there was a softening in the rebel position. This was sufficient to gain the release of Count Louis on 1 December 1325 and caused the nimble-footed Robert of Cassel to change sides.[49] A French army was raised and prepared for a spring invasion, which was forced to wait upon an unusually severe and extended winter. Partly through this accident of weather, treaty negotiations between the French and the moderate Flemings from Bruges and Ypres reached a successful conclusion. Yet the resulting treaty of Arques, while it headed off invasion, reimposed all the terms of its forerunner – Athis-sur-Orge – and piled on new penalties and penances guaranteed to inflame the radicals and undermine the more moderate among the Flemish rebels.[50]

The last act of the revolt of maritime Flanders was played out in a frenzy of violence directed at the aristocracy, urban elites and the hierarchy and fabric of the church as well. Priests became targets of groups led by the peasant leader Jacob Peyt as well as by Nicholas Zannekin, and the radical party led by William de Deken regained the upper hand in Bruges and took over direction of this end phase of the revolt.[51] In 1327 and 1328, de Deken led a series of military actions that sought to impose discipline on reluctant allies, especially in the smaller towns of the Franc of Bruges. In the process, the Bruges militia perpetrated its own list of atrocities, including the storming of the church of Notre Dame in Aardenburg in order to root out the mostly patrician and clerical adversaries who had sought sanctuary there. Not only was the right of sanctuary violated in this attack, but nine of those captured were summarily beheaded as a warning.[52] Terrorist actions also occurred in Bruges, as crowds broke into the houses of patrician families and murdered their occupants.[53] But as he had already shown, de Deken was more than a leader of renegades.

De Deken strove to fulfill a vision of a Flanders cleansed of its fatal division between England and France by proclaiming Edward III of England as the true king of France in the wake of the death of Charles IV, the last

[49] Sabbe, *Vlaanderen in opstand*, 50–51; Nicholas, *Medieval Flanders*, p. 215; TeBrake, *Plague of Insurrection*, pp. 94–98.

[50] See Sabbe, *Vlaanderen in opstand*, pp. 52–53, for the terms of the treaty; also TeBrake, *Plague of Insurrection*, pp. 98–99.

[51] TeBrake tries to dismiss charges of senseless violence (*Plague of Insurrection*, pp. 116–119), but Sabbe, *Vlaanderen in opstand*, pp. 58–59, gives the more balanced account.

[52] Sabbe, *Vlaanderen in opstand*, pp. 60–61.

[53] Ibid., p. 62; among them were Lambrecht Tolnare, Jacob van Oostburg, and Willem van Kokelare.

Capetian king. In one stroke this would undermine Count Louis of Nevers's authority, seal a political and not just economic bond with England, and place Bruges firmly at the head of the other Flemish cities and rural districts as the maker of the new political order and not just the leader of rebellion. In May 1328 de Deken and a delegation left for England in pursuit of a diplomatic conclusion to five years of revolt and civil war.[54] But Edward could not be won over to the idea, and the last hope for military help from Edward's relative and ally, William III of Avesnes, came to nothing. It is possible that the violent actions and extreme rhetoric associated with the revolt had become too much for any churchman or aristocrat to overlook. De Deken returned to the growing certainty of French invasion, in a city and region under interdict, amid growing political defections. There was nothing to do but prepare for war and wait.[55]

The story of the crushing defeat of the Flemish army on the "Cassel mount" (Kasselberg) has been well told elsewhere. In the severe repression that followed, nearly 500 hostages from Bruges were sent to France to guarantee the surrender. Thousands of rebels from Bruges and the Franc had their property confiscated, and hundreds were executed.[56] William de Deken was accorded special treatment. Once he was hunted down and captured, he was taken to Paris to stand trial before the Parlement. Of all the charges preferred against him, the most serious was his trip to England to persuade Edward III to assume the French throne. De Deken was executed in a particularly gruesome manner late in December, 1328.[57] All the punishing exactions of previous treaties were restored and new ones were imposed, along with the annulment of the previous city charter, which was replaced with one restoring the count's right to name all members of the two city councils.[58] A significant chapter in the political history of Bruges was closed.

What that history showed was a nearly-fifty-year period of political action and agitation on the part of a significant segment of Bruges's populace. These sometime rebels had vague and sometimes conflicting goals, but in general they opposed hereditary elites, corrupt financial practices, and exclusion from city office. They were not exclusively craft workers, nor

54 For much of this see Sabbe, *Vlaanderen in opstand*, p. 64.

55 DeVries, *Infantry Warfare*, pp. 100–104, for the battle's preliminaries.

56 H. Stein, "Les conséquences de la bataille de Cassel pour la ville de Bruges et la mort de Guillaume de Deken son ancien bourgmestre (1328)," *BCRH* 68 (1899), 647–664; J. Mertens, "De economische en sociale toestand van de opstandelingen uit het Brugse Vrije wier goederen na de slag bij Cassel (1328) verbeurd verklaard werden," *RBPH* 47 (1969), 1131–1153; Sabbe, *Vlaanderen in opstand*, pp. 79–80.

57 Sabbe, *Vlaanderen in opstand*, p. 82.

58 Nicholas, *Medieval Flanders*, p. 216; Vandewalle and Ryckaert, *Brugge*, p. 42.

were they the poorest of urban dwellers: among the Bruges "Five Hundred" sent as hostages in 1328, the largest group was indeed drawn from weavers and fullers (34.77%), but second on the list were *poorters* and members of the broker/hostelers' guild (18%).[59] Thus the group calling itself the "common" (*Gemeente*) is best thought of as a vertically aligned group of the politically discontented whose goal was to widen the avenues of power to include guildsmen and others employed by the growing commercial sector of the city's economy.[60] The resonance of some of these ideas in the countryside surrounding Bruges is also apparent given the events of the revolt of 1323–1328, which underline the free traffic of people and ideas from city to countryside and vice versa. The revolutionary vision of 1328 that was embraced by many and embodied by William de Deken was of a city and countryside united in opposition to aristocratic and patrician privilege, where political and religious power resided with local leaders, not with count, king, or pope. Never again in the fourteenth century would a Bruges leader either lead such a movement or unequivocally express such ideas. Thereafter Ghent took over the role of arch-adversary of the count of Flanders and the king of France.

The next leader to take up the standard of William de Deken was the legendary figure, Jacob van Artevelde of Ghent.[61] With the increasing hostilities between the French and English, leading to the embargo of 1336 on English wool exports, it was van Artevelde who succeeded in forging a coalition among guildsmen (especially textile workers), disaffected patricians, and others to oppose the pro-French policies of the count. After rising to virtual dictatorship as captain of Ghent, van Artevelde next forged an alliance among the three leading Flemish cities in order to end the embargo and restore relations with England. As a result Bruges was dominated by a pro-van Artevelde, anglophile party, which more or less recreated the urban government of 1326–1328, albeit with van Artevelde controlling policy. The Bruges militia was often called out to aid the Gentenars and the cause of Edward III, who had been proclaimed king of France on the Friday

59 Sabbe, *Vlaanderen in opstand*, p. 77; Maurice Vandermaesen, "De rekening der Brugse Gijzelaars 1328–9/1338–41," *ASEB* 115 (1978), 1–16; Dirk van den Auweele, "De Brugse gijzelaarslijsten van 1301, 1305 en 1328: Een comparatieve analyse," *ASEB* 110 (1973), 105–167.

60 This explains the prominence of brokers among leaders of the revolt. Not only de Deken, but also Jan Bertoen, Maes Dankaerd, Jan Ackerman, and Heinric de Meyere were members of the brokers' guild. On the other hand, Willem van der Stove, the leader of the reactionary party that dominated Bruges politics for the next decade, had also been a member of the brokers' guild in the 1320s. For both see Sabbe, *Vlaanderen in opstand*, pp. 82, 109 n. 384, 111 nn. 413, 423.

61 The similarities between the two went deeper than a shared vision: both were brokers as well as politicians. See David Nicholas, *The Van Arteveldes of Ghent* (Ithaca, 1988), pp. 14–15.

market square in Ghent in January, 1340.[62] For nearly a decade the politics of van Artevelde and his followers dominated Bruges as they did most of Flanders.

Changes in the political alignment came after the deaths of van Artevelde and Louis of Nevers in 1345 and 1346 respectively. Social tensions remained in Bruges, however, especially with the repression of the weavers, who had been the most consistent and radical supporters of the van Artevelde regime. Bit by bit, in place of a policy imposed from outside came support for the new count, Louis of Male, who furthered the economic well being of Bruges above all other Flemish cities.[63] First and foremost, quite unlike his father, he strove to restore and maintain good relations with the English. France he kept at arm's length, at least at first, claiming a neutrality in the French/English conflict that he sought to maintain by pitting one side against the other when necessary. It was only after marrying his only child and heir, Margaret, to Philip, Duke of Burgundy and brother of the French king, that Louis began to look more to Paris than Westminster.

Louis of Male's special relationship with Bruges began early, for the city was the first to recognize the sixteen-year-old as count after his father's death, and continued to support him as he fought to gain recognition throughout the county. Bruges also remained loyal to Louis during the civil war led by Ghent that convulsed Flanders between 1379–1385.[64] The city was rewarded with confirmation of the privileges gained under the van Artevelde regime, which had restored most of the freedoms lost in 1329. The guilds of weavers and fullers, however, lost their seats on both councils.

The uneasy social and political peace achieved by 1350 began to unravel under the hardships that began with the first visitation of the plague in 1349. Bruges was more seriously affected than historians previously thought, although the outbreaks of the 1360s probably caused greater loss of life.[65] Changes in the textile market and steep price rises for grain and other necessities caused unemployment and hunger not seen since the Great Famine of forty years before. Resentment led finally to revolt in 1359, when the weavers of Bruges again made common cause with those of Ypres

[62] Nicholas, *Medieval Flanders*, p. 221.

[63] Louis has been rather harshly judged by historians of Flanders, largely because of his monetary policies and the civil war that marred his last years. Recently a more balanced view of his reign has come to prevail, as in Walter Prevenier and Wim Blockmans, *The Promised Lands: The Low Countries under Burgundian Rule, 1369–1530* (Philadelphia: University of Pennsylvania Press, 1999), pp. 10–13.

[64] Nicholas, *Medieval Flanders*, p. 224.

[65] See chapter 3.

and Ghent, influenced by the example of Etienne Marcel in Paris.[66] But unlike previous outbursts, there was no long-term community of interests or common program to unite the three cities, and each settled the conflict in a different way. For Bruges the final pacification of 1361 meant a more equitable system of representation for the guilds in the central institutions of city government, and a reorganization of government in general that would endure for close to a century.[67] Crucial to the reform was the guarantee to the fifty-five guilds of nine seats on each bench of aldermen according to an agreed division of representation. Seats were apportioned among the guilds according to the size of a guild's membership as well as its general economic and social importance. This hierarchy was recognized by rank order in processions in service in the urban militia, and on any other formal occasion. The fifty-five guilds were further divided into eight groups, each with a dean at its head, with the *poorterij* forming the ninth. Together these nine functioned as a counterweight to the authority of the aldermen, represented symbolically by the ten-keyed strong box that contained the city's charter and seal. Each dean and the burgomaster of the council (*raad*) possessed one of the keys necessary to open it.[68]

Despite all attempts at institutional reform, social and political tensions remained. This was due above all to the fact that despite the show of representation in city government, in reality power remained in the hands of wealthy *poorters*, brokers, and the leaders of the significant guilds. These men were in effect a political oligarchy determined by wealth and social position, and they no doubt had more in common with one another, even across guild boundaries, than with the average guild member.[69] Louis of Male cultivated this political elite by working to ensure stable diplomatic relations with the English and the German Hanse, in return for support for his centralization policies. The result was a decade of considerable prosperity for those Brugeois involved in foreign trade and in the hosting of foreign merchants – the "new economy" in effect. Those who were dependent on the textile industry, however, were caught in a vise of rising prices (exacerbated by Louis of Male's coinage debasements) and diminishing demand for traditional Flemish woolens. The paradox of the 1360s and 1370s in Bruges is that as the city became the real commercial capital of northern Europe, its own social problems continued to simmer, albeit not

[66] The textile workers imitated the French by donning red hoods as they took to the streets to protest ten years of oppression; see *Algemene geschiedenis*, vol. II, p. 433.

[67] Vandewalle and Ryckaert, *Brugge*, p. 43.

[68] Ibid.

[69] For more on this see chapter 3 and *Algemene geschiedenis*, vol. II, p. 434.

in the potent formula of 1328. The close alliance with the count also brought with it considerable tension with the other Flemish cities, especially Ghent, which was struggling with the dislocations caused by changes in the cloth market. This became an explosive mixture in 1379.

To be sure, while the elements were unique to Flanders, revolt was in the air in all of Europe's most economically developed regions. Northern Italy, northern Germany, France, and Flanders all were convulsed with revolts that drew on various combinations of social and economic troubles in both city and country.[70] As the most populous and politically aggressive of Flemish cities, Ghent was struggling to adapt to the harsh new economic realities of the era after 1340.[71] By some estimates, sixty percent of its populace depended on the cloth industry for employment, so the difficulties in that industry struck with particular force.[72] Falling back on Ghent's traditional role as a transshipment center for grain imports, Gentenars, especially the powerful shippers' guild, regarded any threat to the city's grain staple with suspicion. When Count Louis of Male granted Bruges permission to recommence digging a canal to connect the city to the Leie river in 1379, threatening to divert grain barges from Ghent, a Ghent paramilitary band (the White Hoods) attacked the canal workers. This act released all the violent energies still present in both the cities and countryside of Flanders, leading to six years of the most destructive civil war in the war-torn history of fourteenth-century Flanders.[73]

With help from Jan Yoens, dean of the Ghent shippers' guild and captain of the city, a pro-Ghent regime was installed in Bruges and Ypres, dominated by weavers and other cloth workers. The speed of the political shift caught Louis of Male by surprise, forcing him to agree to demands for confirmation of city privileges and to begin a formal inquest into the complaints of his rebellious subjects. He was even forced into exile in France where he began to rebuild his political base. Characteristically, Bruges joined the comital counteroffensive quickly, when the city government was retaken by supporters of the count in May 1380. The tide turned against the

70 Michel Mollat and Philippe Wolff, *The Popular Revolutions of the Late Middle Ages* (Amsterdam, 1978) TeBrake, *Plague of Insurrection*, pp. 1–14.

71 David Nicholas, *Metamorphosis of a Medieval City: Ghent in the Age of the Arteveldes* (Lincoln and London, 1987), pp. 290–293.

72 Walter Prevenier, "Bevolkingscijfers en professionele strukturen der bevolking van Gent en Brugge in de 14de eeuw," *Album Charles Verlinden* (Ghent, 1975), pp. 269–303.

73 There is no general history of the revolt; two authors, however, give a general overview with a particular emphasis. Maurice Vandermaesen (*Algemene geschiedenis*, vol. II, p. 434) emphasizes the cumulative tensions released rather than blaming the war solely on Bruges/Ghent tensions. David Nicholas (*Medieval Flanders*, pp. 227–229) is more traditional in blaming the civil war on the Ghent/Bruges rivalry.

Ghent-led rebellion throughout 1380 and 1381, so that by January 1382 Ghent was under blockade and threatened with starvation as the lone holdout against the count. Desperation led to the radical step of calling as captain Philip van Artevelde, son of the great rebel leader of the 1340s, who seized upon a last-ditch expedition against Bruges, as a means to save the revolt. On 3 May 1382 the Ghent militia approached the outskirts of Bruges, catching the citizens in the midst of the most important religious procession of the year – that of the Holy Blood – which also signaled the beginning of the Bruges fair.[74] Apparently made feckless by drink and reckless by pride, the Bruges militia was called out, and under the leadership of Count Louis himself, marched off to do battle. The Brugeois were quickly routed and in the confusion Louis barely escaped capture. Then began a six-month reign of terror for many in Bruges, as the Ghent-backed regime tried to consolidate its power.[75] Meanwhile, Bruges was practically bereft of its colonies of foreign merchants.

The van Artevelde renaissance was fueled by Philip's desire for vengeance on his father's assassins and adversaries rather than by a vision of a new political order or the genius for diplomacy so conspicuous in his father. Moreover, the very name van Artevelde brought the French into the struggle with an army of invasion led by Louis's son-in-law, Philip of Burgundy. Conversely, van Artevelde's violent actions and rhetoric prevented the rapid enlistment of the English as allies, despite the fact that Philip van Artevelde had had long and friendly relations with the English crown.[76] For the final time in the century, a Flemish militia faced off against a French army composed mostly of mounted knights on a field near the Flemish village of Westrozebeke in the castellany of Kortrijk. There was no repetition of the glorious 1302 victory this time, only slaughter of thousands of Flemings including van Artevelde himself. Bruges and Ypres quickly submitted to the French victors, while Ghent grimly withstood the French and rejected all compromise until 1385. For Bruges and much of West Flanders, however, 27 November 1382 and the battle of Westrozebeke marked the end of a revolutionary century with only the details remaining to be worked out.[77]

[74] For the events of the Ghent war in Bruges see chapter 9 and Nicholas, *Van Arteveldes*, pp. 160–187.

[75] Bruges was placed under the rule of two governors, Pieter van den Bossche and Pieter de Winter, both appointed by van Artevelde; see ibid., p. 175.

[76] Nicholas, *Medieval Flanders*, p. 230 and n. 40; for the failure of Flemish negotiations, *Algemene geschiedenis*, vol. II, p. 438.

[77] Fritz Quicke, *Les Pays-Bas à la veille de la période bourguignonne (1356–1384)* (Brussels, 1947), gives a general sketch; see below chapter 9 for a more extensive discussion.

Initially, Bruges paid the price for its participation in the Ghent war. Philip of Burgundy saved the city from sack by the French army in return for a large cash indemnity. With the passing of the threat of pillage came confiscation and sale of the goods of dead and banished rebels. This occupied much of 1383. With Louis of Male's death in 1384, Philip came fully into power as the ruler of his wife Margaret's inheritance, which placed Flanders firmly in the orbit of France. Yet Philip was sensitive to the need of his new county to maintain good relations with its trading partners, most critically with the English and members of the German Hanse. In return, he demanded much greater control over urban politics, so the independent selection of aldermen ended in Bruges and elsewhere.[78] Yet normalcy was a long time in returning to Bruges. Many areas of the Franc were devastated by the English expedition of 1383, as were the countryside and suburbs of Ypres. Disputes with the German Hanse, many of them a result of war damage suffered by its members, led to the departure of the Hanse and a boycott of Bruges between 1388 and 1392.[79] Political repression of all revolutionary elements was difficult: small weavers' revolts broke out in 1387 and 1391.[80] But through it all a symbol of this new era was rising slowly on the site of the former comital *Ghiselhuus* in the Burg, where the city aldermen had been meeting since the Belfry fire of 1280. This was the new city hall, begun in 1376 when Louis of Male laid the first stone and completed in 1421 during the reign of Philip the Bold's grandson and namesake, Philip the Good. At the end, its great middle tower was literally crowned with a gold-leaf sculpture under which were displayed the coats of arms of France, Flanders, and Bruges.[81]

Yet even such a successful symbol of political resolution leaves a series of questions that the preceding narrative of fourteenth-century politics cannot answer. How could Flanders' most rebellious and intractable city in the period from 1280 to 1330 become the count's greatest ally by the 1340s and accept the new Burgundian prince with scarcely a murmur in 1384? What were the internal political and economic changes in Bruges that might account for this, while at the same time allowing the city to be a more or less willing ally of Ghent after 1340? Might the explanation

[78] For Burgundian centralization policies, see Prevenier and Blockmans, *The Promised Lands*, pp. 14–34. Vandewalle and Ryckaert, *Brugge*, pp. 44–47, covers the internal history.

[79] Werner Paravicini, "Brugge en Duitsland," in Valentin Vermeersch (ed.), *Brugge en Europa* (Antwerp, 1992), pp. 99–127.

[80] Jacques Mertens, "Twee (wevers)opstanden te Brugge," *ASEB* 110 (1973), 5–20.

[81] Vandewalle and Ryckaert, *Brugge*, p. 44.

have something to do with a series of social and economic technologies I will call "cradle capitalism," whose existence depended on foreign and internal tranquility? It is the goal of this book to show that by 1350, Bruges had become a city unlike any other in northern Europe and was blazing a path that in future both Antwerp and Amsterdam in turn would follow.

CHAPTER 2

Navigating a commercial city

> Mester Cely, I pray youw let yowr man do so myche ffor me as to go to the syne off the Ster next onto Flemmyngys Dame [in Bruges] wheras daggers be maid.
>
> Harold Stawntoyn at Calais to George Cely at Bruges, c. 19 July 1480[1]

A circled cross was the geometric form often employed by medieval city officials to symbolize the institution they represented. It was a richly suggestive symbol, for it captured the simple physical reality of the city – the crossroads encircled by walls – while at the same time invoking Christianity's central symbol and its association with biblical and heavenly cities. It contained a paradox – the squared-off space of two lines intersecting "circled" a figure of no lines intersecting. The nature of the medieval city was true to this paradox, for it was at one and the same time a place of commerce and of communion, a meeting place of residents and strangers for the purposes of trade and religion. And it was a place of exclusion where walls and moats kept out would-be conquerors and immigrants, thereby controlling above all access to the space within, subjecting it to imposed conditions. These conditions were invoked at the city gates, or the city harbors, where in return for either identification, payment, or most likely both, the city's streets, buildings, and market squares were opened to the visitor. Here again paradox intervened, for admission was not initiation to a city's geography: all pre-industrial cities were replete with streets without name and houses without number, and the larger the city the more complete the confusion for the first-time visitor was likely to be. Inaccessible accessibility in service to communal division are the opposite poles between which the reality of medieval city life swung.[2]

[1] Alison Hanham (ed.), *The Cely Letters, 1472–1488* (Oxford, 1975), no. 97, p. 86 and Hanham, *The Celys and their World* (Cambridge, 1985) p. 217.

[2] R. S. Lopez used the symbol in the title of an article about the nature of medieval cities, "The Crossroads within the Wall," in Oscar Handlin and John Burchard (eds.), *The Historian and the City* (Cambridge, MA, 1963), pp. 27–43. Brigitte Bedos-Rezak devotes a number of stimulating articles

Bruges in the late thirteenth century was just such a place, with a fuller freight of complexity given its size and the accumulated centuries of development that had given form to the particular challenges of a rapidly commercializing city. There had been many centuries before 1280, some leaving only archeological traces, for Bruges had been a seaside settlement since Roman times, where the needs of both trade and defense had been accommodated.[3] The geographical advantages of the location had led no later than the first century of the common era to a Gallo-Roman settlement upon a sand ridge along the road from the fortified strong points of Oudenburg and Aardenburg.[4] From the beginning there had been some form of a harbor or docking area connected to the North Sea via a tidal inlet allowing for trade with eastern Gaul and England.

Geology also played an important role in the successful settlement of Bruges, for the city's site lay at the intersection of two land forms whose characteristics posed both opportunities and challenges. The first was an area of sandy soil inland from the North Sea, created in the last Ice Age when the flat, cleared land inland from the coast received a layer of sand, which in the course of time became heavily forested. In the region of Bruges, this landscape was roughly six to eight meters above sea level while the city site was marked by three sand ridges separated by slight depressions, stretching to the south.[5] The second geological form that ended in Bruges was the unstable coastal plain, now known as the Polder region, located north of the city. Unlike the sand region, the coast was changeable and unstable, subject to frequent floods due to storm surges and prominently infiltrated

to the question of cities' self-representation on seals; see "The Town on French Medieval Seals: Representation and Signification," in Brian Pullan and Susan Reynolds (eds.), *Town Life and Culture in the Middle Ages and Renaissance: Essays in Memory of J. K. Hyde, Bulletin of the John Rylands Library of Manchester* 72 (1990), pp. 35–48, reprinted in Bedos-Rezak, *Form and Order in Medieval France: Studies in Social and Quantitative Sigillography* (Aldershot, Hampshire, Great Britain and Brookfield, Vt, USA, 1993), number 12. A more exhaustive treatment of the symbolism of cities is Chiara Frugoni, *A Distant City: Images of Urban Experience in the Medieval World* (Princeton, 1991) especially chapter 1, p. 22.

[3] The Roman past of Bruges has been a recent discovery of archeologists, who have yet to unearth the entire story. This of course demolishes the thesis of Henri Pirenne, who placed the origins of Bruges and other Flemish cities in the ninth and tenth centuries with the revival of long-distance trade. On this see Adriaan Verhulst, "Les origines urbaines dans le Nord-Ouest de l'Europe: essai de synthèse," *Francia* 14 (1987), 57–81 and Verhulst, "The Origins of Towns in the Low Countries and the Pirenne Thesis," *Past and Present* 122 (1989), 1–35.

[4] H. Thoen, *De Belgische kustvlakte in de Romeinse tijd. Bijdrage tot de studie van de landelijke bewoningsgeschiedenis* (Brussels, 1978), pp. 142–146; Marc Ryckaert, *Historische stedenatlas van België, Brugge* (Brussels, 1991), p. 23.

[5] F. Mostaert, "De geologische en geomorfologische gesteldheid van de Brugse binnenstad," in H. De Witte (ed.), *Brugge onder-zocht. Tien jaar stadsarcheologisch onderzoek, 1977–87* (Bruges, 1988), pp. 44–45.

by tidal basins that at high tide flooded to considerable depths. The most invasive period of assaults by the sea, known as Dunkirk Transgression III, turned the entire stretch of coastal ground north of Bruges towards the sea into a flood plain and morass, with peat bogs to the north-east, stretching to the very northern tip of the site of medieval Bruges. Most significant for the future of the city was a tidal basin formed by the action of the sea, stretching from Bruges to what became the fishing village of Blankenberghe on the coast. This inlet was kept open by a rearranged geology that caused freshwater from the region around Bruges to flow into the tidal basin and from there to the sea. Thus as the leading historian of Bruges topography has written:

> The city was situated not only on the border between the sandy region and the coastal plain, where hills of sufficient size offered dry ground at the highest tide. It also stood at the border crossed by a considerable source of freshwater (keeping open access to the sea). This favorable combination is largely responsible for the location and future development of the settlement.[6]

The meeting of sea and land would long determine Bruges's future.

Even the name of the settlement owed its development to the twin influences of water and the mixture of peoples that flowed across the former Roman province in the seventh and the eighth centuries. Derived from the name of a watercourse, the *Rogia*, the name underwent an evolution in the course of the eighth century largely determined by the influence of Old Norse.[7] Through the similarity of the word "Rogia" and the Norse word *bryggja* meaning "landing bridge" or "mooring wharf" came the mongrel word "Brygghia," which in various forms and spellings the settlement would retain. That name in a sense symbolizes the period immediately before Bruges reemerges in history, which may have seen considerable contact with a Scandinavian colony and perhaps with Scandinavia in general in the late eighth and early ninth century.[8]

THE WATERWAYS OF BRUGES

Just as the derivation of its name evoked the actions of humans on water, so too did the development of Bruges follow closely the evolution of its internal

[6] Ryckaert, *Stedenatlas*, p. 28.

[7] M. Gysseling, "Etymologie van Brugge," *Handelingen van de Koninklijke Commissie voor Toponymie en Dialectologie* 18 (1944), 69–79 and Gysseling, "Een nieuwe etymologie van Brugge," *Naamkunde* 3 (1971), 1–4; Ryckaert, *Stedenatlas*, p. 39. At least from Francesco Guicciardini's sixteenth-century description of Bruges, the city's name was thought to be derived from the bridges which form such a prominent part of the cityscape.

[8] Nicholas, *Medieval Flanders*, pp. 14–16.

and external waterways. These were after all the main routes of access to medieval Bruges, and the history of their development is a tangled and complex story. As sketched above, nature provided both the tidal basin and the system of creeks draining Bruges's hinterland. All the rest was up to human action, which confronted several challenges in harnessing water to the desired ends. One was the challenge of enhancing navigation, both to the sea and to internal waterways leading inland. Another important use of flowing water was as the power source for mills, and ditches could also serve as lines of defense against invaders. There was also defense against flooding and the desirability of maintaining a steady level in the city's waterways to consider. And there was the always considerable challenge of coping with the unstable and shifting nature of the coastal area, where storms, erosion, and variable offshore currents did their part in changing the face of coastline and navigation through it.

Work on the watercourses of Bruges began so early and was carried through with such effect that historians now find it difficult to establish the "natural" hydrography of the region around the city.[9] This problem is compounded by the newly discovered fact of Bruges's considerably more ancient history than the formerly accepted foundation date in the early ninth century. More than likely, altering the flow of water is as old in Bruges as the first settlement itself, so any definitive history of Bruges hydrography must await the results of more archeological excavation. A number of facts, however, are clear and can be placed in a reasonably coherent order.

The inland hydrography of Bruges – the flow of freshwater to and through the city – was dominated by the south to northward flow of river water that came into the city at the point where the basin known as the Minnewater now collects it. This reservoir, whose name is derived from a water spirit (*minne*), then connected with a small river leading to the nearby village of Sint-Michiels and most importantly with the Reie, the most prominent internal watercourse in Bruges.[10] Not only did the Reie contribute to the name of Bruges, but its name was applied more generally to all the canals in Bruges – the *reien* – a feature of the Bruges dialect to this day.[11] The Reie stretched southward to nearby villages and was itself

[9] There is a considerable literature on Bruges hydrography, beginning with A. Duclos, *Bruges, histoire et souvenirs* (Bruges, 1910), pp. 11–14; A. de Smet, "Het waterwegennet ten noordoosten van Brugge in de XIIIe eeuw," *RBPH* 12–13 (1933–1934), 1023–1059, 83–121; J. De Smet, "De oude hydrografie van de stad Brugge," *ASEB* 86 (1949), 5–22; A. C. F. Koch, "Brugge's topografische ontwikkeling tot in de 12e eeuw," *ASEB* 99 (1962), 5–67; M. Coornaert, "Over de hydrografie van Brugge," in *Album Albert Schouteet* (Bruges, 1973), pp. 23–35; and for a synthesis, Ryckaert, *Stedenatlas*, pp. 28–39.

[10] Ryckaert, *Stedenatlas*, p. 31; A. de Witte, "De werken bij de Reie tusschen Brugge en Damme in de XIVe eeuw," *RBPH* 14 (1935), 859–863; Coornaert, "Over de hydrografie," 23–27.

[11] Gysseling, "Nieuwe etymologie," 2–3.

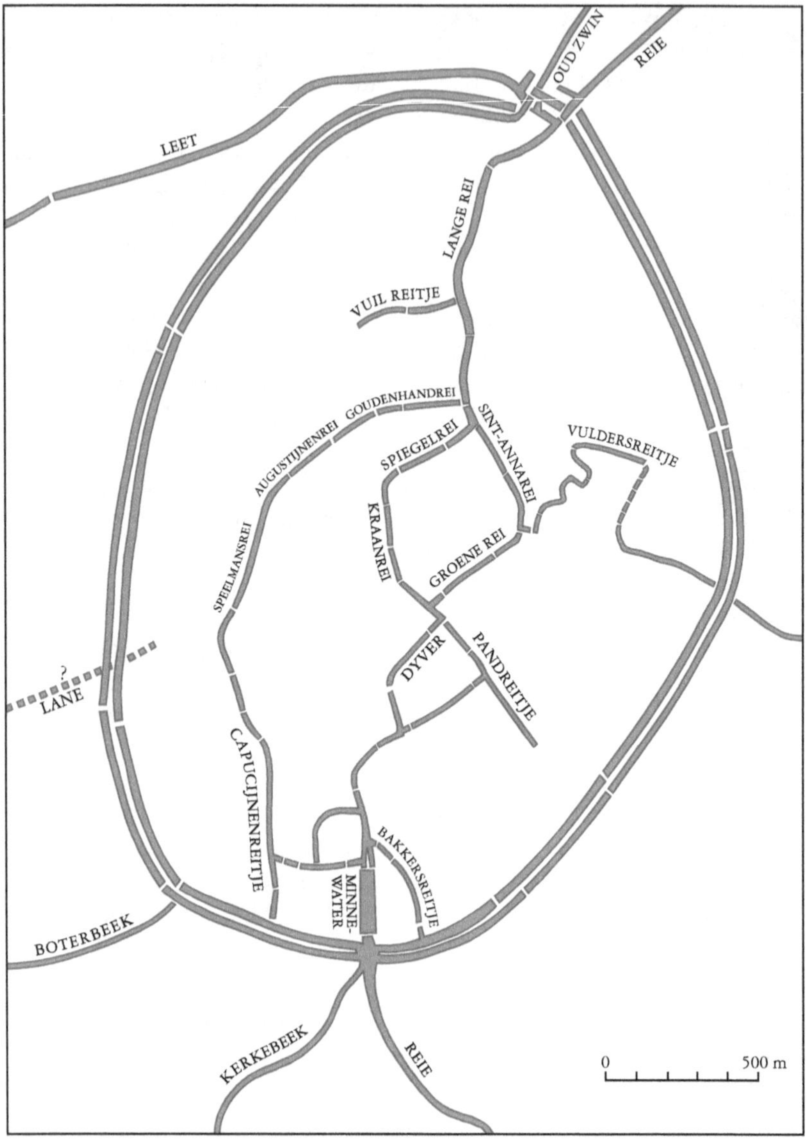

Map 1: The waterways of Bruges. This combination of artificial and natural watercourses features the square formed by the Spiegel-, Kraan-, Groene-, and Sint-Anna-*reien* (canals) and the important north/south connectors to the Damme canal via the Langerei and the Minnewater via the Dyver.

joined by a number of streams in that area. From the Minnewater, the Reie followed a slightly meandering course northwards through what became the city to end up flowing into the tidal inlet from the sea at the point that became the Damme canal (Damse vaart) in the twelfth century. Given the natural topography of the site, with its sand ridges and depressions, the Reie seems to have had arms that flowed through what became the city center, forming the Kraanrei (Crane canal) and eventually what became the Spiegelrei (Mirror canal), which was originally a low-lying marshy area. The need to provide suitable streams for mills seems to explain other features of the enduring internal hydrography of Bruges, such as the Groene Rei and perhaps also the St. Annarei.[12] Although the south-eastern canal, the Dyver, was also once included among the artificial creations intended to power a watermill, it now seems more likely that it flows along some part of the original bed of the Reie.[13] Thus by 1100, not only was the natural course of the Reie the heart of Bruges's internal system of waterways, but it had been "improved" to guarantee that its tributaries maintained a steady water level and provided the water flow necessary to power mills.[14]

The above is a somewhat simplified picture of the reality, however. A number of other secondary streams entered the city from various points, leading to other smaller systems of canals. One of these was formed by the Lane, a small stream that flowed from two south-western villages before entering Bruges. Here its course was probably canalized from an early date, thus forming the course of the Speelmans – Augustijnenrei and Goudenhandrei – that join the Lange Rei at the northern tip of what became the inner city.[15] On the east side of Bruges, the Vuldersreitje (Little Fullers' canal) may also have had its origin as a natural stream, but one whose course was probably altered by early canalization. Its meandering course took it through a significant segment of what became the Vulderstraat, Langestraat, Rodestraat, and Molenmeers before joining the St. Annarei just above the intersection with the Groene Rei.[16]

A look at the map of Bruges's canal system by c. 1150–1200 reveals roughly the shape of internal waterways throughout the Middle Ages, indeed into modern times. It is marked by the overall south-to-north natural flow of the Reie, with larger reservoirs in the extreme south (the Minnewater) and north (the Damse vaart). By 1100 at the latest, these reservoirs, through a system of dams and sluices, maintained a steady water level through what had become

[12] Ryckaert, *Stedenatlas*, pp. 32–33.
[13] Koch, "Brugge's topografische," 18; Ryckaert, *Stedenatlas*, p. 33.
[14] Ryckaert, *Stedenatlas*, p. 38. [15] Ibid. [16] Coornaert, "Over de hydrografie," 31–32.

a strongly human-influenced system of waterways through and around the developing city. These served the various purposes sketched above, including defense, transport, flood control, and supplying watermills. These were (and are) particularly prominent in the south part of Bruges from the Minnewater, narrowing as one follows the system northwards and as canals combine to form the Lange Rei – the longest continuous stretch of what was probably the natural course of the Reie. By the late twelfth century, then, most of the area that was becoming Bruges lay within easy reach of one or more canals, and the ultimate course of these was clearly oriented northwards in the direction of the sea. It was here, in an area of tidal basins and peat bogs, that Bruges's greatest challenge would be faced – providing itself with a harbor.

THE HARBORS OF BRUGES

Perhaps no other part of Bruges's topographic history is as complex as its struggle to be and remain a port city as a settlement inland from an unstable coast subject to storm floods and tides, yet reachable by at least small boats from its Roman origins to the eleventh century. Fragmentary evidence attests to this early phase as a harbor, and several ninth- and tenth-century sources attest to what may have been a busy maritime center.[17] We know of active Scandinavian contact in the ninth century, both from the derivation of Bruges's name and from the likelihood that Bruges served as a send-off point for missionaries to Denmark. The gift from the Carolingian king, Louis the Pious, of a monastery at Torhout to the missionary archbishop Anscharius of Hamburg, to serve as a training center for missionaries, strongly suggests that nearby Bruges was their embarkation point.[18] Traffic with England may have also been busy in the tenth and eleventh centuries, given the marriage of Count Baldwin II to an Anglo-Saxon princess in the early tenth century and the likelihood that Bruges took over the place of the declining trade settlement near Domburg (on the nearby island of Walcheren) which had formerly served the English trade.[19] The strongest evidence of maritime traffic with England dates from the eleventh century, however, and is in the *Encomium* of Queen Emma (c. 1040), which explicitly

[17] Marc Ryckaert, "De Brugse havens in de Middeleeuwen," *ASEB* 109 (1972), 5–27; Ryckaert, "Brügge und die flandrischen Häfen vom 12. bis 18. Jahrhundert," in H. Stoob (ed.), *See- und Flußhäfen vom Hochmittelalter bis zur Industralisierung* (Cologne, 1986), pp. 129–139, esp. pp. 130–131.

[18] Adriaan Verhulst, "Les origines et l'histoire ancienne de la ville de Bruges (IXe–XIIe siècle)," *Le Moyen Age* 66 (1960), 37–63, 60.

[19] Ryckaert, *Stedenatlas*, p. 39.

refers to a "portus Brugensis," although it is not clear whether the classical sense of the word *portus*, "harbor," or the medieval sense of the word, "trading settlement," was intended.[20] In any event, the poem mentions a small fleet mooring not far from the "portus" and that the boats were made fast to pilings.[21]

There is little doubt then that Bruges was a harbor from its origins into the eleventh century, though how important that function was to the development of the settlement in general is unclear.[22] Most likely harbor facilities were minimal, as the brief mention in the *Encomium* suggests, and even the actual site of the mooring place is in doubt. The name "Wic," attached to a place along the Lange Reie, points to an early commercial role linked to a function as a wharf.[23] Even this harbor area did not long survive the gradual sanding in of the tidal basin in the course of the tenth and eleventh centuries. Harbor functions were forced northwards until by the early twelfth century, the Lange Rei was connected to the remnant of the tidal basin, the Sincfal, via a canalized stream bed that probably restricted shipping within the city to small boats.[24] Meanwhile, a great deal of the marshy land directly north of Bruges had been diked and drained in the course of the eleventh century, which probably hastened the shrinking of the tidal basin that had served so long as Bruges's access to the sea. By 1100, for perhaps the first time in her history, Bruges was probably not directly accessible for sea-going craft. Then the unstable sea staged its last great invasion of the medieval period.

This came in the form of a storm surge in the winter of 1134 that struck the coast, but did not penetrate the line of dikes protecting the recently reclaimed land. This channeled and redoubled the scouring force of the invading waters so that the Sincfal became a much-enlarged inlet capable of providing not only easy access to the sea for large craft but a considerable harbor as well. This new "Transgression" (Dunkirk III) created what became known as the Zwin, a body of water that would play a critical role in Bruges's development as a commercial power.[25] But what is often overlooked is that even with this considerable change, the banks of the Zwin still lay some five kilometers (3.1 miles) to the north-east of Bruges. It was only with the construction of a new canal, what became known later as the Damse vaart, and a sluice gate at the connecting point with the Zwin that Bruges

[20] B. A. Campbell (ed.), *Encomium Emmae Reginae* (London, 1949), p. 46.
[21] Ryckaert, *Stedenatlas*, p. 39.
[22] Verhulst, in "Les origines," argued that it was not very important.
[23] J. De Smet, "De Brugse wiic-namen," *ASEB* 85 (1948), 112–117.
[24] Ryckaert, *Stedenatlas*, p. 41.
[25] Ryckaert, "Brügge und die flandrischen Häfen," p. 131.

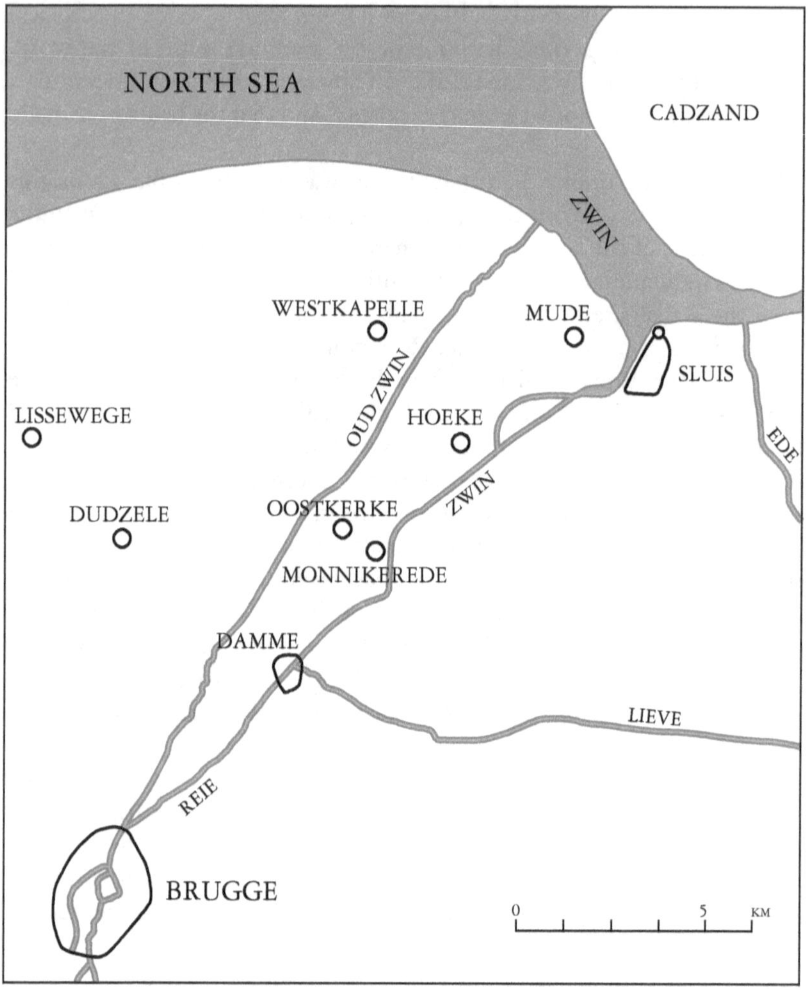

Map 2: The Zwin towns and vicinity. Throughout the fourteenth century and beyond, access to the harbor towns leading to the Zwin basin and the sea was a preoccupation of the Brugeois. The canalized Reie and Zwin formed the vital commercial link leading to Damme and Sluis, with Monnikerede, Hoeke, and Mude playing secondary roles as harbors.

came to possess a new harbor for sea-going ships.[26] However, the canal was not suitable for large vessels so that the Zwin itself had to serve as the transshipment point where sea-borne freight was transferred to smaller

[26] Ibid., p. 133; A. De Smet, "De werken bij de Reie tusschen Brugge en Damme in de XIVe eeuw," *RBPH* 14 (1935), 859–863.

canal boats. It was at this spot that a settlement grew up that received its legal incorporation as the city of Damme in 1180.[27] This established a pattern that would endure for the rest of the Middle Ages: Bruges was a seaport only by means of a series of port cities, of which Damme and later Sluis became the most prominent. As Marc Ryckaert has remarked "it was this [creation of the Zwin and digging of the Reie canal] that marked the beginning of Bruges's development as the late-medieval center of world trade."[28]

The establishment of Damme must be put into the broader range of activities of the Flemish comital house. From 1157, the remarkable Philip of Alsace carried out a number of projects to improve the economic infrastructure particularly of coastal Flanders. These included drainage and diking projects, but also the establishment of harbors. In what must really be called one of the first state economic development policies, he established the harbors of Gravelines, Dunkirk, and Mardijk in southern Flanders, and besides Damme he also founded Nieuwpoort, which became an important access point to the interior cities of the Flemish south-west.[29] All these harbors were meant to serve inland cities – Gravelines for Saint-Omer and Nieuwpoort for Diksmuide.[30] The establishment of Damme provided such a strong attraction for trade that over the next century a remarkable network of Zwin harbors developed, all with a close commercial dependency on Bruges that provided reciprocal prosperity at the cost of any chance for independence. These smaller cities were Monnikerede, Hoeke, and Mude (Sint-Anna-ter-Muiden).[31]

Damme thus owed its origins to legal recognition and financial investment by the count, but it owed its development as a shipping center largely to Bruges and, to a certain extent, Ghent. Not only did Bruges rapidly acquire rights over the comital diking and drainage projects, she quickly added port facilities, thus seizing the opportunity offered by this new access

[27] On the early history of Damme, see Adriaan Verhulst, "Initiative comtale et développement économique en Flandre au XIIe siècle: Le rôle de Thierry et de Philippe d'Alsace (1128–1191)," in *Miscellanea Mediaevalia in Memoriam J. F. Niermeyer* (Groningen, 1967), pp. 227–240; A. de Smet, "L'origine des ports du Zwin, Damme, Mude, Monnikerede, Hoeke et Sluis," in *Etudes d'histoire dediées à la mémoire de Henri Pirenne, par ses anciens élèves* (Brussels, 1937), pp. 125–141; J.-P. Sosson, "Les petites villes du Zwin (XIVe–XVe siècles): des espaces urbains inviables?" in P. Contamine, T. Dutour, and B. Schnerb (eds.), *Commerce, finances et société (XIe–XVIe siècles). Recueil de travaux d'histoire médiévale offert à M. le Professeur Henri Dubois* (Paris, 1993), pp. 171–184.

[28] Marc Ryckaert, "Geographie eines Weltmarktes: Handel und Stadttopographie im mittelalterlichen und frühneuzeitlichen Brügge," in K. Friedland (ed.), *Brügge Colloquium des Hansischen Geschichtsvereins, 26.–29. Mai 1988* (Cologne and Vienna, 1990), pp. 3–12, esp. p. 5.

[29] Ryckaert, "Brügge und die flandrischen Häfen," pp. 134–135; Verhulst, "Initiative comtale," 229–232.

[30] Sosson, "Les petites villes," p. 173.

[31] Nicholas, *Medieval Flanders*, p. 259.

to the sea, continued to pay for the improvement and upkeep of the original infrastructure, and seems to have added docks and other facilities as well.[32] Ghent also recognized the promise of Damme's location on the Zwin, constructing a canal, called the Lieve, which gave Ghent access to the sea.[33] It jealously defended its commercial rights to this waterway throughout the fourteenth century. In the middle of the fourteenth century, as the region was increasingly beset by accumulations of silt, Bruges began a new canal to Damme and rebuilt much of the old sluice gate as well.[34] By the middle of the thirteenth century, Damme had come to fulfill the role of harbor and warehousing center for trade in a strictly limited number of commodities, of which wine was the most prominent.[35] It was also the largest of the Zwin ports until the later foundation and rapid growth of Sluis.

Sint-Anna-ter-Muiden (or simply Mude, as it was known in the Middle Ages) seems to have been established about a generation after Damme, in the first decade of the thirteenth century, beginning in all likelihood as a settlement of merchants and sailors.[36] Its site was along the southern end of the Zwin near the intersection of the old canal to the Sincfal called the "Oud Zwin."[37] It received a foundation charter only in 1242, granting it similar privileges and institutions to those of Bruges, and exemption from tolls at Damme, the Zwin as a whole, and also at Dunkirk.[38] With its command of the Zwin basin's entrance, Mude became the first headquarters of the count's "waterbailiff," the official responsible for collecting tolls and defending comital rights over salvage and shipwrecks.[39] Monnikerede, like Mude, was a settlement on the left bank of the Zwin only a few kilometers north-east of Damme at the point where a connecting canal, the Leugen-Zwin, bridged the Old and New Zwin. Like Mude, it had some decades of vague development before the granting of a city privilege sometime after 1250. The first mention of the town's aldermen dates from 1266.[40]

Hoeke was the last of the trio of left-bank port cities to develop in the course of the thirteenth century. But unlike those of the other two,

32 De Smet, "L'origine des ports," 130.

33 Nicholas, *Town and Countryside*, pp. 129–133.

34 De Smet, "De werken bij de Reie," 861–862.

35 Others were honey, beer, and in general commodities packed in barrels; see Sosson, "Les petites villes," p. 174, and Jan Craeybeckx, *Un grand commerce d'importation: Les vins de France aux anciens Pays-Bas, XIIIe–XVIe siècle* (Paris, 1958), pp. 21–28.

36 The foundation date seems approximate as Ryckaert, *Stedenatlas*, p. 67, has 1213, while Sosson ("Les petites villes," p. 171, n. 4) has 1200.

37 Ryckaert, *Stedenatlas*, p. 66.

38 De Smet, "L'origine des ports," 133.

39 Ibid., 134 and H. Nowé, *Les baillis comtaux de Flandre, des origines à la fin du XIVe siècle* (Brussels, 1929), pp. 409–413.

40 De Smet, "L'origine des ports," 136; Sosson, "Les petites villes," p. 171; J. De Smet, "Monnikerede. Een verdwenen zeestad van het Zwin," *Biekorf* 45 (1939), 1–8.

its foundation and development seem to have been related to the ambitions of the German Hanse to found a permanent trading post along the Zwin itself. These plans were first broached in negotiations with the Flemish countess, Margaret, in 1251–1252, in which it seems that the Hanse diplomats were seeking a grant of land completely under Hanse jurisdiction for the establishment of a trading colony such as those that already existed in London and Novgorod.[41] Cession of territory was refused, but that does not seem to have deterred Hanse merchants from settling in what became Hoeke: a German merchant founded a hospital there in 1280, and in 1299 a bailiff's account from Damme listed only German merchants as the residents there.[42] It must have received its city privilege between 1255 and 1274, identical to that of the other two, and despite the concentration of Hanse residents, it never became a possession of the federation.[43]

The most important port on the Zwin by the fourteenth century was also the last established – Sluis – whose foundation dates from around 1290.[44] Located on the right bank of the Zwin, just facing Mude across the Zwin channel, Sluis was intended to provide the deep-water harbor that Damme could no longer offer due to silting and the increasing size of late-medieval ships.[45] It quickly became the predominant harbor on the Zwin, so that by 1330 most sea-going craft moored there, including of course the French fleet destroyed by Edward III and the English in a battle off Sluis in 1340.[46] Though it outstripped the other Zwin ports in size and importance by 1350, Sluis had the same city privileges and the same toll exemptions as the others. And of course Bruges magistrates kept it on the same tight leash as it did the others.[47]

41 Van Houtte, *Geschiedenis van Brugge*, p. 96.

42 De Smet, "L'origine des ports," 137–138.

43 Ibid., 139.

44 Ibid., 138. Nicholas gives 1280 as the foundation date for Sluis, but later gives 1300 as the date the city is first mentioned (Nicholas, *Medieval Flanders*, pp. 129, 259). Sluis only gradually emerged as the chief port, however. In the forced tax contribution of 1302–1303, Sluis (called by its old name Lammins Vliete) contributed only £160 as compared to Hoeke at £500, Aardenburg at £847, Mude £80, and Monikerede at £100: C. Wyffels and A. Vandewalle (eds.), *De rekeningen van de Stad Brugge*, vol. II (Tweede Deel), part 2, p. 67.

45 Richard Unger, *The Ship in the Medieval Economy* (London and Montreal, 1980), pp. 163–171, describes the evolution of the cog ship, which roughly tripled cargo-carrying capacity by the middle of the fourteenth century. See also Nicholas, *Medieval Flanders*, p. 128. Damme remained a port nonetheless, albeit unreachable by the larger cargo ships.

46 Jonathan Sumption, *The Hundred Years War*, part I: *Trial by Battle* (Philadelphia, 1990), pp. 325–329.

47 As described in chapter 1, it was the violation of the informal staple Bruges claimed on all goods entering the Zwin that caused the city to join in the revolt of Maritime Flanders, resulting in the attack, capture, and burning of Sluis in 1323. Thereafter Sluis was firmly bound by comital privileges giving Bruges staple rights; see Nicholas, *Medieval Flanders*, p. 213; Nicholas, *Town and Countryside*, pp. 118–121, 161.

This distributed harbor network in the Zwin has ingeniously and accurately been called a "Verlagssystem," after the economic organization in which materials are distributed by a merchant to workers who provide the manufacture in return for a piece rate, but the ownership of the product remains with the merchant. In this case harbor functions and transshipment duties were shared out: Damme, as already mentioned, acquired the bulky trade in wines as well as some other minor commodities. Hoeke and Monnikerede handled the pungent trade in dried fish, salt, and wine as well as nautical supplies of all sorts.[48] In every case, however, important commodities had to be transferred to smaller canal boats for the eventual trip to market in Bruges. Admittedly, the Zwin ports had some resident foreigners, and we know that Damme at least had extensive warehousing facilities thus obviating the need for shifting bulky wine barrels. But they remained, even in the case of Damme and Sluis, *villes manquées*, lacking the essential economic and social ingredients for independent viability.[49] This was planned dependence in every respect.

How was this commercial "putting-out system" created and maintained? Control over the infrastructure of sluices, docks, and waterways was one effective measure, and Bruges, as we have seen, was careful to build, acquire control over, and update this costly network.[50] The Zwin ports simply did not have the financial muscle to take on these tasks by themselves. This financial weakness became abundantly clear in the late fourteenth into the fifteenth century, when the increasing tax burden of the Burgundian state along with declining trade sent the smallest ports (Hoeke, Monnikerede, Mude) into severe decline.[51] With populations of 2–4000 around 1350 and half that number by 1400, these small cities did not have the tax base to mount any kind of challenge to Bruges's hegemony. Nor could they summon a diversified manufacturing sector: in the 1390s Damme had seventeen craft guilds spread across six economic sectors; Bruges by comparison had fifty-four guilds and 116 professions in fifteen distinct sectors.[52] Monnikerede had only eight craft guilds, mostly in local supply trades; Hoeke and Mude probably had about the same number.[53] Moreover,

[48] Soisson, "Les petites villes," p. 174 and L. Gilliodts-van Severen, *Coutumes des anciens pays et comté de Flandre. Quartier de Bruges*, 6 vols. (Brussels, 1890–1893), vol. IV, p. 472 .

[49] This is the essential point J.-P. Sosson makes about the "inviability" of these subsidiary cities due to their firm control by Bruges; see Sosson, "Les petites villes," p. 184.

[50] Nicholas, *Town and Countryside*, pp. 133–135.

[51] Sosson, "Les petites villes," pp. 176–177, charts the decline in tax revenues and population in these towns in the first half of the fifteenth century.

[52] Ibid., pp. 182–183.

[53] Ibid., p. 183; the uncertainty in the cases of Hoeke and Mude stems from the fact that no mention of profession is given in their tax returns.

Bruges would not tolerate poaching upon its monopoly over the marketing and finishing of imported cloth. Thus it obtained a comital ban against the efforts of Sluis to become a market and finishing center for imported cloth.[54]

Control was also exercised via jurisdiction, since from their founding all the Zwin ports looked to Bruges as their court of appeal, or their place of *hoofdvaart*.[55] Although this system of appellate justice was in no way invented by Bruges or the two other large Flemish cities, its development worked to the benefit of the larger city in certain circumstances. Bruges seems to have been exceptionally insistent on exercising its rights to hear appeals, to the point of actual intervention into the legal affairs of the smaller cities, especially Damme and Sluis. In the case of Damme, Bruges successfully insisted in 1290 that all cases of any type could be appealed from Damme to the city court of Bruges.[56] Given that the higher court judged according to its own law and not that of the lower court, this gave Bruges abundant opportunity to determine legislation in Damme. Bruges extended this power over Damme after 1352, when it gained the count's ruling to the effect that no city doing *hoofdvaart* to Bruges could obtain a privilege contrary to those of the appellate city. In effect this was an insistence that Damme's laws and privileges be fully subservient to those of Bruges, which was far beyond the original intent and practice of legal appeal.[57] This kind of "passive lordship" over Damme was a deliberate extension of the legal possibilities inherent in Flemish law directed to the imperative of control over the Zwin.

Sluis posed other and more serious challenges to Bruges's control. Unlike the case in Damme, Bruges did not own any of the harbor facilities or any significant real estate in the port city. The site of Sluis was comital land, and the city subsequently became the administrative focus of comital authority with the transfer of the office of waterbailiff there from Mude by the middle of the fourteenth century.[58] Count Louis of Nevers seems subtly to have encouraged Sluis's resistance to Bruges's monopolies. The Brugeois were forced to take another tack with Sluis, one that insisted upon commercial privileges and domination over guilds and commercial functions. The Brugeois were not above fits of violence in insisting on their

[54] Rudolf Holbach, "Brügge, die Hanse und der Handel mit Tuch," in *Hansekaufleute in Brügge, teil 4: Beiträge der Internationalen Tagung in Brügge, April 1996* (Frankfurt am Main, 2000), p. 186; Nicholas, *Town and Countryside*, p. 105.

[55] For the topic in general, Nicholas, *Town and Countryside*, pp. 142–151.

[56] Normally appeals occurred only when the city aldermen of the lower body requested this; Nicholas, *Town and Countryside*, pp. 144–145.

[57] Ibid., pp. 146–147. [58] Nowé, *Les baillis comtaux*, pp. 409–413.

privileges, as the uprising of 1323, mentioned above, shows.[59] Forced to surrender, the count issued a privilege in 1323, enjoining the burghers of Sluis to refrain from making cloth, possessing a large scale for commercial weighing or having a money-changing office.[60] The prevention of money changing in a harbor town was a particularly galling limitation, judging by the repeated attempts to gain its repeal. But on this point the Brugeois remained adamant throughout the fourteenth century, and the ban was repeated in a judgment by Count Louis of Male in 1367.[61] Subordinating the guilds of Sluis to those of Bruges was also a bitter pill, to judge from the constant agitation against it. Bruges complained repeatedly in the 1350s and gained once again a comital prohibition on illegal brokering activity at Sluis and confirmation of its guild control over Sluis in 1368.[62]

The nature of this subservience is illustrated by a case settled in 1423, but of far older vintage, between the barber-surgeons of Bruges and Sluis. The dispute came down to two issues: first that the Bruges guild claimed the right to half the money paid at entry into the Sluis guild by both masters and apprentices; the second was the insistence that any Bruges guild member should have the right to practice freely in Sluis without becoming a member of Sluis's guild.[63] Given that the Brugeois reckoned the unpaid fees at 100 gold crowns, the case had dragged on for a considerable time. In effect, the Bruges barber-surgeons were renewing a claim of precedence that imposed costs and limitations on their colleagues in Sluis, while offering nothing in return. The case was bitterly fought and resulted in only a face-saving compromise for the Sluis barber-surgeons. They admitted their dependence on the Bruges guild and vowed to pay ten shillings for every new master admitted, and they agreed to offer a gift of wine to the Bruges guild every year on the occasion of the Holy Blood Procession.[64] This obligation was to be a permanent ceremonial expression of subservience in return for forgiving the unpaid arrears. With their dominance firmly established, the Bruges guild members willingly let the question of their rights to practice freely in Sluis remain moot.

59 See chapter 1, p. 10.

60 Nicholas, *Town and Countryside*, p. 119; Raymond de Roover, *Money, Banking and Credit in Mediaeval Bruges* (Cambridge, Mass., 1948), pp. 178–179.

61 De Roover, *Money, Banking and Credit*, p. 179. There was another unsuccessful attempt by Sluis in 1441.

62 Nicholas, *Town and Countryside*, pp. 120–121; the documents are found in T. de Limburg-Stirum, *Cartulaire de Louis de Male*, 2 vols. (Bruges, 1898, 1901), vol. I, pp. 641–642; vol. II, pp. 156–158.

63 The notarial instrument of agreement is published in J. M. Murray, *Notarial Instruments in Flanders between 1280–1452* (Brussels, 1995), pp. 304–305.

64 Ibid., p. 305.

Table 1. *Zwin merchants and Bruges money changers*

Place name	Merchants named	Account holders
Aardenburg	18	0
Damme	87	26
Monnikerede	12	0
Sluis	55	6

Source: Account books Ruweel/De Marke

Constant legal vigilance verging on harassment was the tried and true method of Bruges against Sluis. In the 1370s there were comital investigations of Bruges's complaints against Sluis.[65] These continued into the 1380s and 1390s under Philip the Bold and the new Burgundian administration of Flanders. On numerous occasions, Sluis was instructed to respect the privileges and monopolies of its larger neighbor. David Nicholas cites a case that he believes demonstrates the "combined effect" of the privileges Bruges claimed against Sluis. It involved a case of 1389–1390 in which Sluis had gained from the duke permission to annex two suburbs outside the city that lay in the territory of the Franc of Bruges. Bruges objected, insisting it had rights to those areas which could not be abridged by any annexation. The duke ultimately agreed with Bruges's interpretation, severely limiting the economic rights of those inhabiting the annexed areas. Once again, Bruges succeeded in limiting the commerce and industry of its satellite. Moreover, in this case, although the aldermen of Sluis were charged with the enforcement of the duke's edict, the aldermen of Bruges had the right to invoke action if they detected any violations. Thus subservience was insured.[66]

The cumulative efficacy of this policy of control and curtailment is shown by looking at the census of Zwin merchants who frequented the money changers Collard de Marke and Willem Ruweel in Bruges in the 1360s (table 1). Since none of the Zwin towns were allowed their own money changer, their merchants were forced to transact such business in Bruges. And given that money-changing services ran the gamut from simple exchange of one coin for another to banking services such as money transfer and purchase of letters of exchange or credit, the traffic to Bruges was brisk.[67] As the table shows, probably all merchants of any importance in these towns had dealings with Bruges money changers in the period covered

[65] Ibid., p. 79. [66] Nicholas, *Town and Countryside*, p. 121. [67] See below chapter 4.

by the surviving accounts, and many must have had running accounts with them.[68] Surprising, however, is the absence of Hoeke and Mude from the list, particularly given the cluster of merchants from Monnikerede. This anomaly may have more to do with a close commercial relationship between Damme and Monnikerede in the wine trade than with anything else.[69] It is significant that Aardenburg, despite having the right to its own money changer, is still well represented with eighteen merchants, though none had an account with either Ruweel or de Marke. The numbers do clearly show the predominance of Damme and Sluis among the Zwin cities, and the extremely close relationship of Damme and Bruges.

Bruges struggled hard in the thirteenth and fourteenth century to retain ready access to the sea with adequate harbor facilities to handle large ships. As we have seen, this was neither easy nor inexpensive, requiring large outlays for a variety of public works projects and land acquisition. Hand in hand with freedom of access was the necessity for control: Bruges's staple rights had to be protected in the Zwin towns and the count's ambitions had to be handled in return for guarantees of monopolies and redress of grievances.[70] Constant outlay and attention proves the existence of what could only be called a consistent policy on the city's part. The envoys', representatives', legal advisors', and "retainers'" fees expended for business in the comital court alone amounted to a considerable sum. This completely leaves out the sums spent on the canals, sluice gates, and many other items that formed the more visible reminder of these controlling ambitions. In few other places could the paradox of rigorously controlled freedom be better illustrated than in the case of Bruges and its harbors.

INTERNAL WATERWAYS

Access to the sea remained one of the primary goals of Bruges throughout the later Middle Ages, and we have seen the various means and measures it took to ensure this. But Flanders was a country of canals even before the twelfth century, when the comital house of Alsace undertook so many projects to extend and link these waterways.[71] As in the case of Damme and the Zwin ports, the magistrates of Bruges did not stand idly by when their economic interests were at stake, given that access to the rich farm

68 This is particularly likely given that the known accounts are absolute minima, since the accounts of only two money changers have survived.

69 Collart Le Roy was a Damme wine merchant who had an extensive account with Collard de Marke.

70 Nicholas, *Town and Countryside*, pp. 118–122.

71 Verhulst, "Initiative comtale," 229–232; Nicholas, *Medieval Flanders*, pp. 97–100.

and pastoral resources of interior Flanders and Artois was crucial to a populous city. Most of the grain that fed the city before the late fourteenth century came from northern France; much wool was shorn from the sheep of the Bruges Franc, and fuel in the form of peat came by water from the north-east, the "Vier Ambachten."[72] Construction and control of water-links therefore went far beyond those that supported access to the Zwin.

One complex canal project involved a scheme linking the Zwin with the peat-rich areas around the village of Aksel to the north-east of Bruges. Here between 1302 and 1305, Bruges cooperated with Aardenburg in constructing dikes, sluices, and canals. What seems to have occurred is the furtherance and completion of some private initiatives undertaken by wealthy Bruges burghers and the completion of comital projects around Biervliet.[73] The result was a canal that entered the sea at Aksel and ran south to Assenede, following the half moon of a coastal inlet and linking those places. Biervliet became the next link as the canal ran north-west, then onward to connect Aardenburg, which itself was linked to the Zwin via a tributary stream, the Ee. Another canal leading to Ghent was linked via Assenede. An entry in the Bruges city accounts from 1303/1304 lists quantities of peat dug in this area, which was presumably conveyed along this waterway. Thereafter it appears that the city rented out the peat lands to private developers.[74] This interesting mix of public and private initiative is typical of the time.[75]

Control over internal waterways in the Franc as a whole was secured by the city not only by performing maintenance and construction but also by influencing administration. This is clearly shown in the city's successful attempt to control the appointment of the chief supervisor of canals in every administrative district of the Franc. These canals were often created and maintained by local water associations (*wateringhen*) made up of those who owned property along the course of the canal.[76] Of course Bruges, as a large

[72] Nicholas, *Town and Countryside*, pp. 135–136; for the grain trade in general, Georges Bigwood, "Gand et la circulation des grains en Flandres aux XIVe siècle," *Vierteljahrschrift für Sozial- und Wirschaftsgeschichte* 4 (1905), 397–460; M.-J. Tits-Dieuaide, "Les campagnes flamandes du XIIe au XVIIIe siècle, ou les succès d'une agriculture traditionnelle," *Annales E.S.C.* 39 (1984), 590–610; Marci Sortor, "The Ieperleet Affair: The Struggle for Market Position in Late-Medieval Flanders," *Speculum* 73 (1998), 1068–1100, esp. 1092–1094; for wool see Adriaan Verhulst, "La laine indigène dans les anciens Pays-Bas entre le XIIe et le XVIIe siècle," *Revue Historique* 96 (1972), 281–322 and below chapter 7.

[73] Nicholas, *Town and Countryside*, p. 136, and Nicholas, *Medieval Flanders*, pp. 128–129.

[74] Nicholas, *Town and Countryside*, p. 136 n. 69; Wyffels and Vandewalle, *Rekeningen*, vol. II, part 1, pp. 280–281 and p. 320 for renting out of peat lands by the city.

[75] Of course this is not at all surprising given the affinity between the financial interests of the city and those of the aldermen. See chapter 3 below.

[76] In the Franc, a number of monasteries were prominent developers of canals and other water projects; see Nicholas, *Medieval Flanders*, p. 260.

corporate owner of property throughout the Franc, would have been entitled to influence the election of the "master of the sluices" (*sluusmeester*) in many cases, but it insisted on more. In 1380 Bruges received from the count a privilege allowing the city government to choose every *sluusmeester* in the territory of the Franc.[77] In 1385 this legal bridgehead had been widened so that Bruges would no longer pay its share of maintenance costs in a *wateringhe* unless the master were a burgher of Bruges. As David Nicholas has correctly pointed out, this shows a remarkable degree of interest and interference in the politics of local waterways, attesting to the seriousness with which Bruges's magistrates regarded them. More than likely the campaign to control appointments of *sluusmeesters* had occupied some decades before the definitive victory of 1380–1385, adding another instance of steady, inexorable pursuit of the city's transportation interests.[78]

Successful campaigns to guarantee access to the sea coupled with control of the internal east–west waterways, no matter how essential for long-distance trade and distribution, could do little to feed Bruges. Most of the grain consumed by fourteenth-century Brugeois came from the plains of Artois and Picardy, conveyed from the south via the internal waterways in West Flanders, from Saint-Omer to either Dunkirk, or Nieuwpoort, and from there via coastal craft to Sluis or Damme. Another route, albeit less important after 1350, involved shipment from Ypres via the Yperleet canal to Bruges, though the shallowness of this canal probably prevented either large quantities or year-round delivery of grain.[79] In times of famine, such as 1316, large quantities of grain appear to have been shipped from long distances, perhaps even from the Bay of Biscay.[80] England and Scotland also seem to have been a source of foodstuffs in the fourteenth century, but long-distance supplies of grain seem always to have been the exception rather than the rule, and a city could not live by exceptions alone.[81] Bruges could not escape the need in the thirteenth and fourteenth century for ready access to the phenomenally productive grain lands that lay to the

77 Nicholas, *Town and Countryside*, p. 137, n. 73.

78 A full study of the internal waterway system in Flanders is much needed, as David Nicholas has already noted; see *Medieval Flanders*, p. 138.

79 Sortor, "The Ieperleet Affair," 1071–76; even though the canal was only constructed between 1311 and 1320, it was barely navigable for larger canal boats of the type used to transport grain by the late fourteenth century.

80 See chapter 3.

81 Van Werveke, "Bronnenmateriaal," 441, mentions a Scot who sold grain to the city in 1317. This seems to have been exceptional, however, for David Nicholas found no evidence of English grain shipments to Bruges in the 1370s; see David Nicholas, "The English Trade at Bruges in the Last Years of Edward III," *Journal of Medieval History* 5 (1979), 23–61, esp. 25. There seems to have been a lively trade in English beer, however.

south in French Artois, transport from which was controlled by Douai as far as the staple at Ghent.[82] Thus Bruges not only had to absorb the costs levied by Douai but also had to pay costs imposed by Ghent's staple privilege, namely that all grain had to be unloaded at the staple house before being reloaded into boats controlled by Ghent's powerful Free Shippers' guild for the trip along the Lieve canal to Damme. The staple restrictions were applied all the more fiercely by the Gentenars after a reorganization in 1357.[83]

Higher grain prices and uncertain supply were the incentives for the Brugeois to find a better way to obtain their foodstuffs. The most obvious was to lay a canal to the main highway to the interior, the Leie river, upstream of Ghent, thus allowing the Douasiens to proceed directly to Bruges, bypassing the Ghent grain staple. Bruges appears to have taken steps in this direction by the late thirteenth century when it possessed a canal that ran from the Minnewater to a point near Aalter, some fifteen kilometers east from where it connected with the Durme river, over whose course Bruges claimed rights. This brought the Brugeois to Hansbeke, some seven kilometers into the castellany of Ghent, the Oudburg.[84] It was not until 1306 that the first mention of the "New" Leie was made, when three aldermen were sent to investigate the course of the Leie and to inquire after the city's rights along its banks.[85] In the period 1313–1319 a series of improvements followed to this canal system, but all with the intent of improving the amount of water flowing into the Bruges canal system, not making it into an alternative route to the Leie.[86]

The Bruges Leie, or New Leie, disappears from the records for a full decade until a new city initiative to broaden and deepen the course of the canal. Count Louis of Nevers granted a charter to allow the work, pronouncing it profitable "both for us and for our country as a whole," as described by the magistrates of Bruges.[87] In the text of the charter it is clear that the intention for the New Leie was to make it a navigable waterway: "that those of Bruges . . . shall make the said New Leie fit

[82] Nicholas, *Metamorphosis of a Medieval City*, pp. 242–244.

[83] An example of higher grain prices paid in Bruges is cited in Nicholas, *Metamorphosis*, p. 249, n. 58 (text on p. 334): a Gerard de Deckere of Bruges bought grain in Ghent at retail in June 1372, of which the price after transport and markup was considerably higher in Bruges.

[84] This can be dated to 1270–1290; see M. Vandermaesen, M. Ryckaert, and M. Coornaert, *De Witte Kaproenen: De Gentse Opstand (1379–1385) en de Geschiedenis van de Brugse Leie* (Ghent, 1979), pp. 38–39; Nicholas, *Town and Countryside*, pp. 138–139.

[85] Nicholas, *Town and Countryside*, p. 138.

[86] Ibid., p. 140; Vandermaesen *et al.*, *De Witte Kaproenen*, p. 39 with cited texts.

[87] Vandermaesen *et al.*, *De Witte Kaproenen*, p. 41; Nicholas, *Town and Countryside*, p. 139.

for sailing (*mener*) loaded and unloaded boats as well as other things one is accustomed to transport by water." But once again this canalizing of the New Leie did not reach along the entire length of the old canal, and certainly not to Hansbeke or Aalter in the Ghent Oudburg.[88] It may be that the Gentenars successfully dissuaded the Brugeois from continuing the project.[89]

Sometime around 1360 the Bruges magistrates again decided to press on with widening the New Leie, resulting in a new rubric in each year's accounts for "expenditure or the work on the New Leie."[90] In 1362 instructions were given to the new contractor to dig out the canal to the same width and depth as the earlier canal works. Land was acquired from some twenty-eight individuals to allow the expansion.[91] Work continued through the 1360s and by 1368 had crossed the border between Knesselare and Aalter and thus into the region controlled by Ghent. Unaccountably, the work slackened in the 1370s, only to be resumed in 1379, reaching a point north-east of Aalter, when it was violently halted by a militia band from Ghent, the "White Hoods." It is hard to decipher the precise intentions of both cities at this point. According to one scholar, Bruges had received a comital charter allowing the construction of the New Leie to Deinze, where it would meet the course of the main Leie river upstream from Ghent and its staple.[92] This seems unlikely, given the considerable distance from Deinze to the existing canal. More likely was the more modest ambition of pushing the canal bed to a point intersecting the Ghent Lieve canal at Vinderhoute, giving Bruges independent control over a waterway to Ghent. Even this was too ambitious for an increasingly militant and paranoid Ghent, however, and the latter's attack escalated into one of the bloodiest and most destructive civil wars of the entire Middle Ages. Here, for once, the typically unstoppable Bruges quest for access and control collided with the immovable opposition of an equal adversary.[93]

88 Vandermaesen *et al.*, *De Witte Kaproenen*, pp. 41–42, where the text of the quoted document is published.

89 Ghent did achieve a certain hegemony in the county and relatively friendly relations with Bruges in the 1330s and 1340s; see Nicholas, *Town and Countryside*, p. 139 and chapter 1.

90 Vandermaesen *et al.*, *De Witte Kaproenen*, pp. 42–43; Nicholas, *Town and Countryside*, p. 139, has 1361.

91 For this and what follows, Vandermaesen *et al.*, *De Witte Kaproenen*, p. 43.

92 This was the position expressed by Rogghé and rejected by Nicholas, *Town and Countryside*, p. 140, and Vandermaesen *et al.*, *De Witte Kaproenen*, p. 45.

93 Unfortunately confusion over the precise cause of the Ghent war is furthered in an error in the English translation of Prevenier and Blockmans, *The Burgundian Netherlands*, p. 23, where Ghent is incorrectly stated to have approved the extension of the canal.

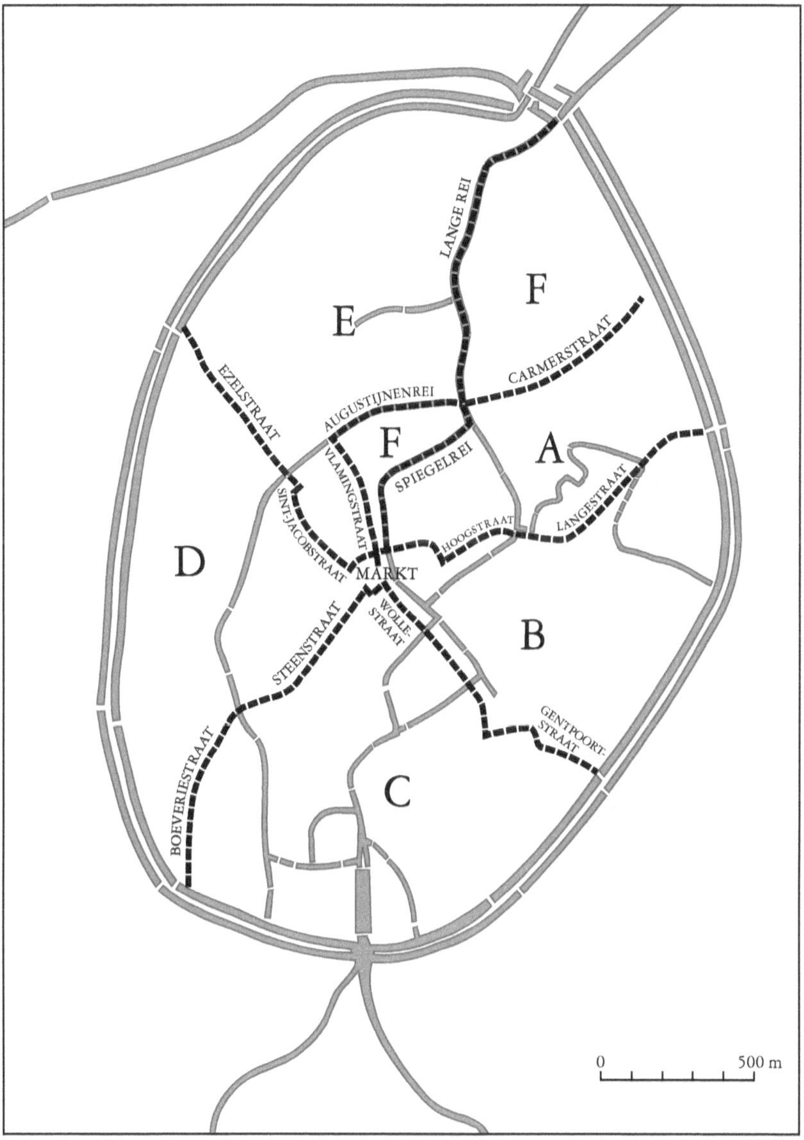

Map 3: The City Quarters (*Zestendelen*). There were six administrative districts in the city: A. Sint-Jan B. Sint-Donaas C. Onze-Lieve-Vrouw D. Sint-Jacob E. Sint-Niklaas F. Carmers. Their boundaries had little to do with parish or other delimiters; rather they were formed by the most prominent streets of the city.

ROADS AND STREETS

The pace of investment in water transport in Bruges appears to have quickened from the late thirteenth century through the late Middle Ages, as ever more money and administrative attention were lavished on the city's shipping infrastructure. Changes in the European economy no doubt spurred on this development, for as several historians have noted, there was a significant shift to sea-borne transport from land routes, especially in the fourteenth century.[94] Add to this the fact that the bulk of documents that survive dates from the age of the ship and the conclusion follows rather too easily that Bruges owed its commercial ascendance solely to its status as a port city. Nothing could be further from the truth, especially for the eleventh and twelfth centuries, which mark the true beginnings of the economic and demographic growth whose momentum was only increased by the later popularity of Bruges's harbors.

There are some important similarities between the development of land and water routes in Flanders, however, and it is important to view them as complementary. This was no doubt how Count Baldwin V viewed the importance of roads when he established a series of fairs, beginning in the south of Flanders in Lille, progressing along the road leading to Mesen, Ypres, Torhout then to Bruges at the northernmost point. Within the city this (probably Roman) road branched to become important arteries – the Steenstraat and the Zuidzandstraat. These Flemish fairs were not established simultaneously, for those of Ypres, Torhout, and Mesen originated in the late eleventh and early twelfth century, followed by the other cities on the southern and northern extremities. The fairs were among the earliest in northern Europe, lasting thirty days each in a cycle extending from February to November with intervals sufficient to allow merchants to shift their wares and themselves from place to place.[95] In this they were aided by improvements in the technology of cart building and horse hauling, with the four-wheeled cart drawn by horses or oxen with padded collars enormously increasing the efficiency of land transport.[96]

94 Herman van der Wee, "Un modèle de croissance interséculaire du commerce mondial (XIIe–XVIIIe siècles)," *Annales E.S.C.* 25 (1970), 100–126.

95 Nicholas, *Medieval Flanders*, p. 110; on fairs in general and their importance to the European Economy, see Edwin S. Hunt and James M. Murray, *A History of Business in Medieval Europe, 1200–1550* (Cambridge, 1999), pp. 28–39, and most recently, M. Yamada, "Le mouvement des foires en Flandre avant 1200," in *Mélanges Georges Despy* (Liège, 1991), pp. 773–789.

96 James Masschaele, "Transport Costs in Medieval England," *Economic History Review* 46, 2 (1993), 266–279.

A second significant land route entered Bruges from the south-east, across the Maria bridge and along the Mariastraat past the Onze-Lieve-Vrouw church. This was the Bruges–Ghent, route which continued eastward through Aalst, Brussels, Leuven, Diest, Hasselt, and Maastricht, ending in the dominant Rhine city of Cologne. The road seems to have come into commercial use around 1000 and followed in part an old Roman road that led to the Rhineland.[97] Thus Bruges was connected via land to two important economic networks well before 1100: the one, leading south, passed through the most Flemish market cities, which in turn offered access to the more economically precocious cities of Arras, Douai, and Saint-Omer. The second extended east through Flanders and Brabant to the important river regions of the Maas and Rhine. These local networks expanded in the course of the twelfth century, when the Flemish fair cycle became integrated with that of Champagne to the south, and Cologne became the connecting point to new German settlements to the east.[98] These land connections had such impact on the topographical development of Bruges that one historian has concluded that access to the sea was of negligible importance in the crucial century between 1050 and 1150. The first commercial city was thus a product of overland trade.[99]

The earliest commercial topography of Bruges was probably influenced by a Carolingian king whose defense against northern attack resulted in the earliest post-Roman fortifications on the site that became Bruges. By the ninth century, the counts of Flanders had inherited and improved upon the work of their royal ancestors, and these fortifications formed the first kernel of the medieval city. Trade and traffic certainly influenced the location of the site, which lay at the meeting point of sea and land routes through the *pagus Flandrensis*, which made early Bruges the administrative and defensive capital of the region.[100] Thus through the barely documented tenth century the Burg of Bruges took shape, growing into a complex of ditches, walls, and buildings enclosing a central square by the end of the reign of Count Arnulf I.[101] The dominant buildings on the Burg were

[97] Jan Dhondt, "De vroege topografie van Brugge," *HMGOG*, new series, 11 (1957), 3–30 and Ryckaert, *Stedenatlas*, p. 64.

[98] Hans van Werveke, "De opbloei van Handel en Nijverheid," in *Algemene Geschiedenis der Nederlanden* (Utrecht, 1950), vol. II, pp. 417–419.

[99] Verhulst, "Les origines," 46–47; Ryckaert, *Stedenatlas*, p. 64.

[100] Verhulst, "Les origines," 41–43; Dhondt, "Vroege topografie," 30.

[101] Nicholas, *Medieval Flanders*, pp. 34–35; Ryckaert, *Stedenatlas*, p. 47, esp. n. 91 for the debate surrounding the foundation date of St. Donatian's church; see also Georges Declercq, "Wanneer onstond het Sint-Donaaskapittel te Brugge?" *ASEB* 122 (1985), 245–257, who makes the case for Arnulf I as founder.

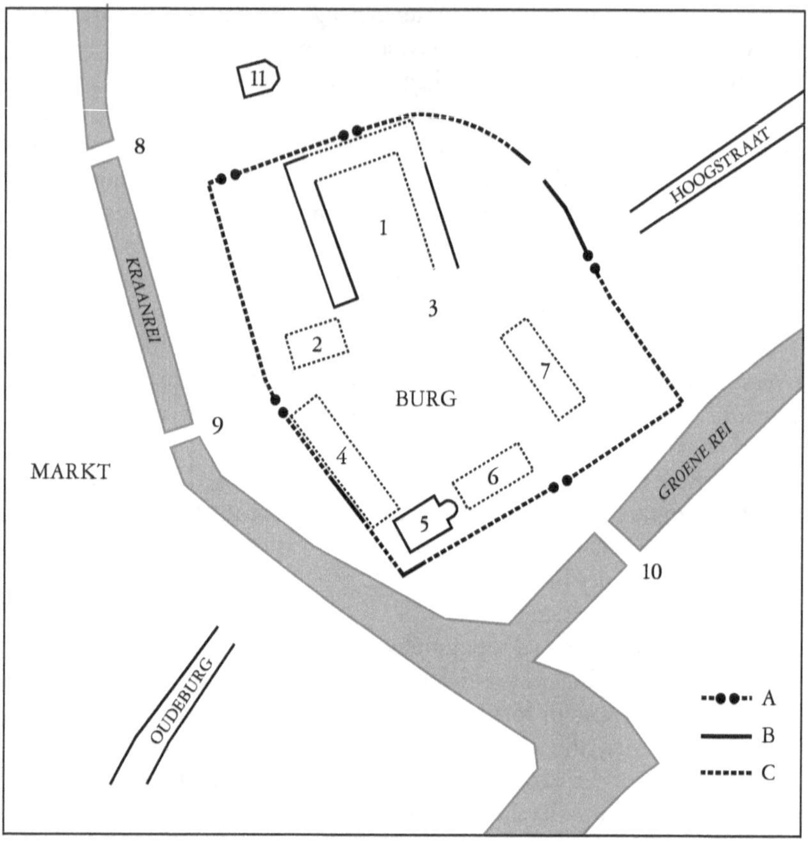

Map 4: The Burg. A reconstruction of the twelfth-century Burg with A. the Burg gates, B. the Burg wall, and C. a hypothetical Burg wall. 1. St. Donatian's cloister 2. Chapter building 3. St. Donatian's church 4. The "Steen" or old comital castle 5. St. Basil's chapel 6. The "Ghiselhuus" 7. The "Love" 8. St. Peter's bridge 9. The "Hof" bridge 10. Oostburg bridge 11. St. Peter's chapel.

well established by the late eleventh century: the comital church dedicated to St. Donatian and the Virgin Mary formed the "clerical" part of the Burg on the north, with the "comital" part lying on the south, east, and west sides of the square occupied by residence-fortifications, the *Love* and *Steen* respectively.[102] The trio of comital buildings was completed with the rather mysteriously named *Ghiselhuus*, which stood on the south side of the square, along the ditch that ran along the entire southern length of the

[102] Verhulst, "Les origines," 42–43; Ryckaert, *Stedenatlas*, pp. 47–48.

Burg.[103] The clerical north side was also built along a defensive ditch, along which the buildings of the Provost and chapter of St. Donatian's later joined the church itself to fill the space between the east and west gates. Through those gates, thus directly bisecting the Burg, passed the extension of the Steenstraat (itself an extension of the road from Ghent) exiting along the "High Street" (Hoogstraat) in the direction of Aardenburg.[104]

The vague, archeologically based image of Bruges's oldest square comes into sharper focus only in 1127–1128, with the vivid memoir of Galbert of Bruges. It was there that that story of tragedy and retribution, from the assassination of Count Charles the Good to the gruesome execution of his murderers, took place.[105] Galbert's account describes the Burg as completely enclosed by stone walls, which were probably begun by Arnulf I and perhaps completed, or certainly augmented, by Count Baldwin V in the middle of the eleventh century.[106] These counts used reclaimed stone taken from old Roman fortifications in nearby Oudenburg for the work, raising a wall of some thirty to thirty-five feet around the square. The walls were pierced by at least three, perhaps four, gates. On the east and west sides, of course, was the major throughway formed by the road leading to the Hoogstraat from the west gate of the Burg. A bridge spanned the canal (the later Kraanrei) leading to the east gate, the Hofbrug. This again marked the division between the clerical and comital north and south. The south gate stood on the modern site of the passage called the Blinde Ezelstraat, which led to a bridge over the Groenerei. In the north there was a gate (later incorporated into the building complex of the chapter of St. Donatian's) leading to the Philipstockstraat, which in turn was linked to the Grote Markt by the St. Peter's bridge.[107]

Galbert as a comital notary probably lived and certainly worked in the Burg, yet he also wrote of "our suburb" ("suburbium nostrum") giving the impression of a well-articulated settlement outside the walls of the Burg.[108]

[103] Verhulst, "Les origines," 46; the name means literally "hostage house."

[104] Ryckaert, *Stedenatlas*, p. 56.

[105] The considerable historiography surrounding Galbert of Bruges and his history is best approached through the introduction in Jeff Rider (ed.), *Galbertus Notarius Brugensis, de Multro, Traditione, et Occisione Gloriosi Karoli Comitis Flandriarum* (Turnhout, 1994), pp. vii–xxviii and Rider, *God's Scribe. The Historiographical Art of Galbert of Bruges* (Washington, D.C., 2001), pp. 1–10.

[106] Ryckaert, *Stedenatlas*, p. 58; Dhondt, "De vroege topografie," is in effect an attempt to piece together the topographical details included by Galbert of Bruges in his diary.

[107] Ryckaert, *Stedenatlas*, p. 60.

[108] This phrase is unfortunately mistranslated in the standard English edition of Galbert as "our town," thereby losing the distinction Galbert intended between the "Burg" or "urbs" and the sub-urbs, the area outside the gates of the count's original fortifications. See J. B. Ross, *The Murder of Charles the Good* (New York, 1967), p. 201, and J. M. Murray, "The Liturgy of the Count's Advent in Bruges, from Galbert to Van Eyck," in B. Hanawalt and K. Reyerson (eds.), *City and Spectacle in Medieval Europe* (Minneapolis, 1994), pp. 137–152, esp. p. 138 and n. 3, p. 149.

This confirms the growth of Bruges as far more than an administrative center by the twelfth century, and the actions stemming from the civil wars of 1127–1128 led directly to both the first formal city privilege granted to Bruges and the first set of city walls. These allow us to see the developing topography of a rapidly growing city. This "first walling" of Bruges had as its basis the ring of "inner canals," those described above as forming the backbone of the inner-city waterway system.[109] To these were added one canal, and two other canals were probably created in the process of straightening and adapting an existing brook. These rather minor alterations to the internal waterways were designed to strengthen the system of what were probably wooden palisades in the initial building, which later became stone walls with half-round towers at regular intervals. This system of walls and defensive waterways enclosed seventy-five hectares and established the political and judicial boundaries of the city for more than a century.[110]

The enclosed area of Bruges was large by twelfth-century standards, but it was neither completely nor densely settled. Given that naturally occurring waterways were used as the basis for establishing the walled boundaries of the city, the built environment may have had little importance in deciding their location. The northern part of the city, the area around the future Oosterlingenplein and the Spiegelrei, was still a veritable marsh in the middle of the twelfth century and would not become habitable until some time after 1200. The area to the south-east, where the St. Jans hospital was founded around 1150 and the Begijnhof nearly a century later, was likewise marshy and sparsely inhabited. It was probably left out of the original ring of fortifications.[111] Thus Galbert's "suburb" did not lie in these marshy extremities of the city, but was most likely the settlement that grew up just south-west of the Burg across the Kraanrei and connected via the Hofbrug on the south side to what was becoming the Grote Markt, or central market place of Bruges.

This was the Oudeburg, a settlement that is now a neighborhood perched on some of the highest ground in the vicinity of the Burg.[112] It was also strategically located at the confluence of the two most significant land

[109] Thus the canals of the St. Annarei to the east, the Groenerei and Dyver to the south-west and south, and to the west and north the Smedenrei, Speelmansrei, Augustijnenrei, and Goudenhandrei provided the outline followed by the walls.

[110] E. I. Strubbe, "Van de eerste naar de tweede omwalling van Brugge," *ASEB* 100 (1963), 271–300.

[111] Van Houtte, *Geschiedenis*, pp. 230–231; Ryckaert, *Stedenatlas*, pp. 63–64.

[112] The precise meaning of the word "Burg" gave rise to a debate among an earlier generation of medieval urban historians. This debate was summarized and resolved by Hans van Werveke, who argued that "Burg" indicated a settlement first and not necessarily a fortification; see Van Werveke, *Burgus. Versterking of nederzetting?* (Brussels, 1965), and Marc Ryckaert, "De Oudeburg te Brugge," in *Album Albert Schouteet* (Bruges, 1973), pp. 155–168.

Map 5: City development to c. 1200. The arrows indicate the direction of urban growth with the Oudeburg and "Great Square" (Groot Vierkant) as the twin nuclei. Later development occurred northward along the watercourse leading to Damme.

routes into early Bruges.[113] The two routes joined at the southern tip of the Oudeburg at what is now the Simon Stevinplein, forming the Steenstraat. By 1127 settlement had expanded considerably from this oldest kernel, stretching along the south side of the Steenstraat to reach 't Zand, and to the south-west following the track of the Ghent road. The two most significant parish churches were founded at the edge of these two zones of expansion: St. Salvator, just west of the intersection of the two roads, and Onze-Lieve-Vrouw, built near the Dyver along the Ghent road.[114] In every respect the Oudeburg and its churches were the result of the proximity of the comital Burg and, perhaps most of all, the important land routes that conveyed the quickening commercial traffic of the eleventh century.

The creation of the Zwin by the flood of 1134, as well as the careful exploitation of its shipping and commercial possibilities by the Brugeois, contributed to an era of rapid growth in the city's population. This began to fill up the vacant land within the first city walls, notably land in the northern part of the city, extending in the direction of the new waterway to Damme and the Zwin. This was no coincidence, for already by 1200, low-lying marshy ground in this part of the city was being drained and filled to provide building sites for the warehouses and residences of merchants who were attracted to the possibilities offered by the new sea route.[115] This new direction of topographical development may have reinforced an earlier commercial settlement that lay north of the Burg in the so-called "Great Square" (Groot Vierkant) formed by the four main canals.[116] Here some historians have hypothesized the existence of a trading settlement linked to the old, pre-1134 harbor site, located around the site of the St. Walburga church.[117]

The combined force of new commerce, new immigration, and the grant of comital privileges over landholding unleashed a veritable building boom in twelfth and thirteenth-century Bruges. One of the desired goals of the Brugeois who intervened in the civil war of 1127–1128 was clearer title to urban property. This they received from the count in the form of direct authority (*dominium directum*) over any land held within the recognized boundaries of the city.[118] This made holding urban land, instead of merely the buildings constructed upon it, extremely desirable. The precise details

[113] Paul Bonenfant, "L'origine des villes brabançonnes et la 'route' de Bruges à Cologne," *RBPH* 31 (1953), 399–447.

[114] Verhulst, "Les origines," 47–50.

[115] Ryckaert, *Stedenatlas*, p. 68.

[116] Ibid., p. 48.

[117] Ibid., p. 49.

[118] The text of the original charter does not survive. The earliest surviving text dates from the period between 1165 and 1177; its most recent edition is R. C. van Caenegem and L. Milis (eds.), "Kritische uitgave van de 'Grote Keure' van Filips van de Elzas, graaf van Vlaanderen, voor Gent en Brugge

of the city's expansion are lost to us, but there remain unmistakable signs of remarkable growth. One was the laying out of a new quarter of the city on land granted the chapter of St. Donatian's church by count Thierry of Alsace in 1155–1157 on condition that it remain undeveloped.[119] The land lay in the vicinity of the "Great Square" between the "High" street and the Groenerei, not far from St. Walburga's church. But between 1170 and 1180, the chapter made a deal with a comital official who absolved the chapter of this condition in return for two-thirds of the profit on subdividing the land and building houses. As a result, considerable care was taken to divide and build in such a way as to pack as many people as possible into the space.[120] Typically these buildings were rows of so-called "rooms" (*cameren*) consisting of a single story, with sleeping lofts built in the rafters. They were usually rented to the new immigrants in the city, whose landlords were often merchants or former merchants profiting from new investments in property.[121]

Demand for housing filled up all available space within the walls in the course of the thirteenth century, forcing the poor and recent immigrants to new neighborhoods outside the city. The Bruges magistrates also took part in the land rush by acquiring territories outside the original walled area. Thus around 1246 the "meadow called Braamberg" was added to Bruges territory, and shortly thereafter the city subdivided and built upon the land in systematic fashion. This resulted in a far more regular, nearly grid-like, series of streets and neighborhoods.[122] Another new neighborhood showed the increasing diversity of the inhabitants of thirteenth-century Bruges. This was a community of religious women who took up residence just outside the city's south-eastern walls in an area of marshy ground called the Wijngaard. In a movement common to a number of cities of the Southern Low Countries, these *mulieres religiosae* received a charter of

(1165–1177)," *BCRH* 143 (1977), 207–257. Since that critical edition was prepared, another text of the privilege has been discovered in the State Archives of Bruges: see Ryckaert, *Stedenatlas*, p. 66, n. 182.

119 Ryckaert, *Stedenatlas*, p. 68. The count's charter of agreement is edited by Thérèse de Hemptinne, Adriaan Verhulst, and L. De Mey, *De oorkonden der graven van Vlaanderen (juli 1128 – september 1191). II. Uitgave – Band I. Regering van Diederik van de Elzas (juli – 16 januari 1168)* (Brussels, 1988), pp. 265–266.

120 Strubbe, "Van de eerste tot de tweede omwalling," 288; Ryckaert, *Stedenatlas*, pp. 68–69 and n. 191.

121 SAB, 271. Confiscatierekeningen, 11 registers, 1302–1305 for the 1380s confiscations, ARA rekenkamer, registers 18244, 48986, and rolrekeningen nos. 1030–1034. For an idea of the contents of the former see M. Vandermaesen and M. Ryckaert, "Een miskende bron voor de sociale geschiedenis van de Stad Brugge bij het begin van de 14de eeuw. De registers van 'forfaiture et sequestre' 1302–1304," *Het Brugs Ommeland* 17 (1977), 143–151, and in general Ryckaert, *Stedenatlas*, p. 69.

122 Ryckaert, *Stedenatlas*, p. 71.

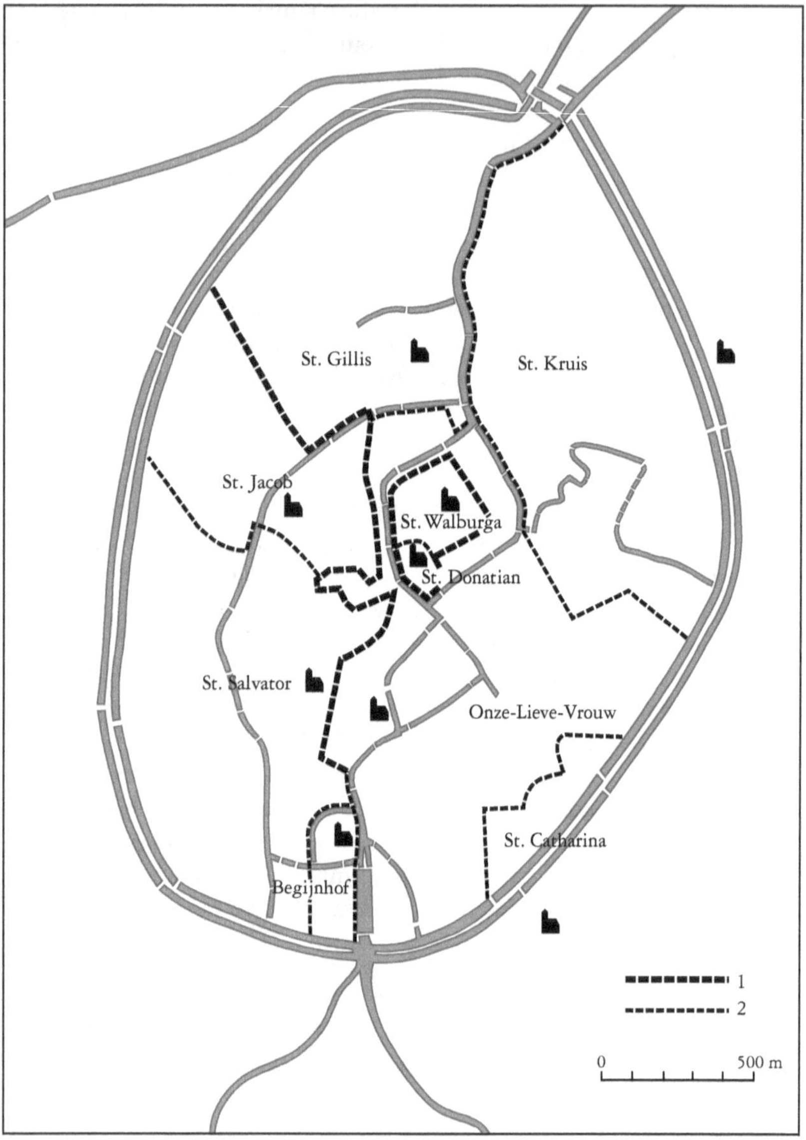

Map 6: The parishes of Bruges. The development of urban parishes was not completed until the early fourteenth century. By that time there were seven churches within the walls, and two urban districts belonged to parishes whose churches lay outside the 1297 fortifications.

incorporation in 1244–1245 from Countess Joanna of Flanders, who made of their foundation an independent parish. Thus their community took on the form of a *curtis beguinage*, with houses grouped around a church, with the entire complex separated from the outside world by walls and canals.[123] In 1299 Philip the Fair, king of France, withdrew the Begijnhof from city jurisdiction, placing it directly under the authority of the prince.

In the absence of more concrete measures, the creation of new urban parishes is the most reliable gauge of rapid population growth. In Bruges, these new parishes were created by division from the two original foundations. Thus the new parishes of St. Walburga and St. Jacob were split off from St. Salvator; those of St. Catharina and St. Gillis came from Onze-Lieve-Vrouw. With the exception of St. Gillis and St. Catharina, all these new parish churches were constructed within the original city wall of 1127–1128. As stated above, St. Walburga's, founded in 1239, incorporated the "Great Square" apart from a few parcels retained by the Onze-Lieve-Vrouw parish. St. Jacob's church was founded the following year, and like St. Walburga's, it had previously been a chapel. St. Gillis was created in an area around the former port of Bruges, outside the 1127–1128 walls, and was also nearly contemporaneous with the others. St. Catharina parish was in fact a semi-rural church, founded between 1270 and 1272 along the road to Kortrijk, south-east of the city.[124] A second rural/urban highbred parish was St. Kruis, whose church lay outside both sets of medieval walls, but whose territory included a significant portion of land enclosed by the 1297 walls.[125]

The decision to locate these new churches within the security of the walls but outside the teeming workers' neighborhoods seems to suggest a failure of imagination in coping with the spiritual needs of these new Brugeois. In comparison with other cities, Bruges was not well endowed with churches, and the insistence on the privileges of the founding church may have stifled and limited the newer parishes in their work. In any event, the shortcomings of the secular clergy were quickly remedied by the arrival

[123] Walter Simons, "The Beguine Movement in the Southern Low Countries: A Reassessment," *Bulletin de l'Institut Historique Belge de Rome* 59 (1989), 67–68; Simons, *Cities of Ladies: Beguine Communities in the Medieval Low Countries, 1200–1565* (Philadelphia, 2001); Joanna E. Ziegler, "The *curtis beguinages* in the Southern Low Countries and Art Patronage: Interpretation and Historiography," *Bulletin de l'Institut Historique Belge de Rome* 57 (1987), 31–40. For Bruges in particular, see Ryckaert, *Stedenatlas*, p. 71.

[124] Van Houtte, *Geschiedenis*, pp. 225–230; Ryckaert, *Stedenatlas*, pp. 86–88; and the classic article by E. I. Strubbe, "De parochies te Brugge voor de XIIe eeuw," in *Album Michiel English: Studies over de kerkelijke en kunstgeschiedenis van West-Vlaanderen* (Bruges, 1952), pp. 355–380.

[125] In 1497 a second church, dedicated to St. Anna, was built within the walls to serve the urban part of the St. Kruis parish; see Ryckaert, *Stedenatlas*, p. 206.

of the mendicant orders, whose mission was precisely to serve the poor and recent migrants to Europe's cities. They would fan out through the new neighborhoods of thirteenth-century Bruges, eventually building six foundations – the most of any Flemish city – before 1300.

Why Bruges received more attention from the mendicant orders than any other Flemish city is a tantalizing question. After all, Ghent was much more populous, and other cities nearly so, suggesting that it was not the mass and density of an urban settlement that was decisive.[126] Most likely it was the unique mix of commerce and merchants in Bruges, for the mendicants had a particular affinity for the money trade – from pawnbroking to banking – that accounts for the large number of foundations.[127] In any event, a look at the topography of the mendicant foundations, which virtually mark the boundaries of the commercial quarter, proves the keen instinct for money these medieval apostles of poverty possessed.

The earliest mendicants to arrive were the Franciscans and Dominicans. The Franciscans had two early establishments – first around 1230 in the area where St. Gillis's church would later be constructed, then in 1246 they moved to city-owned land in the Braamberg.[128] Not far from the Braamberg, the Dominicans began their friary after 1234 with considerable financial help from the countess of Flanders.[129] The Carmelites followed in 1264 with a monastery in the vicinity of the Potterie along the watercourse leading to Damme.[130] The other significant foundation was that of the Augustinians, whose monastery was located on land still owned by the lord of Gistel at the time.[131] Members of the two other mendicant orders were more fleeting figures in the city – the Friars of the Sack and the Pied Friars – neither of whose foundations survived the fourteenth century.[132] This pattern of mendicant settlement shows a relatively orderly division of the city's new neighborhoods, while maintaining contact with the Grote Markt, the central market square, and with a city gate nearby as well.[133]

126 See chapter 3 for the Bruges population in the fourteenth century.

127 This answer was proposed by Walter Simons, *Stad en apostolaat: de vestiging van de bedelorden in het graafschap Vlaanderen (ca.1225–ca.1350)* (Brussels, 1987), pp. 94–95; the question will be taken up in more detail in chapter 4.

128 Walter Simons, *Bedelordekloosters in het Graafschap Vlaanderen. Chronologie en topografie van de bedelordenverspreiding vóór 1350* (Steenbrugge, 1987), pp. 45–53; for the reasons for the move, see Simons, *Stad en apostolaat*, p. 120.

129 P. Meulepas, "De Predikheeren te Brugge," *Biekorf* 45 (1939), 233–234 and Ryckaert, *Stedenatlas*, p. 86.

130 Simons, *Bedelordekloosters*, pp. 112–113.

131 Simons, *Bedelordekloosters*, pp. 99–104.

132 Bruges was the only place in Flanders where the Pied Friars (called "Eksterbroeders" in Dutch) established a community: Simons, *Stad en apostolaat*, p. 62 and *Bedelordekloosters*, p. 121. For the Friars of the Sack, *Stad en apostolaat*, pp. 81–82, 120.

133 Simons, *Stad en apostolaat*, pp. 126–127, notes the semi-circular pattern of the monasteries around the Grote Markt.

Certain individual mendicant preferences are also clear: the Augustinians and Carmelites often favored harbor areas where pawnbrokers were active, which may explain their choice of location in Bruges.[134] The Augustinians showed an early concern for access to the Burg, even to the point of aiding in the construction of a new bridge.[135] The Dominicans were established near the Langestraat in one of the liveliest commercial neighborhoods. All in all, the mendicant houses show both the rapid increase in urban population, especially outside the original walls of Bruges, and the expansion of a money economy in the city as a whole.

The new suburbs outside the walls quickly negated the defensive value of the original fortifications. Not only were many Brugeois living outside these defenses, but the new bridges and streets constructed to facilitate traffic in and out made Bruges essentially an open city by the late thirteenth century.[136] The mendicants were probably representing the interests of their neighborhoods as well as their own in 1268, when the Franciscans aided in the construction of a new road, and in 1294, when the Augustinians received permission to build a new bridge through the city wall.[137] The city also constructed its own bridges to the new Braamberg, and the examples could be multiplied. Several streets were being paved through these new neighborhoods as well.[138] In short, by 1290 the old walls had outlived their usefulness both in defense and in demarcating the actual urbanized area of Bruges. But it required the outbreak of a new age of hostilities for a solution to this defenselessness.

That era began with the preliminaries of war between the French and English kings and the difficult position of the Flemish count, Guy of Dampierre, caught between his liege lord and the monarch of his county's most important trading partner.[139] Count Guy chose the English side, thereby renouncing his feudal oath, and offered his county as a staging area for Edward I's eventual military operations on the continent. Bruges was to be an important part of the English king's plans, owing to both the city's harbor facilities and its ability to store and distribute materials

[134] Ibid., p. 126 and Joseph Marechal, *Bijdrage tot de geschiedenis van het bankwezen te Brugge* (Bruges, 1955), p. 17, and see below chapter 4. Jill Webster notes that as late-comers, Carmelites often were forced into areas frequented by prostitutes and foreigners, as was the case in Majorca and Barcelona; see her *Carmel in Medieval Catalonia* (Leiden, 1999), p. 70.

[135] Simons, *Stad en apostolaat*, p. 120 and Ryckaert, *Stedenatlas*, p. 91.

[136] The term is Marc Ryckaert's in describing the thirteenth-century growth of suburbs, connected to the old city by new bridges: see *Stedenatlas*, p. 91.

[137] Ibid., p. 91.

[138] M. Coornaert, "De middeleeuwse vestingswerken van de stad Brugge," *Het Brugs Ommeland* 31–32 (1991–1992), 177–246, 55–82, esp. 55.

[139] See chapter 1.

of war sufficient to supply an expeditionary English army.[140] In order to be fit for such a role, however, the city needed strong defenses of a kind far beyond those offered by the twelfth-century walls. Edward went so far as to promise to pay half the cost of constructing new fortifications; but the promise went unfulfilled after his retreat and the French invasion of Flanders in June 1297. Bruges was occupied, and the defensive needs of the city became the problem of Philip IV. He ordered the construction of a new set of walls with the entire cost to be borne by the Brugeois. This became one of the largest public works projects ever undertaken by the city, and its relatively rapid completion amid the gathering chaos of war and revolution gives some idea of the depth of financial and physical resources the city could summon.[141]

In about three years, a team of contractors directed by city specialists completed the new defenses. Together they assembled an enclosure of walls and a double moat nearly seven kilometers in length, using at least four million bricks, along with large quantities of limestone, timber, and paving stones, and the labor of carpenters, plumbers, and blacksmiths in addition to that of the hundreds of unskilled workmen.[142] However the city was not then, nor would it ever be, completely surrounded by walls; rather a mixture of heavily fortified gates, palisades, walls and moats made up a true defensive system. King Philip failed, however, to leave an enduring personal mark on the Bruges defenses. As the work neared its end, Philip ordered that a separate bastion or castle be constructed in the south-east of the city, thus controlling the routes to Ghent and Kortrijk as well as providing a strong point for royal troops within the walls. The work began in 1301 and the foundations were complete and the walls begun before the successful uprising, the Matins of Bruges, forced the French to flee the city. The victorious Brugeois destroyed all trace of the hated symbol of occupation, and only a street name and the name of a nearby watermill remained as reminders.[143]

140 Sumption, *Trial by Battle*, pp. 291–318; H. S. Lucas, *The Low Countries and the Hundred Years' War, 1326–1347* (Ann Arbor, 1929), Funck-Brentano, *Les origines de la guerre de cent ans*; M. Ryckaert, *Stedenatlas*, p. 91.

141 Coornaert, "De middeleeuwse vestingswerken," 63–67; Ryckaert, *Stedenatlas*, pp. 92–93.

142 Coornaert, "De middeleeuwse vestingswerken," 64, 67. The surviving city accounts for the years of the construction allow a most precise picture of the work while in progress. The actual length was 6,800 meters according to Ryckaert, *Stedenatlas*, p. 93.

143 Duclos, *Bruges, histoire et souvenirs*, pp. 501–502; Ryckaert, *Stedenatlas*, p. 178. Even though the "French" castle was never completed, its memory remained, as in a charter of 1330, which spoke of "the place where once the king of France had begun to build his castle": OCMW, fonds St. Jans hospitaal, charter 429. My thanks to Marc Ryckaert for helping solve this riddle.

With this second walling of 1297–1300, Bruges attained the dimensions that would remain essentially unaltered until the end of the Ancien Régime.[144] This was not, however, the full extent of the *schependom* – the administrative district of the aldermen – by 1300, nor was all the land enclosed by the walls uniformly under the authority of the Bruges magistrates. Although the walls enclosed an area of some 430 hectares, a large part of the city's jurisdiction remained outside them.[145] This was largely for reasons of practicality and cost, and reflected the fact that much of this land was rural. Much undeveloped land remained within the new walls as well, giving some areas every bit as much a rural aspect as the countryside.[146] Much of the new land enclosed by the 1297 walls, as well as that lying just outside it, had either been purchased from feudal lords or fallen to the city as the result of well-planned aggression. This was the case with land north of the city that was confiscated from its noble owner as a result of his allegiance to the French king in the 1302 war and then attached to the territory of Bruges.[147] Some traces of the past remained even after an area became part of Bruges: the former village of St. Gillis, for example, retained something of its separate identity long after it became an urban neighborhood. And two areas, encompassing land both inside and outside the walls, remained outside the control of Bruges magistrates until after the French Revolution.

The "Proosse" and "Kannunikse" formed one jurisdiction though a double pattern of ownership whose land belonged either to the Provost or canons of the church of St. Donatian's, the original comital church on the Burg square. This land formed a separate jurisdiction in every sense of the word, with distinct laws and privileges, an independent board of governors, and its own law court.[148] The largest bulk of land lay outside the city walls, mostly as enclaves spread among some forty-three villages; however there was much real estate within Bruges itself ruled by this clerical body. Not only was the northern, "clerical" side of the Burg part of this territory; some twelve enclaves of urban land concentrated in the north-east were as

144 F.-L. Ganshof, *Etude sur le développement des villes entre Loire et Rhin au Moyen Age* (Paris and Brussels, 1943), p. 52.

145 Ibid., p. 59; Coornaert estimates ("De middeleeuwse vestingswerken," 82) that at most a third of the settled area was enclosed by defensive works at the end of the Middle Ages.

146 Ganshof, *Etude*, pp. 60–62. Ganshof points out that this was typical of a number of cities in the Loire–Rhine region.

147 Ryckaert, *Stedenatlas*, p. 82; Nicholas, *Town and Countryside*, pp. 57–58.

148 Joseph Marechal, *Inventaris van het Archief der Proosdij van Sint-Donaas te Brugge* (Brussels, 1960), pp. vi–vii; L. Gilliodts-van Severen, *Coutumes des Pays et Comté de Flandre: Coutume de la prévôté de Bruges*, 2 vols. (Brussels, 1887), vol. 1, pp. 1–6.

well. Most lay just inside the walls, but there were some important smaller pockets closer to the city center.[149] As we shall see, this "exceptional" territory within Bruges would have considerable importance in the eventual location of pawnshops, gaming halls, and brothels.[150]

A view of Bruges in 1300 would have shown a star-shaped pattern of building whose arms extended along the routes leading to the most prominent city gates. There were nine of these, and in the course of the fourteenth century they came to be masterpieces of fortification and extravagant building. Most of them were the direct successors to those they replaced from the first walling of the city. But on the city's north side, where the second walling included a noticeable bulge of new territory, there was a quite new situation. This was where the watercourses, Lange Rei, Oude Zwin, the canal to Damme, and the double moat of the fortifications, intersected, making for considerable complication. With great care and expense three new city gates were arranged to allow for both maximum traffic and defense. This complex included a sluice at the end of the Lange Rei, as well as the gate built just inside it, which consisted of two towers and two bridges.[151] This "Speie" or "Sluice" Gate was joined by the St. Nicholaus Gate and the St. Lenaart Gate to form the "Dampoort" complex.[152] This costly and elaborate combining of defense and access is an important indication of the growing power of waterborne commerce from the Zwin. Subtly, yet inexorably, Bruges was growing and reorienting itself towards this new economic stimulus.

Even if the primary motive for building new walls was to provide defense, there were other advantages as well, and these did not elude Bruges magistrates. Some historians have pointed to the attempt to bring unruly workers living on the fringes of the *schependom* within the jurisdiction of the city. In the case of Bruges this seems to have had little importance, however, certainly much less than in Ypres.[153] The desire to wrest control of territory from the various seigneuries surrounding Bruges and to arrange that new territory in coherent blocks was also apparent. Such actions were akin to

149 Ryckaert, *Stedenatlas*, p. 83: among these were St. Jan's and St. Christoffel's churches and their immediate vicinities, both important commercial areas.

150 Guy Dupont, *Maagdenverleidsters, hoeren en speculanten: Prostitutie in Brugge tijdens de Bourgondische Periode (1385–1515)* (Bruges, 1996), p. 66; Nicholas, *Medieval Flanders*, p. 131 and n. 14.

151 Coornaert, "De middeleeuwse vestingswerken," 58–60.

152 The St. Nicholaus and St. Lenaart gates were often called by the name of the land routes leading through them – Koolkerke and Dudzele. St. Lenaart was also called the Watermill Gate; see Ryckaert, *Stedenatlas*, p. 93.

153 E. I. Strubbe originally made this arguement in "Van de eerste naar tweede omwalling," see Nicholas, *Town and Countryside*, p. 54, for further discussion.

Bruges's insistent efforts to control the Zwin ports as well as internal waterways in West Flanders. But commercial motives were also at play in the new walling, with its vast new territory, the increase in the number of city gates by a third, and careful attention to maintaining or enhancing traffic while providing for defense. Consciously or not, the new fortifications also allowed Bruges's city government to fix the places of trade and to profit by them through leasing or direct taxation in a uniform and efficient manner. The result was not only the achievement of the general topography of the city for the rest of the Ancien Régime, but also the establishment, thanks to the market places and commercial buildings of the city, of its economic topography.

Commercial Bruges began at the city gates themselves. Most of these of course connected the city to the prominent trade routes leading to the interior, as we have seen. A tax was collected, based on some estimate of the value of goods, on traffic passing into the city via these routes.[154] The city auctioned off to the highest bidder the right to collect this tax, and this remained a steady, if lesser, source of revenue for the city.[155] Income came also from the moats and defensive ditches of the city, whose fishing rights were also sold to the highest bidder. The city's walls also provided sites for windmills, which numbered at least seven by shortly after 1300. These were joined by at least four city-owned watermills built at various spots along Bruges's inner waterways. All these mills were leased out on annual contracts.[156]

Inside the city the evidence of a new, man-made environment began literally underfoot, for in the course of the fourteenth century the city paved virtually all of its major streets. This was accomplished with large quantities of imported paving stones, of four different types and provenances. Brabant stone seems to have been preferred as a rule, but paving stones from Artois, the Tournaisis, and the upper Landenian (Léau) were purchased as well.[157] Between 1332 and 1398 fifteen contractors shared the work of paving Bruges's streets at a cost of nearly £12,000 par.[158] This was only the beginning of the costs shouldered by the city in providing urban infrastructure.

154 This was known as the Kleine Tol (Small Toll): see van Houtte, *Geschiedenis*, p. 198.

155 See below chapter 3.

156 Fishing rights were divided up into roughly nine areas of the city's canals, which were rented out for varying terms; see L. Gilliodts-Van Severen, *Inventaire analytique des archives de Bruges*, 7 vols. (Bruges, 1871–1885), vol. IV, p. 142; Ryckaert, *Stedenatlas*, pp. 177–178 for windmills, watermills, and further literature.

157 Sosson, *Travaux publics*, pp. 88–92, see especially table 7.

158 See ibid., table 35, p. 172, which gives the list of contractors, of whom three performed the bulk of the work.

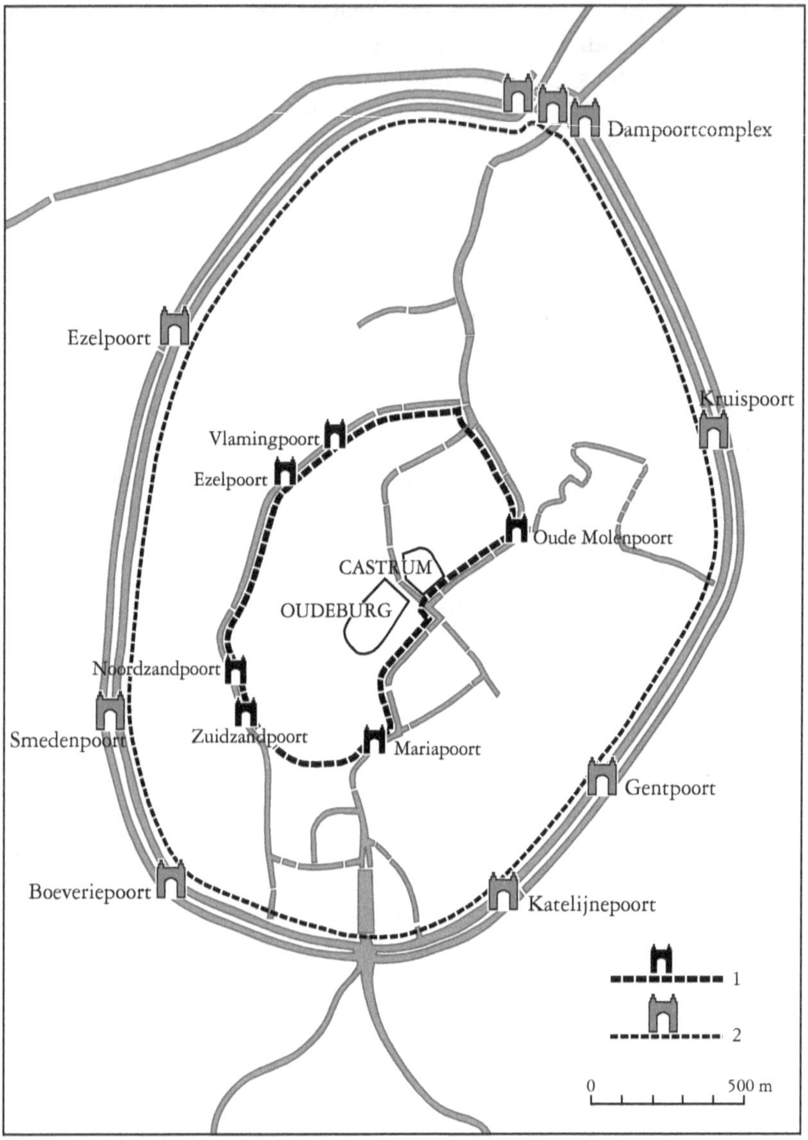

Map 7: The city gates. Shown are both the 1127 (1) and the 1297 (2) fortifications with their corresponding gates. Even after the disappearance of the twelfth-century gates, their names remained as significant streets in the city.

The city accounts are full of bills for providing fountains and the pipes necessary to provide them with water, costs for drainage ditches, and naturally the considerable expenses of improving and maintaining walls, canals, and public buildings. It is little wonder that these expenses in most years accounted for between 13 and 16 percent of the budget and in exceptionally costly years the outlay could total a quarter to a third of the city's expenditure.[159]

The city government's influence on building did not end with the public works it built and maintained, it also extended to private building in the city. Fire and its prevention were important concerns of the Bruges magistrates throughout the Middle Ages, which meant in practice encouraging construction with stone and brick, with roofs made of tile rather than thatch. Bruges lies in a region nearly bereft of quality building stone, and transporting such stone from distant quarries was very expensive. From the thirteenth century bricks offered a partial solution, and were used in enormous quantities in building the new city walls. These bricks were produced in nearby villages of West Flanders, minimizing transport costs. And to reduce costs still further, the city began its own brickyard in 1331 in the nearby village of Ramskapelle, which allowed the heavy cargo to be transported to the city via its own canals.[160] These materials were intended for the most part for city projects, but the decline in the cost of building in brick instead of wood resulted in the appearance of numerous private brick buildings by 1300.[161]

The most direct intervention by the city in building customs came in the selection of roofing material. As dangerous as wooden walled houses could be in a crowded and built-up neighborhood, the greatest danger of rapid ignition and spread of fire came from thatched roofs. As in the countryside, these were probably universal in the earliest houses in Bruges. Wood and thatch may have been responsible for a great fire that apparently destroyed much of the city, including the Burg, in 1184, with much loss of life as well.[162] To counteract this threat, tile, slate, even shake shingles,

[159] Ibid., p. 14; the highest percentages were recorded in 1400–1403.

[160] Ibid., pp. 71–79. In a few years, the city had paid for the construction of four brick kilns, and had made arrangements to improve the canal leading to the city. In a short time, the brickyard was producing 5–8,000,000 bricks per year.

[161] It would be centuries before wooden buildings completely disappeared from the cityscape, however. See Luc Devliegher, *Les maisons à Bruges* (Lanoo/Tielt, 1975), pp. xii–xiii; Ryckaert, *Stedenatlas*, p. 108 and Dirk van Eenhooghe, "De vroegste bakstenen huizen in Brugge." *Het Brugs Ommeland* 38 (1998), 107–128.

[162] Ryckaert, *Stedenatlas*, p. 109 and n. 304.

were preferable, and there is evidence that before 1232 the city had taken steps to require roofs of these materials, at least in the city center. This is the earliest evidence of such a measure in the entire Low Countries, and may have resulted in the majority of buildings in the inner city and along the principal streets and squares being at least more fire resistant.[163] Fire fighting was the responsibility of everyone in a medieval city, and Bruges both required and encouraged its people to combat fires energetically. For this purpose, neighborhood patrols were sent out and lookouts were posted in the Belfort to signal a fire at its earliest appearance. It was then the responsibility of all the able-bodied to turn out for the bucket brigades. City aldermen or other members of the city administration or the comital bailiff supervised, often providing the buckets and ladders for the volunteer fire fighters. Bruges encouraged self-help by setting aside money to pay those who manned the buckets, the so-called "Brandghelde," as well as reimbursing anyone for loss or damage of property used in fighting a fire.[164]

Whether through good fortune or effective preventive measures, Bruges suffered relatively little from destructive fires. The city never had cataclysms such as those suffered by a number of late-medieval and early modern cities, though it had a number of small fires in the course of the fourteenth century. The worst fires of the late-medieval period in Bruges came in 1412 and 1415, when about 120 houses were destroyed in a neighborhood east of the Potterierei, and another two hundred were lost in an area north of the Smedenstraat. Though destructive, it is significant that neither fire struck the inner commercial and administrative districts of the city.[165]

163 The evidence for this comes from a reference in a charter from neighboring Aardenburg; see Marc Ryckaert and W. P. De Zutter, "Brandgevaar en bouwvoorschriften in de Middeleeuwen. Een vroeg Vlaams Voorbeeld: Aardenburg 1232," *Archief uitgegeven door het Koninklijk Zeeuwsch Genootschap der Wetenschappen* (Middelburg, 1976), 14–38; and Marc Ryckaert, "Brandbestrijding en overheidsmaatregelen tegen brandgevaar tijdens het Ancien Régime," in *Het openbaar initiatief van de Gemeenten in België* (Brussels, 1982), pp. 252–255, which puts the Bruges initiatives in the context of other cities in the Low Countries.

164 Ryckaert, "Brandbestrijding," p. 250; for "fire money" see Wyffels and Vandewalle (eds.), *Rekeningen*, vol. II, pt. I, p. 343: "den scouthete ende sin knapen van den brande die was int Maegheden straetkin." Another fire is recorded in 1305 (ibid., 713 and regularly thereafter). From the accounting year 1318, the expenses were listed under a separate rubric: SAB, SR 1318, f. 118r, "Uutgheven van brandghelde." In the same account a special reward was given to the bellringer of St. Donatian's church who spotted a fire and rang his bell in alarm before the city firewatchers spotted it from their perch in the Belfort: ibid., f. 56v. "item doe den clocludere van sinte donaes omme dat hi de clocke cloppede eer dat de wachters wisten up tbeelfroit." Other accounts list such things as payment for the injury sustained by a man from Ypres in fighting a fire (Wyffels and Vandewalle (eds.), *Rekeningen*, vol. II, pt. I, p. 716) and payment of damages to a man whose house was destroyed in order to make a firebreak (SAB, SR 1386–1387, f. 118r).

165 Ryckaert, *Stedenatlas*, p. 109; Ryckaert, "Brandbestrijding," p. 247.

SQUARES AND MARKETS

Care for commercial access was nowhere more apparent than in the creation and maintenance of commercial spaces and buildings in the city. By 1300, these too had become fixed in the cityscape as well as coming under regulation by the *schepenen* and guilds. As in any market, numerous interests were at stake. On the one hand, city residents demanded easy access to foodstuffs and other necessities, while insisting as well on fair and transparent trade. It was also in the interest of public order that grain, in particular was present in abundance and available first to the city's bread and pastry bakers. But as we have seen in the case of the famine of 1315–1317, the city administration was very reluctant to intervene directly in the grain market except in the very greatest necessity. Other interests to be balanced included those of foreign merchants who demanded commercial buildings and honest weighing facilities, standardized brokerage fees, rapid relief in legal and trade disputes, and security for their valuable cargoes and considerable sums of ready money. Guilds demanded control of the manufacturing process of the goods they supervised, including the raw materials, method of manufacture, and in some cases the circumstances of marketing. Over and through all of this lay the city's desire for revenue from the trade transacted in its squares and streets. Bruges's considerable success as a commercial center cannot be understood apart from this provision of the "hard" infrastructure of trade – the buildings, facilities and regulation needed for meeting and balancing the needs of wants of residents and foreigners alike.

The oldest and in many respects the greatest of Bruges's commercial buildings was the Belfry and its attached halls standing on the south side of the Groote Markt ("Great Market"), the central and commanding market of the medieval city. Its location attests to the importance of the intersection of the overland routes from the south and south-east.[166] The building long had a mixed purpose reflected in its architecture: the tower, or Belfort, was the city's symbol and the repository of its archives. Until 1280 it had also

[166] Verhulst underlined the preponderant importance of overland routes in Bruges's early topography – "Les origines et l'histoire ancienne," 48 – especially the intersection of the principal street, leading to the Burg, with the first commercial neighborhood, the Oudeburg. Locating Bruges's signature building at that point on the city map made both commercial and symbolic sense, though by the time of its construction c. 1240 much of the city's commercial growth had moved north and west. By the time of the 1280 fire, some of the Belfry was probably already constructed in stone; and in the wake of the fire, all the rebuilt part was in stone as well. The tower itself was twice heightened, once around 1300 and again in 1345–1350 when it reached two-thirds of its current height. The rest was added in 1482–1486. See Ryckaert, *Stedenatlas*, pp. 160–161.

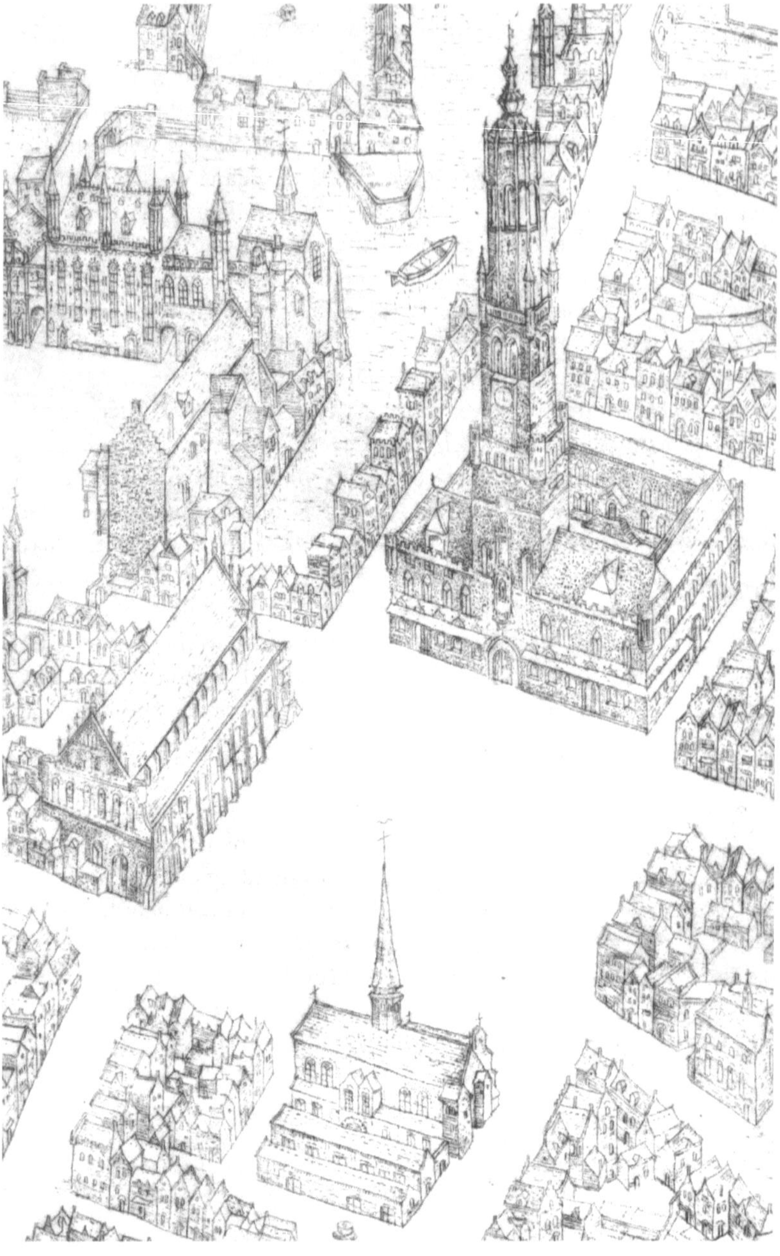

Figure 2: The Great Market (Grote Markt). At the north was St. Christoffel's church, behind which the market in eggs and dairy products was held. At the south was the Belfort and its attached sales halls; on the east was the "New" Cloth Hall or Waterhalle.

functioned as the seat of Bruges's city administration, until the latter was forced out by the fire in that year. The exhibition halls were an integral part of the building; they served a variety of crafts and trades, particularly as sales halls for Flemish cloth, produced either in Bruges or in one of a number of nearby production centers. Another area of the hall served as the "Spice Hall," where despite the name both spices and dyestuffs were sold. Other parts of the halls were given names according to the types of stalls grouped there, such as the "Glovemakers' Hall" or "Mercers' Hall."[167] In the halls' arcades were a number of shops, offering both goods and services. It was at the rear of this building, facing the Oudeburg, that the stands of the money changers were traditionally located.

In contrast to the already venerable Belfry, the "New" Hall, standing on the east side of the Market Square, was completely new in 1300, and its purpose was directly related to the needs of the rapidly growing city. With the increased traffic of small canal boats from the Zwin harbors to Bruges, there was need for a landing place protected from the elements but close to the city center. The "New" Hall, or "Waterhalle" as it was ultimately named, was an ingenious solution, standing squarely between the Burg and the Grote Markt and straddling the canal (Kraanrei) that led eventually to the route to Damme. Begun in 1285 and completed in 1294, the Waterhalle displayed all that the city fathers had learned about building using durable and fireproof materials in a design tailored to the needs of commerce. The city accounts allow a glimpse into the building process, from payments made to surveyors and to contractors for sketches, to the final considerable sums expended for acquiring the land and completing the construction work.[168] The cost in proportion to total annual outlay was enormous: in the accounting year 1283–1284 some £8,113 8s. 2d. out of a total city budget of just over £37,000 went to build the Waterhalle.[169] After the initial building was completed in 1294, new work followed in 1332–1337 that added a covered arcade along the west, facing the market side of the building. In 1366 a second level was added to the arcade along with new windows and alterations to the roof.[170]

The Waterhalle existed for commerce alone, a fact that set it apart from its neighbor, the Halletoren, which continued to serve administrative needs as

[167] For the organization of the halls according to a 1398–1399 description, see Van Houtte, *Geschiedenis*, p. 202.

[168] Luc Devliegher, *Van Waterhalle tot Provinciaal Hof* (Bruges, 1994), p. 9; Ryckaert, *Stedenatlas*, pp. 170–171.

[169] Devliegher, *Waterhalle*, p. 9 and n. 4. The total outlay for the building from 1284 to 1294 was £25,625 16s. $\frac{1}{2}$d. par.

[170] Ibid., *Waterhalle*, pp. 10–12.

Figure 3: The Waterhalle or New Cloth Hall. An architectural symbol of the shift of Bruges's commerce to waterborne freight through its outports, this structure allowed freight to be unloaded and sold without being exposed to the elements.

well as being a sales hall. Not only did the new hall allow goods to be loaded and unloaded: the upper floors were arranged as warehouse space, so that the effort and expense of moving goods from boat hold to secure storage was kept to a minimum. An enormous unimpeded space was created thanks to an extraordinary roofing system that covered an area some twenty-two meters wide without the use of center supports.[171] Its ninety-five-meter length occupied practically the entire east side of the Grote Markt, from the St. Pieter's bridge to the entrance to the Burg. With the addition of the

[171] Ibid., p. 35.

shops on the west side, and the money changers' stalls on the north side along the bridge (soon renamed the Wissel, or exchange, bridge) in the course of the fourteenth century, the new hall markedly shifted the city's commercial center northwards away from the "Old" Hall and Oudeburg towards the links with the Zwin. The clearest sign of this shift is the removal of the "Wissel," the collective location of the money changers' stalls, from the rear arcades of the Halletoren (facing the Oudeburg) to the north side of the Waterhalle.[172]

From the foundation formed by the two halls, the city's market network came to spread out and specialize further. The area in and around the Halletoren and Grote Markt became the center of the markets that provisioned the city. In the Halletoren were of course the Cloth Hall and the Spice Hall, which occupied one of its wings.[173] One of the oldest market sites in the city, formed by the intersection of the Kortrijk and Ghent roads on the south side of the Oudeburg, became the Groot (later the West) Vleeshuis (Meat Hall).[174] The square had originally served as the Friday Market, which was moved (presumably because of increasing size) to a place outside the original city walls, just west of 't Zand.[175] The city administration organized and administered two other important market sites for food. The fruit market was held on the Grote Markt in front of the Belfry, offering in 1318 at least "raisins, figs, and things pertaining thereto."[176] Cheese, butter, and milk were sold at a city-owned "Butterhouse" (*Boterhuis*) that stood on the north end of the Grote Markt, next to St. Cristoffel's church.[177] It contained some eighty stalls, and together with the adjoining square, the "Egg Market" (*Eiermarkt*), and a second, small "Boterhuis" nearby, satisfied the demand for dairy products in the city.[178] The fish market became increasingly important in the course of the fourteenth century, and was held in front of the guildhall of the fish sellers on the north-east side of the Grote Markt.[179] The grain trade shifted in the course of the fourteenth

[172] The significance of this shift will be discussed in chapter 4.

[173] Duclos, *Bruges, histoire et souvenirs*, p. 435.

[174] The building probably belonged to the Butchers' guild, as did the Great Meat Hall in Ghent. See Duclos, *Bruges, histoire et souvenirs*, pp. 494–495; Ryckaert, *Stedenatlas*, p. 174.

[175] Ryckaert, *Stedenatlas*, p. 174.

[176] SAB, SR 1318, f. 1r: "fruitstallen op den maerct, van rosin, fighen ende datter toe behord."

[177] Ryckaert, *Stedenatlas*, p. 162. This may have been synonymous with the "Caeshuus," whose fifty-five sales stalls were rented out to those named in the account of 1304; see Wyffels and Vandewalle (eds.), *Rekeningen*, vol. II, pt. 2, pp. 372–374.

[178] Van Houtte, *Geschiedenis*, p. 198. The second Boterhuis was in the St. Jacobstraat just down the street from the Eiermarkt; see Ryckaert, *Stedenatlas*, p. 160.

[179] André Vanhoutryve, *De vishandel en het visambacht te Brugge tot op het einde van het oud regiem* (Bruges, 1975), pp. 41–50.

century from a site outside the south gates of the Burg to the Waterhalle itself. The site thus vacated became the location of the city's second Meat Hall.[180]

Thus arranged, the city's food markets definitely favored locations in and around the Grote Markt, or, as in the case of both meat halls, near it. There was a good deal of sense in this, given that most of Bruges's food was conveyed either in carts or on the hoof along the roads leading to the city. Grain was probably the exception, and we have seen that it arrived and was sold from the Waterhalle, again along the Grote Markt. Commodities like cloth and domestic wool were also bought and sold in this more southern commercial district, reflecting perhaps patterns that considerably antedate 1300.[181]

Although never a market or "city" square in any strict sense before 1300, the Burg also changed in the course of the century. After the belfry fire of 1280, the city administration began to take up residence in buildings that were gradually being deserted by the count. Thus the *schepenen* moved their judicial sessions to the "Ghiselhuus," the former comital prison that stood on the southern "secular" side of the Burg. For nearly a century the *schepenen* made do with what was probably a ramshackle building, before tearing it down and beginning the construction of the present City Hall (Stadhuis) in 1376. The former comital residence, 't Steen, became in the course of the century the city's prison.[182]

The Burg's commercial side came to be located around St. Donatian's church, in a series of small, enclosed shops built between the pillars of the church facing the Burg square. Apparently licenses to build these were granted to relatives of canons or friends of the church before 1345. By the 1370s there were six of them, which were rented out at an annual rate.[183] During the Bruges fair in May it became the custom to rent out a good deal of space to merchants, particularly around the cloisters where

180 Ryckaert, *Stedenatlas*, p. 164. The increasing numbers and prominence of meat and fish halls in the city attest to those foods' importance in the late-medieval diet.

181 The Wolhuis was the market for native and more common wools. It occupied a part of the old comital castle fronting on the street that became known as the Wollestraat. See Van Houtte, *Geschiedenis*, p. 98.

182 The Steen served as a debtors' prison as well. The Burg square was the city's execution site and ceremonial center; many of the city's scribes and other functionaries were housed in another building taken over from the count, the Love. See Ryckaert, *Stedenatlas*, p. 163.

183 BAB, St. Donaas, A47, Acta Capituli, f. 2r, dated 17 July 1345, states a new policy that no one should obtain a stall unless recommended and examined in full chapter and found worthy of holding such a stall. In December, 1345 a license to construct a stall was given to Jan Withoen and his wife Christinne, and another to two nieces of a perpetual canon in the church (ff. 5–6). The receipts for the six rooms are recorded in BAB, St. Donaas, G2, f. 2v (1375–1380): "Ex sex camerulis infra pilaria ecclesie versus Burgum."

Figure 4: The Burg. The facing buildings – the Stadhuis (begun in the late fourteenth century) and St. Donatian's (Saint Donaas church) – at the south and north corners of the square defined the mixed clerical/administrative nature of the space.

the canons resided. The church even hired its own security guard during the fair.[184] Precisely when the commercialization of these spaces began is not known, but their role and liveliness of trade they brought resulted in some discomfiture for the canons of the church, who lived adjoining the church just east of the Waterhalle. These discomforts came out clearly in

184 Ibid: "Pro locatione claustri in nundinis pro parte eccelsie, £58 15s"; ibid., f. 5r, "Item Johanni van Oest pro claustro custodiens in nundinis Brugensis. 25s." These duties were described in a hiring agreement with Johannes Slabbaerd in October, 1346 (SAB, Acta, ff. 14v–15r) as keeping watch over the cloister during the "tribus noctibus de Brugghemaerct et periculo suo."

discussions held in chapter meetings about what to do about the commerce on their doorstep.

One problem was what types of businesses these rooms and other church properties should house. One of the stalls between the church pillars was built by the sword maker Jan de Bavenkove; other church property, particularly that along the present-day Philipstockstraat on the west side of the Burg at the Posterne gate, was rented out to goldsmiths.[185] A grant in January 1346 to Gerard le Madere, a *poorter* of Bruges, of a market stall built against St. Christoffel's church on the Eiermarkt was made on the condition that he should not permit any quarrels or other "illicit goings-on" that might "violate the church."[186] In 1354 the chapter granted to Georges and Jacob Hauscilt the rear portion of a cellar that they were to open up by cutting a door through to the street, probably so as to use it to store wine. It was sold in 1364 to the hosteller Jacob Visch on the condition that he would not employ it as a tavern or drinking spot.[187] The uneasy relationship between chapter and merchants apparently boiled over in 1362, when the chapter ordered all merchants who frequented the cloister to be ejected by the bailiff, with the exception of sellers of books, eyeglasses, and parchment.[188] This was apparently an idle threat because two years later all merchants selling "in claustro" were ordered to provide one worker to the church for every three feet of space they occupied. Further, they were

[185] BAB, St. Donaas, A47, Acta Capituli, f. 9r, Feb. 1346, grant to Johannes and Hannekin his son. Johannes was dead by 1355: see ibid., f. 95r. The chapter owned houses in the Wapenmakerstraat, rented mostly to armorers; see ibid., f. 73r (14 June 1352), recording the house rented to Stasin de Velde, armorer and barber, "in vico vocato Wapenstrate" next to the house rented to Johannes Hereman, also an armorer. The goldsmiths were clustered in a street called "anteposternam" in the sources, indicating a location along the then "Silversmith" street, now the Philipstockstraat, adjacent to the Posterne gate leading to the cloister. In the 1350s at least half a dozen houses and shops were rented out to goldsmiths there; see BAB, St. Donaas, A47, Acta Capituli, ff. 62r, 71r–v, 73r, 79v, 117r, 157v, 158r. For lists of names, see A. Dewitte, "Goud en zilversmeden in de kerkrekeningen van Sint-Donaas te Brugge, 1251–1587," *Biekorf* 76 (1975–76), 240–241.

[186] BAB, St. Donaas, A47, Acta Capituli, f. 7r; rental was made partly on condition that "non permittat rixam seu aliam illicitam conversacionem in eadem unde possit ecclesia violari . . ."

[187] Visch was a well-known broker/hosteller; see chapter 5. The agreement stipulated that wine could be stored and retrieved there from the first morning bell until the ringing of the bell called "Ave Maria" at dusk. The last item reads: "Item, non tenebit tabernam neque potationes in cellario . . ." See BAB, St. Donaas, A47, Acta Capituli, f. 167v, 6 September 1364.

[188] BAB, St. Donaas, A47, Acta Capituli, f. 147v: "Eodem die [11 August 1362] Cum videretur multis inconveniens tot et tantos mercatores vendere in claustro ordinatum est in capitulo et per ipsum capitulum preceptum et iniunctum ballivo prepositure huius ecclesie, quod ipse eiciat omnis huiusmodi mercatores seu personas alias, res suas vendentes in claustro, eisque inhibeat ne ipsi seu quivis alii de cetero aliquas mercaturas vendant in claustro sub pena amissionis rerum ipsarum . . . Ab hac autem ordinatione et inhibicione excipiuntur mercatores librorum, berillorum et pergameni qui ibidem in claustro fieri conceduntur."

ordered to refrain from quarreling, disputing or "swearing horribly" while selling on pain of a 100 s. par. fine and perpetual banishment from the cloister. Hucksters and vagrant merchants were to be excluded altogether.[189] In 1370 the chapter banned use of the church by merchants selling during the Bruges fair, an act that departed from past tradition.[190]

Merchants and city officials were quite literally within the gates of the Burg in the fourteenth century, causing the chapter of St. Donatian's to try to both profit from and resist these newcomers. But it is difficult to find a spot either in the church or cloisters where business did not reach. Candles were sold in the church, a variety of wares in the cloister, and permanent market stalls were constructed between the pillars of the church arcade in the course of the century. Even part of the cellar at the rear of the cloister was remodeled to serve a commercial purpose. And the chapter was a major landlord in nearby neighborhoods largely occupied by goldsmiths and armorers, as has been mentioned. Yet there are signs of a turn away from such seemingly irreligious commerce. The 1362 ban on all merchants save those selling books, spectacles, and parchment as well as that making the church off limits during the Bruges fair both point in this direction. Eventually this more limited commercial focus won out, for by the fifteenth century the Burg was known for its book merchants, writing offices staffed by trained scribes, and market in art objects. The quarrelsome, swearing, polyglot throng of merchants was directed elsewhere.[191]

189 BAB, St. Donaas, A47, Acta Capituli, f. 169r, [30 October 1364] "In capitulo ordinatum fuit . . . quod illi qui stabunt in claustro cum mercimoniis solvent annuatim magistro fabrice de tribus pedibus unum operarium in opere ecclesie. Item quod non poterunt rixari in vico huiusmodi stantes, nec horribiliter iurare sub pena centem sol. par. et perpetue privationis claustri supradicti. Item quo nulli portantes tafletos per villam stabunt ibidem, et ad huiusmodi personas recipiendas in dicto nostro claustro fuerint ordinati, magister fabrice et dominus Johannes Pachin et persone recepte scriberentur. In dedicatione ecclesie excluderentur omnes quovsque festum fuerit transactum. Item si contingat predictum ordinationem revocari per nos, post ipsam revocationem poterint stare per quindecim dies et non ultra."

190 BAB, St. Donaas, A48, Acta Capituli, f. 4r: "Eodem die [15 June 1370] extitit ordinatum in dicto capitulo quod pro nulla re nundifiant alique vendiciones in nundinis Brugensis in ecclesia et hoc fuit concordatum in capitulo generali." In the margin, "Interdicitur forum nundinarum in ecclesia."

191 A few notaries already seem to have possessed one or another of these rooms at an early date. Jan Abeel is one example; see BAB, St. Donaas, A48, Acta Capituli, f. 86r and Murray, *Notarial Instruments*, pp. 50–51. In the fifteenth century, there were apparently several writing offices there as well as bookshops and artists' shops; see Duclos, *Bruges: Histoire et souvenirs*, pp. 384, 445. In medieval Paris, scribes, bookbinders, and booksellers congregated in the area around Notre Dame; see Richard H. and Mary A. Rouse, *Manuscripts and Their Makers: Commercial Book Producers in Medieval Paris, 1200–1500*, 2 vols. (Turnhout, Belgium, 2000), vol. 1, pp. 19–24.

Where then did they go? We have seen in the course of the thirteenth century a decided turn northward in many of the public buildings and private construction projects in Bruges. This was both a response to the stream of waterborne commerce from the Zwin and encouragement for development along these waterways. With the Waterhalle as terminus, the city constructed an infrastructure in support of trade: 200 meters north along the canal stood the city crane, a large wooden structure powered by the "crane children," youths walking a circular treadmill. The crane was intended for heavy cargoes, like barrels of wine and beer, beyond the capacity of the Waterhalle's equipment. It was a remarkable machine, both visually (as the many late medieval and early modern pictures of it attest) and mechanically, given its ingenious adaptation of windmill technology.[192] The first Bruges crane dates from 1288, but was removed during the work on the Waterhalle. In 1290 the small square adjoining the Vlamingstraat became the permanent site of the crane, and was known thereafter as the Kraanplein as the waterway leading out to the Spiegelrei became the Kraanrei.[193] Along with a similar crane in Damme, this was one of the two oldest city-owned and constructed cranes in the Low Countries.[194]

The other city-provided business infrastructure along the Kraanrei consisted of a series of public scales whose precise location and management was a point of controversy at the end of the thirteenth century. The official city scale lay at the end of the Kraanrei where it intersected the St. Jans bridge at the beginning of the Spiegelrei. There it served the so-called "Great Toll," a feudal right originally held by the count of Flanders that was levied upon goods imported into the city by boat according to their weight. By right this was to be the only scale in the city able to weigh goods of more than sixty pounds.[195] In the late thirteenth century foreign merchants revolted against the inefficiencies and corruption of this system, winning from the count permission both to update the equipment used at the Great Toll and to distribute scales elsewhere in the city. By the end of the fourteenth century there were four public scales: one on the Grote Markt, another at the crane, one granted to the Spaniards on the St. Jans

[192] R. Degryse, "De oudste houten kranen in de Vlaamse en andere Havens (13de–16de eeuw)," *ASEB* 128 (1991), 5–46 and 153–187.

[193] J. A. van Houtte has 1292 as the date, which may have been when the first receipts of the crane are listed in the city accounts – see Degryse, "De oudste houten kranen," 20.

[194] Ibid., 8–10. Damme's crane is actually the first recorded when in May, 1269 Countess Margaretha granted a privilege to construct "ung instrument que ont appelle communement crane . . ." Gilliodts-Van Severen, *Coutumes Quartier de Bruges*, vol. II, pp. 177–178, no. XII. In 1323 Damme and Bruges combined to prevent Sluis from constructing a similar crane, which both cities regarded as a violation of their right of staple.

[195] Van Houtte, *Geschiedenis*, p. 200.

square, and another granted to the English, just off St. Jan's square in the Engelsestraat or English street.[196]

It was along this axis – Market, Crane, Toll – that the great commercial district of Bruges spread out and took shape. With the public buildings as foundation, the private infrastructure supporting trade arose as well. So, for example, St. Pieter's bridge became the "Exchange" bridge with the move of the money changers to the north end of the Waterhalle.[197] The city's hostels, where lodging, warehousing, and a number of other business services were offered, were almost all located within close proximity of this axis. Many were located along the Vlamingstraat, the street that ran parallel with the Kraanrei from the north-east corner of the Grote Markt, past the Crane square to end in a square that took its name from one of the great hosteller families of Bruges, the Beurs square. Some hostels also stood around St. Jan's bridge near the Great Toll.[198] Others, notably that belonging to the Metteneye family, were to be found a little further north, just behind what is now known as the Spinolarei in the Schoofstraatje.[199] Not only was a location in this commercial neighborhood important for the hosteller's guests, it also simplified the hosteller's own business. As we shall see in a later chapter, part of that business depended on the collection and exchange of trade information.

The outer limits of Bruges's trading neighborhood were set off by the four great mendicant houses, forming a rough rectangle with the Franciscans in the south, the Dominicans to the east, the Carmelites in the north-east, and the Augustinians in the north-west. It was in these houses that members of foreign merchant communities established altars and burial places, and were granted the right to use meeting halls and store archives. Between these monasteries and the Kraanrei/Spiegelrei trade artery the communities of foreign merchants settled in what became densely populated neighborhoods. Although certain streets came to bear the names of some of these foreign merchant communities, and hostellers typically specialized in hosting guests of one nation or another, Bruges never had walled-off enclaves consisting of one nation of merchants to the exclusion of all others. To a remarkable and perhaps unique extent, foreign and native merchants mixed and met in their hostels, in the neighborhoods where some of the

196 Ibid.

197 See chapter 4. As mentioned above, the gold- and silversmiths congregated near St. Pieter's bridge.

198 This was the location of Jacob Sconeberch's hostel. A further advantage of a location along one or another waterway was the ease of shifting cargo in and out of the cellar.

199 Heidi Deneweth and Yvette Kemel, "Een verdwenen middeleeuwse wijk tussen Koningstraat, Boomgaardstraat en Verversdijk," *Het Brugs Ommeland* 40 (2000), 156–157.

Figure 5: The Crane square and the Bourse. This section of the Vlamingstraat (Fleming street) connected the important commercial squares of the city crane at right and the Bourse at left. The street was lined with important hostels and warehouses.

better-established foreigners either rented or purchased houses, and of course in the numerous drinking, bathing, and prostitution establishments. All these played a role in the success of Bruges as a commercial city.[200]

Drink was serious business in Bruges, both as a wholesale and retail trade and as the most important source of tax revenue for the city. The location of drinking establishments closely followed the distribution of hostels, since

200 Marc Ryckaert, "Geographie eines Weltmarktes: Handel und Stadttopographie im mittelalterlichen und frühneuzeitlichen Brügge," in K. Friedland (ed.), *Brügge-Colloquium des hansischen Geschichtsvereins* (Cologne and Vienna, 1990), pp. 3–12; Anke Greve, "Vreemdelingen in de stad: integratie of uitsluiting?" in *Core and Periphery in Late Medieval Urban Society* (Leuven and Apeldoorn, 1997), pp. 153–163.

many hostel's also served drink. Their locations showed remarkable stability over time. For example, confiscation records from 1305 mention revenue returned from cellars of properties owned by Bruges Leliaerts, indicating a commercial use. Cellars were most commonly used as taverns, for wine storage, or both. A rental agreement issued by the chapter of St. Donatian's explicitly forbids its tenant to use the cellar as a tavern "in the manner of taverns in the town."[201] These 1305 confiscation records show clutches of commercial cellars in the Vlamingstraat (four), the St. Janstraat (near the Kraanplein) and the St. Jansplein (five cellars), and the Grote Markt (six cellars).[202] Areas to the south-west of the Grote Markt were also represented, such as the Steenstaat (three), the Wulhuusstraat (one), the Oudeburg (one), and the Mariastraat (one), but not to the same degree. Significant as well is the fact that many of the cellars named in the commercial district were attached to houses bearing names drawn from images (e.g. Ten Zwanekinne, "At the Little Swan") or visual puns on a family name (e.g. Ter Buerze, which was both a family and the Flemish name for a purse), which were common ways for inns and taverns to identify themselves on signs and placards.[203]

A complementary source of 1305 fills out some of the information in the town accounts. In a list of fines extracted from owners of "cabarets and cellars" from that year, twenty-seven cellars and seven houses are listed.[204] At least two of the names appear on both the confiscation list and the list of fines, which strongly suggests that the list was drawn up according to the location of the cellars. If this hypothesis is true, then again the bulk of these drinking and entertainment establishments was divided between the Vlamingstraat, the Beurs square area, and the Grote Markt.[205] Joseph Marechal, in tracing the origins of the Bourse of Bruges, was struck by the concentration of inns and drinking establishments, although he did not draw the obvious conclusion that it was precisely this kind of concentration that encouraged, indeed enabled, the foundation of a mercantile

[201] As we have seen, the conditions attached to the sale to Jacob Visch forbade its use as a drinking establishment. A later document (BAB, St. Donaas, A48, Acta Capituli, f. 4r) made clear the connection between cellars and taverns in Bruges: [8 Oct. 1369] "Et primo non poterit tenere tabernam neque potationes in cellario ad modum tabernarum ville."

[202] Wyffels and Vandewalle, *Rekeningnen*, II, pt. 1, pp. 656–661.

[203] Commercial establishments were most often known by a device or some other house name, while personal residences were generally known by the name of a current or past resident.

[204] The list is from a bailiff's account of May 1305 (ARA, RR 1008) of "Des cabres et des chelliers." Notable among the names are "The Lion," "The Silver," "The Cat," "The Egg," and those named after a clutch of well-known Bruges families: "Cellar of Iakemon Bonin, Raven Danwilt," or "li chellier desous Sire Jehan de Hertsberghe."

[205] We know that the "Moppelier" and Winendale were on the Vlamingstraat and "The Cat" was on the Grote Markt, and given that these are separated on the list by fifteen other establishments, some correlation of place on the list and location in the city is likely.

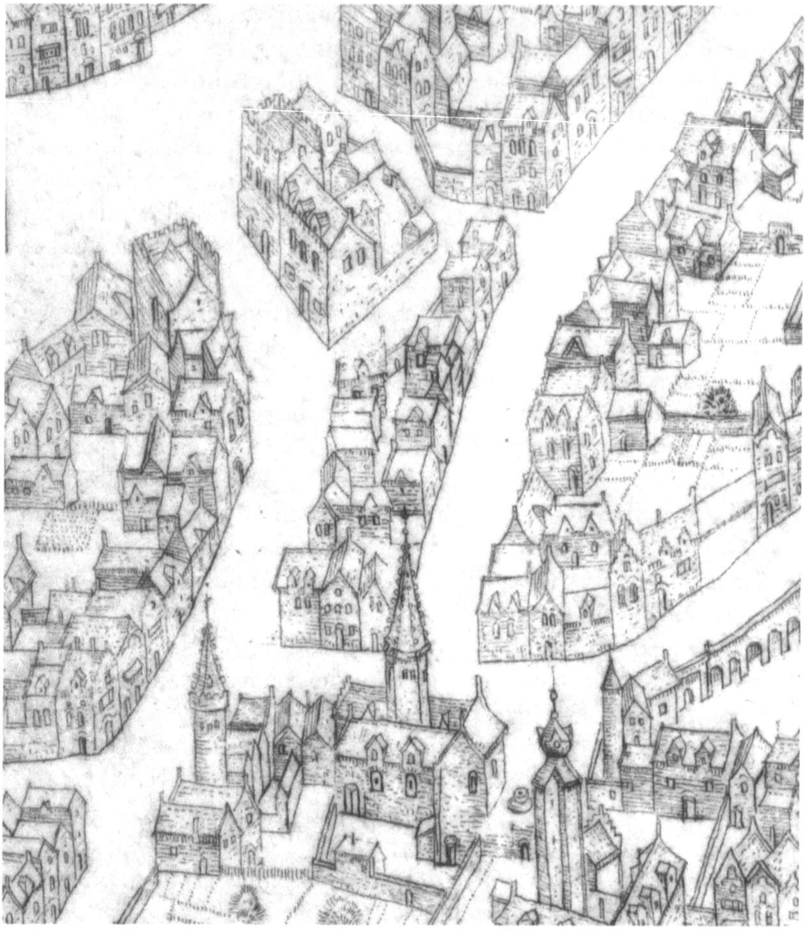

Figure 6: The Bourse and its neighborhood. Pictured is the Bourse square in the upper left with the complex of streets – Vlaming, Grauwerker, and Kuiper – that were its tributaries. Many foreign merchants resided in this area, and later, in the fifteenth century, the Medici bank established itself in the Hotel Bladelin, which is pictured in the centre foreground.

exchange.[206] Long before names and buildings, links of communication between and among merchants were created and renewed in the inns and alehouses of Bruges. In this sense, the creation of "nation houses" for the various groups of resident merchants also merely gives a name to a process long antedating official recognition.

[206] Joseph Marechal, *Geschiedenis van de Brugse Beurs* (Bruges, 1949), p. 38, and see below chapter 6.

Evidence of the longevity of some of these inns and taverns rests in the names, which sometimes remained unchanged from owner to owner. For example, in the Vlamingstraat "Ten Baerze" occurs in both 1305 and 1377, as does the Inn called "In Monpellier" in the Philipstockstraat, adjacent to St. Pieter bridge,[207] and "Te Perone" on the Steenstraat.[208] And place names occur in describing these institutions as well: "in den Wissel" (i.e. near St. Pieter bridge); "Ter Munte" (at the mint off the Geldmuntstraat); and "Ter Colve" in the Hooghstraat.[209] Taverns and hostels also seemed to cluster near mendicant houses: the Caermers bridge was the site of two taverns in the 1380s; another was found "on the canal," "next door to the Augustinians."[210] And the vicinity of churches and their churchyards was a popular location as well.[211]

The mendicant houses of Bruges also seem to have been poles of attraction for illicit or barely licit commerce complementary to that in the commercial district they surrounded. Situated as they were between the central city, with its market squares hostels, and many of the neighborhoods where foreign merchants lodged, and outer Bruges, where the teeming workers' neighborhoods were to be found, the houses of Dominicans, Franciscans, Augustinians, and Carmelites served as landmarks and signposts for situating other elements of the urban landscape.[212] As previously noted, there was also a strong affinity between the choice of location for a mendicant house and the commerce in money, particularly pawnshops. Pawning was the most popular manner of raising cash for a large swath of the urban population, and not only for the poorest, as will be shown in chapter 4. The location of both licensed and unlicensed pawnshops in Bruges had much to do with clerical geography. The licensed pawnshop called the "Great Cahorsin" was located near the site of the original Franciscan house, which

207 ARA RR 1008 (1305) and 1026 memb. 16 (Sept. 1378) and 1032 (1383–1384) "in Monpelier bachten Sint Donaes Clooster."

208 Wyffels and Vandewalle, *Rekeningen*, vol. II, pt. 1, p. 660, and ARA, RR 1029, memb. 12 (1379).

209 ARA, Rekenkamer, RR 1018, memb. 13 (1377) in a list of those who sold wine during the Bruges market, who numbered fifty-four in this year.

210 ARA Rekenkamer, RR 1032 (1383): one belonged to the widow of Gillis van der Leye; the Vrauwe ten Hille owned the inn "vor de Caermers" in the same year, and Jan Cattyn's inn was "up de Reye iuxta Auwestinen." (ARA, RR 1033, "Those who tapped during the Bruges market.")

211 "Pieter f. Willems in kerchof van Sinte Salvators" (ARA, RR 1033); "der Joris Macharis up Onzer Vrouwen kerchof" (ibid.).

212 Two examples of the cloisters as landmarks: SAB, SR 1310, f. 11v: "item van 1 wive die zat voer den Augustinen ter bede die staerf zonder calaenge van aeldinghers 60 lb"; the goods were held by the city until the heirs of this beggar woman came forward. The second is a homicide (SAB, SR 1384–1385, f. 101r) "item ghegheven Lauwersse den Carpere van eenre claghe ende waerhede te scrivene van Michiele f. Willems die doot ghesteken lach bachten Freren."

after their move became the location of the Augustinian house.[213] The "notorious" usurer Jan Pulsers or Pulsere was living behind the Augustinian monastery in 1344.[214] The Franciscans moved to a neighborhood with at least one large pawnshop, the house De Pauw, standing on land under the jurisdiction of the provost of St. Donatian's. The Carmelites looked right across at the pawnshop called "Het Zwaard," in a neighborhood called by one historian "the most notorious [in Bruges]" . . . full of "drinking establishments, bordellos, gaming houses, and bathhouses."[215]

The jurisdictions of the canons and provost of St. Donatian's within the walls of Bruges, the only areas within the walls that were exempt from the jurisdiction of aldermen, were well known as havens for unlicensed pawnshops and other illicit or semi-licit businesses. As mentioned above, the pawnshop De Pauw stood on land called the "Zuudproosse"; at the end of the fourteenth century there were actually two houses by this name serving as pawnshops.[216] In the Oostproosse there were also usurers in a number of houses they rented for that purpose.[217] The chapter of St. Donatian's was aware of the activities of usurers in these enclaves. For example, in October 1358 the General Chapter, led by Provost Jan de Herdsberghe, decreed that from the coming Christmas no usury was to be practiced in their jurisdiction and that known usurers were to return the goods they held in pawn to their owners. If they refused, they would be banished.[218] Whatever the intention behind this decree, it did not rid the jurisdiction of usury.[219] Nor did public excommunication permanently remove usurers from communion with the church. Jan Pulsers's corpse, for example, was accepted for burial by the Augustinians in return for a promise from his widow that she and her fiancé would make restitution to his customers.[220] Nor did the fact that he came from a family of usurers prevent Jan de Roerio from serving as chaplain in the Beguinage from 1342–1360.[221] Social and criminal penalties were apparently light for usurers.

The mendicant neighborhoods were also known for another urban institution that often skirted the law – the bathhouse. In the Bruges conversation manual of c. 1369 the proprietress of the best bathhouse in the city, "pretty

213 Marechal, *Bijdrage*, p. 17; de Roover, *Money, Banking and Credit*, pp. 113–114.

214 Marechal, *Bijdrage*, pp. 23–24; J. Marechal, "De houding van de deken van de Christenheid tegenover een woekeraar en voorkoper te Brugge in 1344," *ASEB* 97 (1954), 73–81, 77.

215 Marechal, *Bijdrage*, p. 17. 216 Ibid., p. 15. 217 Ibid., pp. 15–16.

218 BAB, St. Donaas, A47, Acta Capituli, f. 113v, under the heading "De usurariis." The measure had been discussed in a chapter session on 15 October.

219 Indeed in the fifteenth century explicit privileges were granted to usurers: see Marechal, *Bijdrage*, pp. 24, 102. In 1441 Paulus Masset and "socii" were given exclusive rights to operate as usurers.

220 Marechal, "De Houding," 78–79. 221 Marechal, *Bijdrage*, p. 24.

Natalie," lives "behind the Brothers' wall," i.e. the Dominican convent straddled by the Leertauwerstraten.[222] The 1483 English language version of the same text says of the same Nathalie that "she dwelleth after the walle of the white freres."[223] Of course it was the Carmelites, not the Dominicans, who wore the white habit. An early printed version of this long-lived text contains another variation, reporting that Nathalie now lives "behind the wall of the Augustinians."[224] As Guy Dupont has recently shown, all three of these locations were at the heart of bathing and the prostitution trade in Burgundian Bruges. The question remains, however, whether the topography of these licit and illicit trades was the same in the century before 1385.

Unfortunately, the records are even more unyielding for the earlier period than for the Burgundian period explored by Dupont. Lists of fines assessed against proprietors of bathhouses "where evil is committed" often do not give an exact location. And of course there must have been many bathhouses that were legitimate operations rather than a front for prostitution. Bathhouses after all were important in every medieval city and reached their point of greatest popularity in the fourteenth century.[225] Paris had at least thirty-two bathhouses in the middle of the thirteenth century, some for men and some for women.[226] Bruges seems to have had a similar number in the early and mid-fourteenth century, though the precise number remains unknown.[227] Yet even taking into account the deficiencies of the sources, it is still possible to get a rough idea of the distribution of bathhouses in the city.

It is clear that by 1303, when the records begin, the geography of bathing in Bruges had already been established in a form it would retain until at least the sixteenth century. As the Bruges conversation manual indicates, the neighborhoods around and beyond the chief mendicant cloisters are often mentioned as the sites of bathhouses that were fined for prostitution. So for example, in 1335–1336 the bathhouse "bachten frere chore," i.e. behind the choir of the Franciscan church, was fined as a place of prostitution.[228] Likewise, in 1353–1354, a bathhouse "bachten Jacoppinen"

[222] Gessler, *Livre des mestiers*, p. 38.
[223] Dupont, *Maagdenverleidsters*, p. 149. [224] Ibid., p. 149.
[225] *Lexikon des Mittelalters*, vol. I (Munich and Zurich, 1980), pp. 1331–1333.
[226] Jean Gimpel, *The Medieval Machine* (New York, 1976), p. 91.
[227] Several unreliable figures have been advanced, however. Gilliodts-van Severen (*Inventaire*, vol. IV, p. 151) counts twenty-three bathhouses fined in 1353 for prostitution. A check of the manuscript reveals only fourteen, several of which were fined two or three times (SAB, SR 1353–1354, ff. 27v–29v). Jacques Toussaert, *Le sentiment religieux en Flandre à la fin du Moyen-Age* (Paris, 1963), p. 390, says there were forty bathhouses c. 1300, but gives no reference for what is clearly an inflated number.
[228] SAB, SR 1335–1336, f. 22v.

(behind the Dominicans) was also fined, and from 1353–1356 an establishment known as the "Carmelites' Bathhouse" (sChermers Stove) received the repeated attention of the authorities.[229] Proximity to water as well as potential customers also played a part, for the small streets and alleys of the Oudeburg neighborhood also contained a number of bathhouses.[230] And it was not only the fronts for prostitution that clustered in these neighborhoods, for in nearly every case when the location of an "honest" bathhouse is mentioned, it lay in one of the same neighborhood as the houses of ill repute.[231]

Commercial sex, as we shall see in chapter 8, was an important and flourishing business in Bruges, and its availability was by no means limited to bathhouses. Brothels did, however, have a geographical distribution similar to that of the bathhouses. This is in no way surprising, given the importance of relatively cheap real estate, the proximity of merchant neighborhoods, and the toleration of prostitution by urban authorities. Bathhouses, houses, and rooms where "evil is committed" (to quote the accounts) were common around the three mendicant houses named above, but particularly in the neighborhood of St. Gillis parish, which lay in the vicinity of the Carmelite monastery, very near in fact to the original Franciscan foundation in Bruges.[232] The particular popularity of St. Gillis was due no doubt to the twin influences of the nearby merchant neighborhoods, where many Hanse merchants in particular were to be found.[233] And equally important was the propinquity of the "sailors' neighborhood" along the Potterierei, the last stretch of the Bruges canal leading to Damme. This area basically surrounded the Carmelite monastery and has been rightly termed the "libidinous heart" of Bruges, incorporating parts of the administrative districts of St. Nicholas and the Carmelites.[234] Not coincidentally, it was in

229 Ibid., f. 28v, and for the sChermers Stove, ibid., f. 29v, and SR 1354–1355, f. 25r, and 1355–1356, f. 29v.

230 These alleys led to the Dyver and were intended to provide rapid access to water in case of fire; see Ryckaert, "De Oudeburg te Brugge," pp. 157–159.

231 This was true, for example, in the case of a bathhouse confiscated from Jan Coepman in 1305 located "Bi den Carmers" (near the Carmelite monastery): Wyffels and Vandewalle, *Rekeningen*, vol. II, pt. I, p. 662. In the same account Belen Taysper's bathhouse is mentioned, which was in the Ghistelhof, near the Augustinian monastery. Later she was indeed fined for using her bathhouse for prostitution. SAB, SR 1332–1333, f. 9v. In 1386 an apparently honest bathhouse "en le Carmerstrate" was mentioned in a criminal case: ARA, Rekenkamer 13675, pt. 6, f. 10v.

232 Their presence was long remembered in the place name Freren acker, "the brothers' field."

233 This was near the neighborhood where the Hanse nation house (Oosterlingenhuis) was built in the fifteenth century and where Hanse merchants owned several houses in the fourteenth century. See Georg Asmussen, *Die Lübecker Flandernfahrer in der zweiten Hälfte des 14. Jahrhunderts (1358–1408)* (Frankfurt and New York, 1999), p. 77.

234 Dupont, *Maagdenverleidsters*, p. 147.

these districts that the canons and provost of St. Donatian's held significant enclaves as well, though we have no records from the fourteenth century of any fines levied on brothels in those neighborhoods.[235]

CONCLUSION

By the first decades of the fourteenth century Bruges had acquired, built, paved, and thereby grown into and organized, a space that it would retain for the rest of the Middle Ages. The second walling of 1297 marked the completion of a steady campaign of land acquisition by the city, bringing land both within and without the new set of walls under the jurisdiction of the city aldermen. Only the territory controlled by the ancient chapter and provost of St. Donatian's escaped the inexorable political pressure and abundant means of the city government. But the city acted to control more than land, for a driving imperative for the city was to acquire and dominate its route to the sea. With the application of money to build and maintain the canals, sluices, and dikes, and the dogged insistence on its staple rights, guild monopolies, and appellate jurisdiction, Bruges kept the Zwin port cities both accessible and subservient. In comparison with Ghent and Ypres, Bruges was much less concerned with the rest of its economic hinterland, caring little about clothmaking there for example, which again underlines the importance of the link to the sea.

As the city achieved its greatest expansion, so too did it organize the space within its walls in ways that were to endure for centuries. The development of urban parishes was complete before 1300, as was the construction of the convents of the mendicant orders within the walls. The city government had already begun to infiltrate and supplant comital government in the ancient Burg, leaving the central market as a purely commercial market square. Around and near this square clustered most of the food markets. The Belfort/Old Cloth Hall and the "New Cloth Hall" or Waterhalle continued to house the "traditional" cloth market, as well as the more recently prominent spice market. Just as important was the organization of other commercial space and its infrastructure. These were the spaces and implements used by Brugeois and foreign merchants, including public scales, a crane, buildings such as the toll house and the Waterhalle, and the canals and bridges along and across which flowed merchants and trade goods. By 1300 an obvious tendency of commerce to shift to the north in the

[235] Such records exist in continuous form only from the last quarter of the fifteenth century; see Dupont, *Maagdenverleidsters*, p. 199.

direction of the connection to Damme and the other Zwin ports was well established. Not only did the monumental "New" Cloth Hall straddle the waterway leading to the Zwin, effectively concentrating waterborne trade there, but it brought with it the concentration of business services provided by hostellers and money changers. The shift of the money changers from behind the Old Cloth Hall to the arcade of the "New" Hall and along St. Pieter's bridge neatly symbolizes this move northwards.

It was effectively from the central market square northwards that the financial and commercial heart of Bruges extended: along the Vlamingstraat and its tributaries, the Langhewinkel and Korte Winkel, across St. Jan's bridge to the like-named square and church. It was in these streets, squares, and alleys that the merchant communities and the hostels, taverns, and cabarets that served them came to be. Unlike in other cities, merchants of many nations lived intermingled, sharing churches and the meeting places they provided. It was not until the end of our period that foreign merchants began to acquire meeting houses of their own, sometimes purchasing those they had long rented from Bruges hostellers. This diverse concentration of trade and traders, merchants and merchandise, artisans, hucksters, hostellers, money changers, and innumerable others was responsible for Bruges's success as a great commercial city.

But there was another side to this commercial world, one removed geographically yet intimately related to the workings of the Bruges market. This was the world of the pawnshop and the bathhouse, of the various types of dwellings that served as brothels. Not accidentally these were located in neighborhoods adjacent to those favored by merchants, yet these outer reaches sheltered mostly the artisans and the urban poor. These areas, too, had taken nearly final form in the decades around 1300, and they reflected both the numbers of potential customers they had in the unmarried merchants resident in Bruges and the northward development of the city's commercial space. Thus it was the neighborhoods adjacent to the main watercourses leading out of the city that sheltered most of the "evil" hostels, where gaming, prostitution, and disorder were to be found.

All of this meant in practice that in the great contest in every medieval city between accessibility and impenetrability, it was openness that gained the upper hand in fourteenth-century Bruges. It is important not to exaggerate this quality, however, for as we have seen merchant freedom in Bruges was purchased with rigorous control and restriction upon similar freedoms outside Bruges. But careful attention was paid to ensuring access to the sea, harmonizing a distributed network of port facilities, and welcoming foreign merchants and catering to their needs, while not allowing any one group to dominate a particular part of the city. And last but certainly not least, the casting of a benign eye on the marketing of sex and gambling, seems to add up to a concerted urban policy of letting commerce rule. A fifteenth-century chronicler's description of the city around 1358 as "so flourishing because of trade and so rich in people . . ." indeed captures the pillars of Bruges's prosperity.[236] People and prosperity are a delicate and unstable achievement, however, a fact that accounts for many of the city's struggles in the fourteenth century.

236 Bruges, Stadsbibliotheek, ms 445, f. 20r.

CHAPTER 3

The measure of humanity

> ut ita etiam intelligamus contingere in partibus unius hominis sicut contingit in tota multitudine civitatis, quia singuli subtrahuntur a multitudine per mortem, aliis in loco eorum succedentibus; unde partes multitudinis fluunt et refluunt materialiter, sed formaliter manent, quia ad eadem officia et ordines substituuntur alii a quibus priores subtrahebantur, unde respublica una numero remanere dicitur.[1]
>
> Thomas Aquinas

Urban space and its use say much about a city. The layout of streets, bridges, and buildings reflects, albeit indirectly, the planning and priorities of both public and private enterprise. In a sense they are the city's skeleton, and like most skeletal remains they survive as evidence long after their designers and builders have perished. But what of these "disappeared" – the people who in their aggregate and individual selves animated Bruges in the fourteenth century? What can we know of their numbers? Their geographical origins and professions? And most of all what does this measure of the many, both great and small, tell us about the composition of a cradle of capitalism?

POPULATION

Inevitably urban historians think of producing a city's census – a head count in line with modern metrics of people who "reside" in a place. Clearly there are problems with such an approach. In a pre-statistical age, urban officials rarely bothered to assess the precise number of their city's inhabitants, not so much because they lacked the administrative means (although they sometimes did) as because their conception of number and significance differed from ours. Medieval city dwellers found greater significance in the size of a group defined by function or privilege than in absolute numbers.

[1] Thomas Aquinas, *Opera omnia, iussu impensaque Leonis XIII*, 14 vols. (Rome, 1882–), vol. XII, column 2, lines 67–74; reference in Caroline Walker Bynum, *The Resurrection of the Body in Western Christianity, 200–1336* (New York, 1995), p. 239.

This reflects a more subtle and nuanced understanding of urban residence, for medieval urban populations were very unstable, since they relied so heavily on immigration, both temporary and permanent. And the larger and more commercial the city, the greater the diversity of migrants and the complexity of their "residence" in the city would be.[2] The difficult task of the historian is to square the necessity of absolute numbers with the complex underlying reality of urban dwelling in the Middle Ages. In other words, our problem is to convey an idea of both number and kind, not only how many but simply how people lived and interacted in fourteenth-century Bruges.

There has been remarkably little dispute about the size of Bruges's medieval population and how the city ranked in Flanders and Europe as a whole. This unanimity is not due to an abundance of evidence, however, so the commonly accepted numbers must be viewed as a very rough, minimum measure of the population.[3] Essentially all estimates are based upon a muster role of the city militia dating from 1338–1340, in the heyday of Jacob van Artevelde. This *Register der Herevaerden* (literally "Campaigns Register") consists of lists of men and money collected by administrative district (*zestendeel*) for one of the ten military campaigns launched in that two-year period. Listed are the amounts of money each district gave, the names of leaders of the *poorters* or the guild supplying the men, as well as the names of the militiamen themselves.[4] Fortunately the names of men left to garrison the city in the absence of the general militia are given as well. The total of these "heads of household" amounted to 7,234.[5] This figure has subsequently been modified as uncounted groups were figured in, such as some 431 members of the brokers' guild.[6] Thus Walter Prevenier, in a classic article on Flemish demography, reckoned the city's population in the middle of the fourteenth century at between 36,738 and 45,921, depending upon whether the militia numbers were multiplied by four or five to arrive at the population.[7]

2 For the European city in general, see David Nicholas, *The Growth of the Medieval City* (London, 1997), pp. 178–182.

3 For the historiography of the question, Walter Prevenier, "La démographie des villes du comté de Flandre aux XIVe et XVe siècles. Etat de question. Essai d'interprétation," *Revue du Nord* 65 (1983), 255–275, 256; Jan Dumolyn, "Population et structures professionnelles à Bruges aux XIVe et XVe siècles," *Revue du Nord* 31 (1999), 43–64, 43.

4 J. F. Verbruggen, *Het Gemeenteleger van Brugge van 1338 tot 1340 en de namen van de weerbare mannen* (Brussels, 1962), pp. 6–7.

5 Ibid., p. 80; Verbruggen's correction of de Smet's numbers is n. 1.

6 See Carlos Wyffels's review of Verbruggen's *Gemeenteleger* in *RBPH* 76 (1963), 231–233.

7 Prevenier, "Bevolkingscijfers en professionele strukturen," pp. 279–285, and "La démographie des villes," 256.

A partial point of comparison is provided some fifty years later (1394–96) in one of the few tax lists surviving from fourteenth-century Bruges. Unfortunately these lists survive only for three of the six administrative districts, a fact partly ameliorated by the tendency of tax lists to give more reliable population numbers than militia musters. I. De Meyer, who compiled and analyzed the figures, arrived at a total of 17,914 inhabitants for what she took to be half the population of the city, or 35,828 when doubled.[8] In reviewing this number, Walter Prevenier adjusted this number to include groups exempt from taxation, such as nobles, clergy, and foreigners, resulting in the figure 37,510.[9] This falls within the same population range as preplague Bruges, indicating a remarkably stable population through a period of war and disease. The evidence of long-term stability is strengthened if the population figure of 42,000 proposed by A. Janssens for 1477 is accepted. He based this number on a rather ingenious gleaning of information from town accounts, plus some educated guesswork about groups that did not figure in city records.[10] One other indirect measure of stability is the nearly constant level of tax contribution assigned to Bruges. This was fixed at 15.2 percent in the early fourteenth century, rose to 15.7 percent in 1408 and declined only slightly to 14.4 percent in 1517.[11]

Long-term stability could mask short-term fluctuation, as a study of Bruges's fifteenth-century population has suggested. Jan Dumolyn has shown with the help of chronicle and archival records that the population of Bruges rose and fell in line with economic growth and decline, trends caused or reinforced by the course of war, famine, and infectious disease. Thus the fourteenth-century high reached before 1349 declined by some 18 percent by the end of the century as a result of the Ghent war as well as the serious plague outbreak of 1400–1401. Thereafter population rebounded until the disastrous events of 1438–1440, followed by another recovery during the Burgundian golden age, which itself ended in 1477.

[8] I. De Meyer, "De sociale strukturen te Brugge in de 14e eeuw," in W. Blockmans, I. De Meyer, J. Mertens, C. Pauwelijn, and W. Vanderpijpen (eds.), *Studiën betreffende de sociale strukturen te Brugge, Kortrijk en Gent in de 14e en 15e eeuw* (Kortrijk and Heule, 1971), pp. 7–78.

[9] Prevenier, "Bevolkingscijfers," 284.

[10] A. Jannssens, "Brugse bevolkingsaantal in 1477," in *Van Middeleeuwen tot heden. Bladeren door Brugse kunst en Geschiedenis* (Bruges, 1983), pp. 29–35 and Dumolyn, "Population," 45.

[11] This was the "transport" of Flanders payable to the count; see Walter Prevenier, "De beden in het graafschap Vlaanderen onder Filip de Stoute (1384–1404)," *RBPH* 38 (1960), 346–361, 360–361; Raymond van Uytven, "Stages of Economic Decline: Late Medieval Bruges," in *Peasants and Townsmen in Medieval Europe: Studia in Honorem Adriaan Verhulst*, pp. 261–262, reprinted in van Uytven, *Production and Consumption in the Low Countries, 13th–16th Centuries* (Aldershot, UK, 2001), pp. 259–269. Such stability may have been an optical illusion, however: Bruges's fifteenth-century share may have appeared more significant because of the relative decline of the rest of West Flanders due to natural and man-made disasters.

The picture painted by these numbers therefore shows considerable population stickiness in Bruges at a level between 40–45,000 despite the periodic onslaughts of war, famine, and disease.

Even given this consensus about population trends in Bruges, so unlike those in Ghent and Ypres in the period, there is still a need to look critically at such numbers. First of all, even the best estimate provided by the 1338–1340 data remains an absolute minimum, even if the highest acceptable coefficient is applied. This is due to the omission of the poor, the foreign merchants, the clergy, nobility, and other resident groups who were not subject to militia service. Even if hypothetical totals are supplied for these in the global total, they remain little more than guesses, and, as we shall see they too are probably underestimates.[12] More subtle and serious than adjusting for an undercount is the fact that all commonly accepted estimates for Bruges's population ignore what I call the commercial population of the city – a number that would include the combined population of Bruges's outports.

As shown in chapter 2, the Zwin towns of Damme, Monnikerede, Hoeke, Mude, and Sluis functioned as close commercial satellites. This meant in practice that though they were juridically independent, economically and to a degree socially they were tethered to Bruges in unique ways. Neither Ghent nor Ypres had such close and dependent towns in their vicinity, and those villages near Ypres more often competed than cooperated with that declining industrial center in the fourteenth century.[13] There is abundant if fragmentary evidence of Bruges burghers owning property in Damme, and we have already noted that the craft guilds of Sluis and the other cities had to recognize the supremacy of the Bruges guild over their internal affairs.[14] Thus it is not unreasonable to consider the population of these five towns as significant and relevant to the effective number of inhabitants of their dominant partner.[15]

Unfortunately, there is less evidence about the populations of the five Zwin towns than there is for Bruges in the period. Only in the fifteenth century is there any direct indication of numbers of hearths on which some estimate can be made, albeit for a time when some decay had already

[12] Janssens for example allows 1,000 as the number of foreigners, 500 for clergy and only seventy-four for the poor; Janssens, "Brugse bevolkingsaantal," 32; Dumolyn, "Population," 46.

[13] John H. Munro, "Industrial Transformations in the North-West European Textile Trades, c. 90–1340: Economic Progress or Economic Crisis?," in *Before the Black Death. Studies in the 'Crisis' of the Early Fourteenth Century*, ed. Bruce M. S. Campbell (Manchester, 1991), pp. 110–148 and Stabel, *Dwarfs*, pp. 156–173.

[14] See chapter 2, p. 36 for the incident with the barbers of Sluis.

[15] Sosson, "Les petites villes du Zwin," p. 172.

Table 2. *Population of the Zwin towns*

	c. 1340	1408	1469
Damme	2,000	1,900	1,900
Hoeke	750	580	135
Monnikerede	750	567	225
Sint-Anna-ter-Muiden	900	837	175
Sluis	9,000	10,000	10,000
Totals	13,400	13,884	12,435

Sources: Sosson, "Les petites villes," 175–177; Stabel, *Dwarfs*, p. 38; Prevenier, "Démographie," 263–264.

begun to affect the towns. As the table 2 makes clear, all the Zwin towns were dwarfed by Bruges, but there is a clear hierarchy with Sluis easily at the head, followed at some distance by Damme, with the other three trailing considerably, a trend that accelerated across the fifteenth century. Yet even reckoning conservatively and reading backward from fifteenth-century demographic data, the Zwin towns in effect added 13,400 individuals to the commercial population of Bruges.[16] This fact goes some way to explaining the outsized significance of Bruges in the urban geography of Flanders. As Peter Stabel has observed, when the Flemish urban hierarchy of some sixty-two towns and cities is compared across a range of urban indicators, of which population is but one, Bruges surpasses even the more populous Ghent as an urban center.[17]

CLERGY, MERCHANTS, AND THE POOR

Estimating the numbers of "outsiders" in a city's population is a telling reminder of the imprecision inherent in medieval population figures. By status and definition these three groups did not enter the fiscal or military records of the city, leaving us little if any basis on which to estimate their numbers. This has forced scholars to fall back on very rough estimates:

[16] It must be stressed that the fourteenth-century data are based on backward projections from fifteenth-century hearth surveys. But they are quite conservative given the demographic travails of the middle to late fourteenth century.

[17] Stabel employed a matrix of seventeen data points to rank the urban significance of the various Flemish towns and cities. These include population, tax assessments, political participation, governmental structures, and professional and economic structures. Not surprisingly, Bruges, Ghent, and Ypres, in that order, far outdistanced the other fifty-nine urban communities of the county. See Stabel, *Dwarfs*, pp. 243–249.

Prevenier, for example, puts the number of the "unregistered" at 8.6% of the city's population of 1338–1340.[18] For the later period estimate derived from the 1394–1396 population data, he adds around 1,000 persons to cover the foreigners, nobles, clergy, and ducal officers resident in Bruges.[19] Janssens likewise adds roughly a thousand foreigners, 500 clergy and only seventy-four poor to his more firmly based count of militiamen.[20] Historians have thus arrived at figures of roughly a thousand merchants, half as many clergy, plus another 5 percent (following Prevenier) or less for the poor of the city. But are these reliable figures?

The poor

The medieval urban poor have been the subject of considerable research in the recent past. As a result we now know a good deal more about poverty and poor relief in the fourteenth century. This was a period in which Bruges and other cities sought both to define the deserving poor (and by implication the undeserving) and to establish institutions to provide for them.[21] This did not result in any kind of centralized approach to the problem; quite the opposite, in fact, as Bruges burghers founded hospitals, leprosaria, and parish "poor tables," guilds and confraternities founded almshouses or food distributions, and the city government took upon itself the cost of caring for abandoned children and orphans.[22] As a result an estimated 200–250 households enjoyed regular distributions of food and other necessities from one of the five parochial *dissen* or poor tables, thus becoming the privileged "shame-faced" poor.[23] Applying the same multiplier to these households gives a figure of between 800 and 1250 for these "privileged poor." Figures from the four hospitals that offered housing to transients indicate that they could house roughly 200 indigents.[24] Add to that figure the roughly seventy lepers and perhaps ten residents of the city's house for the insane (*dulhuis*),

[18] Prevenier, "Bevolkingscijfers," 298; Prevenier, "La démographie," 257.

[19] Prevenier, "Bevolkingscijfers," 289–290.

[20] Janssens, "Brugse bevolkingsaantal," 31–32.

[21] Wim Blockmans and Walter Prevenier, "Poverty in Flanders and Brabant from the Fourteenth to the Mid-Sixteenth Century: Sources and Problems," in *Acta Historiae Neerlandicae* 10 (1978), 20–57; Griet Maréchal, "Armen-en ziekenzorg in de Zuidelijke Nederlanden," *Algemene geschiedenis*, vol. 11 pp. 268–280.

[22] Paul Trio, "Armenzorg te Gent. Een onderzoek naar de steunverlening aan armen bij de broederschappen in de late middeleeuwen," in *Feestbundel Achiel de Vos* (Evergem, 1988), pp. 181–187; Griet Maréchal, *De sociale en politieke gebondenheid van het Brugse hospitaalwezen in de Middeleeuwen* (Kortrijk and Heule, 1978) (see pp. 52–53 for the Dulhuis); Michael Galvin, *The Poor Tables of Bruges, 1270–1477* (University Microfilms, Ann Arbor, 1998).

[23] Galvin, *Poor Tables*, pp. 2–3, 46; the Flemish was "scamele huusweken." Galvin notes that for the most part these were workers' households, not those of widows and the elderly.

[24] Maréchal, *Hospitaalwezen*, pp. 11–22–38; Blockmans, Prevenier, "Poverty in Flanders," 42.

plus the residents of almshouses in the city, and one arrives at another 300 or so sponsored poor.[25]

This by no means included all, or even the majority, of the urban poor of Bruges. On the hand there must have been a large group of families always living on the brink of poverty, for whom a workplace accident or the sudden death of the breadwinner meant catastrophe. The second fact that influenced impoverishment rates has to do with the price trends of food staples, particularly for bread. We know from other studies that outlays for food absorbed a considerable percentage of the poor family's income, thus magnifying the impact of any price rises. Recent research has shown that grain and bread prices were subject to medium- and long-term inflation throughout the fourteenth century, with periodic price spikes.[26] Fortunately, it is possible to construct price series that illustrate the trends, based upon data from the Ghent city accounts and from the records of the chapter of St. Donatian's church. The most complete of these is for oats, admittedly a non-bread grain, but one whose price evolution paralleled that of wheat and rye, the chief subsistence grains in Flanders.[27] The price of oats reflects the tendency towards higher prices accelerating after 1340, reaching a peak in 1370 before settling again at roughly 15 gro. per hoed, (see note 74), a price three to five times higher than from 1317 to 1330.[28] Wheat prices in Bruges can be tracked beginning in 1348, and these again show the sudden spike in prices around 1370 before settling into a higher average than 1350 with the exception of a steep fall in the late 1380s, due perhaps to the cumulative effects of the Ghent war and plague mortality.

The impact of such fluctuations could be devastating. For example, in 1362–1363 the purchase of sufficient rye bread for a family required between 27 and 30 percent of the annual wages of an unskilled worker in Bruges. The very next year, however, that same bread required between 40 and 48 percent of those wages, given that the average daily wage rate increased only slightly.[29] This shows rather dramatically that in many years after 1340 wages were not adequate to provide the average working family with the

[25] A rough census of these insitutions can be found in Maréchal's *Hospitaalwezen*, esp. pp. 122–140, and Griet Maréchal, "De Zwarte Dood te Brugge (1349–1351)," *Biekorf* 80 (1980), 377–392.

[26] Erik Thoen, *Landbouw, ekonomie en bevolking in Vlaanderen gedurende de late Middeleeuwen en het begin van de Moderne Tijden*, 2 vols. (Ghent, 1988), vol. I, pp. 238–253 (see figure 14a, p. 248 for the grain prices in Bruges); Adriaan Verhulst, "Prix des céréales, du beurre et du fromage à Bruges (1348 bis 1801)," in *Documents pour l'histoire des prix et des salaires*, 4 vols. (Bruges, 1965), vol. II, pp. 33–53.

[27] Thoen, *Landbouw, ekonomie en bevolking*, vol. I, pp. 240–243, explains the origins and meaning of these data.

[28] Thoen, *Landbouw*, ibid., p. 245 calls 1340–1370 a period of "hyperinflation."

[29] Prevenier and Blockmans, "Poverty in Flanders," table 2, p. 27, shows that the daily wage of unskilled and semi-skilled laborers rose only from 3 to 3.5 gro.

necessities of food, clothing, and shelter. Thus in hard years – "diere tijden" as the chroniclers called them – the ranks of the poor swelled with those who in better times were self-sufficient.

The last and perhaps largest category of the poor was made up of the wandering, uprooted country dwellers whose ranks ebbed and flowed according to conditions in the countryside. This group defies any attempt at measuring, but there is reason to believe that Bruges attracted more than its share of the wandering poor. Certainly this was true in famine years, particularly those of 1315–1317, when consecutive crop failures caused peasants to consume even their seed corn, thus forcing entire families to abandon their homes in search of food.[30] Paupers may also have been attracted to Bruges in other than crisis years owing to the availability of institutionalized poor relief, casual urban employment, or quite likely a combination of the two. It stands to reason that the wealthiest city in the Low Countries could have afforded a living to the street beggar and migrant laborer, as well as the resident poor. For a later period there is evidence that hospitality for the poor was substantially greater in Bruges than in the nearby Brabant town of Mechelen. Not only was the food more varied and substantial, but distributions lasted four times longer in Bruges than in Mechelen.[31] This pattern was probably true of the fourteenth century as well.

Given the above, it is nearly certain that the percentage of the undocumented poor in fourteenth-century Bruges was quite high, perhaps well above the 5–8 percent of the population traditionally allotted by historians. No doubt this was a fluctuating and unstable group whose number could expand spectacularly in famine years and contract during harvest season, when work in the countryside was more easily available for the able-bodied. Indirect evidence of this ebb and flow is provided by the institutions of poor relief, which were never comprehensive or sufficient but did provide something for both the resident and transient poor. And, as we have seen, Bruges could afford to be and probably was more generous to the needy than other cities, perhaps in line with its relative openness to foreigners and desire for social peace.[32] Moreover, an analysis of donors to the parish poor tables has shown that support of poor relief was broadly based among Brugeois,

[30] Jordan, *The Great Famine*, pp. 7–24; David Nicholas, *The Later Medieval City* (New York and London, 1997), pp. 248–257; note as well the evidence from St. Nicholas parish in Ghent in Nicholas, *Metamorphosis of a Medieval City*, pp. 52–58.

[31] Prevenier and Blockmans, "Poverty in Flanders," p. 42; there were 176 days of food distribution in Bruges as compared to forty days in Mechelen.

[32] Ibid., p. 42; Maréchal, *Hospitaalwezen*, pp. 58–153, attributes this to the desire for control and order on the part of urban elite, particularly business people.

with a surprising number of donations coming from those who at best had moderate means.[33]

Clergy

Members of religious institutions – monasteries, churches, beguinages – enjoyed a dual special status in Bruges. The first was a far-reaching exemption from normal taxes (especially those on beer and wine), military service, and other burdens of citizenship. The second was the possibility of receiving donations from the city, for the mendicants and other institutions dedicated to poor relief were frequent beneficiaries of the Bruges aldermen. Yet Bruges has never been known as a clerical city, given that it became the seat of a bishop only in the sixteenth century, and unlike Ghent, had no truly significant monasteries in its immediate environs.[34] Nonetheless, the city did house a significant concentration of mendicant houses, two chapter churches, and a host of smaller chapels and churches, which together may have employed more than the 500 traditionally allotted to the clergy share of the urban population.

By far the most significant churches were St. Donatian's and Onze-Lieve-Vrouw (the church of Our Lady), though we have no firm numbers of how many canons, chaplains, choristers, and other clerical personnel each may have counted. St. Donatian's was no doubt the larger of the two, and it may well have had between fifty and seventy-five clergy; Onze-Lieve-Vrouw had perhaps half that number.[35] Other parish churches – St. Salvator, St. Jacob, St. Catherina, St. Walburga, St. Gillis, St. Kruis – had between one and at most five clergy.[36] Free-standing chapels, which were dependencies of the parish churches, numbered some fifteen in the city.[37] Hospitals, notably St. Jans and the Potterie, contributed some twenty-five to thirty personnel in orders.[38] Beguinages, a house of Beghards, two Augustinian monasteries,

33 Galvin, *Poor Tables*, pp. 179–210, disputes Maréchal's contention that poor relief was an affair of the upper bourgeoisie by pointing out that the donors and administrators of the parish poor tables were drawn from the middle class.

34 Bruges is strikingly different from Ghent in this regard. The most significant monastic establishments in the neighborhood of Bruges were the Cistercian monasteries of Ter Duinen and Ter Doest, both of which lay within fifteen kilometers of the city; see Ryckaert, *Stedenatlas*, pp. 185–187. One should add the Augustinian house of the Eekhout abbey within Bruges.

35 These estimates rest upon numbers known from comparable institutions; see Simons, *Stad en apostolaat*, p. 156. The cathedral at Tournai had forty-two prebends in the fourteenth century, and an unknown number of chaplains. St. Donatian's may have been as large. At the more extreme end of the scale, the cathedral of Laon had about eighty beneficed clergy in the same period.

36 Ryckaert, *Stedenatlas*, pp. 210–218.

37 Ibid., p. 113.

38 Maréchal, *Hospitaalwezen*, pp. 166–176.

and other assorted small cloisters and almshouses probably added another 150 to the number. In sum, these clergy-run and staffed institutions alone may have accounted for close to those five hundred.[39]

Thus far the profile of Bruges's clergy resembles that of any other city in the southern Low Countries, adjusted for population. As mentioned in chapter 2, Bruges stood apart in the number of mendicant monasteries it housed, but how numerous the individuals were who belonged to these communities remains an open question. Some indications point to a considerable number, however. Walter Simons, in his research on the mendicants in Flanders, finds that Bruges was "the center of mendicant establishment in the county of Flanders."[40] Part of this was due to the function of the city as a center of instruction for the region's mendicants. The Augustinians, Carmelites, Franciscans, and probably the Dominicans as well all possessed a *studium generale* there by 1350.[41] Thus there must have been a continual stream of brothers and novices to and from Bruges to attend and teach in them. One extraordinary source, moreover, gives some idea of numbers of brothers, since Edward III made it a practice to give donations to individual mendicants during his visit in January–February 1340. In that month Edward gave alms to 252 members of the four chief mendicant convents.[42] Simons allows a modest 10 percent figure for those who were temporarily absent during that period to arrive at 277 as a rough count. Taking into account the absence of the two lesser mendicant orders and the omission of the female houses, there must have been well over 300 mendicant brothers and sisters in the city before 1350.[43]

Last and most difficult to classify, if not quantify, are Bruges's beguine houses. Beguines were single laywomen who chose to lead a life of religious devotion and simplicity without the formalities of joining an order.

[39] Bruges had one large beguinage, De Wijngaard, which was its own parish in the fourteenth century. There was one other smaller beguinage, St. Obrecht's, and at least eight other so-called "convents of poor beguines," virtually all of which were founded in the fourteenth century. See Ryckaert, *Stedenatlas*, p. 205. For the Beghard house, which became a Third Order Franciscan convent between 1374 and 1376, see Simons, *Bedelordekloosters in het Graafschap Vlaanderen*, pp. 166–170, and Simons, *Cities of Women*, p. 268. For the two Augustinian abbeys – Eekhout for men and St. Trudo for women – see N. Huyghebaert (ed.), *Monasticon Belge*, 4 vols. (Brussels, 1960–1978); vol. III contains the histories of West Flemish monastic foundations.

[40] Walter Simons, "Mendicant Collaboration in the Fourteenth Century: the Bruges Pact of 1370," in P. Chandler and K. J. Egan (eds.), *The Land of Carmel: Essays in Honor of Joachim Smet, O. Carm.* (Rome, 1991), pp. 171–187; the quote is found on p. 177.

[41] Simons, "Mendicant Collaboration," p. 178.

[42] Simons, *Stad en apostolaat*, p. 150.

[43] The Friars of the Sack and the Pied Friars were unmentioned but were probably only small groups. The number of mendicant nuns is unknown for the fourteenth century, but Bruges had convents of Poor Clares (transferred to Bruges 1260–1261) and Dominican sisters (after 1292–1293): see Simons, *Bedelordekloosters in het Graafschap Vlaanderen*, pp. 126–127, 145–150.

By the end of the fourteenth century, Bruges had at least ten beguine establishments, all but two of which were quite small. Of the two "court" beguinages, which consisted of numerous houses grouped around a central square or green, the largest by far was De Wijngaard. Possessing its own parish church, clergy, and independent foundation charter from a thirteenth-century countess of Flanders, De Wijngaard was a veritable "City of Ladies." And thanks to recent research, one can arrive at a reasonable estimate of its fourteenth-century population. Based on the survival of fairly complete data from 1439 to 1455, Walter Simons has shown that the average number of beguines in De Wijngaard was just under 145.[44] There is reason to believe that the fourteenth-century population was higher, even if the 1440 population of Bruges as a whole was about the same. Most beguinages lost population across the fourteenth century as the textile industry declined, and De Wijngaard was probably no exception, even if its beguines tended to come from a higher social class than other beguinages.[45] Thus an estimate of 175 beguines at De Wijngaard and 125 at the other nine institutions results in again a conservative number of around 300 women.

This picture of the Bruges clergy community (including beguines) thus seems larger than the number traditionally assigned to it. The size and significance of the mendicant presence alone argues for a figure closer to a thousand by the middle of the fourteenth century; adding the beguines brings the number to 1,300.[46] But even here one must be cautious, for prebendaries at Bruges churches could be (and often were) absent from the city for a variety of reasons. Chaplaincies could remain unfilled despite the express and carefully worded wishes of their founders. On the other hand, Bruges's role as an educational and administrative center brought additional visitors and short-term residents to the city. The single example of the 1370 convocation of representatives of the four mendicant orders held in Bruges might well stand for many others across the century.[47] Moreover, beguines were known to educate their own children or other children committed to them for instruction.[48] To this one might add litigants in the dean of Christianity's court, as well as those outside of Bruges who resided on lands owned by the chapter of St. Donatian's, St. Jan's hospital, or any of the

44 See Simons, *Cities of Ladies*, pp. 304–305; 267–269 for others.

45 Simons, ibid., p. 93, states that in Bruges beguines were rather exceptionally drawn from aristocratic and patrician families.

46 This figure agrees with that put forward by Dumolyn, "Population," 46, n. 18, except in his omission of the beguines.

47 Simons, "Mendicant Collaboration," pp. 177–180.

48 Simons, *Cities of Ladies*, pp. 73–74; and for beguines as teachers, pp. 80–85.

other large extra-mural landowning religious institutions in the city. These could have only added to the throngs in the streets of a bustling city.

Foreign merchants

There has been until recently only a single numerical description of the presence of foreign merchants in medieval Bruges. The fifteenth-century chronicler Nicolas Despars described the merchant groups taking part in a great urban procession on the occasion of the first entry of the duke of Burgundy after the Bruges revolt of 1436–1438.[49] There were 136 Hansards, 150 Italians, and forty-eight Spaniards, each in their distinctive livery, marching in procession.[50] These figures have often been cited to indicate both the numbers and the proportion of foreign merchants resident in the city. But there is much to criticize about this rather peculiar sampling of the merchant community. First, as J. A. van Houtte has pointed out, the ceremony took place in December, traditionally a low point in the business year at Bruges.[51] This may explain the absence of entire nations of merchants we know to have been active at the time. Even the numbers of participants may have been considerably reduced by the required wearing of costly ceremonial clothing. All in all, the Despars numbers give a very imperfect image of the dimensions of the foreign merchant population of Bruges.

Two new sources, however, can provide considerable additional nuance to the traditional picture, both in detail and in time-period. Interestingly, both were hiding in plain sight as it were, since they are contained in long-familiar sources. The first stems from the grant of a privilege to the members of the German Hanse exempting them from half of the assize on wine and roughly 70 percent of that levied on beer.[52] Quite exceptionally, for a period after 1360 both the quantities of wine and beer granted exemption and the names of the Hanse merchants who were the beneficiaries were noted in the city accounts.[53] These lists permit a glimpse of the number of Hanse

[49] For the revolt, see now Jan Dumolyn, *De Brugse Opstand van 1436–38* (Heule, 1997).

[50] Nicolas Despars, *Cronijcke van den lande ende graefscepe van Vlaenderen*, ed. J. de Jonghe, 3 vols. (Bruges and Rotterdam, 1839–1842) vol. III, pp. 431–432.

[51] J. A. van Houtte, "Handel en nijverheid," in *Algemene Geschiedenis*, vol. IV, p. 90.

[52] These privileges had been won in the treaty of 1307–1309, but had been resecured with added clarity and emphasis in the new treaty of 1360; see Klaus Krüger and Werner Paravicini (eds.), *Hansekaufleute in Brügge, Teil 1: Die Brügger Steuerlisten 1360–1390* (Peter Lang, Frankfurt am Main, 1992), pp. 11–17.

[53] These cover the years 1360–1390, with various degrees of completeness. Some lists include the merchant's name and the quantity of wine; others mention only the quantity and the name of the merchant's hosteller. See Krüger and Paravicini (eds.), *Hansekaufleute*, vol. I, pp. 11–12 for precise descriptions of the accounts.

merchants both *in toto* and as distributed throughout the year. The tax lists vary considerably in number, from a high of 205 names to a low of only two. In total the names of 1,700 merchants are noted, representing approximately 950 individuals.[54] Yet there are clear patterns across the years. For example, the largest number of Hanse merchants always occurs during the second quarter of the fiscal year; thus it is likely that their numbers were typically greatest in the summer months, from the Bruges market in May through July.[55] It was during this period in 1372 that the total of 205 was reached. Werner Paravicini concludes from these data that probably between forty and fifty Hanse merchants were present throughout the year, but their numbers could double or even triple during the late spring and early summer months. An estimate of 100 is therefore an acceptable, if conservative, figure.

More new data about merchant numbers are available in the account books of the money changer Collard de Marke.[56] There de Marke or his bookkeeper often indicated the place of origin of particular merchants, no doubt in an attempt to identify them. When these names are collected from the five ledgers, they run into the hundreds.[57] Of course, as in the case of the tax lists, there are problems of interpretation here. First is the difficulty of identifying person and place, due the wide variety of orthography used in the accounts. Our scribe is also selective in the merchants to whom he assigns place names, for he omits such identification in the case of well-known foreign merchants, making clear that short-term or new visitors to Bruges were chosen in most cases. The list also omits those merchants, such as the Italians, who were not usually customers of the money changers.

Breaking the names down roughly into European regions yields the following: merchants from the Low Countries (chiefly Brabant) numbered 125; Germans, 19; French (including Hainaut, Liège and Tournai), 233; British (Scotland and England), 52; Italy, 20; Iberia (Spain and Portugal),

[54] These numbers are very approximate since in *Hansekaufleute*, vol. 1, p. 21, the number given is c. 1,820 total names representing 1,020 individuals.

[55] Paravicini, "Brugge en Duitsland," p. 101.

[56] De Marke's accounts are in the Stadsarchief, Bruges (SAB), series 305, Koopmansboeken, De Marke, Journals 1–5. They are described more extensively in James M. Murray, "Merchant Account Books in Fourteenth-Century Flanders," in N. Jörn D. Kattinger, and H. Wernicke (eds.), "*Kopet Uns Werk by Tyden*"*: Beiträge zur hansischen und preußischen Geschichte; Festschrift für Walter Stark zum 75. Geburtstag* (Schwerin, 1999), pp. 27–31.

[57] I presented a partial compilation of these data in James M. Murray, "Of Nodes and Networks: Bruges and the Infrastructure of Trade in Fourteenth-Century Europe," in P. Stabel, B. Blondé, and A. Greve (eds.), *International Trade in the Low Countries* (Leuven and Apeldoorn, 2000), pp. 1–14, esp. p. 7 for discussion.

128 and Flanders, 413. There are some surprises here. First, and perhaps most surprising, the number of "Germans" (the scribe describes them most often as "Almant") is far below expectations. This can be explained in part by the rather low popularity of the money changers among Germans, who most often favored keeping accounts with hostellers.[58] But this is not entirely satisfactory, for de Marke's accounts contained a good deal of accounting information about Bruges hostellers, who were popular among Germans. The very tentative conclusion based on these data is that Hanse merchants might not have been as numerous in Bruges as traditionally believed. The second interesting fact contained in these figures is the number of merchants from Spain and Portugal. Their numbers exceed those of nearby Brabant and are significantly greater than English and Scottish merchants. Judged by these figures alone, Iberian merchants were the most numerous distant visitors to the city by the 1360s.

POPULATION CHECKS

Urban living even in the best of times was a deadly proposition: demographers estimate a mortality rate of 3 percent per year in a stable, pre-industrial city.[59] Needless to say, the fourteenth century was far from the best of times in Flanders as elsewhere in Europe; but the challenge remains to measure the impact of violence, famine, and disease on Bruges's population in order to assess their role in shaping the roller-coaster ride in the numbers of residents within the walls.

The danger of violent death was a constant threat, particularly for the male residents of Bruges, or any other medieval city. And above and beyond the normal incidents native to a densely inhabited, lightly policed area, full of knife-toting men and women, Bruges had some spectacular bloodlettings at various times during the century. Battle casualties are impossible to establish with any certainty, though we know they were light at the battle of Courtrai (Kortrijk); but one should remember a host of smaller actions that followed this battle, which required contingents of the Bruges militia to campaign in Zeeland and Tournai.[60] Their luck changed in the rematch fight against the French at the battle of Mons-en-Pévèle in 1304, where the

[58] James M. Murray, "Moneychanging and Exchange in 14th-Century Bruges," in N. Jörn, W. Paravicini, and H. Wernicke (eds.), *Hansekaufleute in Brügge, Teil 4: Beiträge der Internationalen Tagung in Brügge April 1996* (Frankfurt am Main, 2000), pp. 139–149.

[59] Nicholas, *Metamorphosis*, p. 37; David Herlihy and Christiane Klapisch-Zuber, *Tuscans and Their Families: A Study of the Florentine Catasto of 1427* (New Haven, 1985), p. 270 and cited literature.

[60] Nicholas, *Medieval Flanders*, pp. 195–196; DeVries, *Infantry Warfare*, pp. 23–25.

Flemish army, of which the Bruges contingent made up the majority, sustained heavy losses.[61] Given a militia of between 5,000 and 7,000 through the period of the revolt, losses from disease and wounds could well have amounted to 10–20 percent.[62]

The next era of intense fighting in which the Bruges militia figured prominently was that of the revolt of Maritime Flanders, 1323–1328, which was brought to an end by the battle of Cassel in 1328. This was a decisive victory for the French army and a deadly disaster for the Flemish. Again the army that faced the French cavalry was made up of contingents from Ypres, the Bruges Franc, and Bruges itself, and probably numbered some 16,000–20,000.[63] The number of Flemish dead at Cassel probably totaled at least 9,000, of which a quarter could have been from Bruges. Thus probably as many Brugeois militiamen perished at Cassel as were lost during the entire revolt of 1302–1305. Two generations passed before battle casualties of the order of the first third of the century occurred again, but with the onset of the Ghent war of 1379–1385 Bruges and Flanders entered a deadly age. Bruges itself suffered at three specific junctures in the long conflict: the battle of Beverhoudsveld against the Gentenars in May 1382, the subsequent massacres of townsmen, and the great slaughter inflicted by the French at the battle of Westrozebeke on 27 November 1382.[64] Again, precise figures are elusive, but 1,000–3,000 killed at Beverhoudsveld and its aftermath is not out of the question; and confiscation records in the wake of Westrozebeke also suggest 1,000–2,000 Brugeois killed.[65]

The impact of battle deaths or deaths caused in the kind of public disorder common in the Ghent war was often disproportionately great. This was due to the age and importance of the militiamen killed in battle, who were likely to have been in the prime of young adulthood, with young families and other dependents. And since the household was also the key unit of economic production, the loss of its head also could mean permanent loss of production unless the widow could carry on the trade.[66] Victims of urban mobs were likewise often chosen for their wealth and position; in

[61] DeVries, *Infantry Warfare*, p. 43.

[62] No muster rolls survive from 1302 specifically, but the militia numbered 7,234 in 1338; see Nicholas, *Medieval Flanders*, p. 195, n. 36 and cited literature.

[63] DeVries, *Infantry Warfare*, p. 110; for casualties, see p. 108, n. 47.

[64] See below, chapter 9 for more discussion.

[65] One chronicler stated that 3,000 were massacred by Gentenars and their Bruges allies alone – certainly an exaggeration. A. van Oost estimates some hundreds died; see "Sociale stratifikatie van de Brugse opstandigen en van de opstandige ingezeten van de kleinere kasselrijsteden en van de kasselrijdorpen in Vlaanderen van 1379–1385," *RBPH* 56 (1978), 830–877.

[66] For issues relating to widowhood see Marianne Daneel, *Weduwen en wezen in het laat-middeleeuwse Gent* (Leuven and Apeldoorn, 1995), pp. 251–292.

other words their deaths were intended by their killers to have considerable impact. One has to imagine the urban population, especially that of men, could be markedly reduced at least in the short term by losses due to the violence of opposing armies and enraged mobs.

Famine

The Flemings as a whole struck contemporaries as both unusually numerous and unusually well fed throughout the Middle Ages.[67] Whether this was due to agricultural wealth or (as David Nicholas argues) to poverty has been the subject of considerable debate; but there is no disputing the fact that between 1100 and 1400 Bruges suffered only two significant famines.[68] No doubt part of this was due to the largely clement weather and the sophistication of the transport system that brought imported food to Flemish cities even in the twelfth century.[69] Unfortunately for Bruges, the famine of 1315–1317 heralded a new age of adversity in which traditional means of heading off hunger were quickly overwhelmed.

The preliminaries leading to famine are well told elsewhere. Most recently, William Jordan has pointed to the disastrous weather as a trigger, while stressing complex social and geographical factors which determined the actual impact of dearth on populations.[70] In Bruges and Flanders in general, the urban populations depended on food imports, especially from Picardy and the Artois region. The inundating rains of those years did not spare these regions either, resulting in crop losses exacerbated by the off-and- on military expeditions of the French king, Louis X.[71] Reduced supplies and difficulties in transport quickly squeezed both urban and rural populations in Flanders. It is likely that shortage of grain hit the population of the Franc of Bruges particularly hard, given the more specialized

[67] David Nicholas, "Of Poverty and Primacy: Demand, Liquidity and the Flemish Economic Miracle, 1050–1200," *American Historical Review* 96 (1991), 17–41, esp. 28–29; Nicholas, *Medieval Flanders*, pp. 107–109.

[68] Of course these are famines that left a trace in the historical record. The famine during Charles the Good's reign is described in Galbert of Bruges's chronicle: see Galbertus Brugensis, *De Multro, Traditione*, pp. 7–11; Nicholas, "Poverty and Primacy," 31–32; Nicholas, *Medieval Flanders*, pp. 101, 108–109. Certainly the famine of 1197 was very severe as well, though we don't know its effect in Bruges.

[69] See Nicholas, *Medieval Flanders*, p. 101 and Nicholas, "Poverty and Primacy," 32, where he discusses the effective provisioning system developed by Flemish cities.

[70] Jordan, *Great Famine*, pp. 7–23. Jordan cites one mid-sixteenth-century chronicler from Leuven whose retrospective on famine years contains two from the twelfth century (1146, 1197) and then none until 1316. Thereafter follows another two-century gap before the famine of 1530 is noted.

[71] Jordan, *Great Famine*, pp. 20–21; H. S. Lucas, "The Great European Famine of 1315, 1316, and 1317," *Speculum* 5 (1930), 343–377.

agriculture of that region.[72] Unfortunately, little record of food prices survives from Bruges from this period. A single price statistic from the hospital of Oudenaarde in eastern Flanders shows that wheat may have been from three to ten times more expensive than normal.[73] Prices paid for wheat and rye by the Bruges St. Jan's hospital show a similar jump.[74] Chroniclers from equally near-by Brabant describe inflated prices and desperate people.[75] Similar conditions in West Flanders are highly likely.

The crop failures of 1315 led to a rapid spike in mortality in both Bruges and Ypres, commencing in May 1316. Unclaimed corpses were collected from the streets and houses of Bruges at a rate of 116–156 per week from 14 May until 24 July, after which there was a gradual subsidence through August and September. Ypres, on the other hand, reached the peak of mortality slightly later – in August – and maintained it longer than her neighbor to the north-east.[76] The victims in Bruges numbered 1,938, as recorded in the city accounts for 1316, based on the weekly bill presented by Jan Bilherse, the chief gravedigger.[77]

Hans van Werveke was undoubtedly correct in his observation that the Bruges magistrates were taken by surprise by the dimensions of the famine; yet there is evidence as well of a rapid response to the new challenges. The very operation of collecting and burying the dead quickly assumed bureaucratic regularity. In normal times, the city paid St. Jan's hospital to collect the bodies of paupers, whose number was typically relatively small.[78] The extraordinary circumstances of 1316, however, caused the city to hire Bilherse "and company" ("ende sinen gheselscepe") and to pay separately one Boudine Berbise for the use of two flatbed carts pulled by horses "in which the aforesaid dead people were conveyed."[79] Like any city contractor, Bilherse submitted his written, itemized bill each Friday for payment. In

[72] Nicholas, *Medieval Flanders*, p. 264, reports that even though much of Maritime Flanders was given over to grain cultivation, production could not begin to meet demand. Pastoralism was also common in the region.

[73] Thoen, *Landbouwekonomie*, vol. I, pp. 43, 244 and vol. II, p. 1157. Prices may have even reached twenty-four times normal level; see Nicholas, *Medieval Flanders*, p. 207.

[74] Maréchal, "Zwarte Dood," 381, n. 11; the Bruges "hoed" of wheat equalled 1.66 hectoliter and cost 60s. paris. In 1314–1315 the price spiked to 200s. and returned to 65s. in 1317–1318; rye jumped from 48s. to 160s., returning to 50s. across the same period.

[75] Nicholas, *Medieval Flanders*, p. 207.

[76] Van Werveke, "La famine de l'an 1316," 6–7.

[77] Van Werveke, "Bronnenmateriaal," 437–440.

[78] Many churches likewise buried unknown or unclaimed corpses; see Renée Rössner, *Hansekaufleute in Brügge, Teil 5: Hansische Memoria in Flandern* (Frankfurt am Main, 2001), pp. 136–139.

[79] Van Werveke, "Bronnenmateriaal," 440: "Boudine Berbise, van twee scrinen met vallen, daer men de dode lieden in droech." *Scrijn* means literally casket, but in this case probably refers to some kind of open cart resembling a casket, given its purpose. It is certainly not a "sheltering screen" as translated by Jordan, *Great Famine*, pp. 146–147.

other words, judging from the dispassionate and dry language of the Bruges accounts, collecting corpses had become much like any other routine city service by mid-summer, 1316.[80]

Extraordinary measures were seemingly reserved for heading off a recurrence of famine the next year. From April 1317 Bruges magistrates fell back upon the city's growing role as a port and meeting place for foreign merchants, suspending the free market and enlisting a number of foreign merchants as suppliers of imported bread grains, particularly wheat.[81] At precisely a year's distance from the grim work of the gravediggers, the city was able to buy some 19,636 hectoliters of wheat, plus 833 hectoliters of rye, distributing most of it to the city's bakers at a slight loss.[82] According to William Jordan's calculations based on eighteenth-century norms, this infusion of grain represented between 30 and 45 percent of the total required for a population of 35,000.[83] Due to this direct and forceful effort on the part of the Bruges city government, the accounts of 1317 record payments for grain and not for burial expenses.

Thanks to this intervention by city government, Bruges suffered the loss of 5.5 percent of her population due to famine, while Ypres, without such countermeasures, suffered a mortality rate closer to 10 percent. These figures were first stated by Hans van Werveke and have been widely repeated in a variety of works, including William Chester Jordan's.[84] But there are difficulties with these numbers, even beyond the fact that the estimate of Bruges's 1315 population (35,000) is certainly too low. The essential question is: Who were the victims collected from the streets and tenements of Bruges? Were they residents or transients? And did their deaths mark a true demographic disaster for the city? A return to the documents can help us with these questions.

The city accounts are explicit if cryptic in their identification of those buried at city expense: "the dead people . . . who had no friends wishing to lend a hand . . ."[85] Though puzzling at first glance, this tells us quite a lot about these nameless dead. "Friendlessness" was an unnatural condition in an urban community like Bruges, either signifying social breakdown

80 Bilherse was paid sixteen pence parisis per head, "whereof Jan Bilhers aforesaid brought proof written up in a letter at the end of each week . . ." (Van Werveke, "Bronnenmateriaal," 438). Thus the accounts are a much-shortened record of the original "letter" prepared by Bilherse. See Jordan, *Great Famine*, p. 146 for an appreciation of the impact of such numbers of dead in a community of 35,000–40,000.

81 Van Werveke, "La famine," 12–13.

82 Ibid., 13–14; Van Houtte, *Geschiedenis*, p. 110; Jordan, *Great Famine*, p. 159. Losses are detailed in Van Werveke, "Bronnenmateriaal," 447.

83 Jordan, *Great Famine*, p. 159.

84 Van Werveke, "La famine," 8; Jordan, *Great Famine* p. 146.

85 Van Werveke, "Bronnenmateriaal," 437.

or denoting a person who had not yet sunk social roots. The full phrase, "friends and relations" ("vrienden en magen") is loaded with significance in Flemish customary law, for normally, every individual was part of a network of overlapping relationships of kin, guild colleagues, and neighbors who had an obligation to offer advice and assistance at times of decision or crisis.[86] These victims also fell outside the parish, hospital, and guild poor relief systems, which offered food, clothing, and fuel to special categories of the poor, guild members and their families, and also helped in many cases with burial expenses.[87] Given the absence of proof of social breakdown caused by the food emergency, it is nearly certain that the nameless 1,938 were either recent immigrants or transients drawn to Bruges in the last desperate hope of finding food.

In normal times this would not have been an empty hope. There were institutions in Bruges that distributed food to rootless and impoverished travelers – all "passanten" in the terminology of the time.[88] Those who were sick could also hope for a bed at the St. Jan's hospital, which also took in indigent travelers. But these institutions were no doubt quickly overwhelmed by country dwellers and others who likely swarmed into the city in the spring and summer of 1316. Many must have been in an advanced state of starvation when they arrived, thus explaining the dead collected from city streets.[89] Undoubtedly, the resident poor of the city suffered as well in the face of skyrocketing food prices, and they may also have died from deprivation; but it is unlikely that these victims would be among the unclaimed dead. Thus we cannot guess their number.

There are two conclusions to be drawn from the Bruges evidence about the Great Famine. First, the city's successful efforts to acquire additional grain, imported most likely from south-western France, were intended to meet the needs of both the urban poor and a large number of famine-driven refugees in the city.[90] The fact that grain was sold to the major hospitals and other eleemosynary institutions proves this, as does the sale

[86] There is no precise modern equivalent of this group; for Danneels (*Weduwen en wezen*, pp. 76, 132–140), "vrienden en magen" were synonymous with potential heirs of the deceased; Nicholas (*Domestic Life*, pp. 25, 112) equates the term with kindred, but he nuances this by indicating that the term included in-laws of a married person.

[87] Galvin, *The Poor Tables*, pp. 243–249; Maréchal, *Hospitaalwezen*, p. 269.

[88] Maréchal, *Hospitaalwezen*, pp. 243–260, with descriptions of the help provided.

[89] The accounts speak of them being gathered from "houses and backstreets" (Van Werveke, "Bronnenmateriaal," 437); Jordan, *Great Famine*, pp. 86–123, describes the pressures and effects in the European countryside: these could lead to abandonment of holdings by the marginals and the rise of bands of beggars, whose natural destination was towns.

[90] I agree with Jordan that the Bordeaux region was the most likely provenance of grain, which was relatively easy to ship in ships used in the wine trade; see *Great Famine*, pp. 159–162.

of grain to the nearby town of Hulst.[91] In other words, the city magistrates made use of the commercial networks that typically brought a wide variety of commodities to the city to increase the grain supply at a critical time. Secondly and most importantly, the number of corpses buried in 1316 tells us little or nothing about the famine's demographic impact on the city. There is every reason to believe that the victims were recently arrived outsiders to the city who had no claim to urban poor relief, and whose numbers overwhelmed the institutions that sheltered and fed transients. On the other hand, there is the possibility of numerous deaths among the average urban poor, whose swelling numbers may also have quickly exceeded the capacity of the poor tables and other relief sources to prevent starvation. Either way, there is simply no basis for an estimate of mortality among Bruges residents. On the contrary, the city may have actually attracted large numbers of food seekers in the spring and summer of 1317, at least temporarily, when there was bread to be had at the city bakeries and hospitals.

Plague

While food scarcity was unquestionably more common and severe in the fourteenth century than in the thirteenth, it is likely that disease killed many more Brugeois than did hunger. Even in the aftermath of the 1316 famine there is evidence that outbreaks of disease – chiefly fevers and enteric disorders – cut a wider swath through the urban populace than did starvation.[92] Here famine was the handmaid of pestilence, given the weakening of those suffering chronic hunger, the roaming bands of the starving who spread disease, the "strange diets" consumed by the desperate. Griet Maréchal found some indication of the possible effects of disease outbreaks in her study of the personnel of the St. Jan's hospital.[93] The hospital accounts report an unusual number of vacancies (filled with new staff) and between 1315 and 1318, likely caused by extreme mortality.[94] She speculates that these were caused by the deaths of the incumbents, a likely result of exposure to famine victims brought to the hospital.

Even if disease was never a stranger in Bruges, no one could have anticipated the deadly novelty of the first onslaught of bubonic plague, which

[91] Van Werveke, "Bronnenmateriaal," 435 and 442, for the sale of 100 hoeden to Hulst at cost and grain provided to St. Jan and St. Marie Magdalene hospitals.

[92] Jordan, *Great Famine*, pp. 142–146, discusses the health effects of famine-induced "strange diets."

[93] Maréchal, "De Zwarte Dood," 377–392.

[94] Ibid., 380; there were fourteen in these years, three to four times the average of other periods.

reached Bruges sometime before August, 1349.[95] It arrived via the city's link with Sluis, carried, like so much cargo, into the area near the Potterie. Recognition of the disease seems to have been slow, for there are no descriptions or casualty reports as in 1316, although city magistrates applied to the count for permission to lay out two new cemeteries.[96] By late in the year, the chronicler Gillis li Muisit reported processions of flagellants arriving in his city of Tournai from Bruges.[97] Yet there is no clear voice of alarm from Bruges itself.

This silence caused Hans van Werveke to conclude that Bruges along with the other major cities of Flanders was spared the worst effects of the first plague outbreak.[98] Although he was certainly correct to point out the varying mortality rates across Flanders and Europe in general, van Werveke's conclusions have been substantially revised. Griet Maréchal's careful sifting of the Bruges evidence provides evidence that the first outbreak of plague killed roughly 10 percent of the city's population.[99] She bases this estimate on a number of indications of abnormally high mortality rates among Bruges institutions. Again in 1350–1351, the St. Jan's hospital recorded the largest number of new personnel since the famine year of 1317.[100] Expenditures on extra medical care were also abnormally high, and staff members disappeared inexplicably from the accounts.[101] In an account book of life rent and orphan money payments made by the city, there is also evidence of high mortality. By December 1349 twice as many of these contractual payments lapsed as was usual.[102] The other public hospital, the Potterie, recorded the dates and numbers of deaths in late 1349. These

95 W. P. Blockmans, "The Social and Economic Effects of Plague in the Low Countries 1349–1500," *RBPH* 50 (1980), 833–863, 838; by tradition the plague entered Bruges via Sluis, according to the chronicler de Meyere (Meyerus) in his 1561 *Annales*. His source is unknown.

96 Paul Rogghé, "De Zwarte Dood in de Zuidelijke Nederlanden," *RBPH* 30 (1952), 834–837; Blockmans, "The Social and Economic Effects of Plague in the Low Countries 1349–1500," *RBPH* 50 (1980), 833–863, p. 838; Nicholas, *Medieval Flanders*, pp. 265–266. The timing of this request seems too early to have been intended to inter plague victims, indicating perhaps more fear of the disease's arrival than actual body counts. Hans van Werveke pointed this out, in "Nogmaals: de Zwarte Dood in de Nederlanden," *Bijdragen voor de Geschiedenis der Nederlanden* 8 (1954), 251–258, pp. 252–254, in a debate with Paul Rogghé.

97 Maréchal, "De Zwarte Dood," 386 and n. 38.

98 Findings he first published in *De Zwarte Dood in de Zuidelijke Nederlanden, Mededelingen. Konink. Vlaamse Ak., Kl. Letteren* 12, no. 3 (1950).

99 Maréchal, "De Zwarte Dood," 377–392; 389 is her estimate. David Nicholas judged this to be perhaps too conservative; see *Medieval Flanders*, p. 266.

100 Maréchal, "De Zwarte Dood," 380 – the nine vacancies in 1317–1318 is the greatest number for the whole of the fourteenth century, with that of 1350–51 (7) in second place.

101 Maréchal points out that in the plague year five bursers in succession made the daily payments in place of the usual one: ibid., 382–383.

102 Ibid., 383–384.

show that the first plague cases began as early as late July, with numbers of dead recorded in September and October. The numbers fell in November, with only one recorded death in December.[103] This was time enough, however, for the hospital's entire personnel to have fallen victim to the disease.

Less direct indications of population loss come from reduced income from rents and indirect taxes. Van Werveke first pointed out that the auction price for collecting the tax on beer (the commodity most likely to show immediate effects of a drop in demand among average people) fell only 10 percent between February 1347 and February 1350, indicating little plague-induced effect on demand.[104] Yet other sources point to an opposite conclusion. The copy of an appointment letter recorded among the *Acta* of the chapter of St. Donatian's, dated 30 September 1350, indicates considerable losses in tithe income due to the "Great Mortality" then raging, as well as damage caused by war and inundating rain.[105] While no accounts survive from the church allowing us to put numbers to these words, those of St. Jan's hospital are more complete. These show a disastrous harvest in 1349–1350 from the farms directly exploited by the hospital, as well as a considerable loss of income from rented land.[106] All these indications, however fragmentary, support the conclusion of considerable plague mortality, on the order of 10–15 percent, in and around Bruges from the autumn of 1349, with some economic effect on both city and countryside apparent by the following spring and summer.[107]

This new information about the first incidence of plague in Bruges effectively sweeps away the traditional belief that this angel of death passed over the cities of the southern Low Countries.[108] Unfortunately, if anything,

[103] Ibid., 385. [104] Van Werveke, "Nogmals: de Zwarte Dood," 24.

[105] Adriaan Verhulst first discovered this text during his research on prices in Bruges; he passed a transcript on to David Nicholas, who published it for the first time in his important article "Economic Reorientation and Social Change in Fourteenth-Century Flanders," *Past and Present* 70 (1976), 3–29, esp. 18. Yet he fails to give a full citation or explain the context. The original of the letter does not survive; what the Acta contain (BAB, St. Donaas, A47, Acta Capituli, f. 60v) is a more or less complete copy of a directive by the chapter and provost of the church establishing Johannes de Herdsberghe, a canon of the church, as "obedientarius," the chief fiscal officer of the church. The letter goes on to state that the chapter fears the loss of income may be long-term or permanent, indicating serious damage to the population and productive capacity of the countryside around Bruges.

[106] Maréchal, "De! Zwarte Dood," 390; the largest farm in Zuienkerke had its first losing year in its recorded history in 1349–1350; rented lands returned from 10 to 30 percent less that year, proving themselves less variable.

[107] Bruges mortality may thus have been on the low side of David Nicholas's estimate that Flanders as a whole lost between 17 and 25 percent of its population as a result of the 1349 plague outbreak (*Medieval Flanders*, p. 266).

[108] Blockmans, "Social and Economic Effects," 845.

evidence about the renewed outbreaks of the disease later in the century is even more scattered and fragmentary. There were serious revisitations of the plague in 1358, 1361 and 1368–1369, with ever gathering ferocity judging from mortality records in other cities and towns. Ghent, in particular, was very hard hit by the epidemics of the 1360s, recording death rates two to two and half times above normal.[109] These succeeded in greatly reducing the city's population by 1385. In Bruges there is no official record of plague in any of the sources that were so eloquent earlier in the century. David Nicholas noted rates of turnover of fiefs similar to Ghent's in the Bruges Franc and in the city as a result of the epidemic of 1368–1369.[110] Spikes in the price of grain and rises in the wages paid to skilled craftsmen also point in the direction of unusual population loss.[111] Several customers and a business partner of the money changer Collard de Marke disappeared in the accounting years covering the epidemic; the apparently unexpected deaths of the hosteller Jacob Sconebergh and his wife were probably due to the 1368 outbreak.[112] But strangely, the acts of the chapter of St. Donatian's are silent about the plague until August 1399. Thereafter the chapter's canons regularly lodged their applications to leave the city until the epidemic had passed.[113]

The population history of Bruges is nothing if not full of gaps and uncertainties. This alone demands a certain tentativeness in any conclusions that might be drawn. One must avoid in particular the modern tendency to dwell on the horrors of the plague outbreaks, for there is no contemporary document that indicates that the Black Death was any worse than death in battle or from starvation in terms of its effect on the city's population. Peaks in mortality there certainly were, especially in 1302, 1328, 1382–1383, 1316–1317, and of course the plague years 1349–1350, 1368 and

109 Nicholas, *Medieval Flanders*, p. 266; Nicholas, *Metamorphosis*, pp. 24–40; he argues for a decline by more than half by 1385.

110 Nicholas, "Economic Reorientation," 18 n. 54.

111 Blockmans, "Social and Economic Effects," 862.

112 For Sconebergh, see below pp. 202–205. Apparently the plague also carried off Sconebergh's brother, Jan, and his mother died later that year as well; see Anke Greve, "Jacob Sconebergh and His Short Career as a Hosteller in Fourteenth-Century Bruges," in W. Blockmans, M. Boone, and Thérèse de Hemptinne (eds.), *Secretum Scriptorum: Liber Alumnorum Walter Prevenier* (Leuven and Apeldoorn, 1999), pp. 213–224, esp. 216–217. For de Marke's partner, Pieter van le Finghe, see below p. 182.

113 The first instance of these "plague leaves" has heretofore escaped the notice of historians: BAB, A49, Acta Capituli, f. 33r: "die xxva dicti mensis [August] in capitulo me Balduino absente actum fuit per dominos decanum et capitulum . . . propter epidimiam pestilencialem que nunc incipit vigere . . ." Canons who feared plague infection were granted a leave of absence until Christmas, 1399. This may indicate the hard-won knowledge that plague was most active in warm-weather months, falling off rapidly in the winter. For later applications by the canons, see Blockmans, "Social and Economic Effects," 852 nn. 47, 57, 58.

1399, on top of the "normal" high death rates of any medieval town. Yet mortality rates were one of many fluctuations influencing the population within the walls at any given time. There were the annual rhythms of trade that drew merchants in greater or lesser numbers depending on the season; the agricultural seasons must certainly have affected others. And we must not forget the occasional grand occasions, like the visit of a king of France, the residence of the count of Flanders or duke of Burgundy, meetings of diplomats or church dignitaries: any and all of these could add or subtract scores or hundreds of individuals.[114] To paraphrase Aquinas' comment from this chapter's beginning, individuals flow in and out of the urban multitude leaving undisturbed the whole entity which is the city. Thus Bruges's population remained in the range from 40,000 to 50,000 throughout our period. But it only did so by attracting thousands of new residents in a near-constant stream of immigration. To know fourteenth-century Bruges then is to learn something about those who abandoned their previous homes to come and live in a merchant city.

IMMIGRATION

Surprisingly little has been written about the immigration history of Bruges beyond the commonplace assertion that there as in every medieval city dwelt a population of immigrants.[115] While J. A. van Houtte and J. P. Sosson have made some partial and preliminary studies, it is only recently, with the work of Erik Thoen, that a beginning has been made on answering questions about the numbers, origins, and professions of Bruges immigrants in the fourteenth century.[116] However, here again there is a problem of sources sufficient to provide a reliable picture of this important part of the urban population. In essence we have only the lists of immigrants who purchased full citizenship rights in the city, or *poorterschap*, and whose names were

[114] This list is far from hypothetical, since Bruges was the site of a visit of Philip the Fair, of negotiations between the English and French in the early 1370s of relatively frequent visits from Philip, duke of Burgundy, from the 1360s, and of course of the intermittent presence of the count of Flanders, who in the person of Louis of Male had his favorite country residence just a few miles from the city walls.

[115] Robert Bartlett, *The Making of Europe: Conquest, Colonization and Cultural Change, 950–1350* (Princeton, 1993), p. 233; on urban populations in general, R. Mols, *Introduction à la démographie historique des villes d'Europe du XIVe au XVIIIe siècle*, 3 vols. (Leuven, 1954–1956).

[116] Van Houtte, *Geschiedenis*, pp. 156–157, discusses new *poorters* and compares the fourteenth and fifteenth centuries; Sosson, *Les travaux publics*, pp. 206–216, has a valuable discussion of the origins of Bruges construction workers. Erik Thoen, "Verhuizen naar Brugge in de Late Middeleeuwen," in Hugo Soly and René Vermeir (eds.), *Beleid en bestuur in de oude Nederlanden. Liber Amicorum Prof. Dr. M. Baelde* (Ghent, 1993), pp. 329–349.

Table 3. *The number of immigrant* poorters *in Bruges (1331–1409)*

Decade	Number of months	Global total	Annual total
1331–1339	108	878	98
1340–1349	87	1394	192
1350–1359	96	595	74
1360–1369	96	1200	150
1370–1379	60	647	129
1380–1389	64	312	59
1390–1399	112	508	54
1400–1409	112	757	81

Source: Thoen, "Verhuizen," p. 332.

then transcribed in the city's accounts.[117] Certainly this does not give us a complete list of immigrants, for many newcomers did not have the means to pay, nor is there complete agreement about the reliability of what survives.[118] Nonetheless, from the 1330s there is enough reliable information available, including careful notations of individual professions and origins, to provide the material in table 3.

It is immediately apparent from the table that the rate of immigration reflects some of the same peaks and valleys as outbreaks of unusual mortality. The rather remarkable rise in registrations between 1340 and 1349 is followed by a steep drop, again followed by a two-decade long swell in the numbers until the difficult 1380s and 1390s brought a crushing downturn.[119] These numbers show the close relation between the health of the urban economy and the numbers of newcomers, and the period after 1360 stands out as indicative of an economic peak for Bruges in the century. On the other side stands the considerable damage of the Ghent war from 1379 to 1385,

[117] It was not until the fifteenth century that a separate register was kept for these enrollments: see André Vandewalle, *Beknopte inventaris van het Stadsarchief van Brugge* (Bruges, 1979), p. 73. There was a number of ways to gain *poorter* status: inheriting it from one's parents, of course, but purchase, gift, and long residence were all sufficient to gain recognition. The primary motivation for many immigrants was the necessity of *poorter* status in order to join a guild in the city; see Thoen, "Verhuizen," 330–331.

[118] Dirk van den Auweele rejected the lists of new *poorters* as a source because of their unreliability; see "Schepenbank en Schepenen te Brugge (1127–1384): Bijdrage tot de studie van een gewone stedelijke rechts- en bestuurs instelling," doctoral dissertation (University of Leuven, 1977), vol. 1, pp. 14–22.

[119] The post-1349 fall-off may be attributable to the bureaucratic confusions caused by the temporary regime of Jacob van Artevelde rather than a real decline in the number of immigrants (Thoen, "Verhuizen," p. 336).

from which the urban economy and hence the immigration rate only very slowly recovered. If these numbers indeed reflect a demand for labor within the Bruges guilds, we have a good, if indirect, picture of the urban labor market across at least two-thirds of the century.

An equally important and suggestive fact about Bruges immigrants is the distance their place of origin was from their destination. Again Thoen's study provides some interesting data: in the two decades from 1331 to 1359 about 22 percent of immigrants came from places outside the county of Flanders, a rate that fell by more than half in the following two decades. Erik Thoen observed that the higher the number of migrants in any given period the farther the average distance of their moving to Bruges.[120] Correspondingly, the more immigrants in total, the fewer who migrated from the adjacent countryside. But even given such periods of strong attraction, the majority of immigrants came from places within twenty miles of Bruges. Yet nuance must be added to the evolution of immigration across the century. For example, it is striking that despite the fall in the percentage of those from outside Flanders in the period 1360–1389, the number of immigrants from French Flanders was very high. This may have had more to do with a crisis in the agrarian economy, caused or exacerbated by war damage, than with the economic attraction of Bruges alone. Striking as well is the near absence of immigrants from England or Germany, despite the presence of large numbers of merchants from those countries.[121]

Two other characteristics of immigrants to Bruges are ascertainable in the records: the percentage who came from another town and the profession of the enrolled immigrant. The data show that town dwellers (all either from Flanders or areas immediately adjacent) became an increasingly important source of new residents: from roughly 40 percent in the period 1331–1356 they increased to over half of the immigrants by 1460.[122] In other words, by the end of our period, nearly half of Bruges's immigrants came from a town within a radius of twenty to thirty miles from the city. A look at the professions of these immigrants helps to complete the picture. The roughly 1,000 immigrants from the period 1331–1375 can be divided into sixteen professional categories depending on the industry their craft served. The totals show the considerable importance of cloth and clothing production in the city: 26.2 percent produced articles of clothing; 18.7 percent produced cloth, and a significant number worked in the luxury sector (gold, silver smithery, rosary makers); construction workers make up the last

[120] Ibid., p. 339. The peak of this phenomenon came in the period 1440–1459, in which more than 50 percent of immigrants came from outside the county of Flanders.
[121] Ibid., pp. 340–341. [122] Ibid., p. 341.

significant group with some 11.9 percent.[123] As we shall see, the professional profile of immigrants mirrors closely the overall division of labor in the city.

PROFESSIONAL AND POLITICAL STRUCTURES

The core of social and political identity in any medieval city was formed by an individual's membership in or exclusion from one or more corporate groups. The privileges of full citizenship, of course, could only be obtained through *poorter* status. If not obtained by birth, or in rare cases by gift, it could be purchased, as in the cases of those whose names appear in the city's accounts. Last but not least, a *poorter* could also be made through marriage to a *poorter*.[124] No one knows how many of those permanently resident in the city were *poorters* – certainly the poor were not, who made up perhaps 25 percent of the residents. On the other hand, as shown among immigrants to the city, non-*poorters* suffered a number of legal impediments, including exclusion from guilds and from certain professions, as well as from employment or service in city government or the militia.[125]

However important to one's political or economic position, it was membership of a guild or professional association that did the most to define identity in late-medieval Bruges as in most medieval cities. Far from being purely economic associations, guilds were the points of entrance for many into urban politics, defense, even poor relief.[126] Guilds reflected in miniature the hierarchies of power that concentrated money and influence in the hands of the ruling few. Guilds also vied with one another for power and precedence within city government, the city militia, and popular pageants and processions.

At the end of the fourteenth century there were some fifty-four guilds and 116 professions divided among fifteen large economic sectors of the

[123] Ibid., table 6, pp. 344–345.

[124] R. A. Parmentier, *Indices op de Brugsche Poorterboeken*, 2 vols. (Bruges. 1938), vol. I, p. vii; for legislation regarding *poorterschap*, Gilliodts-van Severen, *Coutume de la ville*, vol. I, pp. 20–24, 114–115, 153, 238, 298–299, 405–406; 552–554; vol. II, pp. 20–22, 46, 53–55, 80–81, 123–125, 326, 353–359, 753–774.

[125] Non-*poorters* were barred from such professions as money changing, for example, which belonged specifically to a class of employment which, while not controlled by a guild, was reserved to Bruges *poorters* alone – the so-called *poortersneringen*; on this see de Roover, *Money, Banking and Credit*, pp. 171–175.

[126] Marc Boone, "Les métiers dans les villes flamandes au bas moyen âge: images normatives, réalités socio-politiques et économiques," in J.-P. Sosson and P. Lambrechts (eds.), *Les Métiers au Moyen Age: Aspects économiques et sociaux* (Louvain-la-Neuve, 1994), pp. 1–21.

Table 4. *Distribution of professions**

Merchants	20.1%
Construction trades	13.65%
Textile production	12.53%
Producers of tools, furnishings	12.69%
Food	10.71%
General manufacture	10.65%
Luxury production	7.81%
Broking/money changing	2.85%
Transport	2.54%
Administration	2.25%
Police and security	2.25%
Health care	1.76%
Military	0.29%
Agriculture	0.19%
Education	0.09%

* Adapted from I. de Meyer, "De sociale strukturen te Brugge in de 14e eeuw," *Standen en Landen* 54 (1971), 9–78.

urban economy (see table 4). These numbers are at the very best a crude approximation given the nature of the source, but they reflect *grosso modo* the social and professional reality of a great merchant city. Unique among Flemish cities of the time were the numbers of merchants and producers of luxury articles. This underscores the reality of economic development in Bruges away from cloth production in favor of a more diverse collection of trades catering above all to the desires of the rich. Yet this professional profile was itself a product of a century of change, a change that can be measured through comparison with earlier moments in time.

Unfortunately, data drawn from earlier in the century are not entirely commensurate with the late-fourteenth-century tax records. First they are derived from militia rolls and thus are likely to overstate the numbers in prominent guilds like weavers and brokers (tax records have the opposite tendency, since many weavers earned too little to pay tax). Secondly, their numbers do not seek to count the same things as a tax record, whose goal is to list every fiscally significant household. Nonetheless, the lists of 1302, 1316, and 1338–1340 provide time-lapse photographs of the professional structure of Bruges society across the century (table 5). Even giving a wide margin for imprecision there are certain clearly discernible tendencies at

Table 5. *Professional structure**

	1302	1338–1340
Merchants	2.25%	3.61%
Building trades	11.28%	10.13%
Textile production	44.63%	37.15%
Tools, furnishings	4.06%	5.78%
Food	10.5%	11.62%
General manufacture	10.10%	12.62%
Luxury production	3.83%	7.98%
Broking/money changing	8.36%	6.89%
Transport	2.25%	2.47%
Health care	0.81%	0.78%

* Adapted from de Meyer, "Sociale strukturen te Brugge," vol. I, p. 34.

work. First is the relative decline of textile workers, especially of weavers, as a percentage of the population. From other records Jan Dumolyn has calculated that the participation of weavers in the urban militia fell by two-thirds between 1340 and 1382.[127] Their numbers were no doubt partly made up by an increase in the numbers of those in the cloth finishing trades, which better withstood the structural changes in the industry, as chapter 7 will show. Yet the fact remains that Bruges had many fewer textile workers, both in absolute numbers and as a percentage of the population, than did either Ghent or Ypres.[128]

Guilds were once often mistakenly associated with "democratic" urban politics and opposition to economic and technological innovation. The great Henri Pirenne was the best known of the historians who identified the guilds with "democratic" agitation in late thirteenth and early fourteenth-century Flanders. Their sworn enemies have been traditionally portrayed as the urban "capitalist" patrician elites whose political monopoly was broken by the revolutionary era of 1280–1302.[129] The situation in Bruges, as other research has shown elsewhere, belies these old certainties. In the first place

[127] Dumolyn, "Population," 53.

[128] Prevenier estimated the figure for Ghent at 60 percent of the labor force and that for Ypres at 50 percent; see Prevenier, "La démographie," 256.

[129] Pirenne, *Histoire de Belgique*, vol. III, p. 220, for guilds as enemies of innovation. For more on the fate of Pirenne's ideas, see Walter Prevenier, "Henri Pirenne et les villes des anciens Pays-Bas au bas moyen âge," *Archives et Bibliothèques de Belgique* extra number, 28 (1986), 40, 45–49; and see Boone, "Les métiers," pp. 6–7 and n. 18.

the dynamically expansive urban economy of fourteenth-century Bruges was every bit as guild-based as in any other town or city. Secondly, lumping together under the same "revolutionary" banner guilds as different as weavers and brokers/hostellers distorts a much more complex reality. Lastly, viewing guilds as "democratic" in either their inner workings or in their participation in the larger operations of urban government is a fundamental error.

As elsewhere in Flanders, guilds in Bruges were descended from older forms of association representing a cross-section of the rich, the middling, and even the relatively poor whose first job was organizing the conduct and provisioning of local markets.[130] The London Hanse was the name traditionally given to this dominant association in the city before 1300. But, as Carlos Wyffels has pointed out, it was hardly made up exclusively of rich capitalists involved in the wool trade with England. Instead, it included many traders in the local market – butchers, bakers, brewers, and others who would form some of the most powerful fourteenth-century guilds.[131] Thus the violence and agitation of the "revolutionary" decades around 1300 should properly be understood as a breakthrough of existing or incipient guilds, both in obtaining power in urban government and in organizing themselves into formally constituted guilds. In short, the larger oligarchy of the "Hanse" was divided and recreated in the numerous miniature oligarchies of the guilds. Whatever the formal result, however, power tended to remain with the rich. For example, brokers and hostellers, who in many cases had the relationship of employee and employer, formed a single guild in which hostellers quickly gained political prominence.[132] Even the notoriously "democratic" weavers formed a guild in which wealthier "weaver/drapers," who bought much of their cloth from other weavers and sold it in the cloth hall, held dominant positions.[133]

By the 1350s, at the end of Bruges's revolutionary period, a lasting balance of power had been achieved among guilds and members of the *poorterij* – itself a mélange of "patriciate" families and those exercising a profession not formally organized in an independent guild. This balance was translated into proportional possession of seats on the two aldermanic benches,

[130] Carlos Wyffels, "De vlaamse hanzen opnieuw belicht," in *Academiae Analecta. Mededelingen van de Koninklike Academie voor Wetenschappen, Letteren en Schone Kunsten van België, Klasse der Letteren* 53 (1991), 8–13.

[131] Carlos Wyffels, "De vlaamse hanze van Londen op het einde van de XIIIe eeuw," ASEB 97 (1960), 5–30 and Boone, "Les métiers," p. 7.

[132] For the Bruges hostellers, see chapter 5.

[133] See chapter 7.

whose members were the result of a many-stage selection process. First, each guild and neighborhood held elections, followed in most cases by elections among guilds who were grouped together for representative purposes in city government, with the winner of that election becoming the occupant of an alderman's seat.[134] Next, the members of the first bench of aldermen (the *schepenen*) selected their colleagues on the second bench (*raad*), who acted as advisors to the *schepenen* but also undertook some administrative tasks of their own.[135] After 1304 four of the thirteen seats in each bank were apportioned to the *poorterij*, with the remaining nine allotted to the guilds. The fifty-four guilds were in turn divided into nine groups, each in theory with a seat to fill.[136] All officeholders in both city and guild government served for one year, which commenced at Candlemas (2 February) for most of the century, and after 1383 on 2 September.[137]

Six additional ruling councils operated in the urban neighborhoods (*zestendeelen*) of Bruges, also composed of *poorters* and guildsmen, headed by a dean, who was usually a *poorter*. These local councils had considerable responsibilities, including military organization, land and building disputes, tax collection, and any other tasks delegated by the *schepenen*.[138] Many of these local leaders also directed the poor relief efforts of one or more of the parish churches in their district.[139] The internal governance of guilds strongly resembled that of the neighborhood councils, since they too consisted of elected "deans" assisted by four to eight councilors. Unlike the city magistrates, however, individuals in both guild and neighborhood could serve consecutive terms in office without a mandatory interruption.

In theory this governmental system seems representative to a fault, given its emphasis on proportionality and short terms of office. And indeed the

[134] W. Prevenier and M. Boone, "De steden in de Zuidelijke Nederlanden in de late middeleeuwen: stedelijke identiteit en corporatieve solidariteiten," *Het Tijdschrift van het Gemeentekrediet* 183 (1993), 25–42, esp. 36.

[135] The Burgomaster of the Raad acted as city's representative in prosecutions and bankruptcies; see K. Vanhaverbeke, "De reële machtsstructuren binnen het stadsbestuur van Brugge in de periode 1375–1407. Verslag van een prosopografische studie," *ASEB* 135 (1998), 3–54, esp. 9 and n. 21.

[136] J. Mertens, "De verdeling van de Brugse schepenzetels op sociaal gebied," *Wetenschapelijke Tijdingen* 21/10 (1961), 451–466, p. 460; Vanhaverbeke, "De reële machtsstructuren," 10.

[137] Annual terms were typical across Flanders and northern France and seem to have been inspired by practices of the mendicant orders; see Marc Boone, "Verfassungsnorm und Verwaltungswirklichkeit im spätmittelalterlichen flämischen Raum, das Beispiel Gent," in W. Ehbrecht (ed.), *Städtische Selbstverwaltungsorgane vom 14. bis 19. Jahrhundert. 21 Kolloquium des Kuratoriums für vergleichende Städtegeschichte* (Münster, 1990) and Boone and Prevenier, "Steden in de Zuidelijke Nederlanden," 35.

[138] Gilliodts-van Severen, *Coutumes Quarties de Bruges*, vol. 1, pp. 327–362.

[139] Galvin, *Poor Tables*, pp. 211–229.

system seems to have addressed many of the complaints voiced by protestors against the "Old Regime" that was in place before 1302.[140] But appearances are deceptive, for in Bruges, as in all medieval Flemish cities, real power was held by a relatively small group of self-recruited and too often self-enriching men whose influence extended into every corner of the city. Unfortunately, there is no definitive study of the Bruges oligarchy, but enough is known to give a rough idea of the workings of power in the city.

A recent prosopographical study of city officeholders between 1375–1407 reveals the true dimensions of the urban power structure. In this period the possible 1,172 city offices were held by a total of 260 individuals, an average of 4.5 each. But a closer look reveals that two-thirds of the 260 held only one to three offices, but the other third occupied in total a whopping 75 percent of the total. And within this small group, eighteen men, or 30 percent served fifteen or more times. In effect urban government was controlled by a pyramid, with a relatively rapidly shifting base of those who served only once or twice, ascending to a more or less permanently fixed group of the most powerful.[141] The men at the top, whether they ostensibly represented a guild or the *poorters*, had a similar social profile: they were wealthy, from well-connected families, and were disproportionately drawn from among the brokers/hostellers and other merchants.[142]

The clearest proof of this domination by the mercantile and wealthy few is in the management and awarding of the city's public works projects and taxation. As in many medieval cities, the majority of tax revenues came from indirect or excise taxes on commodities such as wine, beer, and mead, as well as the sale of the right to collect tolls or other customary taxes.[143] By far the greatest single source of revenue was the tax on wine, which was consumed in far larger quantities in affluent Bruges than elsewhere.[144] Every thirteen weeks the right to collect excise taxes was auctioned to the highest bidder, who was required to pay the purchase price in cash before

[140] Walter Prevenier, "Inzicht van kritische tijdgenoten in de sociale facetten der fiscaliteit en in sociaal-politiek onrecht in Vlaanderen (13de–15de eeuw)," in *Arbeid in veelvoud. Een huldeboek voor Jan Craeybeckx en Etienne Scholliers* (Brussels, 1988), pp. 51–60.

[141] Vanhaverbeke, "De reële machtsstructuren," 13–15.

[142] The most egregious pluralist was Jan van der Beurse of the well-known hosteller family; another was Niclais Barbesaen, who served many consecutive terms as city treasurer. For both see below and Vanhaverbeke, "De reële machtsstructuren," 15 and 19–21.

[143] Vanhaverbeke, "De reële machtsstructuren," 21.

[144] For beer and wine consumption as an index of population and economic decline, see Raymond van Uytven, "Stages of Economic Decline," in J-M Duvosquel and E. Thoen (eds.), *Peasants and Townsmen in Medieval Europe: Studia in Honorem Adriaan Verhulst* (Ghent, 1995), pp. 259–269, esp. 263–265; reprinted in *Production and Consumption* XII.

receiving a penny of actual revenue. The treasurers of the city presided over these auctions, and the successful bidders were usually partnerships formed from the most affluent of Bruges burghers. But what is striking about the tax farmers is that they were themselves drawn from former officeholders, either aldermen or treasurers. Dirk van den Auweele in fact observed that it had become almost customary for an alderman rotated out of office by the annual change of office to appear the next year as a farmer of an excise tax.[145] Given the crucial calculation of the difference between purchase price and potential revenue, city administrators and successful bidders formed a nearly closed circle with a monopoly on privileged information.

There were many other ways to profit from city officeholding. J.-P. Sosson has shown that most city building contracts were awarded to a small group of guild leaders who also served in city government as aldermen.[146] Contracts to supply city officials and employees with cloth also went to well-connected weaver/drapers, as did purchases of fish and other comestibles.[147] Though this subject is far from exhausted, certain facts about money and power emerge clearly. As in most medieval cities, governmental and economic power was in the hands of a small elite which circulated in and out of city office, often profiting from city contracts at the same time. Money was certainly a prerequisite for entry into the elite, a fact that then linked individuals across professional and even social boundaries, so that the rich weaver/draper had much more in common with his opposite number in any other guild than he had with the ordinary weaver. This is a familiar story to any student of late-medieval urban society. What makes Bruges different, however, is the dominance of those directly involved in international trade. These were the great broker/hosteller families, the van der Beurses, Metteneyes, Honins and Bonins; the wool-brokering van den Walles, and the important draper families, the de Vos and de Munteres. Generation after generation of these families fanned out into nearly every facet of economic and political life in the city. They served as aldermen and treasurers; negotiated commercial treaties; were dispatched as ambassadors to foreign courts; and above all profited from the rich and growing role of

[145] Van den Auweele, "Schepenbank en schepenen," p. 404. Similar conclusions for Ghent were drawn by Marc Boone, "Triomferend privé-initiatief versus haperend overheidsoptreden? Over pachters van indirecte belastingen in laatmiddeleeuwse steden," *Tijdschrift voor Sociale Geschiedenis* 15 (1989), 113–138.

[146] Sosson, *Les travaux publics*: see chapter 4, "Un syndicat de patrons," pp. 189–201.

[147] This was certainly true of cloth; see below chapter 7. Vanhaverbeke, "De reële machtsstructuren," 23, notes that in the year when Jan de Muntere was burgomaster of *schepenen* (1387–1388), all cloth purchased by the city came from him.

Bruges in international trade and finance. Yet Bruges seems overall to have been less dominated by clans of ancient lineage than Ghent, for example. There remained a fluidity of power and influence amenable and open to men of business and administrative ability.

CONCLUSION

As in all medieval cities, the streets and squares of Bruges were filled with immigrants and strangers – but here a merchant from Gdansk could jostle one from Genoa, as an immigrant from Lille might move next door to one from Utrecht. In other words, both resident merchants and immigrants came from farther away and probably remained longer than in many other cities. Vigorous immigration was necessary in the fourteenth century, both to fill the empty ranks left by famine, war, and disease and to do the work of ensuring that Bruges became and remained a great merchant city. And immigration, population, and professional patterns showed the effects of economic change and development. The overall percentage of the population involved in cloth manufacture fell throughout the century, as opportunities for artisans of luxury products increased. Guilds multiplied, becoming the organizing principle for much of urban social and political life; the poor lived literally and figuratively on the margins – packed into the outlying neighborhoods, part of no corporate body except perhaps that of the "shame-faced" or parish-supported poor.

Bruges's exceptionality among Flemish and other cities of the era is subtle but important. While elsewhere plague and other mortality reduced populations for considerable periods, population in Bruges seems to have rebounded quickly to a range between 42,000 and 50,000. While every city had its merchant visitors, particularly during fair time, Bruges had far more both short and long-term merchant guests, whose number no doubt peaked during the Bruges fair in May. And unusual size seems to have characterized the clergy population of the city, whose number could also rise due to student visitors or visitors for councils or other clerical gatherings. Bruges city politics also had traits of the typical and exceptional. As elsewhere, an oligarchy ruled, yet in Bruges its members were typically drawn from the ranks of rich merchants and guildsmen, where money made the man. The most subtle yet profound trait of all was the feeling of speed and flux, clear even at the distance of seven centuries. Bruges was a city of the rootless, where the vast majority rented their rooms or houses, few could count on extended family or kin networks, and many found short lives and scant comforts. Life, to quote Huizinga, had a fierceness to it – a ferocity of newness and opportunity in the market places and hostelries, and one of despair, disease, and death on view in the streets, almshouses, and hospitals. Thousands came forward in that century to wager with their lives and fortunes on the success of Bruges as a commercial city. So perhaps the best measure of their humanity is to assess what they created.

CHAPTER 4

Money and its discontents

Monnoyer et cangeur ont ore l'aventure,
car en monnaies est li cose moult obscure.
Elles vont haut et bas, se ne set-on que faire;
Quand on quide wagnier, on troeve le contraire . . .[1]

Gilles li Muisit, abbot of St. Giles Abbey, Tournai

No single group in medieval society had a keener nose for money than members of the mendicant orders. This was due in part to their very foundation and development, which to a greater or lesser extent eschewed using or possessing money in any form. St. Francis emphatically renounced money and lineage, thereby pointing to their power over the eventual mission of his friars and those of the other orders.[2] For paradoxically, while shunning money, mendicants congregated around and drew near to those who possessed it. There was no duplicity or hypocrisy in this, only the realization that the work of salvation lay precisely in the morality of the market, in influencing money and its use. Thus no place was more in need of the religious care of souls that the mendicant orders were created to provide than the great money centers of the Middle Ages, places like Bruges.[3]

Predictably then, Bruges had more mendicant foundations within its walls than any other city in Flanders by 1300. As pointed out in chapter 2, the dominant orders – Franciscans, Dominicans, Carmelites, Augustinians – built their cloisters in effect to frame the commercial district of the city, while at the same time connecting it to the outer neighborhoods of Bruges

[1] Joseph Kervyn van Lettenhove (ed.), *Poésies de Gilles li Muisis*, 2 vols. (Leuven, 1882), vol. II, p. 156; quoted in Marc Bloch, *Esquisse d'une histoire monétaire de l'Europe* (Paris, 1954), p. 40.

[2] Lester Little tells the story of Francis in the context of economic change in his *Religious Poverty and the Profit Economy in Medieval Europe* (Ithaca, NY, 1978), pp. 146–152.

[3] Walter Simons points to the differences between a commercial and industrial city to explain the difference in the number of mendicant houses in Ghent and Bruges. Ghent's population exceeded that of Bruges by nearly a third, yet there were six mendicant houses in Bruges versus five in Ghent; see Simons, *Stad en apostolaat*, pp. 92–93.

Figure 7: *Man Weighing Gold* by Adriaen Isenbrant, c. 1530. Metropolitan Museum of Art, New York, The Friedsam Collection, Bequest of Michael Friedsam, 1931. Money changers were specialists in the evaluation of coinage according to a fixed weight in bullion. By law they were required to cull out underweight coins and send them to the comital mint for recoinage, but abuse was common.

where the poor resided and vice – especially prostitution and usury – flourished. But do we really know what brought the mendicants and kept them in Bruges? In other words, had money really achieved a level of prominence and sophistication in the city beyond that of even neighboring Ghent, a more populous and industrialized city of considerable wealth? This chapter will argue that the mendicants were correct in choosing a place where the money business achieved a measure of size and complexity sufficient to pique the interest of anyone who sought to curb money's moral danger or harness its economic power.

MONEY AND ITS ORGANIZATION

As economists have long recognized, "money" takes any number of forms according to the economic complexity of the context.[4] Of course some forms of money are used nearly exclusively by rather small groups within an economy: for example, even now only a minority of Americans are direct holders of company stock shares. Part of Bruges's success as a commercial city lay in the number of discrete groups of people within her walls, with their incessant need for a flexible and powerful payment system. Such a system had to be able to accommodate foreign bullion and coinage, supply Flemish and other gold and silver coins of a startling range of face values, provide short-term, long-term and consumer credit, and solve the problems posed by distance and politics in transferring funds from one place to another. For trade to flourish, no part of this system could be wanting, for the participants and specialists in the money economy of Bruges formed an interdependent whole bound together by mutual trust and opportunity. Foreign and native, male and female, noble or commoner, all played a role as makers and users of a financial system of unique power and flexibility.[5]

Envisioning the structure assumed by such a system in fourteenth-century Bruges has proven an elusive task. Raymond de Roover, its first great historian, pictured it as a rigid hierarchy, with vertically ascending rungs occupied by moneylenders, pawnbrokers, money changers, with Italian merchant bankers at the summit. The activities of each profession were rigidly separated and sealed off by law and privilege, so that there could

[4] On money in the medieval economy, see the preliminary remarks of Peter Spufford, *Money and Its Use in Medieval Europe* (Cambridge, 1988), pp. 1–4.

[5] Of the literature on finance and financial systems in pre-modern Europe, see Herman van der Wee, "Monetary, Credit and Banking Systems," in M. M. Postan and H. J. Habakkuk (eds.), *Cambridge Economic History of Europe* second edition, 8 vols. (Cambridge, 1978), vol. v, pp. 290–392, is still the best introduction. On the reciprocal influence of money and the "accounting" mentality, see Joel Kaye, *Economy and Nature in the Fourteenth Century: Money, Market Exchange, and the Emergence of Scientific Thought* (Cambridge, 1998).

be little talk of a cooperative, inter-professional money and credit system. Instead he argued for a largely "local" division of specialization between pawnbrokers and money changers on the one hand, and on the other an "international" cadre of Italians who handled long-distance money transfers via bills of exchange. Bruges thus became a great money city in part because of the number of its money changers, some of whom became deposit bankers in the course of the fourteenth century; but most of all because it became the seat of the great Italian banking companies of the late Middle Ages. To a large extent this was a fortuitous occurrence, in de Roover's view, with only vague reference to, and dependence on, the specific urban context.[6]

De Roover's vision is fundamentally flawed, however. Driven by a desire to find the "origins of modern banking," as well as a predisposition to emphasize Italian business techniques, he forced the medieval money professions into their various categories based on their proximity to mid-twentieth-century definitions of banking and finance. In so doing he denied to both Bruges pawnbrokers and money changers any significant involvement in long-distance financial networks, and he was unclear about the very great importance of investment in local and long-distance trade by each.[7] This anachronism caused him to miss the organic unity of the system, which was defined not by changing money or lending on pawned

[6] De Roover, *Money, Banking and Credit*, pp. 345–354. De Roover's ideas still largely condition recent studies, as for example the introduction to Peter Spufford's *Handbook of Medieval Exchange* (London, 1986), pp. xix–lviii, attests. De Roover spelled out his ideas not only in *Money, Banking and Credit in Mediaeval Bruges*, but also in a series of articles and book chapters, most notably in "The Organization of Trade," in vol. III of the *Cambridge Economic History of Europe* (Cambridge, 1963), pp. 42–118. Because of the long delay in the publication of his Bruges book, the first articulation of his ideas was in "Le contrat de change depuis la fin du treizième siècle jusqu'au début du dix-septième," in *RBPH* 15 (1946–1947), 115–118. This rigid hierarchy of discrete specialties has had its critics, especially Roberto Lopez ("The Dawn of Medieval Banking," in *The Dawn of Modern Banking* (New Haven, 1979), p. 7 n. 6) and other historians, who have criticized some of its specifics. Nonetheless, the vision has remained virtually unchallenged in histories of Bruges and Flanders. The best discussion of the question is Erik Aerts, "Middeleeuwse bankgeschiedenis volgens Professor Raymond de Roover," *Bijdragen tot de Geschiedenis der Nederlanden* 63 (1980), 49–86, with an English summary.

[7] Ibid., 55–57. These errors had serious consequences both for de Roover's work and for general understanding of the development of banking institutions. For, as Aerts points out (73–74), the work of Herman van der Wee and John Munro has proven that the crucial breakthrough leading to the creation of modern banking, the discountable bond, was developed in England and Antwerp, the lineal descendants of Bruges as banking centers. See John H. Munro, "English 'Backwardness' and Financial Innovations in Commerce with the Low Countries, 14th to 16th Centuries," in Peter Stabel, Bruno Blondé and Anke Greve (eds.), *International Trade in the Low Countries (14th–16th Centuries): Merchants, Organisation, Infrastructure* (Leuven and Apeldoorn, 2000), pp. 105–167, and Herman van der Wee, *The Growth of the Antwerp Market and the European Economy (Fourteenth–Sixteenth Centuries)*, 3 vols. (The Hague, 1963), vol. II, pp. 348–352; van der Wee, "Sporen van disconto te Antwerpen tijdens de XVIe eeuw," *Bijdragen tot de Geschiedenis der Nederlanden* 10 (1955), 68–70; and "Anvers et les innovations de la technique financière aux XVIe et XVIIe siècles," *Annales E.S.C.* 22 (1967), 1085–1088.

articles, but by mobilizing money for investment. Money changers, merchant bankers, and pawnbrokers alike probably profited more from trade than anything else. With this in mind, the structure that these financial professionals created most resembles a honeycomb and not a hierarchy. Besides being a favorite symbol of medieval intellectuals, the honeycomb evokes a structure that allows for specialization in tasks, while recognizing unity of purpose. In short, all moneymen and women should properly be thought of as merchants first and money changers, pawnbrokers, hostellers, or bankers second. Moreover, rigid specialization and separation of tasks in the money business simply did not exist in fourteenth-century Bruges, despite comital and municipal legislation intended to impose them. As we shall see here and in a later chapter on long-distance finance, many merchants might grant credit, hold deposits, or change money if business demanded. But the foremost concern of all was to profit from the abundant business opportunities coursing through the streets and waterways of Bruges.

"READY" MONEY

For the vast majority of residents in fourteenth-century Bruges, money meant coined silver, gold, or copper/silver alloy, bearing a sovereign's symbol and struck at a weight, fineness, and value stipulated by that same sovereign power. This was what contemporaries called "ready" or "clinking" money.[8] The first rule of such money was that it existed at the pleasure and for the profit of the lord who issued it and not for the utility of the people who used it.[9] This could be the chief source of discontent with money. Of course no sovereign prince could be completely indifferent to public opinion even in

[8] Modern Dutch preserves the medieval forms *gereed geld*– ready money – and *klinkende munt*, i.e. cash money, especially in coin form.

[9] This fundamental fact of medieval coinage in the context of the medieval economy is discussed by Hunt and Murray, *History of Business*, pp. 11–30. Essential as well is Spufford, *Money and its Use*, pp. 240–263. For Flanders, the work of Olivier Elsen, "La monnaie des comtes de Flandre Louis de Nevers (1322–1346) et Louis de Male (1346–1384) d'après les comptes et les ordonnances monétaires', *Revue Belge de Numismatique et Sigillographie* 141 (1995), 37–183, has superseded earlier works. Still valuable are Hans van Werveke, *De muntslag in Vlaanderen onder Lodewijk Van Male* (Brussels, 1949) and "Munt en politiek. De frans–vlaamse verhoudingen vóór en na 1300," *Bijdragen tot de Geschiedenis der Nederlanden* 7 (1953–54), 1–19; these and other works were collected in *Miscellanea Mediaevalia: Verspreide opstellen over economische en sociale geschiedenis van de Middeleeuwen* (Ghent, 1968) with an introduction by F. L. Ganshof. In English, see John H. Munro, *Wool, Cloth and Gold: The Struggle for Bullion in Anglo-Burgundian Trade, 1340–1478* (Toronto, 1972), pp. 20–21 and Nicholas, *Metamorphosis of a Medieval City*, pp. 120–133. Also useful is Frans Blockmans and W. P. Blockmans, "Devaluation, Coinage and Seignorage under Louis de Nevers and Louis de Male, Counts of Flanders, 1330–84," in N. J. Mayhew (ed.), *Coinage in the Low Countries (880–1500): The Third Oxford Symposium in Coinage and Monetary History* (Oxford, 1979).

the Middle Ages, and in the fourteenth century intellectuals like Nicholas Oresme sought to convince princes that maintenance of a strong and reliable currency was an affair of the common good and not private profit. His arguments, set out in a learned treatise, reportedly had some success with Charles V of France, but he remained an exceptional figure.[10] Charles's contemporary and vassal, Count Louis of Male of Flanders, was a notorious manipulator of the coinage of his county, a fact that compounded an already complex monetary system.[11]

For simplicity's sake the history of Flemish coinage is best divided into two periods: the first, from roughly 1269–1322, saw the introduction of the "groot" coin and the struggle with the increasing interference from the French kings. The second period encompasses the reigns of Louis of Nevers and Louis of Male, when Flanders produced both enormous quantities of coin and carried out a continuing policy of debasement, continuing until the draconian reform carried out in 1390 by the Burgundian prince, Philip the Bold. These divisions mark significant shifts in the kinds of coins minted, but they did not diminish the large number of different coins in circulation or the complexity of their use. In part this had to do with the split identity of Flanders, at once a fief of the French king and a part of the empire by virtue of territory held by the Flemish count east of the Scheldt river.[12] Flemish coinage reflected this reality by embracing French monies of account and often imitating actual French coins, while the counts defended their right to strike coins in the face of increasing Capetian objections to the practice. While a satellite of France politically, the Flemings were heavily influenced by the coins of their other neighbors and trading partners. This is well illustrated by the fact that even as Countess Margaret of Constantinople imitated the gros tournois of King Louis IX as the central coin of her Flemish monetary system in 1269, she instituted a different monetary regime in her county of Hainault, a part of the empire.[13] Her son and successor, Guy of Dampierre, attached Flanders even more firmly to the French royal monetary system throughout his reign, imitating the gros tournois exactly in weight and fineness while at the same time

10 Spufford, *Money and Its Use*, pp. 300–308.

11 Hans van Werveke, "Currency Manipulation in the Middle Ages: The Case of Louis of Male, Count of Flanders," *Transactions of the Royal Historical Society* series 4/31 (1949), 115–127.

12 On the territorial origins of Flanders see Nicholas, *Medieval Flanders*, pp. 56–96. It should be stressed, however, that the French influence was always supreme in the county. This is reflected in the money of account system, which was originally based on the parisis system of northern France and a real coin, the penny or denier. Even after this system was superseded, the penny parisis remained the money of account in the Bruges city accounts and in those of many other Flemish cities.

13 Elsen, "La monnaie," 42–43; for the reign of Margaret in general, see Nicholas, *Medieval Flanders*, pp. 156–158.

striking large quantities of imitation English sterlings. In fact, coin hoards from the southern Low Countries suggest that the most widely circulated coin in Flanders during the late thirteenth into the early fourteenth century was the English sterling and its imitations. In effect, as Peter Spufford points out, Flanders had a "multi-tiered" currency system in which two or three denominations of coins were struck at any one time to satisfy different needs.[14]

The same apparently chaotic minting practices continued under the reign of Robert of Béthune (1305–1322). On the one hand he continued the step-by-step assumption of the French monetary system, so that in effect the gros tournois became the basis of the Flemish system. He also continued the practice, initiated by Philip the Fair in his brief occupation of Bruges, of striking French gros in clear contravention of the royal ordinance against such imitation by the barons. On the other hand, Robert continued to strike imitation sterlings at his mints in Ghent and Aalst, and he introduced a new gros coin, struck on imperial territory in Aalst, with design characteristics that would be continued by his successors. However, contrary to the opinions of earlier historians, Robert was not the initiator of the Flemish gold coinage. What can be said with certainty, however, is that by 1312 at the latest, the system of monies of account and their relationship to circulating coins had been fixed, so that the money of account most frequently used was the pound parisis, which had a fixed relationship with the Flemish pound gros or groot of twelve to one. Thus one groot always equaled 12 d. parisis.[15]

The Flemish monetary regime from 1322 to the last decade of the century is both noted and notorious. It is justly famous for the wide diversity of coins issued, especially gold but also silver; by the quantity of coins produced and the high artistic quality of their design; and last but not least by the widespread influence of Flemish coins on neighboring states.[16] However,

[14] Spufford, *Money and Its Use*, pp. 229–232; Elsen, "La monnaie," 44. So great was the demand for imitation English pennies, or "esterlins" as they were called in the Low Countries, that ten times as many imitations were struck there as in England; see Spufford, *Money and Its Use*, p. 231; N. J. Mayhew, "The Circulation and Imitation of Sterlings in the Low Countries," in *Coinage in the Low Countries*, p. 61; John H. Munro, "Mint Policies, Ratios and Outputs in the Low Countries and England, 1335–1420," *Numismatic Chronicle* series 8, 1 (1981), 71–116.

[15] For the substance of the paragraph see Elsen, "La monnaie," 42–45. A complementary change was the shift from reliance on the *marc* of Cologne to the *marc* of Troyes as the measurement of silver bullion. According to John H. Munro this occurred sometime in the early fourteenth century; see "The Maze of Medieval Mint Metrology: Determining Mint Weights in Flanders, France and England from the Economics of Counterfeiting, 1388–1469," *The Journal of European Economic History* 29 (2000), 173–199, esp. 175, n. 5.

[16] Elsen, "La monnaie," 46 and n. 39.

Louis of Male is maligned as an arch- "false moneyer" who systematically debased his coins for his own profit. In the period from 1337 to 1364 the bullion content of the Flemish groot was reduced by half across a possible nineteen different coin issues.[17] The differences between issues were often so minute so as to be detectable only by money changers or other money specialists.[18] The resulting monetary chaos brought reform with a new silver coin, the double groot, which ironically marked a further debasement over the coin it replaced and contained in fact less silver than the original single groot of 1337. In this period of the "Double *Groot*" from 1365–1384, six issues of coins were struck, resulting in the huge sum of thirty-seven million double groots in circulation. Again, debasement in the form of reductions in the silver content of the alloy from which coins were struck was the rule: the 1384 double groot contained 25 percent less silver than that of 1365.[19]

Less troubled by debasement, though no less complex, was the history of Flemish gold coins from the mid to late fourteenth century. As in Italy, where gold coins were struck from the middle of the thirteenth century, gold coinage came to replace silver as the preferred exchange medium of international commerce in northern Europe by 1350.[20] Much of this new wave of gold was brought on by war expenditure and massive borrowing from Italian merchant companies. Flanders in general and Bruges in particular became a collecting place for gold coins of various provenances, providing Louis of Male with an added opportunity for profit if he could direct foreign coins to his mints. Nonetheless foreign gold coins continued to circulate in Flanders throughout the fourteenth century, indicating that even Louis's best efforts fell short of meeting demand.[21]

Just as Flemish coins moved from imitation to original in the case of silver, gold coinage in Flanders also began with an imitation of the Florentine florin, struck by Louis of Nevers in 1335.[22] Louis added imitations of French

17 Ibid., 118 and 120 n. 401.

18 Although debasement usually appeared to subjects as a purely economic decision, in effect it was a form of taxation with important political motivations and ramifications as well. On this see Munro, *Wool, Cloth and Gold*, pp. 13–22. Elsen ("La monnaie," 61 and n. 111 and 113) discusses the sometimes minute differences among different issues of the same coin and the clues money changers could use to establish their fineness.

19 For the substance of this paragraph, see Elsen, "La monnaie," 126, 146–147.

20 Spufford, *Money and Its Use*, pp. 267–288.

21 In 1357 Louis complained of "le grant grief, blasme et damage" caused by foreign coins current in Flanders: Elsen, "La monnaie," 107 and n. 330.

22 Spufford, *Money and Its Use*, pp. 276–278, on importation of Florentine florins to Bruges c. 1300 and first minting of gold coins, and Elsen, "La monnaie," 62–63.

coins, notably the écu, royal, and mouton, and an original coin, the angel.[23] Louis of Male continued his father's practice of imitating foreign coins, while adding new ones of original design. These included imitations of the English noble, continued imitations of the chief French gold coins of the era, notably the French franc, and the new gold "Flanders" and "Lion" coins.[24] By the end of Louis of Male's reign, fifteen different Flemish gold coins had been minted, both imitations and originals. Perhaps recognizing this unbearable richness of choice in 1361 Louis again tried to ban circulation of "foreign" gold coins.[25] Despite the promise of confiscations and fines, the ordinance had no effect.

The quantity and (design) quality of the Flemish coinage were indeed striking characteristics of Louis of Male's reign, but the true emphasis lay on profit. In some years 20 percent of the count's revenues were derived from mint profits, with a noticeable shift of emphasis from silver to gold.[26] What Louis succeeded in creating after 1350 was a very nearly closed system of minting, recalling and reminting silver coins in circulation in Flanders and neighboring regions. One such issue, a double groat coin of 1368 was coined from bullion of which 40 percent was supplied by recycled coins. Louis of Nevers had also achieved this thirty years before, but on a far smaller scale.[27] For gold bullion, Louis of Male could not count on recapturing coins from Flanders itself, so he tried by every means at his command to divert and capture the gold of his neighbors. To do this he offered a premium for gold brought to Flemish mints. In 1357 he offered the English wool merchant and financial adventurer John Goldbeter a special bonus for all English gold nobles and sterlings he delivered to the mint.[28] Louis also operated a mint in the annexed city of Mechelen, with the clear intention of capturing as much bullion from Brabant and his other eastern neighbors as he could. Louis fully grasped the fact that an aggressive minting policy was war by another means, and many of his tactics were carried on by his successor, Philip the Bold of Burgundy.[29]

[23] Elsen, "La monnaie," 157–158.

[24] These were the first entirely original Flemish gold coins: ibid., 126.

[25] These were defined as coins both gold and silver, issued by sovereigns other than the king of France or count of Flanders, ibid., 115. According to this ordinance, only the mouton and franc coins were to circulate, at the rate of 28 groot and 27 groot respectively.

[26] Elsen, "La monnaie," 163–164; van Werveke, "Currency Manipulation," 123.

[27] Elsen, "La monnaie," 134–135 and n. 456.

[28] de Limburg-Stirum, *Cartulaire de Louis de Male*, vol. 1, pp. 572–573, and Elsen, "La monnaie," 99. The document calls him Jehan Goudbetel, but there is no doubt about his identity; for more on Goldbeter, see chapter 7.

[29] In this as in many other things, Louis of Male paved the way for his Burgundian successors. For the later period see Munro, *Wool, Cloth and Gold*, pp. 43–63.

By 1350, then, the bimetallic hierarchy of silver and gold was established in Flanders, and its mints were among the busiest and most productive in Europe, churning out coins by the million. Yet the true coinage of the people was "black money," so called because of its high copper content and the color it acquired in its passage through many hands.[30] Whether or not such "fractional" coins were produced in sufficient quantities to meet local demand is a difficult question. Indeed, just defining "sufficient" in the context or an urban economy is virtually impossible.[31] What is clear is that the mites and double mites (struck after 1375) of the Flemish monetary system were significant and useful coins, given that a mite represented a constant fraction ($^{1}/_{24}$) of a penny gros/groot, and that a wide variety of purchases required coins of small denomination. Just a glance at commodity prices in Bruges from 1350 to 1390 shows the great buying power that even the mite enjoyed, given that a penny gros was sufficient to buy five pounds of cheese. Utility was not reflected in mint production, however, for there is no evidence in the surviving mint accounts that any petty coinage was struck between 1339 and 1375.[32] Given the number of foreign visitors and residents, and the highly developed market structure of Bruges, it is very likely that "black money" was eagerly sought after. Possible shortages could only be averted through efficient distribution and increased velocity of exchange of the existing stock of coins, with money changers as the essential link.[33]

The confiscation record of the Hanseatic tavern-keeper Heinrich Erembrecht, from 1383, provides evidence that tends to confirm this picture of rapid circulation and consequent wear on the existing stock of petty coins in Bruges.[34] When what remained of the contents of his tavern was

30 On "black money" and small change in general see Spufford, *Money and Its Use*, pp. 328–333. Quite typical is the case of grain imports organized by the city to head off the famine of 1317. In the accounts the city paid for the grain from the foreign merchants with silver *groten*, but the bakers who purchased it from the city paid in mites; see Van Werveke, "Bronnenmateriaal," 436.

31 John H. Munro, "Deflation and the Petty Coinage Problem in the Late-Medieval Economy: The Case of Flanders, 1334–1484," *Explorations in Economic History* 25 (1988), 387–423.

32 This is not absolute proof that none were struck, however; see ibid., 395. Munro, moreover, is convinced that the Flemish mint accounts "grossly understate the amounts of petty coin in domestic circulation" (ibid., 416).

33 Yet even money changers could not command an inexhaustible supply, as in 1316 when, during the city-organized grain distribution, the changers ran out of mites which the bakers were using to purchase grain, so that they had to seek out other merchants; see van Werveke, "Bronnenmateriaal," 436 and 508–509.

34 His name is spelled Heinricx Herbrechts in the confiscation accounts (ARA, Rekenkamer, RR 2017, membrane 6). He was a native of Cologne and a long-time importer and retailer of wine in Bruges. For a biography, see Ingo Dinck, Sonja Dünnebeil, and Renée Rössner, *Hansekaufleute in Brügge Teil 3: Prosopographischer Katalog zu den Brügger Steuerlisten (1360–1390)* (Frankfurt am Main, 1999), pp. 229–231.

carried off, an enormous pile of mites was found. These were assessed with the help of Erembrecht's *cnape*, Gheerkin, who counted to 7,050, which he (or the comital officials) estimated to represent a quarter of the total. Thus they entered the number 28,200 mites in their accounts. This should have given them the value of the coins, since the mite was equal to 0.044 of a groot ($^{1}/_{24}$). But the condition of the coins in effect demonetized them, and they were delivered to the keepers of the shrines of the Blessed Virgin in the churches of St. Donatian's and Onze-Lieve Vrouw, where they were weighed and sold by the pound.[35] Needless to say, this represented a fraction of their nominal value, indicating that their "link" to the Flemish coinage system was tenuous indeed.[36] It is also possible that the best mites were culled out of circulation and sold, though this was officially banned.[37]

The business of coining money in fourteenth-century Flanders brought certain profit to the counts and hope of profit to mint-masters and others involved in bullion delivery and coin manufacture, but much frustration and insecurity to the majority of coin users. Without a doubt, the combination of a fiscally rapacious count, active international trade, and the political ambitions of French and English kings contributed to the most complex monetary situation in northern Europe. Nicholas Oresme's scholastic treatise captured real outrage and dissatisfaction in its learned Latin and mildly reproving tone.[38] But there were winners as well as losers in the mint policies and politics of the Flemish counts, and on balance Bruges derived more profit than loss from the monetary situation. Aggressive debasement induced larger bullion flows, encouraged dishoarding, and increased exchange velocity, all of which benefited trade far more than income derived

[35] ARA, Rekenkamer, RR 2017, membrane 6: "ende mits dat zy [the mites] quade ende bessulfert waren, so waren se ghelevert tloncwyf van Onser Vrouwen te Sinte Donaes ende tloncwyf van van[sic] Onser Vrouwen in Onser Vrouwe kerke te Brucghe, bi ghewichten ende woughen £36 ende 1 vierendeel ponds, elc pond ghepríst bi hemlieden ghelyc dat zi copen de offranden van der kerke, 20 gr. valent £36 5 s. parisis. Hierof ontfaen in minderinghen £19 10s. ende tsourplus blyft noch onder haren handen." This represented a discount of one third over the face value of the coins, since £36 5s. parisis would ordinarily purchase only 18,720 mites. The fact that the church officials were accustomed to receive such coins in their collection boxes strongly suggests that much, if not most, black money was in poor condition even after the recorded resumption of minting of black money in 1375. It should be noted that mites were both the coin of everyday purchases and the coin most suitable for alms-giving; see Spufford, *Money and Its Use*, pp. 330–331.

[36] This case suggests that much if not most of the black money in circulation functioned in practice as token coinage. On tokens, see Spufford, *Money and Its Use*, pp. 331–333.

[37] In 1388 a Jehan le Oysel was fined for trading "monnoye de billon dedans le ville de Bruges . ." ARA, Rekenkamer, 13677 pt. 2, f. 10r.

[38] Of course Oresme was writing with specific reference to the quite sudden and drastic debasements of the French coinage by Philip VI; but the sentiments were no doubt shared by many in Flanders, particularly those dependent on money rents. See Spufford, *Money and Its Use*, pp. 304–308.

from land or industry. Merchants had a strong incentive to invest in trade goods and not to leave profits in coin or bullion. Arbitrage could also be profitable, either through direct contract with the mint (as in the case of John Goldbeter) or simply in closely following the mint price and acting as a broker when selling bullion was profitable. Trading in bullion and coin, however, demanded highly specialized skills as well as ready access to the comital mint, a fact that benefited money changers above other merchants. In fact, as we shall see, Bruges money changers were the most numerous and well-connected with the mint of all Flemish cities. Such skills in assaying and amassing coins and bullion could be useful to the count in turn. Thus mint-masters and members of the council of oversight of the coinage were recruited by Louis of Male from among either Bruges burghers or the Lucchese merchant community of Bruges.[39] Bruges became known across northern Europe as a place to acquire not only cloth and spices, but gold and silver as well, despite the fact that for most of the century no coins were actually minted there.[40] In 1341 for example, when the city of Lübeck needed gold bullion in order to mint its first gold coin, it sent two representatives to Bruges to acquire it.[41] But in Bruges coins and bullion were just the beginning.

MONEY SUPPLY

Ready money was in short supply in fourteenth-century Bruges, despite the massive quantities of bullion and coin that flowed in and out of the city. There were many reasons for this: the above-mentioned incentive for merchants to avoid tying up capital in coin; the difficulties posed by distance and laws against exporting bullion or coins; difficulty in obtaining the proper coin for the intended use; and last but certainly not least the chronic shortage or absence of coin among Bruges residents of all social levels, caused by either choice or poverty. To a greater or lesser degree,

[39] Bruges burghers included Bernard Priem, master of the gold coinage in 1352; Thideman van de Berghe, "garde de la monnaie" at the Mechelen mint, Clais Rapesaert, "garde de la monnaie" in Ghent, and Bauduin de Vos, a commissioner of the coinage; the Lucchese included Percheval du Porche, Aldrigo Interminelli, and Jehan Interminelli. More will be said about these men in the course of this chapter.

[40] The Bruges mint fell victim to the disputes between the king of France and count of Flanders over sovereignty and was closed for much of the century. Louis of Male reopened it briefly for the striking of gold coins from 1349 to 1354; see Elsen, "La monnaie," 83–93; De Roover, *Money, Banking and Credit*, pp. 220–239.

[41] Asmussen, *Hansekaufleute in Brügge*, pp. 62–63. Interestingly, much of the gold was acquired from Lübeck merchants resident in Bruges.

these problems affected foreign merchants, the clerical community, city government, the city elite, and the common people alike. Where Bruges differed from other cities was in its relative success in providing a payment system equal to the demands of its varied publics, and whose reach extended even far beyond the city walls.

Measuring the incidence of coin possession among natives and visitors to Bruges is difficult. There are virtually no systematic estate inventories extant for the fourteenth century, and surviving confiscation records are few and incomplete. Confiscations from French sympathizers (Leliaerts) in the wake of the battle of the Golden Spurs are difficult to assess because they are haphazardly recorded in the city accounts. But the impression they give is that these Bruges burghers kept most of their wealth in trade goods, rents, and properties.[42] There were notable exceptions however, such as the £1,000 parisis' worth of "assorted money" confiscated from Clays van Coelkerke and company.[43] Quite exceptional was the case of money, bullion, and plate seized from an establishment called "ten Cortscovinghers," possibly a pawnbrokerage.[44]

The confiscation records that resulted from the defeat at the battle of Westrozebeke in 1382 are more extensive and better organized. They offer the advantage of listing the confiscated goods from a cross-section of the Bruges populace, particularly of its lower reaches, though again we do not know how representative the sample is.[45] What these records reveal is the rather astonishing rarity of coins among the confiscated goods, even allowing for the fact that money was more portable and more easily hidden

[42] Wyffels and Vandewalle, *Rekeningen*, vol. II, pt. 1, pp. 132–137; for the 1302 dossiers, Vandermaesen and Ryckaert, "Een miskende bron." The invaluable "Wezenboeken" – inventories of deceased parents' possessions drawn up for the benefit of surviving children – survive only from 1398; see Marianne Daneel, "De Brugse wezenboeken als bron. Mogelijkheden en beperkingen (late middeleeuwen–vroege moderne tijden)," in F. Daelmans (ed.), *Bronnen voor de geschiedenis van de materiële cultuur: staten van goed en testamenten. Handelingen van de studiedag te Brussel, 24 Oktober 1986* (Brussel, 1988), pp. 34–36.

[43] Wyffels and Vandewalle, *Rekeningen*, vol. II, pt. 1, p. 505, "in alrehande ghelde die Clays van Coelkerke ende sijn gheselscap hadde £1,000."

[44] The account does not identify the place further. But there was a family of Bruges pawnbrokers active at the time whose name was variously spelled Cosere, Scozers, or Cosericghe, all reasonably close to Cortscovinghers; for this family see Marechal, *Bijdrage tot de Geschiedenis*, pp. 114–115. The money they had on hand included gros tournois (£1,699 15s. worth at 27d. each); king's "sysainen" (sixths?) at 8d the piece (£556 8s.); English sterlings (10d. each, £786 10s.); "black" pennies *tournois* at 3½ obules each (£1,254); in assorted money ("alrehande ghelde," £543 17½ s.); and "parisisen" at 2d. each (£101 8s.): Wyffels and Vandewalle, *Rekeningen*, vol. II, pt. 1, p. 504.

[45] For a discussion of this source, see chapter 9 and J. de Smet, "De repressie te Brugge na de slag bij Westrozebeke, 1 december 1382–31 augustus 1384," *ASEB* 84 (1947): 71–118.

than other kinds of property.[46] Only the relatively wealthy seem to have kept any quantity of coin on hand, men such as the weaver-draper Jacop van der Colve, who had 156 nobles among his possessions.[47] The wool merchant Willem Kouck, had £30 groot in cash listed among his possessions, but his was an exceptional case.[48] Other incidents involving confiscated cash were relatively small amounts such as £1 groot taken from the Genoese merchant, Morvel Damaer, or the contents of a poor box hung in front of a stand in the West Meat Hall.[49] More popular among those with liquid wealth was uncoined silver, which is far more common than coined silver in the confiscation records. This may indicate either a strategy to avoid the uncertainty of coinage debasements or an abiding conservatism in keeping money.[50]

An interesting, albeit isolated, example of coins possessed by a well-to-do canon of St. Donatian's church occurs seemingly by chance in the chapter's *Acta* in September, 1365. By a decision of the chapter, the late Honorius de Hodyc's goods were inventoried and registered, perhaps for fear of a lawsuit or some other dispute over his estate. Significant among his possessions were a chest and purse sealed with his seal containing a number of gold coins. The most numerous of these were Brabantine moutons (108), followed by

46 The comital bailiff did his best to discover hidden caches of money, including paying rewards to informers. One example concerns £15 groot given secretly ("hemelic") to Joncvrouw sVrients by the wife of Pieter Winter, one of those indicted for treason. Martin den Ardre reported the arrangement to the bailiff and received £6 *groot* as his reward: ARA, Rekenkamer, RR 2018.

47 Van der Colve had a complex web of investments and holdings that took the bailiff some time to unravel. Besides the 156 nobles, he had eighty-nine marks of silver stored in his house, a debt of another twenty-five nobles owed by Jan den Waghenare, and a debt of £29 groot owed by Moreel de la Mer. Also in his house were two lengths of cloth: ARA, Rekenkamer, RR 2017 and ARA, Rekenkamer, 18244, f. 3r–v. For van der Colve's business as a draper, see chapter 7.

48 Willem Koucke's case was settled for £600 parisis or £50 groot, representing roughly half of its value given that his wife was still alive. Thus the £30 groot in cash was a considerable part of his estate, but his status as a Bruges *poorter*, born in the city, yet having died in England and whose heirs were English according to the accounts, makes him an anomaly. A quantity of wool was also listed in the inventory: ARA, Rekenkamer, 48986, f. 7r–v.

49 Jan van Bouchoute, apparently Damaert's host, surrendered the money (ARA, Rekenkamer, RR 2017); ARA, Rekenkamer, RR 2018, records the £13 8s. that the rebel Jan van Varssenare had in a box hanging in the Meat Hall during Philip van Artevelde's reign in the city ("ontfaen uter busse die Jan van Varssenare hilt hanghende int Vleeschuus bi Lippins tiden . . ."). Most likely this refers to an alms box kept by the butchers' guild in a prominent place. We know that the brokers kept such boxes in their favorite taverns, and that the collection was used to support the guild chapel; see Murray, *Notarial Instruments*, p. 288.

50 Silver bars were the customary means of payment for large sums prior to 1300 in Flanders, and the habit may have persisted among some in the city despite the closing of the city's silver smelting facilty, or *barnecamer*, before the middle of the century; see Spufford, *Money and Its Use*, p. 2735, and de Roover, *Money, Banking and Credit*, pp. 230–231. Both historians agree that merchant use of silver bars in international trade disappears after the introduction of gold coinages in the fourteenth century.

"royals" (23), "lions" (19), Florentine florins (10), French francs (6), French moutons (4), "old" écus (2), and a single Flemish mouton.[51] All the silver Hodyc possessed, apparently, consisted of plate and silver vessels of various kinds.[52]

The fortunate survival of a coin tally inserted and forgotten among the folios of the money changer Collard de Marke's account book gives another look into the contents of a coin box just a few years after the inventory of the late canon of St. Donatian's church.[53] The list is hurriedly scrawled across a sheet of scrap paper and is difficult to decipher in parts, but it is clear that De Marke's inventory contained 2,000 lions, 2,400 double moutons, 2,000 "doubles de Castille," 12,400 francs and 1,000 francs "à rosette." Once again, it is impossible to know how representative this tally was, but it gives an interesting idea of the coin stock of one of the more important Bruges money changers of the 1360s.

Knowing something about the coins visitors brought to Bruges poses even greater problems caused by the scarcity of evidence. Again, the disincentives to carrying a great deal of either bullion or coin – especially dangers posed by thieves and the bullion restrictions imposed by princes – make it likely that travelers came to the city with little in the way of ready money. Possessing the right type of coins was another problem, since, unlike gold coins, foreign silver coins did not circulate. This forced the visitor to visit the money changer or perhaps his hosteller to exchange for current coin. Moreover, anyone making small purchases in Bruges would need small denominations half groots, or mites and double mites. We shall see in a later chapter that these problems were solved by local and foreign merchants in a variety of ways, usually through letters of exchange or book transfers arranged through hostellers, money changers, or Italian merchant companies. These "discontents" and disadvantages of coins were dealt with in a number of ways by the visitors and natives of Bruges.

[51] BAB, St. Donaas, A47, Acta Capituli, f. 183v. The coins' total value was £237 5s. parisis. The types and value of coins correspond closely to the those actively traded by the money changers at the time.

[52] Besides the plate, Hodyc possessed only a large cloak made of English cloth, which was much motheaten ("vermibus vastata"). The house he possessed from the chapter was apparently far gone with age as well, since it was let to Lambert de Waghenare and his wife, Catherine, in July, 1365 for a low rent because it was in a ruinous state ("quia ruinosa est"), which they were to repair in return – BAB, St. Donaas, A47, Acta Capituli, f. 173r. Hodyc had apparently held the house since before July, 1347, when he was confirmed in its possession despite his temporary absence because of the political troubles then racking Flanders – BAB, St. Donaas, A47, Acta Capitulli, f. 25v.

[53] The single sheet was inserted between folios 295 and 296 in the second of De Marke's account books (SAB, Koopmansboeken, De Marke) and must date from late 1367. It appears among scraps of accounts belonging to Edele de Rudevorde and Jehan van Timeskin, both important customers of de Marke. The inventory also includes the amount of "avaintaige" charged for the gold coins; for example "ii mille de lion a 12s. le mille somme 24s . . ."

CREDIT AND DEBT

The simplest remedy for a shortage of ready coin was to circulate the existing stock as rapidly as possible. Lending and borrowing were the most efficient means to achieve this, directing the coins from those who possessed them to those who needed them. In Bruges this led to a plethora of loan instruments and an ubiquity of debt.[54] This is shown clearly in the confiscation records of the early 1380s where practically every inventory shows debts of one kind or another. This is true not just of the poor, as for example the weaver Jan Keyser, who lived with his wife and children in a heavily mortgaged half-house near the Eekhout bridge. His debts included unpaid sums for merchandise, rent, and a number of personal loans.[55] It was also the case with the relatively affluent, like hosteller Pieter Huerel and the draper Jakop van der Colve. Huerel paid two mortgages on his inn "Ten Hane" located along the expensive Vlamingstraat, which was his only recorded indebtedness.[56]

Most loans seem to have been secured by real estate, usually the house or other structures since the land was most often owned separately.[57] Many owners of houses paid a perpetual ground rent to the literal "land lord" of the space their house occupied. This seems to have been a rather quiescent market, perhaps because much urban land remained in patrician families for generations and because inflation had deprived the rents of much of their value. What the land market lacked in volatility and inventiveness, however, was more than made up by the housing market, which offered a variety of debt instruments and financing schemes. Chief among these was the *renten* – a mortgage of a house with a variety of shorter or longer terms. There was the "life rent" in which a sum of money was advanced to the homeowner in return for a semi-annual payment. A variation of this was the *ervelike rent*, literally the "inheritable rent," which might run for two or three generations. These seem to have been relatively low-risk investments,

[54] F. Irisigler noticed the same thing in fourteenth-century Cologne, where he was stuck by the "stark need for loans and lenders" on the part of all levels of society; see "Juden und Lombarden," 130.

[55] ARA, Rekenkamer, 48986, f. 11r–v.

[56] ARA, Rekenkamer, 18244, f. 2r–v. The inventory records that he lived at his place of business, which was stocked with a considerable list of furniture and other objects. Among these were found, in his "contoir" or strong box, many small parcels containing spices: "vele dinx van specerien." There was no ready money in the chest, however. For more on Huerel and Bruges hostellers, see chapter 5.

[57] Guillaume Des Marez, *La propriété foncière* (Ghent, 1898, reprinted, Mégariotis Reprints, Geneva, 1978), pp. 2–5; Nicholas, *Metamorphosis*, pp. 213–223; Hans-Peter Baum, "Annuities in Late Medieval Hanse Towns," *Business History Review* 59 (1985), 24–48, and for Bruges, Michael Galvin, "Credit and Parochial Charity in Fifteenth-Century Bruges," *Journal of Medieval History* 28 (2002), 131–154.

favored by religious foundations and families seeking to provide for dependent members. Of course, real estate was only one form of *renten*, as this was also the name given to the city debt sold in return for annual payments.[58]

Another important form of private investment resulted from the Flemish legal custom mandating an inquest and financial settlement in the case of the death of one or both parents children. This put a cash value upon an estate, which in effect was "borrowed" by the surviving parent or guardian, who was to administer it with an eye to maintaining or increasing its value. This *wezengeld* (orphan money) was given extraordinary legal standing in Flemish cities, being the only form of investment legally entitled to attract interest.[59] In Bruges, after the failed early attempt to form a central investment fund, perhaps in imitation of the Italian *Monte* system, "orphan money" was loaned out for any number of purposes. Management of this money could last for some time, as in the case of Claissekin Petiit, killed at the battle of Westrozebeke, whose father still held the money left to his son on the death of the former's wife some years before.[60] The broker Pieter Witscaerd had a portfolio of debts of various kinds, including a mortgage on the three quarters of an inn he owned and a loan of orphan money owed to Jan sMeisters's children, but he was also owed money by the city and several individuals.[61] The brewer Mathijs Bouts was owed money for various properties he owned and for beer sold on credit, and among his debts were considerable sums of *wezengeld* plus interest owed to his own children and those of Jan Buers.[62] Most other individuals tended to fall between these two examples.

Even more common than debt secured by real estate or inheritance was a neighborhood network of casual moneylending. This ran the gamut from loans of a few shillings from neighbor to neighbor, or credit extended by a tradesman, to loans of considerable amounts secured by written

58 Baum, "Annuities," 25–27, Galvin, "Credit," 139–142.

59 David Nicholas, *The Domestic Life of a Medieval City: Women, Children and the Family in Fourteenth-Century Ghent* (Lincoln and London, 1985), pp. 13–132, and *Metamorphosis*, pp. 207–213.

60 ARA, Rekenkamer, 48986, f. 2v "Claissekin Petiit f. Clais, doot te Rosebeke. Clais Petiit zijn vader hadde in zinre handen van svorseide Claykins goede van ziinre moeder dood, £4 groot."

61 ARA, Rekenkamer, RR 2019: Witscaerds' properties all lay in the vicinity of the Waterhalle, including his house of residence "an den Wissel" i.e. on St. Pieter's bridge, which he rented from the chapter of St. Donatian's church.

62 ARA, Rekenkamer, 48986, f. 13v. Both debts were spelled out in charters sealed by Bruges aldermen. He had failed to pay interest on the sum he owed Jan Buers's children for four years, so he owed £9 gro. on top of the principal of £30 gro. This translates in simple interest to a rate of 7.5 percent per annum – fairly typical for loans of this type, judging from the Ghent examples cited by Nicholas, *Domestic Life*, pp. 131–132. More exceptional was the fact that his brother Jan distilled Mathijs's finances into a single chirograph, of which one copy went to the bailiff and the other was kept by Jan.

instruments, called "loans by charters."[63] Much of this activity is impossible to trace, but again the confiscation records of the 1380s convey some impressions. The knifemaker Hannekin Meeus had loans owed him "secured by charters."[64] The heirs of the weaver Pieter den Grave received an estate encumbered with loans attested by "legal charters."[65] The pursemaker Jacop den Buersemaker may stand as an example of the small tradesman/shopkeeper. He was relatively well off, possessing a sword and some armor, indicating he served in the Bruges cavalry.[66] Nine individuals listed in the accounts owed him money, perhaps as customers. The amounts were small, averaging 4–6 s. groot. Among his debts was rent for his house, taxes, and money owed the wetnurse of his bastard child.[67]

More casual types of moneylending of course left no written evidence behind. Apparently much use was made of neighbors' knowledge of each others' affairs for accounting purposes. The bailiff was careful to question such sources in cases where there was no one to represent the victim of confiscation.[68] He was seldom disappointed. Neighbors knew a great deal about the financial affairs of those they lived among. The weaver Jan de Clerc, a battle casualty, owned little other than the simple furnishings of his house. His wife apparently refused to cooperate in drawing up the inventory; but the neighbors knew she was heavily in debt.[69] The same was true of the drayman Stevin van Auderve, whose few household possessions were joined by a number of coffins as if in premonition of his own fate. The neighbors said also that he was heavily in debt.[70] A feel for neighborhood credit is also conveyed by the case of Jan Godscalc, nicknamed the Pepperer, who also died in battle. He was owed small amounts by two individuals, and he or his wife were owed 2s. 5d. groot

[63] These loans secured by charters sometimes fell foul of the ban on usury: see Marechal, *Bijdrage*, pp. 11–24.

[64] ARA, Rekenkamer, 48986, f. 9r: "Item es men hem sculdich in onghereede schulden ghewet up charters £10 groot."

[65] ARA, Rekenkamer, RR 2019, "Ende deze parseelen belast met £14 groot van uutsculden also bleect bi wetteliken charters."

[66] ARA, Rekenkamer 48986, ff. 6v–7r: "Item 1 halsberghvel, 1 boorst plate, 1 ketel hoete met eenre houtskuevelen, 1 paer pipen, 1 paer platinre handscoen, 1 zwaerd." For the organization of the Bruges militia see J. F. Verbruggen, "De organisatie van de militie te Brugge in de XIVe eeuw," *ASEB* 87 (1950), 163–170.

[67] ARA, Rekenkamer, 48986, ff. 6v–7r: "Eerst van huushueren van 2 jaer tachter loopt 30s. groot. Item van sconinx ghelde 5s. groot; Item van eenen bastaerden kind dat Jacob vorseid achter hem heift ghelaten ende dat Sconin zijn breed nu houdt, moet betael[en] der voestere 6s. groot."

[68] Murray, *Notarial Instruments*, pp. 93–95 for reliance on written and oral testimony in Flemish cities.

[69] ARA, Rekenkamer, 48986, f. 4v: "Jan de Clerc de wever, doot te Rosebeke . . . ende die weduwe es vele sculdich also hare ghebuers zeeghen."

[70] Ibid., f. 5v: "Stevin van Anderve een draeyere, doot te Rosebeke . . . Item vele doot kisten . . . de weduwe vele sculdich es also die ghebuers zeiden."

by "the neighborhood" for what appears to be treatments for wounds.[71] The widow owed money to the baker and 14s. to a carpenter for wood used to repair the house. This pattern is recognizable in many places in Europe, closely following what William Jordan has called the "networks of sociability."[72]

Neighborhood moneylending was perhaps kept purposefully in the shadows because of the official ban on lending at interest. Apparently some operators throughout the century became so obvious to local officials as to incur a fine for usury. What the threshold was for imposing a fine is unclear early in the century, as the accounts employ an abbreviated and imprecise heading.[73] By 1350, however, the ban on usury explicitly declares that the crime is committed by those who lend at interest rates greater than two pennies in the pound per week (43.3 percent annualized). The fine seems also to have been fixed at £50 parisis at this time.[74] As we shall see with the licensed usurers, they were given the monopoly of lending at interest at that rate of interest in the area ruled by the aldermen, so the greater precision may have had as much to do with enforcing a legal monopoly as with discouraging illegal moneylending. Greater precision and equality was also brought to the amount of the fine assessed against wrongdoers. While the fines might vary from 9s. to £25 parisis in the accounts of 1304; they varied "only" from 9 to £33 in the 1360s.[75] Perhaps fewer casual moneylenders were caught out and fined as the century wore on.

The lack of recurrence of names in the lists of fines also tends to support the impression that on the whole moneylending was an amateur business. However, some usurers apparently made a profession of the practice, and were willing to pay the fines as part of the cost of doing business. This group included Bruges burghers such as the Cosere family from 1304 to 1312, the Ram family from 1355 to 1376, and individuals such as Thomas Ghildolf and "Lady" Heile.[76] A group of immigrants from northern France represented another significant body of illegal professionals. Among them were men from Lille and Tournai, who were almost a constant presence throughout

[71] Ibid., f. 12v. The debts owed him and his wife were specified as three and six "scilden," which must refer to the small silver coin that also went by the name given to the gold coin. The account mentions: "Item noch es men haer sculdich int Ghebuerstijp[?] van corten penewonden ontrent 45 gro."

[72] William C. Jordan, *Women and Credit in Pre-Industrial and Developing Societies* (Philadelphia, 1993), pp. 24–32. The issue of women and moneylending in Bruges will be dealt with in chapter 8.

[73] The earliest accounts speak of "de core prester a husure" or simply "Ontfanghen van den woukerars."

[74] De Roover, *Money, Banking and Credit*, pp. 102–108; Marechal, *Bijdrage*, pp. 105–119, gives excerpts from the accounts.

[75] Marechal, *Bijdrage*, pp. 105–110.

[76] Ibid., pp. 114–116.

the fourteenth century.[77] The numbers of those fined for usury, however, remained small on the whole from 1304 to 1390.[78] Yet this does nothing to dispel the impression that loans and credit were constantly on offer in the neighborhoods of Bruges, and even the city made use of these sources on occasion.[79] The neighborhood moneylender was a fixture in Bruges, as everywhere else, and was probably the first and most frequented remedy for an empty purse.

LICENSED AND UNLICENSED USURY

To remedy the chronic shortage of ready coin was one purpose of the licensed usurers of Bruges, although their business was not limited to extending consumer credit. They were variously and confusingly called lombards, Cahorsins, or simply usurers (*woekeraars*).[80] The confusion does not end with names in this case, however, for although lending at interest was illegal in fourteenth-century Bruges, it was permitted in return for

77 Ibid., pp. 117–119. Unlike the Bruges natives, these were all men, such as Gillise Musschet, who was active from 1335 to 1338, though his wife and daughter were fined for usury in the 1340s and 1350s. We know from the accounts of Collard de Marke that Jan Moreel and Jaquemard de Blandain, both from Tournai, were active in various kinds of business and not just usury. Moreel, in fact, may have acted as a money changer at times since he is named as such at one point in the De Marke accounts (4, 301v, "Moriel cangeur"); also for Moreel see de Roover, *Money, Banking and Credit*, pp. 289, nn. 91, 306. Both Moreel and Blandain settled permanently in Bruges and bought citizenship rights for themselves (Marechal, *Bijdrage*, pp. 118, 119). Blandain seems to have fallen on hard times at the end of his life, since he received alms from the city in 1398.

78 There were very rarely more than two or three fines per term. For published examples see Wyffels and Vandewalle (eds.), *Rekeningen*, vol. II, pt. 1, pp. 446.

79 Georges Bigwood, *Le régime juridique et économique du commerce de l'argent dans la Belgique du moyen âge*, 2 vols. (Brussels, 1921–1922), vol. I, p. 336. The wealthy *woekeraar* (usurer) Wouter de Smet contributed to a forced loan to the city in 1379. He belonged to the highest category of contributors; see De Meyer, "De sociale strukturen," 65.

80 Raymond de Roover insisted on the distinction between "lombard" and "Lombard" – i.e. a usurer and an individual from northern Italy. But contemporaries seem to have made no distinction in their use of the term. A similar confusion arose over the name "Cahorsin" as applied to usurers. The English chronicler Mathew Paris wrote in the middle of the thirteenth century that they came from Italy, while Giovanni Boccacio a century later insisted that they were from the southern French town of Cahors. Leaving aside controversy, it is clear that by 1300 in Bruges, both names – "lombard" and "Cahorsin" – indicate the profession of licensed usurer and sometimes geographical origin as well. See Marechal, *Bijdrage*, p. 13, and de Roover, *Money, Banking and Credit*, pp. 99–100. More recently C. Tihon has criticized de Roover's too rigid categorization of the original lombards, who were from Italy, as rigidly excluded and separate from other Italian merchants. As for the Cahorsins, he argues that they were from northern Italy not France; see "Aperçus sur l'établissement des Lombards dans les Pays-Bas aux XIIIe et XIVe siècles," *RBPH* 39(1) (1961), 334–343. For discussion of Cahorsins, see *Lexikon des Mittelalters*, vol. V, s.v. "Kawer(t)schen)," with bibliography. C. Vornefeld also found a mix of Italians and native usurers in his prosopographical study of a list of French usurers from the early fifteenth century; see his "Einheimische und lombardische Wucherer im Frankreich von Charles VI. Eine neue Quelle zur Sozialgeschichte des Wuchers," *Journal of Medieval History* 15(3) (1989), 269–287.

fines, loans, and taxes, which amounted to licensing fees. These "licensed" usurers differed from the social or casual moneylender both in quantity of money loaned and by the fact that they lent money on pledges, left with them in return for a loan, with interest payable by the week until the repayment of the principal.[81] By 1350 there were at least three groups of licensed pawnbrokers operating in Bruges: one with privileges from the count and city under the aldermen's jurisdiction, and two others in areas under the jurisdiction of the provost and canons of St. Donatian's church. Their numbers and financial clout argue for an unusually robust demand for consumer credit on the one hand, and a well-developed and sophisticated network of services and commercial involvement on the part of pawnbrokers on the other. Historians have long overlooked and downplayed the considerable importance of this profession to the commercial infrastructure of Bruges.[82]

The origins of officially recognized pawnbroking in Bruges date from before 1244, when *Caorsini* are mentioned in a comital charter.[83] Sometime between the middle of the century and 1281 these "Cahorsins" took up residence in an area then outside the city's jurisdiction called popularly 't Wiic, a name that suggests its role as a harbor.[84] Thus these professional moneylenders found a welcome amid the shippers and merchants on the margins of the growing city. By the time of the formal grant of privileges by the count in 1281, these Cahorsins or "Lombarden op 't Wiic" occupied a complex of three houses, providing room for the loan office as well as

[81] This by no means excludes casual moneylenders, who may have also taken in objects as collateral for loans; but this is less likely given the logistical demands of a pawnshop.

[82] This modern scorn of pawnbroking as a small-scale and financially insignificant part of the history of money in medieval cities is due in no small part to Raymond de Roover's characterization of it as a marginal business with little direct involvement in other commerce; see de Roover, *Money, Banking and Credit*, pp. 151–155, a view largely accepted by Joseph Marechal, who nonetheless amassed considerable material unknown to de Roover that modifies the traditional picture (see Marechal, *Bijdrage*, pp. 11–24).

[83] De Roover was unaware of the earlier presence of lombards of Bruges, mentioned in a charter published by T. Luykx. In it Countess Johanna of Flanders lists her debtors as of December 1244, including "caorsini" of Oudenaarde, Kortrijk, Veurne, Poperinge, Mons, and Bruges. The amounts are identical, £100 tornois, except for the Bruges Cahorsins, who were owed £100 tornois and £50 artois, and those of Mons, who were owed £29 6s. 8d. artois. This proves that by the middle of the thirteenth century, lombards were already well established among the credit-granting institutions of Flanders, and strongly suggests that Cahorsins of various cities and towns in west and east Flanders were already cooperating in granting large loans to favored individuals. They are mentioned alongside well-known financiers like Robert Crespin of Arras, as well as burghers from Lille, Ghent, Ypres. For the charter, see Theo Luykx, *Johanna van Constantinopel, Gravin van Vlaanderen en Henegouwen* (Antwerp, 1946), pp. 606–607; Marechal, *Bijdrge*, p. 13; Tihon, "Aperçus," 340, mentions transactions other rulers, both religious and secular, had with lombards in the middle of the thirteenth century.

[84] Ryckaert, *Stedenatlas*, p. 88.

storage of the pawned articles.[85] With the passing of this by now urbanized area from the jurisdiction of the lords van Praet to that of the city in 1283, some sharing of authority between the count and city officials became the rule, but no formal agreement survives. Due to the size of the establishment, as well as its importance, it became known as the "Great Cahorsin."[86] Fixity of place and size of operation thus decisively separated this business from the neighborhood moneylender.

Comital privilege conferred on these pawnbrokers a number of guarantees and protections that taken together made them the most secure of all foreign groups in the city. Like foreign merchant groups, they were granted security of person and property; moreover they came to enjoy further rights after the 1283 annexation of the area by Bruges.[87] These granted all rights of citizenship to the lombards including freedom from tolls and most communal taxes. These rights went beyond protection and exemptions to include the right to trade without a broker, a privilege denied every other foreign merchant group.[88] Thus these lombards were simultaneously wards of the count and burghers of Bruges, a remarkable and unique status that suggests their value to both city and county.

That value can be measured in pounds, shillings, and pence. For the counts, the syndicates of lombards spread throughout his significant towns and cities proved a trusty source of loans and taxes for himself and for members of his family.[89] The most famous debtor of the Bruges lombards was Yolande of Flanders, countess of Bar.[90] For the city government, the lombards were both a source of emergency credit, as in 1316 when a loan was

[85] This was a large establishment consisting of three houses in 1281 and two in 1302, and was sometimes called a "hof" or "hostel" (Marechal, *Bijdrage*, p. 14). For this terminology and its business importance, see chapter 6. This remained the site of a pawnshop until the sixteenth century, when it became the first site of the Mons Pietatis, or public pawnshop. Into the twentieth century the house on that site was known as "De Woeker," "The Usurer."

[86] Some alternation or combination of the name "Gran Lombard" or "Grote Caorsinen" was used throughout the Middle Ages. In Willem Ruweel's accounts they are called "le Gran Lombards," in those of Collard de Marke they are "le grans Lonbars des Caoursin." SAB, Koopmansboeken, Ruweel, f. 121v; De Marke 3, f. 109v.

[87] These were spelled out in a privilege granted by the city in 1306 (Marechal, *Bijdrage*, pp. 18–19). Operators of this pawnhouse became full *poorters* of the city with all the attached privileges and exemptions, despite de Roover's assertion that they enjoyed only partial citizenship rights (de Roover, *Money, Banking and Credit*, pp. 103–105). Before 1306, most lombards had purchased citizenship rights.

[88] Trading without a broker was still widely practiced, as will be shown in chapter 6.

[89] Bigwood, *Le régime*, vol. 1, pp. 11–95. Philip the Bold also borrowed in 1371 and 1390 from Bruges lombards.

[90] For Yolande, de Roover, *Money, Banking and Credit*, pp. 125–126, Bigwood, *Régime*, vol. 1, pp. 445–449, and most recently Jacques Sabbe, "Yolande van Vlaanderen, gravin van Bar en vrouwe van Cassel, en het huis de 'Casselberg' in Brugge (1373)," *ASEB* 138 (2001), 33–55.

arranged in order to pay the city's contingent of crossbowmen, who were on campaign.[91] A long-term loan was made to the city in 1340, relieving another liquidity crisis in that politically stormy period. But it was above all as a source of an annual tax that the lombards of the "Great Cahorsin" provided their steadiest contribution to the urban treasury. Indeed, the tax was even indexed to the decline in value of the Flemish currency, moving from £133 6s. 8d in 1307 to £216 in 1390.[92]

Who were these highly privileged and useful usurers? Most of the Great Cahorsins came from the Piedmont region of northern Italy, from Asti and Chieri in particular, and belonged to a handful of extended families. These were the di Caloccio, Roerio and Deal families, who effectively controlled the Bruges pawnshop from 1281 to 1420.[93] Though managed by a single factor/partner, ownership was divided into shares held by family members and closely allied outsiders. Some individuals owned shares in several pawnshops in different cities, and there is evidence that syndicates of these shareholders pooled their resources to provide loans to the count of Flanders and others.[94] In short, the count licensed these "lombards" to disperse and operate the pawnshop business throughout Flanders from which the loosely affiliated families could mobilize large amounts of capital for loans and investments.

The other group of licensed pawnbrokers in Bruges received their privilege from the provost and canons of St. Donatian's church, the holders of jurisdiction in those scattered enclaves within and without the walls of the city, called the Proosse and Kannunikse. These establishments offered similar advantages of location – away from the center, yet well situated amid busy neighborhoods and streets. Both areas in fact offered not only a workers' neighborhood, but also proximity to a mendicant convent frequented by one or more nation of foreign merchants.[95] Yet unlike the

91 Marechal, *Bijdrage*, p. 20; de Roover stresses the occasional nature of city borrowing from the lombards, which he attributes to the availability of cheaper credit through the sale of annuities (*Money, Banking and Credit*, p. 126).

92 From 1307 to 1312 the amount was £133 6s. 8d.; in 1316 £144, in 1318 £160; from 1332 to 1355, £144 par.; from 1361 to 1395, £216 par.; and it was raised to £288 in 1396 (Marechal, *Bijdrage*, p. 19).

93 Marechal, ibid., pp. 93–100, gives a complete list of names of those associated with this pawnshop, including known factors and employees; see also de Roover, *Money, Banking and Credit*, p. 116.

94 As was the case as early as 1244. Little is known of the organization and modus operandi of these lombard associations. C. Tihon used Vatican documents to point out the case of the liquidation of the business of a Brabant lombard, Benedict Royer, who was probably related to the Bruges lombards of that name. This case revealed that Duke John I of Brabant owed the "lombards of Brabant" the considerable sum of £100,000 tornois, suggesting a collective loan to the duke. Other evidence from the fourteenth century confirms this ("Aperçus," 350–353).

95 Marechal, *Bijdrage*, p. 17.

Great Cahorsin, the professional moneylenders licensed by St. Donatian's rented or more rarely purchased houses according to need or opportunity without the centuries-long permanence of the city/comital licensed pawnshop. Thus these houses were known by a name – De Pauw – or by a sign affixed to it – De Zwaan – or by some reference to the house's location – Ter Muelne, Ter Poort. Some pawnshops did have considerable longevity in the same location: that owned by Alard Bataille operated from 1379 to 1405 in the South "Proosse". In the other enclave, the East "Proosse," the house known as "The Sword" (Het Zwaard) served a number of pawnbrokers from at least 1363 until the 1460s. The ease with which moneylenders came and went, and moved from house to house, gives the impression of a less settled, more opportunistic business in the relatively free-wheeling jurisdiction of the provost and canons.[96]

The geographical origins of these pawnbrokers also differed from that of those who owned and ran the "Great Cahorsin." Although a few were Bruges natives, the majority came from the cities or rural districts of northern France and French Flanders, especially Tournai and Lille.[97] Like the Piedmontese pawnbrokers, they typically either purchased citizenship or became official residents of the St. Donatian's jurisdictions, acquiring thereby many of the same rights and privileges. Thus by the middle of the fourteenth century there were at least three areas of Bruges harboring pawnshops, at three compass points (north, south and east), well removed from the city center yet well situated along thoroughfares in neighborhoods of artisans, manual workers with a high number of bathhouses, bordellos, and drinking establishments as well.[98]

Pawnbroking as a business bore considerable social stigma as well as popular animosity, but it is mistaken to consider its practitioners as either complete social or business outcasts for that reason. On the contrary, beyond the annual sentence of excommunication pronounced against usurers from the pulpit, pawnbrokers and their families entered freely into the money market and the wider commercial life of the city. In one notable case, a member of the De Roerio clan was a notary public, priest, and chaplain

96 Ibid., pp. 15–17. This case of an ecclesiastical jurisdiction sheltering more vice than the aldermen's is similar to the case of Southwark and London, yet the literature shows no unusual development of pawnbroking/moneylending there. See Martha Carlin, *Medieval Southwark* (London and Rio Grande, 1996), pp. 253–257. Perhaps the essential difference is that St. Donatian's jurisdictions were not suburbs in the way Southwark and Westminster were.

97 Marechal, *Bijdrage*, pp. 14 and 117–119. Marechal found ten moneylenders from the area who were active in Bruges in the fourteenth century. He does not, however, explain why there was this particular affinity between the region and profession of moneylender in Bruges.

98 De Roover, *Money, Banking and Credit*, pp. 162–163; Marechal, *Bijdrage*, p. 17.

for the parish of the Wijngard, the city's chief beguinage.[99] The core of the business remained short-term loans (less than one year) with personal articles taken as security and interest charged up to the legal maximum of two pence per pound per week. Pawnbrokers of the Proosse and Kannunikse may have loaned at even higher rates.[100] Interest rates could vary, from high rates for individuals, to institutions and powerful individuals, which borrowed at rates from 15 to 20 percent. No doubt much of the pawnshop operator's time and effort went into organizing pawned articles, arranging the sale of those left unclaimed, making loans and issuing pawn tickets. These demands may explain why the loan operations were often entrusted to assistants or factors.[101]

This traffic in objects and small loans filled a need for cash in urban society, but to some degree it disguised a much wider array of business activities, especially in the case of the Great Cahorsin. It is clear that this operation was a financial power to be reckoned with and sought after, as examples drawn from the city government of Bruges and count of Flanders have shown. The ability of the Bruges Cahorsins to satisfy the credit demands of the always impecunious countess of Bar speaks to both their financial power and the financial desperation of some of the region's nobility. In 1370 alone, the countess borrowed in a single transaction 5,000 French francs, 3,000 Hungarian florins and 3,000 common florins from the Bruges pawnbrokers.[102] Five years earlier her loans amounted to 1,010 moutons; another transaction found her pawning gold and silver figurines for 6,000 francs. This is an impressive demonstration of the Cahorsins' ability to produce ready coin for an important customer.[103] Even more impressive is the fact that most of these large loans were made in gold while the bulk of the pawn business was transacted in silver.

Businessmen were also keenly aware of these financial resources. When the English wool merchant and Bruges denizen John Goldbeter was raising money for his king, Edward III, he searched Flanders for money to borrow. Between late 1346 and early 1348, Goldbeter brokered six loans worth at least £25,000 sterling. One source was a Hanse merchant and Bruges denizen,

[99] This was Joannes de Roerio, whose qualifications as a notary public indicate that he probably studied abroad before taking up his post. For the education of notaries in Flanders, see Murray, *Notarial Instruments*, pp. 17–31, and Murray, "The Profession of Notary Public in Medieval Flanders," *Journal of Legal History* 61 (1993), 1–29.

[100] De Roover, *Money, Banking and Credit*, pp. 125–126, 162–163, discusses various rates of interest that were charged depending on the customer and security offered, and points out that higher rates predominated in pawnshops in St. Donatian's enclaves.

[101] Marechal, *Bijdrage*, 99–100. This was particularly true of a large operation like the "Great Cahorsin."

[102] De Roover, *Money, Banking and Credit*, p. 119; Bigwood, *Le régime*, vol. 1, pp. 447–449.

[103] De Roover, *Money, Banking and Credit*, p. 119.

Tideman Blomenrod; the other Bruges connection was the pawnshop of the Great Cahorsin. There Goldbeter borrowed £5,333 6s. 8d., the single largest loan of all, for a term of six months at an interest rate of 30 percent. The security was wool, cloth, and silver plate. The four other sources of loans were Italian and English merchant companies and three Ghent drapers.[104] These lombards also served merchants in financial difficulties, as the case of the well-known Lübeck merchant Hildebrand Veckinhusen shows. After establishing a successful business with his brother, Siverd, in Bruges in 1390, he developed a fur trading business with Venice after 1407, before returning to East/West Prussian trade around 1414. In this business, however, he began to lose money, then exhausted his sources for loans among other Hanse merchants. By 1420 he had gone to the Bruges lombards, whose loans came at such a high rate of interest that they caused more financial problems than they solved. After fleeing to Antwerp to escape creditors, he was prevailed upon by his hosteller to return to Bruges and face his debts. This resulted in a three-year imprisonment as a debtor.[105] Given the loan amounts for the countess of Bar and John Goldbeter, the lendable resources of the Great Cahorsin were probably the largest among all the pawnshops of Flanders, and perhaps the largest of any private institution.

The example of the Cahorsins of Bruges reveals a business with an impressive reach. From pawn transactions amounting to pennies to large sums paid out in gold with precious stones and jewelry as collateral, this alone documents a complex traffic in pawned goods. But this business may have been merely the most visible (and best-documented) aspect of pawnbroking. There were other, darker sides to the business. The pawnshop was often the destination for the desperate and the criminal in medieval Bruges. Desperation for money seems sometimes to have led to "borrowing" and pawning of articles belonging to guilds or other institutions. This was the case in 1372 when officials of the weavers' guild sent a clerk to check the pawnshops for missing ceremonial gowns.[106] Guild members were also guilty of pawning military equipment they were required to own – in 1371 members of the weaver's guild could not answer a military summons until the deans

[104] E. B. Fryde, "Some Business Transactions of York Merchants: John Goldbeter, William Acastre and Partners, 1336–1349," *St. Anthony's Hall Publications*, 1966, table 2; reprinted in *Studies in Medieval Trade and Finance* (London, 1983).

[105] Asmussen, *Lübecker Flanderfahrer*, pp. 797–798, and Rolf Hammel, "Hildebrand Veckinchusen," in *Biographisches Lexikon für Schleswig-Holstein und Lübeck*, vol. IX (Neumünster, 1991), pp. 358–364.

[106] Georges Espinas and Henri Pirenne, *Recueil de documents relatifs à l'histoire de l'industrie drapière*, 5 vols. (Brussels, 1906), vol. I, pt. I, pp. 587–88: "Item gheven den deken ende sine ghezworne metgaders den oftmannen van sambacht clederen te soukene te wouckerars huse 12s. gro."

of their guild had redeemed their pawned weapons and armor.[107] Sacred objects were also not spared the pawnshop, as in 1369 when St. Jan's hospital redeemed a silver chalice and two silver plates from the "Couwertsinen."[108] No doubt among the first places searched when an object disappeared were the pawnshops.

Indeed petty thieves often made the pawnshop their first stop in order to sell their stolen goods. In 1378 Griel, daughter of the Bruges *poorter* Jan Gremme, stole a silver bowl and then pawned it at an unspecified shop, where it was later recovered.[109] Another case of the same year found Philippa, daughter of Griele Slabbaerd, stealing two silver bowls and pawning them.[110] Two other cases show other forms of theft. An Italian clerk or merchant apparently swindled his Italian partners and a Bruges hosteller when he made off with cloth purchased in the cloth hall and left in the care of his host, Jan Calf. He then took it to the pawnshop, received twelve francs for it and "went on his way," leaving his two companions to answer to the Bruges aldermen.[111] An entry in the city accounts from early in the century proves how routine and fruitful the search of pawnshops for stolen goods could be: two valuable goblets were recovered from the Great Cahorsin.[112]

Though used by the dishonest and desperate, there is scattered but convincing evidence that lombards of the Great Cahorsin, at least, preferred to channel money and effort into the whirl of Bruges commerce. In 1366 records show them involved in frequent shipping of merchandise via the Spanish fleet to Bruges.[113] Confiscation records of 1371 also show the Great Cahorsin as owners of merchandise impounded in the general seizure of English trade goods.[114] The lombards sometimes joined other merchants in business arrangements. This seems to have been the case in 1376, when

[107] De Roover, *Money, Banking and Credit*, p. 122 and n. 59; P. de Stroop, "Particularités sur les corporations et métiers de Bruges," *ASEB* third series, 1 (1843), 158; Espinas and Pirenne, *Recueil*, vol. I, p. 587.

[108] Emmanuel van der Elst, *L'hôpital Saint-Jean de Bruges (de 1188–1500)* (Bruges, 1975), p. 59.

[109] ARA, Rekenkamer, RR 1026, membrane 13. Her status as *poorter* saved her from confiscation of property but not from imprisonment in the Steen. Her case was settled for £48 parisis.

[110] ARA, Rekenkamer, RR 1026, membrane 14. A third case from this year involved the theft by Maye Gheerkins of unspecified property belonging to her employer, which she then pawned (ibid., membrane 13).

[111] ARA, Rekenkamer, RR 1014 (May–September 1375), membrane 11. The two dupes were Anthone de Lompaeinge and Vidaen de Beyoene, who were questioned by the Bruges aldermen then released because the latter could find no evidence that the former were at fault, and they were vouched for by "good people." They escaped with a fine on top of their business loss.

[112] Wyffels and Vandewalle, *Rekeningen*, vol. II, pt. 1, p. 243 – 1303/04 "Item bi den selven [Denarde] van 2 nappen die waren vonden ten Cauwerchinen up Sint Gillis dorp £54."

[113] Childs, *Anglo-Castilian Trade in the Later Middle Ages*, p. 181.

[114] Nicholas, "English Trade," 32.

the operators of the Great Cahorsin, Otto Garet and Bonifacius Royer, joined the Lübeck merchant Arnold Lewerke in a complaint against the Dortmund merchant Johann Suderman. They succeeded in having him thrown in prison for an enormous unpaid debt. Though the affair is complex and dragged on for years in the Bruges courts, with intervention by officials of the German Hanse, it indicates an intimate relation of Bruges lombards with foreign merchants.[115] Somewhat later, but still relevant, was the bankruptcy of the Great Cahorsin in 1457, brought on by unsuccessful speculation in the trade in English wool. Rather than the exception that proves the rule of lombard indifference to trade, this case completes the picture of a financial institution long accustomed to dealing in the central commodities traded in the Bruges market.[116] Why else would their failure cause a commotion great enough to merit discussion by the Burgundian chronicler Chastellain?

Pawnbrokers were also the providers of financial services associated with banking. By the terms of their 1281 privilege, the lombards of the Great Cahorsin were forbidden to engage in money changing. This was unique to Bruges, for in all other Flemish towns pawnbrokers were permitted to exchange coins, which indicates the respect for the monopoly granted the licensed money changers in the city.[117] Nonetheless, it is unlikely that pawnbrokers, any more than ordinary merchants, completely refrained from exchanging one gold coin for another. More significant was the practice of accepting monetary deposits, or investments, from non-partners and paying interest on them. This was clearly a business of long standing when the financial records of the Great Cahorsin were examined as a result of the bankruptcy of 1457. In the investigation by the aldermen, the numerous depositors were found to be widows, orphans, and religious men and women of Bruges as well as a number of wealthy individuals. By custom, interest could be paid on money invested for the benefit of widows and orphans, but the aldermen were indignant to find wealthy individuals profiting from usury as well.[118] Given these depositors, such an investment must have been perceived as a very safe haven for money, of long and proven performance.[119] Yet all in all, the most convincing proof of the importance

[115] The case is summarized with bibliography in Dierck *et al.*, *Hansekaufleute in Brügge, Teil 3*, pp. 271–273, though they do not make clear whether it was Johann Suderman or his brother, Arnold (p. 417), who was imprisoned for the debt.

[116] De Roover, *Money, Banking and Credit*, pp. 135–136.

[117] Bigwood, *Régime*, vol. 1, p. 391.

[118] De Roover, *Money, Banking and Credit*, p. 135.

[119] Traditionally the safest forms of investment were considered to be life or hereditary rents derived from real property. It is possible that in the fourteenth and fifteenth centuries, placing money with the lombards or money changers became another favored investment for those seeking both profit and security.

of pawnbrokers in the local Bruges economy is their financial relations with money changers.

As we shall see, money changers were the system managers of the Bruges financial world in a sense, for they alone offered clearing accounts for individuals and institutions seeking to access a wider range of services. Pawnbrokers entered into financial relationships with money changers both through business partnerships and as account holders. For example, at his death around 1363, the lombard Jacques Mancegas possessed an estate worth £463, three quarters of which was invested with the money changer Jacob Reubs.[120] The text of the charter states that these funds belonged to the lombards as a business and not to Mancegas personally.[121] We know that Mancegas was a partner in the Great Cahorsin, and as such held what amounted to a share of the capital as his own, but probably served as the manager of the shares of other stock holders as well. Some of this he must have invested with Reubs, through either direct partnership or simple deposit. The dividing line may have indeed been thin between the two. There was no protest about the novelty of this, or because Mancegas had acted improperly. It was simply that his erstwhile partners believed he was investing their money. Further support for this relationship as typical business practice is the account this same group held with the money changer Collard de Marke from 1366 to 1369.[122] This was not a particularly significant account, in either volume or activity, because they probably retained Reubs as their chief banker. But this strongly suggests that the lombards kept accounts with a number of money changers, perhaps all the most significant ones, thus following the practice of other Bruges merchants, most notably the hostellers. Once again, these lombards of the Great Cahorsin acted just like any other large-scale merchant company of the time.[123]

Jakemard Blandain provides at least one additional example from among the unlicensed moneylenders, in his case from the city of Tournai.[124] It is difficult to know whether he was a moneylender/pawnbroker by profession, or only as a sideline of a more general career as a merchant. He was fined for

[120] De Roover, *Money, Banking and Credit*, pp. 153 and 158 n. 25; Bigwood, *Régime*, vol. I, p. 316 and vol. II, p. 352, no. 48; he was "compagnon" in the "maison des lombars de Bruges."

[121] "£332 gro. lesquels lis dis lombars rechevoient et comptoient sur le change Jacob Reubz": Bigwood, *Régime*, vol. II, p. 352.

[122] De Marke 3, f. 109v is typical of an account that was minor and episodic. Its holders are described as "Les grans Lonbars des Caoursin."

[123] Raymond van Uytven observed similar merchant activities among lombards in Leuven and Antwerp, as well as close relations between lombards and money changers in those cities, albeit in the fifteenth and sixteenth centuries. In one case, a member of a family of lombards became a money changer in Leuven. See Raymond van Uytven, *Stadsfinanciën en stadsekonomie te Leuven van de XIIe tot het einde der XVIe eeuw* (Brussels, 1961), pp. 462–463.

[124] Marechal, *Bijdrage*, p. 119.

usury, and we also know that he bought citizenship in the 1360s and 1370s. He also maintained an account with Collard de Marke, which reveals him to have been an active merchant with financial interests across a surprising range of geographical areas and foreign merchants.[125] Once again, his case warns against an expectation of specialization among these merchants, even the operators of the Great Cahorsin. They, like, Blandain, were alive to the possibility of profit offered by the Bruges market. Access to services and information was crucial, and this they sought and acquired with their business relationships with money changers and others.

All in all, it is important to keep separate and distinct the social stigma and religious exclusion incurred by pawnbrokers from their financial importance. They certainly served as a major conduit of gold and silver coin to individuals at every rung of the social hierarchy. They also played the role of lender of last resort at times for the city government of Bruges. Well-connected foreign merchants, like John Goldbeter, came to them in order to raise money to fund the political adventures of the English king. But perhaps most significant was the involvement of these privileged foreigners in the finance and organization of local trade. They held a particular and protected niche in the credit system on the one hand; but the profits they earned were invested in the wider world of business. This was a typical and not an exceptional response to opportunity, and it made the Bruges pawnbrokers, especially those of the Great Cahorsin, a force to be reckoned with. And even socially, what separated them from other foreign merchants, to quote C. Tihon, was no more than a bamboo curtain, certainly not an iron one.[126]

MONEY CHANGING: EARLY HISTORY

Medieval money changing was an amalgam of a variety of business functions and services, from the relatively uncomplicated manual exchange of one coin for another to deposit banking and investments in trade, industry, and urban finance. The money changer was also a quasi-public figure since the license to operate an exchange was, in Flanders and elsewhere, a fief held of the sovereign power which carried with it certain duties relating to the control and maintenance of the coinage. Lastly, the money changer

[125] Snapshots from Blandain's account activities (De Marke 3, 152r, 4, 131r, 4, 197r) from August 1368 to May 1369 reveal numerous purchases of coins, and a payment made via another Bruges money changer to a creditor of Blandain's in Tournai.

[126] Tihon, "Aperçus," 335, n. 2 ("un rideau de bambou assez léger"), p. 335, n. 2, and Erik Aerts, "Middeleeuwse bankgeschiedenis," 56.

occupied a precarious middle ground as a purveyor of coins and an expert in finance, between usury, or suspicion of usury, and being a respected and useful member of the merchant community. Public suspicion and mistrust of professional moneymen was proverbial in medieval society, and the money changer did not escape from it, perched as he was between the lawful and the illegal use of what some medieval moralists stamped the "root of all evil." And although almost every city of any importance on the continent possessed money changers, Bruges exceeded most of them in the number of changers per capita, the complexity of their business and the significance of their role as the lynchpin of the Bruges financial system.[127]

This being said, much has been published in the past half century to diminish the claim of uniqueness made on behalf of Bruges money changers. While Bruges counted more changers than any other city in Flanders in the fourteenth century, Leuven in nearby Brabant had a similar or superior number. Moreover, money changers in that city, as well as elsewhere, had public roles as city treasurers and finance officers unknown in Flanders.[128] The European south presents further complexity, with Florentine money changing remaining a modest affair, well removed from the financial complexities of the merchant companies, while in Venice changers provided a variety of financial services very similar to those in Bruges.[129] In England, of course, money changers were banned altogether after 1344, reflecting a deep mistrust of the profession on the part of the king and his officials.[130] Moreover, it is clear that "ordinary" merchants engaged in exchange of coins, effecting payments for others and accepting money on deposit. In short, it is now less clear whether the origins of deposit banking, book transfers,

[127] The locus classicus remains Raymond de Roover's chapters on Bruges money changers in *Money, Banking and Credit*, pp. 171–330. Points of detail omitted in his monograph de Roover supplied in several preparatory studies that are often overlooked. These are "Quelques considérations sur les livres des comptes de Collard de Marke (1366–1369)," *Bulletin d'Etudes et d'Informations de l'Ecole Supérieure de Commerce St Ignace* 4 (1930), 445–475, and "Le livre de comptes de Guillaume Ruyelle, changeur à Bruges (1369)," *ASEB* 72 (1934), 15–95.

[128] Van Uytven, *Stadsfinanciën*, pp. 38–43. In Brussels in 1370 there were ten money changers, and in 1404 there were eight in Antwerp: Herman van der Wee, *The Growth of the Antwerp Market*, vol. II, pp. 355–357. This public role was true of Geneva and Barcelona as well: see A. P. Usher, *The Early History of Deposit Banking in Mediterranean Europe* (Cambridge, Mass., 1943), pp. 256–257.

[129] See Richard Goldthwaite, "Local Banking in Renaissance Florence," *Journal of European Economic History* 14/1 (1985), 5–55, reprinted in *Banks, Palaces, and Entrepreneurs in Renaissance Florence*, (Aldershot, 1995). For Venice, Reinhold C. Mueller, *The Venetian Money Market: Banks, Panics, and the Public Debt, 1200–1500* (Baltimore, 1997), pp. 6–37. With Mueller's work we have the only full-fledged comparison with the situation in Bruges.

[130] T. F. Reddaway, "The King's Mint and Exchange in London, 1343–1543," *English Historical Review* 82 (1967), 1–23; Munro, *Wool, Cloth and Gold*, p. 30 n. 58.

and other financial practices are attributable to the money changer. More than ever the particular urban context of which money changing formed a part must be analyzed as well.[131]

In a city increasingly connected to the quickening pace of north European trade in the high and late Middle Ages, professional money changers appeared early in the documented history of Bruges. But it is clear from the earliest records that money changing in its most complex mix of coin exchange, deposit taking, and investment did not long antedate 1300, though the fragmentary state of the surviving records makes greater precision difficult. Most of what we know about money changing in Bruges in the thirteenth century comes from a dossier of documents copied around 1325 by four holders of the right to keep a money exchange (the so-called "free" money changers) and presented to the count of Flanders, presumably as evidence in an investigation of the count's rights in the matter.[132] There are several instructive points about these documents. First, as early as 1224, there was an explicit link between watching over the currency and holding a money exchange, as Countess Johanna expanded the fief of the aptly named Andreus Monetarius of Bruges from operating the comital mint to include opening a "tabula campsoria," literally an exchange table, to be located between those held by Gervasius de Ponte and Arnulphus Monetarius. For the next hundred years the four "free" money changers of Bruges, all vassals of the count, appended the title "Muntmeester" ("Mintmaster") to their office as money changers.[133] The countess also stipulated the physical dimensions of this new money exchange: it was to be fourteen feet long by twelve feet wide (3.84 meters by 3.29 meters), thus only about 170 square feet in floor area. When a fifth fief was created sometime between 1311 and 1325, the exchange was to be a wooden structure on four wheels with the dimensions of twelve feet by twelve feet (3.29m. × 3.29m) and presumably able to be wheeled to wherever there was demand for its services.[134]

The second document dating from the first quarter of the thirteenth century hints at another truth about early money changing in Bruges: it

[131] Some of these points are made in Hunt and Murray, *History of Business*, pp. 63–67 and 209–212.

[132] Marechal, *Bijdrage*, pp. 79–80: "omme huleiden te informeerne van deser zake," i.e. to inform them (the count's officials) of the history of money changing in Bruges relevant to the dispute.

[133] Ibid., p. 79; this is made explicit in the addendum to the copy of 1325, "Dit sijn de copien van den letteren van den wissele ende van den muntmeesterscepe ende dat daer toebehord," which explicitly links exchange, "wissele", and the office of mintmaster, "muntmeesterscepe."

[134] Ibid., p. 47; Bigwood, *Régime*, vol. 1, p. 413. Raymond de Roover inexplicably overlooked the existence of the wheeled exchange office, as he did the shift of the "Wissel" to the St. Pieters bridge from the Oude Burg around 1300; see De Roover, *Money, Banking and Credit*, p. 200.

may not have been very lucrative. In January, 1229, the heirs of Arnulphus Monetarius, Roger, and Anna his wife were granted permission to sell their exchange to the *poorter* Nicholaus Calkere, because of their evident poverty. But Calkere must have been buying on the prospects of the fief, for the exchange was to remain in the Calkere family for the next three generations, contributing no doubt to the wealth and influence of the family. Perhaps it is no coincidence that the Calkere clan was one of the most powerful in Bruges throughout the thirteenth century, counting a number of aldermen before either dying out or fleeing Bruges by 1302.[135]

The clearest sign of growth in the money changing business, and by extension of the commercial importance of Bruges, is the increasing number of "unfree" exchanges, which sprang up around and among the four licensed tables in an area defined by the Grote Markt, the Belfort/Cloth Hall, and the Burg with its Mary chapel, with perhaps the greatest concentration on or at the foot of the Hofbrug, the bridge that spanned the Kraanrei and thus connected the Burg (via the Breidelstraat) with the Grote Markt.[136] This was squarely astride the major roads passing through the city, with the then most important market places – the Burg and Grote Markt – as the twin hubs. The holders of these "unfree" exchanges were supposed to acknowledge the primacy of the four "free" exchanges, and in token of this they paid each the holders of the fief 20s. parisis per year perpetual rent. But sometime between 1297 and 1302 the four free money changers lodged an appeal with the king of France, alleging that they had been disenfranchised by the holders of the twelve unfree exchanges, many of whom both refused to locate their exchange tables within the boundaries described above, and to obtain the permission of the aldermen and four mintmasters (i.e. free money changers) to open their exchange. This request was supposed to be accompanied with a payment of the required perpetual rent.[137] What alarmed the free money changers was apparently that the growth in the number of exchanges was exceeding their power to control the business, in terms of both their rights to customary payments and the geographical

[135] From 1250 to 1302 there was almost always a member of the de Calkere clan (also spelled Calkra, Calkre) on one of the two ruling councils of the city, sometimes as its leader or burgomaster. At least two of these were money changers: Nicholaus, son of Nicholaus, alderman from 1250 to 1251 (Marechal, *Bijdrage*, p. 80), and Willem, who was alderman in 1280–1281, 1283–1284, 1286–1287, and 1288–1289; councilor and burgomaster in 1290–1291; and alderman 1291–1292. The last de Calkere to hold office was Nicholaus (III), who was alderman in 1301–1302. These facts are from van den Auweele, "Schepenbank en Schepenen," vol. IV, pp. 6–58. Representatives of the clan were also members of the London Hanse: see Wyffels, "De Vlaamse Hanze van Londen," 13 n. 22.

[136] Marechal, *Bijdrage*, p. 47.

[137] Ibid., pp. 80–81.

location of the unfree exchanges within the boundaries known as the "Wissel."[138]

The outcome of the appeal is not known, but it offers a glimpse into some of the tensions within the Bruges financial community during a period of rapid growth. It also indicates the mounting pressure to relocate the "Wissel" from its traditional boundaries to new quarters off the north corner of the Grote Markt bordering the important new commercial building, the New Cloth Hall, and the thriving commercial neighborhoods extending along the Vlamingstraat and the future Bourse square. After 1307, the "Exchange of Bruges" shifted to another bridge across the Kraanrei, St. Pieter's bridge, which passed along the north end of the New Cloth Hall and connected the new financial heart of the city with the Grote Markt. The dispute between the free and unfree money changers about location was probably a harbinger of this definitive move.

Not all money exchanges were to be found in one location even after the final transfer of the accustomed spot from the vicinity of the Old Cloth Hall to the New. For one thing, the count granted the right to one fief holder to operate an exchange "on four wheels" – thus freely transportable throughout the city. The other scrap of information confirms the complaint about the reluctance of some money changers to fix their business in the proximity of all the others. Jan de Maerc's business, for example, was located on the east side of the Bailiestraat in 1361, some distance away from the "Wissel" bridge.[139]

The picture of money changing as a shifting and changing profession in the early fourteenth century is confirmed when one compares the three surviving city accounts for the years 1303–1306. In all three years there were sums collected from money changers: in 1303 a fine was collected from

[138] The four free money changers described the "Exchange" of Bruges very precisely as sixteen in number, "which stood on the Market of Bruges behind the Old Belfort, both the structures and the ground between the late Gillis Blancardz property and St. Mary's chapel." It is clear as well that the collectivity was known as the "Wissel" in an abstract sense, for the charter states that "no one may maintain an exchange, nor exchange [money] anywhere in the castlery of Bruges unless in the aforesaid Exchange . . ." The document dates from between 1297 and 1302 and survives only in a summary from a 1325 copy (Marechal, *Bijdrage*, pp. 80–81).

[139] RAB, fonds St. Walburga church, 399, f. 6r: "Johannes de Maerc wisselare soluit viginti solidos par. in termino nativitatis Domini et sunt assignati supra fundum suum super quem sue camere situantur in vico appelato Baeliestrate a parte orientali ab uno latere et fundum Jacobi Boets ab alio latere." The fact that this entry clearly refers to his "room," coupled with the fact that he owned a house in the Steenstraat where he probably resided, means this was his business location. For the house in the Steenstraat: RAB, Aanwinsten, no. 256, f. 34v, describes a house belonging to "Jans wedewen van Maerc swisselaers." At the end of the fifteenth century, the money changer Collard de May's establishment stood just off the Bourse square, in the Grauwwerkersstraat, well north of St. Pieter's bridge: Marechal, *Geschiedenis van de Brugse Beurs*, p. 38.

fourteen of them; likewise in 1304 a general fee, or fine (*boete*), was assessed against thirty-two; and in 1305, a forced loan was collected from some changers and a fine from others. The total number of changers named was twenty-eight. Only four names appear on all three lists; thirteen names appear on the lists of 1305–1306; thus in the space of just three years, the majority of money changers either ceased their activities in money changing, or changed professions altogether.[140] Even of those changers of "Gheleenden Gheld," whose loans to the city suggest that they were wealthy and well established, only five of the eleven appear on both lists.[141] Thus if we eliminate the anomalous years of 1305–1306, we are left with the number of between thirteen and sixteen public money changers in the city.[142]

The number of practicing money changers shows remarkable continuity if we take the long view across most of the fourteenth century. From sixteen in 1306, the number fell slightly to fourteen by 1310. After a gap in our information lasting from 1311 to 1345, we again see fifteen exchanges in 1346, and the figure remains more or less at that level until after 1370 when a sudden and prolonged decline in their number becomes apparent. By 1378 there were only eight exchanges, and by the fifteenth century, these dwindled to the original five fiefs held from the count.[143]

Money changing had probably not reached its most developed form by the time of the shift from the Hofbrug to St. Pieter's bridge, that is around 1300, but had remained largely confined to simple exchange of coin. This suspicion is supported by the description of the activities of the money changer in the 1297–1302 appeal as "holding an exchange" or "exchanging" "within the city or territory of Bruges."[144] There is no sign here of the two crucially important adjuncts, deposit banking and book transfers, which were to be so much a part of the money changing business in the fourteenth century.

140 Wyffels and Vandewalle, *Rekeningen*, vol. II, pt. I, pp. 305, 507, 600–601.

141 It is interesting to note that in a loan to the city in February 1305, four of seven individuals who contributed were money changers in "gheleenden gheld," two were irregular money changers (*ghukellaers*), and one was Gillise den Juede, a Jew; ibid., pp. 599–600.

142 De Roover, *Money, Banking and Credit*, p. 206.

143 Bigwood, *Régime*, vol. I, p. 394; Gilliodts-Van Severen, *Inventaire*, vol. II, p. 347; de Roover, *Money, Banking and Credit*, p. 175. The reasons for the decline in money changers under the Burgundians, not only in Flanders but also in Brabant, have been in dispute since De Roover's time. Certainly the official hostility of the Burgundians played a role, as de Roover maintained, but whether it was decisive is difficult to say. Van Uytven argued that money changers were simply a stage in the evolution to merchant bankers at the end of the Middle Ages; see van Uyven, *Stadsfinanciën en stadsekonomie*, p. 456, and Aerts, "Middeleeuwse bankgeschiedenis," 60.

144 Marechal, *Bijdrage*, p. 80.

FROM EXCHANGE TO DEPOSIT BANKING

Raymond de Roover found the earliest evidence of the development of deposit banking among the money changers of nearby Lille, which was at the time still a part of Flanders. In a charter granted by Count Guy of Dampierre in August, 1294, six burghers of Lille were granted permission to "be changers and to receive money." The charter went on to make clear that "receiving" money was in effect accepting deposits from customers and making payments on demand.[145] What the charter's language is struggling to express is that the job of money changer had become three-fold: "changing" or the manual exchange of one coin for another; the responsibility for monitoring coinage; and delivering bullion to the royal mint. In this the Lille money changers acted as royal deputies. Last and beyond these traditional functions, the changers were also granted license by the count to "receive" and make payments, i.e. the financial services of accepting money on deposit and directing it in accordance with the wishes of the depositor. This business was not in the grant of the king (whether it was in the grant of the count is unclear) and thus could not be abrogated by him.[146] On the one hand the count was granting protection and monopoly to the Lille changers, while at the same time defining his rights at a time of growing hostility between the count and the king of France.

De Roover could find no similarly clear line of demarcation in the evolution of money changing in Bruges. Here he missed a valuable clue left in the Bruges town accounts of 1305. This was a period in which the after-effects of the revolt against the king of France were still wreaking havoc on the city's finances, requiring loans, fines, and taxes from a number of professional groups in the city. Among these were the money changers, who are divided into two groups: "Wissellaers in gheleenden gheld" and "Wissellaers die men heet ghukellaers." These two lists appear on the same folio of the same account and there is no duplication of names.[147] What does this difference in terminology mean? In the first instance, the manuscript itself offers some help in resolving the ambiguity about whether they were "Changers in borrowed money" i.e. a description of their function), or simply "Changers, in borrowed money" (a loan to the city). To prevent just this confusion, noticed perhaps when the accounts were audited, a

[145] De Roover, *Money, Banking and Credit*, pp. 202–203.

[146] Ibid., p. 203; Bigwood, *Régime*, vol. II, pp. 304–305, #20. The actual language speaks of "loial cange, loial rechoite et loiaux a paiemens."

[147] Wyffels and Vandewalle, *Rekeningen*, vol. II, pt. 1, p. 600. Earlier in the accounts (p. 507), changers had been listed without differentation.

hand contemporary with, yet different from, that of the account added the word "Prest" so that the amended entry reads "Prest vanden Wissellaers in Gheleenden Gheld." A changer in borrowed money was thus a kind of money changer in this case, and the identifier "in borrowed or loaned money" defines their function as accepting deposits.[148]

The evidence for a system of book transfers among the Bruges money changers is much more straightforward, although it has remained unnoticed until now. In 1309 there was an attempt by the Bruges aldermen to control the trade in bullion in the city, and to regulate the profession of money changer as well. As in the earlier description of 1297–1302, there is a clear statement about the geographical confines of the Bruges "Wisssel"; but the list of permitted activities has changed: "No one is to change money, have money changed or to *make payments* (my italics) through exchange, in the administrative district of Bruges other than in the public exchange."[149] Using the exchange to effect payments is a clear reference to book transfers, where a verbal order is issued to draw on funds in one account and deposit them in another either with the same or another money changer. Another document from the same year also establishes that deposit taking and book transfers were well established in the city. This was a privilege granted to merchants of the German Hanse, which clearly provides for repayment of money lost while on deposit "in the Exchange of Bruges."[150] Both deposit taking and book transfers were established practices in Bruges by 1309.[151]

ORGANIZATION AND SUPERVISION OF MONEY CHANGING

Authority over money changers in Bruges was shared between the city government and the count in ways that are not entirely clear. The count granted as fiefs the five licenses of the "free" money changers, and in practice these were passed on through several generations of the same family.[152] Transfer of the fief came either through the death of the previous holder, or through sale to someone outside the family. Possession of one of these fiefs

[148] Among the eleven "changers in loaned money" are all the "free" money changers and other recognized "unfree" changers. The term *ghukellaer* referred to irregular and illegal exchanges.

[149] Gilliodts-van Severen, *Inventaire*, vol. I, #237, pp. 300–301; Bigwood, *Régime*, vol. I, p. 416.

[150] De Roover, *Money, Banking and Credit*, pp. 336 and 342 n. 26, quoting *Hansisches Urkundenbuch*, vol. II, p. 68, no. 154, art. 24.

[151] This accords well with the practices in other cities we know of. In Venice, Reinhold Mueller dates the availability of deposit banking and transfers around 1300 (*Venetian Money Market*, pp. 8–9).

[152] Marechal provides a number of examples, besides the Calkere family: the Adorne family, the van Heeden family, the Ruseleide family, and the van Curtrike family, to name but a few; see *Bijdrage*, pp. 120–140.

entitled the holder to operate or rent out a money exchange and to collect an annual fee from the "unfree" money changers of the city.[153] How these money changers were licensed and supervised is unclear. It is possible that the city granted licenses and either collected bonds from money changers or required sureties from them.[154] The fief holders also seem to have claimed some additional authority along with the city, as a document from c. 1300 states that unfree money changers had to petition the aldermen and mint-masters for permission to operate and pay additional fees to secure entry.[155] All money changers were required to be *poorters* of the city, making the profession a *Poortersneringe* as distinct from a guild.[156] However, in 1305, "Doyens de le Cange" confiscated money in Sluis, presumably in the course of enforcing the ban on money changing in that city.[157] The title "dean" was that given to the chief officials of a guild, though in this case it probably referred to mint-masters. All in all, money changers seem to have been largely self-governing, with mint policies being enforced by the bailiff and a vague supervisory role played by the city's aldermen.

Responsibility in cases of bankruptcy of money changers clearly lay with the city, however. There were at least three examples of bankrupt money changers in the fourteenth century, with a fourth, Collard de Marke, a near certainty. Early in the century, the case of Boiden Weghebedde tells us something of bankruptcy proceedings in Bruges. Sometime in 1314 or 1315, Weghebedde's exchange was forced into bankruptcy as he was unable to honor his obligations. Imprisonment for himself and his sureties in the "Steen" was the result, until he arrived at a settlement with the city. This involved a deal converting the uncovered losses of the exchange into a long-term debt to be paid off in annual payments to the city.[158] The city in this case must have initially paid off his creditors.

153 The book of fiefs wherein these transfers were recorded clearly states the circumstances of transfer: see ARA, Rekenkamer, RR 1071–1074.

154 The city does not seem to have been very consistent in its financial security requirement for Bruges money changers. Only in 1347, when three money changers paid £24 in order to "maken die wissele," is there clear evidence of posting bond (SAB, SR 1347–1348, f. 33v). In the case of Diederic Urbaen's widow there were at least two sureties, who were pursued after she went bankrupt. See de Roover, *Money, Banking and Credit*, pp. 334, 361–363. In Ghent sizable bonds were required of both money changers and hostellers; see Nicholas, *Metamorphosis*, pp. 200–202.

155 These were entry and quit fees – "ingane ende van uutgane" – Marechal, *Bijdrage*, p. 81.

156 Ibid., p. 49; De Roover, *Money, Banking and Credit*, p. 173.

157 ARA, RR 1007, membrane 8: "les Doyens de le cange en monoye prise a Lesscluse, £4 10s." For the conflict over rights to change money in Sluis, see chapter 2.

158 The only particulars we have of the case appear in the city accounts: "Van Boiden Weghebedde van dat hi der stede jaerlix sculdich es als van fauten van sinen wissele waen of dat hi ende sine borghen inden Steen laghen, bi Janne Cante sine sweer £70" (SAB, SR, 1315, f. 2r). He is mentioned in passing by De Roover (*Money, Banking and Credit*, pp. 175, 193 n. 41). The third certain bankrupt was Nanne, widow of Diederic Urbaens (ibid., pp. 361–363).

By the middle of the fourteenth century, supervision of bankruptcies had been entrusted to the "burgomaster of the Course," the chief of the second bank of Bruges aldermen.[159] He typically presided over the seizure of records and properties of the failed money changer. He then proceeded to an audit of the assets and debts owed on the basis of records and testimony, and supervised the distribution of a proportionate share of the recovered funds to creditors. In so doing he was obliged to observe privileges that granted some foreign merchants a right of full restitution; he could also move against anyone who had stood as a surety for the money exchange.[160] Fines for infringements of the monopoly of money changing in Bruges were collected by the comital bailiff and shared between the city and count.[161]

The business

As we have seen, with the shift of commercial activity caused by the construction of the Waterhalle, the exchanges shifted too, while retaining the strategic location between the Burg and the Grote Markt. But from the north end of the Waterhalle they also commanded the commercial corridor along the Kraanrei, leading to the Tolhuis and the dense concentration of hostels on either side. And as we have also seen, a changing booth may have been wheeled around and between the market centers of the city, a reminder of the shifting geography of Bruges money changing.

Most of the face-to-face business of money changing probably took place on St. Pieter's bridge. Here merchants came to exchange coins and bullion, open accounts, and make payment orders for book transfers. The location was also ideal for weavers to collect money owed them by Bruges drapers for cloth they had delivered to the Old Cloth Hall, as we shall see in a later chapter. And it was near the seat of urban and comital government, which lay only steps away through the Posterne gate and St. Donatian's cloister. The church's chapter rented houses and shops to a number of gold and silver smiths, whose close proximity to the "Wissel" must have facilitated

159 Two charters from the bankruptcy of Willem Ruweel illustrate the procedure. The first reports that Lamsin de Vos, "burgmeester vanden Course," had reached agreement based on precedent in Bruges and agreement with Willem Ruweel that his goods be confiscated and used to satisfy his creditors: SAB, St. Salvator, S722, 278a published in James M. Murray, "Family, Marriage and Money Changing in Medieval Bruges," *Journal of Medieval History* 14 (1988), 123–124. The other is identical in language and is edited ibid., 123.

160 As stated above, Hanse merchants acquired right of restitution for all deposits held by Bruges money changers in 1309. Other foreign merchant communities gained this guarantee only much later in the century: Spaniards in 1380 and Italian communities also late in the century.

161 Bruges Bailiff accounts for 1303–1306 are representative: that for 1304–1305 contains only two names; that for 1305–1306 contains twenty-one; see ARA, RR 1001, 1003.

trade in gold and silver bullion. Yet with the virtual closing of the Bruges mint in the 1330s, as well as the dismantling of the city's smelting facility, the overall importance of bullion in the business must have diminished.[162] This may account for the disappearance of the title "mintmaster" formerly claimed by the "free money changers" around the same time. Thereafter a dwindling number of Bruges money changers had accounts at the Ghent mint, which served as a bank and clearing house for bullion and coins. The flight of the Master of the Money of Flanders in late July 1357 provides an indication of the percentage of money changers with active mint accounts, and the relative importance of Bruges money changers in the county. In the accounts of the debts he left behind, five Bruges money changers were owed more than 40 percent of the undelivered gold moutons.[163] One money changer alone held more than a fifth of the debt.[164] In comparison, three Ypres money changers were owed 5.7 percent and twenty Ghent merchants accounted for 14.6 percent. The largest creditor was the Bruges native Baudouin de Vos, who also served as a comital official.[165] Ten years later the Bruges "unfree" money changer Collard de Marke seems to have specialized in the delivery of bullion to the Ghent mint and the return of coin to Bruges. His accounts show that he single-handedly supplied about 10 percent of all the coined metal in 1369–70.[166] These figures indicate an overall decline in the importance of mint deliveries to the average Bruges money changer in the course of the century.

Money changers were still obliged to serve as (unpaid) guardians of the coinage, responsible for culling out of circulation seriously underweight, worn, or demonetized coins and delivering them to the mint for reminting. For gold coins, market forces often conflicted with these legal obligations, as changers sometimes exchanged coins at rates exceeding those decreed by the count, resulting in legal action against money changers. This was the case in 1366, when nine money changers were fined by the city for accepting and issuing gold nobles at a price above that set by the count's mint ordinances.[167] The return of a strong money policy in 1390 also had profound

[162] The smelting facility closed before 1350 and the Bruges mint virtually ceased operations, except for a brief period in the 1340s when gold coins were minted there; see de Roover, *Money, Banking and Credit*, pp. 230–231, and Elsen, "La monnaie," 83, 85 n. 233.

[163] De Roover, "Le livre de comptes de Guillaume Ruyelle," 39–40; Elsen, "La monnaies," 100.

[164] This was Evrard Goederic, one of the most successful of mid-century money changers, at least judging from his political importance; see de Roover, *Money, Banking, and Credit*, pp. 188–190.

[165] Ibid., p. 39, Elsen, "La monnaie," 101 n. 299; it should be noted that these two differ slightly in their report of the coin totals.

[166] For more discussion on the Bruges bullion market, see chapter 7.

[167] SAB, SR 1366–1367, f. 16r: "Ontfanghen van wisselaers die noble dierre ontfanghen hebben ende uteghegheven danne zie doen moghe na der cuere . . ."

repercussions on money changers and their business practices. Breaking with a tradition of relative laissez faire, the bailiff investigated charges that certain Bruges money changers were accepting gold coins that were not to circulate as legal tender in Flanders and then failing to "cut" them for bullion.[168] In company with two Bruges aldermen he searched the exchanges and found two changers in violation of the ordinance.[169] A request sent to the money changers of Paris by the Bruges city government shows another facet of a money changer's competence. The aldermen wanted to know the history of the French coinage for the previous twenty years so that they could negotiate with French royal officials in some unnamed dispute.[170]

Just how great a level of skill was required of money changers? On the one hand, the ability to collect coins, convert their value into money of account, and enter the result in the "paper" of the exchange (as the account book was commonly called) required fairly basic skills. Given that the language of many transactions, as well as the written language of the accounts, was French adds another degree of difficulty since that was not the first language of most Bruges natives.[171] More daunting must have been the ability to recognize and properly assay the many different kinds of gold and silver coins that passed across the counter on a typical business day. De Marke's and Ruweel's account books, though silent on silver coins, list the large number of kinds and quantities of gold coins they dealt in. Even given this level of complexity the daily running of an exchange office probably did not require the constant attendance of the license holder. We know in fact that in 1389–1390, Baltazar Langherard operated the exchange belonging to his uncle, Jacob Langerards. In the fifteenth century at least one exchange was leased to its operator, and there is abundant evidence that the exchange of Willem Ruweel was run by his wife.[172]

168 A money changer was obliged to have a set of shears so that he or she could deface a non-current coin, thus rendering it suitable only for reminting.

169 Gilliodts-van Severen, *Inventaire*, vol. IV, pp. 186–187; ARA, Rekenkamer, 13679, ad. 1392.

170 SAB, SR 1333–1334, f. 91r "Claikin Longius ysent te Parijs toten wisselaers omme te wetene tcoers vander munte binnen 20 jaren omme te rekenne ieghen sconinx liede die hier laghen up den 22sten dach van den ouste, 36s." The dispute may have been over the debts owed the king of France, resulting from the wars early in the century and the treaties arising from them; see Werveke, "Les charges financières issues du traité d'Athis."

171 Instruction in the French language was an important part of business training in the Dutch-speaking areas of Flanders; see Nicholas, *Domestic Life*, pp. 127–129. The survival of a bilingual conversation manual, which probably belonged to a Bruges schoolmaster, also suggests French language instruction in the fourteenth century. See Gessler, *Brugsche Livre des Mestiers.*

172 ARA, Rekenkamer, 13677, pt. 1, f. 10v: "Item Baltazar le fils Willem Langherards, qui tient le change de Jaques Langherards en le ville de Bruges . . ." (mentioned by Marechal, *Bijdrage*, p. 136); the mention of a leased exchange dates from 1409 (ibid., p. 132).

Book transfers and auditing required the attention of a specialist, however. Most book transfers were effected through verbal orders either delivered in person or by an assistant. Records were kept of the transaction by both the money changer and, presumably, the customer. Therefore at regular intervals the customer – or his agent – and money changer compared accounts and reconciled balances. While careful merchants apparently kept independent records, many did not, and in disputed cases the money changer's account book had the force of legal record.[173] There is also mention in de Marke's account books about account balances being written on "square" pieces of paper. These mostly involved small amounts of money and may have been intended as a kind of paper currency recognized among Bruges shopkeepers.[174] The system was not perfect, as errors are mentioned from time to time in the surviving accounts, particularly of de Marke.[175] In the case of possible error, a search was sometimes made of the ledgers of another money changer, with appropriate adjustments to accounts when the error was discovered.[176] Accounts were also adjusted if the coins tendered were later found to be worthless.[177]

In a very real sense, the crucial business of money changing took place away from the daily trade in coins, in the hostels and market places of Bruges. For as de Roover proved long ago, the bulk of the deposits left with

[173] This reliance on the changer's ledgers is explicitly stated in the bankruptcy case of the widow Urbaens, whose sureties insisted that they "need not answer for the debts aforesaid because they are not recorded in the Ledger of the Exchange" ("'t Panpier van den Wissele"); see de Roover, *Money, Banking and Credit*, p. 363.

[174] This is a curious practice noted at least half a dozen times in the de Marke ledgers. Typical is the account of a Jehan de Wet in mid-December 1368 (De Marke 2, f. 228v): "Jehan de Wet me doit que jay mis en 1 petit papier quaret, £2 gro." The amounts vary from 5s. to £20, with most being less than £1. Raymond de Roover was puzzled by this "square" paper or notebook as well, but he believed it was part of de Marke's own financial record keeping (*Money, Banking and Credit*, pp. 211 and 219 n. 68). But all the entries suggest that the paper or notebook were taken by the customer, which seems to indicate some kind of local use for such a thing, for example to make small purchases with Bruges shopkeepers.

[175] Examples of errors from de Marke's accounts: 2, f. 171r, the account Sire Piere Teste, "item me doit il ale cause de Jehan Kerler, almant, lesquels nous li aviesmes payet sans raison et il les a trouves Pieter Daudenarde 6.9.10."

[176] Errors could be simple instances of miscopying, as in the broker Pieter van Collekierke's account of October 1369: (De Marke 5, f. 221v): "item me doit il par cou quil dist a 1 octobre somme £13 9s. 5d. ou 100 francs par cou quil ne conte que cent a lui que 260 et jay escrit 360 francs." Or they could be errors such as forgetting a transaction (ibid., 34v): "Jak. de Gerart me doit il que je avoie oublyet aconter a lui lesquels je li prestay 21 mart . . . 30 nobles a 55 gro." An example of searches of another changer's ledger (ibid., 2, f. 171r): "Sire Piere Teste . . . item me doit il a le cause de Jehan Kerkere, almant, lesquels nous li aviesmes payet sans raison, £6 9s. 10d., et il les a trouves a Pieter Daudenarde."

[177] These adjustments are indicated by the word "refus," as in the account of the Italian Thumas Sarlande (De Marke 3, f. 4v): "item me doit il par Andrius pour refus 3s. 5d. et 10 francs franc." This indicates that large deposits of silver coins would be immediately credited to an account while the coins themselves were kept together, probably in a sack pending closer scrutiny.

money changers – up to 75 percent – were invested in trade.[178] Thus the success or failure of a money exchange depended on the investment and business skill of the money changer. Besides the detailed information we possess about the business interests of de Marke and Ruweel (about which more will follow), we also have scattered evidence about the business activities of other money changers. Farming the city's excise taxes was one popular investment option. Acquiring the right to collect these consumption taxes on wine, beer, and mead required a sometimes large investment of ready money in return for a flow of cash over the course of the term, which was usually seventeen weeks. Thus besides ready capital, some expertise about the likely consumption of the commodity was required to turn a profit. We will see that Willem Ruweel was either unskilled or unlucky in his farming of the wine excise. But his contemporary Jacob Reubs appears to have been better suited by experience or chance to derive a profit from his investments. Reubs is also known to have invested in trading ventures, as in the case mentioned above with the lombard Jacques Mancegas. There is strong evidence that Bruges money changers invested heavily in the cloth trade, both in its manufacture and in the import of cloth for sale in Bruges.[179]

Moneylending was also certainly an important part of the money changing business, though its precise importance is difficult to make out from the sources. One form of a loan could be the right to overdraw an account, which the evidence of the de Marke account shows was a common practice.[180] However, the de Marke accounts also show that overdrafts were tightly circumscribed, granted only to the best customers for small amounts, which were rapidly repaid. Some tradesmen, like drapers, were allowed to overdraw their accounts as a matter of course, owing perhaps to the nature of their business in which cash flow could be a problem.[181] Were Bruges money changers making loans at interest? This is difficult to determine. Collard de Marke rarely mentions loans in his accounts, which is understandable given that usury was illegal and his accounts were public documents, at least in case of bankruptcy. But he did mention at least a handful of loans in the accounts. More significantly, in his journals, the daily running accounts from which the definitive entries in the ledgers were drawn, there are more frequent mentions of small loans to trusted customers. These suggest that

[178] De Roover, *Money, Banking and Credit*, pp. 204–205.

[179] One indication of Jacob Reubs's investment in cloth survives in the de Marke accounts, De Marke 2, f. 343r: "Jakop Reups me doit . . . sen doit mettre sur sen conte en ce papier £21 12s. 4d. et £10 16s. 2d. sur le conte de dras en me petit papier." This topic will be taken up again in chapter 7.

[180] De Roover, *Money, Banking and Credit*, pp. 294–305, where he discusses overdrafts and the customers who were granted them by de Marke.

[181] See the discusion, chapter 7 pp. 285–288.

de Marke supplied on occasion the type of small consumption credit usually extended by pawnbrokers and other moneylenders.[182] Of course we cannot know if and at what rate interest was assessed on these loans, but the "odor of usury" seems quite close. De Marke may have made a distinction between these loans and advances intended for business investments. These he called "finanches," and most seem to have had a business purpose. For example, the Bruges furrier Jehan van de Walle's account was debited for the large sum of £76 for a "finanche" advanced to two Italians, Lucadine and Dine Malapris.[183]

The line between money changers and pawnbrokers was also sometimes overstepped. As we have seen, pawnbrokers were those who made loans on the pledge of personal property, and most were licensed usurers. Notwithstanding the implied monopoly of these licenses, there are examples of changers lending on pledge. In 1366–1368, Jehan Moreel of Tournai, called "le cangeur" in the account he kept with de Marke, was fined for pawnbroking in Bruges without a license.[184] There is also a very clear fifteenth-century case when Maximilian of Austria pledged jewels as security for a loan with two Bruges money changers.[185] Thus money changers acted on

[182] One loan (or *prest*) made by de Marke sounds very much like an emergency advance for consumption purposes: (De Marke 3, f. 127r): "Nicollas Outremarin . . . item me doit il par Gilles Crestien 24 juinguet pour 1 prest quil li fist pour le leuwier de leur maison de le Nostre Dame lan 68 en aoust iusques a le Nestre Dame en aoust lan 69 apries, £14 gro." This advance of rent money from Assumption day 1368 to 1369, at the request of a frequent customer, seems very much like a personal loan. A similar case occurred on 8 April 1367 when another foreign merchant customer, Catain Pimiel, secured a loan of £50 gro. for Jehan Contemin (ibid., 2, f. 280r). No interest charges are mentioned in either case.

[183] De Marke 3, f. 203r: "Jehan van de Walle peletier . . . item me doit il pour Lucadine a Dine Malapris pour une finance 21 decembre (1368) £75 gro." De Roover thought both men were Italian, possibly from Lucca; see *Money, Banking and Credit*, pp. 287 n. 39, 372, 303, 370, 378. A similar case occurred in April 1368 (ibid., 4, f. 173r): "Sire Jehan Baille me doit par Sire Jehan de Concorighe pour une finance £75 gro." And again in the business of Jehan van de Walle in November 1369 (ibid., 5, f. 157v): "Hugelin Adelaise doy [credit to] par Jehan van de Walle 20 novembre pour une finanche qui eskei 18 novembre, £119 13s. 4d."

[184] Moreel apparently immigrated to Bruges, purchasing citizenship in 1366. He was fined for operating an unlicensed pawnshop in 1368 where he lent money at an interest rate above the legal limit; that year he held an account with de Marke, which was grouped among those of the money changers, but was open only between January and February with very few transactions. It is impossible to know whether he was operating a pawn or exchange shop or if the distinction really applied in his case. See Marechal, *Bijdrage*, pp. 117–118 and De Marke 4, ff.302r, 308r. De Roover called him "a shady money-monger because he had not succeeded in earning a living by reputable and legal means" (*Money, Banking and Credit*, p. 306).

[185] O. Mus, "De Brugse Compagnie Despars," *ASEB* 101 (1964), 5–118; see 34 n. 134, case of Maximilian of Austria making use of his jewels as security for a loan from two Bruges *wisselaars*, Jan Nutin and Colard de Mey. The jewels were later sold to the king of England. Thus there was no clear distinction between pawnbrokers and money changers. Collarde de Mey went bankrupt in 1482; see Hanham, *The Celys*, p. 188. George Celys banked with him on occasion.

occasion as high-order pawnbrokers. If usury and money changing were not quite synonymous in the cities of the late medieval Low Countries, they were close neighbors both in fact and popular estimation. The distinction, of course, made all the difference, for even "licensed" usurers were social and religious outcasts and the even more numerous "unlicensed" moneylenders were committing a crime as well as imperiling their souls. Given this close professional proximity, is there any evidence that money changers suffered any kind of social stigma or ostracism?

SOCIAL AND LEGAL POSITION OF MONEY CHANGERS

To be a money changer required the legal status of *poorter* – a bundle of rights and privileges claimed by only a small percentage of the political and economic elite of the city. It could be acquired through inheritance, purchase or marriage to another *poorter*, so it was possible for outsiders to participate in the profession. As a result money changers were a diverse group, which included elite families and foreigners, with a majority originating from the middling ranks of Bruges society. Money changers from truly patrician families seem to cluster at the beginning of the century, including members of the Calkere, van der Matte, Metteneye, Utezacke, and van Wulfsberghe clans.[186] As the fourteenth century progressed, however, money changing seems to have become more an avenue for foreigners to enter Bruges than a respectable profession for a member of the elite. Notable was the Lübeck merchant Tideman Blomenrod, who was expelled from membership of the German Hanse and thereafter purchased Bruges "citizenship" and became a money changer. For the best part of a decade he pursued business with relatives and friends in Lübeck (despite the Hanse ban) in partnership with the hosteller Matheus van der Beurse, who catered to the Hanse merchant community.[187] He also mixed with powerful financial figures in Flanders, including the widow of Simon de Mirabello, with whom he joined in advancing a large loan to the city of Ghent. In 1359 he joined a number of his colleagues in a loan to Bruges government as well.[188]

[186] Marechal, *Bijdrage*, p. 49.

[187] This liaison with one of the most important of Bruges hostellers argues for the simple continuation of a long-standing business relationship between the two. For an extensive biography of Blomenrod see Asmussen, *Lübecker Flandernfahrer*, pp. 294–299, whose works supersedes de Roover, *Money, Banking and Credit*, pp. 171–173.

[188] Asmussen, *Lübecker Flandernfahrer*, pp. 297–298. Simon de Mirabello (or van Halen) was the bastard son of a Lombard from Asti, and he followed his father into the moneylending business before taking up a political career during the dictatorship of Jacob van Artevelde. His family remained both wealthy and well connected with the aristocracy of Flanders; see Nicholas, *Medieval*

Other money changers of foreign origins include Willem Ruweel, Pieter Adorne of Genoa, and his son Joris. In the fifteenth century, foreigners made up an even higher percentage of Bruges money changers.[189]

Measuring the social status and respectability of a profession is always difficult, but one sure indication is the frequency its members held the office of alderman. The de Calkere clan is a notable example of eminence gained through urban office holding. But there is no comparable case in the fourteenth century. Only two money changers held the alderman's office in the entire century, and one of these, Evrard Goederic, had already given up the profession by the time he entered city politics. Goederic indeed went on to a distinguished career of city service, including terms as alderman, ambassador, and representative at the wedding of Philip the Bold and Margaret of Flanders in 1369.[190] But Goederic seems rather the exception than the rule, for there is considerable contrary evidence about the social position of money changers. Even the count's "guardian of the money," the Bruges changer Clais Rapesaert, never held city office.

There was considerable official hostility to money changers, particularly from the beginning of the Burgundian regime. An annual oath was required of all changers from 1389, and searches as well as confiscations were carried out from time to time in order to enforce adherence to monetary ordinances.[191] Popular attitudes are more difficult to assess. In Ghent there was a clear connection between social protest and hostility towards money changers. Philip van Artevelde was no doubt giving vent to popular mistrust of money changers when he decreed in January 1382 that there should be only one exchange in Ghent and that it would "value each penny according to its worth."[192] This reproduces almost word for word a

Flanders, p. 221 and Ellen Kittell, *From Ad Hoc to Routine. A Case Study in Medieval Bureaucracy* (Philadelphia, 1991), pp. 150–161, and most recently, D. Kusman, "Jean de Mirabello dit van Haelen (ca. 1280–1333). Haute finance et Lombards en Brabant dans le premier tiers du XIVe siècle," *RBPH* 77 (1999), 843–931.

189 Marechal, *Bijdrage*, p. 49. These included men and women from Lille, Amiens, and Sint-Winoksbergen, as well as Genoa, Florence, and Milan. The most common origin was from Lille or its surrounding territory.

190 De Roover, *Money, Banking and Credit*, pp. 189–190.

191 The Burgundian dukes in effect took over the supervision of changers after 1389, which was a small part of their overall program of state centralization; see Marc Boone, "Geldhandel en pandbedrijf in Gent tijdens de Bourgondische periode: politieke, fiscale en sociale aspecten," *RBPH* 66 (1988), 770–772.

192 Ibid., 770 n. 12: "Voordt, dat maar eene wissele in Ghent ne zoude ghehouden zijn, ende die zoude elken penninc valuweren naer zijne weerde." For the historical context, see Nicholas, *Van Arteveldes*, pp. 164–165.

proposal brought forth in Bruges during the turbulent times leading up to 1302.[193] The famous abbot from Tournai, Gilles li Muisit, lumped usurers, moneyers, and changers together as those who risk all for money.[194] These expressions of popular suspicion suggest widespread misunderstanding of the market in coins as well as a reaction to sharp practices by changers who stood to profit in times of widespread debasement, accompanied always by the tinge of usury.

Bruges provides some additional evidence of hostility towards the money changing profession. In the early fourteenth century two *Keuren* or edicts sought to ban changers from the office of alderman, together with usurers, clerics, tax farmers, grain and wine dealers, and toll collectors.[195] Though these were never adopted into law, we have seen that changers were very rarely appointed to one of the banks of aldermen; nor were they called upon to serve as city treasurer, a very powerful position for which their professional competence would seem to fit them. In addition, exclusion from these offices walled them off from the important and lucrative areas of urban finance like tax farming.[196] It was also from the city accounts of 1305 that the word *ghukellaer* emerges, which must have been a popular nick-name for some changers. In all Middle Dutch, this term as applied to money changers occurs only in Bruges at this time. It was anything but complimentary, for it is etymologically related to the word for gambler or magician, as in the contemporary translation of the New Testament in which Simon Magus is called a *gokelare*. The word resembles the term for usurer, *woekeraer*, as well.[197] All together, then, there is good reason to darken the rather too sunny traditional view of the social and political standing of money changers in Flemish urban society.[198]

193 "Ende hierbi zo zal elc wisselare jugieren den penninc na zire waerd, iof goed iof quaed . . .": SAB, politieke oorkonden 1e reeks, #237. The ordinance dates from 1309.

194 Gilles li Muisit, *Poésies*, vol. II, p. 72: "Userier wagnent tout, cangeur et monnoyer; / C'est tout leur, che dist-on; or voit-on envoyer / A ches fausses monnoies, les florins employer; / Pluseur qui les aportent, en ont malvais loyer."

195 The texts are edited in full by Espinas and Pirenne (eds.), *Recueil de Documents*, vol. I, pt. I, pp. 532–552.

196 See chapter 3, pp. 115–116.

197 E. Verdam and E. Verwijs, *Middelnederlansch woordenboek*, 12 vols. (The Hague, 1998), vol. II, columns 2052–2053: "Daer hi vant een gokelare . . . die gokelare hiet Simon Magus . . ." Even though *ghukelaer* and *woekeraer* are similar they were not synonymous, as another entry from the same city account proves: "Item, Pelskine, up sinen dienst van der stede, als dat hi die huse verhurde ende woukerars ende ghukelars toe brochte: £20."

198 De Roover, *Money, Banking and Credit*, p. 173. There is no doubt, however, that the most successful changers were among the wealthiest of Brugeois, which in the course of generations could result in social mobility; see de Meyer, "Sociale Strukture," 69.

Bank deposits, depositors, and book transfers

The practice of opening what amounted to a demand account with a money changer and depositing in it money and bullion whose Flemish money equivalent was then noted in the changer's ledger, and from which one could make payments in current coin, was a well-established practice in Bruges in the fourteenth century. Its popularity was due to the security and ease it provided customers in making and receiving payments, two qualities often missing in dealings with cash. The advantage for the changer was the ability to use depositors' funds for his or her business purposes while their money was literally "on the books." In short, deposits with the money changer functioned as money without the drawbacks of cash; for the changer deposits functioned as a source of investment capital. Given peace and good fortune, this was an advantageous relationship for both parties.

But just who were the money changers' customers? There has been a good deal of nonsense written and repeated in answer to this question.[199] Part of the confusion arises from the failure to distinguish between depositors and users of this part of the Bruges financial system; and there were many more of the latter than the former. Depositors were simply not drawn from among the average residents of Bruges. This should come as no surprise, since they would be unlikely to deposit money that would receive no interest; nor would the other services offered by the changer be of much use to the average Brugeois. We have seen that petty cash was raised by lending to or borrowing from neighbors, or visiting the local pawnbrokers. Overwhelmingly, depositors were the city's hostellers, important merchants, moneylenders and a great variety of (but certainly not all) foreign merchant residents and visitors. On the other hand, a large number of ordinary Brugeois did receive payment for their goods and services at the "Wissel," either in cash or in the form of a book transfer to a temporary account. Thus money on deposit with money changers was part of the local and regional money supply, even if relatively few Bruges residents were account holders.[200]

Collard de Marke's accounts provide a rough idea of the proportion of foreign merchants who held accounts with Bruges money changers. As

[199] This involves unfounded extrapolation of the numbers of Bruges residents who possessed a bank account.

[200] There has been a good deal of discussion about the relative importance of "bank money" in the money supply of the late Middle Ages. The recent consensus notes its existence but downplays its importance. See Peter Spufford, *Money and Its Use*, pp. 258–260, and Aerts, "Middeleeuwse bankgeschiedenis," 57–58.

discussed in chapter 3, de Marke or his clerk sometimes added a place of origin to the name of a foreigner as a means of identification. By noting those who also had accounts with him some surprising facts emerge. Account holding clearly varied from group to group, though generally speaking the greater the distance from the merchant's place of origin and the closer the commercial ties with Bruges the more likely he (rarely she) was to be an account holder. Iberians banked with money changers to a much greater degree than did Hanse merchants. For example, eleven of twenty-eight Portuguese merchants were account holders as were eighty of 181 Spaniards; but with the exception of long-term Bruges residents, only six Hanse merchants held accounts. Yet English merchants (who may have been mostly Londoners by the 1360s) were frequently depositors as well, perhaps because of the well-developed credit triangle of Calais–Bruges–London.[201] Within Flanders, both Damme and Ghent had the largest percentage of their merchants who held accounts with de Marke.[202] Even allowing for national preferences and the crudeness of the figures, the fact remains that Bruges changers were more important for the payment system they offered than as deposit bankers. Book transfers, in other words, were one of the most sought-after remedies for the shortcomings of coin.

Equally interesting is to count the number of Bruges hostellers, drapers, and members of professions and crafts who were depositors. Hostellers as a block were by far the most numerous and active of the changers' customers, as virtually all of them held an account with de Marke, and many had accounts with Ruweel too. We cannot know whether the same held true for the ten other changers in Bruges at the time, but it is quite likely that hostellers held clearing accounts with all the largest changers while favoring one with the bulk of their business.[203] The goal here was a seamless system of book transfers across both the hostel and the exchange. Other types of merchants and craftsmen had more or less obvious reasons for holding an account. The general rule seemed to be: the greater the degree of involvement with long-distance trade, the greater the likelihood the merchant would hold an account. Thus drapers and brokers are well represented; weavers, the construction trades, and crafts intended for the local market are not.

[201] See below, chapter 6, pp. 236–238.

[202] The proportion was fourteen of sixty-one for Ghent and twenty-four of eighty-two for Damme. Merchants from the cloth towns of Brabant were also well represented: twenty-five of 110 from Mechelen, four of nine for Leuven and six of twenty-six for Bois-le-Duc.

[203] Close business relationships, such as that already noted between Matheus van der Beurse and Thideman Blomenrod, must have been common. This question will be further explored in chapter 5.

Uses and users of the payment system

When we turn to those who used the payment system offered by the money changers, we see its true impact. By the time of the Ruweel and de Marke ledgers, Bruges drapers had come to use their accounts with the changers to pay for cloth they sold from their stalls in the Cloth Hall. Thus the weaver who delivered the finished cloth to the draper received a chit or some other form of proof redeemable for cash upon presentation to the money changer. The proximity of the exchanges to the Cloth Hall made delivery and payment for cloth a simple errand. Drapers obtained the considerable advantages of management of their accounts payable, smoothing out their cash flow and affording occasional overdrafts when money was tight. Literally hundreds of Bruges weavers, in turn, received immediate cash for their one or two bolts of cloth, products of many hours of labor, enabling the rapid replenishment of raw materials for further production.[204]

Payments to other Bruges professionals and artisans do not seem to have equaled in number or organization those to the cloth industry. Surprisingly, a number of artisans in the building trades were paid through the changers. Cheese merchants and a single fish dealer represent the food business; furriers, a hatmaker, paternoster makers, and a leather tooler represent the luxury trades. The sporadic nature of these payments argue against any significant role for the money changers in the financial affairs of these segments of the Bruges business. Other occasional customers were members of the clergy, aristocrats or their agents (who used Bruges as a shopping emporium or finance center), and city governments.[205]

Payments made through book transfers worked in quite a different manner for most foreign merchants of Bruges. Except for merchants either long resident or highly adept, who dealt directly with the changers, many foreigners dealt through the hosteller with whom they lodged. Hostellers also accepted deposits of cash and bullion and were able to credit an account in a ledger for their customers, thus freeing them from the necessity of

[204] Money changers' involvement in cloth production in Bruges will be analyzed further in chapter 7.

[205] Clergy who are mentioned in the de Marke accounts include the curate of St. Jacob's church, a chaplain of St. Donatian's, and a cleric of Onze-Lieve-Vrouw church. Aristocratic account holders tended to be either knights en route to the Prussian crusades (a group that will be discussed in chapter 6) or those represented through their agents, who include the countess of Bar and Flanders, the count of Blois and the Lord of the Gruuthuus in Bruges. One interesting instance of a city government using these payment services was a payment of 6,000 French francs made to the account of the Lucchese merchant Forteguerra di Forteguerra by the aldermen of Douai; see De Marke 3, f. 222r.

dealing in coin. This was a parallel but not competing service to that of the money changers, since both cooperated through clearing accounts managed by the changers, who were the crucial link in the system, since there is no evidence that hostellers maintained their own clearing accounts with one another.[206] Thus for example if merchant X, lodging with hosteller X, wished to draw on his account to pay merchant Y lodging with hosteller Y, hosteller X would send an order to his money changer to debit his account the necessary amount, with directions to credit the account of hosteller Y naming merchant Y as the eventual recipient. As far as the merchants were concerned, this complex operation was invisible, resulting in the simple shift of goods from the warehouse of one hosteller to the other. The system was open to a number of other possibilities as well. A partner or factor could also direct payments, as could an order delivered by letter, and account balances themselves could be exchanged to complete business deals in distant places.[207]

As the nature and intention of each money changing business differed, so too did the numbers of depositors. When Nannen, Diederic Urbaen's widow, went bankrupt sometime before 1350, there were twenty-six depositors (plus one money changer) whose accounts were found in the exchange's ledgers. Sixteen others (plus two money changers) also made claims, but they were not regular depositors according to the accounts. There is good reason to believe that the sixteen had other kinds of business dealings with Nannen, but allowing half their claim to have been depositors results in a total of only thirty-four account holders.[208] This was a very small operation in its final days. At the other extreme is Collard de Marke, whose business was expanding during the period covered by his surviving ledgers, from 134 open accounts on 16 April 1366 to an impressive 305 accounts at the opening of his last account book on 20 May 1369. Willem Ruweel seems to have been somewhere between these two, though his business had certainly diminished by the period covered by his surviving ledger. In May 1370, there were eighty-two open accounts on his books.[209]

With an average of fifteen or sixteen changers at work in Bruges throughout the fourteenth century, and a very rough average of eighty or ninety depositors, each represents a total of between 1,200 and 1,440 individuals with accounts at any given time. There are a number of cautions to be made with regards to these figures. First, it is likely that hostellers and other

[206] The large number of broker/hostellers may have made this impracticable.
[207] This will be treated in chapter 6 below.
[208] My numbers differ slightly from those of de Roover; see *Money, Banking and Credit*, p. 251.
[209] Ibid., p. 252.

merchants had accounts with more than one changer. Secondly, many accounts in the surviving ledgers are of very short duration; some indeed existed only a few days and should probably be considered more a suspended cash payment than a true "bank" account.[210] Thus a direct correlation of these numbers with the population of Bruges gives a very misleading impression of ubiquity of account holders. The fact is that the most numerous and active bank customers were drawn from a small group of foreign merchants, hostellers, drapers, and wool merchants. However, far larger numbers of individuals, such as Bruges weavers, were beneficiaries of the payment system without holding accounts. Thus the reach of the Bruges banking system is both smaller and larger than previously thought.

TWO CASE STUDIES

We owe much of what we know about the money changing business of fourteenth-century Bruges to the survival of two sets of business records. Since their discovery and the later researches by Raymond de Roover, no other records of this type from any other area of northern Europe have surfaced.[211] It is probably now safe to say that they are unique and unrivalled as the oldest sources of their kind to survive from any of the commercial cities of the north. They are voluminous, difficult, and, despite their rarity, neglected sources, which were not completely inventoried in the Bruges city archives until 1979 and even then not with complete accuracy.[212] What the several thousand folios of accounts, two indexes, two journals, and a few fragments contain is a window both into the internal workings of two very different businesses and through them into the internal workings of the Bruges market. Reviewing these micro-histories is therefore essential to understanding the whole.

The Ruweel exchange was the result of a marriage between the Brugeoise Margaret van Ruuslede, whose family had possessed one of the "free" exchanges for two generations, and Willem Ruweel, whose original name was probably Guillaume Ruyelle. Given that his name was unknown in Bruges before 1350, and that his descendants are the only known

[210] De Roover made the same point: ibid., p. 253.

[211] Murray, "Merchant Account Books," pp. 27–31.

[212] In Vandewalle, *Beknopte Inventaris*, the Ruweel and de Marke materials are assigned #305 in the classification of "Koopmansboeken," with a brief description of each item. Unfortunately in the course of time a quire of the fourth de Marke ledger became detached and so was listed as an unknown fragment rather than as part of the de Marke ledgers. This oversight has now been corrected. The more extensive descriptions by de Roover remain the best introductions; see *Money, Banking and Credit*, pp. 210–212, 218–219 n. 57–68, for de Marke and de Roover, "Le livre de comptes de Guillaume Ruyelle," 15–95, with additions in Murray, "Merchant Account Books," pp. 29–31.

Ruweels until they disappear from the records early in the fifteenth century, Guillaume was probably an immigrant.[213] If he was true to the general rule, his origins may have been Walloon Flanders, Hainault, or the Tornaisis.[214] A plausible career before his marriage may have brought him first to Bruges to trade or as an apprentice and later to live. Ruweel was probably a skilled and knowledgeable merchant by the time he chose a bride, and Margaret brought her husband not only *poorter* status but the opportunity to operate an exchange as well.

After their marriage, which occurred some time shortly after 1350, the exchange took the name of Willem, though as we will see in a later chapter it continued to be operated by Margaret, their children, and Ruuslede relatives.[215] And despite the name change, as dower property the license legally belonged to Margaret.[216] Willem's importance was no doubt as an established man of business. Depositors would only be attracted to the exchange by the confidence they had in him as a merchant and investor. Risk of loss is always a possibility when money is entrusted to someone else, and in medieval Bruges deposits were hazarded on the personal prestige of the money changer alone. Only privileged foreigners could claim their full deposits from the city government in the event of a bankruptcy. Despite the considerable role played by women in the economy of Bruges (the subject of chapter 8), it is unlikely that a young woman could elicit this kind of trust. Margaret Ruweel's dowry was thus worth what the strength of her husband's reputation could draw in customers, as well as his luck and skill in managing their investments.

In this Ruweel was much like any other merchant, for it is clear from other evidence from Flanders and elsewhere that common business strategy called for agility and quick judgment in pursuit of profit. Specialization was often fleeting as merchants adjusted to radical swings in the business climate. And above all, everyone sought to cut costs and achieve security.[217]

[213] The Flemish form of his name is most likely a phonetic spelling of the French. The scribe who drafted de Marke's accounts preferred the French form of his name.

[214] Marechal, *Bijdrage*, pp. 14–17, de Roover, *Money, Banking and Credit*, p. 308.

[215] See chapter 8 for more on the operation of the exchange under Margaret.

[216] This is an important detail (more fully treated in chapter 8), for it removed a significant portion of family assets from the reach of creditors in the event of Willem's business failure.

[217] For the business climate of late-medieval Europe, see Hunt and Murray, *History of Business*, pp. 132–150. For the mentality of northern businessmen and women in the same period, Jenny Kermode, *Medieval Merchants: York, Beverley and Hull in the Later Middle Ages* (Cambridge, 1998), pp. 15–21; Nicholas, *Metamorphosis*, pp. 178–197, Martha Howell, "Fixing Movables: Gifts by Testament in Late Medieval Douai," *Past and Present* 150 (1996), 3–45; Erich Maschke, "Das Berufsbewusstsein des mittelalterlichen Fernkaufmans," in *Städte und Menschen: Beiträge zur Geschichte der Stadt, der Wirtschaft und Gesellschaft 1959–1977* (Wiesbaden, 1980).

Most Bruges money changers kept their exchange as part of either trading or innkeeping establishments, as a way to spread risk and seek profitable investments. By the 1360s the Ruweels seem to have opted for trade, though admittedly the surviving evidence is fragmentary. A charge for a pack animal recorded in one account hints at overland trade, and a recorded partnership with a Spanish shipmaster points to long-distance business interests.[218] This evidence suggests a largely passive business role, particularly in comparison with Collard de Marke, as we shall see.

Other traceable investments held by Ruweel were in real estate. Ordinarily, real property would be a poor investment for a medieval money changer because it was not easily convertible into specie and could therefore be of little use in case of a run on the bank. To mitigate this drawback, Ruweel seems to have preferred commercial properties, particularly around the Grote Markt, the city's premier market square. Two adjoining houses on the north side, where fish was sold at the time, represented a major investment by Ruweel in a commercial area, albeit one burdened with debt.[219] Ruweel seems also to have owned a third house on the Grote Markt, which may have served as his residence and business headquarters, since it was only a short walk from the exchange.[220] Another considerably smaller investment was a mortgage that Ruweel held on a house in the Langestraat, a busy shop-lined street traversing one of the city's most densely populated quarters.[221]

Public finance was another possibility for the medieval financier, and in this regard Bruges offered great opportunities, as shown in chapter 3. The assize on wine, of course, was both the most potentially remunerative and the most prestigious, given the city's wealth and the social prestige attached

[218] SAB, Koopmansboeken, Ruweel, f. 42v; De Marke 2, f. 195r, from the account of the Spaniard Nicollas Iaves, 9 November 1367: "Persendo mestre de naves de Saint Jehan de Mortrike." The £40 gro. payment was split between Persendo (£27 gro.) and Iaves (£10), with the balance paid to Willem Ruweel.

[219] RAB, Ambachten, fishmongers' cartulary, Roobouck, f. 1r–v, edited in Murray, "Family, Marriage," 122–123. The debt amounted to £22 10s. par. (£1 1s. 6d. gro.) per annum "landcheins."

[220] ARA, Rekenkamer, RR 1072, f. 1v: "Item zo houd Jacob Alverdoe vorseide een leengoed van minen vors. Heer van £5 parisis erfelik renten siaers ende staet beset up Willem Ruweels huus staende te Brucghe an de maerct . . ." This house is clearly different from those purchased by the Fishmongers, since on f. 6r of ARA, Rekenkamer, RR 1074 (1384), "Jan vanden Berghe houd een leengoed van minen vors. Heer van £8 10s. parisis siaers legghende up thuus dat wilen was Willems vander Rouwele staende up de Vischmaerct te Brugghe . . ." differs from f. 6v of the same source: "Jonfrauw Margriet f. Jan Alverdoens houd een leengoed van minen vors. Heer van £5 parisis erfeliken renten siaers ende staet beset up Willem Ruweels huus staende te Brugge an de maerct . . ." His ownership of the third house seems to have continued after his bankruptcy.

[221] BAB, fonds St. Salvator, s722, f. 278a, edited in Murray, "Family, Marriage," 123–124. This mortgage was also sold to satisfy Ruweel's creditors.

to drinking wine instead of beer or mead.[222] Obtaining the tax farm on wine was the pinnacle of the Bruges world of high finance, and only the very wealthy and well connected were able to bid for it. Changers were seldom among the successful bidders, with the exception of Ruweel and his contemporary, Jacob Reubs. But Reubs was one of the two richest money changers in Bruges at the time.[223] The other tax farmers typically belonged to the higher reaches of the business/social elite that dominated much of Bruges's business and politics. Ruweel looks distinctly out of place in such company, as if he were overreaching his social and financial standing in leasing the assize.

Ruweel leased the wine assize three times in his last three years in business, each time paying a higher price.[224] Whatever his expectations for this business venture, Ruweel booked very meager profits. According to de Roover's calculations, he made only 2 percent profit on the more than eleven thousand pounds he collected in the summer and early autumn of 1369; and it is likely that if administrative costs were figured in, the Ruweel tax farm was a distinct financial failure.[225] Failure also occurred in a third investment area carried on in partnership with the hosteller Jacob Sconebergh. Although the precise nature of their business is unknown, Sconebergh was active in trade with Catalonia, England, and France, and offered lodging to Hanse merchants in his inn near St. Jan's bridge.[226] Sconebergh's insolvency became apparent after he and his wife died, probably of the plague, in the summer of 1368. Dozens of unsatisfied creditors were left after the heirs refused to assume the debts. Among them was Ruweel, who had to settle for less than a quarter of the sum owed him by his late business associate.[227]

The roots of Ruweel's failure actually predate his forays into tax farming. Although we do not know the details, one indicator of decline is a

[222] Craeybeckx, *Un grand commerce d'importation*, pp. 8–10, 40–43.

[223] Reubs's account in the de Marke ledgers often records hundreds of transactions involving thousands of pounds, while Ruweel's might have ten or twelve transactions involving small sums. On this basis and the fact of his ascent in amount he contributed in the forced loan of 1362, de Roover called him "perhaps the leading money-changer in Bruges" by 1369 (*Money, Banking and Credit*, p. 208).

[224] In Bruges the right to collect the assizes was sold quarterly to the highest bidder, who had to then immediately advance a significant portion of the sum to the city treasurer. Thus the tax farmer wagered that his collections from the sale of wine would exceed his expenses. On this aspect of urban finance in Flanders see Hans van Werveke, *De Gentsche Stadsfinanciën in de Middeleeuwen* (Brussels, 1934), pp. 212–216 and Marc Boone, *Geld en Macht: De Gentse stadsfinanciën en de Bourgondische staatsvorming (1384–1453)* (Ghent, 1990), pp. 129–152.

[225] De Roover, *Money, Banking and Credit*, pp. 282–283.

[226] SAB, SR 1368–1369, f. 80r, where Sconebergh's assets and creditors are listed. See also Greve, "Jacob Sconebergh," and chapter 5.

[227] He received £21 9s. gro. on a debt of £78 gro.: SAB, SR 1368–1369, f. 80v.

comparison of forced loan assessments of money changers in the 1350s and 1360s. In 1359, of the fifteen money changers listed, Ruweel was tied for fifth in the amount assessed, paying only a fifth of the amount of the highest assessment. Three years later, when the city treasurers again called upon the changers to advance money, Ruweel was third on the list, paying two thirds as much as his presumably wealthier colleagues.[228] This may signal an improvement in his business. By 1366, however, when the de Marke accounts allow a clear look into Ruweel's business, he is clearly no longer among the leading changers in Bruges. The critical measure of this decline is activity in the account Ruweel kept with de Marke. There were forty-one transactions in the six-month period from April to October 1366, increasing to sixty-eight for the same period in the following year, and reaching a peak of eighty-eight transactions in April to October, 1368. From this peak transactions fall to forty-six in October to April 1369 and remain at that level through December 1369.[229] More significant is the fact that as the number of Ruweel's transactions climbed, so did his deficit with de Marke, erasing the earlier surplus. From April 1367 through October 1368 Ruweel ran a £318 deficit with de Marke before returning to rough balance thereafter. Not only does this indicate financial distress, it also proves that changers acted together at times to cover the temporary shortfalls of their colleagues in the interest of market stability.[230] Even this safeguard broke down in Ruweel's case by the summer of 1370, when he could no longer fight off bankruptcy.

Willem Ruweel and Collard de Marke shared the same profession, but their business operations differed sharply. Differences are apparent even in the way they kept their books: Ruweel used the ledger of the exchange to post the results of his business ventures to separate accounts. De Marke preferred to keep separate ledgers for his major business ventures, though he frequently shifted money back and forth from the ledger of the exchange to his auxiliary accounts. De Marke's ledgers are also a much more voluminous source, providing an uninterrupted flow of information about his exchange across the years 1366–1370, while the survivals for Ruweel amount to a single ledger covering the last year of his already considerably reduced

[228] De Roover, "Le livre de comptes de Guillaume Ruyelle," 88–89.

[229] Murray, "Family, Marriage," 122, Appendix 1. As a comparison of relative size, the changers Jacob Reups and Pieter van Oudenaarde had accounts with de Marke that ran to many hundreds of entries in the same period. This probably reflects bigger and more active money changing businesses that Ruweel's had become.

[230] This possibility was mentioned in the already cited case of Nanne Urbaens. There loans among changers were excluded from those with rights of reimbursement; see de Roover, *Money, Banking and Credit*, p. 363.

business. Part of this difference is due to the flourishing of de Marke's exchange business, while that of his colleague floundered. In fact there is no solid evidence of the failure of the de Marke exchange at all. Given these differences, recounting the micro-history of the de Marke exchange is also of value in a chapter on money and its discontents.

Unlike Ruweel, de Marke operated an "unfree" exchange, one that did not enjoy a direct license from the count. There is no evidence that this hampered his operation in any way, certainly not in maintaining relations with the comital mint in Ghent. Somewhat ironically, in fact, Ruweel probably broke off direct dealings with the mint, perhaps as a result of the disaster of 1357 when Ruweel and other Bruges changers were faced with considerable losses after the flight of the mint-master.[231] But de Marke seems to have taken over from his colleagues the role of main deliverer of bullion to the mint and conveyor of finished coins to changers and hostellers in Bruges. The Lucchese mint-master of the time held an account with de Marke in what amounted to a inter-city transfer arrangement.[232] De Marke maintained other regional financial contacts as well, including Antwerp and Valenciennes. He also had active partnerships in cloth importing, the bullion trade, and in Bruges cloth manufacture.[233] De Marke thus exceeded Ruweel in both the breadth and the activity of his business endeavors both in Bruges and beyond.

Differences between Ruweel and de Marke should not be exaggerated, however. Like Ruweel, de Marke was assisted by family members, notably his son, Collard. Like the staff of the Ruweel exchange, de Marke's son was just coming to maturity in the late 1360s. The expenses for the wine consumed at his wedding appear in the surviving account, indicating that he was married in May 1368.[234] By this time the young Collart had assisted his father in Bruges and he was entrusted with trade and banking during the Antwerp market in 1368–1369 and then took over the management of the cloth importing business at the death of his father's partner.[235] Judging from two account entries, de Marke's wife may have had a business role as

[231] See above, p. 158. [232] On this see chapter 6.

[233] These businesses will be discussed in chapter 7.

[234] De Marke 4, f. 146v (account of the hosteller Pieter van Ake) "pour Will. Rapebaut a le cause de Collart de Marke pour le vin de ses neuches, £8 gro."

[235] Unfortunately we cannot follow the earlier stages of the young de Marke's apprenticeship, but we know that Bruges was a popular training ground for young Hanse and Italian merchants; see Asmussen, *Lübecker Flandernfahrer*, pp. 115–118 and de Roover, *Money, Banking and Credit*, pp. 20–23. Relations between Bruges hostellers and their Hanse clients were so cordial that sometimes young Germans were taken as apprentices by Bruges hostellers; see Asmussen, *Lübecker Flandernfahrer*, pp. 117 for several examples.

well, but its precise nature is unclear.[236] Even more enigmatic is an account from 1366 in the name of Jakemart de Marke, apparently a relative involved in Collart's business. His account includes an errand performed in Tournai in March 1367, charges for his stay with a Bruges hosteller, and the price of "absolution" obtained in Tournai, presumably after his death.[237]

In common with Ruweel, de Marke kept track of domestic building expenses in his ledgers. Until 1368 he apparently rented a house from the well-known hosteller Sir Flipre Ramvis. When the house needed work, he had it done and charged the account of his landlord for the cost as a deduction from his rent.[238] A sign of de Marke's improving business fortunes was the purchase of a house for the considerable sum of £200 gro. from the estate of Simon van Artrike, a member of a wealthy and important family in Bruges.[239] Perhaps this acquisition of a patrician's house was for de Marke what bidding on the wine assize was to Ruweel – a step up the ladder of social advancement.

A flourishing and a failing money changing operation are visible in the account books of de Marke and Ruweel. They also serve as a reminder of the profound differences and similarities within a single profession. Both exchanges relied on family and were organized and run along lines established by local legal and social custom. De Marke's exchange seems to have been more nimble and entrepreneurial, displaying a keen sense of the possibilities of the Bruges market. Yet it appears to have vanished without a trace in the early 1370s. There is a larger number of partial histories, some like that of Jacob Reubs, who ran a very large business operation with the money exchange at its center, and others like the business run by "Lady" de Witte, which combined a hostel and small changing operation. All these seem to confirm the diverse and different pattern shown so clearly by Ruweel and de Marke.

What was common to all money changing in Bruges, however, was intense involvement in the Bruges market in one or many ways. Even though changers were not the dominant players in the urban economy (that honor belonged to the hostellers), their system of book transfers and

[236] De Marke 3, f. 166r, notes a payment made to Henric van Asenede "pour plusieurs coses quil a payet pour nous ale cause de Medemiselle, £1 18s. 3d."

[237] De Marke 1, f. 199v, which contains evidence that he was ill, since one account was audited by him "en se lit" and £3 gro. were spent on a nurse for him: "pour se gouvrenante."

[238] De Marke 1, f. 2r: "Ramenbranche que jay payet sur me hostaige de lan lxvii au machon qui fist le keminiee contet 30s. gro. Item, ai je payet a Jakop de Semet, carpentier, £2 gro. Item ai je payet par Sire Jehan le carpentier, £1 gro. somme £4 10s. les quels jay escrit sur le conte Sire Flipre."

[239] Ibid., 4, f. 204v, account of Sir Joris van Artrike: "Doy, par Collart de Marke ale cause dune maison qui fu Sire Simon van Artrike quil accata au hoirs, 17 mai [1369]."

clearing accounts was a crucial business service to both native and foreign merchants. By receiving coins and bullion on deposit and making transfers on demand, they brought some order to the periods of chaos caused by the count's policy of debasement, particularly after 1350. Their expertise allowed a remarkable number of different kinds of gold coins to circulate as legal tender, and their role as intermediaries with the mint kept a flow of gold, silver, and billon coins available for use. While relatively few residents or natives of Bruges either held or needed accounts with the money changers, many made use of the exchanges to draw payment, make transfers, or trade coins or bullion. Thus there was a multiplier effect at work, resulting in a far greater importance for the changers of Bruges and their services than their relatively small number and limited resources might suggest.

CONCLUSION

Medieval money offered many reasons for discontent – from its bulkiness to its manipulation by princes for their own enrichment to the persistent scarcity of coin. A measure of the success of any business city, this chapter has argued, is how resourceful its people were in overcoming the limitations of coin and bullion as the medium of exchange. On this score Bruges must count as the most diverse and sophisticated money market in northern Europe. Nowhere else could the challenge of scarcity and debasement have been met with a greater number of professionals whose various specializations complemented each other, with the Bruges city government by and large encouraging market freedom while acting as a guarantor of last resort, at least in cases of bankrupt money changers. This is not to claim uniqueness or innovation for Bruges in any single category of moneylending, changing, or neighborhood bartering. Rather, it was the extent and interrelatedness of the whole that conferred the singular quality to the Bruges payment system. And while money remained a mysterious thing to most – a "cose moult obscure" in the words of li Muisit – it could at least be bent to suit the devices and desires of those who thronged the streets and market places of Bruges.

CHAPTER 5

La Bourse et la vie

> Aliud est forum, ubi conveniunt mercatores: die boers dictum. Ubi inquam Hispani, Itali, Angli, Almani, Ostrogotti, et omnes naciones conveniunt.
>
> Hieronymus Muenzer, 1495[1]

There is some mischief in this chapter's title. Not only does it refer to a book about the medieval economy, it contains a verbal/visual pun of great significance to the history of Bruges and the subsequent merchant history of northern Europe. Rather typically the story was best told by an outsider, the Florentine merchant and historian Ludovico Guicciardini, in his *Discrittione di tutti i Paesi-Bassi*:

> In one of the squares of Bruges, a large and old house had been built by the noble family called van der Buerse; carved in stone above the door appeared their coat-of-arms – three purses. As frequently occurs in such cases, the square was named after the aforesaid house, family, and coat-of-arms. The merchants that used to dwell in Bruges had chosen this square or "Bourse" as a place to gather in order to transact their business. And when they traveled to the annual fairs of Antwerp and Bergen-op-Zoom, they applied the name "Bourse" to similar locations in those places, where they also used to come together to do business.[2]

By the sixteenth century, these increasingly formalized meetings of merchants at a set place and time were already ancient enough to require a foundation myth that prominently featured geographical and genealogical facts about Bruges. There was indeed such a square, located at the end of the oft-discussed Vlamingstraat, with its hostels and taverns, from which emerged the Zouterstraat leading to the Tolhuis, St. Jan's bridge, in

[1] E. Ph. Goldschmidt, "Le voyage de Hieronimus Monetarius à travers la France, 17 septembre 1494–14 avril 1495," *Humanisme et Renaissance* 6 (1939), 55–75, 198–220, 324–348, 529–539; quoted by Marechal, *Geschiedenis*, p. 8.

[2] Jacques Le Goff, *La bourse et la vie: économie et religion au Moyen Age* (Paris, 1986). Ludovico Guicciardini, *Descrittione di tutti i Paesi Bassi* (Antwerp, 1567), p. 67; see also J. A. Goris, *Les colonies marchandes méridionales à Anvers de 1488 à 1567* (Leuven, 1925), p. 604.

Figure 8: "Byrsa Brugensis." A seventeenth-century view of the Bourse square, with the Genoese and Florentine lodges indicated, both buildings that had once been hostels.

short the heart of the merchant's quarter. There was indeed such a family, prominent from the middle of the thirteenth century, who were owners of a complex of houses on the square where they operated as brokers and hostellers from 1290 until their establishments were split off and sold to other owners around 1400.[3] In that time at least ten members of the family stretching across five generations became brokers/hostellers. Certainly no better example could be found of a patrician family throwing itself into trade than this one.

Yet one thing is at risk of being lost in all the scholarship devoted to the history of commercial exchanges (Bourses) – the alleged competition between Bruges and Antwerp as the cradle of the Bourse, or the separate fixations with guilds, brokers, and active/passive trade: the fact that the origins of such commercial exchanges lie in the fourteenth century. They

[3] Marechal, *Geschiedenis*, pp. 25–29. The house known as "Ter Ouder Beurse" referred to by Guicciardini became the headquarters of the Venetian colony from 1397 until their departure for Antwerp around 1505. For the building history of this commercial corner of Bruges, see Devliegher, *Les maisons à Bruges*, pp. 418–421. For the chronology of merchant departures from Bruges, see Joseph Marechal, "Le départ de Bruges des marchands étrangers (xve et xvie siècles)," *ASEB* 88 (1951), 26–74, reprinted in *Europese aanwezigheid te Brugge*, pp. 180–210. Marechal's genealogy of the van der Beurse family (*Geschiedenis*, pp. 15–24) is completed in a review by J. A. van Houtte, *RBPH* 29 (1951), 275–279.

are in turn deeply rooted in the social and institutional processes behind the brokers'/hostellers' guild and the customs of foreign merchants who lodged, rented, and resided in Bruges. And they are ultimately fixed in urban space, leading to the choice of one square among all the squares of Bruges as the place merchants met to do business. The purpose of this chapter is to unravel the various strands that make up the pre-history of the Bruges Bourse.[4]

Separating out the activities of the later commercial bourses of pre-industrial northern Europe reveals important facets of these exchanges. First, long before they were places or buildings, bourses were simply opportunities for merchants to gather and exchange information about prices, politics, and markets. This fact anchors the early modern Bourse firmly in the medieval past of regional and international fairs, which existed as much as exchanges of news as of merchandise.[5] Fourteenth-century Bruges marked a stage in the development of merchant gathering in that fairs remained significant, especially the Bruges fair in May and those of Brabant. Yet a core contingent of foreigners chose to reside in the city in a more permanent way, using it as a geographical, financial, and even social base for their business elsewhere. Second was the commercial infrastructure of Bruges, which came to be distributed in close proximity to the "Beurse" square with its hostels, money exchanges, notaries, and law courts, but whose reach extended considerably further, even into the home cities and regions of the foreign merchants themselves. Thus Bruges brought together in a lasting way what the great fairs of Champagne only achieved temporarily: the merging of far-flung merchant networks at a precise place, and time. From Bruges news of prices and exchange rates, gossip about politics, news of shipwrecks and lost cargo, could be collected, included in letters, disseminated by messenger, and acted upon in a constantly replenished circle of communication and trade.[6]

Which brings us again to a house on a square; or rather a hostel called "Ter Beurse" – which loosely translated means "At the Sign of the Purse." This

[4] As a prehistory, this chapter will not pursue the debate about the "character" of the Bruges bourse, which properly belongs to the fifteenth century. For a useful summary of the historiography of European bourses, see Geert De Clercq (ed.), *Ter Beurze: Geschiedenis van de aandelenhandel in België* (Bruges and Antwerp, 1992).

[5] Hunt and Murray, *History of Business*, pp. 52–60; on the Champagne fairs, R. H. Bautier, "Les foires de Champagne: recherches sur une évolution historique," in *La Foire. Recueils de la Société Jean Bodin pour l'histoire comparative des institutions*, vol. v (Brussels, 1953), pp. 133–145; republished in *Sur l'histoire économique de la France médiévale: la route, le fleuve, la foire* (Aldershot, 1991).

[6] On the subject of merchant communication in general, see Gunnar Dahl, *Trade, Trust, and Networks: Commercial Culture in Late Medieval Italy* (Lund, Sweden, 1998).

is a literal evocation of place, for it was customary to mark off a commercial house with a sign or banner indicating its identity. It was quite common for this name to refer in some way to a current or past owner, sometimes by using a visual pun on the owner's name, as with the van der Beurse family whose name means literally "from the purse" or "from the sack."[7] A hostel, like a money exchange, was an amalgam of many businesses combined or omitted as the owner desired or business demanded. Whatever the mix of business, however, every hostel by definition occupied a substantial house of many rooms and stories, frequently with annexes and outbuildings as well.[8] The Middle French and Flemish words – *ostel* and *hof* – signify size in the indication that the building possessed a courtyard, a space walled off from the street, equipped very probably with a stable at the least and with cellars and other buildings suitable for commercial purposes. Very quickly this architectural fact was translated into a sense of corporate identity: the count had an "ostel," which referred not so much to a building as to the collection of courtiers and officials who embodied his interests. Thus a first fact to remember is that a hostel was a significant building or assemblage of buildings, whose space conveyed significance in size and prestige, which in turn could engender a corporate identity to those who worked or resided there.

The second fact to remember about commercial hostels is that in all their variations they were loci of trade. This sets the hostel apart from the inn, whose first purpose was to offer lodging, food, and drink, and from the taverns, cabarets, brothels, churches, or other places where merchants met and business was occasionally transacted.[9] This also unites the two groups of hostellers in Bruges, which are too often regarded separately by historians. These were both the foreign merchants who either purchased

[7] These visual elements became a symbolic vocabulary drawn upon by merchants in constructing seals, merchant marks, and notarial signs, which in turn became legal identifying marks. There is no general study of these; for notaries see Murray, *Notarial Instruments*, pp. 118–119; for merchant marks in Bruges c. 1370, Nicholas, "English Trade," 23–61; for marks of the town clerks of Ypres, Guillaume Des Marez, *La lettre de foire à Ypres au XIIIe siècle, contribution à l'étude des papiers de crédit* (Brussels, 1901).

[8] The van der Beurse family's holdings, for example, included three substantial buildings by the late thirteenth century: "Ter Beurse," "De Cleene Beurse," "Ter Ouder Beurse," which together formed an elbow of contiguous buildings stretching around the Grauwwerkersstraat, fronting on the Vlamingstraat. See de Vliegher, *Maisons*, p. 418, and Marechal, *Geschiedenis*, pp. 26–31. By 1302, one or more of the houses had already passed out of the possession of the family without affecting the name. After 1350, several van der Beurses operated independent hostels out of one or more of these buildings.

[9] I have followed David Nicholas in his preference for the use of the word "hostel" to denote a place where commercial deals were brokered as a primary role, while recognizing, as he does, that the distinction is a difficult one to draw; see Nicholas, *Metamorphosis*, pp. 142–143.

or rented their own "hostel" as a residence and business location while in the city, and those members of the brokers guild wealthy enough to afford the investment in a large establishment of their own, including a staff of brokers and other experts, such as money changers and notaries. As two parts of one body these individuals operated the institutions aptly called by J. A. van Houtte "the Ignition Points" of the Bruges economy.[10]

There was no hard and fast boundary between what we might call the "free" and "unfree" hostellers of Bruges, despite guild regulations and some political agitation across the century.[11] Some foreign merchants acquired "hostels" in order to pursue a very specific avenue of trade. This was the case with Collard de Marke's business partner, Pieter de la Fine, who specialized in importing cloth from northern France before succumbing, probably to the plague, in 1368.[12] The English wool merchant William de la Pole also rented substantial quarters in Bruges in order to pursue the wool trade. From 1339 to 1340 he rented no fewer than eight houses for sixty-five weeks.[13] There he distributed and stored more than 2,400 sacks of wool at a cost less than one-third of that in his native Hull. The well-known Hanse merchant Siverd Veckinchusen owned a complex of houses in the Krom Genthof, which later became the site of the Oosterlingenhuis, the seat of the Hanse

[10] J. A. van Houtte, "Herbergswesen und Gastlichkeit im mittelalterlichen Brügge," in H. C. Peyer (ed.), *Gastfreundschaft, Taverne und Gasthaus im Mittelalter* (Munich and Vienna, 1983), pp. 177–187. Van Houtte has been the principal authority on Bruges hostellers, having dedicated his doctoral thesis, unfortunately unpublished, to the subject in the 1930s. The results of that work appeared in two major articles: "Les courtiers au moyen âge: origine et caractéristiques d'une institution commerciale en Europe Occidentale," *Revue Historique du Droit Français et Etranger* series 4, 15 (1936), 105–114, and "Makelaars en waarden te Brugge van de 13e tot de 16e eeuw," *Bijdragen voor de Geschiedenis der Nederlanden* 5 (1950), 1–30, 177–197. The latter was reprinted in van Houtte, *Essays on Medieval and Early Modern Economy and Society* (Leuven, 1977), pp. 19–47. Recently, Dr. Anke Greve of the German Historical Institute of Paris has completed a doctoral thesis on Bruges hostellers. Early results of this research have been published as "Gast und Gastgeber: Hansekaufleute und Hosteliers in Brügge im 14. und 15. Jahrhundert," in V. Henn and A. Nedkvitne (eds.), *Norwegen und die Hanse. Wirtschaftliche und kulturelle Aspekte im europäischen Vergleich* (Frankfurt a. M., 1994), pp. 95–107; "Brügger Hosteliers und hansische Kaufleute: ein Netzwerk vorteilhafter Handelsbeziehungen oder programmierte Interessenkonflikte?" in Nils Jörn, Werner Paravicini, and Horst Wernicke (eds.), *Hansekaufleute in Brügge, Teil 4*, pp. 151–172; "Vreemdelingen in de stad: Integratie of uitsluiting?" in Carlier *et al.*, *Core and Periphery in Late Medieval Urban Society*, pp. 153–163.

[11] This borrows contemporary terminology, for guild-organized crafts and trades called themselves the "free" as opposed to outsiders – the "unfree." I must emphasize that this was not the terminology actually used by contemporaries. There is no evidence in the fourteenth century that foreign merchants could not freely lodge with whomever they wished. In the accounts of Collard de Marke, in fact, there is absolutely no distinction made between a "ostel" holder who was a member of the Bruges guild and one who was not. It was only in the revised Hosteller/Broker privilege of 1477 that foreigners were forbidden to offer lodging to anyone but their direct employees and family. See van Houtte, "Herbergswesen," p. 180.

[12] For further discussion, see chapter 7.

[13] E. B. Fryde, *William de la Pole, Merchant and King's Banker* (London, 1988), p. 28.

merchant community of Bruges.[14] Sometimes these merchants rented their accomodation from Bruges hostellers, as did the Spaniard Goris Enpereal in 1368–1369.[15] There is every reason to believe from these examples and many others that merchants with long-term interests in Bruges rented or purchased "hostels" where they stored their goods and housed themselves and their households, without encroaching on the "free" hostellers' business by serving as brokers.[16]

If most foreign merchants were content to pursue specific commercial use of their space without challenging local monopolies, there were those who insisted on broader rights to use their commercial space. Part of this may have been due to differences of interpretation and vagueness of distinctions. How after all could one distinguish between offering lodging to business associates or to a run-of-the-mill fellow countryman? How large did a merchant's household have to be before it aroused the suspicions of the brokers' guild? And how could that guild possibly determine whether a foreigner was renting commercial storage to fellow countrymen in his warehouse? As a result of conflict and a desire for reasonable accommodation, most privileges granted to foreign merchant communities contained provisions allowing rental of lodgings and warehouse facilities to fellow countrymen.[17] This in effect legalized what I have called "unfree" hostels, allowing foreign owners or renters of spacious commercial premises to sublet these at will as long as the sublessors were members of the same merchant community. Since nearly all hostellers, both free and unfree, specialized in merchants from one region or city anyway, this restriction was hardly onerous. There can be little doubt that Bruges was dotted with unofficial inns, which probably appeared and disappeared according to the vagaries of demand. They may also have given a start to immigrants who later became legitimate members of the Bruges guild.

[14] Asmussen, *Hansekaufleute in Brügge*, pp. 803–804 and n. 19; Luc Devliegher, "Het Oosterlingenhuis te Brugge," in *Hansekaufleute in Brügge, Teil 4: Beiträge der Internationalen Tagung in Brügge*, pp. 13–32.

[15] His landlord was the broker/hosteller Pieter van de Wijngarde: SAB, Koopmansboeken, De Marke 5, f. 82r: "[Debit] pour Pieter van de Wingarde pour lacomplisement dune maison quil a leuwet a ladit Gor[is] pour le primiere anee, £5 10s. [gro.]"

[16] It was explicitly the act of serving as broker without being a member of the Broker/Hosteller guild that incurred a fine. In the bailiff's account of 1305–1306 this was referred to as violating "De coere estrainge marchans ki ont achate et vendu en le castelrie de Bruges" (ARA, Rekenkamer, RR 1003, membrane 10). Later the crime was "Van den gonen die makelardie ghenomen hebben ende gheene makelars zijn ghecocht ende vercocht hebben zonder makelare" (ibid., 1012, membrane 13), which explicitly adds the intervention of a sworn broker as well as restating the prohibition on foreigners freely buying and selling in Bruges.

[17] Van Houtte, "Herbergswesen und Gastlichkeit," p. 180.

How many of these establishments were there? Of course precise figures for the entire century are impossible to adduce; we do not know the actual number of "free" hostels operating in Bruges, let alone those that had an interest in remaining clandestine. The only possible indication surviving is due to the habit of Collard de Marke's scribe of referring indiscriminately to all large commercial buildings as "ostels," regardless of whether or not their operators were members of the brokers' guild. This sample is slightly skewed, however, by the fact that mentions of such hostels nearly always occur as attempts to identify individuals as either employees or residents of a particular hostel.[18] Most likely this omits some of the unfree hostels that did not offer lodging. Be that as it may, we can at least arrive at a number of the "unfree" for the period 1366–1369, and compare it to the number of the free hostels in the same period.

The numbers offer some surprises. Sixty-three unfree hostels are noted in the de Marke accounts, a total that exceeds by eight the number of free hostels. Within this group there are distinct differences. The vast majority – forty-seven – seem to fit the description of a temporary residence rented by a foreign merchant for a specific period of time. The "guests" (*hostes*) they may have housed were few in number, though judging from surnames (a hazardous call), they were not always of the same city or region.[19] This suggests enforcement of this provision was haphazard at best. A handful among the total may have been "inns" in the sense that they seem to have had a corporate existence, but there is no evidence of brokerage or other commercial activity there. These were the hostels Cambron, van Asberghe, Louis, and van Pouke.[20] Quite another group

[18] For many foreign merchants their hostel functioned as their address and bank account; thus de Marke's scribe was following an old tradition in identifying foreigners by their place of residence in Bruges; see van Houtte, "Makelaars en Waarden," 19–30.

[19] One example is Piere Coulet, who hosted Martin Sense from Lisbon (De Marke 2, f. 77r, 23 March 1369); another French surnamed example is Jehan Crestien, who also hosted Iberians, Grasie de Getaire and Piere Jehan, "espaignart" (ibid., ff. 328r and 24r); Renier de Sellande hosted Collart de Boutenaire, "escot" (ibid., f. 169r), and Gilles van de Wachst hosted Jehan Scot, "escot" (ibid., f. 93v, 20 April 1369). Others seem to have abided by the stipulation: Jehan Angevin hosted Laurent de Saint Tiebaut and Hulon de Rambiert Villers (De Marke 1, ff. 199v and 152r); France dAvesnes hosted Collart Vrekart and Jehan de Melleville of Abbeville (ibid., 3, ff. 350v and 293v); Andrius van de Pape hosted Jehan Doreguy of Saint Quentin and Simon de Bekout of Amiens (ibid., 2, f. 294r, and 3, f. 241v).

[20] These are the only four not associated with a particular individual and none had more than one guest mentioned, leading easily to the conclusion that they were not very significant. Only the van Pouke hostel can be associated with a Bruges family of the time: see A. Schouteet, *Regesten op de oorkonden*, 4 vols. (Bruges, 1978), vol. III p. 504. Pamela Nightingale notes the frequent complaints of foreigners keeping hostels in fourteenth-century London: see Nightingale, *A Medieval Mercantile Community: The Grocers' Company and the Politics and Trade of London, 1000–1485* (New Haven, 1995), p. 200.

was the eight "pure" merchants, all of whom had separate accounts with Collard de Marke, which bear witness to businesses anchored in trade. One of these, the English wool merchant John Goldbeter, hosted only a business associate, John Lindesay.[21] Only Gelfe Desus, who may have of been of French or Spanish origin, clearly was in the business of lodging as well as trading in cloth.[22] Most of the rest seem to have been in the cloth trade, either as importers of northern French cloth – Pieter van le Fine and Willem se Probien – or exporters of Flemish cloth to Spain and Portugal – Ector Picamiel and Jehan Duc. Two German merchants, Henric van Berove and Albrec Kesere, were in the wool and wine trade respectively.[23] All in all, it is safe to conclude that at any given time there were as many significant commercial establishments – hostels – belonging to foreign merchants as there were free hostels, operated by members of the brokers' guild. Most of the unfree hostels did not seriously encroach upon the monopoly of the free hostellers, and some were involved in trade, which required possession of significant commercial and living space during their residence in Bruges.

Even though most of this admittedly small sample left few or no lasting traces of their time in Bruges, others came as visitors and remained permanently, becoming legitimate brokers and hostellers. Of the sample group, only John Goldbeter married a local woman and made Bruges his home and burial place. But he had no children, so his business wealth was dispersed in building his tomb and endowing local charities.[24] Other foreigners used their experiences as merchants in Bruges to establish dynasties of brokers and free hostellers, which became fully integrated into the Bruges elite. Notable among these were the Adornes from Genoa, who progressed along the professions from broker to hosteller, finally operating both a prosperous hostel and a money exchange. By the fifteenth century they had passed into the ranks of the Burgundian nobility, leaving their

[21] John Goldbeter is discussed extensively below and in chapter 7.

[22] Desus shared the business with a brother, Aubiert. In May 1367 a Jakemart de Marke was charged for "son hostaige au frere Gelfe Desus . . ." (2, f. 2r) and in January 1369 he hosted Ser. Feyes, "mestre de le nave de le Coutonne," probably a Spanish or Portuguese ship (ibid., 4, f. 54r).

[23] Henric van Berove had an account with de Marke that ran across all but the first ledger. He employed two varlets as assistants. He is not traceable among the Hanse merchants known to be active in Bruges. Albrec Kesere (or Albrecht de Keÿser) appears on the tax lists of Hanse merchants recorded in the Bruges city accounts; see Paravicini, *Hansekaufleute in Brügge, Teil 1*, 8 #8, 21 #5, 22 #42, 23 #1, 30 #42, 32 #43; for a biography see Dierck *et al.*, *Hansekaufleute in Brügge, Prosopographischer Katalog*, pp. 109–110.

[24] Goldbeter and his wife Clare endowed a funeral chapel for themselves in St. Donatian's church, and made gifts to the St. Jans hospital as well; see chapter 7 and E. van der Elst, *L'hôpital Saint-Jean*, p. 87.

merchant roots behind.[25] The Barbezaens from Lucca are another notable example of a foreign merchant dynasty making its way through these merchant professions on the path to full incorporation in Bruges society.[26] So striking did this stream of foreigners into Bruges brokers' guild become that in 1339 there was a nativist backlash. Apparently at the urging of some in Bruges, the count issued a charter establishing the fundamental by-laws of the guild, one of which forbade anyone born outside Flanders to become a merchandise broker in Bruges in future, even if he had purchased citizenship.[27] But the list of those of foreign birth who were exempted from this restriction proves the cosmopolitan character of the guild had already been established. In fact, among those who witnessed the charter were the hosteller Dominghe de Saint Arin and Jan de Witte, both from families of "foreign" origin, who represented only two of the twenty-nine foreign members.[28] However determined the nativists, this cosmopolitanism was never rooted out of the guild.

THE CORPORATION OF "BROKERS/HOSTELLERS"

It was not only the significant presence of "foreigners" among their members that made the Bruges brokers'/hostellers' guild exceptional among

[25] The first Adornes arrived in the 1340s; two, Pieter and Jacob, were brokers in the 1360s, and by 1390 the family had succeeded in combining a hostel and money-changing operation. For more on their subsequent history see Noël Geirnaert, "Het archief van de Familie Adornes en van de Jeruzalemstichting," *De Leiegouw* 28 (1986), 289–297, and Noël Geirnaert, *Het Archief van de Familie Adornes en de Jeruzalemstichting te Brugge*, 2 vols. (Bruges, 1987), vol. 1, pp. 7–8 and geneaological table, pp. 167–168. For the fifteenth century see also M. Boone, M. Danneel, and N. Geirnaert, "Pieter IV Adornes (1460–ca. 1496): Een Brugs Patricier in Gent," *HMGOG* new series 39 (1985), 123–145.

[26] Barbezaen was a Flemish version of the Italian Barbagialla. By the 1370s, Nicolaas (or Claes) had become one of the wealthiest hostellers in Bruges, while maintaining close relations with Lucchese merchants. In 1385 he was the "official" host of Lucchese merchants in Bruges; see van Houtte, "Makelaars en Waarden," 14–15 and n. 1; see also Raymond de Roover, "La communauté de Lucquois," *ASEB* 86 (1949), 23–89, 60.

[27] L. Gilliodts-van Severen, "Les anciens règlements de la corporation des courtiers de Bruges," *La Flandre* 13 (1881), 145–146, 254–255. The broker candidate born in Flanders had to have resided for a year and a day in Bruges before he became eligible. The seventh clause of the charter explicitly banned anyone born outside of Flanders from eligibility no matter how long his residence in Bruges. Note that J. F. Verbruggen, "De Getalsterkte van de ambachten in het Brugse Gemeenteleger (1297–1340)," *Belgisch Tijdschrift voor Militaire Geschiedenis* 25 (1984), 461–480, mentions that a number of foreigners, apart from the twenty-nine, were forced to leave the guild, and that its members complained that such a large number of foreigners had "sickened" ("verkrankt") the guild.

[28] Dominghe was obviously of Iberian origin, while the de Wittes were from Germany. Descendants of the de Wittes also managed an ascent into the Burgundian aristocracy in the fifteenth century; see Gilliodts-van Severen, "Les anciens règlements," 246 and van Houtte, "Makelaars en Waarden" 6.

other guilds in the city, or indeed in any city of Flanders.[29] For despite its traditional organization and trappings, the guild was based upon an internal contradiction from its very beginnings. Like all guilds, it depended on a legally guaranteed monopoly, in this case the exclusive right of its members to broker exchange between buyers and sellers in the Bruges market. Yet as early as 1293 its members were both "makelaers," the traditional brokers, and "hosteliers," those whose business combined brokerage, innkeeping, warehousing, and investing on their own account. This brought tension between the two types of members, for the interests of brokers lay in the rigorous control of trade, while those of hostellers lay more in its expansion, which brought them more foreign merchant guests and investment opportunities. Differences in wealth and social origins reinforced these differences, for (as shown in chapter 3) hostellers often came from rich and powerful families and became in turn significant political figures. This divergence may also have stood behind the 1340 ban on foreign members as well as explaining the guild's internal stresses and strains.[30]

Two facts stand out in the evolution of the guild across the fourteenth century. The first is its enormous popularity, due no doubt to the expansion of trade in Bruges. Unfortunately the lack of membership lists makes precise knowledge of this increase impossible. But there are plenty of indirect indications. In 1297, brokers received the third largest share of a bribe from the king of France.[31] In 1302, the guild provided nearly 10 percent of the horses for an expedition of the urban militia, trailing only the weavers and fullers in number.[32] By the 1330s the demand to join the guild had grown to such a point that the city government intervened to supervise it. The city accounts for 1332–1339 record 116 new members enrolled.[33] In the Bruges militia of 1338–40, at least 431 brokers served, five more than the contingent sent in 1321–22, and one of the largest contingents among the guilds.[34] In

[29] Van Houtte, "Courtiers au moyen age," 134–135, points out that in many cities the combining of innkeeping with brokerage was explicitly forbidden by law.

[30] Close ties with foreign merchants were characteristic of hostellers: indeed, they may have conferred a competitive advantage on some, as the case of Claes Barbezaen shows. On the social class differences of hostellers and brokers, see van Houtte, *Geschiedenis*, p. 206 .

[31] Verbruggen, "De Getalsterkte," 462. Nonetheless, they received less than a fifth of the share of the weavers and less than half that of the fullers.

[32] Van Houtte, *Geschiedenis*, p. 206; van Houtte, "Makelaars en waarden," 5 and n. 1.

[33] Verbruggen, "De Getalsterkte," 479; the number differs from the 124 new members counted by van Houtte (*Geschiedenis*, p. 206; "Makelaars en waarden," 18, n. 4). Walter Prevenier estimated the number of brokers at between 431 and 862 by the middle of the fourteenth century: see Prevenier, "Bevolkingscijfers," pp. 296–300.

[34] Van Houtte, *Geschiedenis*, p. 206. Carlos Wyffels and Verbruggen disagreed on the total number. In his review of *Het gemeenteleger* (*Tijdschrift voor Geschiedenis* 76 [1963], 232–233) Wyffels pointed

1379, the contingent of brokers in the militia was still among the largest of all the guilds.[35] The combination of numbers, wealth, and influence made the guild unique not only in Bruges but in any other commercial city of the time.[36]

The political and economic struggle between brokers and hostellers is the second notable fact. This began very early, before the official establishment of the guild itself, in the split between the two in the civil war of 1298–1302. Many more hostellers chose the side of the French king and the patriciate of Bruges than did brokers, who sided with the weavers and other artisans of what Pirenne called the "democratic" party.[37] The hostellers very much embodied the interests and behavior of a merchant guild, and in fact many of them had been members of the so-called "Bruges" or "London" Hanse before 1300.[38] The defeat of the French in 1302 brought with it what may have been a forced merger of brokers and hostellers into a single guild, but this did not long submerge the political tendencies of the hostellers. In every other outbreak of civil strife thereafter, the vast majority of guild members chose the side of the political establishment and not that of the more radical elements of Bruges society. This was true in 1339, when a riot broke out between brokers and *poorters* on one side and weavers and fullers on the other. In a sign that Ghent had come to the fore among revolutionaries in Flanders, the Bruges weavers and fullers summoned their brethren from Ghent, who defeated their adversaries, "slaying many brokers in the Vlamingstraat and on the Bourse."[39] Again in 1380, a similar uproar brought a similar result – brokers/hostellers fighting against weavers and their followers, with reinforcements from Ghent winning the day.[40] When Bruges fell to the Ghent militia in May 1382, it was again the brokers who were sought out and slain by the victorious Gentenars in the aftermath.[41] In other words, the Bruges broker/hostellers guild behaved consistently more like a collection of merchants than workers.

out that missing folios listing members of the brokers' guild taking part in campaign meant that their numbers must have been around 800. Verbruggen, ("Getalsterkte', 479") answers this challenge convincingly.

[35] Van Houtte, *Geschiedenis*, p. 206, providing some 6 percent of all the guildsmen and more than 5 percent of the entire army.

[36] Van Houtte, "Les courtiers au moyen âge," 122–124.

[37] Pirenne, *Histoire*, vol. II, pp. 63–65.

[38] For the Hanse, see chapter 3 and A. van den Abeele and M. Catry, *Makelaars en handelaars* (Bruges, 1992), p. 15 for a list of names of families which were both.

[39] Quoted from MS 437 City Library of Bruges, *Cronycke van Vlaanderen*, published by Gilliodts-van Severen, "Anciens règlements," 148.

[40] Van Houtte, "Maakelaar en waarden," 17, n. 1; J. J. de Smet, *Corpus Chronicorum Flandriae*, 4 vols. (Brussels, 1837–1865), vol. I, p. 236. For the political context see Nicholas, *The Van Arteveldes*, pp. 160–187.

[41] See below chapter 9.

There were sound economic reasons for this. Before 1302 most brokers had actually worked as employees of the much richer hostellers, who provided the brokers with their customers and paid them wages. This practice ended with the new regime installed after 1302, when fees were established and brokers could seek out their own customers.[42] But hostellers had considerably more opportunity to profit from the increasing stream of merchants, enabling them to gain an increasing financial advantage in the city, in effect reducing brokers to dependency once again. The brokers also suffered from the constant debasements of the mid-fourteenth century since their fees were legally fixed. There is no clearer sign of this hosteller predominance than a look at the lists of the guild's deans and captains, which were recorded at the commencement of every governmental year and survive from 1363.[43] Almost without exception these men operated their own hostels, and many were carrying on what had been a family enterprise for generations.[44]

The hostellers' ascendancy in their own guild was only a single, and in some ways minor, part of a grander project, which was nothing less than to help create and capture the full wealth-generating capacity of the new Bruges economy. Breaking with a past as traveling merchants, yet remembering its lessons, Bruges hostellers chose the much more complex game of go-between, entrepreneur, or to use the contemporary word, masters of *coopmanscepe*.[45] This avenue to profit demanded from its practitioners dedication to the goal of creating an urban business environment of surpassing openness to foreigners, great efficiency in allocating capital and matching buyers and sellers, and perhaps most of all, ease of access to

42 The decree established that no merchant, be he burgher or foreigner, could seal a transaction without the help of a broker; see van Houtte, *Geschiedenis*, p. 207; "Makelaars en Waarden," 19; and Gillidots-van Severen, "Règlements," 220 for the text. The politics from 1293 to 1303 are described in van Houtte, "Makelaars en waarden," 4–5. For Bruges brokers/hostellers in general, see Nicholas, *Medieval Flanders*, pp. 297–300.

43 SAB, Wetsvernieuwingen, 1363–1374; those of the broker/hostellers are printed in van den Abeele and Catry, *Makelaars en handelaars*, pp. 95–97. These lists record the annual swearing in of aldermen and deans of the city's guilds.

44 Besides the van der Beurses and de Wittes, there were the Metteneye clan, whose inn stood for several generations on the east side of the Schoofstraatje near St. Martin's square and the Cromme Wal in a neighborhood favored by English and Spanish merchants in the middle of the fourteenth century. From the 1360s, the hostel was operated by Jakop Metteneye, whose customers were predominantly Spaniards; see Heidi Deneweth and Yvette Kemel, "Een verdwenen middeleeuwse wijk tussen Koningstraat, Boomgaardstraat en Verversdijk," *Brugs Ommeland* 40 (2000), 143–168; for his accounts with Collard de Marke see J. M. Murray and Anke Greve (eds.), *The Hosteller Accounts*, forthcoming in the series *Hansekaufleute in Brügge*.

45 The term literally means "merchantship," although the full sense of the Flemish is difficult to capture in English; perhaps it is best conceived as describing both the mechanics of trade and the general business culture that underpins it.

important information. Achieving this was the true focus of Bruges society and politics in the fourteenth century, and the foundation of Europe's first "Bourse" is but one achievement in the course of a much greater undertaking.

Given the unique audaciousness of the task – building what I have called a cradle of capitalism – it is surprising how little attention, and less praise, it has received from historians. Traditionally, the era has suffered from the label of decline and retrogression, as Flemish merchants were forced to abandon centuries of active, direct trade especially in England and the North Sea and Baltic regions, to fall back behind their own borders and become "passive" traders only.[46] The defeatist tone of this historiography probably stems from a romantic image of the swashbuckling, fiercely individualistic merchant, whom Pirenne brought forward as the agent of urbanism and savior of Europe from the backwardness of the feudal regime. This illusion of a heroic past has blinded historians to the subtlety of the economic achievements of fourteenth-century Bruges largely under the leadership of its hostellers. But what precisely were the elements of this undeclared program of economic change, and why was it unique to this particular city?

TOWARDS THE NEW ECONOMY

The greatest single difference of the economy that was taking shape by 1300 was that instead of Brugeois or Flemish merchants journeying to their customers, their customers were journeying to them. What is more, economic well being depended on attracting the largest possible number of foreign merchants, from the greatest diversity of places with the greatest variety of trade goods. The *deus ex machina* of such a trading system was an increasing force of attraction to the Bruges market that made it imperative for a merchant to have a presence there. The statistics presented in chapter 3 attest to the success of this new economic emphasis for the city.[47] In another way, Geoffrey Chaucer's choice of Bruges as the natural destination of his merchant of the *Shipman's Tale* while the monk seduced his wife is another indication of the success of this evolution toward a different economy. Bernardino of Siena completes the picture of Bruges's success in becoming

[46] Pirenne, *Histoire*, vol. II, pp. 429–438, J. A. van Houtte, *An Economic History of the Low Countries 800–1800* (London, 1977). Also Hans van Werveke, *Bruges et Anvers: Huit siècles de commerce flamand* (Brussels, 1944), pp. 27–28. David Nicholas presents revisions of the traditional views in *Medieval Flanders*, pp. 286–289.

[47] See census data (drawn from the de Marke accounts) on foreign merchants in Bruges in chapter 3.

the proverbial merchant destination by including in a sermon an anecdote about merchants traveling to Bruges.[48]

Visiting merchants were not always welcome in most European cities of the time, and the tendency was for even greater xenophobia and intolerance in the course of the fourteenth century. Violent incidents in English cities, in particular, can stand as examples of the worst that could befall visiting and resident foreigners; Bruges was perhaps the best place.[49] Reception of foreigners – merchants, nobles, clergy – became the chief job of Bruges hostellers, and ensuring their comfort, satisfaction, and security required the lion's share of their effort. And not by chance: seeing to these needs offered the hosteller the greatest opportunities for profit.

One clear adjustment made by the hostellers was to specialize in the types of foreigners they hosted. As a general rule, a hosteller catered for a single community of merchants as guests, though not always as business partners, as we shall see. In some ways this was a logical result of the economic and immigration history of Bruges. It was quite natural for a family of England traders to open a hostel where English merchants would be welcomed in their own language and with some understanding of the business and political conditions of their homeland. A remarkable example of this attachment is the Scuetelare clan. Members of this family were active as merchants in English wool from the 1320s. A Jacob Scuetelare gained the title of "king's merchant," perhaps in exchange for several loans he made to Edward III in 1340.[50] Several generations of the family probably continued in this trade, and by the 1370s a Pieter Scuetelare was operating a hostel catering to English merchants as well.[51] As we have seen,

[48] Geoffrey Chaucer, *The Riverside Chaucer* (Boston, 1987); Amleto Spicciani, *Capitale e interesse tra mercatura e povertà nei teologi e canonisti dei secoli XIII–XV* (Rome, 1990), p. 128, where in a vernacular sermon, the famous preacher sets out four visions of everyday life, one of which has "molti mercanti che vengono di verso Brugi . . ."

[49] English xenophobia was often inspired by politics and trade disputes, beginning with the despised Italian bankers of Edward I and Edward II, then with simmering tensions and intermittent violence against Hansards, climaxing with widespread killing of foreigners during the 1381 revolt. Bruges, and later Antwerp, were also exceptional among cities chosen by the Hanse for their operations; see Rössner, *Hansisiche Memoria*, pp. 226–239.

[50] Bryce Lyon, Mary Lyon, and H. S. Lucas, *The Wardrobe Book of William de Norwell: 12 July 1338 to 27 May 1340* (Brussels, 1983), pp. 75, 221, 286.

[51] Walter Prevenier, "Les perturbations dans les relations commerciales anglo-flamandes entre 1379 et 1407. Causes de désaccord et raisons d'une réconciliation," in *Economies et sociétés du Moyen Age. Mélanges Edouard Perroy* (Paris, 1973), pp. 482–484. The Scutelares, especially Lubrecht Scutelare, also proved themselves of inestimable value in Flemish–English diplomacy in the aftermath of the Ghent war of 1379–1385. But anglophilia had its political price as well, for Jacob Scuetelare, probably the son of Pieter, was banished for treason in 1383; see ARA, Rekenkamer, RR 2019. Both Pieter and Lubrecht Scuetelare had accounts with Collard de Marke; see also Nicholas, "English Trade at Bruges," 42 for Coppin and Pieter de Scuetelare.

the profession of broker/hosteller had a natural affinity with immigrants to Bruges, who of course offered merchants from their homeland many advantages of shared culture and local insight. And there is evidence that links with the homeland endured for generations: the Adornes family was still choosing godparents from among Genoese merchants in Bruges a century after their immigration.[52] These hostellers became established figures in the merchant community they served, with reputations that extended far beyond the walls of Bruges itself.[53]

Besides knowing their guests' language and customs, the hosteller provided food and shelter for the merchant and his party. This could mean as little as a shared bed and an occasional meal, or as much as renting a self-contained "hostel" with room for an entire household, complete with warehousing and stabling facilities as well. It is difficult to know what a Bruges hostel of the fourteenth century might have looked like and how it was equipped. Most were named either after their owners – Ter Sconeberch, Ter Beurse – or after a device or sign either built into the house or displayed on a banner outside it, or both.[54] Some apparently allowed merchants to bring their own furniture and buy and prepare their own provisions.[55] The seizure of the hostels of Pieter Huerel and Joris van Roengeville in 1383 provides some idea of the size and contents in at least two examples. Roengeville's hostel stood in the Naaldenstraat, a side street of the Grauwerkerstraat, which itself entered the Bourse square from the west. It was a substantial house of seven bedrooms, kitchen, pantry, dining hall, and cellar.[56] Roengeville had a total of twenty-seven beds shared out among these rooms, with twenty-two divided among only four bedrooms. If the best bed was for his and his wife's use, his hostel still offered considerable sleeping accommodation even if there was only one guest to a bed. Huerel owned and lived in the well-known hostel Ten Hane on the Vlamingstraat,

[52] This was clearly the case with Anselm Adornes, whose sixteen children offered him many opportunities to maintain friendly relations with Genoese merchants, though the immediate result of this was not economic but cultural, as a means to introduce humanist culture to Bruges in the 1460s and 1470s. See M. Boone *et al.*, "Pieter IV Adornes," 2–5.

[53] The German merchant Muenzer, whose description of the Bruges Bourse opened this chapter, spoke of his lodgings on the Bourse square ("foro mercatorum, Boers dicto") with Jan Francke, who was the host of merchants of upper Germany ("hospes est mercatorum Almanie alte"): see Goldschmidt, "Le voyage," 344. Lubrecht Scuetelare is an example, which could be multiplied, of the diplomatic uses a hosteller's contacts could be put to.

[54] The best-known example – the old van der Beurse inn – bore both a name and a visual pun on it. A century later, when the letters left by the English Cely family allow an intimate look into Bruges, their knowledge of the city was synonymous with the names of such hostels as the "Sheep's Hoof," the "Star," and the house of "Two Horns": see Hanham, *The Celys*, pp. 54, 81, 218–220, 278, 281.

[55] Van Houtte, "Makelaars en waarden," 178–179.

[56] Smedt, "De Repressie na Westrozebeke," 31; van Houtte, "Makelaars en waarden," 179, n. 2.

which ran through the Bourse square from south to north. The inventory of his hostel's contents is less extensive than that of Roengeville's, showing only eleven "narrow" beds, but a much more elaborate kitchen and greater dining capacity, with enough dishes and accoutrements to serve 48–74 persons. The much greater stocks of food and fuel also suggest that Huerel may have specialized in food and entertainment rather than lodging.[57] We know that in 1386 the Marshal of Burgundy was entertained there by the aldermen, in the "cabaret."[58]

The issue of rooms, beds, and guests leads naturally to the question of how many people Bruges hostellers could accommodate. Any calculation based on extrapolating numbers of hostels and beds will surely be an underestimate, for hostellers rented out houses as well as rooms, and we know that some beds accommodated more than one person even if they were unrelated. Even admitting these drawbacks, a rough calculation of fifty "free" hostels in operation – a figure quite likely in the decades after 1350 – with an average of fourteen to eighteen beds yields capacities from 700 to 900 guests. With the addition of rented and owned houses, this number accords well with the rough census data contained in the de Marke accounts.[59]

Just as a hosteller's identity was inevitably tied to the nationality of the merchants he served, his guests in turn derived a part of their legal identity from the hostel where they resided. In the de Marke accounts, for example, many merchants are identified as "hoste" of a particular hosteller or hostel, or whose residence there is indicated by the preposition *à* or *de*.[60] In essence this functioned both to confer identity and to provide a local address, sufficient for both semi-legal and legal documents like

57 Smedt, "Repressie," 31–32: "4 dousinen platelen, 26 andere platelen . . ."

58 SAB, SR 1386–1387, f. 130v: "item ghegheven ten Hane int cabaret van costen ghedaen bi den borghmeesters ende eenighen wethouders van costen aldaer ghedaen doe zii festeirden den maerscalc van borgoengen 34s. gro. somme £20 8s." This reputation as a prime entertainment property may also explain why the count retained half ownership of the hostel as part of the settlement with Marien, Pieter Huerel's wife. See Smedt, "Repressie," 32: "Vercocht mijns heeren deel, hute ghedaen de helt van den huus die mijn heere behout metten laste . . ." The word "cabaret" seems to have been applied to places of legitimate entertainment. These, like taverns, were sometimes run in conjunction with a hostel.

59 See chapter 3 for census data. In another context, Guy Dupont estimated that each house of prostitution sheltered fourteen prostitutes; see chapter 8. Katherine Reyerson gives estimates of between ten and twenty beds per inn for a number of southern French towns including Avignon, Montpellier, Marseille, and Toulouse; see Reyerson, "Medieval Hospitality: Innkeepers and the Infrastructure of Trade in Montpellier during the Middle Ages," *Proceedings of the Western Society for French History: Selected Papers of the Annual Meeting* 24 (1997), 38–51, esp. 45.

60 In practice it seems that the preposition *à*, literally "at," most often indicated a guest of the hostel, while *de* ("of") usually referred to an employee.

accounts and court proceedings. Often documents were drawn up in hostels with the hosteller serving as witness. Bruges hostels had an analogous legal existence even outside the city: documents from Hanse cities, for example, often refer to them as commonly known landmarks.[61] Merchants in turn made themselves very much at home in their rented lodgings. They left furniture and personal effects behind when absent on trips.[62] In one case from 1376, two Florentines felt so much at home in their hostel that they used a room there to imprison and hold hostage a fellow merchant from Florence until he agreed to pay his debts.[63] Thus conscious specialization on the part of hostellers created loyal customers, who in turn carried the name and reputation of that hostel homeward. And to complete the virtuous circle, once a hostel was rooted in merchant custom it could then exercise financial influence far beyond Bruges, as debts and deposits at the hostel became common currency among its merchant guests.[64]

Another important facet of the hosteller–merchant relationship was the shaping of a fair and efficient legal environment for merchant visitors of every nation. Grants of legal rights, of course, could only be an act of the sovereign prince, and as we have seen the count of Flanders was solicitous in accommodating the desires of foreign merchants throughout the century. Even after the grant of privileges, however, subtle conflict and constant negotiation were the rule. Sometimes this led to suits for redress of grievances, in which hostellers often functioned as advocates for their merchant guests. This was the case in 1358, when the Hanse merchant Niclaus Roden appeared in the comital court accompanied by the aldermen of the Hanse Kontor in Bruges and his hosteller, Clais Hauscilt.[65] More common was intervention in the Bruges aldermanic court, both as advocate and on

61 For examples of financial transactions, see chaper 6.

62 Van Houtte, "Makelaars en waarden," 178.

63 ARA, Rekenkamer, RR 1017, membrane 13; edited version in L. Gilliodts-van Severen, *Cartulaire de L'ancienne estaple de Bruges. Recveil de documents*, 2 vols. (Bruges, 1904–1906), vol. 1, no. 360, referenced in van Houtte, "Makelaars en waarden," 178 and n. 6. These two Florentines, Lucas Hevainges and Renier Dominges, seem to have rented their own establishment or "herberghe" in St. Jans street, known as "Ter Stroche," where they held Ledenard de Benison captive. Taking separate rented quarters seems to have been typical of Florentines and other Italian merchants in Bruges. The Lucchese banker Dino Rapondi had his own house in the Kuiperstraat, very near the Bourse square (Marechal, *Bijdrage*, p. 69, n. 68.) The two Florentines were represented by two hostellers in their trial, however, as will be discussed further below.

64 This will be discussed more fully in the next chapter.

65 *Hanserezesse: Die Recesse und andere Akten der Hansetage*, 8 vols. (Leipzig, 1870–1897), vol. 1, 3 no. 240:5 4, p. 234, August 1358: "Des nam ich de oldermannes unde minen wert, Clais Howesscilt, ende ghinc vor den grave van Vlaendren met der uutscrifte onser prevelege." An alternate spelling of this name is Aoskilt, and his accounts are edited in Murray and Greve, *Hosteller Accounts*, p. 00.

occasion to post bond for the guest. Sometimes these were cases of violation of the intricate trade laws of the city, as in 1378, when a Catalan merchant, Willaume Sigales, bought saffron in the Spice Hall for more than the legally set price.[66] Considerably more serious were criminal cases, as in the affair of the Florentines and their captive compatriot. This exercise in do-it-yourself commercial justice resulted in the imprisonment of the two Florentines in the Steen, where they languished for a month before two Bruges hostellers posted the considerable sum of £1000 par. each to secure their release. Unfortunately for the hostellers, both men apparently took to their heels, failing to appear at their court hearing, thus causing their hostellers to forfeit the pledged money. One hosteller dutifully paid up; the other offered to stand in for his delinquent guest. But before that could be acted upon, he departed for Florence apparently in full pursuit. Whether he bagged his quarry or not is unclear, but he did end up paying the bulk of the forfeited sum.[67]

Much of this legal representation and behind-the-scenes negotiating went unrecorded, however. After all, the basis of Flemish law and punishment was a kind of deal making between the parties, in which the central question was not so much innocence or guilt as the amount of the fine.[68] Evidence of such deals abounds, and a 1379 case is particularly revealing. Somehow the Bruges bailiff got wind of a case from six years previously, in which the English merchant Robert Ekelsteen allegedly raped a prostitute. The affair seems to have been rapidly covered up because the bailiff found all parties were "satisfied" with the deal and did not wish to reopen the case. Realizing his position was weak and that more than a year and a day had elapsed, the bailiff settled with Ekelsteen's hosteller, Pieter de Scuetelare, for £60 par. This was certainly just another in a whole series of "settlements" resulting from this sexual attack.[69]

[66] ARA, Rekenkamer, RR 1027 (1378–1379), membrane 15, "Calaengen van diveersen aventuren . . . Willaume Sigales de Catteleengere ghecalengeirt omme dat hi ghecocht soude hebben sanffraen boven der kuere, twelke de scoutheet ghecalengierd hadde bi den deken vander Cruuthalle over verbuerd, pais ghemaect van mijns heren dele ter beide van den heer Jacob Metteneye den houden omme £48." Thus Metteneye senior acted to settle the complaint.

[67] ARA, Rekenkamer, RR 1017, membrane 13; the two were Lucas Hevainges and Renier Dominges, both of Florence. Tideman van den Berghe posted bond for Hevainges and Franchoys van Zinghene did so for Dominges. Van den Berghe paid the sum upon the failure of his guest to appear in court; van Zinghene made his promise but then departed for "de Florentyne."

[68] David Nicholas, "Crime and Punishment in Fourteenth-Century Ghent," *RBPH* 48 (1970), 289–334, 1141–1176; Nicholas, *Medieval Flanders*, pp. 341–345.

[69] ARA, Rekenkamer, RR 1028(1379), membrane 12: "Robrecht Ekelsteen dinghelsce ghecalengiert dat hi een wyf van lichtervoere vercracht soude hebben wel 6 jaer verleden daer partyen of vernoucht waren ende de Scoutheet ducht hadde dat hem ontgaen soude bi wette omme dat jaer ende dach

From such examples one can better understand the link that bound merchant to host, and host to an entire foreign merchant community. The tie could be abused, as the story of the fugitive Florentines well shows, but clearly the benefits flowed both ways. Relying on the legal influence of one's host was a sure bet for the merchant, given the political standing most hostellers enjoyed in Bruges. This political clout could even extend to the comital court – the supreme court of the land – since Bruges hostellers served as diplomats from time to time, and profited from their experience as aldermen as well. The payoff for the hosteller for the exercise of his or her influence is not so readily apparent, except that it shaped the generally receptive atmosphere for trade in the city. Yet advantages there were, which only become apparent when we lay open the inner workings of the hostelling business.

THE BUSINESS OF THE HOSTELLER

The later Middle Ages throughout Europe were a golden age for the operators of hostels and inns of every kind.[70] Although some facets of the business were common to most places, there was much variation as well, given the differing economic makeup and role of particular cities. Thus hostellers in some cities specialized in arranging transport and warehousing for goods passing through their city. Others, like those in Rome, were much more active in providing hospitality to pilgrims and tourists. As stated earlier, I have chosen the term "free" hostels to describe establishments that, while offering meals and lodging, tended to emphasize commerce and commercial customers. Their owner/operators were invariably members of the brokers' guild, which they came to dominate completely in the course of the century. Kathryn Reyerson has called them "merchant-innkeepers," a literal translation from the Montpellier statutes of the fourteenth century.[71] In perhaps no place in Europe other than Bruges were there such numbers of hostels with such a varied merchant clientele, whose owners so tried to

verleden war. Pays ghemaect bi de heer Pieter de Scuetelaere sinen wert omme £60." According to Verwys and Verdam, *Middelnederlandsch woordenboek*, vol. IX, pp. 722–723, 2466, the description "loose woman" ("wyf van lichtervoere" or "quader voere") was most commonly attached to prostitutes (e.g. "Dat sijn vele hoeren die nu ommegaen met quader voeren . .") but could also mean immoral women in general.

70 Van Houtte, "Les courtiers," 105–141; Murray and Hunt, *History of Business*, pp. 151–177, where responses to the challenges to business posed by the fourteenth century are discussed; the solutions in many cases required a greater role for hostellers.

71 Reyerson, "Medieval Hospitality," 39.

orchestrate the rhythms and flows of commerce. In other words, in Bruges the business of hostelling was *business*.

This was not an unregulated business, however. While it evolved into more of a merchants' guild than a trade guild, the regulating customs of guild life and organization, as well as urban controls, were very much in evidence in Bruges. The brokers had their deans and captains, who were installed and sworn in annually along with the urban government and the other guilds. As with other guild leaders, they policed and supervised the practice of brokerage in the city, reporting violators and receiving a portion of the fines imposed.[72] They also administered the guild's property and presided over its corporate religious services and poor relief. In the course of the fourteenth century, the guild purchased two farms in the St. Gillis parish, not far from the Carmelite monastery where the guild continued to hold its formal sessions, in a boisterous neighborhood of taverns and bordellos.[73] By 1376, the guild had completed construction of a chapel and may have completed a "Godshuus" for impoverished members as well.[74] The chapel was large and ornate, with an organ and expectation that singers would be employed to sing masses on principal feast days and for funerals and anniversaries.[75] Rather typically, the chapel seems to have been completed before the club house, called in the fifteenth century the "brokers' pleasure garden," suggesting an early concern with the religious, confraternal aspect of the guild.[76] Such efforts may have been warranted, for there is evidence that hostellers shared in the violent tenor of the market

[72] The fines were split among the city, the comital bailiff, and the guild.

[73] For the St. Gillis "dorp" see chapters 2 and 9. The charters of purchase are described in A. Schouteet, *Regesten op de oorkonden, 1089–1300*, 4 vols. (Bruges, 1973), vol. II, pp. 453, 640; vol. III, 422, 603; 628, 632, 641; vol. IV, 617, 618, 636, 639; van den Abeele and Catry, *Makelaars en handelaars*, p. 20.

[74] OCMW, Dis St. Anna #38, 20 April 1364 (os), a charter mentioning a house "buter vlaminc porte" called Te Doteins, "toebehorende der neringhe van den makelaers." In an agreement of 1376, the provost of Onze-Lieve-Vrouw, vicar of St. Gillis parish, and the guild agreed upon the division of charitable donations made to the guild chapel, dedicated to Our Lady of Bethlehem ("Onser Vrauwe te Bethleem"). By the sixteenth century the land held not only the chapel but almshouses (*Godshusen*), gardens, and a meeting and recreation complex, as well as other houses. The 1376 agreement speaks of monies that were to go to the "poor and sick" of the guild, so there may have been by that date at least forerunners of the houses pictured on the map of Marcus Gerards in 1562.

[75] Murray, *Notarial Instruments*, p. 289; given that Onze-Lieve-Vrouw church had St. Gillis's church and the brokers' chapel in its gift, musicians from that church may have been the obvious choice to sing at such services. For the musical history of Onze-Lieve-Vrouw, see Reinhard Strohm, *Music in Late Medieval Bruges* (Oxford, 1985), pp. 42–50. Strohm does not consider the role of guilds in sponsorship and production of polyphonic music, which may have been considerable.

[76] The 1376 charter suggests that guild members typically met in two taverns, "sPapen Hant" and "ten Bardekinne," for socializing, suggesting that the "pleasure garden" had not yet been constructed; see Murray, *Notarial Instruments*, p. 288.

place. In 1389, for example, the prominent hosteller Lubrecht de Scuetelare intervened in an argument between his brother, Joorge, and another hosteller, Clais de Teemseke, by grabbing a club and hitting de Teemseke over the head.[77] Maintaining peace in the guild may have required quite a few masses.[78]

Supervision and regulation of hostellers and brokers did not begin and end in church, however. The city reinforced and broadened the restrictions imposed by the guild on its members in ways that point to the reciprocal relationship of hostellers, urban government, and the interests of trade. These included guaranteeing the competence and neutrality of brokers and hostellers, as well as preventing conflicts of interest in the pursuit of their business. The 1303 privileges were explicit in forbidding the practice of both brokerage and business – *coopmanscepe* – by the broker, except for purchasing horses, peat, and herring.[79] However, this ban was only on retail trade by brokers; involvement in foreign trade was permitted. But partnerships with foreign merchants in pursuit of such trade were also banned in the 1303 privileges, and this restriction was further reinforced by an oath required of brokers in 1360.[80] The strenuousness of such restrictions may in fact indicate widespread evasion, but they remained the ideal in legal theory at least.

Above all else, hostellers were liable for the goods and money left in their care. Hostellers of course had the incentive, common to all medieval merchants, to maintain an honorable reputation. Beyond this, the city itself required all brokers and hostellers to assume financial responsibility for all goods left in their care. Their liability was broadened in 1359 in the privilege granted to the German Hanse to include goods left with their clerks and apprentices as well.[81] What is more, the hosteller could be held financially liable for goods purchased on credit by guests. Once the date of repayment came and went, the creditor could come to the merchant's hostel and demand repayment. This was the case when an English merchant left town with his purchases of copper ware and did not honor his bond or *recognoissance*. His hosteller, Jan Honin, was forced to pay up in his absence.[82]

[77] ARA, Rekenkamer, 13676, pt. 3, f. 12r, under "Calaenges de debat, £11 Primiers Lubrecht le Scuetelare souchonnies quant il voy le debat entre Joorge le Scuetelare son frere, et Clais de Teemseke, priust ung boffet et se frappa le dit Clais sour son tiest ainsy quon dist; prius delle dite calaenge £7."

[78] Donations made to resolve such quarrels were foreseen in the statutes of foundation of the chapel: "Wart oec so dat eenich zoendinc ware ghemaect, ende men in dat zoendinc ter kerke ende capelle of den zieken ende aermen [die] daer zullen sijn eenich goed gave . . .": Murray, *Notarial Instruments*, p. 289.

[79] Gilliodts, "Règlements," 225; van Houtte, "Makelaars en waarden," 183–184 and n. 2.

[80] Van Houtte, "Makelaars en waarden," 186 and n. 2.

[81] Ibid., 188 and n. 1.

[82] Ibid., 188.

Unforeseen disasters and the financial capriciousness of guests could leave the hosteller vulnerable to bankruptcy. In theory the city guarded against this eventuality by requiring hostellers to post bond, as was the rule in Ghent; but this requirement seems to have quickly fallen into desuetude at Bruges, before the middle of the century.[83] A number of bankruptcies from the 1360s put city officials in a difficult position *vis-à-vis* the creditors of a hosteller. Members of the German Hanse, under the terms of their 1359 privilege, were to be reimbursed from the city treasury if necessary for any losses suffered as a result of a hosteller's bankruptcy. This required of city administrators not only the time and expense of foreclosure and sale of property, but also pursuit of the assets of family members and those who had stood surety for the hosteller, and auditing of financial claims and eventual repayment. But given that the city was forced to pay 100 percent of any losses by Hanse merchants, this meant that the claims of other creditors might be only partially satisfied.[84] This must have led to some ugly scenes. By 1400 the city seems to have learned to pre-empt such bankruptcies whenever possible, for in that year it assumed the liabilities that the prominent hosteller Jacob van de Walle owed to Hanse merchants, in return for his promise to repay the amount over a twenty-six-year term.[85]

There is reason to believe that hosteller bankruptcies in the last half of the fourteenth century stemmed in part from a new audacity in response to business opportunities. Rather than acting as passive service providers, many Bruges hostellers joined in the business of their customers in new and complex ways, which offered greater rewards and greater risks. In so doing, they made use of systems and structures they had helped create, especially the credit and payment system that they operated with money changers, and the network of taverns and cabarets where merchants exchanged information and closed deals. Being at the literal center of exchange put into the grasp of hostellers the most potentially profitable commodity of all – information.

[83] For Ghent, see Nicholas, *Metamorphosis*, pp. 142, 146: there the amount was huge, £250 gro., suggesting a serious attempt to cover any anticipated losses, and unlike in Bruges, the practice continued; see Walter Prevenier and David Nicholas (eds.), *Gentse stads en baljuwsrekeningen* (Brussels, 1999), pp. 865–76. Posting bond is mentioned in 1331 (ARA, Rekenkamer, RR 1009, February–November 1331, membrane 21) "de tenir hosteil contra le cuere sans faire seurteyt." This requirement seems to have been ignored, as was that required of money changers. Posting bond was reimposed in the fifteenth century on all hostellers; see van Houtte, "Makelaars en waarden," 190 n. 1.

[84] Two examples from the 1360s and 1370s were Jacob Sconebergh and Edele de Rudevoorde; for the latter see Greve, "Jacob Sconebergh," pp. 213–224.

[85] Van Houtte, "Makelaars en waarden," 189 and n. 5.

To some extent hostellers and brokers were forced to expand their search for profitable adjuncts to their business, because their traditional sources of revenue were drying up due to rate fixing and currency debasement. Ordinarily, brokers were paid for their services not on a percentage of the value of the goods they brokered, but by a set sum per piece or weight.[86] In Bruges this resulted in lists of goods issued by the city government indicating the permissible brokerage fees that could be charged. Only trade goods not mentioned on such lists could be charged a brokerage fee based on a percentage of the selling price.[87] The trouble was that the list of goods became ever longer as foreign merchant groups succeeded in their insistence on fixed brokerage rates. By 1379, the list included all the usual commodities exchanged in Bruges as well as newer ones like dried fruit and dyestuffs.[88] Moreover, enforcement of these fees seems to have been uncharacteristically strict and thorough, as lists of fines show.[89] Fixed fees not only made brokers/hostellers subject to the inevitable inelasticities that price fixing brings, particularly in a highly volatile era; they also subjected them to the full force of coinage debasement. Add to this the fact that most brokerage fees were split between brokers and their employers – hostellers – and the dimensions of the problem become clear. One could not live by brokerage alone.

Hostellers had two other traditional sources of income in the fees paid by guests for lodging and warehousing, called hostage and hostelage. Rates at which these services could be sold also came under scrutiny by city officials. As early as 1267, a commission composed of representatives of the five Flemish cities with annual trade fairs established the price of lodging during each city's fair. Since Bruges was one of the five, it seems likely that such price controls remained the rule in the fourteenth century as well. We know that in 1547 room rates were fixed again, with additional fixed fees for stabling horses.[90] What the price of lodging might actually have been in practice is difficult to determine. Prices could vary considerably: in 1302 the nobleman William of Juliers and his entourage were lodged at city expense, which ranged from 9s. 3d. par. per day for the commoner Gilion de Mesnil to 41s. 7d. per day for Sir Henri de Petresem.[91] Horses

[86] This was largely true throughout Europe: ibid., 191.

[87] Gilliodts-van Severen, "Règlements," 234 – which van Houtte calculates ("Makelaars en waarden," 191 n. 6) at 3.33 percent or 2 gro. per pound.

[88] Gilliodts-van Severen, "Règlements," 229–334.

[89] Van Houtte, "Makelaars en waarden," 193 and n. 3.

[90] Ibid., 195; the rates were 2d. groot for the person, 7d. for the horse.

[91] The text is published in full in Wyffels and Vandewalle, *Rekeningen*, vol. II, pt. 1, pp. 848–852. The total amount expended for dou Mesnil and a "compagnon" was £13, thus 18s. 6d. per day each.

cost just over 1s. per day extra for boarding, with an additional shilling required for incidentals.[92] In 1386, the hosteller Trude Braems (Broems) was paid 13s. 1d. per day for lodging a squire who had been injured in an All Saints' Day riot. She received an additional £42 par. (or 24s. per day) for miscellaneous expenses probably resulting from his medical care.[93] In 1382, Margaret, widow of hosteller/money changer Peter van Oudenaarde, lodged a complaint of non-payment against a canon of St. Donatian's, Jacob de Vos, for £10 gro. (£120 par.) for room and board for himself and his servant, £2 4s. for cloth, and £4 gro. for his horse.[94] All these fragments seem to show that the price of lodging varied according to the quality of food and accommodation, and the breadth of services offered. It may well have offered considerably more opportunity for profit than did brokerage.

Renting and supervising warehouse space may also have been a profit center for Bruges hostellers. Unfortunately virtually nothing is known about the rates charged or the profits made from this important part of the business. It is possible that the advantages of warehousing were compounded by the increased likelihood that the hosteller or one of his employees would also serve as broker for the sale of the stored merchandise. But guests were not required to use their hosteller as the broker for goods stored with him.[95] One clue is provided by the hosteller Nicolaas Barbesaen, who in the late 1390s was forced to disclose his yearly income as a result of his prosecution for malfeasance as city treasurer. He declared that he earned between five and six hundred francs from brokerage and a thousand French crowns from warehouse fees per year.[96] This is a stunning level of income, even

De Petresem's lodging cost £25 5s. in total, leading to the conclusion that Plume ran one of the more opulent establishments in town. Other charges, like that for Sir Jehan dou Markiet and Boidin Braem at the hostel of Gherard Hals, amounted to 15s. 2d. per day each.

92 The figures for the horses come from a separate account for feed, blacksmithing and harnessmaking fees, and various unspecified incidentals amounting to £30 12s. 6d. par. (Wyffels and Vandewalle, *Rekeningen*, vol. II, pt. I, p. 848). The widow Ricovart, hosteller, boarded twenty-two mares for one night at a cost of 22s. 6d.

93 SAB, SR 1386–1387, f. 129v: "Item ghegheven Truden Henric Broems wyf van dat zoe costen ghehadt heift den vorseiden sciltcnape te houdene in hare herberghe 5 weken lanc bi beveilne van borghmeesters 15s. gro. [or £24 par.] Item noch ghegheven der zelver Truden bi beveilne van borghmeesters van costen ghedaen in hare herberghe bi den vorseiden sciltcnape £3 10s. gro. somme £42. (These expenses were for the care of the above squire, who was wounded in a "remour" on All Saints' day.)

94 BAB, St. Donaas, A48, Acta Capituli, f. 95r, 19 May 1382: Margaret appeared before the canons in a chapter meeting, along with a number of de Vos's creditors seeking payment. She handed over an itemized list of these expenses ("tradidit unam cedulam") whose text is copied out into the acts: "Meester Jacob Vos es mii sculdich £10 gro. van zire tafle ende cnape tafle die hem toebehoren. Item 54s. gro. Willem de Bouc van lakine. Item £4 gro. Barthelmeus den Fachelare van eenen parde." This is the only text of a hotel bill known to survive from fourteenth-century Bruges.

95 Van Houtte, "Makelaars en waarden," 195–196.

96 Gilliodts-van Severen, *Inventaire*, vol. IV, p. 12.

for one of the leading members of the guild, who came from an immigrant family that had spent several generations establishing its position.[97] On the other hand, Barbesaen had every incentive to exaggerate his wealth in order to aid his defense, so the figures must be regarded with some skepticism.

There is an additional reason to doubt Barbesaen's self-disclosure, which mentions only the traditional sources of hosteller earnings. For it is clear from analysis of several bankruptcy cases that Bruges hostellers developed and maintained complex financial relationships with their guests and other clients. These ran a gamut of roles from factor, with power to buy and sell in a client's name, to full partnership in trade ventures by virtue of investment. They developed out of the traditional roles played by hostellers as representatives of their guests in the market and law courts, as well as administrator of goods and money deposited with them on a long-term basis. And these new roles were not discouraged by a city administration that had in fact banned direct involvement in trade by brokers/hostellers earlier in the century as a danger to their neutrality in the market. This evolution of hostellers into investors and commission agents, a unique development at the time, thus points to fundamental changes in the politics of trade and to its inner workings in the Bruges context. The unusual freedom allowed brokers/hostellers strongly suggests recognition of the value of their new role in maintaining the economic growth of the city on the one hand, and the ability of hostellers in particular to create and capitalize on new business opportunities on the other.

The Bruges hosteller Jacob Sconebergh provides one example of how these various strands might come together in a particular business. Little is known of his origins, though there are strong indications that he was either an immigrant or the son of German immigrants.[98] We know that by the 1360s he and his wife Marie operated a hostel near the St. Jans bridge, specializing in lodging Hanseatic merchants. Their sudden deaths in the summer of 1368 left a business heavily encumbered with debt, which resulted in the refusal of Jacob and Marie's heirs to assume it.[99] The case landed in the city's bankruptcy court, where the claims of

[97] Anke Greve's biographical index notes that Barbesaen was active from 1372 to 1407 and had served in every office of the guild as captain and treasurer; he had also served numerous times as an alderman on both benches of the city council, and as burgomaster as well. He was banished from Flanders in 1407 as a result of these allegations; see Anke Greve, "Hansen, Hosteliers und Herbergen. Studien zum Aufenthalt hansischer Kaufleute in Brügge im 14. und 15. Jahrhundert," unpublished doctoral dissertation, University of Ghent, 1998, part 2, Catalogue.

[98] Greve, "Jacob Sconebergh," pp. 215–217; Greve notes the incidence of his last name among Hanse merchants.

[99] Surviving Sconeberghs were a brother, Jan, his mother, Zoetin, his sister-in-law, and a daughter whose name is obscured by damage to the account document. By 1370, Jan and his mother had died (SAB, SR 1369–1370, f. 80v; Greve, "Jacob Sconebergh," 216).

thirty-eight Hanse merchants and thirty-four Bruges burghers and other foreign merchants were reviewed. Simultaneously all the Sconeberghs' remaining assets were impounded and sold, bonds posted by their sureties were collected, and even Jacob's sister-in-law was assessed for her late brother-in-law's share of the family estate.[100] Still the proceeds covered barely half of Sconebergh's liabilities, and the city was forced to expend nearly half of the budget surplus of 1379 to cover merchant losses.[101]

Thanks to this bankruptcy and the account Sconebergh kept with the de Marke exchange, we can learn a good deal about the nature of his business. Judging from the list of his guests, Sconebergh clearly did specialize in lodging merchants from the Hanse cities.[102] However, given that only two of the twelve guests filed claims for losses with the city authorities, Sconebergh had a much larger circle of associates than those who merely lodged with him. A total of thirty-eight Hanse merchants were paid more than £528 gro. to settle their claims against Sconebergh.[103] This amounted to full repayment for losses as guaranteed by the commercial treaty of 1359. What this considerable sum represents in terms of business activity is less clear. The city accounts called them simply "debts" – did they represent more than simply deposits left with him for safekeeping? Surely the wide variety of individual sums owed (from £3 to £60 gro.) might suggest multifarious business activities; the lack of overlap between Sconebergh's recorded guests and list of creditors supports this, as does a look at the list of Bruges and other merchant creditors. Thirty-two individuals were described as *poorters* and "resident" foreign merchants.[104] Among them were prominent Bruges cloth merchants like Jacop Bave, Jacop van Roesselare, Jakop Thibelin, Jan Gaderpenninc, and the weaver/drapers Jan van Berneem and Diederick Minnen.[105] Three money changers were also among the creditors, two of

[100] SAB, SR 1369–1370, f. 83r: "Ontfanghen van Jans Sconeberchs weduwe als van der inhave die ver Zoetinne Ians ende Iacobs Sconeberchs moeder toebehoorde van alse verren als up Iacobs Sconberchs deel cam £120."

[101] These were only a portion of the total, those guaranteed by treaty. Thus Hanse merchants received 100 percent of proven losses; all others received only 5s. 6d. in the pound groot – just over a quarter. Thus from the total of £4765 19s. 4d. parisis (£397 3s. 3d. gro.) the city advanced some £2025 17s. 5d.

[102] This list is drawn from those named as his guests in the De Marke accounts and brought together in Murray are Greve, *Hosteller Accounts*, 296.

[103] The final amount listed in SAB, SR 1368–1369, f. 81r, was £528 15s $5\frac{1}{2}$ d.

[104] SAB, SR 1368–1369, f. 81r: "poorters ende vreemden cooplieden wonachtich binnen der stede van Brucghe . . ." He also owed tax to the farmers of the city's scale, "dien van den pondere" (f. 81v).

[105] The Bave clan (Clais, Jakop, and Jehan) were all prominent drapers in the 1360s and 1370s; in 1363 alone Clais Bave sold thirty-two Bruges cloths to the city government (SAB, SR 1363–1364, f. 42r). Thibelin was a member and official of the weavers' guild as well as a cloth seller to the city (SAB, SR 1362–1363, f. 43v; SAB, Wetsvernieuwingen, 1370, f. 59r, an inspector of the weavers' guild); Van Berneem and his wife Lizebette are both mentioned in the Bruges city accounts as drapers (SAB, SR 1369–1370, f. 35r).

whom had significant sums invested.[106] If the extent of losses sustained by Bruges merchants indicates wider business contacts, the size of the losses sustained by non-Hanse merchants proves them. These fourteen "resident" foreigners included men from Spain, England, Italy, Catalonia, and France, who together held 45 percent of Sconebergh's bad debts as opposed to 32 percent for Hanse merchants and 23 percent for Brugeois. His largest creditors were not Hanse merchants; they came from Catalonia and France, and included his two Bruges bankers.[107] It is thus an over-simplification to call him simply a hosteller who specialized in Hanseatic trade.

Analysis of Sconebergh's debts reveals an overly ambitious business that literally connected the Mediterranean and the Baltic. Evidence of a partnership in a ship indicates at least minor interest in direct trade, but on the whole it was probably partnerships and brokering trade – perhaps in wool and Flemish cloth – that made up most of his business. His circle of creditors far exceeded those who lodged with him, and it is tempting to regard hostel keeping as a minor part of his business. Given that his liabilities exceeded his assets by nearly three to one and that his entire hostel and furnishings were worth just over £382 gro., his exposure in trade was far greater than the worth of his real and business property.[108] Unfortunately, Sconebergh's account with de Marke adds little new information other than confirming the importance of Hanse merchants and containing some of the names of those who lodged claims against his estate.[109] He never ran a deficit in his account with de Marke, who does not appear among his creditors in the city's list.

With Sconebergh we see the possible dimensions of the hosteller business, as well as the part played in it by money changers and their cooperative book transfer system. Yet the sums lost by the three money changers in the bankruptcy reveal some form of equity or debt participation in the Sconebergh business, suggesting that a book transfer system was only a part of the business relationship of changer and hosteller.

[106] Griele sWitten (or de Witte), Pieter Potter, and Willem Ruweel (SAB, SR 1368–1369, f. 81v).

[107] The Catalan Willemme van St. Gales was owed £116 15s. 4½d., followed by the presumably French Janne Bustin with £112 gro. Ruweel and Pieter Potter were owed £78 and £76 respectively: SAB, SR 1368–1369, f. 81r–v.

[108] Their total debt was £1647 4s 8½d; total assets were £677 1s. 1½d. Subtracting the £150 surety paid by three of Sconebergh's backers gives a remaining deficit of £527 9s. 6½d.

[109] His accounts are edited in Murray and Greve, *Hosteller Accounts*. The Hanse merchants were Diederic Rupelbonde, Radekin Vrauendourpt, and Geuble Coullelaire; two members of the Bruges Bave clan, Clais Bave, junior and Paskier Bave, as well as the Italian merchant Conrart Boin Adone are mentioned both in De Marke and among his creditors in the City case.

The bankruptcy of the Sconebergh hostel puts into sharp relief the close financial interdependence of hostellers and their foreign and Bruges clientele. Investments, partnerships, banking, and trading were all part of the hosteller's business by the time death took Sconebergh and his wife unawares. But it still leaves unanswered the question of how such a closely intertwined system came about and was maintained. In essence this takes us back once again to the enigma of the Bourse square – named for a hostel, but developing even by 1390 into a meeting place of merchants, transcending the narrowing traditions of urban monopoly and regulation. The key to understanding this evolution is embedded in two hosteller-managed networks: merchant sociability and payment/credit.

THE "EVIL INN"

As a business genre, medieval inns had a bad reputation. Too often in both literature and legal ordinances they are harbors of all vices on offer in the city – violent crime, sedition, gambling, drunkenness, and prostitution. Medieval preachers created the topos of the church and inn poised at opposite ends of the same public square, ideological enemies locked in struggle for the souls of those who passed.[110] Religious women were in particular peril, as a charter granting parish status to the beguinage of Tongeren warned: "they [beguines] live so far away from these [parish] churches that they must pass market squares and streets and even by inns . . ."[111] The reality was much more complex, of course, for as I have tried to show by attaching the name "hostel" to the commercial inns of Bruges, many if not most such establishments were involved in businesses considered licit even by the most hard-bitten moralists. And yet the taint of the immoral was never entirely absent in Bruges. Even there, crimes committed against morality took place in "evil inns" whose very name seemed sufficient to obviate the need for further description.[112]

Bruges hostels of all sorts were not completely innocent of these charges, for there were sound business reasons for offering drink and entertainment in or near the hostel itself. The hundreds of foreign merchants who frequented Bruges were for the most part young, single or unaccompanied

[110] Reyerson, "Medieval Hospitality," 38–39, points to the work of W. C. Firebaugh, *The Inns of the Middle Ages* (Chicago, 1924), as a modern expression of the traditional view.

[111] Simons, *Cities of Ladies*, p. 114.

[112] To select just one rubric from a city account (SAB, SR 1368–1369, f. 28r): "Onfanc van den ghenen die quade herberghe ghehouden hebben." The Flemish word *herbergh* is close to the English "inn" in meaning, denoting a place where primarily food and lodging were on offer, while not excluding other sidelines.

men, far from home often for extended periods. Their habits, to paraphrase Erich Maschke, rode a circuit from rationality to lust and back, in both their business and entertainment. Indeed, many a business deal was struck in a tavern, where not coincidentally most gambling also took place.[113] Hostels, taverns, cabarets, and gaming houses (*speelhuizen*) were the places merchants met to strike deals, exchange information, and enjoy themselves, often in a seamless continuum. And it is often unclear whether the boundaries between such venues were anything but vague, for hostellers often stood behind them all.

We have already seen in the hostel of Pieter Huerel – Ten Hane – a case of the use of a "hostel" as a "cabaret," a place specializing in serving wine and food. There is considerable evidence that this was true of many hostellers, either as operators themselves or in partnership with others in the operation of a separate establishment. While we cannot know with any certainty how many hostellers chose to follow Pieter Huerel's example, there is evidence of close cooperation between hostellers and Hanse merchants in operating taverns where wine, beer, and mead were served.

"Tavern" was a word common to all the vernaculars spoken in medieval Bruges, meaning first and foremost a drinking establishment.[114] But it was not the only term used, especially early in the fourteenth century. In the Bruges bailiff's accounts of 1305 the terms were "cabarets" and "cellars," with cellars in the majority by nearly three to one.[115] The 1308 city accounts also have a similar list, but the term "cabaret" is applied to all establishments.[116] Only some of these can be firmly tied to hostellers by name, but many of the rest bear names of known hostels or places that were most likely hostels.[117] Thus it is very likely that the classic setting for a drinking establishment was the spacious cellar beneath the sizable buildings occupied by hostels. Clearer evidence of hostellers selling drink occurs in 1331, when six prominent

[113] Katelijne Geerts, *De spelende mens in de Boergondische Nederlanden* (Bruges, 1987), pp. 40–41; Maschke quote from Martha Howell, *Women, Production and Patriarchy in Late Medieval Cities* (Chicago, 1986), p. 121.

[114] Of course medieval Latin was the ultimate source of the word *taberna*, made famous by the Goliard poets of the thirteenth century. For the retail sale of wine in the Low Countries in general, see Craeybeckx, *Un grand commerce*, pp. 186–192.

[115] ARA, Rekenkamer, RR 1007 (May 1305), membrane 6, "Des cabres et des chelliers." Twenty-six are explicitly called "chellier"; one is not but it appears among the cellars so was very likely one; the seven others, presumably the "cabres," are called simply after their owner/operators.

[116] SAB, SR 1308, f. 3r: "Van cabaretten te borghene tieghen de cuere": there are twenty cellars and six real cabarets.

[117] The cellars that can be definitely associated with known hostellers are Raven Dauwilt, Jakemon Bonin, Watier Dauwilt, de le Hanghele, Jehan Balke, Dierman Caufin, Jan van Curtrike; the cabarets of Lambsin de le Wale can as well. Most of the others are identified by the device or symbol by which the building and/or cellar was known.

guild members paid fines to the comital bailiff for selling wine.[118] Four "taverniers" who were fined for not surrendering the keys to their wine cellars in 1367 may have been either hostellers or members of a clan of hostellers.[119]

Yet the most abundant evidence of the hostellers' role in serving drink dates from the mid-1370s, when the comital bailiff either instituted or revived a regalian right to collect a license fee from all those who wished to sell wine at retail during the Bruges fair.[120] Not only do these records show the continuing involvement of hostellers in wine sales: they reveal as well an extensive partnership between hostellers and Hanse wine dealers in the operation of Bruges taverns.[121] This unique sharing of a lucrative urban market by those who could have excluded outsiders reveals in fact their common interests. High taxes assessed on their wine and interference in their selling at retail had long been a complaint of Hanse merchants, particularly those from Cologne.[122] After the Hanse boycott and issue of new privileges in 1359, however, not only was the right to import wine tax-free for personal consumption confirmed, but an explicit guarantee of the right to sell wine at retail was added, requiring payment of the accustomed excise tax and no more.[123] Though we have no actual partnership agreements, the role of the hostellers is made clear when they are named together with many of these "taverners" and wine merchants in the Bruges city accounts.[124] As a result, as Anke Greve has shown, Hanse merchants from the 1360s were in the unique position of being able to import and

118 ARA, Rekenkamer, RR 1009 (February–November 1331), membrane 22. These were Jehan Alverdoe, Fransoys Metten Eye, Clais Leken (Greve, Jan Laicken), Jacob Goederic (Evraert Goederic), Pieter Dardoye, and Jehan Caufin.

119 ARA, Rekenkamer, RR 1010 (September 1367–January 1368), membrane 7. These were Jan Marck, Ricart Bolcx, Andres Francois, and Pieter de Scotelare. The reason for the order to deliver up the keys is a mystery. The broker/hosteller Jacob de Visch was also fined in this year for selling wine at a price higher than the set maximum.

120 The count was the author and guarantor of the fair in May, which coincided with the procession of the city's holiest relic, the Holy Blood. But strangely there is no evidence of a fee paid for the banner that was required to be displayed by any wine seller.

121 ARA, Rekenkamer, RR 1014 (May–September 1375), membrane 12. Of the eighteen "taverniers die wine ghetapt hebben in de Brucghemaerct," ten were called "Osterling" and the remainder were known hostellers, like Victoor van den Eede, Gilis van den Bussche, and the Metteneye family hostel Ten Eye on the Vlamingstraat.

122 In 1358, for example, Hanse merchants complained that they were being forced to pay a higher than accustomed rate of excise tax on red wine, and were also being taxed for wine they consumed themselves. See K. Koppmann, *Die Recesse und andere Akten der Hansetage*, vol. 1, pt. 3 no. 240:9 1–7, 237–238. The right to consume their own wine free of tax in Bruges was guaranteed in the 1309 privilege: *Hansisches Urkundenbuch*, vol. II, no. 154, 21, p. 68.

123 The crucial expression indicating retail sale is not only "to sell" (*vercopen*) but also "to tap" (*wine ten tappe*): Gilliodts-van Severen, *Inventaire*, vol. II, no. 532, p. 50.

124 Krüger (ed.), *Brügger Steuerlisten*, pp. 15, 63, 64, 69–72.

profit from wine in three distinct ways: tax-free for their own consumption; wine for retail sale, taxed at half rate; and wine for reexport, taxed at the usual rates.[125] Hostellers not only aided them in the diplomacy resulting in the agreement, but also stood to profit by joining with Hanse merchants in vertically integrating the retail sale of German wine in Bruges by providing them with premises. Thus the *Weinkeller* became a common sight in the commercial landscape.

The example of the Cologne wine merchant and Bruges taverner Heinric Erembrecht can stand for many. We know a good deal about him and his wine shop because of confiscation records and his protracted legal battles to secure compensation for his losses.[126] His case and other records show that a tavern was far from a one-man operation. Customarily, a tavern employed two men or boys to shift and tap barrels, two men to serve, a "wine measurer," and a "winescroder" to do the accounting and delivery work.[127] Erembrecht's establishment seems to have been in the cellar of the hostel Ter Matte, which he had operating by 1375.[128] He was still actively involved in the wine trade in Cologne, Dordrecht, and elsewhere in the 1370s and 1380s.[129] Meanwhile he operated his tavern in Bruges continuously at the same location until 1382, when calamity struck. In the lawlessness of that year, three of his assistants were arrested and imprisoned on a trumped-up charge of evading the wine excise tax, Erembrecht later alleged.[130] Moreover, the tavern was broken into and looted by the victorious Gentenars in May, and what little remained was confiscated by the count in 1383. For unknown reasons, Erembrecht was branded an enemy of Flanders, and his wine cellar never reopened.[131] Whatever losses he suffered in his retail business, his greatest loss stemmed from a debt owed him by

[125] Greve, "Hansen, Hosteliers und Herbergen."

[126] His name is spelled Heinricx Herbrechts in the confiscation accounts (ARA, Rekenkamer, RR 2017, membrane 6). He became a burgher of Cologne and a long-time importer and retailer of wine in Bruges. For a biography, see Dierck *et al.*, *Hansekaufleute in Brügge*, pp. 229–231.

[127] This description is derived from the 1358 complaint, in *Hanse Recesse*, vol. 1, pt. 3, no. 240, p. 238. Erembrecht had at least one assistant who aided the comital officials in drawing up their inventory.

[128] This was a venerable location, since a "kelnare ter Matte" was in operation in 1308: SAB, SR 1308, f. 3r.

[129] Judging from Dutch toll records, which record shipments under his name; see Dierck *et al.*, *Hansekaufleute in Brügge*, p. 230.

[130] Erembrecht paid for the license to sell during the Bruges market between 1375 and 1379; see ARA, Rekenkamer, RR 1014, membrane 12; RR 1017, membrane 14; RR 1018; RR 2023, membrane 14; RR. 1026, membrane 15, where his establishment is "ten Toolnare"; RR 1027, membrane 17, "ter Matte"; RR 1029, membrane 13. See also Dierck *et al.*, *Hansekaufleute in Brügge*, p. 230.

[131] The confiscation accounts are ARA, Rekenkamer, RR 2017, membrane 6.

the Bruges city government for a large quantity of Rhine wine.[132] Thus his retail shop may have been at best a sideline to his main interests in the wine trade.

Though exceptionally well documented, Erembrecht's case was hardly exceptional. Even after the disaster of 1382, Hanse merchants remained as operators of Bruges taverns, though to a diminished degree. Some had a much greater stake in the retail end than did Erembrecht: for example, Vrauwin Steppin operated three wine cellars in 1379. And others, like Diedric Riperband and Sander and Jacob Scimmelpenninck, had much longer careers as taverners, suggesting it was their sole livelihood.[133]

Yet Bruges hostellers remained throughout the period the most consistent operators of taverns in the city, serving wine, mead, and presumably beer to their guests and other customers. Why would this have been so uniformly true for so long? One answer is the natural extension of a hostel into a specialized drinking establishment, particularly if roomy subterranean space were easily available. In this case, however, the obvious answer is incomplete, for it fails to account for the inclusion of Hanseatic wine merchants and taverners as easy partners in a system of drinking establishments whose main customers were probably foreign merchants. It also begs the question of why hostellers, who were so occupied with investments in trading ventures, would have been interested in another retail operation. After all, a tavern was labor intensive and involved a good deal of regulation, as well as tax and fees levied on both the product and the right to sell it. I think part of the answer lies in a desire to influence merchant sociability. The hostel and the tavern were natural places for drinking, eating, and business. If the hosteller rented the room, provided the meals, offered warehousing and brokerage, and, last but certainly not least, operated a convenient wine cellar, the merchant stranger need never go off in search of services. Not

132 The quantity was 5 roeden 40½ zesters (about 9,400 liters) of "Rhine" wine with a value of £819 7s. parisis: ARA, Rekenkamer, RR 2017, membrane 5.

133 Steppin had taverns in the hostels "in 't Ghenthof," "in Werregaren," and "in den Ketele." In the same year the "osterlinc" Coene Molensteen had two taverns, one "in den Raemhout" the other "ten Crauwele": ARA, Rekenkamer, RR 1029, membrane 12 and Dierck *et al.*, *Hansekaufleute in Brügge*, 292–293. Riperband's origins were the Hanse city of Emmerich, but he was permanently resident in Bruges seemingly from the 1360s, as he appears in the accounts of de Marke and was among the creditors of Jacob Sconebergh; see Dierck *et al.*, *Hansekaufleute in Brügge*, pp. 332–334. In 1384 he was fined by the Bruges bailiff for using improper bottles ("omme dat hi wederzeide flasschen toe te stelne die vergiert zijn," ARA, Rekenkamer, 48652, f. 10r). The Scimmelpennincks operated from "ten Slotelle" from 1377 until 1390 (ARA, Rekenkamer, RR 1027, membrane 15 and ibid., 48651, f. 14r; 48653, f. 10r). They came from Zutphen. They may have imported wine as well, since there is evidence that they paid tolls for wine imports through Dordrecht in 1383–1384; see Dierck *et al.*, *Hansekaufleute in Brügge*, p. 368.

only was the hosteller enriched by his guests' money, but he profited more subtly as a broker of information.

THE BRUGES CREDIT/PAYMENT SYSTEM

The de Marke/Ruweel account books are not only outstandingly useful in understanding the operations of money changers, they are of equally great value as records of the business and financial activities of Bruges hostellers. With their help, we can view the daily functioning of a payment and credit system that formed another of the great business tools of Bruges. Taken individually, the accounts illustrate how central business partnership and investment were to the hostelling business. Taken together, the accounts reveal the enormous economic power of this group, as tens of thousands of pounds passed through their accounts with the money changers, sums far exceeding those controlled by any other business, even city or comital government. And it was a system offering advantages to both customer and host.

In the five-year period from 1366 to 1370 covered by the accounts, fifty-five hostellers routinely banked with one or both money changers. It is probable that this group included nearly all of the hostellers with significant involvement in the Bruges commercial market. Other hostellers without such involvement are mentioned in connection with their guests but have no account of their own.[134] There were differences as well among the fifty-five, as only twenty held accounts with both Ruweel and de Marke, while the majority banked with de Marke alone. This preference is understandable given the greater size and commercial importance of the de Marke exchange by this time. One suspects that most hostellers maintained accounts with all the four or five most important Bruges money changers. Probably each hosteller favored one particular money changer with the bulk of his or her business, as Edele de Ruddevorde, for example, clearly did with de Marke.[135]

The chief purpose of the accounts was to facilitate a book transfer payment system whose foundation was the clearing accounts the Bruges money changers kept with each other.[136] Though this fact was recognized long ago, the importance of hostellers in expanding the reach and usefulness of Bruges

[134] This is true primarily of the hostels I have called "unfree," such as the "lostel Laires," "lostel de Cambron," "lostel van Asberghe" and "lostel Lonis."

[135] Hostellers resembled most merchants in having closer financial links with one or two changers. As we have seen, Jacob Sconebergh owed Willem Ruweel and Pieter Potter considerable sums at the time of his death.

[136] For the nature of these accounts see chapter 4 and de Roover, *Money, Banking and Credit*, pp. 272–276.

banking has escaped notice. In effect, hostellers and money changers cooperated in building a network of linked accounts, which permitted book transfers among changers, hostellers, and their customers, and facilitated a number of other financial services as well. This close cooperation is attested by the fact that two money changers also kept or acquired a commercial hostel in the second half of the fourteenth century.[137] In effect, changers acted as the common denominator; since nearly all hostellers kept clearing accounts with them, though not with their competitors, a hosteller could transfer a sum via book transfer to another hosteller with a verbal order to his changer. This also opened the book transfer system to a hosteller's guests, who often held accounts with the hosteller, by using his host's account with a changer as a means to effect money transfers.

The utility of such a system for foreign merchants is apparent in any number of examples. In 1368, the hosteller Edele de Rudevorde secured an advance of £19 gro. from the Rapesaert exchange for a guest described only as "a man from Paris."[138] These kinds of advances, secured by the good name of the hosteller, alone might very well rescue a victim of robbery or some other misfortune suffered on the journey to Bruges. Such relationships with money changers also smoothed the exchange of coin as hostellers forwarded foreign coin and uncoined bullion to the changers and in return received credits in their ledgers, which could then be easily transferred at the stroke of a pen in payment for goods and services.[139] Guests could also obtain from the hostel the small-denomination "groots" and "mites" necessary to make small purchases in the local economy. Hostellers kept their cash repositories stocked with these through purchases from money changers.[140]

Links with money changers were only a logical extension of the already long-standing tradition of taking deposits from lodgers. Then as now, guests

[137] These were Jan and Griele de Witte, who had a clearing account with de Marke; Jan van Courtrai or Kortrijk, likewise an account holder and contemporary of de Marke; and the well-known merchant clan, the Adornes, who purchased an exchange around 1390: Marechal, *Bijdrage*, p. 49, 121.

[138] De Marke 3, f. 150r.

[139] Some of this transfer of coin is virtually seamless in the accounts. For example, the hosteller Demiselle Isoie deposited 70 nobles, 48 double moutons, 35 lions between 7 and 9 March 1369, as recorded in de Marke's second journal (f. 3r). But when the resulting balance was posted to her account in the general ledger, there is no mention of coins: De Marke 5, f. 14r.

[140] As noted in the previous chapter, Collard de Marke specialized in delivery of coin from Ghent to Bruges, so his accounts are full of such references. One example is (De Marke 2, f. 263r) the account of Raoul dou Coumin: "me doit pour Jehan Soriel sen hoste de Diepe pour francs, 28 fevrier [1367] £30 13s. 6d." And again the same hosteller the following July: "item me doit il par se femme et par Jehan Olleron que je li envoiay en se maison 17 juinguet [1367] 200 francs franc. a 3s." (ibid., 3, f. 279r). The trade in coins could be in both directions, as in an account of the hosteller Pieter van Ake (ibid., f. 79r) in which de Marke paid 33 nobles out to van Ake's varlet on 1 July, but collected 300 Brabant moutons and 100 heaumes on 5 August [1368].

could put money or objects for safe keeping in the hosteller's strong box.[141] Over time money on deposit became running accounts, conferring certain financial advantages on both the hosteller and the customer. Of course for the hosteller there was new capital to invest; for the customer there was ready money in Bruges to be spent or traded at his command. As Bruges increasingly became a financial and commercial center, deposits with hostellers and money changers in the city came to function as a means of exchange. Thus merchants could complete a sale by exchanging a letter of credit drawn on a Bruges hosteller or changer even if the transaction took place far from Flanders.[142] Even within Flanders, the account held by de Marke at the Ghent mint allowed letters of credit to be issued to the guests of Bruges hostellers.[143] Transfers to Antwerp were also easily arranged.[144]

Allowing book transfers through both hosteller and money changer accommodated the various regional practices and preferences of the resident foreign merchants as well. For whatever reasons it is clear that Hanse merchants, for example, held accounts in their own names with Bruges money changers far less often than did merchants from the Mediterranean.[145] This by no means hampered their use of the Bruges payment system; it simply meant they obtained access through their hostellers. Given the close intertwining of the commercial interests of Hanse merchants and many Bruges hostellers, there is considerable logic in this arrangement. It may also explain in part the tendency of hostellers to specialize in one foreign merchant community or another. Acting as a transfer agent and banker was just another link that made Bruges hostellers the business agents and partners of their guests.[146]

The flexibility allowed by cooperation also suited the sometimes complex web of business partnerships kept up by merchants in the Bruges market. One aspect of this complexity was the increasing role of the hosteller as

[141] The confiscation inventory of Pieter Huerel's hostel mentions a chest (*contoir*) in which he stored packets of spices, letters, and other things "done up in small parcels": ARA, Rekenkamer, 18244, f. 2r and Jacques Martens, "De beschuldigingen tegen Pieter Huerel opstandig Brugs Hostelier," in *Album Albert Schouteet* (Bruges, 1973), pp. 111–116.

[142] For numerous examples, see chapter 7 and Greve, "Jacob Sconebergh," 219 and n. 31.

[143] This was the case in December 1369 when Martin de Scans, guest of Raoul de Coumines, received "une lettre adreche a le monnoie" in the amount of £27 10s. groot (De Marke 5, f. 284v). This topic will be covered in the next chapter.

[144] See below chapter 6. [145] See below chapter 6.

[146] Thus the conclusion drawn by Raymond de Roover, that Hanse merchants' "backwardness" prevented them from opening bank accounts, must be revised. The crucial difference seems to have been the degree of familiarity with the Bruges market and the degree of business cooperation with Bruges hostellers. For a similar revision to the tradition that Hanse merchants were also reluctant to use credit, see Stuart Jenks, "War die Hanse kreditfeindlich?" *Vierteljahrschrift für Sozial- und Wirtschaftsgeschichte* 69 (1982), 305–338.

local representative and consignment agent for various foreign merchants. This role is often indicated in the de Marke accounts by payments made "at the command of X" or simply "for X" – in other words, decisions to buy and sell were executed in the absence of the merchant in whose name they were performed.[147] There is also abundant evidence that hostellers were partners in many of these business deals, as the accounts sometimes state their share of the particular payment.[148] Some of the permutations in business relationships as revealed in the accounts could reach levels of considerable complexity. For example, in 1368 a man referred to simply as "Rosendalle," acting as the agent for Melis Scepstien and Piere Teste, ordered a payment be made from Teste's account with the changer Jan van Marc, to the account of Demiselle de Witte kept with Collard de Marke.[149]

The firmest evidence of the interdependence of hostel and exchange bank in Bruges is revealed in table 6. The table shows the combined credit and debit balances of the nineteen most prominent hostellers who held accounts with Collard de Marke. Admittedly the record is incomplete, since we do not have the accounts of the other money changers (except in the abbreviated form in the de Marke ledgers). Still, the persistence of credit balances (with only one significant exception) maintained by the hostellers is abundantly clear.[150] In effect, not only did the Bruges money changers owe a large portion of their exchange business to the hostellers, they were also obliged to them for a share of their operating capital. In effect, the hostellers provided much of the liquidity that was the lifeblood of the Bruges market. There was a good deal of mutuality in the financial relationship, however, because there are numerous examples of changers covering short-term deficits in a hosteller's account.[151] Thus for hostellers,

[147] There are abundant examples in Murray and Greve, *Hostellers' Accounts*. De Roover also cites example of these operations, as in his discussion of Vicko van Geldersen (*Money, Banking and Credit*, pp. 277–278).

[148] To cite a few examples: (De Marke 1, f. 101v) the hosteller Jakop van den Acre share a payment with Jehan le Blanc, a Spaniard; (ibid., 2, f. 25v) Franke Aloet and his guest Wautier Demies share a payment; the examples could be multiplied many times. David Nicholas also found much evidence of partnership and other forms of cooperation between Bruges hostellers and foreign merchants; see "English Trade," 41.

[149] De Marke 3, f. 296v, dated 5 May 1368.

[150] The large deficit of the de Witte hostel is quite exceptional and rather puzzling. There is no evidence that the hostel went bankrupt – the fate of Jacob Sconebergh in 1368 and later of the de Rudevorde hostel as well. Perhaps the deficit indicates de Marke's capital investment in the de Witte business and trade investments.

[151] In the account of Edele de Rudevorde, for example, it was out of balance in the period of April, 1367 to April, 1368, before recovering in the next accounting year. Then again from December 1368 to May 1369 there was a shortfall of £200 gro. (or 6 percent), a deficit made good in the last half of 1369.

Table 6. *Hosteller Accounts with de Marke, 1366–1370*

Name	Credits	Debits	Balance
van de Acke	1443.0.2	1459.5.3	(16.5.1)
van Ake	2593.4.2	2049.16.4	543.7.10
Peter Aoskilt	1645.17.0	1551.18.8	94.18.4
Jehan Balke	832.16.2	813.0.10	49.15.4
van Bassevelde	1568.11.1	1236.18.1	331.13.0
Jehan Bonin	1619.0.0	1420.19.9	198.0.3
van Collekierke	4024.4.8	3213.6.9	810.17.11
de Coumines	15,557.8.1	12,927.11.7	2,629.16.6
Jakop Crakebeen	1657.17.9	1531.4.9	126.13.0
Lieven Everbout	646.16.6	614.12.0	32.3.8
Giles Honin	2513.2.0	2310.7.8	202.14.4
van der Leke	714.12.2	694.5.11	20.6.3
Jakop Metten Eye	1615.5.5	1332.18.7	282.6.10
Ernout Poultus	1841.2.4	1696.12.0	144.10.4
de Ram	2962.4.6	3105.9.5	(143.4.9)
de Rudervorde	18,924.18.7	18,601.17.0	323.1.7
Jehan Utebrouke	1468.2.0	1437.12.6	30.9.6
Gilles Valensine	6,212.1.1	5,639.4.3	572.16.10
de Witte	9,477.11.9	10,532.3.7	(1,054.11.10)

as well as drapers, as we shall see in a later chapter, money changers worked to bridge periods of interrupted or decreased cash flow. With all its advantages, the Bruges credit/payment network is a fitting capstone to a commercial system created to further trade and the central position of Bruges hostellers in it. Amidst much self serving, hostellers offered their guests and clients the advantage of credit, book transfer, and currency exchange, all seamlessly connected via the money changers.

CONCLUSION

It is not at all far-fetched to see in the hosteller-led commercial system of fourteenth-century Bruges the embryo of future "Bourses" in Antwerp and Amsterdam. There was a group of more or less permanently resident merchants, places of accustomed meeting, a commercial infrastructure consisting of lodging, warehousing, credit/payment services, and an already developed tradition of joint business enterprise reaching across national and cultural boundaries. Commodity and currency prices were freely available, though we do not know precisely how they were noted.

Thus the needs of exchange were met in every way but one – the provision of a specialized building, which through a process of transference became known as the "Bourse." In light of this chapter, then, the construction of the "New" Antwerp Bourse in 1531 marked the end of an era in which the hosteller so often presided over the meetings of businessmen.[152] Thereafter it became first the city, then the state government that provided the facilities where merchants met for the purpose of doing business. Yet the name has remained that of a Bruges family, affixed to an old house, perched along a city square.

[152] Hunt and Murray, *History of Business*, pp. 213–215.

CHAPTER 6

Bruges as node and network

> . . . Cioe Bruggia e Guanto e Ipro e Lille e Doagio, ma parlereno il piu di Bruggia pero ch'ella a quella terra ove piu stanno i risedenti mercatanti a fare la mercatantia e cambi in Fiandra.
>
> Francesco Pegolotti, c. 1340

> . . . and lete me understande wat ready mony I have at Brygys.
>
> Richard Cely, senior, 1478[1]

All cities are tangles of human networks. This observation is not new, given that for quite some time, historians of the late-medieval and early modern economy have embraced the concept of urban networks covering sometimes vast areas of geographic space in order to model economic change. Works like those of Braudel and his followers have not only caused historians to think in terms of systems and their integration, but also brought both theoretical refinement – one thinks of Immanuel Wallerstein's "Core and Periphery" – and the introduction of network thinking on the more "micro" level, for example the level and dynamics of urbanization in the Low Countries and Northern Italy. This post-war migration to new conceptual models, often borrowed from the social sciences, has played a great role in the expansion of economic history as a discipline, but has brought with it several problems as well. Among these is a tendency to trust too much in inflexible models, or quantification, turning a blind eye to the historical forces of disequilibrium and sudden change so characteristic of the fourteenth century.[2]

[1] Francesco Pegolotti, *La pratica della mercatura*, ed. Allen Evans (Cambridge, Mass., 1936), p. 236; Hanham, *The Celys*, p. 217; Alison Hanham (ed.), *The Cely Letters, 1472–1488* (London and New York: Oxford University Press, 1975), p. 26, #27.

[2] Some of these issues are discussed in Carlo Cipolla, *Between Two Cultures: An Introduction to Economic History* (New York, 1991), pp. 3–13. An interesting application of network theory to Flemish urbanization is in Stabel, *Dwarfs among Giants*, pp. 237–241. For a discussion of merchant diasporas and functions of cities, see Philip D. Curtin, *Cross Cultural Trade in World History* (Cambridge, 1984), pp. 1–11.

It is a commonplace to view Bruges as a "network" based system, but too often this has been viewed as a simple hierarchy or "meeting" place of different geographical areas or trading commodities.[3] What we have lost sight of is the behavior of the Bruges merchants themselves, and by this I mean all those merchants who visited or resided in the city to carry on trade. The complexity of their behavior simply cannot be approximated by static or purely hierarchical models (Bruges as "gateway"), for they, like nodes, were capable of complex and varied trading behavior. Moreover, fourteenth-century merchants were confronted with a swiftly changing and frequently hostile business environment. War was the most significant disrupter, but one should not forget plague, famine, trade embargoes, and boycotts. I argue that in response to these and other threats merchants, however unknowingly and haltingly, came together as a trading community within the walls of Bruges in ways very much like an artificial neural network. They did so to profit from the speed and flexibility such an arrangement afforded them – in the survivability, swiftness of information exchange, and sheer possibilities of dealing offered by the network.

Past historians attributed the abandonment of the Champagne fairs in favor of year-round trade at a fixed location to improvement in business techniques, allowing the rise of the "sedentary merchant."[4] This certainly overstates the importance of Italian business, for the majority of northern businessmen and significant numbers of those from the south must have traveled regularly to the important commercial cities of Europe.[5] Moreover, there is no evidence that the Champagne fairs suffered in direct proportion to Bruges's gains. Certainly the Champagne fairs were affected by the greater insecurity of land transport across France due to the Hundred Years' War

[3] This observation refers to the well-known debate between J. A. van Houtte and Wilfried Brulez about the nature of the Bruges market in the fourteenth century. Van Houtte argued that Bruges was essentially a national market for distributing Flemish products and purchasing articles for local consumption from foreign merchants, while the Antwerp market of the fifteenth century was more truly "international." Brulez disagreed, pointing out the valuable services the brokers and changers of Bruges provided the foreign merchant community, a view seconded by David Nicholas in his study of English trade at Bruges. My view is that an analysis of the network function of Bruges in the fourteenth century reveals more similarities than differences between the Bruges and Antwerp markets. See J. A. van Houtte, "Bruges et Anvers, marchés nationaux ou internationaux du XIVe au XVIe siècle?" *Revue du Nord* 34 (1952), 89–108, and "The rise and decline of the market of Bruges," *Economic History Review* 2nd series, 19 (1966), 29–47, esp. 36–37; Wilfred Brulez, "Brugge en Antwerpen in de 15e en 16e eeuw: een tegenstelling?" *Tijdschrift voor Geschiedenis* 83 (1970), 15–37, translated in a slightly shortened form in *Acta Historiae Neerlandicae* 6 (1973), 1–26; Nicholas, "English Trade," 45.

[4] De Roover, *Money, Banking and Credit*, pp. 11–13.

[5] Even such complex firms as the Peruzzi often required travel from its partners and factors. See E. S. Hunt, *The Medieval Super-Companies: A Study of the Peruzzi Company of Florence* (New York, 1994), pp. 206–211.

as well as the shift to waterborne transport to connect North and South. Yet dwelling on the negative dynamics of decline has caused historians to overlook the positive attributes of a fixed trading location like Bruges: it allowed far greater possibilities for finance and transport, offered more security, and was relatively freer from the exactions and interference of the French monarch. In short, a merchant community drawn from all corners of Europe, permanently resident in the same city, supported by trading and financial institutions, resulted in far greater trading possibilities, just as a hundred networked computers are far more powerful than a hundred isolated ones.[6] Yet like a computer network, Bruges as a network city derived its power in proportion to its use by individual merchants and merchant communities. In other words, Bruges's European importance owed much to the sum of the networks it incorporated.

As we have already seen, crucial to Bruges's importance was the fact pointed to by Francesco Pegolotti: that among the five great "Flemish" cities, Bruges stood out as the residence and base of operations for foreign merchants.[7] What forms did the presence of foreign merchants take in fourteenth-century Bruges, and how did they contribute to the city's emergence as a great outpost of trade? There is no easy answer to this question, for no doubt the ways merchants came to the city ran the gamut from brief visits to long residence and even outright settlement. When groups of merchants gathered to decide important matters, as the English did in 1344, they were described as either "being in" or "frequenting" Bruges.[8] A slightly earlier document speaks of all English merchants "tunc moram trahentes in villa de Bruges," a phrase implying residence.[9] The seal of the nation of Catalonia/Aragon of 1386 also speaks of a "Universitas mercatorum Catalanorum Brugis comorantium."[10] Thus it seems that both frequency and length of stay marked out those merchants who carried political weight in their community. Even so, frequent visits or long residence are very imprecise indications of a merchant's "presence" in a city. To return to the English for a moment, the York merchant John Goldbeter frequented Bruges from as early as 1337 until sometime after 1370. He had an adventurous career

6 Ph. Wolff, *Automne du Moyen Age ou Printemps des Temps Nouveaux? L'économie européenne aux XIVe et XVe siècles* (Paris, 1986), p. 156.

7 Bruges was also alone among the five in not being primarily a cloth production center. One should note that at the time Pegolotti wrote Douai and Lille were no longer legally part of Flanders due to their annexation by the French crown.

8 Joseph Marechal, "De kapel van de Engelsen te Brugge, 1344–1563," in *Europese aanwezigheid*, p. 46.

9 H. S. Lucas, "Diplomatic Relations between England and Flanders from 1329 to 1336," *Speculum* 11 (1936), 59–87, 79: "mercatores diversarum parcium Anglie in villa de Bruges tunc moram trahentes . . ."

10 Marechal, "La colonie espagnole de Bruges du XIVe au XVIe siècle," in *Europese aanwezigheid*, p. 113.

as a wool merchant, financier of Edward III's continental adventurers, and high-level political schemer.[11]

No doubt Goldbeter was the exception, and most foreign merchants in Bruges were short-term visitors, who, like Chaucer's merchant, came to "by[eth] and creaunc[eth]."[12] As we saw in the last chapter, while in the city they resided in a hostel, taking advantage of the business contacts and services offered there. Thus most individual merchants were in a sense "network takers" and not "network makers," for their presence lacked the permanence necessary to contribute much to the infrastructure and mechanisms of trade. What contributed most to the Bruges network were the institutions that organized merchants and conditioned their trading and social contacts. Among these were the hostels, money changers, taverns, mendicant houses, and to a lesser extent parish churches and charitable institutions. These in effect granted presence in Bruges to those merchants who were in fact absent from the city most of the time. They also created or enabled credit and business relationships extending far beyond the walls of Bruges. And it was the number and complexity of these institutions and their contacts that made Bruges the first "network" city in European economic history.

This presents us with a chicken and egg problem: which came first, the foreign merchants or the institutions of permanence? Of course the merchants did, and we know that they were numerous throughout the thirteenth century. But neural network theory posits that the importance and power of a network (and by extension the value of Bruges as a trading center) increases as the square of its members. Hence what we need to examine is the numbers, organization and geographical location of foreign merchant communities in the city.

THE MAKING OF A MERCHANT COMMUNITY

As shown in chapter 3, we have only a fragmentary knowledge of the number of foreign merchants present in Bruges at any given time. There was a natural ebb and flow of merchants throughout the year, with numbers reaching a high tide during the Bruges fair in May. Again, the figures derived from the de Marke accounts from the 1360s are persuasive in showing the size and diversity of the foreign merchant population of the city. Thus in terms of network theory, Bruges combined geographic breadth with density of numbers in a way achieved nowhere else in the European north.

[11] For more on Goldbeter, see chapter 7.

[12] *The Riverside Chaucer*, p. 206.

In the absence of precise statistics, there are indirect measures of the growth of Bruges's foreign merchant communities, beginning with the history of merchant privileges. These were charters granted by the count of Flanders, which spelled out the economic and political rights the corporation or any member of a specific merchant community could claim across Flanders.[13] Though county wide, such privileges were based on conditions in Bruges owing to its importance for merchants. Logically, initial grants of trade privileges, as well as renegotiation and regranting of new privileges, signal change and growth in the kinds and volume of trade between two areas. Thus a brief review of the merchant treaties enjoyed by the prominent foreign communities of Bruges can serve as a contour map of development.

Undoubtedly the most frequently contentious merchant community in Bruges came from the member cities of the German Hanse. In part this was a determined strategy of the whole urban confederation, which always portrayed itself as an embattled advocate for trade.[14] In reality the Hanse leadership seized upon any means to gain or extort additional privileges for its members, particularly in the few places like Bruges that became seats of the confederation's trade organization. Given this obduracy in negotiation and instability within the confederation itself, the history of the German Hanse in Flanders is full of negotiation, conflict, embargo, and new privileges. The first charter of privileges dates from 1252–1253, concluding a period of desultory use of the Bruges market on the part of Germans other than Cologne merchants. It was foundational in another sense, since it did not contain permission to construct an exclusive Hanse enclave in one of the Zwin ports. This broke with Hanse practice elsewhere (London, Novgorod, Bergen, Venice), where the confederation built a trading compound on land granted by the sovereign.[15] Thus Hanse merchants always lived among and not apart from the people and other resident merchants of Bruges. This was no guarantee of amity, however, as disputes caused the Hanse community to leave Bruges for nearby Aardenburg in 1281, leading to a grant of new privileges in 1282. This pattern was repeated in 1307–1309. The most serious disruption in the relations of Bruges and the German Hanse occurred in 1358–1360, during which the Hanse not only left Bruges and Flanders for nearby Dordrecht, but also embargoed the entire county of Flanders with

[13] Typically these included justiciability of the merchant, individual and corporate responsibility for debts, legal protection of person and property, taxes, weights and measures, and their determination.

[14] Hunt and Murray, *History of Business*, pp. 164–166.

[15] Paravicini, "Brugge en Duitsland," pp. 99–127; Philippe Dollinger, *The German Hanse* (Stanford, 1970).

an effectiveness gained from the reorganization of the confederation in 1347.[16]

The revised and much expanded privilege of 1360 symbolizes the greater size and complexity of the trading colony and trade in Bruges and throughout Flanders. Of particular note were the guarantees granted Hanse merchants in their financial relationships with Bruges hostellers and money changers. These gave the Hanse the greatest trading privileges they were ever to enjoy, and made them the most "privileged" merchants in Bruges bar none. A practical result of these protections was the right of Hanse merchants to full repayment, at city expense if necessary, of any losses suffered by members in the failure of a hostel or money exchange.[17] The more than century-long history of Hanse–Flanders trade privileges describes a steady increase in the numbers of merchants and the complexity of trading and financial relationships among members of both communities. Certainly by 1350, Hanseatic trade and traders were of the very greatest importance for Bruges. Ironically perhaps, all this occurred before the Hanse possessed its own meeting house, which was only built as a means to halt the ebbing away of Hanse trade after 1450.[18]

English merchants had an even older, though less tempestuous, trading history with Bruges by the fourteenth century. Trade between Bruges and England existed already by the time of the oldest London toll records of 991–1002. Two centuries of trade relations resulted in the first trade agreement between Bruges and England in 1216; its text has not survived. By the 1230s, Bruges had surpassed Ghent and Ypres as the most important English trading partner.[19] In the fourteenth century, Bruges became for two short periods the staple, or monopoly, of English wool exports to the continent.[20] After the departure of the staple in 1359, a new privilege was drawn up that determined both the internal organization of the English colony in Bruges and its relationship with Bruges officials. Conflicts between the two sides

[16] Paravicini, "Brugge en Duitsland," pp. 100–103; Van Houtte, *Geschiedenis*, pp. 168–169.

[17] ". . . ende waer dat eenich coopman scade ontfinghe van den hostelier, daer voor zal de stede ghehouden ziin daer de coopman leicht." This inclusion of city financial responsibility for losses suffered at the hands of hostellers marks an expansion of the 1309 privilege, which only guaranteed accounts with money changers. The 1360 privilege was also extended to all of Flanders as it was issued by Count Louis of Male. The text of the privilege is Gilliodts-van Severen, *Inventaire*, vol. II, #532, p. 51.

[18] The rather complex history of various "Hanse houses" in Bruges is presented by Luc Devligher, "Het Oosterlingenhuis te Brugge," *Hansekaufleute in Brügge, Teil 4, Beiträge*, pp. 15–17. What became known as the "Hanse house" was built around 1478 on a square that was thereafter known as the "Easterling" square (Oosterlingenplein), not far from the Bourse square in a neighborhood of merchant hostels.

[19] Van Houtte, *Geschiedenis*, pp. 89–90.

[20] For the Bruges wool staple, see chapter 7.

were not uncommon, however, particularly after the outbreak of hostilities between England and France in 1338. These often brought pirate attacks, confiscations, and embargoes in their wake.[21]

Despite the relative rarity of Anglo-Flemish commercial treaties, English merchants left many traces on the face of the city. One of these was the "English weigh house," which was a special facility granted to English merchants for the purpose of weighing their trade goods. This was a special mark of favor for the English, given that disputes about the accuracy and honesty of weights and measures were common.[22] While the two scales that made up the weigh house's complement were installed in the cellar, a room on the first floor was reserved for meetings of the English merchants.[23] There was also the "English street," which owed its name to the weigh house and is first recorded in 1330.[24] The nearby "English square" and the "English quay," both located just east of the Burg, the Crane square, and the Grote Markt, completed the anglicized parts of the city. Similarly, Scottish merchants and settlers left their marks on the Bruges cityscape in the same period as the English. There was the "Scottish dike," a few hundred yards east of the "English street," and the connecting streets and squares – Boomgaardstraat, Verwersdijk, Spiegelrei, and Sint Jansplaats – were favored by Scottish and Irish merchants.[25] The Scots seem also to have favored a handful of hostels as lodging places.[26]

[21] For a general history of the period, in which English–Flemish relations played an important part, see Sumption, *Trial by Battle*, pp. 146–147, as well as the older work of Quicke, *Les Pays-Bas à la veille de la periode bourguignonne*, pp. 139–174, and Nicholas, *Medieval Flanders*, pp. 285–305.

[22] First mention of the house dates from 1315; it was rebuilt in 1331; see Marechal, "Duizend Jaar Britse Aanwezigheid te Brugge" in *Europese aanwezigheid*, p. 17.

[23] The "weigh house" was actually a cluster of buildings that the city leased out. A charter of 1376 describes the obligations of the lessee: OCMW, Dis St. Gillis, #64, records a gift by Jan Francke and his wife Lisebette of an eighth part and a sixteenth part of "den huusinghen die men heet tInghelsche weghe huus staende in de niewe Inghelsche strate . . . Behouden dies dat Jan Francke, Lisebette zijn wyf vors . . . sculdich zijn tvorseide weghe huus dats te wetene den kelnare van den vors. huus hopen te houdene ende te leverne Inghelscher cooplieder goed in te weghene ghelike dat men tote den daghe van heiden der inghweghen heift, ende ene stede, iof camere binden zelven huusinghen soffisant te hebbene omme den inghelschen cooplieden hare court der in te hebbene ende te houdene tallen tiden alst te doene zal wesen." This was done by the Bruges aldermen on the last day of February 1376. Note also that a Hanse merchant, Heinric van Herenst or Herresten, donated rents drawn on the English weigh house ("Inghelsche weichuse") to the poor tables of St. Jacob's, Sint Gillis's and Sint Salvator's churches: RAB, fonds St. Jacobskerk, Oud archief, 646, f. 2r–v and OCMW, fonds Dis St.-Gillis, 61; OCMW, Dis St. Salvators, 126, f. 124r–124v. I owe this reference to the kindness of Dr. Michael Galvin.

[24] G. Dumon, *De oude straatnamen van Brugge. Een handleiding* (Bruges, 1997), p. 8 #56.

[25] Marechal, "Duizen jaar Britse aanwezigheid te Brugge," in *Europese aaanwezigheid*, p. 15. The Sint-Maartensplein was also known in the late fourteenth century as the "Scottish" square: see Dumon, *Oude straatnamen*, p. 36 #272. In Bruges the term "Scottish" was used to describe natives of both Scotland and Ireland.

[26] In the 1360s they favored those of Jehan Scot, and the hostel Laires.

The surprising number of Spanish and Portuguese merchants who frequented Bruges in the 1360s, as recorded in the de Marke account books, attests to a long history of trade between Iberia and Flanders. The first commercial privileges granted the "nations" of Spain were granted in a charter of August 1280 and closely paralleled those of the German Hanse. However, the fact that a great number of Iberian visitors of the 1360s were shipmasters belonging to organized fleets grouped according to "nations," whose order was maintained by the fleet commander, indicates that more of them were transients. Both the fleet of the kingdom of Castile (from 1343) and that of Aragon (from 1389) visited Sluis and conducted business in Bruges.[27] Permanent "consulates" began in 1330, when the "nation" of Aragon-Catalonia was organized. That of the "Castilians" followed only in the fifteenth century and incorporated at first all merchants who were subjects of the king of Castile.[28] Between 1357 and 1396 the consulate of Aragon-Catalonia possessed a house on the Bourse square.[29]

Italian merchants organized themselves differently from any of the other merchant colonies, because of the prominence of their home cities as makers of identity. By the fourteenth century there were five organized Italian merchant colonies representing Lucca, Genoa, Florence, Milan, and Venice.[30] Trading privileges accorded to these different groups were remarkably similar by the end of the fourteenth century, though the Venetians were the most zealous in the pursuit of privileges at first.[31] In two trade agreements of 1322 and 1332, Venetian merchants obtained wide-ranging privileges guaranteeing security of person and property and allowing their consul power over the adjudication of disputes and custody of property of deceased members.[32] The charter granted to the Genoese in December 1395 proves that the other Italian merchant colonies had gradually achieved the same privileges as the Venetians, with certain modifications and additions according to need. The Genoese colony, for example, insisted upon detailed protection from interference in the conduct and discipline of its fleet while at anchor in the Zwin.[33] Yet only the merchant community of Lucca has left more

27 Marechal, "Colonie espagnole," in *Europese aanwezigheid*, p. 97.

28 Marechal (*Europese aanwezigheid*, pp. 101–103) believed that all those called "Spaniard" in Bruges documents were really from Castile, which could include those from Biscay, Navarre and Andalusia. These split into the "nations" of Castille and Biscay after 1455.

29 Marechal, *Europese aanwezigheid*, pp. 114–115; Spanish merchants favored the hostel of Jacob van de Buerse in the first part of the fifteenth century and during the 1360s they typically lodged with Jakop van den Acre, Pieter and Trude van Ake, or Clais Aoskilt.

30 De Roover, *Money, Banking and Credit*, p. 13; Marechal, "De Metropool van het Westen," in *Europese aanwezigheid*, p. 216.

31 De Roover, *Money, Banking and Credit*, p. 15.

32 Ibid., p. 16.

33 Ibid., pp. 14–15.

than a fragmentary record of its presence in Bruges. Organized rather late – in 1369 – the "Community of Lucchese Residing in Bruges" had a consul and three-man ruling council whose purpose was to encourage the cult of the *Volto Santo*, maintain their chapel dedicated to it, and ensure "peace, concord, and union" among their members.[34] An undeclared objective was of course to represent the interests of the community in altercations or negotiations with local officials.

The three dominant Italian colonies also left architectural landmarks behind, albeit late in their histories in Bruges. The location of these *Loges* closely reflected their traditional preferences for lodging near the commercial heart of the city. The Venetian *Loge* was in operating on the Bourse square by 1397. The Genoese *Loge*, also on the Bourse, followed two years later, but that of the Florentines was not in place on the Bourse until 1420 and was rebuilt a decade later.[35] The smaller Lucca merchant colony also had a house just off the Bourse square purchased from a Lucca merchant in 1394.[36] This replaced an earlier *Loge*, mentioned in 1377, whose location is not known. Thus in varying tempos all the important Italian merchant communities of Bruges evolved into self-governing, privileged bodies whose center of communal and presumably individual activity lay in the heart of commercial Bruges.

The lack of trading privileges or *Loges* did not indicate a complete absence of merchants from other areas of Europe, however. We have seen, for example, that merchants from France frequently settled in the city, most often as a result of long-term trading visits there. Other merchants, such as the Irish, Pisans, and Piacenzans, were subsumed into other nations. Still others, like the Danes and Poles, certainly came to Bruges, yet their presence left few traces.[37] The Bruges *Livre des mestiers* contains a hypothetical list of foreign merchants, including those from Hainault, Friesland, Normandy, Zeeland, and Holland.[38] This lack underlines the differences between the greater and lesser merchant colonies: the degree of organization and corporatism varied in direct proportion to the number of more or less permanently resident merchants and the age of the colony.

[34] De Roover, "La communauté des marchands lucquois," 42 and n. 64. The inscription on the community's seal was "Sigillum Lucensium Communitatis Brugis Commorantium"; see also Eugenio Luzzarreschi (ed.), *Libro della communità dei mercanti lucchesi in Bruges* (Milan, 1949).

[35] Ryckaert, *Stedenatlas*, p. 106.

[36] De Roover, "La communauté des Lucquois," 85; Ryckaert, *Stedenatlas*, p. 106.

[37] Henryk Samsonowicz, "Die wirtschaflichen und politischen Beziehungen zwischen Flandern, Polen und Preußen," in *Hansekaufleute in Brügge*, pp. 309–318.

[38] Gessler, *Brugsche Livre des mestiers*, vol. II, p. 39, where Olivier the "ostelier" lists the guests he may and may not have.

Religious foundations by foreign merchant communities provide a last important measure of their degree of development. As these nations grew in coherence they most often sponsored an altar or chapel in a local church or monastery as the site of joint worship and other facilities as well. The custom of corporate worship, often coupled to veneration of a saint of particular individual significance, was an important catalyst for medieval groups of all sorts. And significantly in the case of Bruges, places of worship could also serve as meeting places for foreign merchants.

Of all the foreign colonies, the merchants of the German Hanse developed the closest relations with Bruges religious institutions, particularly with the Carmelites. They were perhaps the first to display the marked preference for the mendicants that became characteristic of most merchant colonies. This tendency was either caused by, or itself reinforced, the decision taken by the leaders of each order to make their Bruges monasteries the de facto centers of their respective provinces, where both general and provincial chapters were held. Bruges also became the site of *studia generalia* for the Franciscans, Carmelites, and Augustinians, thus drawing students from all provinces of the orders.[39] This monastic cosmopolitanism may have more easily attracted foreign merchants. In any event the Hanse "nation" used the Carmelite refectory for meetings, especially the annual festivities involving the election of the consul, his installation at an elaborate banquet, and a sung Mass of celebration.[40] Tradition even attributed to the Hanse a hand in the foundation of the order in Bruges.[41] The nation's archives were also kept in the monastery, as were the master weights used to calibrate the official scale used by Hanse merchants.[42] Other Bruges mendicants enjoyed similar, if not quite so extensive, relations with the Hansards. With the Augustinians, Hanse merchants had negotiated burial space for their members in the monastic church.[43] The Bruges Franciscans

39 Walter Simons attributes the large size and signficance of the Bruges mendicant houses *vis-à-vis* any other foundation in Flanders to a conscious choice on the part of religious leaders; see his *Stad en apostolaat*, p. 154.

40 Herman Leloux, "Kirche und Caritas im Leben der Genossenschaft des Deutschen Kaufmanns zu Brügge," *Hansische Geschichtsblätter* 91 (1973), 34–45, esp. 36–37. The Hanse merchants possessed no private chapel in the church, but were allowed use of the main altar for special services. They apparently also possessed burial rights in the church; see Marechal, *Europese aanwezigheid*, p. 67; Asmussen, *Lübecker Flandernfahrer*, p. 244; and most recently Rössner, *Hansische Memoria*, pp. 203–219.

41 B. Vermaseren, "De Carmel van Brugge en de buitenlandse kooplieden," *Carmel* 3 (1950), 19–31, esp. 24, mentioning the work of Rudolph Häpke, "Der deutsche Kaufmann in den Niederlanden," *Pfingsblätter des hansischen Geschichtsvereins* 7 (1911), 35, who did not cite a source; for the entire bibliography see Asmussen, *Lübecker Flandernfahrer*, p. 76, n. 230.

42 Leloux, "Kirche und Caritas," 36.

43 Gilliodts-van Severen, *Cartulaire de l'ancienne estaple*, vol. II, p. 95; Leloux, "Kirche und Caritas," 39.

and Dominicans also enjoyed annual gifts from the Hanse. Remarkably enough, even the parish churches of Bruges shared in the German Hanse's largesse. At least three of them owed stained glass windows to Hanseatic generosity, and last but not least there were also contributions for relief of the parish poor made by both the society and individual Hanse merchants.[44] Through these gifts and relationships, the German Hanse colony in Bruges both defined itself and established ties with the broader Bruges community.

The English merchant community also enjoyed a special relationship with the Bruges Carmelites. Already in 1334 the English nation met in their refectory; and in 1344 a chapel dedicated to Thomas Becket was constructed alongside the Carmelite church to house a brotherhood dedicated to that saint and to offer burial places for twelve of its members.[45] The Scots followed the English example in 1366 with a gift of land to the Carmelites for the construction of a chapel dedicated to St. Ninian. They, too, gained burial rights in the chapel, whose construction commenced in 1369.[46] There is also evidence that the merchant community of Catalonia/Aragon had use of a chapel in the Carmelite church, probably from the mid-to-late fourteenth century.[47] The Bruges Augustinian church held the chapel of the Lucchese nation from the 1360s as well as that of the Venetians and Genoese.[48] The Florentine merchant community established an altar dedicated to St. Francis in the Franciscan church shortly after 1400.[49] They were joined there by the Biscayans and Castilians after 1414.[50]

Last but not least among those Bruges institutions that served as organizing centers for foreign merchants were the hostels. That certain hostels specialized in hosting merchants from a particular city or region has long been known, but the importance of this to the organization of the merchant communities themselves has been missed. As we saw in a previous chapter, hostels served as places of legal record, where foreign merchants often sealed

[44] These were the "Armendissen," constituting a lay-administered fund to support the parish's "worthy" poor; see Galvin, *The Poor Tables of Bruges*, who notes (p. 149) the important gifts made to Bruges poor tables by the Hanse merchants Heinric van Herresten or Herenst, Tideman Rebbe, and Conraed Zuderman. Asmussen (*Die Lübecker Flandernfahrer*) mentions gifts of Johan Oldevere to the Carmelites, Franciscans, Augustinians, and Dominicans in 1361 and endowments given to the poor tables of Onze-Lieve-Vrouw and St. Salvator's church by Boldewin van der Brugghe. Jacob Plescow also made important gifts to Bruges parish churches in his testament of 1361–62.

[45] Marechal, "De kapel van de Engelsen," in *Europese aanwezigheid*, pp. 41–50. The leading forces in the foundation of the chapel were London merchants. For the meeting of English merchants in the Carmelite refectory during trade negotiations in Bruges, see Lucas, "Diplomatic Relations between England and Flanders," 67.

[46] Marechal, *Europese aanwezigheid*, p. 51.

[47] Leloux, "Kirche und Caritas," 28.

[48] De Roover, "La communauté des marchands lucquois," 50–51.

[49] Simons, *Stad en apostolaat*, p. 228

[50] Marechal, *Europese aanwezigheid*, pp. 94–95.

contracts with each other while in or outside of Bruges. There is also evidence that the foreign community itself chose a particular Bruges hosteller to serve it exclusively.[51] Whether such conscious awarding of monopoly is true of other groups is unknown. The distribution of hostellers specializing in one merchant group or another suggests that some combination of selection and the law of supply and demand is at work. For example, of the fifty-five hostellers holding an account with Collard de Marke, seven hosted Spaniards, four French, thirteen Hansards, one South Germans, two Portuguese, three English, five Scots and one Hainauters.[52] These numbers closely mirror the proportion of foreign merchants collected from the accounts, though significantly no hostel catering for Italian merchants is mentioned.[53] The fact that two or three generations of a single hostelling family could serve the same merchant nation is also suggestive of long-term stability.[54]

The community building and definition created by the cooperative work of foreign and native merchants in Bruges must have had its effects on those involved. We have traced the creation of an influential class of Brugeois, those operating hostels or exchanges, or working as brokers.[55] But were there effects among the foreigners themselves? In other words, did travel to and residence in Bruges produce distinct communities among foreign merchants? The answer seems to have varied from group to group. For Italian merchants, time in Bruges was often a stage in their apprenticeship as businessmen; only a few regarded the city as any more than a way station in a corporate career leading back to Venice, Florence, or Genoa.[56] For French merchants, residence with one hosteller or another probably

51 De Roover, "La communauté des marchands lucquois," 60: Claes Barbagialla, or Barbezaen to use his Flemish name. Typically it involved the son of an immigrant to Bruges, who had married a native woman establishing a family of brokers/hostellers, in this case with a natural affinity for Lucca.

52 SAB, Koopmansboeken, De Marke; see Murray and Greve, *Hosteller Accounts*, for edition.

53 Italians seem to have rented or purchased their residences in Bruges rather than rent a room in a hostel. De Roover attributed this to the fact that Italians were apt to be long-term residents, given the nature of their business and distance from home, while those of other nations came and went more frequently. This may also explain the awarding of the monopoly to the Flemish/Lucchese Barbazaen, who provided services other than lodging to the Lucchese community. The Adornes must have served in a similar role for the Genoese in the last quarter of the fourteenth century: see Noël Geirnaert, *Archief van de familie Adornes en de Jeruzalemstichting te Brugge*, 2 vols. (Bruges, 1987–1989), vol. 1, pp. 5–12; Ryckaert and Vandewalle, *Brugge*, pp. 100–101.

54 One examples is the van der Beurse family, who were a particular favorite of Hanse merchants over several generations (Marechal, *Geschiedenis van de Brugse Beurs*, p. 24). The Scuetelare family catered for the English for generations: see Prevenier, "Les perturbations," pp. 482–484.

55 See chapter 3.

56 For the education of Italian merchants, see Dahl, *Trade, Trust and Networks*, pp. 67–76 and Richard K. Marshall, *The Local Merchants of Prato: Small Entrepreneurs in the Late Medieval Economy* (Baltimore, 1999), especially chapter 4.

conferred a sense of identity. The hosteller Jakop Crakebeen, for example, clearly specialized in merchants from La Rochelle and Gascony, while Raoul de Coumines hosted Parisians and northerners.[57] With so many Portuguese and Spanish visitors being mariners as well as merchants, Bruges was probably just a port of call. But with the Hanse city of Lübeck, the fact of belonging to the group of merchants known as "Flandernfahrer" (literally "voyagers to Flanders") conferred a virtual civic identity.

Parallel to the formation of the Hanse Kontor in Bruges was the rise to dominance of Lübeck among the leading cities of the German Hanse.[58] So thoroughly dependent on trade did Lübeck become in the course of the thirteenth century that groups of merchants became identified with the area of their chief trading activity. Thus there were groups of "Stockholmfahrer" and "Bergenfahrer" as well as those who journeyed to Flanders. The Flanders merchants distinguished themselves in several ways from the others. First was the fact that a higher percentage of them belonged to the urban elite of Lübeck.[59] Second, despite the presence of members of the merchant elite, most *Flandernfahrer* were not natives of Lübeck but chose to settle there, often after a successful trading career. This reinforces the image of Hanse merchants as a footloose group whose long residences in various cities often resulted in resettlement.[60] As a city of immigrants – the original settlers came from over 220 different places – Lübeck continued both to attract and send out merchant settlers throughout the fourteenth century.[61] In this "immigrant swarm" of a population, Lübeck much resembled Bruges. The last significant fact to emerge from recent research is the absolute preponderance of Bruges as destination and residence of *Flandernfahrer*. Of the 200 Flanders merchants identified from the half century from 1358 to 1408, 163 resided in Bruges, and another twenty resided in one of the Zwin outports.[62] Thus Bruges as destination and residence for many of Lübeck's leading citizens had a profound influence upon this leading Hanse city.

We can draw several conclusions from the evidence presented thus far: the existence of merchant corporations in Bruges depended on both numbers of merchants in general and the length or permanence of their residence. Thus the series of privileges and foundations from 1330 to 1390 and the

57 Murray and Greve, *Hosteller Accounts*.

58 Asmussen, *Lübecker Flandernfahrer*, p. 34

59 Ibid., pp. 84–87. Asmussen believes this may be due to the greater amount of capital necessary to conduct trade in Flanders.

60 Ibid., p. 88 and especially see the map of the origins of Flanders merchants, p. 89.

61 Notable examples of settlers were the Veckinchusen brothers: ibid., pp. 98, 117.

62 Ibid., table 5, p. 105.

de Marke data indicate that a critical mass of merchants had been reached from three crucial areas of Europe by this period. This afforded an unprecedented variety of merchandise and business contacts to any merchant visiting Bruges around 1350, and supports the conclusion that the merchant network, and correspondingly the Bruges market, had achieved a significant level of maturity. In other words, the more long-distance trade required dealing in Bruges, the larger and more diverse the numbers of merchants and their merchandise, attracting more merchants. Large trade volumes in turn resulted in accumulated credits available for transfer or exchange. A "virtuous circle" was the result, propelling Bruges from strength to strength even through the difficult last decades of the fourteenth century.

A large part of what made Bruges unique among cities was the use her foreign merchant communities made of their presence there. Each merchant group brought not only trade goods, but also financial practices and networks, of which Bruges became a part. These expanded the reach of the city, making it a node in networks that stretched from the Levant to Ireland and east through the Baltic to Novgorod, the German Hanse's furthest outpost. Of course no one group of merchants had direct access to networks stretching to every corner of Bruges's trading hinterland: only by maintaining a presence in Bruges could a merchant tap into this economic powerhouse.

BRUGES AS AN INTERNATIONAL BANKING CENTER

The impressive body of writing by the great Belgian/American historian Raymond de Roover was nothing if not "insistent and repetitive," particularly on the point that it was the Italians in general and the Florentines in particular who made Bruges a center of international banking.[63] As in so much else, he was largely, but not completely, correct in this assertion. There is no denying that Florentine and to a lesser extent Lucchese companies were the masters of long-distance banking and short-term credit through the perfection of the bill of exchange. This "delicate invention," as the fifteenth-century Ragusan merchant Benedetto Cotrugli described it, met the considerable challenge of distance and payment in conducting long-distance trade. Given that Bruges was the point where English wool, Flemish textiles, eastern spices and dyestuffs, and northeastern furs (to name but a few commodities) were bought and sold, Italian companies

[63] This was Reinhold Mueller's very canny characterization of de Roover's work: see *Venetian Money Market*, pp. 288–290. This is also the source of the Cotrugli quotation.

accumulated considerable credit balances there. Converting these to bills created at a stroke a means to trade currency without physically transporting it, a credit instrument for the period required for the bill to be transported from one banking center to another, and a means to profit from a loan without falling foul of the church's usury prohibition.[64]

But the Italian network and its bill of exchange was not the only credit/payment mechanism in Bruges, nor was it necessarily the most widely used when viewed by the standards of the time rather than those of modern finance. The English and the Hansards, for example, developed their own solutions to the challenge of distance and payment, in which Bruges also played a central role. De Roover was remiss in dismissing these as "primitive" and therefore unworthy of the historian's notice. In so doing, one completely misses the importance of the multiplicity of financial systems available in Bruges, each with its own possibilities.[65]

Perhaps in no other merchant community was the relationship between trade and exchange closer than the Italian. As the Florentine businessman and former employee of the Bardi company stated so clearly in his handbook for merchants, Bruges was a place of trade and "il cambio" – which was essentially the trade in money.[66] Bruges and to a lesser degree London became essential collecting points for the credits accumulated by trade in spices, wool, textiles, and other commodities, from where they could be remitted to another banking place or traded in furtherance of some other business deal. In other words, as a result of far-flung Italian, especially Florentine, trade a true money market was created in Bruges.

"Exchange is a most subtle activity to investigate," warned one fifteenth-century merchant, and modern historians would rush to agree with him.[67] Yet the essential instruments and preconditions for the development of the medieval money market are now fairly well understood. The bill of exchange began its evolution in the thirteenth century, and had reached maturity in the first decades of the fourteenth century in tandem with the development of what one historian has called the medieval "super-companies."[68] These large merchant organizations had their roots in the agricultural commodity trade within Italy, yet success in this business enabled several companies, notably the Bardi, Peruzzi, and Acciaiuoli, to expand to unprecedented size,

64 There is a huge bibliography on the history of the bill of exchange. See Spufford, *Money and Its Use*, pp. 262–63, 393–5 and especially, Mueller, *Venetian Money Market*, pp. 288–355.

65 Hunt and Murray, *History of Business*, p. 57.

66 Pegolotti, *La pratica della mercatura*, p. 236; the full quotation is found as the heading of this chapter.

67 The words are those of Benedetto Cotrugli, Ragusan merchant, quoted by Mueller, *Venetian Money Market*, p. 288.

68 Hunt and Murray, *History of Business*, pp. 65, 99–122; Spufford, *Money and Its Use*, p. 254.

encompassing trade from England to the Levant. Controlling commerce on this scale required a number of company branches, each staffed by either a factor or a partner of the firm. The economic importance of a particular city to a firm can often be measured by whether it was headed by a partner; we know the Bruges branch of the Peruzzi company was always run by a partner.[69] Whoever was the manager, all Italian companies worked abroad as self-contained entities, employing fellow countrymen and most often either leasing or purchasing a suitable building. In Bruges their preference was for a location on or just off the Bourse square. Company communication took the form of a constant stream of letters in which details of business were relayed and essential currency and commodity prices noted.

Having branches in far-flung corners of Europe, buying and selling in tempo with the season and the market, presented Italian companies with challenges and opportunities. The bill of exchange was an answer to both, since it served to transfer balances from branch to branch or across companies, and it did so in a form that supplied a need for short-term credit. Essential to this exchange system, however, were pairs of exchange rates in different places and different currencies, which changed in predictable and calculable degrees.[70] Thus a Florentine merchant could be fairly certain that a bill purchased in Florence in florins could be redeemed in Bruges in Flemish pounds groot four to six months later at a rate likely to turn a profit. By 1330, Florentine merchants used Bruges and Venice as important points of their exchange network. In fact, these banking places almost became merchant abstractions, since many bills were never actually sent. All that was really necessary to the initiating party was a quote of the exchange rate in Bruges on the day of maturity of the bill. By the 1360s bills drawn on Bruges were often "dry" – that is issued but not sent – thus emphasizing the use of the bill as a credit instrument.[71] The power of the Bruges market was thus extended to the exchanges of northern Italy.

69 De Roover erroneously stated that factors directed the Bruges office, an error he corrected in a later publication; see de Roover, *Money, Banking and Credit*, p. 32 and Hunt, *Medieval Super-Companies*, pp. 145–146. The Acciaiuoli company, however, had two factors in Bruges, two in London and one in Paris: de Roover, *Money, Banking and Credit*, p. 39. In general see the discussion in Hunt and Murray, *History of Business*, pp. 54–60 and 107, with diagram of Peruzzi company branches and organization.

70 Mueller, *Venetian Money Market*, p. 289.

71 Albeit an instrument with the severe limitation of not being discountable: Mueller, *Venetian Money Market*, pp. 291–292; John H. Munro, "Die Anfänge der Übertragbarkeit: Einige Kreditinnovationen im Englisch–Flämischen Handel des Spätmittelalters (1360–1540)," in Michael North (ed.), *Kredit im spätmittelalterlichen und frühneuzeitlichen Europa* (Vienna and Cologne, 1991), pp. 39–69.

A concrete example of the workings of this banking system is given in Reinhold Mueller's recent work on money and banking in medieval Venice. Using as examples two bills of exchange from 1360 as well as later bills from the Datini archives, Mueller has shown that the exchange relationship between Venice and Bruges in the fourteenth century involved two different ways of quoting rates. In the former example, a Venetian merchant quoted exchange rates based on Venetian and Flemish gold coins converted into moneys of account. Thus a Venetian ducat (of twenty-four *denari grossi a oro*) equaled one Flemish gold royal (of twenty-four Flemish groats).[72] In the opposite direction, a bill from Bruges drawn on Venice, curiously enough, quotes the Venetian ducat in deniers tournois and at a percentage over par.[73] In the accounts of the changer Collard de Marke ducats and florins are always quoted in Flemish groats. One suspects that Italian merchants depended on Bruges money changers to report the fluctuations in exchange rates, which were then used to either draw up bills of exchange or report back to the home office.[74] By the time of the Datini accounts at the end of the fourteenth century, Bruges was quoting Venice in groats Flemish per ducat, while Venice similarly gave the equivalence of the Flemish gold franc in *grossi a oro*.[75] Obviously there was homogenization at work between the two exchange markets.[76]

It goes without saying, then, that by the middle of the fourteenth century, every Italian merchant company of consequence was represented in Bruges. By the 1390s complex systems of bill brokering and foreign remittances had evolved. Barcelona, for example, became the other point in the trade triangle embracing Florence and Bruges. Raymond de Roover found many examples of this among the records of Francesco Datini. In his company, credit balances in Barcelona were frequently used by the Datini factors in Bruges to make payments in Italy. The trade could also work in reverse, as in February 1400, when the firm Bernardo degli Alberti of Venice drew on

[72] Mueller, *Venetian Money Market*, pp. 594 and 637; he is incorrect in stating that the Flemish royal was in 1360 simply a money of account. Royals were struck by Count Louis of Male, although they were not a very successful coin. In 1359–1360, in fact, a royal of 24 groats was struck at Ghent, intended as an imitation of the French coin of the same name and value; see Elsen, "La monnaie des comtes de Flandre," 109, 174.

[73] Mueller, *Venetian Money Market*, p. 594; on 13 October 1360 the denier tournois was 28.25 percent over par – thus each ducat was worth 16.5 gros tournois.

[74] Raymond de Roover, *The Bruges Money Market around 1400 with a Statistical Supplement* (Brussels, 1968); de Roover, "Renseignements complémentaires sur le marché monétaire à Bruges au XIVe et au XVe siècle," *ASEB* 109 (1972), 51–91, esp. 52.

[75] Mueller, *Venetian Money Market*, p. 595. Here again the rate is based on two real gold coins.

[76] Mueller also mentions the important trade triangle Barcelona–Bruges–Venice; see *Venetian Money Market*, pp. 596–597.

the Datini firm of Barcelona in the amount of 400 ducats at the rate of 16s. 8d. Barcelonese per ducat, with the final charge to be made on the Alberti company branch in Bruges.[77] This complex joining of Bruges and Venice by way of Barcelona was due in part to the contours of the spice trade, of which Venice was the major supplier and Bruges the major northern market. It also may have reflected a persistent trade imbalance between the three regions, with Italian merchants faced with the problem of remitting credit balances from Flanders.[78]

The international banking system created by Italian companies existed mainly to serve the needs of the companies that created it. But it was in no way exclusive or closed to other opportunities to profit or offer service to prized customers. Most important among these was the papacy, which had need of the Italian banking system in order to collect monies from far-off corners of Europe. Given that Bruges was the western-most prime banking place in the north and was a natural point of destination for merchants from regions without extensive banking facilities, it was logical for trade goods and bullion used to pay fees owed the papacy to be exchanged there. And owing to the fourteenth-century papacy's major concern with revenue, especially in the Avignon period, much care and attention were devoted to recovering these funds efficiently.[79]

The examples of Scandinavia and Poland are the best known. From Italy or southern France these two regions seemed hopelessly distant – "in the most remote parts of the world," as one letter to Clement VI described Sweden.[80] Together with Denmark and Norway this country had ancient ties to the papacy, but financial contacts were a different matter. In the course of the fourteenth century, however, Scandinavian merchants became the intermediaries for papal collectors through the purchase of trade goods in their home region, which would be carried by them to Bruges for sale.[81] The funds could then be deposited with a branch of the bank favored by

[77] De Roover, *Money, Banking and Credit*, p. 65; Mueller, *Venetian Money Market*, pp. 596–597.

[78] De Roover, *Money, Banking and Credit*, p. 65, a point he developed further in "La balance commerciale entre les Pays-Bas et l'Italie au quinzième siècle," *RBPH* 37 (1959), 374–386. His arguments were criticized by W. B. Watson, "The Structure of the Florentine Galley Trade with Flanders and England in the Fifteenth Century: Some Evidence about Profits and the Balance of Trade," *RBPH* 39 (1961) and 40 (1962) and by E. B. Fryde, "Anglo-Italian Commerce in the Fifteenth Century: Some evidence about profits and the balance of trade," *RBPH* 50 (1972), 346–355.

[79] In general see Yves Renouard, *Les relations des papes d'Avignon et des compagnies commerciales et bancaires de 1316 à 1378* (Paris, 1941) and Guillaume Mollat, *The Popes of Avignon, 1305–1378* (London and New York, 1963).

[80] Georges Despy, "Bruges et les collectories pontificales de Scandinavie et de Pologne au XIVe siècle," *Bulletin de l'Institut Historique Belge de Rome* 27 (1952), 95–109, esp. 97 n. 4, quoting U. Berlière, *Suppliques de Clément VI (1342–1352)* (Rome, 1906), p. 300 n. 1149.

[81] Despy, "Bruges et les collectories," 99 and n. 3.

the papacy for remittance to Rome. The reverse was also true, as shown by a case in 1335. In that year a Norwegian bishop entrusted money bound for the papal treasury to Lubertus Howoschild, "burgher of Bruges," who was apparently in Norway on business.[82] Lubertus or Lubrecht was a member of a notable hosteller family with close ties to the German Hanse.[83] Hanse merchants seem to have largely taken over the role of merchant intermediaries for Scandinavian churchmen after 1350, for it is likely that they were the most reliable visitors to Bruges by that time.[84]

Poland was a firm papal ally in northeastern Europe, and here too the solution Bruges offered to the problem of remittances to Avignon was quickly seized. From 1325 until the end of the fourteenth century, papal collectors in Poland regularly confided the funds they had collected to Polish merchants bound for Bruges, where they met the pope's Italian bankers. Once in Bruges these funds were sometimes remitted, but were also frequently used to purchase Flemish or Brabant cloth for the papal court.[85] Here once again interests of trade and finance came together.

Evidence that Italian companies in Bruges were used for other financial transactions in the fourteenth century is extremely scarce. Although we know that letters of credit could be obtained from Italian companies in Bruges, there is little record of them.[86] One clear example dates from 5 March 1380, when a letter of credit was issued to a canon of St. Donatian's for 200 francs, at the rate of 38½ groats per franc. The letter was drawn up by Giovanni Christofani, a Lucchese merchant resident in Bruges, and was to be paid in Rome by Andrea Tysi.[87] This was probably intended as expense money for de Bosco (or van Praet) to pursue the church's affairs in Rome, during the early years of the Great Schism.

82 Ibid., 101; this is certainly a corrupted form of the surname Auscilt or Aoskilt, a well-known hosteller/merchant family.

83 The family may indeed have originated in Lübeck although Lubrecht's sons, Clais and possibly Pieter, both became important hostellers in the 1360s. Lubrecht was dead by 1353, when his children laid claim to a house in Lübeck; see Asmussen, *Lübecker Flandernfahrer*, p. 116 and n. 369. The family name is spelled Aoskilt in the De Marke accounts.

84 Despy, "Bruges et les collectories," 101; Renouard, *Les relations des papes d'Avignon*, p. 309.

85 Despy, "Bruges et les collectories," 104; Henri Laurent, *Un grand commerce d'exportation au moyen âge. La draperie des Pays-Bas en France et dans les pays méditerranéens (XIIe–XVe siècle)* (Paris, 1935), pp. 176–177. For a list of Polish merchants (mainly from Cracow), see Despy, "Bruges et les collectories," 106–107; see also de Roover, *Money, Banking and Credit*, pp. 60–61.

86 De Roover did not consider them significant: ibid., p. 83.

87 BAB, St. Donaas, A48, Acta Capituli, f. 78v: "mccclxxix die quinta mensis marcii positi fuerunt in manibus Johannis Christofoni Brugis commorantis et socii de Luca, ducenti franci recipiendi in manibus magistrum Rassonis de Bosco, canonici huius ecclesie in Roma ad opus suum et capitulum nostrum ibidem ab Andrea Tysi socio de Luca . . ." A Giovanni Cristofani was a counsellor of the Lucchese community in Bruges in 1378–1379, and an Agnolo Xristofani was a factor of the Rapondi company of Lucca in Bruges in 1385; see de Roover, "La communauté des Lucquois," 87, 76.

Notwithstanding the paucity of evidence of transactions involving private individuals, Italian companies in Bruges were active in the local market in other ways. There is scattered evidence of loans made to the city government, for example. One well-known case involved the Peruzzi company of Florence. This began with a large indemnity imposed on the city by the count of Flanders as part of the settlement of the revolt of Maritime Flanders in 1328. Through a series of intermediate steps involving Donato de Peruzzi, who was both a partner in the company and the count's General Receiver, the obligation became the property of the Peruzzi company. This was a considerable sum – £20,000 Parisis, equivalent to 33,333 florins. The bulk of the debt was repaid by 1333, although a part of it remained unaccounted for until 1345, two years after the company's bankruptcy.[88]

Urban finance was never more than an occasional, even accidental, sideline for Italian companies in Bruges, but it does prove the degree of Italian involvement in the local market. Some resident Italians became important local figures in their own right as well as significant sources of loans and cash advances to the city government. Forteguerra di Forteguerra, a Lucchese merchant banker, is a good example. In 1379, during the crisis of the Ghent war, he lent the city £300 gro. In the war's aftermath the debt remained unpaid until 1385, when a payment schedule and a decrease in the principal were worked out.[89] Forteguerra was much more than a source of cash; his account with Collard de Marke shows that he and his company were fully occupied with buying and selling in the Bruges market. The Forteguerra company had factors or partners located in London, Paris, and Bruges, but was directed by Forteguerra from Bruges.[90] This structure remained in place even after Forteguerra returned to Lucca to a rather brief and tragic political career.[91] A figure similar to Forteguerra, though of grander success, was Dino Rapondi. The Rapondi company had a history in Bruges from the time it was the seat of the company's northern activities under Guglielmo Rapondi in the 1360s. The principal branches of the company were located in Bruges, Lucca, Paris; and Avignon. Guglielmo, like Forteguerra, was

[88] De Roover, *Money, Banking and Credit*, pp. 84–85, discusses the chain of transactions with some thoroughness. Hunt, *Medieval Supercompanies*, p. 161, refers to it as well. Murray, *Notarial Instruments*, pp. 194–195, edits a record of payment of part of the debt to Angolus Montis Aquerelli, procurator for the Peruzzi, witnessed by Francesco Baldouini of the Bardi company. For Italian merchants in the service of Count Louis of Nevers in the 1320s and 1330s, see Kittell, *From Ad Hoc to Routine*, pp. 150–160.

[89] De Roover, *Money, Banking and Credit*, p. 85.

[90] De Roover, "La communauté des Lucquois," 79–80.

[91] Leon Mirot, "Forteguerra Forteguerra et sa succession," *Bibliothèque de l'Ecole des Chartes* 96 (1935), 308–309; de Roover, "La communauté des Lucquois," 80.

a frequent customer of Collard de Marke. His brother, Dino, eventually became head of the company and simultaneously an important counselor of Duke Philip the Bold and John the Fearless.[92]

By the second half of the fourteenth century a close symbiosis had developed between Bruges and her resident Italian merchants. Based on trade, especially the lucrative flow of wool from England and spices from the Mediterranean, their activities extended to a number of parallel and subsidiary businesses. Among these were banking, shipping, and more specialized buying of export items such as manuscripts, art, and jewelry.[93] As a "banking place" Bruges became more than just an entrepôt for goods – it became a money market where data about exchange rates and prices of commodities were collected and communicated to other outposts of the Italian trading network. In this way Bruges came to play a role in the trade of bills of exchange even in the local financial markets of Florence, Lucca, and Venice.[94] In this sense, the Bruges market became more significant than the simple sum of its trade. Add to that the role of the city as a remittance spot for papal revenues from northeastern Europe – again thanks to the presence of Italian companies – and one begins to appreciate the important role played by Italian merchants in making Bruges a great commercial city.

Yet it is important to stress that this was not the only financial game in town; it was not even the most popular, if we judge from the number of potential merchant customers. Different kinds of trade brought with them different credit and finance arrangements, some connecting with the Italian, others not. Bruges was above all rich in the numbers of such networks, as well as the multiplicity of options they offered for doing business.

The most obvious and long-standing trade/credit network through Bruges was with England. Of course England and Flanders had been close trading partners for many decades before 1280: Flemish merchants had traditionally come to Britain in search of medium- to high-quality English wools with which to supply Flemish looms. The economic relationship survived the blow dealt by the onset of hostilities between France and England

92 Ibid., 76–78; de Roover, *Money, Banking and Credit*, pp. 85–86. In his role as financial advisor to the Burgundian dukes, Rapondi became the first in a line of Bruges-based merchants who lent, and profited by, their aid and advice to the Burgundian dukes; see Blockmans and Prevenier, *The Promised Lands*, p. 166.

93 De Roover, *Money, Banking and Credit*, p. 89; see below chapter 9 for the development of trade in luxury goods.

94 Mueller points out that by the fifteenth century rechange on Bruges and London served as a medium-term credit instrument, for four- to six-month periods. He gives examples drawn from the Borromei and Medici companies and the Venetian merchant Andrea Barbarigo; see Mueller, *Venetian Money Market*, pp. 326–337.

after 1270, even though the Flemish had been largely driven out of the direct trade in wool by the 1290s, leaving this role to the Italian companies and other privileged foreigners.[95] Even as the English crown worked to consolidate the export and sale of wool at a single staple, Bruges set out to be the chief market for English wool on the continent, with or without the formal title of staple.[96]

This new trading pattern was made possible by two factors. The first was the domination by the Italian merchant companies of both the export of English wool and the import and distribution of Mediterranean spices. This fact made Bruges the primary market for spice, which included dyestuffs, in northern Europe. The second was the emergence of London as the most important trading and financial city of England, and the increasing role of its guild of pepperers in the spice and wool trades. As Pamela Nightingale puts it, "The link between London and Bruges became the main axis of the Italians' northern trade. At Sluys . . . the Genoese dromonds and galleys unloaded the bulk of their dyes and alum to supply the Flemish textile industry, and then sailed to England to ship wool there in return."[97] Thus after 1310 both English and Flemish merchants cooperated with Italians in organizing trade and its financing.

After 1350 the exchange of wool and spices with Bruges as its center developed into its mature and enduring form. Bruges had enjoyed several brief periods as the English wool staple until it surrendered the role to Calais in 1362. This in no way ended Bruges's function as the chief market for English wool, however, for English merchants still had need of exchange credits to purchase spices as well as imports brought by the Hanse to the Bruges market. Londoners in general and the pepperers' guild in particular set out to dominate and direct this trade. They profited from the proximity of Calais to London and from the fact that Calais lay so close to Bruges that it effectively entered its financial orbit. By 1370, if not before, Calais and Bruges money changers could effect book transfers from city to city.[98] After 1345, this guild had both drawn together into a tighter corporation and taken the first steps from mere retailers and distributors of commodities to exporters and importers.[99] The breakthrough had come with the revival of the English cloth industry, which created demand for alum and

[95] T. H. Lloyd, *The English Wool Trade in the Middle Ages* (Cambridge, 1977), pp. 25–59.

[96] See below, chapter 7. [97] Nightingale, *Medieval Mercantile Community*, p. 122.

[98] Nicholas, "English Trade," 32.

[99] The reorganization and founding of a pepperers' fraternity occurred in 1345, which began the evolution of the business in the direction of importing and exporting; see Nightingale, *Medieval Mercantile Community*, pp. 178, 187 and 160–163.

dyestuffs in various English cloth districts.[100] These commodities London pepperers could best obtain in return for exports of English wool, with either themselves or Italians serving as middlemen. With a ban on wool export licenses for native merchants in the 1350s, many wool merchants joined the "Fraternity of St. Antonin" in order to resist the ban through collusion with foreign merchants and other measures.[101] Ultimately, the result of this fundamental realignment of the wool trade was a highly profitable opportunity for the grocers' fraternity to export wool and import cargoes of alum, woad, sugar, pepper, and brazil-wood – their stock in trade.[102] The reorganization of the fraternity of St. Antonin in 1372 and its reemergence as the Company of Grocers the following year only cemented the three-way relationship of Bruges, London, and Calais.[103]

Meanwhile a second financial network involving England and Bruges had developed from the northern wool outposts of York and its nearby port cities of Hull and Boston. Wool was once again the medium of exchange, especially the much-prized fleeces of Lincolnshire, Shropshire, and Yorkshire. By the fourteenth century, of course, trade relations between northern England and the Low Countries had a decades-long, if not centuries-long, tradition, but the credit system this trading network gave rise to is best understood through the careers of two men, William de la Pole of Hull and John Goldbeter of York.

De la Pole is well known as merchant banker to Edward III, banneret and baron of the exchequer. His rise was spectacular, given that no native Englishman had ever played such an important role in the king's financial affairs, and his fall was just as spectacular.[104] Much of this success was due to his virtuosity in the wool and credit trade with Bruges and Brabant. This is revealed most clearly during Edward III's continental expedition of 1338–1340, a grand invasion resting upon weak financial foundations.[105]

100 Pamela Nightingale, "Capitalists, Crafts and Constitutional Change in Late Fourteenth-Century London," *Past and Present* 124 (1989), 10–12; for developments in English cloth production, see John H. Munro, "Cloth Manufacture and Trade," in P. Szarmach, M. T. Tavormina, and J. T. Rosenthal (eds.), *Medieval England: An Encyclopedia* (New York, 1998), pp. 194–197.

101 Nightingale, *Medieval Mercantile Community*, p. 210.

102 Nightingale, "Capitalists, Crafts," 12.

103 This is clearly shown by the arrest of English merchants and merchandise ordered by the Flemish count in 1371. Of the twenty-one boats arrested, nineteen were bound for London with cargoes of woad, madder, alum, almonds, soap, olive oil, iron, ashes, flax, and spices. Nicholas, "English trade," 37–39; Nightingale, *Medieval Mercantile Community*, p. 235.

104 Fryde, *William de la Pole*, pp. 101.

105 See E. B Fryde, "Financial Resources of Edward III in the Netherlands, 1337–1340," RBPH 40 (1962), 1168–1187. The cost of Edward's residence in the Low Countries was some £350,000; less than half was supplied by Englishmen, most was borrowed. See also Fryde, "Some Business Transactions of York Merchants," 7 reprinted in *Studies in Medieval Trade and Finance*, XI.

It was the job of de la Pole and others to keep these foundations from complete collapse, and this they did by tapping every possible source of credit. Political considerations forced Edward to spend most of his time in Antwerp, but de la Pole's actions prove that Bruges and the connections he made there contributed a good deal to his success as a fund raiser. Despite the king's choice of residence and a promise to the duke of Brabant to shift English imports to a Brabantine city, English merchants continued to market the bulk of their wool in Bruges. De la Pole rented warehouse space in Bruges to store his wool, maintained three agents there, and carefully monitored the fluctuations in wool prices between Antwerp and Bruges in order to improve his profits.[106] He also brokered royal licenses to export English wool, using business relationships no doubt gained in Bruges. This is especially true with a group of influential Hanse merchants, who obtained royal export licenses and who in turn advanced money to the king both directly and through de la Pole.[107] Much of this business de la Pole performed by correspondence, but he had opportunities also during his occasional visits to Bruges.[108]

John Goldbeter did not approach the stature of de la Pole, which makes his contacts in Bruges perhaps more representative of those of the less prominent. Saving all the details of his colorful career for another chapter, it is clear that Goldbeter had an intimate knowledge of the credit market in Bruges and Flanders. Between 1346 and 1348 Goldbeter brokered at least six loans whose proceeds were intended for the royal coffers. Two were made with Italian companies with offices in Bruges on security of English wool. A similar loan was contracted with a London merchant and a Hanse merchant turned Bruges money changer and financier.[109] The security was once again English wool. The last two significant deals came

106 Fryde, *William de la Pole*, pp. 106–108 and 28. De la Pole leased eight houses for sixty-five weeks at £10 sterling per year to store the 2,409 sacks of wool he brought to the Low Countries for sale under his name between 1339 and 1340. In December 1339 his close watch on prices led to sales in Antwerp of sixty-one sacks of Lincolnshire at £1 14s. 4d. more than they would have fetched in Bruges.

107 Among these were the Dortmunder merchants Johann, Henry and Hilderbrand Suderman, whose family was for several generations active in the England/Bruges trade: see Dierck *et al.*, *Prosprographischer Katalog*, pp. 416–417. Another Dortmunder of importance in Bruges enlisted by de la Pole was Johan Clippinc – ibid., 114. For their links with de la Pole, see Lyon, Lyon, and Lucas, *Wardrobe book of William de Norwell*, pp. 52–53; loans to the king, pp. 71 and 76; and see for activities in wool export from England, Lloyd, *English Wool Trade*, p. 142.

108 Such as that during March 1339, when he conducted negotiations for Edward with Jacob van Artevelde and others of the pro-English party in Bruges – Fryde, *De la Pole*, p. 107. He was still in Bruges in April, May and June, according to the accounts of Norwell: see Lyon, Lyon, and Lucas, *Wardrobe Book*, pp. 281, 282

109 Fryde, "Some Business Transactions of York Merchants," 24.

from a fictitious sale of Ghent cloth with two prominent drapers from that city, and a loan from the Cahorsins of Bruges, with wool as security. In all Goldbeter advanced some £20,000 sterling as a result of such borrowing between 1347 and 1348. Moreover, E. B. Fryde has estimated that Goldbeter and his associates raised almost one-sixth of the £126,000 conveyed to the king by the Chiriton company of London.[110]

The founding of the Calais staple marked the decisive shift away from York and Hull to London in the history of English trade at Bruges. The trade flow of Spanish and Italian-borne goods, chiefly spices and dyestuffs from the south, augmented with trade goods from the Hanse region, perfectly matched the credits earned through wool sales in Bruges. By the 1370s, the grocers' guild of London had managed to combine the wool export trade with the import of spices, mordant, and dyestuffs from Bruges and the distributive trade into the English countryside. As Pamela Nightingale put it, "What had started as a fraternity turned into something more akin to a joint-stock company organizing naval convoys . . . [bound for the Calais staple]."[111] This commercial order remained largely intact for much of the next century, as the surviving Cely papers prove. The Celys were a family of shippers and wool merchants, or "staplers" as they became known in the fifteenth century. Their economic world still revolved round London, Calais, Bruges, and Antwerp in the 1470s and 1480s. Bruges remained the financial linchpin; its valuation of coins set the standard and its money changers handled drafts and transfers for staplers and their foreign customers alike.[112] In turn, London mercers often "took up" credits owed to the Celys in Bruges to cover their purchases in Bruges.[113] This sales/credit system was "the main source of English commercial credit and a source of funds which the crown could exploit through a series of 'forced' loans," according to one historian, and remained intact until the triumph of the Antwerp money market in the middle of the sixteenth century.[114]

The achievement of this interdependence had far-reaching consequences for both trade patterns and the political history of London. The grocers and later the staplers rapidly became powers to reckon with in city and county politics in England.[115] An example of how trade was influenced

110 Ibid., 4, 6. 111 Nightingale, *Medieval Mercantile Community*, p. 240.

112 Hanham, *The Celys*, pp. 186–188. 113 Ibid., p. 196.

114 Ian Blanchard, "English Royal Borrowing at Antwerp, 1544–1564," in Marc Boone and Walter Prevenier (eds.), *Public and Private Finances in the Late Middle Ages* (Leuven/Apeldoorn, 1996), pp. 57–73, esp. 64. This system was not replaced until the middle of the sixteenth century with the definitive replacement of Bruges by Antwerp as the Low Countries' financial center.

115 This is one of the major themes of Pamela Nightingale's "Capitalists, Crafts and Constitutional Change," especially 16–35.

is the fact that many English merchants purchased articles from Spain in Bruges, ignoring the fact that Spanish ships often called at Southampton.[116] In Bruges, English and Spanish merchants met on neutral ground in a market capable of absorbing or offering any kind of trade good and offering a large variety of credit and payment arrangements. This was a powerful inducement to make their exchanges there rather than in the narrower confines of an English port city. Yet so close did Bruges seem to England that English merchants could bring suit in its aldermanic court against Spanish merchants for failure to fulfill contracts to deliver goods to England.[117] Easy access and familiarity with Bruges had other important results for England. As the examples of de la Pole and Goldbeter show, English merchants learned the ways of borrowing and syndicating loans in Bruges and throughout the Low Countries. With a warrior king like Edward III, these skills could lead a man to the highest positions of power and influence. For de la Pole's family they led to a position among the landed gentry for one branch, and even to baronial rank for another.[118]

To a similar degree, the credit/payment systems of the Italian and English merchant communities were "members only" networks, whose services were most freely available to other English or Italians. Outsiders could on occasion avail themselves of their advantages, but this appears always to have been the exception rather than the rule. Yet the possibilities of the Bruges market begin with the English and Italians rather than end there. For every merchant community brought its own credit and payment needs and desires; and each in turn added to the possibilities on offer. Nowhere is this more apparent than in the far-reaching and powerful network offered by the Bruges hostellers and money changers.

As discussed in a previous chapter, foreign merchant communities had their own customs in choosing lodging in Bruges. Many Italian and English merchants chose to rent their own establishments, though their landlords were also commonly operators of inns.[119] This probably discouraged the close dependence on the hosteller for banking and other services. For those groups who customarily lodged with hostellers – notably the Portuguese, Spaniards, and Hanse – the credit/payment system offered by their hosts

116 Wendy R. Childs, *Anglo-Castilian Trade in the Later Middle Ages* (Manchester, 1978), pp. 180–181.

117 Ibid., p. 181.

118 William's sons, Richard and William, followed their father into business careers yet succeeded in acquiring enough land to enter into the gentry. The eldest son Michael mounted even higher – to become the king's chief adviser, Lord Chancellor of England and earl of Suffolk. See Fryde, *William de la Pole*, pp. 230–231.

119 There were hostellers who specialized in Italian or English merchants, however – one thinks of Scutelare and Barbezaen – but not in numbers sufficient to accommodate all of the resident merchants from those areas.

acquired importance even beyond the walls of Bruges itself. For as Bruges rose ever larger as an important center of regional and long-distance trade, merchants who often journeyed and lodged there found that money or goods on deposit with a well-known and trusted hosteller could function as currency. With a simple written order, a hosteller could honor a client's wish to transfer funds to the bearer of the letter. Unfortunately for historians, these transactions have left little or no record, given the absence of any significant cache of private business documents surviving from the fourteenth century in northern Europe.[120] Enough fragments survive, however, to convey some idea of how the system functioned.

Merchants from Iberia were the most heterogeneous among the geographically distinct communities of Bruges, and many of them came from areas with well-developed traditions of local and long-distance banking. Barcelona, for example, was both an important link in the Italian system and the possessor of its own system of deposit banking.[121] Nonetheless, there are scattered indications of the financial importance of Bruges hostellers to the Spanish community. One tantalizing example occurs in the de Marke account books from June 1368. A Spaniard named Pelegrin de Palmes (or Palhias) arrived in Bruges in that month on board the *Star of Navarre*. He opened an account with de Marke and received payments of nearly £300 gro. from a Lady d'Esne and a Sir Justin de Haveskierke, both for "ransom."[122] The most plausible explanation for these accounts is the ransom of French knights captured while on campaign with the French marshal du Guesclin in Spain. Bruges served as the collection and shipment place for the money. Completion of the deal came on the debit side of de Palmes's account, where the entire sum was deposited to the account of his hosteller, Jakop van le Fine, who specialized in hosting Spanish and Portuguese merchants.[123] Probably de Palmes intended to use the balance of this account

120 For the fifteenth century there are of course the Cely papers, and in the Low Countries surviving fragments like Wouter Ameyde's account book.

121 Usher, *Early History of Deposit Banking*, pp. 237–268.

122 The d'Esnes were a noble house from near Cambrai in what is now the Département du Nord; the Haverskerque dynasty was from the area around Dunkerque just to the west of Flanders, now also in the Départment du Nord. For both see Ernest Warlop, *De vlaamse adel voor 1300*, 3 vols. (Handzame, 1968), vol. II, pt. 2, p. 600 and vol. II, pt. 1 #106, 279–283. For mentions of these two, see M. le baron Kervyn de Lettenhove (ed.), *Œuvres de Froissart*, 25 vols. (Brussels, 1867–1877), vol. XXI, under "Esne"; for Haveskierke see vol. XXII, p. 323; my thanks to Werner Paravicini for the citations. The account is found in de Marke 3, f. 97v, "cause de le rencon de mesire Mansart d'Esne, 22 juin (1369)" £214 1s. 3d., and "Item li doige par mesire Justin de Haveskierke pour le cause de se rencon a ce jour, £85 12s. 6d."

123 Le Fine was not a member of the brokers'/hostellers' guild, so he belonged to the "unfree" segment of the business. He also maintained a business in cloth import and export in partnership with Collard de Marke; on this see chapter 7.

to secure payment in local currency upon his return to Navarre through exchange with a merchant who needed funds in Bruges.

More evidence of the long-distance value of the hosteller/money changer network has survived from merchants of the German Hanse.[124] As shown above, they were probably the most numerous guests of the Bruges hostels and were long accustomed to trust their hosts with their business affairs, as either factors or partners. The two main sources of day-to-day evidence of the working of this system are preserved in the ledgers and business correspondence of Vicko von Geldersen and Hildebrand Veckinghusen. Von Geldersen was a draper from Hamburg, who probably never visited Bruges but was nonetheless affected by the city's role in the business and credit transactions of Hanse merchants. For example, in early 1375 von Geldersen noted that he had purchased from Heyne Vorrad of Hamburg £6 gro. that he had on account with the hosteller Joncvrouw Thyze, in Bruges.[125] Von Geldersen maintained this account for at least three years, noting that his balance stood at £12 gro. in 1377, and he replenished the account with the dispatch of sixty nobles in the summer of 1378.[126] The bonds of a partnership also led to Bruges for von Geldersen. Albrecht Lunenborch was von Geldersen's partner in the cloth trade between 1370 and 1379. Lunenborch seems to have done the traveling: he was in Bruges at least three times between 1369 and 1372, lodging with the hosteller Evraerd Goederic.[127] Goederic was perhaps of German origin himself, and he became in succession a money changer and hosteller in Bruges. He is also noted in the von Geldersen ledgers as someone who held accounts for other Hanse merchants.[128]

Von Geldersen was probably only one of many Hanse merchants who exported large quantities of Flemish cloth eastwards. This trade no doubt

[124] Rolf Sprandel, *Das mittelalterliche Zahlungssystem nach hansisch-nordischen Quellen des 13.–15. Jahrhunderts* (Stuttgart, 1975) writes in general about a payment system among Hanse cities, with curiously little attention to the preponderant role of Bruges.

[125] Hans Nirrnheim, *Das Handlungsbuch Vickos von Geldersen* (Hamburg and Leipzig, 1895), p. 92; Anke Greve, "Hanseatic Merchants: Banking Customs in 14th Century Bruges," in *Public and Private Finances*, pp. 6–7; de Roover, *Money, Banking and Credit*, p. 278. Thyze had an account with Collard de Marke: see chapter 8.

[126] Nirrnheim, *Handlungsbuch Vickos von Geldersen*, pp. 103, 104. Von Geldersen notes that the £12 gro. represents money from Vicko Sankenstede, perhaps a business partner. Sixty nobles represented about £16 10s. gro. at then current rates of exchange. Von Geldersen's messenger was another Hanse merchant, Christian Rodenborghe, who was later a frequent guest of Thyze; see Krüger (ed.), *Brügger Steuerlisten*, pp. 175–176, from 1387 to 1388.

[127] Greve, "Hanseatic Merchants," p. 7; Krüger, *Brügger Steuerlisten*, pp. 80, 114, 124.

[128] For Goederic see chapters 4, 5; de Roover, *Money, Banking and Credit*, pp. 188–89. Von Geldersen recorded that a "Lord" Albertus de Geldersen (a relative?) had £20 gro. on account "with Heer Evrerd Ghudenrik in Flanders" (Nirrnheim, *Handlungsbuch Vickos von Geldersen*, pp. 92–93) which he sold to Albert Hoyers, whose agent Make Screyghe collected it. Heyne Vulsikesone also had a sum of money with Goederic in the summer of 1377 (p. 104).

began in the late thirteenth century, but its growth becomes apparent in the middle of the fourteenth, with many of the cloth purchases financed through credit extended by the Flemings.[129] By 1350, many of these transactions were financed through exchange, as the surviving account books of the Lübeck firm of Wittenborg show. There is also evidence of three-corner credit arrangements from Hanse sources, between Bruges, Rostock, and Zutphen, for example.[130] These links and practices intensified from the late fourteenth into the fifteenth century, and came to include the furthest eastern regions of the Hanse network.[131]

The Veckinchusen family show another side of Hanseatic business with Bruges as a base. Thanks to the survival of a considerable cache of business documents including account books and letters, one can follow the family's business activities, which were spread among Reval, Riga, Dorpat, Lübeck, Dortmund, Cologne, and Bruges. Sivert Veckinchusen possessed a house in Bruges before 1395, and his brother Hildebrand joined him there from 1395 to 1398. Hildebrand moved himself and his family definitively to Bruges in 1401 in a large rented "Hof" that housed both his business and his seven children. Hildebrand's Bruges era marked the height of his fortunes, for by 1418 he had moved his family to Lübeck to escape the importuning of his creditors. His largest debts were to the hosteller Jacob Scuetelare and the Genoese merchant banker Joris Spinghel (Spinola). This says something about the nature of his business activities, seeking to profit from the spice trade out of Genoa with far-reaching credit and partnership relations with prominent Bruges hostellers. It ended badly for Hildebrand, however, as his creditors succeeded in having him imprisoned, and three years passed before he succeeded in regaining his freedom.[132]

Hanse merchants shared in credit operations associated with English wool passing through Bruges. In the fourteenth century, these merchants had increased their role in the export of wool from England, eventually becoming second only to the Italians in procuring export licenses. Many English merchants entered partnerships with colleagues from the German Hanse, as we have seen in the case of William de la Pole in the 1350s, when wool export was forbidden to denizen merchants.[133] The creation of credit based on wool delivered to Bruges seems as natural an extension to Hanse business activities as it does to English ones. For the Hanse, however, it was

[129] Sprandel, *Zahlungssystem*, p. 104. [130] Ibid., pp. 104–105 and n. 496.
[131] Ibid., pp. 105–108.
[132] Paravicini, "Brugge en Duitsland," p. 109; M. P. Lesnikov, *Die Handelsbücher des hansischen Kaufmannes Veckinchusen* (Berlin, 1973), pp. xiii–xxiii.
[133] Lloyd, *English Wool Trade*, pp. 141–143.

exchange of wool for finished Flemish cloth as return freight, as an example of 1382 shows. A number of drapers from Mechelen had brought finished cloth to the Cloth Hall in Bruges as repayment for English wool purchased from Hanse merchants.[134] We know about the incident because the cloth was lost in the looting that followed the capture of the city by the Ghent rebels. A case in 1398 of Hanse merchants trading in England accepting English cloth as payment of a debt there also suggests a similar role for that increasingly valuable product in the credit/payment system of Bruges.[135] And as with the English, Hanse merchants maintained this credit system linked to wool well into the fifteenth century.[136]

One common element to all the credit/payment networks discussed this far is the role of Bruges as payment place. This also continued in the line of succession of the Champagne fairs, which, like those in Flanders, had functioned as places and times of payment. Earlier Flemish fairs, such as that at Ypres, had instituted a formal system of registering obligations between merchants. These so-called "fair letters" (*lettres de foire*) constituted formal promises of payment, usually at the interval of the next fair.[137] Even though Bruges had an important fair, it never led to the same kind of record keeping as in Ypres, though merchants no doubt settled accounts and issued "reconnaissances" there as well. What did occur at Bruges was the replacement of the episodic and roving nature of the fair by the fixity of a single place, which in turn led to new possibilities such as the letter of exchange. Yet that invention of Italian merchants was not the only creative use of Bruges as an endless trade fair.

An unexpected instance of a long-distance payment system with Bruges as an important node grew in support of the pilgrimage journeys of hundreds, if not thousands, of western European knights and retainers to Prussia. In the fourteenth century, "le voyage de Pruce" became in every

[134] Mechelen merchants, as well as those from other Brabant cloth towns, depended on Bruges as the purchase point for English wool; see David Nicholas, "English Trade," 30–32, and chapter 7.

[135] This despite the fact that import of English cloth was forbidden in Bruges. Not only was this ban widely evaded, but the Hanse had gained the explicit right to transship English cloth through Bruges as long as it was not displayed for sale. See John H. Munro, "Industrial Protectionism in Medieval Flanders: Urban or National?" in H. A. Miskimin, David Herlihy, and A. L. Udovitch (eds.), *The Medieval City* (London and New Haven, 1977), pp. 229–268; Nicholas, "English Trade," 28 for the illegal import of English textiles, and Rudolf Holbach, "Brügge, die Hanse und der Handel mit Tuch," *Hansekaufleute in Brügge, Teil 4*, pp. 183–203.

[136] This is abundantly clear from an English source of 1457–1459, which shows Hanse merchants in London heavily involved in the credit market as borrowers to finance purchase of export articles, chiefly wool; see Jenks, "War die Hanse kreditfeindlich?" 307.

[137] Des Marez, *La lettre de foire à Ypres au XIIIe siècle*; Carlos Wyffels, *Analyses de reconnaissances de dettes passées devant les échevins d'Ypres, 1249–1291* (Brussels, 1991); *Cambridge Economic History* (Cambridge, 1965), vol. III, p. 137.

way comparable to earlier wanderings of chivalric youth to the Holy Land or to Spain to fight the Saracens. In this case, however, the fighting was in alliance with the Teutonic Knights against the "Saracens of the North," the Lithuanians of eastern Prussia.[138] Fighting there reached its peak between 1351 and 1382, drawing knights from every rung of the chivalric hierarchy from the Low Countries, England, France, Scotland, even from Portugal and in at least one case, from Florence.[139] They were not drawn by the lure of riches or booty, or proximity to holy places; they came in pursuit of those two seemingly irreconcilable attractions of crusading: serving God and acquiring fame through the exercise of arms. So irresistible was the combination that Werner Paravicini estimates that at least in the second half of the fourteenth century, "practically every nobleman had been at least once to Prussia."[140]

In short, traveling to fight in Prussia became another item of conspicuous consumption among the European chivalric class. Viewed purely as an economic proposition, it required the mobilization of significant financial, lodging, and transportation resources both in the home country and en route. This meant a passage through Bruges for most knights from west of the Rhine. Sometimes this passage was a literal one, as knights bound for Prussia boarded Hanse ships moored off Sluis for the sea voyage to Gdánsk.[141] For others Bruges became a place to finance the costs of transport, equipment, lodging, and other expenses of the eastward journey and the return home. Because the campaigning season was as a rule during the winter months, with a month each way required for travel, a trip of six months to a year had to be paid for.[142] And as so often with Europe's aristocrats, crusading was paid for with borrowed money.

The critical links in the financial network supporting the Prussian crusade were Hanse merchants and Bruges hostellers and money changers. The merchants came for the most part from the great merchant and aldermanic families of Elbing, Thorn, and later Gdánsk, Königsberg, and Marienburg,

138 Werner Paravicini, "Die Preußenreisen des europäischen Adels," *Historische Zeitschrift* 232 (1981), 25–38; "Edelleute, Hanse, Brügger Bürger: Die Finanzierung der Westeuropäischen Preussenreisen im 14. Jahrhundert," *Hansische Geschichtsblätter* 104 (1986), 5–19; *Die Preußenreisen des europäischen Adels*, 3 vols. (Sigmaringen, 1989, 1995).

139 The list of those undertaking the Prussian crusade is an honor roll of notable figures: Henry Grosmont, duke of Lancaster; Henry Bolingbroke (the future Henry IV of England); Gaston Phoebus, count of Foix; Duke Albert III of Austria, and the great adversary of the early Medici, Maso degli Albizzi, who was dubbed a knight while in Prussia in 1378. See Maurice Keen, *Chivalry* (New Haven, 1984), p. 172 and Paravicini, "Edelleute," 7. On the northern crusades in general, see Eric Christiansen, *The Northern Crusades* (Minneapolis, 1980), especially chapters 6 and 7.

140 Paravicini, "Preußenreisen," 26.

141 Paravicini, *Preussenreisen des Europäischen Adels*, vol. 1, p. 265.

142 Christensen, *Northern Crusades*, pp. 150–160; Paravicini, "Preussenreisen," 31.

and acted as guarantors and brokers of loans whose principal came from the coffers of the Teutonic order itself.[143] These loans might be contracted in Danzig or Königsberg to cover the immediate costs of lodging while waiting for the expedition to form up. The terms of repayment were drawn up in the form of a *reconnaisance* or *Schuldbrief* wherein the quantity of money received was stipulated, usually in silver marks, with repayment to be in gold coins current in Bruges. This arrangement obviated the need for transport of large quantities of silver, although some knights chose to carry their money with them: in 1369 Jean de Blois was forced to hire a wagon pulled by six horses in which to carry his money.[144]

In Bruges the hostellers who specialized in the Hanse trade served as collectors of money, issuers of quittances under their seal, and arrangers of book transfers and exchange through a Bruges money changer. A number of examples of this loan/repayment arrangement are preserved in the Collard de Marke ledgers, but only one has independent confirming documentation. A surviving account book of this same Jean de Blois, lord of Gouda and Schoonhoven, records his expenses while on crusade in Prussia.[145] In it his clerk records a loan of 2,000 marks taken out just before Easter 1369, with repayment stipulated by mid-June of the same year, a term of some eighty-five days.[146] On 24 June, de Blois's agent paid the Hanse merchants Herman von Rode and Baernt Amerov a total of 1,000 nobles, the equivalent of half the principal.[147] The second payment was to the Bruges hosteller Clais van der Beurse, drawing upon de Marke's exchange and the resources of another nobleman, Foukaut d'Artiaus, resulting in the deposit of 300 old écus to van der Beurse's account with de Marke.[148] This is the classic pattern of funds advanced in Prussia through the offices of Hanse merchants, who

143 Paravicini, "Finanzierung," 12; Paravicini, *Preussenreisen des Europäischen Adels*, vol. II, pp. 163–310.

144 Paravicini, *Preussenreisen des Europäischen Adels*, vol. I, p. 13. Prussia did not have a gold coinage until 1394, thus transport of large quantities of silver was often necessary.

145 Ibid., vol. I, p. 289 and vol. II, p. 178.

146 Easter fell on 1 April in that year, and the term was to end on the feast of St. John the Baptist, which was 24 June.

147 Paravicini, *Preussenreisen des Europäischen Adels*, vol. II, no. 19b, 24 June 1369: "Item die twee dusent marc, die mijn heer in Pruussen na ontleende onlanghe voor Paesschen, waren betaelt in der manieren dat hier na volghet, dats te weten, dat her Aelbrecht daer of een dusent marc betaelde te Brugghe te Sinte Jans misse voirscreven na den voorwaerden, die daer of ghemaect waren, daer hi voor betaelde dusent noble, daer Herman von Rode of ontfinc als leggher 600, ende Baernt Amerov als zaecwouder 400, ende gaf voir elken nobel 66 gr. 4 miten, loept £275 13s. [. . .] vlaemsch payments." Von Rode and Amerov were apparently the taker and drawer of what amounts to a bill of exchange.

148 Ibid., vol. II: "Item op die selve tijd betaelde her Aelbrecht Clais van der Buerze in Colaerts wissel van Marc, die mijn heer gout voir heren Focken van Archiyac te borchtochte, daer mijn heer Focken voirs., 300 ouder scilde, voir elken scilt 38 gr." The corresponding entry is SAB, Koopmansboeken, De Marke 5, f. 86v, edited in Murray and Greve, *Hosteller Accounts*, HII.6, 6–7. It is not clear what the relationship of de Blois and d'Artiaus was.

in turn used the financial facilities of Bruges to complete the deal. Similar cases appear regularly across the de Marke ledgers, unfortunately without the equivalent entry in another account book. These again involve the prominent Bruges hostellers Lievin Evrebout, Tideman van den Berghe, Jan de Witte, and others.[149]

Although primarily an affair of Hanse merchants and Bruges hostellers and money changers, financing crusaders did involve the Italians of Bruges and their far-reaching financial network. A notarial instrument of 1363, composed by an Italian notary resident in Bruges, records a quittance drawn up in Bruges, closing a transaction between Prussia and Poitou via Bruges, Paris, and La Rochelle.[150] In 1378 the Bruges factor of the Rapondi company paid the debts the duke of Lotharingia had incurred with a number of merchants of Thorn while in Prussia. Likewise in 1380–1381, Dino Rapondi himself paid in Bruges and Paris sums owed by a French knight to an Elbing merchant for a journey to Prussia on behalf of the duke of Burgundy.[151] These few mentions prove that the Italians had very much a secondary role in this financial system, although their presence added to Bruges's attractiveness.

That money and credit flow along with trade is the lesson to be drawn from the examples discussed thus far, for only where merchants traveled could there be the kinds of financial infrastructure that could enable journeying knights, papal collectors, and others to tap or transmit money over great distances. Bruges abounded in merchants and merchandise, thus opening up the possibilities sketched above, which added up to an overlay of payment/credit systems reaching from Prussia to Italy. Yet it might well be asked what role did Bruges merchants play in regional and long-distance finance? "Little to none" was the answer of the redoubtable

149 For Evrebout, De Marke 1, f. 41v on 26 June 1366, involving Sir Surijen des Kaines and Nicolles de Stouteville. The Hanse intermediary in this case was Radekin Vrauwendourpt (Vrouwendorp), a well-known merchant from Elbing; see Dierck *et al.*, *Prospographischer Katalog*, pp. 447–449. Vrouwendorp served in this capacity in 1357, 1358, and 1363 for various French noblemen on crusade in Prussia. De Marke's second register (f. 354v) records a large payment of £373 6s. 3d. gro. "pour le cause demoriaumes de messire d'Esebourc et pour messire Tiestart de Honkourt," dated 21 June 1367, which most likely refers to lodging costs incurred while on crusade. Werner Paravicini has collected data about financial transactions related to the "Prussian road" and finds that a number of Bruges hostellers and (more rarely) Bruges money changers served the credit needs of traveling knights; see Paravicini, *Preussenreisen des europäischen Adels*, vol. II, table 92, pp. 228–229.

150 Published in Ch. Higounet, "De La Rochelle à Torun: aventures de barons en Prusse et relations économiques (1363–64)," *Le Moyen Age* 69 (1963), 529–540; the document was republished in *Preußisches Urkundenbuch*, vol. VI, 1, nos. 100, 161, 253, 309, 328. For the notary public Bartholomeus d'Arquato, see Murray, *Notarial Instruments*, pp. 59, 85–86, 92.

151 Paravicini, "Die Finanzierung," 16–17; Paravicini, *Preussenreisen des europäischen Adels*, vol. II, p. 279, and vol. III, document 71.

Raymond de Roover, who insisted that it was the presence of Italian merchant bankers that made Bruges an international money market. The local money changers and pawnbrokers had no share in this, since they served only the local needs for consumer credit and simple banking services.[152]

This picture must be modified if not abandoned altogether, both in light of the payment systems described above, and because the predominant internal system – that formed cooperatively by Bruges hostellers and money changers – also functioned as a regional system, again following established patterns of trade.[153] We have already discussed evidence of cooperation between money changers in Calais and Bruges soon after the shift of the wool staple. But the accounts of Collard de Marke once again reveal a far larger pattern of interlocking personal and institutional contacts, stretching from Hainault to Antwerp, Ghent, and even farther afield on occasion. Thickest in Hainault and northern France – the region of de Marke's cloth trading interests – this web of contacts also extended to Ghent and Antwerp, where many of his customers had business interests. The accounts of Willem Ruweel provide no evidence of similar business or credit contacts outside of Bruges, which is understandable given the different business interests of the two money changers.[154] This again underlines the very personal nature of a credit/payment function, and points out that not all – perhaps not even most – Bruges money changers served as links in a larger financial system.

Ghent and Bruges were allies and competitors across nearly the entire range of fourteenth-century politics and economics. And though Ghent took over the political initiative from Bruges from the 1330s, the two cities could not escape their geographical proximity or their mutual dependence for markets and raw materials. The looms of Ghent were largely supplied with wool acquired in Bruges, its dyers used dyestuffs and mordants from the same source, and in turn Bruges depended on its larger industrial neighbor for certain textiles and grain.[155] Cooperation among Ghent and Bruges merchants must have been intense and far-reaching, as traveling to,

152 De Roover, *Money, Banking and Credit*, pp. 345–354. For a critical appraisal of de Roover's work, see Aerts, "Middeleeuwse bankgeschiedenis," 49–86. Aerts points out problems with de Roover's definition of the three "orders" of money dealers in Bruges. David Nicholas has shown as well that lombards in Bruges were heavily involved in trading ventures: Nicholas, "English Trade," 32. See also Murray, 'Hanse Merchants and the Bruges Money Market', pp. 139–149.

153 De Roover stated flatly that "the Bruges money-changers had no correspondents abroad": *Money, Banking and Credit*, p. 238.

154 On these differences, see chapter 4 and de Roover, *Money, Banking and Credit*, pp. 210–215.

155 Nicholas, *Metamorphosis*, pp. 9–10, 249: "Bruges was obtaining much of its grain through the Ghent Staple" (in 1372); for purchases of Ghent cloth by the city government, see chapter 7.

or doing business with, Ghent must have been frequent among the foreign merchants resident in Bruges. And beyond simply business, Bruges and Ghent were joined together in another way after the closure of the Bruges mint, making the mint at Ghent the closest source of coined money.[156] The Ghent mint became a crucial institution for Bruges money changers, both for the regular flow of coinage and as a financial institution that could serve very much like a deposit bank.

As quasi-public officials, Flemish money changers had the duty of removing defective or non-current coins from circulation and arranging to transport them to the mint for recoining. A pair of shears was therefore supposed to be standard equipment at a money exchange along with a scale, strong box and ledger, in order to mark coins whose value was to be only that of bullion. Earlier in the fourteenth century, it is likely that Bruges money changers had a much more direct role in the melting down and recoining of demonetized coins. But by the time of de Marke's accounts, it appears that he was the chief specialist in transport of coins to and from the mint.[157] De Marke's financial relationship with the mint, however, was much more complex than simply the delivery of bullion and return of coin. It is clear by various entries in the accounts that de Marke "banked" some of the bullion, using a positive balance with the mint-master to make payments to customers and agents in Ghent.

There is evidence that this practice was not confined to either de Marke or the 1360s. In 1357, the comital mint-master, the Lucchese Bardet de Malpelys, fled the county, leaving a tangle of debts behind him.[158] Chief among his creditors were five Bruges money changers, whose share amounted to more than 65 percent of Malpelys's liabilities. While historians have traditionally interpreted these debts as simply resulting from undelivered coins, they may have been more than that. For example, de Marke paid

156 Bruges had long served as a minting center for the Flemish counts, in keeping with the commercial importance of the city. But quarrels with the French king over sovereignty resulted in the closure of the mint and the founding of a much larger operation in Ghent in 1334 on the right bank of the Leie, thus on imperial territory (Elsen, "La monnaie des comtes de Flandre," 55–57); the Bruges mint was used sporadically to strike gold coinage in the 1340s and 1350s.

157 This suspicion is supported by the fact that two of the most important changers at that time, Pieter van Oudenaarde and Jacob Reubs, both purchased coins from de Marke, apparently fresh from the mint: De Marke 4, f. 309r, account of Jakop Reubs: "item me doit il quil rechut pour 1 kareton qui vient de le monnoie." Ibid. 3, f. 321r, account of Pieter Daudenarde: "par lui contet que je li portay a sen cange en 1 sac 10 novembre, £50 gro. et encore en 1 sac par Hanekin contet a 10 november £50 gro." Ibid. 4, f. 315r, account of Pieter Daudenarde: "item me doit il quil recut en 1 tonniel qui vient de le monnoie 26 mart, £158 3s. 10d." De Roover, *Money, Banking and Credit*, p. 233.

158 Elsen, "Monnaie des comtes de Flandre," 100–102; de Roover, *Money, Banking and Credit*, pp. 235–236; Bigwood, *Régime*, vol. 1, p. 230.

an unspecified debt for the Ghent merchant Jakop Wilbart on 7 December 1368 by simply drawing on his credit balance at the Ghent mint.[159] A similar payment was made the following day for a Martin de Scaus, and the examples could be multiplied.[160] Clearly balances in Ghent at the mint could be exchanged in Bruges, presumably to finance purchases there. Thus the mint could and did function as a bank, at least for the privileged few (mostly money changers) who held bullion accounts there.[161]

De Marke kept track of his dealings with the mint in two ways. He maintained a separate account book of his bullion transactions, a "papier de le monnoie," which has not survived; and he had a clearing account with the mint-master himself, who in the accounts is called Jehan Interminelli, or sometimes simply "mestre de le monnoie."[162] These rather intermittently kept accounts show some large transfers, as in December 1367 when Jehan Dais, a guest of the Bruges hosteller Jehan Duc, was credited with £134 17s. 11d. via Interminelli's account, representing a book transfer of Ghent-held credits.[163] Another sizable transfer occurred in February 1369, when Roulot Rambone of Leuven received £415 4s. 3d. gro. from Interminelli's account via a letter presented to de Marke in Ghent. De Marke records an offsetting credit in the account, which he received at the mint a week later.[164] Transactions could also be handled through the accounts of one of Interminelli's business associates. Thumas Sarland, for example, a merchant banker of Lucca and a partner of Forteguerra di Forteguerra, apparently acted for Interminelli in a series of rather hazy business dealings, as did Forteguerra himself on occasion.[165] And there is a single instance of a payment made

[159] SAB, De Marke 3, f. 278v: "Sire Jak. Wilbart de Gant me doit pour que je li fu payer a le monnoie 7 en decembre [1367] £60 gro."

[160] Martin was a foreign merchant who probably lodged with Raoul Doucemin while in Bruges. Almost exactly a year later, on 4 December 1369, his host was charged £27 10s. on Martin's behalf, "pour une lettre adrechee ale monnoie": De Marke 5, f. 284v.

[161] De Roover suspected that there might have been more to the relationship of money changers and the mint: see *Money, Banking and Credit*, pp. 233–234. In the fifteenth century many English "merchants of the staple" had what Postan called "something in the nature of a current account with the [Calais] mint": see M. M. Postan, "Private Financial Instruments," in *Medieval Trade and Finance* (Cambridge, 1933), pp. 49–51; Kermode, *Medieval Merchants*, p. 310.

[162] He was the Lucca merchant banker Jehan Interminelli or Enterminelly; on him see Bigwood, *Régime*, vol. 1, pp. 230–234, and Elsen, "La monnaie," 104–105.

[163] De Marke 3, f. 277v, "Le mestre de le monnoie me doit, pour Jehan Dais de lostel Jehan Duc 4 en decembre £134 17s. 11d."

[164] Ibid., 4, f. 103r: "Jehan Terminiel me doit, pour Roulot Rambone de Louvain par une lettre quil menvoia, £415 4s. 3d." and "doy que je rechut ale monnoie 2 mart, £415 4s. 3d."

[165] Ibid., f. 3v: "Thumas Sarlande a le cause dou mestre de le monnoie me doit;" and De Marke 5, 3v, Thumas Sarlande "me doit a le cause de Jehan Terminiel pour une reste que on me devoit ale monnoie dou 17 jour davril et dou 28 jour davril et dou 7 may contet lan lxix, a ces journees a Jehan Jourdain si quil appert par me papier de le monnoie. £501 19s. 7d." De Roover also could

through the "garde" of the mint.[166] Without further documentation it is difficult to be certain, but it appears that Interminelli's activities as master of the mint were only part of broader financial dealings involving Lucchese merchants resident in Bruges.

De Marke's contacts and activities in Ghent went beyond those at the mint. It is clear from his accounts that he went personally to the city from time to time, or sent his son, Copin, to act on his behalf.[167] This could not have been practicable very often, however, so de Marke sometimes called on the services of money changers or hostellers in Ghent. Two changers are mentioned by name in the accounts: Jehan Use "cangeur de Gant" and the well-known Lievin Zegres.[168] The Ghent hosteller, Zeger van Loeve, had an account with de Marke through his clerk, Bauduin de Winderote.[169] It is impossible to make out how frequent such financial contacts might have been, since the account entries provide few details. An exception occurs in one of the two surviving journals of de Marke, where in an entry of 25 September 1368 de Marke writes a memorandum that he owes Lievin Zegres £10 gro. for money he paid on behalf of one of De Marke's customers, a Sir Joris van Tielt.[170] Conceivably this just skims the surface of the close contacts between Ghent and Bruges, which a more exhaustive comparison of the de Marke accounts with contemporary documents surviving in Ghent would probably augment. Nonetheless, it proves that a Bruges money changer drew upon his credit balance at the Ghent mint via book transfers, maintained active correspondence with Ghent money changers

not explain what these accounts represented (*Money, Banking and Credit*, pp. 233–234). An account entry for the money changer Jakop Reubs suggests something of this broader financial network (De Marke 2, f. 302v, 31 May 1367): "Jakop Reups me doit par Fortegerre ale cause dou mestre de le monnoie, £200 gro. en or."

166 De Marke 2, f. 279r, "Gilles Springaut me doit, item me doit il par le clerc sire Jehan de le Faucille [or van Zidielen], 22 en fevrier [1367] a le monnoie a Gant par une lettre, £18 gro." De la Faucille's name was actually Symon; he had been appointed by the count in 1359. See Elsen, "La monnaie." 112.

167 An example is in the account of Joris Wandelaire of March 1369: "Doy par sen varlet que je rechut a Gant, 9 mart, £41 gro. (De Marke 4, f. 102r). A French merchant, Renier Campion seems to have been frequently in Ghent, judging from his accounts in ledgers 3–5 of de Marke. He delivered bullion to the mint there with Copin de Marke as broker: De Marke, 4 f. 121r: "Renier Campion, doy par Copin contet a Gant 7 avril [1368] item li doige par Copin quil recut a Gant 28 avril pour 68 marcs a 8d. somme £32 18s. 8d."

168 De Marke 1, f. 173v, account of Franche van Singhe: "Doy par Jehan Use cangeur de Gant, 24 jan. [1367] £28 11s." and ibid., 3, f. 239r, account of Mestre Jehan Beste, "Item me doit il pour Davit de Coumines 13 nov. [1368] contet a Gant a Will. van Saint Jakophus par le cange de Lievin Zegres." For Zegres, see Nicholas, *Metamorphosis*, pp. 128, 313, n. 16.

169 The accounts call him "Zegre se Love"; I am indebted to David Nicholas for this identification.

170 SAB, De Marke, Journal 1 (unfoliated), 25 September 1368: "Je doy Lievin Zegres pour Sire Joris van Tielt £10 lesquels je li ay payes pour lui a Gant."

and at least one hosteller, and traveled there both in person and through an agent to pursue business.

A similar pattern of cooperation also existed in Antwerp, the other great merchant city near Bruges. Antwerp in the fourteenth century was still a far cry from the thriving commercial metropolis it would become in the sixteenth century, but its development attracted the notice of Bruges merchants and politicians nonetheless. The fact that the English chose Antwerp as their wool staple in the Low Countries between 1296 and 1315 and again in 1338 was enough in itself to cause concern.[171] The increasingly easy access to Antwerp by water and land routes also fostered the twice-yearly Antwerp fairs, which even before the middle of the fourteenth century had become a real threat to Bruges's commercial interests. There was thus much common interest between the merchants of Bruges and Louis of Male, count of Flanders, in his pursuit of hereditary claims in Brabant whose successful conclusion led to the annexation of Antwerp to Flanders in 1356.[172] During the ensuing half century Flemish policy, led by the interests of Bruges, set out to place Antwerp among the satellite cities of Sluis, Damme, and the others through a nurturing control of the Antwerp fairs. Confiscation records from 1382 prove the success of this policy, as Bruges maintained a flourishing trade with both Antwerp and other Brabantine towns along the Western Scheldt.[173] As long as Antwerp remained a "city of fairs" and not of permanent residence for foreign merchants, Bruges's hegemony would remain secure.[174]

This prominence accorded the Antwerp fairs is already apparent in the de Marke accounts just a decade after annexation. De Marke's customers, both Bruges merchants and foreigners, demanded access to their money held by de Marke while visiting the Antwerp fairs. De Marke was able to satisfy this demand either by cooperating with an Antwerp money changer or by sending a representative to act in his name. This was very much what he did in Ghent, though it is clear that he offered such services only during fair time in Antwerp. For example, the foreign merchant Bauduin de Meureville ordered a payment made in Antwerp, which Collard accomplished by sending a letter with his son to a Pieter Sucrebouc, who was probably an Antwerp merchant or money changer.[175] A Flemish merchant,

[171] Van der Wee, *Growth of the Antwerp Market*, vol. II, p. 19; Brulez, "Brugge en Antwerpen," 15–37.

[172] Quicke, *Les Pays-Bas*, pp. 41–62; Nicholas, *Medieval Flanders*, pp. 224–226.

[173] David Nicholas, "The Scheldt Trade and the 'Ghent War' of 1379–1385," *BCRH* 154 (1978), 189–359, esp. 260.

[174] Van der Wee, *Growth of the Antwerp Market*, vol. II, p. 104.

[175] De Marke 3, f. 170r: "Bauduin de Meureville me doit que je li fit payer a Anwiers par Collart par 1 brievet quil porta 12 septembre [1368] £4 7s. payet pour Pieter Sucrebouc."

Jakop Pocof, had his Bruges account credited with £93 gro. through the Antwerp exchange of Hermant "cangeur."[176] And the Bruges furrier Jan van de Walle was able to sell his wares in Antwerp and deposit the money directly in his account in Bruges.[177] Apparently there arose a demand for additional services from de Marke, for in 1369 he sent his son and namesake to the Antwerp fairs both to market cloth and to represent the de Marke exchange. Thus young Collard was able to supply Jehan Stadevourde with £70 gro., supply the Hanse merchant Thideman Rebbart with 45 French francs, and lend the Tournai merchant Jak[emes] dou Pouchiel £40.[178] When the full roll of de Marke customers with business transactions in Antwerp is tallied, some thirty-seven names appear, with Bruges money changers, hostellers, and drapers, and Hanse and other foreign merchants among them.[179] The de Marke accounts thus give clear evidence that Bruges money changers at least periodically knit Antwerp into the fabric of their financial system.

Ghent and Antwerp occupied special positions in relation to the Bruges market, and the financial network of money changers and hostellers was able to include them in its sphere of operations, although we can only guess at the frequency and intensity of these contacts. The evidence of the de Marke accounts, however, gives the impression that his services in the two other cities were customer-driven and not natural adjuncts to his other business interests. This may account for the sparseness of evidence of commercial contact with Ghent or Antwerp. When attention shifts to the ring of cities from which he purchased cloth, especially Tournai, Mons, and Valenciennes, data are abundant, proving once again that money and credit accompanied trade. In this case, de Marke's cooperative business relationship with three other money changers offered access to the Bruges market

176 Ibid., 3, f. 90r: "Jakop Pocof, doy par lui contet a Anwiers a Hermant cangeur £9 gro. et £85 gro." This was also in September 1368 during the St. Bavo fair.

177 Van de Walle and de Marke had extensive business dealings, with de Marke standing as surety for the furrier on several occasions. The Antwerp payments could be large: £164 9s. 5d. in September 1369 (De Marke 5, f. 174v) and £212 1s. 1d. in May "a le fieste" (ibid., f. 6r; £150) during the Whitsun fair of 1368 (De Marke 3, f. 66r). For more on van de Walle, see de Roover, *Money, Banking and Credit*, p. 287, n. 39.

178 De Marke 5, f. 53r: "Jehan Stadevourde me doit que Coll[ard] li delivra a Anwiers." It is significant that "li delivra" is inserted above the crossed-out "li preste" in this account. Ibid., f. 52r: "Thideman Rebbart me doit, par lui contet a Anwiers 45 francs francais." For Rebbart, or Rebber, a merchant from Thorn, see Dierck *et al.*, *Prospographischer Katalog*, p. 329. De Marke 5, f. 44v: "Jak[emes] douPouchiel me doit, par Jehan de Velaine de Tournay les quels Collart li presta a Anwiers, £40 gro."

179 Among the prominent Bruges names, the hostellers Joris Eurle, Pieter van le Fine, and Raoul Doucemin; the drapers Jehan van Ianbeke and Mikiel van de Horne; and the money changers Clais Rapesart and Bauduin van de Meersch. Foreign merchants are more difficult to distinguish, but to Rebbart can be added Jehan Kerleman and Ernout van Roede.

to a number of foreign merchants while affording de Marke additional business opportunities, notably in the bullion market.[180]

The means for this cooperation between money changers in distant cities was the same as that between Bruges changers: individual clearing accounts kept in one another's ledgers. This allowed direct book transfers between exchanges, as well as transactions in the name of a customer. For example, in April 1367 the Bruges merchant and alderman Jehan Bonin received a payment of £17 gro. on behalf of a Nicaise Cartiel of Mons in neighboring Hainault. The money was not delivered to de Marke by Cartiel himself, but arrived via a letter drawn on the Mons money changer Lottart de Tournay.[181] The messenger apparently carried a number of such letters, for a similar payment was made to the Bruges merchant Willem se Proibien.[182] In Douai, de Marke had an account with Jakop (or Copin) Velaine, who shared the operation of the exchange there with his brother Adrien. Both of them had clearing accounts with de Marke.[183] The same system worked in reverse as well. On an unspecified date in 1368, de Marke's customer Jehan Duc was able to pay Jehan Gallon fifteen "petits moutons de Brabant" with coins advanced to him by Lottart in Mons. De Marke simply credited Lottart's account with that number of coins.[184] On the whole, this was not an intense business relationship, as Lottart had only a handful of accounts, and only a few customers seem to have used the inter-exchange transfer possibilities. The same was true for the money changer Jehan de Lingina of Geraardsbergen, who has a single account with de Marke in February 1369.[185]

Two other money changers left their marks in the de Marke accounts as well. Jehan dou Gardin of Tournai had only a few personal accounts, but he apparently served as an intermediary for a number of Tournai

180 For the bullion business, see chapter 7.

181 De Marke 2, f. 284v: "Sire Jehan Bonin, Doy: item li doige pour une lettre de Lottart de Tournay par Nicaise Cartiel de Mons, £17 gro."

182 Ibid., f. 285r, "Will. se Proibien Doy: li doige par Jehan Creste pour une lettre qui vient de Lottart de Tournay, 6 avril [1367] £19 9s. 11d." This Jehan Creste was a frequent customer in these types of exchanges. In May 1368 his account was debited 200 "francs dou roy" worth £24 17s. 2d. 2 mites "par Lottart de Tournay par une lettre escrit sur Jehan Creste" ibid., 3, fol. 63r.

183 They were still operating Douai's only exchange in the 1380s; see Bigwood, *Régime*, vol. 1, p. 396. Their clearing accounts are de Marke 1, ff. 255v, 256r, 260r–v, 271r, 272v. I have found only one transaction drawing upon the Douai exchange (ibid., f. 44v, account of Simon Ongeriet): "Doy item li doige pour Jehan le Cuer par le cange Copin Velaine a ce jour (18 July 1366) £6 gro."

184 De Marke 3, f. 358r: "Lott[art] de Tournay cangeur a Mons en Hain[aut] Doy: pour Jehan Duc quil a paia a Jehan Gallon a Mons 15 moutons petis de B[rabant]."

185 Ibid., 4, 90r, "Jehan de Lingina (Lingnia) cangeur de Grammont." The largest entry in the account is a payment to Lingina in the name of the Bruges merchant Willem Senaillart, whose own account with de Marke is debited that amount ibid., f. 86v.

drapers who sold their cloth in the Bruges Cloth Hall and made their own purchases there as well.[186] Dou Gardin may have worked out of an inn, for de Marke addressed a letter to him at a place called "le Fleur de Lis Karolus" in August 1366.[187] By far the most important operative in de Marke's long-distance network was the money changer Thierry Brochons of Valenciennes. His accounts attest to a long-standing and intensive trading business in cloth and gold and silver bullion as well as exchange. These involved the by now familiar pattern of using clearing accounts for book transfers, though with some interesting twists. An example is a charge made to the account of the Bruges hosteller Jakop Metteneye on behalf of his guest, the Spaniard Biernaert Disiaus, to effect the delivery of 1,277 francs to him in Valenciennes. This was accomplished with a letter to Thierry Brochons.[188] For his part de Marke was able to advance a considerable sum to Jakemes Brochons, Thierry's brother and business partner, to "take with him to the fair of Ypres."[189] The cloth trade occasioned more business between the two, both through transfers in the name of Valenciennes drapers, and for direct purchase of cloth by de Marke.[190] And one entry concerns a rather small sum advanced by Brochons to a Flemish nobleman via a letter of credit from de Marke.[191] The level of trust between the two men must have been high, judging from a memo de Marke wrote to himself in his first journal dated 19 June 1368, which records the collection of a very large payment that he was to make on Brochons's behalf to a Bruges hosteller.[192]

There is a good deal of predictability to connecting the dots outlining de Marke's regional network – from neighboring Ghent and Antwerp to the

[186] Accounts are ibid., 5, ff. 415r and 416r for the group of Tournai merchants. Note as well that a Simon dou Gardin was a changer in Valenciennes; see Bigwood, *Régime*, vol. 1, p. 407, where he finds that a Renier dou Gardin was a changer in 1353 and a Simon in 1381.

[187] De Marke 1, f. 293r, "Jehan de Crespin me doit: pour une lettre que je li delivray adrech[ee] a Jehan dou Gardin le 19 jour en aoust a le Fleur de Lis Karolus 722 francs et £17 14s. 2d."

[188] Ibid., 167r: "Sire Jakop Matenaie me doit: que je fis delivrer a Biernaert Disiaus espaignart, a Valenc[iennes] par une lettre a Tiery Brochons, 19 janvier [1367] 1277 francs."

[189] De Marke 2, f. 363v, "Thiery Brochons me doit: item me doit il pour Jak. Brochons contet pour porter a le fieste dIpre £180 gro." Brochons built up a considerable credit balance with de Marke, for the same account lists a £195 credit made via letter carried by Jakemes. Upon his return from the Ypres fair, Jakemes made a £30 6s. 9d. deposit and a delivery of £53 9s. 8d. of gold bullion and £167 4s. 3d. of silver bullion.

[190] Ibid., 3, f. 356v, lists a number of payments credited to Brochons for Valenciennes drapers, among them Kak. de Montauban and Jehan de Crespin, "drapier." An account of August 1369 records a payment made to Brochons for "8 dras quil menvoia" worth £9 13s (ibid., 5, f. 145v).

[191] Ibid., 2, f. 130v: "Mesire de Dikemue me doit, que je li fit avoir a Valenc[iennes] par le cange Tiery Brochons, 6 aoust par une lettre, 52 francs franc[ais]."

[192] Ibid., 1, under 19 June: "Memore que je doit recevoir pour Tiery Brochons a Jakop van deniede £391 16s. 8d."

significant cities of the regions from which he bought and sold. And while the resulting sketch refutes the long-held belief that the network of book transfers run by Bruges money changers ended at the city gates, it falls short of a convincing demonstration of a powerful, long-distance aid to business. The absence of any evidence of such a network in the Ruweel accounts also points to the fact that not all and perhaps only a few, Bruges money changers had the far-flung business contacts necessary to form similar networks. Is there evidence in de Marke of a wider network of greater utility to Bruges and foreign merchants alike? The answer is a tentative yes, with appropriate caution due to the fragmentary nature of the evidence. It appears that de Marke could effect payments in both London and Paris, though it is by no means clear in the accounts how he accomplished this. Paris and London were to a degree financial satellites of Bruges at the time, at least in the view of Italian merchants.[193] In these three cases the men involved were a Hanse and an Italian merchant, so it is difficult to judge what business lay behind the transactions.[194] Other tantalizing hints of even longer-distance connections occur twice in the accounts. In 1368 the clerk of the nobleman Watier de Monstruelcourt secured a letter of credit from de Marke to be redeemed in Rome at the office of the Galberti company.[195] A last mention of long-distance exchange seems to point to Genoa, since the account of an Ivo Fio Daviguolo was debited for £8 12s., a portion of which was used there.[196] Given the rarity of these transactions, it is unlikely that financial transfers of this type were anything but exceptional. They serve however to show the range of this Bruges financial network.

Again only a single example can be drawn from de Marke's accounts documenting a business relationship involving a Flemish merchant performing a long-distance trading operation. This fact is probably due more to the lack of specific information in the accounts than to any shortage of

193 De Roover, *Money, Banking and Credit*, p. 55; Mueller, *Venetian Money Market*, pp. 594–596.

194 On 15 November 1369 the presumably Italian Baudouch Belenat was paid £105 11s. 1d. "pour 1 cange a Paris" for which the account of Piere Bregadin was debited (De Marke 5, f. 271r). Two other items relate to the business of the Dortmund merchant Lambrecht or Lambert Berswort. In October 1367 he had a payment made to an Andrius Franchois in London (ibid., 2, f. 177r): "Lambrec Beswot me doit, pour Andrius Franchois 12 oct. [1367] pour une finanche quil li fist a Londres £120 gro. se li doit faire le dis Andrius avoir sen argent 18 jours apres le sain Martin [18 November 1367]." The second entry refers perhaps to a later payment involved in the same deal: ibid., Journal 1, under 16 December [1367]: "Andrius Francois doit pour Lambrec Beswort a payer a Londre 30 jour apres le nouel [30 December 1367] 420 nobles." For Berswort, see Dierck *et al.*, *Prosopographischer Katalog*, pp. 38–40.

195 De Marke 3, f. 351v "Jehan le Wette me doit, par lui par le cause de Mesire Watier de Monstruelcourt pour aler a Romme 237 francs lequel devrer fur. delivrer a le compaigne de Jak. de Galbert."

196 Ibid., 5, 144r, "Ivo Fio Daviguolo me doit £8 12s. pour Mathiu £5 pour 1 cange a Genues, 30 aug. [1369]."

Flemish-run trade. The merchant was Jakemes or Jakes de Wallers, whose company organized trade with Brittany and Spain. De Marke accepted drafts from Brittany for rather small amounts in 1368, and advanced de Wallers 200 French francs for a journey to Spain.[197] Apparently de Wallers was involved in trade in the Bay of Biscay with at least one Spanish partner.

CONCLUSION

One of the magical qualities of networks is that their power grows exponentially as the number of connections increases, to the point that they become greater than the sum of their parts. The interleaved and interwoven financial networks that once existed in Bruges are symptomatic of the successful achievement of volumes of trade, numbers of resident merchants from enough different European regions to make of the Bruges market a place that not only could not be bypassed, but could actually draw those whose desire was perhaps not to so much to buy and sell goods as to buy those letters of exchange or credit. This constituted the financial power of a city of merchants: that its inns and banks were places known and trusted far beyond Flanders, that its resident merchants developed their own financial systems in which Bruges played a central role, among whom the financially precocious Italians played the leading, albeit not the solo, part. Bruges was first a city of commerce and then a city of finance, and it owed its success in both these roles to the presence and involvement of merchants, native and foreign, present and absent, all part of a great virtuous circle that expanded throughout the fourteenth and survived to the end of the fifteenth century.

[197] The clearest indication of the organization of de Waller's business is in de Marke's second journal (f. 5r), which speaks of "li compaignie de Jak. de Wallers" and mentions Sire Gabryel dAgovegre, who was apparently an active partner in the traffic between Brittany and Bruges. He arrived with letters of exchange calling for the Flemish equivalent of 30 French moutons, and equal number of francs – SAB, De Marke, Journal 1, f. 5r (my foliation). The corresponding account is De Marke 2, f. 287v, written to Gabryel Dagovegre, 2 March 1367. On 29 July 1366, Jak. de Wallers was able to draw out 200 French francs "pour porter en Espengne": ibid., 1, f. 287v.

CHAPTER 7

Wool, cloth, and gold

But ye Fflemmynges, if ye be not wrothe,
The grete substance of your cloothe, at the fulle,
Ye wot ye make hit of youre Englissh wolle . . .
For the wolle of Englande
Susteyneth the commons Flemmyngis . . .[1]

Vego molti mercanti che vengono di verso Brugia con molti muli carichi di lane, e di panni, e d'oro, e d'argento, e di molte belle cose.[2]

Bernardino di Siena, 1425

Bruges may have been the first northern European city to develop an intricate network of exchange, bridging coinages, distances, and political barriers – but it was not to be the last even in its immediate neighborhood of the Low Countries. By the sixteenth century Antwerp, followed by Amsterdam in the seventeenth and London in the eighteenth and nineteenth centuries, *seriatim* stood at the head of ever larger and more intricate economic and banking networks. And surely the great commercial metropolis of the industrial and post-industrial age, New York (once Nieuw Amsterdam), shows that there is a kind of genetics to this succession of commercial capitals. Yet in this family tree the least is known about Bruges, particularly how its status as the host of foreign merchants, the central node in a network of exchange, this great city of *marchandise*, affected other economic structures within the city. For Bruges, in common with all its descendent cities, was also a city of manufacture, consumption, and local trade. How these economic sectors coexisted, interrelated and in some cases were revolutionized is the subject of this chapter.

The opening quotation is taken from a tendentious pamphlet of the early fifteenth century in which the English boast of Flemish dependencee

[1] G. Warner (ed.), *The Libelle of Englysche Polycye* (Oxford, 1926), pp. 5–6.
[2] Spicciani, *Capitale e interesse tra mercatura e povertà*, p. 128.

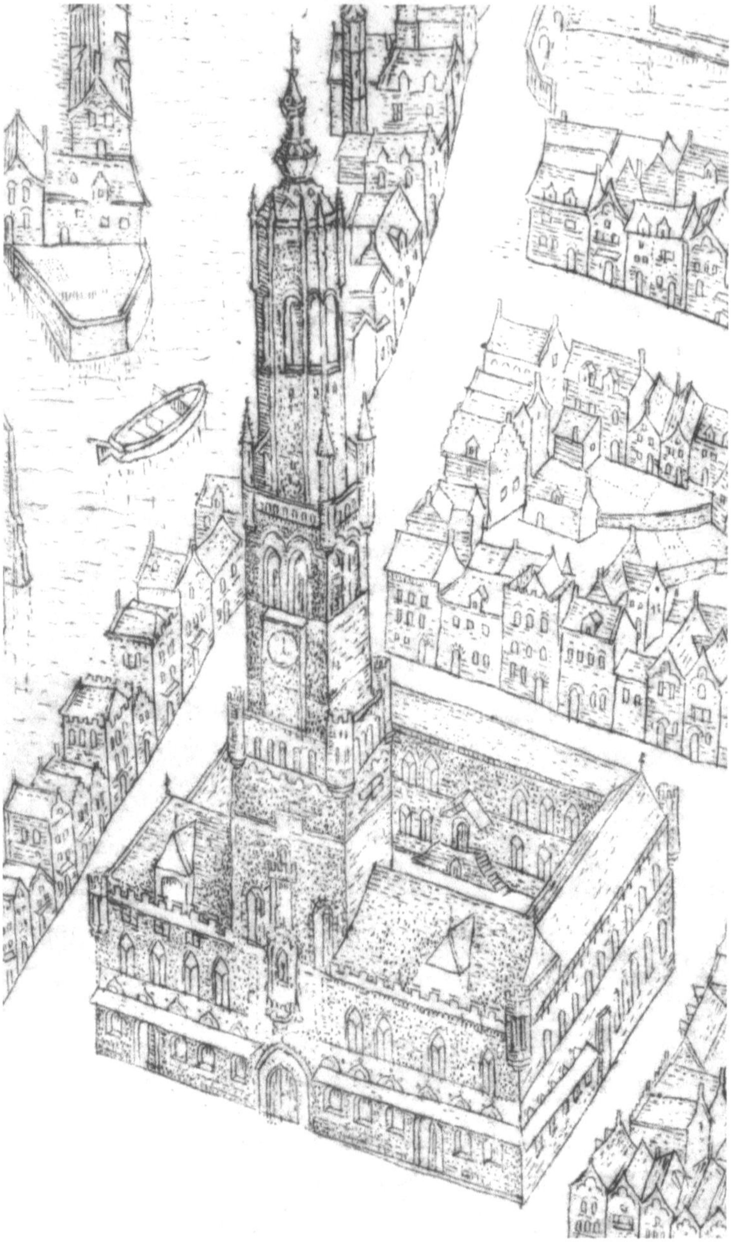

Figure 9: The Belfort and "Old" Cloth Hall. This sixteenth-century view includes the spire added to the belfry in the late fifteenth century.

on English wool. The second is drawn from a sermon by the popular Florentine preacher Bernardino of Siena, who drew on popular images to drive home his theological point. However late in date, the anonymous English writer states the truth in praising both the quality of English wools and the dependence of Flanders on them in order to produce cloth. It was especially the wools of Herefordshire and the "March" wools of Shropshire and Staffordshire, equaled also by those of the Cotswolds that were used to produce the famous cloths of Ypres, Ghent, and Douai.[3] By 1400, the symbiosis between English fleece and the looms of Flanders as well as Brabant and Holland was already at least two centuries old, though the quantities shipped from England to the continent had suffered significant reductions.[4] By that date the wool trade had also passed through at least three distinct phases, all of great significance for the economy of Bruges.

WOOL

There is a good deal of hyperbole, however, in the above English declaration, for by no means all Flemish cloth was woven from English wool, particularly from the finer sorts. Wool produced in other areas in Europe is all too often overlooked. For example, the earliest and most continuous source of wool for Flanders was produced in Flanders itself, particularly along the coastal polders – recently diked and reclaimed land still too salty to support crops.[5] Other sources were Scotland, Ireland, and even Spain. It is certain that these wools were woven into cloth for domestic consumption in Flanders, and in the thirteenth century were also exported along with the much higher-priced luxury cloth sorts as far south as the Mediterranean and as far east as the Baltic.[6] Of course, commencing in the fifteenth century and lasting into the modern period, it was the merino wool of Spain that replaced English wool as the most sought-after fiber in Europe.[7]

[3] Munro, *Wool, Cloth and Gold*, pp. 2–6.

[4] For the history of the English wool trade, see Lloyd, *English Wool Trade*, especially chapter 8, "The decline of the wool trade." The rather gradual decline of the last half of the fourteenth century accelerated after the introduction in 1429 of the bullion and partition ordinances, which severely limited credit and imposed bullion requirements in payment for English wool. See Munro, *Wool, Cloth and Gold*, pp. 84–86.

[5] Verhulst, "La laine indigène," 281–322.

[6] Hilmar C. Krueger, 'The Genoese Exportation of Northern Cloths to Mediterranean Ports, Twelfth Century', *RBPH* 65 (1987), 722–750; Patrick Chorley, "The Cloth Exports of Flanders and Northern France during the 13th Century: A Luxury Trade?" *Economic History Review* second series 40 (1987), 349–379.

[7] Munro, *Wool, Cloth and Gold*, p. 4; Carla Rahn and William D. Phillips, *Spain's Golden Fleece: Wool Production and the Wool Trade from the Middle Ages to the Nineteenth Century* (Baltimore, 1997), pp. 238–239.

Nonetheless it was the trade in English wool that was one of the defining economic forces in Flanders in the thirteenth and fourteenth centuries, and in ways beyond the purely economic. In a number of west Flemish cities, but particularly in Bruges, the social and political elite was drawn essentially from a trading organization known to historians as the Flemish Hanse. Though its members traded commodities other than wool, it was wool that had the upper hand in terms of both value and prestige.[8] This pattern of fixing social and political hegemony with reference to English trade was only eroded by the gradual democratization of the Hanse itself and its ultimate demise in the wake of trade embargoes and social revolution by 1300.[9] But wool and wool merchants lost little of their importance to the Bruges economy in the process.

This "first period" of the English wool trade was marked by what historians have called "active" Flemish trade. In other words, Flemish merchants traveled to the source of English wools, purchased them, often paying in advance for the next year's clip, and then shipped them to Bruges or via Nieuwport to Ypres.[10] This created a true "interdependence" between the pastoral economy of England and the urban, textile-driven economy of Flanders. It certainly enriched many an English Cistercian monastery, as well as a fair number of Flemish merchants.[11] This era came to an abrupt and definite end between 1270 and 1300.

The reasons were political and not economic. From the 1270s, the English crown grasped the revenue and political opportunities offered by wool exports and control of the wool trade. First by embargoing exports to Flanders in the early 1270s and thereafter by taxing them, Edward I and later Edward III ousted Flemish merchants from their previous role as purchasers and exporters of wool and impeded trade with ever higher export duties. By the late fourteenth century, such taxes made up about a third of the price of a sack of English wool.[12] At the same time, Italian merchants took over the active trade in wool, in part as revenue agents for the crown.[13]

[8] See Wyffels, "De Vlaamse Hanze van Londen," and Chapter 3.

[9] Van Houtte, *Geschiedenis*, pp. 90–91; Ryckaert and Vandewalle, *Brugge*, p. 41.

[10] O. Mus, "Het aandeel van de Ieperlingen in de engelse wolexport, 1280–1330," in *Prisma van de geschiedenis van* Ieper (Tielt, 1974), pp. 332–355, and in general Lloyd, *English Wool Trade*, chapters 1 and 2.

[11] The best documented of these tend to be merchants of Douai, such as the infamous Jehan Boinebroke. See Georges Espinas, "Jehan Boine Broke: bourgeois et drapier douaisien," *Vierteljahrschrift für Sozial-und Wirtschaftsgeschichte* 2 (1904), 383–412, and more recently, Martha Howell, "Weathering Crisis, Managing Change: The Emergence of a New Socioeconomic Order in Douai at the End of the Middle Ages," in *Drapery Production in the Late Medieval Low Countries: Markets and Strategies for Survival (14th–16th Centuries)* (Leuven and Apeldoorn, 1993), pp. 85–118.

[12] Munro, *Wool, Cloth and Gold*, p. 7.

[13] See Hunt and Murray, *History of Business*, pp. 102–105; Lloyd, *English Wool Trade*, pp. 60–98.

The English wool trade remained crucial to the developing commercial hegemony of Bruges in the fourteenth century, however. With the intervention of the English crown in the market, a new system of stapling was created. A staple was a fixed point of sale for a commodity or product, where buyers, sellers, and royal tax agents could meet to do business.[14] Ordinarily, no English wool could be exported other than to the staple market, although in practice some wool was exempted from this requirement either because it was of low quality, or through special royal license granted individual exporters. Needless to say, Bruges, both because of its long history as a wool market and because of its growing commercial importance, was an eager and logical site for the English wool staple.

Nothing came easily in the commercial politics of King Edward I or III. Though Bruges was not the primary site of the first staple in 1294, it functioned as a secondary market with royal approval in 1297, though only for a year. Bruges became the sole continental staple in 1325–1326 and again in 1340, demonstrating the continued interest in the English wool trade in the city.[15] But political troubles and disputes restrained the English from fixing the staple in Bruges. At first it was the economic blackmail exercised by Edward I in his struggles against Philip the Fair of France; later the Flemings insisted on permitting wool sales only to other Flemings. Finally, the Flemings, led by Bruges, first objected to, then banned, the import and sale of English cloth in Flanders.[16] Only under considerable pressure from merchants of the German Hanse did the Flemings back down enough to permit transshipment of English cloth through Flanders. The ban on sale of such cloth, however, remained in force until 1489.

One result of these conflicts was the removal of the wool staple to Middelburg in neighboring Zeeland in 1348, from where it returned to England in 1353. The most important transfer of the staple came in 1363, when it was moved to English-occupied Calais where, with the exception of two brief periods, it was to remain until the expulsion of the English in 1558.[17]

The Calais wool staple by no means meant the end of either important Flemish/English trade or of Bruges's role as an important wool market. In fact, it is striking that in the course of the fourteenth century, a certain

[14] For the development of an English wool staple, see ibid., pp. 193–224.

[15] Nicholas, "English Trade," 23–61; Nicholas, *Medieval Flanders*, pp. 172–179, 273–276.

[16] Munro, "Industrial Protectionism in Medieval Flanders," pp. 229–268; Munro, "Bruges and the Abortive Staple in English Cloth: An Incident in the Shift of Commerce from Bruges to Antwerp in the Late Fifteenth Century," *RBPH* 44 (1966), 1137–1159; reprinted in John H. Munro, *Textiles, Towns, and Trade: Essays in the Economic History of Late-Medieval England and the Low Countries* (Aldershot and Brookfield, Vermont, 1994); Nicholas, *Medieval Flanders*, pp. 290–291.

[17] Nicholas, "English Trade," 23. Somewhat ironically, the staple returned to Bruges one final time in 1559 after the English loss of Calais, before being given up altogether by the 1560s.

synchronicity arose linking sectors of the English economy with the payment and exchange system of Bruges. As previously noted, English merchants came almost exclusively to Bruges to acquire the Spanish products imported by merchants from Iberia, despite the fact that the Spaniards regularly called at English ports, particularly Southampton, throughout the century.[18] The reason for coming to Bruges was to take advantage of credits derived from wool sales, thus allowing for payment by letter of exchange, obviating the need for payment in ready coin. Given the difficulties of exporting coin or bullion from England in the late Middle Ages, such services could only enhance the appeal of the Bruges market.

There is also considerable evidence that Bruges remained a favorite destination and overseas residence for English merchants after the establishment of the Calais staple. As described in chapter 6, the English colony in Bruges had its corporate beginnings in the early fourteenth century, growing apace in the 1320s and 1330s as the wool staple came and went from the city.[19] It is in the 1360s, however, that the Bruges money changers' accounts give us an idea of the relationship between Bruges and its English merchant visitors. As mentioned previously, the names of eighty Englishmen are listed in the de Marke accounts between 1366 and 1370, twenty-four of whom had accounts with the money changer.[20] This is in no way proof of a permanent English colony of this size, for no doubt some of the merchants were only temporary and occasional visitors. However, given that the scribe indicated nationality only in cases where the merchant was unfamiliar to him, and that de Marke is only one of ten or more money changers, eighty is certainly too low a figure to represent all English merchants who may have passed through Bruges. The de Marke accounts also imply an easy, familiar relationship between these English merchants and Bruges, for unlike the Scottish merchants listed in the accounts, the English rarely seem to have lodged with one of the official hostels of the city.[21] This means that the English either rented their own accommodation in Bruges or lodged with fellow countrymen. We know that William de la Pole rented houses in Bruges in order to store his wool shipments in 1339–1340.[22] In either case

[18] Childs, *Anglo-Castilian Trade*, pp. 181, and above chapter 6.

[19] Marechal, "Duizen jaar Britse aanwezigheid te Brugge," in *Europese aanwezigheid*, pp. 13–33 (originally published in 1966).

[20] SAB, Koopmansboeken, De Marke 1–5: the account holders were John Apelot, William Banby, Adam Becsuelle, John Bemestre, John Bonston, Thomas Bourbas, Rogier Branseby, John Cousin, Simon Elizem, John Goldbeter, Animon Hastet, John Lovee, and John Massal of London.

[21] The sixty Scottish merchants lodged in ten hostels, many of them run by well-known business figures in Bruges. The hostels of Jan Metteneye, Zegher Honin, Lambesin van de Walle, Pieter Scuetelare, and Franche van Singhe had English merchant guests. Not coincidently these broker/hostellers also dealt in English wool.

[22] Fryde, *William de la Pole*, p. 28, and above chapter 6.

this argues for a more developed English trade infrastructure in Bruges, akin to that of the German Hanse.[23]

One English merchant of the mid-fourteenth century, John Goldbeter, has a career well documented enough to give some indication of the continuing importance of English wool to the Flemish economy, and in which Bruges plays an especially important role. It is a remarkable story that reveals much about the nature of trade and the role of Bruges in it. John Goldbeter was a native of York, who in the course of a thirty-five-year career as a wool merchant and political adventurer came to call Bruges his second and even eternal home:[24] eternal because of an agreement sealed in March 1370 between Goldbeter together with his wife, Clare, and the chapter of St. Donatian's church in Bruges, establishing and endowing a chapel which would serve as the burial place of both Goldbeters.[25] But this is just the end of the story. The beginning was some thirty-four years before, during the summer of 1337. A trade war had been declared between Flanders and England the previous autumn, and Goldbeter had been unlucky enough to be in Bruges when a general arrest warrant was issued for all English merchants and their goods.[26] He wrote a plaintive letter to his cousin and protector, Henry Goldbeter of York, complaining that he was "lying in a deep and dark prison among thieves and murderers." He was indeed being held in the old comital castle called 't Steen (the Rock), located on the north side of the Burg at the heart of Bruges. He was right to complain, for the common name for the prison in Flemish was "de Donkere Kamer" – the Dark Chamber – and donations for the relief of its inmates were a common form of charity.[27] Goldbeter displayed his talent for escape in this first instance, for by the autumn he had embarked on another escapade.

This involved a venture organized by Henry Goldbeter to collect and sell English wool in the Zeeland port of Dordrecht, since the English wool

[23] See chapter 3 for the German Hanse, whose members certainly owned considerable real estate in Bruges, but who were also frequent lodgers at commercial hostels and inns. The English were granted the much-coveted privilege of their own weighing facility, the "Engels Weeghuis," first mentioned in 1315 (Marechal, "Duizend jaar," p. 17). This was a city-owned building, usually leased out to a private individual who nonetheless agreed to operate it according to agreed procedures and to keep a room for meetings of the English merchant community. For the conditions of Hanse and other foreign merchants, see Anke Greve, "Vreemdelingen in de stad: Integratie of uitsluiting?" in Carlier, *et al., Core and Periphery in late Medieval Urban Society*, pp. 153–163.

[24] Much of the English documentation about Goldbeter is gathered by Fryde, "Some Business Transactions of York Merchants."

[25] The original is BAB, St. Donaas, D 40bis, number 30 with a copy in St. Donaas, A48, Acta Capituli, ff. 22v–25v. It is edited in Murray, *Notarial Instruments*, pp. 279–285.

[26] On the series of events leading up to this general arrest, see Lloyd, *English Wool Trade*, pp. 144–147.

[27] Fryde, "Some Business Transactions," 5. For the debtors' prison, the "Dark Chamber," see Galvin, *Poor Tables of Bruges*, pp. 163–166, and Van Houtte, *Geschiedenis*, pp. 303–304.

staple at Bruges had been closed due to the trade war.[28] Some 1,800 sacks (ten of which belonged to John Goldbeter) had been collected by October 1337, but in December, as a result of a quarrel with royal agents, the whole lot was seized by the king. Afterward it was discovered that some 300 sacks were missing, including those owned by John. Eventually it came out that he, in cooperation with other owners of the wool, had spirited away those sacks and sold them to Flemings through his agents in Bruges, in defiance of the royal ban. For this he was fined £200 sterling by the king, but true to his talent for escape, Goldbeter was pardoned by Edward while he was abroad in Antwerp in October 1338.[29] Already Goldbeter had perfected the pattern his subsequent career was to take: wool was his business, Bruges his market, audacity, risk, and a genius for getting out of tight corners his trademarks.

A wool merchant during the reign of Edward III was faced with a trade situation of considerable challenge, yet in the hands of someone like Goldbeter, of almost unlimited opportunity as well. The key figure was King Edward, whose consuming passion was to gain land and honor in France at whatever cost.[30] His continental expeditions thus became a series of financial improvisations, a sort of borrow-as-you-go and repay-if-you-must plan in which wool was the key commodity. Wool was taxed at export; seized and sold by the crown and its agents; blockaded and traded; and like Arabian sweet crude in the 1970s, wool could either make your fortune or ruin you. The key was knowing how to break the law and escape the consequences. It was, to quote one historian, "a unique period of opportunity and danger."[31]

The ruinous duty on wool exports, some 40s. st. per sack, imposed by Edward after 1338 practically forced English merchants to play a double game as smugglers and lenders to the king. Frequent large loans both bought pardon and purchased tax exemptions, for the loan principal and interest were invariably repaid by a license to export wool tax-free, or some other assignment on the customs.[32] Loans or other services rendered to the king also could result in lucrative rewards to the merchant with good

[28] Lloyd, *English Wool Trade*, pp. 146–152 for the general background.

[29] Fryde, "Some Business Transactions," 6. Goldbeter's pardon is *Calendar of Patent Rolls, 1338–40*, 16 vols. (London, 1891–1916), vol. 1, p. 191.

[30] On Edward in general, see Scott Waugh, *England in the Reign of Edward III* (Cambridge, 1991), pp. 14–16, 231–232 and Sumption, *Trial by Battle*, pp. 113–114.

[31] Waugh, *England in the Reign*, p. 186.

[32] This was the coin used to pay the Italian merchant companies, the Bardi and Peruzzi. See Hunt, *Medieval Supercompanies*, pp. 190–211. In 1337–1340, English merchants were given a £2 exemption for each sack exported by them: Fryde, "Some Business Transactions," 7, see also E. B. Fryde, *Wool Accounts of William de la Pole, A Study of Some Aspects of the English Wool Trade at the Start of the Hundred Years' War* (York, 1964).

timing. In the decade from 1338 to 1348, encompassing the period from Edward's first expedition to the Netherlands to the siege and capture of Calais, Goldbeter played the game for all he was worth. From 1338 to 1340 he provided loans, and with his partner and eighteen men-at-arms served in Edward's army during the Cambrésis campaign of 1339.[33] Meanwhile he was smuggling wool, attempting to avoid customs payments by loading a small boat with wool. In the ensuing inquiry, Goldbeter apparently bribed members of the first jury, which was dissolved and a new one called.[34] He was convicted in 1341, but again pardoned in view of his services to the king. He and his partners had again advanced the king money in 1340 in anticipation of the tax on wool voted by Parliament. But it was not until 1341 that the Goldbeter Company was able to make good their promissory note and turn a handsome profit on the sale of 664 sacks of wool valued at £4188 st. Trouble came again in 1343 as a result of another bit of sharp trading by John. He had purchased the bond of a deceased wool merchant issued by the king on the wool confiscated at Dordrecht in 1337. Such debt could often be purchased at a steep discount, and then used at full face value in the form of tax exemptions on the export of wool. The cheek of this (a merchant convicted of evading the order, then profiting by it) apparently enraged the now powerful William de la Pole, who denounced Goldbeter to the Exchequer; this led to an inquiry and lengthy court case.[35] Ultimately, in 1346 Goldbeter was summoned to appear before the court of the Exchequer, a summons he defied, but before a sentence of outlawry could be brought against him, he had already found a way out.[36]

Once again the king's taste for war intervened, this time the eleven-month siege of Calais that was devouring great stores of treasure even as Goldbeter's case before the Exchequer reached a crisis point. Again, Edward sought ready money by farming out the customs, on this occasion to an English firm, Walter Chiriton and Company. Goldbeter in effect became a loan broker for Chiriton, employing his knowledge gained in the wool trade and contacts in Flanders to come up with the sizable sums needed by the king in a hurry. Documents from Chiriton's bankruptcy case permit a clear view of Goldbeter's financial artistry in pursuit of the king's war and his own profit. Between late 1346 and early 1348, Goldbeter brokered six loans for Chiriton, raising at least £25,000 sterling Where he got the

33 Fryde, "Some Business Transactions," 8–9. Lyon, Lyon, and Lucas, *Wardrobe Book*, pp. xcvii, 350.

34 Kermode, *Medieval Merchants*, pp. 194–195.

35 Fryde, *William de la Pole*, pp. 186–187.

36 He did serve some time in the Fleet prison, however; see Fryde, "Some Business Transactions," 8–10; Fryde, *William de la Pole*, pp. 158–160.

money and on what terms reveal much of Goldbeter's remarkable knowledge of Flemish finance and its possibilities.

Of the six loans, two were contracted with Italian companies in Bruges in return for promises of English wool.[37] By then Italians had the leading role in the marketing of English wool, particularly through Bruges, so a deal with them, particularly for the finest quality northern wools, which Goldbeter promised, made sense. These loans were in effect futures contracts, with promised dates of delivery and interest assessed in case of tardiness.[38] Bonds were also given by Chiriton, giving amounts two to three times greater than the value of the wool. Another deal involving wool was sealed with a London merchant and a Hanse merchant and soon-to-be Bruges money changer and financier. Their partnership agreed to advance money against the delivery of 700 sacks of wool to them in Bruges.[39] A consortium of York merchants made the last loan on the security of 100 sacks of wool.[40] It was the smallest of the four, resulting in only a little more than £500 for Chiriton's coffers. Goldbeter clearly reveals his knowledge of where the money was in the market for English wool. Between Italian companies in Bruges, partnerships between the English and a naturalized Bruges merchant, and the York merchants living near the source of supply, the flow of wool and money could be effectively tapped by someone who knew how to deal.

The other two loans reveal more of Goldbeter's artistry at raising money quickly despite the cost. The first involved a sophisticated loan in the form of a fictitious sale of Ghent cloth. The creditors were three Ghent cloth merchants, two of whom came from wealthy and prestigious clans, the uten Hove and Braem. They in effect advanced £1,300 st. to Goldbeter in return for their Ghent cloth, which was declared to be worth £1,850 st. The cloth would be held by the three Gentenars in pledge until a payment for the full declared value of the cloth was received. Goldbeter even volunteered to remain as a hostage in Ghent until the loan was repaid, an offer that seems

[37] These were Francis Venture and Co. and Massy Johan and Gabriel Lyprandi, whom the documents surviving from the bankruptcy of Chiriton and Co. describe as residing in Bruges; see Fryde, "Some Business Transactions," 24.

[38] Ibid., table 11, 24; that for Venture was for the value of 2,000 sacks of wool. The precise conditions of the loan to the second two Italians are not known.

[39] Henry Causton of London and Tideman Blomerode or Blomenrode of Lübeck eventually refused the wool and took a money payment instead (ibid.). They represent the sometimes close cooperation between English and Hanse merchants in the English wool trade of around 1350, though it is likely that Bruges was their meeting place. Blomenrode at least became a Bruges burgher after 1350 and spent a decade as a money changer and financier. On him see Asmussen, *Lübecker Flandernfahrer*, pp. 294–299.

[40] This was John Sakelok and Co.; see Fryde, "Some Business Transactions," 24.

to have been more rhetorical than real.[41] The final loan was contracted with the largest pawnbroking house of Bruges in a deal combining aspects of the previous five loans. Wool was used as the pledge in this case, but wisely perhaps, the Bruges pawnbrokers demanded additional security. Therefore Goldbeter, an English associate, and a Bruges partner put up an additional £2,000 sterling worth of wool, cloth and silver plate as security. This single transaction raised over £5,000 sterling for Chiriton.[42]

Goldbeter's financial talent is unmistakable in the above business deals, and the Chiriton company was fulsome in its thanks for the cash flow. But by 1349, the interest rates and other conditions agreed to by Goldbeter proved to be ruinous. For example, the loan from the pawnbrokers of Bruges was higher than above the prevailing rate – 5 instead of 3.6 percent per month – and the other loans, when the penalties for late payment began to mount, proved to be just as costly. Chiriton and Company simply could not derive enough cash from their control of English customs to pay the enormous costs of borrowing, so the firm was forced into bankruptcy and prolonged litigation. Goldbeter and associates did very well out of it all, even taking into account their payment of some of the interest and principal of the loans Goldbeter brokered. In return for his services and cash, Goldbeter had received tax benefits on wool exports; these he either resold or used himself while Chiriton was still solvent. Thus it is estimated that Goldbeter made roughly a 25 percent profit from his work for Chiriton, at the same time securing the king's pardon for his smuggling offenses. It was also around this time that Goldbeter received land in recently conquered Calais as additional reward for his services.[43]

After Chiriton and Co.'s bankruptcy case has worked its way through the Court of Exchequer in 1352, Goldbeter fades from view for a time. He seems to have taken up more or less permanent residence in Bruges by the 1360s, for in 1361 he was named governor of the king's merchants in Flanders. This office made him the king's agent in Flanders in cases of debtors fleeing the king's justice, and other affairs. He was still active in business, this time in trade from Nantes to Bruges, for a ship he owned in partnership with an Englishman and a Fleming was captured by pirates on its return voyage in 1361. But the appearance of model behavior was more illusion than

[41] For the above, ibid., 12–13, 24. For the Uten Hove and Braam clans in Ghent, see Nicholas, *Metamorphosis*, p. 146, where he mentions a Jan Uten Hove, a broker, and p. 81, with mention of the Braem family.

[42] This case is discussed above in chapter 5 in the context of credit in Bruges. For the precise terms of the loan, see Fryde, "Some Business Transactions," 24.

[43] Dorothy Greaves, "Calais under Edward III," in George Unwin (ed.), *Finance and Trade under Edward III* (Manchester, 1918), p. 314.

reality, for in 1362 Goldbeter was denounced for defying the ban on wool exports by native merchants between 1353 and 1356. Specifically, Goldbeter had allegedly organized a phony corporation fronted by two Flemings, thus escaping the ban, but in reality the wool belonged to Goldbeter and the powerful and well-connected Sir William de la Pole. When de la Pole was summoned before the King's Bench, he charged Goldbeter with masterminding the operation.[44] Goldbeter defied a similar summons to appear and was outlawed as a result. Bruges thus became both haven and home by 1362. There was yet one more escape, however, when in 1364, through the mediation of the Flemish count, Louis of Male, Goldbeter was pardoned by Edward. This is the last record of him in England.[45]

As a merchant of Bruges, Goldbeter, now certainly in his fifties or sixties, continued many of his accustomed ways. His interest in bullion and finance continued unabated. We know that in 1357 he was offered a bonus for delivery of bullion to the comital mint.[46] Records are fragmentary, but we know of a complaint, dated January 1366, lodged against him and two others, the Englishman John Salomon and Antonio de Alberti, likely of the famous Italian merchant family, denouncing them as notorious usurers who advanced "large sums of money under usurious conditions." Such charges, lodged in the local church court and sent on in the form of a supplication to Pope Urban V, were sufficient to result in Goldbeter's excommunication.[47] His activities as a moneylender are confirmed by large advances he made to the duchess of Brittany in the spring of 1366. These resulted in a lawsuit in the Parlement of Paris, before the debt was finally discharged. Other evidence of his business activities in Bruges is less spectacular. Judging from the account he kept with the money changer Collard de Marke, Goldbeter continued his interest in the wool trade. Several large payments to English merchants and from Italian and French merchants as well as Bruges innkeepers indicate this, but the small number of transactions across the four-year period from 1366 to 1370 – a mere thirty-three – suggest that the pace of Goldbeter's business was beginning to slow.[48] Goldbeter died

44 Fryde, *William de la Pole*, pp. 159, 226–227 and Fryde, "Some Business Transactions," 20–21, where citations are to be found for Goldbeter's ship and the incidents leading up to the suit in King's Bench. For the general history see Nicholas, *Medieval Flanders*, p. 290.

45 Fryde, "Some Business Transactions," 21.

46 A variant of his name current in Flanders – Goudbetel – is used in the document, whose text is found in Limburg-Stirum, *Cartulaire de Louis de Male*, vol. II, pp. 181–182 and Elsen, "La monnaie," 99.

47 D. Ursmer Berlière (ed.), *Suppliques d'Urbain IV (1362–1370)* (Rome 1914), p. 613; Marechal, "Duizend jaar," p. 230 n. 2.

48 SAB De Marke 2, f. 293r, 10 March 1367: there is the large payment of £ 841 16s. 3d. to the Englishman Tumas Wist, presumably for wool; likewise in July 1369 (ibid., 3, f. 138v) a payment of £60 gro. to

sometime before 1371; his wife Clare's body was interred beside him in 1380 in the chapel they had founded in St. Donatian's church.[49]

This leads us to the creation of Goldbeter's burial chapel in the chapter church of St. Donatian's, located ironically only a few hundred feet from the dungeon in which he had languished nearly thirty-five years before. An additional irony, of course, is what became of his excommunication as a notorious usurer. The location was remarkable: the church was the most aristocratic in the city, with ancient ties to the comital house and a leading role in maintaining the cult of the martyred Count Charles the Good. Remarkable as well is Goldbeter's choice to pass up burial in the chapel dedicated to St. Thomas Becket, founded by English merchants in 1344 in the Carmelite church. Clearly, as a wealthy, status-conscious, and well-connected foreigner, Goldbeter was making a dramatic gesture in creating a chapel for himself and his wife Clare. Fear of advancing age and sudden death due to plague may also have played a role, for Bruges had been hard hit in 1368–1369 by a recurrence of the plague that had carried off a number of prominent merchants.[50] The foundation document attests to Goldbeter's unusual status, given that it is drawn up in French, presumably by a clerk of the chapter, sealed by the great seal of St. Donatian's, but attested to not by a notary public from the chapter, of whom there were several, but by Bartholomeo de Arquato, an Italian notary whose customers were drawn from the foreign merchant community of Bruges.[51] The deal involved an extant chapel, dedicated to St. Julian, which according to the terms of the agreement would be completely refitted by the Goldbeters. Carefully

Tumas Draieton, another Englishman and a business partner of the Bruges money changer Pieter Daudenarde. Italian merchants involved in large transactions with him were Barde Menchine (ibid., 4, f. 96r 21 February 1369) and Dimenche Dandree (ibid., 5, ff. 180v, 304v). Their involvement in the wool trade is proven by confiscation records of 1371 (see below and Nicholas, "English Trade," 31). In November 1369, a fellow countryman, John Lindesay, was lodging with him, and he also had dealings with the Bruges hostellers and wool brokers Pieter Scuetelare (De Marke 5, f. 270r, 12 November 1369) and Jakop van den Eede (ibid., f. 315v, 24 December 1369). Goldbeter's varlets through these years were William Maison and Henric Loptus.

49 Unfortunately, before the inscriptions on the monument were transcribed in the eighteenth century, they had been damaged in the iconoclastic riots of the 1560s, thus effacing the dates. Chapter documents of St. Donatian's and the city give some parameters, however. In the city accounts of 1371, Clare received a refund for three barrels of wine consumed by the Cardinal of England and his entourage, who stayed with her while in Bruges for a peace conference (SAB, SR 1371, f. 74v). Given that John is not mentioned, he was probably dead by this date. Clare died sometime shortly after May, 1380, since the expenses for her funeral fall just after the receipts from the Bruges fair in May: BAB, St. Donaas, G2, f. 53r "Ex sepulturis . . . pro redemptione panni albi iacentis super corporem uxoris Goubetels £20 par." The transcription on their monument, with their coats of arms, is found in J. Galliard, *Inscriptions funéraires et monumentales de la Flandre occidentale, avec des données historiques et généalogiques*, 3 vols. (Bruges, 1861–1866) vol. 1, pp. 152–153.

50 See chapter 3.

51 For Arquato, see Murray, *Notarial Instruments*, p. 92.

stipulated as well were the services to be performed, including an annual sung requiem mass as well as a daily mass said by the chaplain. These services were to begin in 1372 or after the death of either of the Goldbeters, whichever should come first. Moreover, funeral services were to be performed even if the Goldbeters were interred elsewhere. Apparently there were no children born of the marriage, since none are mentioned on the list of those to be prayed for and none among those to have rights of appointment of the chaplain. The chaplain could also be of "whatever nation" according to the terms of the agreement, thus allowing an Englishman.[52]

Goldbeter's career and adventures provide much qualitative evidence of the continuing importance of Bruges in Anglo-Flemish trade, and the role of wool as the stuff and lubricant of that trade. Although an exceptional case, he also shows the financial and personal possibilities of long acquaintanceship with Bruges and Flanders. Marriage into an important Bruges family, as well as personal friendship with the count of Flanders, were not the experience of many English merchants. Yet Goldbeter was far from alone in knowing how to raise money in the city, or how to rent commercial property for storage and sale of wool. And he was far from alone in his dealings with the important Bruges brokers and wool merchants – the de Scuetelares, van de Walles, and others. Rescuing his biography, however, does nothing to establish in quantitative terms how much wool actually passed through Bruges, particularly after the establishment of the Calais staple. But fortunately, we can also rely on confiscation records to provide a complementary quantitative indication of the size and extent of the trade in English wool contemporaneous with the last decade of Goldbeter's life.

The politics of the wool trade after 1350 are as significant as the growing importance of the best English wools to Flemish and other cloth manufactures. While the Calais staple certainly eased the difficulties of organizing and taxing the sale of English wool bound for export, it also concentrated its control into the hands of a few merchants. These "Staplers" became by the 1370s largely London men, usually members of the guild of grocers, who were bent on enhancing the status of Calais by making it a staple for all English merchandise going to the continent.[53] In this they were unsuccessful due to opposition from northerners and English coastal towns, who feared for their Flemish trade.[54] It must also be kept in mind that stapling

[52] Ibid., pp. 282–283.

[53] Nicholas, "English Trade," 29, Nightingale, *Medieval Mercantile Community*, pp. 235–262; Lloyd, *English Wool Trade*, pp. 250–253.

[54] Greaves, "Calais under Edward III," pp. 341–342; Robert L. Baker, "The government of Calais in 1363," in W. C. Jordan, W. C. McNab, and T. F. Ruiz (eds.), *Order and Innovation in the Middle Ages. Essays in Honor of Joseph R. Strayer* (Princeton, 1976), pp. 207–214.

regulations did not apply to all wool exported from England. Inferior grades, mostly from northern England and Scotland, could be exported from the port cities of Berwick and Newcastle directly to Bruges or Middelburg.[55] As mentioned previously, the second stream of wool to escape the staple laws was that whose export was granted by special royal license. In the 1330s and 1340s as we have, seen these were given to both Italian and native merchants in return for money advanced to the crown. In the 1360s and 1370s such licenses were routinely granted to Italians who planned to export the wool directly to the Mediterranean, though many may have broken this promise and taken the wool to Bruges for resale.[56] This was certainly the case in 1375 when a Florentine merchant was arrested for murder and a large quantity of wool was found in the house where he lived.[57] The quantity of wool from these sources that ultimately passed through the Bruges market is unknown.[58]

What happened to the wool once it reached the Calais staple has not received much scholarly attention until recently. Traditionally, historians have assumed that after 1363 continental purchasers were forced to travel to Calais for their wool, which was the case in the fifteenth century.[59] Yet David Nicholas noticed the persistent complaints and regulations issued by the Staplers in the late fourteenth century forbidding resale of wool by Italians, presumably operating out of Bruges. Then he went to little-noticed confiscation documents that prove Bruges's role as the major resale center for English wool on the continent. This means that other merchants from the Low Countries regularly journeyed to Bruges to purchase wool and often made use of the Bruges financial and shipping network in the process. Last but not least, this transshipment and

[55] Eileen Power, "The Wool Trade in the Fifteenth Century," in E. Power and M. M. Postan (eds.), *Studies in English Trade in the Fifteenth Century* (New York, 1966), pp. 43–44. In 1379 a petiton was introduced in the English parliament by representatives of Calais that stated: "All the wools of England, Wales, Ireland and Berwick should be sent to its staple"; Lloyd, *English Wool Trade*, pp. 226–228.

[56] Lloyd, *English Wool Trade*, p. 227.

[57] ARA, Rekenkamer, RR 1013, membrane 13; the case involved a Aubert Caroutse of Florence who was accused of murdering his wife, Agnees, near Tournai, which resulted in the confiscation of all the wool found in his house by the comital bailiff. His two partners, Philip de Nerle and Philip Wake, however, appeared before the aldermanic court and proved that only one poke of the confiscated wool belonged to Caroutse. Unfortunately, the exact quantity of wool is not stated in the account.

[58] But given the popularity of Bruges as a purchase point of wool by producers of lower quality woolens in the Leie cloth towns, its volume was probably considerable. For these production centers see below, pp. 289–295.

[59] Nicholas, "English Trade," 29; J. P. Peeters, "Bouwstoffen voor de geschiedenis der laatmiddeleeuwse stadsdraperie in een klein Brabants produktiecentrum: Vilvoorde (1357–1578)," *Handelingen van de koninklijke Commissie voor Geschiedenis* 151(1985), 1–48, esp. 3; Power, "Wool Trade," 60.

resale reveals widespread cooperation among English, Italian, Flemish, and German merchants in the exploitation of this most valuable of medieval commodities.

It is useful at this point to analyze some of Nicholas's conclusions and extrapolations based on the surviving evidence. There are two major sources for measuring the English wool trade at Bruges after 1363. The first resulted from a seizure of ships in Sluis, Bruges's outport, ordered by the count of Flanders in 1371 in retaliation for alleged English piracy.[60] The seizure was supervised by comital officials, led by the counselor and notary public Lambert Vromond.[61] He supervised the inventorying of the trade goods as well as the questioning of merchants and ship captains about their cargoes, destinations, and recent voyages. Four notebooks survive from this work, which together give an invaluable snapshot of the size and nature of Anglo-Flemish trade at least on and around 27 August 1371. Some thirty-nine boats of various types and sizes were caught in the round up, nine of which carried English wool.[62] None of the 356.5 sacks of wool temporarily impounded was confiscated, however, since none of its owners was English. Thus ownership of the wool had passed from its producers to its customers by the time it reached the Zwin.[63] The identities of the wool's owners tell us much about the organization of the wool trade at that time: 216.5 sacks were owned by Italian merchants; forty belonged to merchants of Mechelen in Brabant, who had purchased it through wool brokers in Bruges.[64] Seventy-five sacks belonged to Bruges merchants, among whom was Jan Bryselay, who was heavily involved in the London trade, and the hosteller and wool merchant Lamsin van de Walle.[65] Van de Walle and several of the Italians cooperated in hiring transport for the wool from Sluis to Bruges, underscoring the close relations among merchants from various nations in the wool trade.[66]

60 The records are inventoried under a single number, SAB, politieke. oorkonden, first series, 616. They were extensively described in Gilliodts-van Severen, *Inventaire*, vol. II, pp. 188–227.

61 For Vromond's career, see Murray, *Notarial Instruments*, pp. 78–80.

62 The craft were of various types, ranging from "cog" to ordinary fishing boats. Several were *scuten*, the small boats used to convey cargo along the Zwin estuary to Bruges. See Nicholas, "English Trade," 37.

63 Nicholas, "English Trade," 30.

64 Their broker in this instance was Michiel de Joncheere, who personally vouched for the ownership of the wool, agreeing to stand surety for its value and to secure letters from the aldermen of Mechelen to vouch for the wool's ownership within fourteen days: SAB, politieke oorkonden, first series, 616, f. 31v.

65 For Lamsin van de Walle, see chapter 5. Bryselay or Briselay's English contacts and allegiances cost him his property in the commercial district between the Cromme Wal and Ververs dijk; see Gilliodts-van Severen, *Inventaire*, vol. III, pp. 281–285.

66 SAB, politieke oorkonden, first series, 616, f. 5v

Twenty-five sacks were owned by Dutchmen, who were using one of their own merchants to broker and arrange transport for wool out of Bruges (not Calais!).[67]

The testimony of many of the ship captains confirms the picture of Bruges as a major market for English wool despite the existence of the staple at Calais. The Sluis-based Jan Willekin Wouterszoon reported that he had loaded twenty-four sacks of Calais wool in the Zwin in order to convey it to Bruges. His customers were all Italian merchants living in Bruges.[68] Captain Jan Zuereweys, also of Sluis, loaded twenty-six sacks in his ship at the order of the Bruges wool broker Jan Bryselay. The wool had been in the charge of Jan's "knape," who had brought it either from London or Calais to Sluis. Zuereweys was loading it for the trip from Sluis to Bruges at a fixed rate per sack. The wool's owners were "lombards," Bryselay and Lamsin van de Walle.[69] Italian merchants also arranged transport of English wool from Calais to Bruges on their own. Jaqueme Franchois and his brother maintained a complex trade operation between the Calais staple and Bruges, whereby the brother resided in Calais to arrange the wool purchases. His brother syndicated those purchases, and arranged wine shipments from Damme and book transfers of money to cover the cost of the wool.[70]

[67] Nicholas, "English Trade," 30.

[68] SAB, politieke oorkonden, first series, 616, f. 5r: "die heift gheladen xxiii zacke wullen die van Calays camen die hi loet int Zwin omme te voerne te Brucghe, lombaerden toebehorende . . ." One of the merchants was lodging at the inn "Ter Baerdze;" another lived in the "English street" near the crane and the English weigh house.

[69] Ibid., f. 5v: "Eerste 26 zacke wullen die hem ingalf Jan Briselais knape, ende huerdene omme van der Sluus te Brucghe te voerne de vorseide wulle omme 3 gro. de zac, ende behorde toe zom Lambaerden, zom Bryselaye ende zom Lamsin van der Walle te Brucghe weerd van Inghelschen . . ." It is safe to conclude that a network of wool importing was in place in Bruges that was organized cooperatively across merchant communities, with native Bruges brokers playing a key role. Both Bryselay and van de Walle had accounts with Bruges money changers – van de Walle with Collard de Marke and Bryselay with Willem Ruweel (ff. 45v, 69r, 81v, 86r, 128r).

[70] Ibid., ff. 16v, 31r: this case involved ten sacks of wool that were impounded and unclaimed by Franchois for a time, after which it was entrusted to the Florentine wool merchants Barde Manchin and Zundach, who promised to sell it for at least £20 gro. the sack. When Franchois returned he reported that half the wool belonged to Franchois Donat, presumably another Italian merchant, and the other half belonged to him and a partner, Andrieu Johanni. With the wool as security, however, Franchois had already sent his brother in Calais £120 gro. and twenty vats of wine with the Bruges broker Jan Tygry as surety. Presumably a Bruges money changer had advanced the £120 gro. and the wine was also shipped on credit. Folio 31r: "Ende zedert quam Jaquemon Franchois vorseide zecghende dat de heltsceede daer of toebehorde Franchois Donat ende andre heltsceede hem ende Andrieu Johanni. Ende dede vort informatie dat hi daer omme ende anne ander goed zende zinen broeder te Calays £c xx gro in vorme van cambye, ende vorte xx vate wyns ende vort heift hem Jan Tygry borghe ghestelt . . ." These kinds of Calais/Bruges shifting operations designed to evade the ban on Italian sales of English wool at Bruges became quite common in the 1370s and 1380s; see Lloyd, *English Wool Trade*, pp. 255–256.

This use of Bruges by Italian wool merchants was not new, judging from a confiscation case of 1347.[71]

The confiscations of 1382 confirm the general picture painted by the records of the 1371 seizure. In this case six boats were seized plying the Scheldt after having been loaded with English wool in Bruges, then occupied by rebels against the count of Flanders.[72] Some 117 sacks were impounded at this time; of these twenty-two were redeemed by their owner, a merchant from Dortmund, and another six were redeemed by their owner, an Englishman. Eleven sacks belonged to merchants from Brussels, and most of the rest was apparently owned by merchants from Mechelen.[73] Other confiscation records from the same period prove the importance of Italian, especially Lucchese, merchants in the transshipment of English wool through Bruges.[74]

There are several conclusions that can be drawn from the above evidence. First, Bruges remained one of the chief markets for English wool throughout the fourteenth century, both before and after the establishment of the Calais staple. As revealed by the confiscation accounts of 1371 and 1382, Bruges supplied English wool to drapers in Brabant, Holland as well as in Bruges and other parts of Flanders. Based on projections made by David Nicholas, Bruges may have marketed about half the total of wool exported from England in these years.[75] Secondly, the wool trade was the indirect means of exchange and collateral that underlay trade in spices and other commodities, taking advantage of the payment and credit mechanisms offered by Bruges hostellers and money changers. The example of John Goldbeter, though admittedly exceptional, shows the possibilities of intimacy inherent in Anglo-Bruges trading relationship. He was not the only Englishman to find in Bruges not only a place to do business, but also a place to live and remain in. And thirdly, the wool trade involved Italian, Hanse, and English merchants and also some from the Low Countries, often working cooperatively to accomplish the transport and sale of this valuable commodity. Thus this was both a domestic

[71] SAB, SR 1347–1348, which records the confiscation of ten out of twenty-four sacks of wool owned by "lombards" who had smuggled them into Bruges "tieghen die ordinandse van den Ghemeener Lande . . ." The de Marke accounts contain a single mention of a wool transaction involving an Italian (De Marke 3, f. 187r): "Jehan Conteurin me doit pour Barde Menchine pour 12 sarpelier de lainnes 26 september (1368) £129 et 6s. 8d." Note that Barde Manchin is mentioned in Nicholas, "English Trade," 51 as a wool merchant.

[72] Nicholas, "English Trade," 33; Nicholas, "The Scheldt Trade," 192–260; and below, chapter 9 for the Ghent War in Bruges.

[73] Nicholas, "Scheldt Trade," 262–265.

[74] Ibid., 260.

[75] Nicholas, "English Trade," 31.

and international trading endeavor for the merchants who frequented Bruges.[76]

CLOTH

Bruges the cloth city is an image out of kilter with many of the fourteenth-century developments traced thus far. After all, it is quite clear that the percentage of cloth workers among the city's population was in steady decline throughout the century, with economic and political power increasingly monopolized by those in commercial sectors of the urban economy. Ghent, in contrast, stands as the fourteenth-century cloth city par excellence in Flanders, with cloth workers making up the majority of the working populace and providing the revolutionary spark and fervor that so dominated urban and regional politics. Ypres, perhaps the predominant cloth town of the thirteenth century, clearly trailed Ghent in importance by the early fourteenth.[77] Throughout the century, in fact, Bruges was always a distant third behind Ypres and Ghent in the defense of traditional Flemish cloth production. Yet appearances can be deceiving, for as Rudolf Häpke remarked long ago, Bruges was one among an archipelago of cloth towns.[78] Moreover, cloth production remained an important occupation of many within Bruges's walls as well as a significant source of investment opportunity. The combination of cloth import, production, and sale – both for export and domestic consumption – as we shall see, remained one of the three props of the Bruges urban economy throughout the fourteenth century. And the size and power of Bruges's commercial sector proved invaluable in financing the greatest reorientation of cloth production in the history of that industry.

Cloth has rarely been absent from any discussion of the origins of capitalism or the history of Flemish cities. Henri Pirenne put long-distance trade in wool, dyestuffs, and finished cloth at the forefront of causes of the urbanization of northern Europe from the twelfth century.[79] In Pirenne's

[76] Thus the wool trade disproves the distinction J. A. van Houtte drew between the Bruges and Antwerp markets at their height – that the one was "national," the other "international" – as well as calling into question the characterization of Flemish merchants as merely passive; see Nicholas, "English Trade," 45–46.

[77] Nicholas, *Town and Countryside*, pp. 203–221.

[78] Rudolf Häpke, *Brügges Entwicklung zum mittelalterlichen Weltmarkt* (Berlin, 1908), pp. 30–31.

[79] Henri Pirenne's arguments were outlined in his *Histoire de Belgique*, and in more detail in various articles brought together by Emile Coornaert (ed.), in *Histoire économique de l'occident medieval* (Bruges, 1951); the most influential statements of his views in English has been *Economic and Social History of Medieval Europe* (New York, 1937) and *Medieval Cities: Their Origins and the Revival*

classic argument, it was merchant-entrepreneurs who came to dominate the production of cloth as well as the import of wool and other raw materials, gaining vertical control of the product virtually from sheep to sales hall. By the thirteenth century, these merchant capitalists – and Pirenne is emphatic in describing them as such – imposed a form of industrial capitalism on the textile crafts, enabling both rapid growth in the size of the industry and a concomitant increase in the sophistication of the production process and thereby the quality of the finished cloth. Increasing production of high-quality cloth bound for export also shaped social relations, creating an industrial proletariat out of the traditionally independent urban cloth workers, and drawing rural immigrants to the city to man the looms and fulling vats of the burgeoning industry as demand for labor increased. Thus the classic equation was first merchant capital, then capitalistic organization of the cloth industry leading to urban growth with prosperity for the few at the cost of economic and political oppression of the many.[80]

Several generations of research have eroded belief in Pirenne's vision without really replacing it with an alternative.[81] Gone are many of the old certainties, such as the belief in the all-encompassing control of production by a group of individuals; the exclusive attention to luxury woolens produced from fine English wools; the rigid demarcation between urban and rural cloth production; or any direct link between the organization of cloth production and early forms of capitalism. It is now impossible to speak of a straight line between "early" merchant capitalism and the development of a highly specialized, export-based cloth industry. The historical reality seems to have been much more complicated than earlier theorists and historians realized, and to have varied depending on the particular city, its economic makeup, and the stage of its economic development.[82]

of Trade (Princeton, 1925). Important recent commentary on Pirenne's influence can be found in G. Despy and A. Verhulst (eds.), *La fortune historiographique des thèses d'Henri Pirenne* (Archives et Bibliothèques de Belgique, Brussels, 1986) and in Verhulst, "The Origins of Towns in the Low Countries and the Pirenne Thesis."

80 The best description of Pirenne's model and the work done by Georges Espinas, Hans van Werveke, and others to support it is Renate Martins, *Wertorientierungen und wirtschafthiches Erfolgstreben mittelalterlicher Grosskaufleute: Das Beispiel Gent im 13. Jahrhundert* (Cologne, 1976), pp. 101–106.

81 In fact Pirenne's ideas live on unchanged in the new version of the *Cambridge Economic History*, in the essay by E. M. Carus-Wilson.

82 The assault on some aspects of the traditional model was begun by Emile Coornaert, *Une industrie urbaine du XIVe au XVIIe siècle: L'industrie de la laine à Bergues-Saint-Winoc* (Paris, 1930), whose critique was largely ignored by scholars. More recent and influential criticism has come from Alain Derville, "Les draperies flamandes et artésiennes vers 1250–1350," *Revue du Nord* 54 (1972), 353–370, esp. 356–357. Denille denies the existence of the merchant-entrepreneur both in theory – denying that there was any vertical integration of the industry in the thirteenth century – and in fact by disputing the commonly accepted example of Jehan Boinebroke of Douai as an early industrial capitalist. He

It is now generally recognized that the Flemish cloth industry was not specialized in the production of luxury cloth before the fourteenth century. Instead, it appears that cheaper and lighter fabrics, especially "says," were the most frequent Flemish exports to the Mediterranean in the twelfth century according to Genoese shipping records.[83] Patrick Chorley has shown that in the thirteenth century, cheap Flemish and northern French cloth exports to the Mediterranean exceeded luxury cloth not only in volume but also in total value.[84] These fabrics were woven largely of native Flemish, Irish, and Scottish wools, and received little or no finishing.[85] An era of crisis for Flemish woolen production commenced with the breakdown of order along the overland and oversea trade routes between Italy and the Low Countries as well as disruption of the sea routes in the Mediterranean itself. Beginning around the time of the first English wool embargo (1270s), these disruptions loaded additional transport and security costs onto the price of every export item. Cheap Flemish and French woolens simply could not bear these added costs and thus disappeared as products for export. Cloth producers were forced to reorient production towards cloth capable of bearing the higher costs, which were invariably cloth types woven exclusively from the highest quality English wools and finished with thorough fulling, stretching, raising, and shearing. This flight to quality represented a reorientation of stunning proportions, requiring

restates his views in "L'héritage des draperies médiévales," *Revue du Nord* 69 (1987), 715–724, where he nonetheless insists that capitalism, albeit commercial capitalism, existed in Flemish and northern French cloth towns in the fourteenth century (723). The most sophisticated and far-reaching criticism of Pirenne issued from an article by Robert DuPlessis and Martha C. Howell, "Reconsidering the Early Modern Urban Economy: The Cases of Leiden and Lille," *Past and Present* 94 (1982), 49–84, where an alternative model of non-capitalist economic organization is proposed: small commodity production, characterized "by independent master artisans who owned their means of production and worked in individual small shops" and who dominated the complex, export-oriented cloth industries of Lille and Leiden in the fifteenth century. This was not a predecessor to capitalism, they argue, but a "stable alternative" to industrial capitalism. Y. Fujii, "Draperie urbaine et draperie rurale dans les Pays-Bas méridionaux au bas moyen âge: une mise au point des recherches après H. Pirenne," *Journal of Medieval History* 16 (1990), 77–97, summarizes the new consensus about rural/urban cloth industries, as does the chapter by Rudolpf Holbach, "Some Remarks on the Role of 'Putting-out' in Flemish and Northwest European Cloth Production," in Marc Boone and Walter Prevenier (eds.), *Drapery Production in the Late Medieval Low Countries: Markets and Strategies for Survival (14th–16th Centuries)* (Leuven and Apeldoorn, 1993), pp. 207–250.

83 Krueger, "The Genoese Exportation," 722–750, which completes the earlier work of R. L. Reynolds, "The Market for Northern Textiles in Genoa, 1179–1200," *RBPH* 8 (1929), 831–850.

84 Chorley, "The Cloth Exports of Flanders," 349–379 and in general, John H. Munro, "Industrial Transformations in the North-West European Textile Trades, c. 1290–1340: Economic Progress or Economic Crisis?" in Campbell (ed.), *Before the Black Death*, pp. 110–148.

85 The distinction between lesser-quality cloth and its betters was often signified by its being either "greased" or "ungreased" – in French "draperie ointe" or "draperie sèche," Flemish "gesmouten" or "ongesmoute draperie." On this distinction, see John H. Munro, "Textile Technology," in Joseph Strayer (ed.), *Dictionary of the Middle Ages*, 26 vols. (New York, 1982–1989), vol. XI, pp. 693–711.

considerable flexibility from the guild-dominated clothworkers as well as massive outlays of capital for costlier raw materials and more complex production processes.[86]

Faced with such far-reaching challenges to the transport and marketing of their cloth, Flemish producers were also faced with new competitors. Barcelona and other Catalan towns, for example, developed products that competed with the medium-grade Franco-Flemish woolens. These were woven from good-quality wools from Majorca and Burgundy, which were first augmented then replaced by Castilian merino wools and English wools.[87] Languedoc woolens also competed in this medium-to-fine-grade market. Two additional regions offered perhaps the greatest competition to the Flemish. The Lombard and Tuscan textile industries developed from producers of cheaper cloth sorts into competitors at the luxury end of the scale. Woven of the finest English wool in imitation of the finest Franco-Flemish cloths, these Italian woolens, especially those of Florence, became the most highly prized (and priced) textiles of all in some European markets.[88]

Serious as these new competitors were to the Flemish, they paled in comparison with the potential of the English and Brabantine cloth industries, which became clear after 1350. England had long been a producer of coarse worsted fabrics, but by the middle of the fourteenth century the production of these had fallen off, replaced by the highly prized broadcloth. This was a true luxury woolen, woven of the highest-quality English wools and dyed and finished with the best materials and utmost care. The key competitive advantage for the English, however, was the considerable price advantage given them by staple and taxation policies imposed by Edward III in support of his war finance. As we have seen, the cumulative effects of attempts to control and tax wool exports resulted in a near-tripling of export duties levied on every sack of wool.[89] Given that wool represented between 60 and 70 percent of the price of the unfinished textile, English taxation had an

[86] Munro, "Industrial Transformations," pp. 114–116; Munro, "Urban Regulation and Monopolistic Competition in the Textile Industries of the Late-Medieval Low Countries," in *Textiles of the Low Countries*, 41–52.

[87] Munro, "Industrial Transformations," p. 131. Barecelona was using English wool to imitate Flemish and English woolens by the early fifteenth century.

[88] Hidetoshi Hoshino, *L'arte della lana in Firenze nel basso medioevo: il commercio della lana e il mercato dei panni fiorentini nei secoli XIII–XV* (Florence, 1980); Munro, "Industrial Transformations," pp. 132–133.

[89] These amounted to a rise from 6s. 8d. per sack to nearly £3 st. a sack. John Munro has calculated that this burden amounted to about 44 percent of mean export prices in the last half of the fourteenth century: "Industrial Transformations," p. 135 and Munro, The "Industrial Crisis' of the English Textile Towns, c. 1290–c. 1330," *Thirteenth-Century England* 7 (1999), 133–135.

enormous impact on the purchase price of Flemish woolens.[90] Moreover, the export duty assessed on English broadcloth was less than one-tenth the average export value of the cloth, conferring a cost advantage for English producers of between 25 and 35 percent, according to John Munro.[91]

The wrenching changes in the political and economic environment after 1300 put the efficiency and resilience of every Flemish cloth town to a severe test. Ypres has to be considered one of the victims of the new Darwinian era, since it experienced considerable decline throughout the century, compounded by population and material losses caused by famine, disease, and war.[92] The city's efforts to adapt relied excessively on vigorous if not ruthless action against nearby cloth producers, especially Poperinge, as well as a failed pursuit of a grain staple for West Flanders.[93] Ghent, on the other hand, though equally ruthless in enforcing cloth bans in its vicinity, managed to weather the storm by both concentrating resources in the production of high quality cloth and reemphasizing its traditional role as a grain market.[94] Ghent paid a high price for such change beyond the mere business costs, given the incidence of social revolution, much of it driven by weavers and fullers.[95] Smaller cloth towns chose other strategies. Some sought out cheaper wool varieties and used them to imitate or counterfeit the products of the bigger cloth cities.[96] Others, notably the "new drapery" towns of Wervik, Armentières, Kortrijk, and Menen, both experimented

[90] John H. Munro, "The Medieval Scarlet and the Economics of Sartorial Splendour," in N. B. Harte and K. G. Ponting (eds.), *Cloth and Clothing in Medieval Europe: Essays in Memory of Professor E.M. Carus-Wilson* (London, 1983), pp. 13–70; see especially table 3.2, p. 52.

[91] Tax on broadcloth exported by English denizens amounted to an average of 1s. 2d. per cloth after 1347; see Munro, "Industrial Transformations," p. 135 and n. 89, and Munro, "Anglo-Flemish Competition in the International Cloth Trade, 1340–1520," *Publication du Centre Européen d'Etudes Bourguigonnes* 35 (1995), 37–60 (*Rencontres d'Oxford (septembre 1994): L'Angleterre et les pays bas bourguignons: relations et comparaisons, XVe–XVIe siècle*, ed. Jean-Marie Cauchies).

[92] The classic article on the decline of Ypres is Henri Pirenne, "Les dénombrements de la population d'Ypres au xve siècle (1412–1506). Contribution à l'histoire statistique sociale au moyen âge," *Vierteljahrsschrift für Sozial- und Wirtschaftsgeschichte* 1 (1903), 1–32, reprinted in Mus and van Houtte, *Prisma van de Geschiedenis van Ypres*, pp. 359–390. On the attempts of Ypres magistrates to reverse or stem the tide of decline, see Sortor, "Ieperleet Affair," 1069 n. 4.

[93] Ibid., 1090–110; on the Poperinge affair, see Munro, "Industrial Transformations," pp. 115–116. Such actions against cloth producers continued into the Burgundian period: see Marc Boone, "L'industrie textile à Gand au bas moyen âge ou les resurrections successives d'une activité réputée moribonde," in *Drapery Production in the Late Medieval Low Countries*: *Markets and Strategies for Survival* (Leuven and Apeldoorn, 1993), pp. 15–58, esp. 18.

[94] Nicholas, *Metamorphosis*, pp. 291–292.

[95] Boone, "L'industrie textile à Gand," p. 42 Nicholas, *Metamorphosis*, pp. 6–8, 154–164.

[96] In a 1373 law suit before the Council of Flanders, representatives from Poperinge defended their adoption of production methods that closely imitated the cloth of Ypres by stating that the towns and villages of Comines, Warneton, Menen, Kortrijk, Deinze, Dendermonde, Linselles, and others had done the same; see Munro, "Industrial Transformations," p. 116.

with Spanish merino wool as a raw material and courted and cooperated with foreign merchants, especially from the German Hanse, by producing cloth to meet their demands.[97] Other less nimble or more unlucky secondary cloth towns such as Aardenburg, Dendermonde, and Diksmuide suffered decline and even complete collapse of their textile export trade. What made the difference between survival and failure was the number of internal resources a place possessed, plus success in opening and maintaining markets and adaptability to changing patterns of fashion and demand.[98]

If every cloth producer was forced to either change or perish in the fourteenth century, and change depended on internal resources, what could Bruges with its growing commercial sector bring to a struggling industry? One answer of course is that a declining cloth sector spurred investment and activity in commercial ventures. In this scenario, Bruges's commercial development was compensatory – a reorientation away from tradition. But it is altogether too easy to explain away the differences among the three great Flemish cities – Ypres, Ghent, Bruges – by saying the first two were cloth cities and Bruges was not. Granted Bruges's fame as a commercial center, it is nonetheless crucial to remember that it was and remained a cloth town amid cloth towns. This fact is often overlooked by modern historians, as it was by Geoffrey Chaucer, who in his egregious boast about the clothmaking abilities of the wife of Bath claimed that she surpassed in skill the weavers of Ypres and Ghent – not Bruges, certainly the third great Flemish cloth town at the time he wrote.[99] But in fact, when Chaucer wrote, Bruges had only just reached the top rank of cloth producers in terms of quality, and even then, when the city magistrates sought an impressive gift for Edward III, they purchased Brussels "scarlet" cloth to be tailored into a suit of clothes by Bruges tailors.[100] Despite impressions to the contrary, cloth production was

[97] Boone, "L'industrie textile à Gand," pp. 33–34; Peter Stabel, *De kleine stad in Vlaanderen. Bevolkingsdynamiek en economische functies van de kleine en secundaire stedelijke centra in het Gentse kwartier (14de–16de eeuw)* (Brussels, 1995), pp. 124–138. Paradoxically, as noted by Stabel, Menen and Kortrijk switched from Spanish to English wool in the course of the fifteenth century, so wool replacement was not always predictable based on price. For Hanse and secondary cloth towns, see Hans van Werveke, "Die Stellung des hansischen Kaufmanns dem flandrische Tuchproduzenten gegenüber," in *Beiträge zur Wirtschafts- und Stadtgeschichte. Festschrift für Hektor Ammann* (Wiesbaden, 1965), pp. 296–304.

[98] For fashion as an element in textile change see Raymond van Uytven, "Cloth in the Medieval Literature of Western Europe," in *Cloth and Clothing*, pp. 151–183, reprinted in van Uytven, *Production and Consumption*, x.

[99] *Riverside Chaucer*, p. 323.

[100] SAB, 1360–1361 (n..s.), f. 49r: "Item ghegheven Clais Huerle van ene roden Bruecelsche scaerlakene ende van enen peersen esel Bruecelsce laken der sie cledren of maecten die te Calays voeren toten Co[inc] van Ingheland costen £228 par." This Brussels scarlet cloth was probably the finest available anywhere at the time; for "scarlet" as a luxury cloth see Munro, "Medieval Scarlet," pp. 13–70.

central to the urban economy in the fourteenth century, with a production estimated by one historian at 15–20,000 export textiles in 1371, admittedly far less than Ghent's output, but probably not much behind an already declining Ypres.[101] More telling than production estimates is the leading role played by Bruges in gaining a ban on the sale of English broadcloth in Flanders in order to protect Flemish industry, a notable departure form the general freedom of the Bruges market, where cloth from a number of cloth towns was sold.[102]

This measure of concern about cloth production in a commercial city shows a clear realization on the part of Brugeois that cloth was the one commodity crucial to both the city's industry and its trade, offering employment for textile artisans and an extremely attractive return cargo for the foreign merchant. Bruges thus played a complex role: first as a producer of quality cloth for export; secondly, as an entrepôt for the cloth of other Flemish and northern French cloth towns and as a market for both local and regional cloth sales. Evidence from the middle of the fourteenth century proves that the commercial sector of Bruges, its money changers and hostellers, played a significant role in many of these facets of the cloth trade.

The Bruges cloth industry had experienced its own travails after the late thirteenth century. Never a producer of cloth of the quality of the finest Douai, Ypres, or Ghent varieties, Bruges weavers had specialized in the production of "dry cloths," i.e. those woven of coarser long-staple wools, which did not require the application of fat after the initial scouring.[103] These cheaper cloth sorts covered a range of products from rays to biffes and says. A 1222 Barcelona toll entry takes "Bruges cloth" to be synonymous with ray, and it was taxed at half the rate of a Ypres woolen cloth.[104] The Bruges *keuren* or regulations governing the production of cloth, which were revised in the late 1280s, mention a number of cheaper cloth sorts belonging to the "worsted" variety, though it implies that some value was added to cloth by a more elaborate dyeing than was typical in other production centers.[105] Nonetheless, among the seventeen cloth-exporting towns of

[101] Nicholas, "English Trade," 30; van Uytven, *Stadsfinanciën en stadsekonomie*, p. 356.

[102] Munro, "Industrial Protectionism," 229–268.

[103] Munro, "Industrial Transformations," pp. 114–116; Chorley, "The Cloth Exports of Flanders," 373–379. The wool used was probably either native Flemish wool or the coarse wools of Scotland or Ireland: Verhulst, "La laine indigène," 285–286. The most complete technical description of medieval says and say production is John H. Munro, "The Origin of the English 'New Draperies': The Resurrection of an Old Flemish Industry, 1270–1570," in N. B. Harte (ed.), *The New Draperies in the Low Countries and England, 1300–1800* (New York, 1997), pp. 35–127, esp. 87–93.

[104] Chorley, "The Cloth Exports of Flanders," 363.

[105] Georges Espinas Henri Pirenne, *Recueil de documents relatifs à l'histoire de l'industrie drapière en Flandre*, 5 vols. (Brussels, 1906–1966), vol. 1, pp. 348, 359–360; Chorley, "The Cloth Exports of

Flanders and northern France before 1300, Bruges belonged solidly among those producers of cheaper cloth, which we now know made up the majority of shipments to the Mediterranean and presumably to other markets as well.

Once crisis struck, the traditional woolens of Bruges suffered along with all the rest. John Munro has shown that the fate of most of these products was virtual extinction by the second or third decade of the fourteenth century. Lumping all the cheap cloth sorts under the generic name of *sayetterie*, he has shown that mentions of such cheap cloth disappear from the export records almost entirely. In Bruges the last ordinance referring to production of *ghistelsayen* – a formerly important type of "dry" drapery – occurs in 1314.[106] The last mention of the deans, or urban supervisors, of the *sayetterie* dates from the account year 1298–99. Say-making apparently disappeared from Ypres and Douai around the same time, with all mention of sales stalls for says ceasing by the 1320s in Ypres, and in Douai the last regulations mentioning biffes and says dating from 1305.[107] Ypres and Douai at least had their quality woolens to cushion the blow of change; although, as it turned out, even this only delayed the inevitable for both cities. Bruges, on the other hand, faced the challenge of reinventing and not simply reorientating its traditional cloth industry.

How the challenge was met has never been explained. Bruges, by tradition a producer of low-cost, low-quality cloth, became in the course of the fourteenth century a center of quality production of true woolens. Evidence of the change is both anecdotal and documented from the municipal accounts of Bruges itself. Among the literary references collected by Raymond van Uytven, Bruges cloth was referred to as clearly of the second grade as compared to Ghent or Ypres.[108] The Bruges city accounts from 1331 to 1390 tend to support this traditional cloth hierarchy, yet increasingly across the period, Bruges cloth was favored for the liveries of the city's clerks and police force.[109]

Flanders," 365; Guy de Poerck, *La draperie médiévale en Flandre et en Artois. Technique et terminologie*, 3 vols. (Bruges, 1951), vol. 1, pp. 246–257.

106 Ghistelles say was itself probably an imitation of the product of a smaller cloth center: de Poerck, *Draperie médiévale*, vol. 1, pp. 255–256 Coornaert, "Draperies rurales," 64.

107 Munro, "Industrial Transformations," pp. 111–112; Howell, "Weathering Crisis," pp. 90–99. Alain Derville disagrees slightly with Munro's terminology, arguing that says in the thirteenth and fourteenth century were cheap imitations of true woolens ("wet" drapery) rather than a separate genre unto themselves – see Derville, "Les draperies flamandes et artesienne," 363–365.

108 Van Uytven, "Cloth in Medieval Literature," p. 160.

109 This is not the place for an extensive analysis of these account data. But it is clear that in cases when cloth was to be given to an important figure, such as the count of Flanders or a king, Bruges cloth was never given. For the period before the 1360s, such presents were usually Ypres or Ghent

By the middle of the fourteenth century, the production of Bruges cloth was in the hands of weaver-drapers, who were not merchants, but rather medium-to small-scale entrepreneurs who both produced cloth themselves and organized cloth production. This blurring of boundaries between producers and entrepreneurs in cloth manufacture is typical throughout Flanders, although in Bruges it is possible to identify a number of weaver-drapers whose role approached that of wholesalers who bought from local weavers and sold in the cloth halls.[110] Their social status and economic power did not place them in a commanding position in the city however, certainly not in comparison with Ypres. Limitations on the number of looms any one draper could control, with the inevitable effect on the amount of capital any one draper could accumulate, placed drapers in Bruges much closer to ordinary weavers than to the powerful broker/hostellers of the city.[111] De Marke's records call these men and women simply "drapers."[112] Drapers, in the terminology of the time, seem to have been those who rented a stall in one of the cloth halls of Bruges and sold cloth produced on their looms as well as cloth purchased from other weavers. What also set Bruges drapers apart from ordinary weavers is that many of them had accounts with one or more money changers, using these banking services to further their business. It was here that the worlds of capital and industry came together.

At least twelve drapers held accounts with Ruweel or de Marke (or both) at some time in the period from 1366 to 1370. Seven of these drapers had

cloth obtained either from one of the Flanders markets (SAB, SR 1332–1333, f. 52r, where Ghent scarlet cloth is purchased at the Lille market) or obtained from a Ghent merchant resident in or visiting Bruges. By the later half of the fourteenth century, the cloth of Mechelen and particularly Brussels was being chosen for these costly presents, indicating a profound shift in the geography of high-quality cloth production.

110 Hans van Werveke, *De Koopman-ondernemer en de Ondernemer in de Vlaamsche Lakennijverheid van de Middeleeuwen* (Antwerp and Utrecht, 1946), pp. 1–7. Van Wervete emphasized the draper's industrial role with trade activities held to a minimum. For Ghent see Nicholas, *Metamorphosis*, pp. 155–157 and for Ypres in 1382, Nicholas, *van Arteveldes*, p. 179. The situation in Leuven was similar; see van Uytven, *Stadsfinanciën*, pp. 346–353.

111 Van Werveke, *Koopman-ondernemer*, pp. 15–19 Stabel, *Dwarfs; Among Giants*, p. 151. The surviving regulations governing cloth production in Bruges (all from the late thirteenth century) are found in Espinas and Pirenne, *Recueil*, pp. 347–608, and are a miscellany of normative documents and a few comital privileges. As the editors point out in the introductory section (pp. 342–347), other documents relating to the drapery that once existed have not been preserved.

112 That is, in most cases. The de Marke accounts rarely indicate professions: only Jan Artrike, Willem van den Eke, and Jan van Jabeke are explicitly called drapers in their accounts or elsewhere in the de Marke ledgers. The other "drapers," Willem and Kateline Marizoen, Jakop van de Kolve, Jan de Pinkere, Jakop Dommele, Jan and Jakop van den Eke, Jan Tibelin, and Lamsin de Vos, though not explicitly called drapers in the accounts, were named as weavers, shearers (in the case of Jan van den Eke), or fullers (in the case of Jakop Dommele) in de Marke's accounts or in other documents, and/or are found in the city accounts as sellers of Bruges cloth to the city. In the case of Jan van Artrike "weaver" and "draper" are used interchangeably, e.g. De Marke 3, f. 159v, "Jehan van Artrike, drapier"; ibid., 5, f. 45v, "Jehan van Artrike, tisserant."

accounts extensive enough to be carried over several years; one, Willem van den Eke, had a very active account running to hundreds of entries across all five volumes of de Marke's surviving ledgers. These records are of considerable importance; they are probably the only surviving private financial records of drapers anywhere in Flanders in the fourteenth century.[113] An analysis of these accounts shows clearly that Bruges drapers utilized at least two important financial services offered by the money changers.

First, money changers served as paymasters for the drapers, supplying ready coin to pay their creditors. In fact, a draper's account served almost exclusively to pay for cloth purchases from other weavers, who apparently delivered their cloth to the draper in the sales hall, received their prices, and then collected the money from the money changer's stall located just outside the New Cloth Hall (or Waterhalle).[114] All twelve of the drapers made use of this service; thus if we consider that Bruges had at the time some fifteen money changers, it is quite likely that all Bruges drapers made use of the banking system offered by money changers.[115] In some cases, this strikingly modern relationship between exchange bank and customer extended to the granting of a line of credit to the draper through the use of overdrafts, whereby payments would be made beyond the amount of a draper's balance if the shortfall were made up in a reasonable period.[116] Willem van den Eke again made good use of this service, for although his account was usually in balance, there was a seven-week period from November 1367 to January 1368 when his deficit was allowed to climb to

113 I first noted the existence of these in 1990: James M. Murray, "Cloth, Banking and Finance in Medieval Bruges," in John H. Munro and Erik Aerts (eds.), *Textiles in the Low Countries in European Economic History* (Leuven, 1990), pp. 24–31, esp. 28–29. Raymond de Roover noted the accounts of Willem van den Eke in *Money, Banking and Credit*, p. 287 n. 39, but did not analyze them.

114 The credit side of each draper's account contains lists of names, many of which can be identified from surviving guild records as weavers. The amounts of the recorded payments to them average out to be very close to the price paid for Bruges cloth by the city government – roughly £2 12s. the piece – further strengthening the case that they represent the purchase price of cloth. A surprising number of the weavers were women, and for this see chapter 8 below.

115 Allowing, of course, for differences among the bankers and drapers. De Marke's ledgers show that he had many more drapers as customers than did Ruweel, and it is likely that the larger and more important bankers in Bruges counted most of the drapers among their customers. There is also one example of a shearer-draper, Jan de Pinkere, who had an account with both De Marke and Ruweel. De Pinkere apparrently came from a family of weavers, as a Jehan li jeune appears as a weaver in 1328 (Gilliodts-van Severen, *Inventaire*, vol. I, p. 393). The Jan of 1366 was probably his son; he is mentioned in 1379 as a representative of the shearers: "Den here Jan den Pinkere over de scerers . . ." (ibid., vol. II, p. 370). Other examples of joint account holding are Jakop vander Colve, (Ruweel, f. 12v); Jan vanden Eke (Ruweel, ff. 34v, 142r, 152v); Mikiel Crakebeen (Ruweel, ff. 32v, 43r); Jakop Dommele (Ruweel, ff. 68r, 76v); and Willem vanden Perebome (Ruweel, f. 167r); doubtless others have gone undiscovered.

116 For the use of overdrafts in general, see de Roover, *Money, Banking and Credit*, pp. 294–304.

£50 gro. (equal to twenty to twenty-five textiles) before being paid off.[117] He ran smaller deficits at other times.[118] Van den Eke was apparently the only draper de Marke allowed this overdraft privilege, attesting both to his importance as a customer and perhaps to de Marke's caution as a banker. But the important point is that for some drapers a bank account could also be a source of short-term credit, offering an enormous advantage in a business in which purchases of cloth were frequent for relatively small sums of money, while sales were apt to be less frequent for comparatively large sums – the classic cash-flow problem.[119]

The second banking service drawn upon by Bruges drapers is a logical extension of the practice of short-term credit. The surviving drapers' accounts show that Bruges money changers were either investing substantial amounts in many drapers' businesses, or buying large quantities of cloth, or most likely both. This is clear from the credit side of the accounts, in which the names of Bruges bankers far outnumber those of foreign merchants, who were purchasing cloth for export. Willem van den Eke, for example, had credits of £848 gro. from January 1368 to January 1369, of which £145 (17 percent) was paid in by foreign merchants, £163 (19 percent) came from Bruges hostellers, £165 he deposited himself, perhaps from sales completed in the Cloth Hall, and £372 (43 percent) came from Bruges money changers. Not all the drapers' accounts show the same preponderance of bank money; but as a rule, the larger and more active the draper's account, the greater the share of money changers in it.[120]

There are at least two explanations for these large sums advanced by money changers to the drapers. The first is that money changers were acting as heads of cartels, in which capacity they bought large amounts of cloth on behalf of other silent partners, or purely on their own accounts, as a form of commodity speculation. If this was their intention, they did quite well in the 1360s, for the price of Bruges cloth rose at a pace that easily

[117] SAB, De Marke 2, f. 204r, 213r.

[118] Ibid., 3, f. 220r for the period from October to November, 1368.

[119] The cash-flow problem could only have grown more acute with the reorientation to luxury cloth production. This required the expenditure of more capital for acquiring the necessary raw materials – English wool in particular – and additional production steps, especially in the finishing of the cloth. It is unlikely that even wealthy drapers financed the entire production process. The changers' accounts make clear that drapers purchased cloth from weavers, though it is not known whether or not they then paid for further dyeing, fulling, napping, and shearing of the cloth.

[120] This is true of van den Eke, Jacop van de Kolve, and Willem and Kateline Marizoen, though less true for Jakop Dommele, and not characteristic of the accounts of Jan van Janbeke, Jan de Pinkere, or Lamsin de Vos. The smaller drapers seem to have sold all of their cloth to foreign merchants. Lamsin de Vos, who was one of the most important drapers of the time, is a special case in that he sold large quantities of cloth to the city government in the 1360s as well as to foreign merchants. He probably had little need of outside capital to conduct his business.

exceeded the depreciation of the Flemish coinage due to debasement.[121] A second possibility is that Bruges money changers were simply investing in the actual production of cloth, much as de Marke invested in the import of cloth, with an eye towards reaping profits from a dynamic industry that was in need of capital to compete and survive in a period of great change and uncertainty. In many ways this was a favorable match for both parties. The changer obtained a potentially profitable investment for capital gained from his depositors – no easy task given the constrictions of an economy without stocks, bonds or other securities. The draper was able to tap a source of working capital and financial services, enabling him to maintain a stock of cloth, pay his suppliers, and survive the gap between constant outgoing of payments and an infrequent income from sales.[122]

The example of cloth in fourteenth-century Bruges drives home the dynamism and uncertainties of that medieval market. As hundreds of foreign merchants flocked to the city, Bruges struggled to maintain its traditional role as a center of the wool trade. As the appeal of its financial system held onto a great deal of English trade, its cloth industry faced the challenge of adapting to rapidly changing market conditions by reorienting its production away from its thirteenth-century tradition and towards high-quality wool textiles. The strength of Bruges's financial sector helped here as well, first in maintaining diversity of cloth supply, as shown by de Marke's import business, and just as importantly supplying credit and financial services to the drapers of the city. Perhaps nowhere else was the relationship of finance and industry so close and profitable as in fourteenth-century Bruges.

Bruges as cloth emporium

With the decline of the Champagne fairs, Bruges emerged as the center of trade in a wide variety of Flemish and French textiles. Of course it

[121] As described in chapter 4, this was a decade of steady debasement. In 1361 the relationship of the Floretine florin and the Flemish groot was 22 groten to the florin; in 1370 a florin cost 32 groten (+ 45 percent); exchange rates are taken from Spufford, *Handbook*, p. 215. In the same period, the price of blue and white Bruges cloth (which I use as a benchmark) rose from £ 2 1s. gro. to £3 6s. gro., or + 61 percent.

[122] Gerard Sivery has observed that cloth lost none of its allure for the rich investor in the fourteenth century, and I agree with him that "les détenteurs de gros capitaux ne se desinteressaent pas totalement de la draperie . . . mais ils ne le feraient plus que de manière indirecte en prêtant de l'argent aux drapiers, aux artisans, aux gros acheteurs, étrangers surtout . . ." ("Capitaux et industrie textile," 731) Yet in the case of Bruges, most bank loans went to the drapers and perhaps to foreign merchants; there is no evidence of loans to others in the chain of cloth production. The apparent financial sophistication of Bruges drapers resembles that found by Marshall in Prato; see *The Local Merchants of Prato*, esp. pp. 34–38, 101–110.

periodically shared this role with one of the Flemish fairs; but the city remained the one permanent sales point for a large variety of cloth, and during the Bruges fair in May the choice of cloth must have been unsurpassable.[123] Exactly what kinds of cloth were available for sale in the Bruges cloth halls is not entirely clear. Some indication is given by the *Livre des Mestiers*, the French/Flemish conversation manual of c. 1369, which lists fifteen types of cloth available in the Bruges market. A slightly later edition of the same work (c. 1380) lists twenty-three cloth sorts, including those of Douai, Valenciennes, and Maubeuge.[124] Anecdotal evidence comes from the Datini archives as well, which record the purchase by an agent of Francesco Datini in 1387 of 2,000 Wervik and Kortrijk textiles in Bruges for shipment to Sicily.[125] In the de Marke accounts there are tantalizing mentions of Diest, Frisian, and Poperinge cloth.[126] And we know that Hanse merchants used Bruges as both a purchasing and a transshipment point for their cloth trade to the East.[127] The account books of the Hanse merchant Vicko von Geldersen (1367–1392), in fact, enumerate some forty sorts of cloth he traded in, mainly through Bruges.[128]

Evidence that Bruges served as the major sales point for West Flemish and northern French cloth abounds in the de Marke accounts. Weaver-drapers from Kortrijk are particularly numerous, which is not surprising given the rise to prominence of that city's cloth industry after the middle of the century.[129] Smaller production centers of the same region along the Leie

[123] The four other fairs of Flanders remained viable throughout the fourteenth century, as even the city government of Bruges purchased cloth at the Ypres and Torhout fairs. This practice seems to have become rarer after c. 1350 for example in 1332 cloth for the hangman's uniform was transported from Torhout (SAB, SR 1332–1333, f. 52v: "Van desen vors. lakene te beslane ende van Thorout te bringhene te Brucghe 5s. par."). The following year (ibid., 1333–1334, f. 58r): "van den vorseiden lakene van Ypre te Brucghe te bringhene van draghene van beslane ende van deelne 35s. 6 d. par." The examples could be multiplied.

[124] Van Uytven, "Cloth in Medieval Literature," p. 165; Gessler, *Brugsche Livre des Mestiers*, p. 96.

[125] Prevenier and Blockmans, *Burgundian Netherlands*, p. 104.

[126] De Marke 5, f. 112r: (account of Nicoll. De Marin) "me doit pour Henric de Semit. 19 July (1369) pour 2 dras et demy de Diest, £ 19 2.s. 6d."; ibid., 5, f. 154r: "Jak. Scaramp pour drap de Frise que jay payet a couquil dist. 18s. 6d."; ibid., 2, f. 91v (account of Jacop van la Fine): "me doit pour se femme (12 July 1367) pour payer dras de Poperinghe £49 17s. gro."

[127] That was the reason for the special exemption granted them from the ban on the importation of English cloth; see H. Amman, "Deutschland und die Tuchindustrie Nordwesteuropas im Mittelalter," *Hansische Geschichtsblätter* 72 (1954), 1–63, especially 38–40.

[128] Nirrnheim, *Handlungsbuch Vickos von Geldersen*, p. xxv. The Hanse merchant H. Veckinchusen exported more than 2,000 Flemish textiles from 1401 to 1420, with those of St. Omer predominating by four to one over second-place Ypres, followed by Poperinge as a distant third. See Simone Abraham-Thisse, "Les draps de Flandre en Europe du Nord: Faut-il encore parler du déclin de la draperie flamande au bas moyen-âge?" in *Drapery Production in the Late Medieval Low Countries*, pp. 167–206, esp. 178–180.

[129] A partial list of Kortrijk drapers edited from a now largely illegible manuscript can be found in Espinas and Pirenne, *Histoire de l'industrie drapière*, vol. 1, pp. 689–694.

river are also common in the accounts: Wervik, Comines, and Armentières sent their drapers and cloth to the Bruges market.[130] Drapers from not-so-flourishing Diksmuide are also much in evidence, as are those of the West Flemish towns of Poperinge and Roeselare.[131] Ypres cloth of course was brought in large quantities to the Bruges cloth halls, especially during the Bruges fair in May, and many Ypres drapers opened accounts with de Marke during that time of the year. Even the cloth-producing village of Langemark, near Ypres, sent its drapers to Bruges.

Perhaps the best source to gauge the cloth varieties available in Bruges is the nearly complete series of city accounts from 1331 to 1390.[132] These record city purchases of a vast array of goods and services, from crossbows to the services of wet nurses. But cloth occupies a special place, for it was acquired by the city to serve as an extravagant gift, as was the Brussels cloth intended for Edward III mentioned above. It also formed a part of the regular compensation for city officeholders and employees. The particular value of these purchases is not only their regularity – cloth was purchased twice a year, at Easter and on the feast of St. Bavo (1 October) – but how closely they correspond to the social hierarchy of the time. Cloth was chosen for purchase running from that literally fit for a king to that intended for the lowliest city lackey. Not all this cloth was available for sale in the Bruges market at any one time, so the city sometimes dispatched purchase agents to acquire it or reimbursed city officials who purchased it while on another mission. The kinds of cloth purchased also changed over time, reflecting perhaps changes in the market place or in fashion.

Table 7 shows the geographic spread of city cloth purchases across a fifty-year period. Of course purchases of Bruges cloth were most common, followed by those from other West Flemish producers. Ghent cloth was frequently purchased, particularly for the liveries of aldermen and city clerks. Rather surprisingly, other East Flemish producers are represented as well: Oudenaarde and Dendermonde stand out here. More surprising is the frequency of purchases of Brabant cloth, particularly that of Brussels, Leuven, and Mechelen. After 1360, it is clear that Bruges officials chose cloth

130 Cloth from the Leie region (including Kortrijk) enjoyed a wide popularity with foreign merchants from both northern and southern Europe: see Charles Verlinden, "Draps des Pays-Bas et du nord-ouest de l'Europe au Portugal au xve siècle," *Anuario de Estudios Medievales* 2 (1966), 235–261, who finds evidence of the popularity of cloth from Ypres, Bruges, Wervik, and Kortrijk after 1350 in both Portugal and Castille (pp. 239–242); Verlinden, "Draps des Pays-Bas et du nord de la France en Espagne au xve siècle," *Le Moyen Age* 47 (1937), 21–36; and especially Frederigo Melis, "La diffusione nel Mediterraneo occidentale dei panni di Wervicq e delle altre città delle Lys attorno al 1400," in *Studi in onore di Amintore Fanfani* (Milan, 1962), pp. 234–243.

131 Stabel, *Dwarfs Among Giants*, pp. 144–145; Derville, "Draperies flamandes et artsiennes," 354.

132 SAB, SR 1359–1370.

Table 7. *Cloth purchases by Bruges city government, 1331–1381*

Years	Sources of supply in descending order of importance
1331–1340	Bruges, Ghent, Ypres, Diksmuide, Leuven, Mechelen, Vilvoorde, Gistel, Brabant
1341–1350	Bruges, Ghent, Brussels, Gistel
1351–1360	Bruges, Ghent, Ypres, Brussels, Mechelen, Vilvoorde, Dendermonde, Oudenaarde
1361–1370	Bruges, Ghent, Ypres, Brussels, Kortrijk, Mechelen, Dendermonde, Vilvoorde, Oudenaarde, Diest, Komen, Wervik, Brabant
1371–1381	Bruges, Ghent, Brussels, Ypres, Mechelen, Kortrijk, Dendermonde, Vilvoorde, Wervik, Roesselare, Komen, Diest

Source: SAB, SR 1331–1381.

from Brabant when only the finest would do. All in all for the period from 1351 to 1371, the city purchased cloth from at least sixteen different cloth producers, ranging from the venerable Ypres and Ghent to newer, smaller producers such as Wervik. And last but not least, the number of different cloth types increased across the century, judging from these account records.

Answering the question of where and from whom the city acquired its cloth brings other significant facts to light. Some of the non-Bruges cloth was acquired directly from drapers who came to Bruges to effect the sale. For example, much Ghent cloth was acquired directly from drapers from that city, either purchased directly in the Ghent Cloth Hall, or brought by Ghent drapers to Bruges.[133] The Bruges city government also sent purchasing agents to the fairs of Torhout, Ypres, Lille, and Mesen, which obviously still functioned as gathering places of cloth merchants from across Flanders and northern France.[134] For special cloth either agents would be specifically sent to the place of production itself, or one or another city offical would dispatch cloth while on a diplomatic or business visit.[135]

[133] Before 1350, Bruges agents apparently visited the Ghent Cloth Hall directly, e.g. SAB, SR 1359–1360, f. 50r, in which a purchase of three striped Ghent cloths is translated from the "hall money" of Ghent into moutons, the then-current gold coins of Flanders. Thereafter, well-known Ghent drapers, such as members of the Ser Sanders clan, appear regularly. (On this well-known Ghent family, see Nicholas, *Metamorphosis*, p. 326, n. 26). Throughout this period, Ghent cloth was the most frequently purchased after that produced in Bruges.

[134] SAB, SR 1359–1360, f. 49v, cloth purchased at the Mesen market; ibid., 1332–1333, f. 52r, "2 brunen scaerlakenen . . . die Clais Bonyn cochte ter Ryselmaerct . . ."

[135] This was frequently done in the case of Brussels cloth, which seems to have been the finest obtainable after 1350, and was reserved for gifts to the most important personages. In 1384, Willem van Melane was sent to Brussels "omme lakene te copene" (ibid., 1384–1385, f. 76v); while in that city, the city clerk Ghiselbrecht van Roeselare dispatched a Brussels cloth which cost fifty-five gold moutons (ibid., 1362–1363, f. 43v).

Sellers of cloth to the city were of course those visiting drapers, but more significant were the sellers of Bruges cloth. These individuals were drawn from the well-connected and powerful drapers and cloth brokers. A disproportionate number had served or would serve as alderman, so that in many ways those who sold cloth resembled in social status and background the city building contractors and providers of other goods and services. In all these, money flowed and circulated among a relatively narrow business and political elite corresponding to the new governing class that emerged after 1302, as described in chapter 3. Lamsin de Vos is a good example. The de Vos name is a common one, so family affiliations are difficult to identify; but a relative, Baldwin de Vos of Bruges, was for some years one of the most important officials of Count Louis of Male.[136] Lamsin was repeatedly dean of the weavers' guild and city alderman in the 1360s. It cannot have been coincidence that he was also the single largest provider of Bruges cloth to the city during that time.[137] As in so many facets of city government, those who governed profited from their officeholding in both overt and subtle ways.

All the figures and anecdotes agree that Bruges excelled in the sheer range of choice it offered to the potential cloth buyer. This could be a crucial power of attraction for foreign merchants who came in search of buyers for their imported goods, and sought attractive exports to make the return or continuing journey profitable as well. Recent research has shown that Flemish cloth retained much of its traditional allure as an item of export despite competition and market change.[138] But even the considerable variety

136 This Baldwin was called a "valet" of the count in 1357, when he aided in the repair of the disaster caused by the flight of the count's chief mint offical, Bardet de Malpelys. He possessed enormous resources, since he was the single largest creditor at the time, being owed nearly a third of the total number of gold moutons outstanding. He was given the proceeds of the seigneurage to pay this debt and he assisted in keeping the mint open by the delivery of 175 marks of gold in a single week (6–13 October 1357). de Roover's speculation that these amounts were drawn from public funds must be rejected out of hand, given the very private arrangements for repayment granted by the count. See Elsen, "La monnaie des comtes de Flandre," 100–101 and n. 299, and de Roover, *Money, Banking and Credit*, pp. 235–236. Baldwin may have been the son of the Lamsin de Vos who was an immigrant to the city and became a broker before 1339 (Schouteet, *Regesten*, vol. III, p. 294, #785). He may have been a broker himself, for he had close contacts with at least two broker families, the Baves and the van den Ackeres (ibid., p. 198, #516). He had a close relationship with the convent of the Bruges Beghards and died sometime before 1381 (ibid., p. 245, #649 and pp. 258–259, #689). It is impossible to determine whether the weaver-draper Lamsin de Vos was Baldwin's brother, but it is likely. In any event, a Lamsin de Vos was dean of the weavers' guild in 1346.

137 One example that can serve for many is the sale in 1362 of twenty-eight lengths of Bruges cloth that Lamsin and his fellow draper, Jan van Roden sold to the city for the uniforms worn by the city militia's archer corps. Each cloth was £ 2 10s. gro; see SAB, SR 1362–1363, f. 40v.

138 Abraham-Thisse, "Les draps de Flandre," p. 195.

of Flemish cloth was not likely to satisfy the demands of every buyer in the Bruges Cloth Hall. And it is interesting to learn of at least one clear example of the efforts the money changer Collard de Marke to augment and profit from importing other kinds of cloth.

As stated already, the "flight to quality" tendency of Flemish drapery in the fourteenth century effectively removed Bruges from the list of producers of low-cost textiles. This could not have meant the elimination of demand for such textiles, however. Simply the need to clothe the populace would have required considerable quantities of cloth, most of it necessarily of cheaper quality – the says, biffes, and other cheap worsteds of long tradition. The costlier woolens of Flemish manufacture were simply out of the question for most Brugeois, given that the purchase of enough cloth to make a suit of clothes required many days' wages of a master mason.[139] And surprisingly, there is evidence of sustained demand for says and other cloth types intended for export. In the exports of Hildebrand Veckinchusen in the early fifteenth century, for example, says outnumber the finer cloth sorts by a narrow but important margin.[140] Where was this cloth to come from?

There was no shortage of producers in the vicinity it turns out, for besides the smaller producers of the Leie valley, whose woolens were not cheap enough to be affordable for most, says continued to be produced in a number of places in the nearby county of Hainault. In ways that prefigure the fifteenth-century development of say production in West Flanders in the fifteenth century, de Marke organized a considerable trade in these textiles both on his own and in partnership with a broker/hosteller, Pieter van le Fine. And true to form, de Marke's exchange business complemented this import venture, as both changers and drapers from Hainault gained access to the Bruges market through him.[141]

De Marke organized a classic business operation to bring Hainault and northern French cloth to the Bruges market. Apparently he provided the working capital for his partner van le Fine, though de Marke kept accounts

139 Masons and other construction workers were among the highest paid of day laborers in Bruges. John H. Munro has compiled extensive data on how much buying power was required to purchase various grades of Ghent cloth as well as says produced in other cloth cities. From his 1360s data, a suit of clothes from even a middling grade of Ghent "striped" cloth would require fifteen to twenty days' wages – see Munro, "Textiles as Articles of Consumption in Flemish Towns, 1330–1575," *Bijdragen tot de Geschiedenis* 81 (1998), 275–288, esp. table 3, 280.

140 Abraham-Thisse, "Le draps de Flandre," pp. 179–183; he purchased 2,445 says of unnamed provenance versus 2,087 bolts of Flemish drapery.

141 For more on this, see chapter 6.

for the operation.[142] Two features stand out in this use of commercial capital to import "foreign cloth"; the first is the size of the business. Van le Fine handled the "active" part of the partnership and recorded the results in an account he held in de Marke's exchange. Adding up the receipts from cloth sales allows us some idea of the size of the trade. In one account, recorded on 12 April 1368, van le Fine had receipts of over £700 gro. from the sale of Valenciennes and Maubeuge cloth.[143] This represents between 650 and 700 textiles, based upon price data found elsewhere in de Marke's ledgers.[144] In the late summer of 1368, van le Fine imported at least 400 additional textiles. Thus even these admittedly fragmentary records document the import of 1,100 textiles by van le Fine from April to September 1368.[145]

The second significant fact about this trade was that it involved a type of cloth that, while still produced in Hainault and northern France, was no longer made in Bruges. Light-weight, unfulled, relatively cheap cloth had once been a Bruges specialty, but for economic reasons the production of these "says" was abandoned by the middle of the fourteenth century. De Marke was thus very cannily importing relatively cheap cloth of a type no longer made in Bruges (or anywhere else in Flanders for that matter) to meet the continuing demand for cheaper cloth. The additional fact that most other Bruges money changers appear as purchasers in van le Fine's accounts, alongside foreign merchants, suggests that Hainault cloth attracted the interest of other brokers or investors, even if they did not actively organize the trade and transport of the cloth itself as de Marke did.[146] We know

142 Accounting for the cloth import business was kept separate from the money exchange, in a "papier des dras," though a number of postings were made in his regular ledgers. None of the records from the cloth business survives. In various places in the surviving accounts charges for "voiture de dras" are found, proving that de Marke was actively engaged in purchase and transport of the cloth; see SAB, De Marke 4, f. 405r, and f. 403r attesting to expenses de Marke incurred in shipment. De Roover briefly discussed de Marke's cloth import business: see *Money, Banking and Credit*, pp. 308–09.

143 De Marke 3, f. 10r "Pieter van le Fine me doit pour plusieurs parties de dras de Valenchiennes et de Maubuege qu'il avoit vendus . . ."; see also de Roover, *Money, Banking and Credit*, p. 326 n. 77.

144 Valenciennes cloth is quoted at £10 13s. 10d. gro. per bale of ten textiles in de Marke's accounts (De Marke, Journal I, f. 6r) and at £1 gro. the cloth in another entry (ibid., f. 12r, 18 August 1368). This is about a third of the price of a Bruges broadcloth or medley cloth in 1368, and less than a tenth the price of a piece of Ghent scarlet cloth. Van le Fine's imports in the late summer are known because de Marke charged his account for transport costs (De Marke, Journal I, f. 6r, 12 July 1368, 18 July 1368, 15 September 1368).

145 For futher discussion of the cloth-importing business of de Marke and van le Fine, see Murray, "Cloth, Banking and Finance," 30.

146 De Roover overlooked the importance of bankers among van le Fine's customers. In one account listing purchases from 7 June to 6 November 1368 (De Marke 3, f. 81r), van le Fine's credits totaled £956 gro, of which foreign merchants accounted for £363 and Bruges bankers £307. Significant as well is the fact that in the thirteenth century, Valenciennes says, as well as those of St. Omer, were counterfeited in Bruges; see Häpke, *Brügges Entwicklung*, p. 29.

from other sources that Hainault drapers themselves counted on the market afforded them by Bruges if their cloth failed to sell at a fair.[147] Even the death of his partner from the plague did not deter de Marke from continuing the trade, which he entrusted to his son, Collard.[148]

De Marke's business venture suggests that Bruges's role as a cloth entrepôt complemented its cloth production during a time of fundamental reorientation of the Bruges cloth industry away from one of its traditional products in favor of higher-quality and more expensive cloth.[149] Recent research has shown that most of the Flemish cloth towns reoriented their cloth production in similar ways, abandoning says and worsteds that had been so important as exports in the thirteenth century, and concentrating on luxury cloth, woven from quality English wools and finished with fulling, napping, and shearing. While not alone in this new emphasis, Bruges was extraordinarily effective in climbing from the second rank of cloth producers (in terms of quality) in the thirteenth century to among the top three or four by the middle of the fourteenth.[150] This reorientation was a result of the steeply rising costs of exporting cloth due to the warfare and piracy endemic in the fourteenth century. But any industrial change of this magnitude required considerable capital to bring about, in order both to acquire the costlier raw material and to accommodate the more complex manufacturing process necessary to produce luxury cloth. It was here that Bruges money changers played an important financial role.

GOLD

If wool and cloth formed the ancient foundations of the Bruges economy, gold was the newcomer in the fourteenth century. The return of gold coinage is one of the classic stories of the mature medieval economy, though

147 Georges Espinas and Henri Pirenne (eds.), *Documents relatifs à la draperie de Valenciennes* (Paris, 1931), pp. 298–305: "li Ordenanche des Porteurs des Dras," p. 303: "Et s'aucun drap demoroient a vendre en aucune des fiestes de Flandres a drappier, u a drappiere u a autrui, il les puet faire mener a estachon a Bruges, a fin telle que depuis on ne les puet ramener en Valenchiennes, ne en nulle des fiestes de Flandres . . ." Thus Bruges was the market of last resort for Valenciennes drapers.

148 Van le Fine died in the summer of 1369 and although his widow continued the business, de Marke shifted most of the responsibilities to his son.

149 That there is no necessary incompatiblility between commercial and industrial functions in an urban economy is missed by Raymond van Uytven, who explains the absence of Bruges cloth from the fourteenth-century *Dit du Lendit* as follows: "because in so great an international market, the town's commercial functions had largely superseded cloth-making for export:" "Cloth in Medieval Literature," p. 163.

150 Chorley, "The Cloth Exports," 373; John H. Munro has written extensively about this reorientation. Many of his papers are gathered in *Textiles, Towns and Trade* (Aldershot, 1994).

little attention has been paid to Bruges's role in it.[151] Gold coinage was rare in Bruges before the end of the thirteenth century.[152] By then gold florins and ducats had been used for several generations in Mediterranean commerce. Eventually Italian merchants brought large quantities of gold coins into their English trade, with much of it finding a ready use in Edward III's war preparations. Large infusions of gold led finally to the minting of large numbers of gold coins in Flanders by 1336.[153] The immediate impact of the return of gold coins was that they replaced silver in large transactions. Bruges's silver smelter, or *barnecamer*, whose function was to produce silver ingots of certified fineness for trade, ceased operation shortly thereafter, as did the one in Ghent.[154] In the half century after 1340, gold not only became a common medium of exchange across northern Europe, it became an important business commodity in highly commercial Bruges. There is no clearer example of this new role than the dispatch of agents by the city of Lübeck to Bruges to purchase sufficient gold so that the city could proceed to strike its own gold coins, which it did after 1340.[155]

Bruges money changers must have taken the leading role in organizing the market in gold and silver.[156] To a large degree their business became supplying gold to those who had silver and silver to those who had gold. Both the de Marke and Ruweel accounts take note of whether a deposit or withdrawal was made in gold or silver, and a fee – called *avaintage* – was assessed on the customer who exchanged one precious metal for another.[157] Gold no doubt continued to flow into Bruges via Italian merchants, supplemented perhaps with direct imports from the mines of Hungary; the great traffickers in silver continued to be German and Hanse merchants, whose gold coinages did not quite replace silver ingots as a means of exchange.[158]

151 Classic articles are Andrew M. Watson, "Back to Gold – and Silver," *Economic History Review*, 2nd series 20 (1967), 1–34; Robert S. Lopez, "Back to Gold, 1252," *Economic History Review*, 2nd series, 9 (1956), 219–240.

152 For this and what follows see Spufford, *Money and Its Use*, pp. 277–78.

153 Ibid., p. 278.

154 Bigwood, *Le Régime*, vol. 1, pp. 424–426; de Roover, *Money, Banking and Credit*, pp. 230–231; Spufford, *Money and Its Use*, p. 279.

155 Werner Paravicini, "Lübeck und Brügge. Bedeutung und erste Ergebnisse eines Kieler Forschungsprojekts," in H. Menke (ed.), *Die Niederlande und der europäische Nordosten: ein Jahrtausend weiträumiger Beziehungen (700–1700)* (Neumünster, 1992), p. 120 n. 141; Asmussen, *Lübecker Flandernfahrer*, pp. 62–63; Spufford, *Money and Its Use*, pp. 280–281.

156 Bruges goldsmiths would have had some form of bullion market of their own to satisfy their need for workable precious metal for jewelry. Given that both gold and silversmiths were found in large numbers in the area adjacent to the "Wissel," they may have acquired their metal directly from the money changers. For Bruges topography, see chapter 2.

157 De Roover, *Money, Banking and Credit*, p. 231 and examples on p. 233.

158 De Roover disparagingly referred to this as a symptom of continued German backwardness (*Money, Banking and Credit*, p. 244 n. 73); Spufford, *Money and Its Use*, pp. 282–283, notes that "it was not until the 1420s and 1430s that the circulation of silver marks generally gave way to Rhinegulden in the Baltic."

Little about the inner workings of the bullion business and Bruges's predominant role in it has come to light. On the one hand, mint accounts record the reworking of bullion into coins. Of course bullion delivery was an important responsibility of money changers, as they were de facto deputies of the mint when it came to quality control of coins in circulation and prompt dispatch of worn or demonetized coins to the comital mint.[159] Some idea of the prominence of Bruges as a collection point for bullion is revealed by the list of creditors left by the flight of the count's mint-master in 1357. Bruges money changers were owed 45 percent of the coins the mint had failed to deliver in exchange for gold bullion; and if the share of Baldwin de Vos, a Bruges merchant and comital counselor, is included, Bruges may have supplied nearly 88 percent of the gold minted at that time.[160] Unnoticed by historians is the fact that de Marke, for one, also conducted a thriving business in bullion – uncoined gold and silver not only collected at his exchange but purchased from others. We have looked at his business relationship with the comital mint in Ghent and with his money changer colleagues with regard to coin delivery. His pursuit of gold and silver bullion was a complement to his other businesses in coin and cloth, and its history as revealed in his accounts gives some idea of its organization.

His chief customer in the business was the Valenciennes money changer and cloth merchant Thierry Brochons.[161] Brochons functioned almost as a partner from nearby Hainault, shipping de Marke cloth as well as gold and silver. De Marke's accounts prove that Brochons delivered considerable quantities of gold and silver bullion, most of it bound for delivery to the comital mint at Ghent.[162] In effect, de Marke served as both purchaser and broker for Brochons, who was most likely profiting from the higher mint prices in Flanders.[163]

The bullion arrived in various forms: coined, plate, or in other worked forms. It was also on occasion delivered directly to the Ghent mint, resulting

159 For statistics and information about mint accounts in Flanders, see John H. Munro, "Bullion Flows and Monetary Contraction in Late-Medieval England and the Low Countries', in J. F. Richards (ed.), *Precious Metals in the Later Medieval and Early Modern Worlds* (Durham, North Carolina, 1983), pp. 97–157.

160 This percentage is certainly too high, since de Vos may have been owed for gold from other sources, though it is unlikely that he was merely the conduit of public tax monies, as de Roover believed, for he was granted the receipts of various taxes in order to repay the 1357 debt. See above, p. 158, and note Schouteet, *Regesten*, vol. III, p. 134, #340.

161 For material on the Brochons family see Espinas and Pireme, *Documents relatifs à la draperie de Valenciennes*, p. 262; a Watier Brochons was one of the thirteen aldermen of Valenciennes in June 1346.

162 For the history of minting in Flanders in general and in Bruges in particular, see chapter 4.

163 As a rule, gold was more valuable the further north it reached, value being defined as its exchange value in silver; on this rule see Spufford, *Money and Its Use*, pp. 271–288.

in the dispatch of a letter from the mint-master to de Marke in Bruges, and the crediting of Brochon's account with the equivalent in Flemish money.[164] This is the only example we have of such regional trade in gold and silver bullion, but it is highly unlikely that it was unique to this time and to these two money changers.[165]

The quantities of precious metal exchanged by these two men were considerable. Between March 1367 and December 1369, for example, de Marke purchased £3,369 2s groot Flemish worth of bullion, £2,325 of it silver, £1,044 gold. To get an idea of the magnitude of this trade, in the decade 1365–1374, the total silver coinage output of Flemish mints amounts to roughly £210,000 groot Flemish. Thus in this single two-and-a-half-year period, the silver bullion exchanged by de Marke and Brochons was 1.1 percent of this total. If we extrapolate it for the entire decade, it amounts to nearly 4.5 percent of the total silver minted by the comital mint. This is new evidence of the importance of Bruges as a market and conduit of gold and silver, both to the Flemish mints and to the commercial market of northern Europe.

CONCLUSION

No three commodities capture the essence of the Bruges urban economy better than wool, cloth, and gold. They all required the full ingenuity of the commercial infrastructure of brokers, innkeepers, and money changers. Their presence and exchange in Bruges brought other merchants laden with spices, furs, amber, and scores of other products and commodities changing hands. By circuitous routes, English wool was ultimately exchanged for spices brought from Italy; Flemish cloth filled the Hanse cogs on their voyages to the Baltic, and gold collected in the coffers of Bruges changers and brokers. Given their importance, it is no wonder that both aldermen and Bruges merchants (often the same men) devoted much money and effort to maintaining and increasing the market in wool, cloth, and gold. Collard de

164 For example, on 14 October 1367, £115 gro. of bullion was delivered to the Ghent mint, resulting in the dispatch of a letter to de Marke in Ghent and a corresponding credit to Brochons's account; see De Marke, 2 f. 357v. This example could be multiplied many times.

165 There are hints in the de Marke accounts of a varied and complex trade in coins and bullion. Some of it came via Bruges hostellers, as was the case in an entry from Willem Ruweel's accounts (SAB, Ruweel, f. 167v) in which the hosteller Jacob Meten Eye the younger delivered 114 marks of silver worth £76 19s. gro.; there is also the account of Joris Huerel, the "silversmith," again with Ruweel, who purchased twelve marks of silver (ibid., f. 162v). There was also an account of the mint-master Jehan Terminiel (Interminelli) that mentions a delivery of bullion from Roulof Raberone of Leuven in January 1369, worth the considerable sum of £395 12s. 4d. "que le dis Roulof livra ale monnoie [at Ghent]" (De Marke, 4 f. 69v).

Marke's cloth business, the accounts of wool brokers who banked with him, and of course his bullion business that so closely paralleled his cloth trade, all point to the continuing centrality of these commodities in the Bruges market. On a grander scale, Bruges changers and other merchants helped finance the redirection of Bruges's woolen manufacturing to a successful specialization in luxury cloth. As the traditional say industry disappeared due to the changing competitive and political conditions of the fourteenth century, Bruges drapers were able to call upon the growing commercial and financial strength of the city to make possible such a change of direction. And of course Bruges played the politics of the Hundred Years' War to the utmost in order to insure the continued flow of English wool into the city. A great commercial city could afford to do no less.

CHAPTER 8

Women in the market and the market in women

. . . la città mercatrice, ma che dico, meretrice!

Aeneas Sylvius

This chapter title is meant to be provocative, though it is by no means original. Already in the middle of the fifteenth century, the future Pope Pius II, Aeneas Sylvius, had equated a "città mercatrice" with a "città meretrice" – a merchant with a meretricious city.[1] In this he merely echoed a long tradition of righteous indignation over wealth derived from commerce in European cities and the easy and seemingly natural equation with prostitution. Mendicant preachers made rather a specialty of condemning some aspects of commerce, notably usury and prostitution, while admitting the potential virtue of others. In the Low Countries Guibertus of Tournai, active between 1290 and 1300, when preaching on Luke 19:13–14 admitted the virtue of trade, except for usury and prostitution, which he saw as the clearest evidence of the devil's intervention in human affairs.[2] John Calvin, strangely enough, joins this medieval chorus in his commentary on Ezekiel (23:17) when in the midst of the Old Testament's most graphic description of "harlotry" he observes that the life of the merchant closely resembles that of the harlot, "full of tricks and traps and deceits and many new and unheard of contrivances for making gain."[3] Thus even the man Weber credits as the creator of the spirit of capitalism echoes Sylvius' equivalence of merchant and prostitute.

[1] Quoted in Richard Trexler, "La prostitution florentine au xve siècle: patronages et clientèles," *Annales E.S.C.* 36 (1981), 983–1015.

[2] Simons, *Stad en apostolaat*, pp. 204–205.

[3] Discussed by Ronald S. Wallace, *Calvin, Geneva and the Reformation* (Edinburgh, 1990), p. 86. Linking usury and prostitutes seems to have become a commonplace in the writings of thirteenth-century theologians, such as Thomas of Cobham: "Ecclesia persequitur feneratores sicut alios fures quia assument sibi officium fenerandi publicum ut inde vivant, sicut meretrices": quoted from Spicciani, *Capitale e interesse*, p. 77 n. 73.

Figure 10: Bathhouse scene. A fifteenth-century miniature from a Bruges master shows a scene of mixed bathing of prostitutes and clients, which was often the prelude to sexual intercourse, pictured in the bedchamber at left.

A preacher's commonplaces, medieval or contemporary, seldom make for satisfying history, however. There is no way of telling by these blanket condemnations whether all cities are equally culpable, or just Florence and Geneva? Are the most populous cities the most shameless? Or is it the richest? Do certain social and economic conditions set certain cities apart? And if so, which conditions are they? Moralists also tend to lull us into the easy assumption that the merchants are always male and the prostitutes always female, and that prostitution is somehow less a business than other forms of trade. Is there a more historically accurate way to examine the relationship of a city's social and business infrastructure and the prevalence of paid sex? I will argue in this chapter that commercialization of a particular city, Bruges, in the fourteenth and fifteenth centuries brought numerous women into the market as traders, manufacturers, bankers, and brokers, while at the same time creating the demand for, and toleration of, scores of houses of prostitution.[4]

By now the argument for the dominance of commerce over many aspects of social and political life in Bruges is familiar to the reader. Yet stretching it to state that the nature of a particular urban economy might simultaneously both bring women to the center of that economy, and, in the case of female prostitutes, push them to the social margins, challenges the reigning assumption about women's work in the pre-industrial economy. This sees "patriarchy" as the ubiquitous system limiting women's work, enforcing women's inferiority by requiring male guardianship of person and property, especially in the public sphere of court and market. And the power of patriarchy is directly proportional, in this formulation, to the degree of commercialization of a craft or industry. Judith Bennett, who has done the most to formulate and popularize this view, uses the example of the English alewife to document the physics of a female trade in the central Middle Ages, which became ever more male-dominated as it was commercialized and gradually shifted from the household to the brewery.[5] Bennett believes this case to be typical of work in all sectors of the medieval economy: as any craft or trade becomes of interest to men it falls under the organizing logic of a guild, which *ipso facto* results in the exclusion of women from what

[4] Much more is now known about the various patterns of women's work in the medieval city than was the case when Syvia Thrupp wrote about medieval London. A good starting place is the introduction and articles in Barbara A. Hanawalt (ed.), *Women and Work in Preindustrial Europe* (Bloomington, 1986).

[5] She first sketched the argument in a short chapter, "The Village Ale-wife: Women and Brewing in Fourteenth-Century England," in *Women and Work*, pp. 20–36. This was later expanded into a monograph: *Ale, Beer, and Brewsters in England: Women's Work in a Changing World, 1300–1600* (Oxford, 1996).

Martha Howell has called "high labor status," and their concentration in the more marginal jobs of any given industry.[6] The classic example is of course the textile industry, which after millennia as a female occupation became a full-fledged urban industry in the course of the high Middle Ages. In the process women were excluded from the high-status jobs of weaving, dyeing, and fulling and forced into the "marginal" jobs of wool washing, combing/carding, and of course spinning.[7]

There is no doubt that medieval society, including urban society, was patriarchal, but it is important not to prejudge outcomes as a result or to see all patriarchies as alike. For example, fourteenth and fifteenth-century Florence is a clear-cut example of a commercial city run by men, which clearly excluded women from high-status roles in the urban economy. Florentine women were very explicitly governed by either their husbands or their male relatives in their legal or economic affairs. There simply was no question of an independent woman organizing and managing a business on her own without reference to a male. Interestingly enough, even prostitution had to submit to male organization in Florence, when in 1403 the Florentine government established the Onestà (Office of Decency), a bureaucracy specifically charged with controlling prostitution through the foundation of public houses of prostitution in the city as well as general governance of prostitutes. Thus the conduct and organization of prostitutes became the affair of city officials.[8] Bruges, by contrast, was every bit as commercialized and "patriarchal" as Florence, yet women were neither under the strict guardianship of men, nor absent from the market place. Moreover, prostitution in Bruges never became subject to city control except for the levying of fines that became in effect licensing fees. In short, attributing all the limiting or enabling factors in women's work to "patriarchy" seriously oversimplifies the reality. Local economic, social, and legal conditions were more important.

Several unusual aspects of Bruges's business and social history had important consequences for women. The strength of its trade and industry undoubtedly attracted female migrants in large numbers. In the absence of

[6] Howell, in *Women, Production, and Patriarchy*, pp. 23–26, defines labor status as control over a product from purchase of raw materials to distribution and sale, regardless of occupation. Marginal jobs were those with no power over the product.

[7] David Herlihy, *Opera Muliebria: Women and Work in Medieval Europe* (New York, 1990), pp. 185–191.

[8] Trexler argues that the primary reason for the Onestà's founding was combating homosexuality. John Brackett, on the other hand, argued that it was first founded to control prostitution but then evolved into a means to exploit prostitutes for the benefit of the convent of the Convertite. See John Brackett, "The Florentine Onestà and the Control of Prostitution, 1403–1680," *The Sixteenth Century Journal* 24 (1993), 273–300.

complete demographic data, however, we are reduced to considering indirect measures. We know from chapter 3 that Bruges attracted more immigrants from longer distances than other Flemish cities, and more from the countryside than other cities in Flanders.[9] Many of these new burghers came from more than fifty kilometers away, with the areas of Holland and French Flanders most prominently represented as places of origin. Of the thousand or so new immigrants between 1331 and 1375 whose professions were listed, a significant group – some 26.2 percent – were tailors, leather workers, harness makers, or stocking makers; another 18.7 percent practiced a textile trade; 13.4 percent were in the "luxury" trades of silver and goldsmithing, miniature painting, or panel painting. What is also striking about Bruges immigration is simply the high number of new residents. Between 1281 and 1408 some 20,000 people purchased the right of citizenship and were registered. In most years more than 100 and often more than 200 new heads of household were registered. And these represented at best a partial list, for most new Bruges immigrants neither wished for nor could afford the payment required to purchase full citizenship rights. Most of those who did, did so in order to practice their craft. Single women occur in these lists with unusual frequency as well. Between 1331 and 1460 women made up about 10 percent of newly enrolled citizens; in several years they made up 20 percent.[10] All in all, in a city whose total population numbered some 42,000, the percentage of immigrants was quite remarkable, and among them no doubt were many single women.

The other highly unusual aspect of the Bruges community with important consequences for women was the number of foreign merchants living within the walls. Witnesses from the time were struck by this fact. Francesco Pegolotti, the Florentine businessman, mentions Ypres, Lille, Douai, and Ghent as important Flemish cities but reserves most of his attention for Bruges because it is there that "foreign merchants reside."[11] Another indication of Bruges's status comes roughly a half century later from Geoffrey Chaucer, the English courtier and merchant's son, who made Bruges the logical destination for the merchant of his *Shipman's Tale* who resided long enough for the rascally monk to seduce his wife. Besides these qualitative

9 Thoen, "Verhuizen naar Brugge," pp. 341–44.

10 Martha C. Howell, "Citizenship and Gender: Women's Political Status in Northern Medieval Cities," in M. Erler and M. Kowaleski (eds.), *Women and Power in the Middle Ages* (Athens, Georgia, and London, 1988), pp. 37–60, esp. p. 41. As explained in chapter 3, these purchasers of *poorter* status were a very small minority of immigrants, representing those with both the need and means to invest in this privilege.

11 Pegolotti, *La pratica della mercatura*, p. 236 "Cioe Bruggia e Guanto e Ipro e Lille e Doagio, ma parleremo il piu di Bruggia pero ch'ella a quella terra ove piu stanno i risedenti mercatanti a fare la mercatantia e cambi in Fiandra . . ."

judgments of contemporaries, the data presented in chapter 3 are striking. Taken as a percentage, foreign merchants probably represented between 4 and 6 percent of the Bruges population at any one time.[12] Yet the characteristics of their presence gave these numbers disproportionate impact in a number of ways. First was the frequent coming and going of merchants who formed the clientele of the city's hostellers. Second was the period of peak activity falling in May during the Bruges fair. This event certainly brought additional hundreds of short-term visiting merchants. Also not to be forgotten are the long-term residents from abroad who might remain for extended periods in rented or purchased quarters. The majority of these visitors to Bruges came without family, which meant a constant abundance of single men within the walls.

The unusual prominence of trade, the hosting of merchants, the changes in urban industry, and unique patterns of immigration including female immigration, combined, as we have seen, to give Bruges a kind of rollicking energy and instability. Further indications of this were the fluid, money-dominated social and political elite of the city, in which brokers/hostellers exercised considerable power. All these things gave Bruges a social profile uniquely its own even in comparison with other commercial centers.[13]

The second essential background element to understanding women's work in a commercial metropolis was not unique to Bruges, but was common to all Flemish cities, i.e. the web of customary law governing family law, especially with regard to the rights it allowed women. There were several unusual aspects to Flemish law which are of importance: the first was partible inheritance, which guaranteed female children equal shares of an estate.[14] Women also continued to have absolute right to any property they brought into a marriage, though the husband could and ordinarily did manage it. Any increase in the family's fortunes achieved during the marriage, however, belonged equally to the husband and wife. In contrast, any debts or losses incurred by the husband could only be made good from either his assets or community assets; those assets brought into the marriage by the woman were normally inviolable.[15] There was also the unusual custom of "orphan money" whereby upon the death of either spouse in

[12] See figures and discussion presented in chapter 3, p. 96.

[13] Cologne was probably the most similar to Bruges, as the work of M. Wensky establishes; see *Die Stellung der Frau in der stadtkölnischen Wirtschaft in Spätmittelalter* (Cologne and Vienna, 1980).

[14] For an explanation of the system current in Ghent see Nicholas, *Domestic Life*, pp. 21–32, and 76–83. The Flemish system was perhaps among the most liberal in its allowances for women, but some degree of control over property was common all across northern Europe. For this see Howell, *Women, Production and Patriarchy*, pp. 14–21.

[15] Renouncing responsibility for a husband's debts did require legal action by the woman, however. David Nicholas cites cases in which either ignorance or poor judgment on the part of a widow resulted in her continued liability for a late husband's debts; see Nicholas, *Domestic Life*, pp. 77–78.

a family with children, an inventory would be drawn up before public officials detailing the property that now belonged to the children. The surviving spouse could have use of that property, but only in exchange for guaranteed maintenance of the children (including provision for education and training) and return of the capital when the child or children reached the age of majority. Normally orphan money was invested, and it was one of the few investments legally exempted from usury prohibitions.[16] Whatever the reasons for this unusual body of family law, the fact remains that especially in the cities of medieval Flanders, women enjoyed considerable power over their property, they were accustomed to acting on behalf of their husbands or family in economic and legal matters, and family assets were monetized (as in orphan money) to a considerable degree. Money and property changed hands rapidly in this society and women were fully part of the decisions governing the exchange.[17]

WOMEN IN THE MARKET

One of the strange novelties of Bruges for the colony of Florentine and Lucchese businessmen living there must have been the near equality of men and women in the market places, brokerage houses, and money exchanges of the city. This was a far different state of affairs from what they knew from their hometowns, or anywhere else in Mediterranean Europe for that matter. Only the fifteenth-century Spaniard Pietro Tafur has left us a direct reaction to this equality when he expresses his amazement at the custom of men and women going to bathhouses together.[18] A literary evocation of the ubiquity of women in the Bruges market place is a bilingual

In Bruges the custom seems to have been to lay the keys of the family house on the husband's casket or grave, or to give them to the city clerk in charge of inventorying their goods; see M. van Coppenolle, "Een verdwenen uitvaartgebruik: de sleutels op de put leggen," *Biekorf* 50 (1949), 3–7. Marianne Danneel traces in considerable detail the choices fifteenth-century widows in Ghent faced after the death of a spouse. These included not only how a widow could receive and use property, but what responsibility she bore for her husband's debts. Unlike David Nicholas, however, Danneel finds that in fifteenth-century Ghent widows remained fully liable for their husband's debts, very unlike the case in Bruges: see Danneel, *Weduwen en wezen*, pp. 264–302, esp. 292.

16 Nicholas, "Of Poverty and Primacy," 17–41. For the investment of "orphan money" (*wezengeld*) in Ghent see Nicholas's *Domestic Life*, pp. 131–134 . Marianne Danneel refines some of Nicholas' findings in *Weduwen en wezen*, pp. 23–130, and she devotes an excellent section to the investment and management of orphan money, pp. 148–166.

17 Ellen Kittell, "Guardianship over Women in Medieval Flanders: A Reappraisal," *Journal of Social History* 31 (1998), 897–930; Martha Howell, *The Marriage Exchange: Property, Social Place, and Gender in Cities of the Low Countries, 1300–1550* (Chicago, 1998), p. 107.

18 Men and women bathing together was strictly illegal in Spain. For women in the Mediterranean economy, see Katherine Reyerson, Women in Business in Medieval Montpellier *Women and Work in PreIndustrial Europe*, pp. 117–144, reprinted in *Society, Law, and Trade in Medieval Montpellier* VIII (Aldershot, 1995).

conversation manual of around 1369, which names women as cooks, seamstresses, spinsters, combers, parchment sellers, and, unforgettably, "Natalie, la belle dame, tient boine estuve: li plus soufissant de la ville y vont estuver" – Natalie of the baths.[19]

The best way to grasp the reality of women's work in Bruges is to divide the urban economy into sectors. The extant evidence for each is uneven in both quantity and quality, so the intention here is just to refer to it briefly by way of illustration. Selling foodstuffs has always been a job closely associated with women in most medieval cities and Bruges was no exception.[20] All evidence points to their near monopoly on the retail food trades in the city, with the exception of the Meat Halls. Even in cases of joint ownership of a retail foodstall, where the man was the actual guild member, it was the woman who most often did the actual selling.[21] Clear indications of this come from lists of those paying rent for city stalls in the Cheese Market (Caes Huus) and for those who rented outside stalls for the sale of figs and raisins. Of the fifty-five stalls listed in the hall in 1304, fifty were held by women.[22] Similarly, of the ninety-three fruit stalls rented by the city during Lent, eighty-three were held by women in 1305–1306.[23] A further indication of female dominance in the sale of dairy products is a list of fines from 1379 assessed for forestalling: five women and two men were charged.[24] Another instance of women falling foul of city regulations occurred in 1363, when an unstated number of women were fined for setting up their sales stalls on the bridge near the Carmelite monastery.[25]

[19] Gessler, *Livre des mestiers*; Myriam Greilsammer, *L'envers du tableau: mariage et maternité en Flandre médiévale* (Paris, 1990), pp. 24–25; Peter Stabel, "Women at the Market. Gender and Retail in the Towns of Late Medieval Flanders," in Blockmans *et al.* (eds.), *Secretum Secretorum*, pp. 259–276, esp. 259–265.

[20] Martha Howell found that in Leiden, Cologne, and Douai women were concentrated in a few occupations, many having to do with the preparation and sale of food and drink: *Women, Production, and Patriarchy*, p. 176. David Nicholas noticed the same in Ghent; see *Domestic Life*, p. 84.

[21] This was true of the fishmongers' guild, which became increasingly influential and wealthy in fourteenth-century Bruges as elsewhere, but it is significant that in 1384 Maye Tuts, the fishmonger, lodged a complaint against a woman competitor, Bele van Winghene: ARA, Rekenkamer, RR 1033, membrane 4. For the history of the fishmongers' guild in Bruges, see Vanhoutryve, *De Vishandel en het Visambacht te Brugge*, pp. 59–62.

[22] Wyffels and Vandewalle, *Rekeningen*, vol. II, pt. 1, pp. 372–374 and 507–509. We only know about the details of hall rental in years when it was not leased out to a *pachter* – someone who paid a flat fee for the right to manage the hall.

[23] Ibid., pp. 758–760. These were temporary stands allowed on the Grote Markt, apparently only for the forty-day period of fasting. Interestingly, only four of the women are described as either wives or widows, lending further credence to their independence as sellers.

[24] ARA, Rekenkamer, RR 1029 (1379): "Boete van den ghonen die gaen buter stede omme zuvel te copene eer datter bin der stede ter maerct, de boete £3." This enforcement of a city's right to have rural products sold only in its market is quite common in medieval Europe.

[25] SAB, SR 1363–1364, f. 20r ("diverse boeten") "Item van wiven die stonden up tscaermers brugghe met cramen ieghen tghebod vander stede 10s."

Women also appear quite often as sellers of drink, even though they apparently did not dominate this professional category to the same degree as in foodstuffs. Of the twenty-four persons fined in 1305–1306 for selling short measures of wine, only five women appear.[26] In a complaint lodged with the comital bailiff in 1374, the attorney for the Lord of the Gruuthuus alleged that seven individuals were selling illegally brewed beer from stands around the city. Five of the seven were women.[27]

The largest guild-dominated industry in Bruges was the cloth industry. Though not nearly as dependent on it as its neighbors Ghent and Ypres, Bruges nonetheless had about 25 percent of its male inhabitants employed in the industry in one guild or another.[28] The role of women is problematic, however. Accepted wisdom is that with the domination of guilds, particularly the dominant guilds of weavers, dyers, and fullers, women were forced into the very labor-intensive, but marginal, tasks of washing, combing/carding, and spinning wool. There are two indications that this was not the case in Bruges. First are the considerable bodies of *Keuren*, the regulations promulgated by the city to govern the production and sale of cloth.[29] These are full of examples in which women are clearly described as part of the production process. Often the dyad *mester/mestrigghe* is used to indicate male and female masters. Another more direct source is a list of weavers who sold cloth to one of the drapers who had a bank account with the money changer Collard de Marke between 1366 and 1370. Of the 440 weavers mentioned in the accounts, 222 were women, 184 were men, twelve were married or widowed women, twenty-two were husband and wife teams.

There is also evidence that women dominated other areas of textile and clothing manufacture. The city accounts have numerous instances of payments made to seamstresses for tailoring cloth given to city officials into clothing.[30] There are also scattered references to washerwomen, wet

[26] Wyffels and Vandewalle, *Rekeningen*, vol. II, pt. 2, pp. 760–761. One of five of those selling short measures of mead was a woman in the same account.

[27] The Lord of the Gruuthuus enjoyed a monopoly on the sale of "gruut," the herbal mixture used to brew beer in Bruges before the advent of hopped beer making. The inventory of all seven was ordered to be destroyed as a result and they were each fined £6 par. as well. The seven were Clemencie, the widow of the Hanse merchant Aelbrecht Musepenninx, Aleit van Cleven, Jan Sneeuwers, Lysbette sGrooten, Marie van Houtkerke, Heinric van de Scake, and Kateline van Praet: ARA, Rekenkamer, RR 1011, membrane 7; on beer brewing in Bruges, see Raymond van Uytven, "Beer Consumption and the Socio-economic Situation in the Franc of Bruges in the Sixteenth Century" in *Production and Consumption* XIII, esp. pp. 5–7.

[28] As discussed in chapter 3, the percentage of the population employed in the textile industry declined across the century; see above, p. 000.

[29] Pirenne and Espinas, *Recueil*, vol. I, pp. 342–608.

[30] Part of the compensation given city officials and employees consisted of a semi-annual distribution of cloth. Usually the tailoring costs are not stated in the city accounts; an exception was in 1333,

nurses, and a host of other rather marginal workers common in all medieval cities.[31] Unfortunately, what we know about female servants in fourteenth-century Bruges comes only from a few cases of theft recorded in bailiffs' accounts.[32]

Another sector of the Bruges economy in which women were active, if not predominant, was unlicensed moneylending. A recent book by William Jordan has brought attention to the activities of women in this area of the medieval economy. He argues that links of sociability – the informal links of households – could lead to non-professional or casual moneylending.[33] Most of this is rendered invisible due to the lack of records. But in Bruges there were those who crossed the line between casual and professional, and just broke the law banning loans at excessive rates of interest. In practice these were most likely rag-tag pawnshops, where small loans were made against the surrender of a household article or an article of clothing. Of the list of fines preserved in the city accounts of Bruges, women made up typically a third of those found guilty of lending money above the legal maximum rate of interest. In the first part of the fourteenth century an entire family of women, the Cosericghen, were moneylenders.[34]

The most impressive sector of the Bruges economy in which women were involved was the business service sector, primarily money changing and brokering/innkeeping.[35] By and large this was a sector of little guild

when the seamstress Kateline sReepers was reimbursed for the cost of extra cloth needed to line some Bruges striped cloth, because the two cloth types were of unequal length (SAB, SR 1333–1334, f. 61r: "Kateline sReepers van 13 ellen gheminghet lakens die hem [sic] gheborsten omme dat die strijpte bruxsche lakene langher waren dan die gheminghede, £5 4s. par." The next year Griele Nerinx was paid for some additional cloth used to make the clothes of the city policemen (*scerwetter*): SAB, SR 1335–1336, f. 59r: "Griele Nerinx van 9 ellen blaeus lakens ter scerwetters boef . . ."

31 Ibid., 1309–1310, f. 32r: "Item enen wive van 1 vondelinghe bi beveelne van scepenen, 20s"; 1315 (f. 58r): "lysken van ekelo van enen vondelinghe te houdene dat schepenen vonden int coren van den jare 43s. 4d." In 1310 the city listed under its receipts the property of a beggar woman who died without heirs: ibid., 1310, f. 11v, "item van 1 wive die zat voer den augustinen ter bede die staerf zonder calaenge van aeldinghers £60 de welke peneghe ontfanghen waren ter stede waerd toter wile dat recht aelding quame."

32 ARA, Rekenkamer, RR 1026 (1378) found that Maye Gheerkins stole goods from her master and then pawned them. In 1383 Godelief Veldams from Leffinge was briefly imprisoned for the theft of some of her master's jewels: ibid., 1032. Servants were probably the most numerous among single women working in Bruges, but we know the least about them. For female servants in an urban economy, see the discussion of Paris by Herlihy, *Opera Muliebria*, pp. 142–149; for Paris as well see Sharon Farmer, "Down and Out and Female in Thirteenth Century Paris," *American Historical Review* 103 (1998), 345–372. Florence is another interesting example, as discussed by Christiane Klapisch-Zuber, "Women Servants in Florence during the Fourteenth and Fifteenth Centuries," *Women and Work* , pp. 56–80. For England, see P. J. P. Goldberg, *Women, Work, and Life Cycle in a Medieval Economy: Women in York and Yorkshire c. 1300–1520* (Oxford, 1992).

33 Jordan, *Women and Credit*, pp. 13–42.

34 Marechal, *Bijdrage*, pp. 13, 114–115.

35 De Meyer lumped together these professions with that of usurer, which together formed the "money brokers" in the city; see de Meyer, "Sociale strukturen," 69.

control, much emphasis on the family as the organizing unit of business, and in turn a large independent role for women. Nowhere was this truer than in the money changing profession.

As shown in previous chapters, money changing in Bruges had evolved into a complex business by the fourteenth century. Far from being simply the exchange of one coin for another, it also came to include related activities such as deposit banking, inter-bank transfers, investments in trade and real estate, and bullion arbitrage, to name just a few.[36] It remained a financially risky venture, however, since most money changers operated on a fractional reserve system in which the majority of their deposits were invested. In the absence of a central bank and a securities market, any unanticipated loss or financial panic could quickly lead to bankruptcy. Yet in the fourteenth century a significant minority of money changers were women, and probably a greater number partnered their husbands in the operation of a money exchange.[37] In the lists of money changers preserved in the city accounts of Bruges, women are nearly always present. There are also at least two cases of a mother/daughter team at the head of a money-changing operation early in the century.[38] And many of these came from wealthy and powerful families: Calkere, van de Walle, van Curtrike, Danwilde, and others.[39] Understanding why that was the case can teach us much about the close relationship of business and family life.

[36] De Roover, *Money, Banking and Credit*; Murray, "Family, Marriage and Money Changing," 115–125.

[37] De Roover noticed this as well, though he did not explore it in any depth – see *Money, Banking and Credit*, pp. 173–174. Bruges was far from unique in this affinity of women with money changing: in Paris in 1313, two of twenty-three money changers were women (Herlihy, *Opera Muliebria*, p. 149); Cologne also had female money changers in the fourteenth century (Wensky, *Die Stellung der Frau*, p. 122). The fact that partnerships of husband and wife were common in the running of exchanges is clear from an ordinance of Duke Philip the Good, duke of Burgundy and count of Flanders, published in 1434 and addressed not only to money changers but to "leurs femmes, clercs, varles ou familliers . . .": Gilliodts van Severen, *Inventaire*, "table analytique," under "changeur".

[38] These were Jan Calker's wife and her daughter, who contributed to a forced loan from money changers in 1305, and Lijsbet Raloos and her like-named daughter in 1312; Wyffels and Vandewalle, *Rekeningen*, vol II, pt. 1, p. 600, "Van Jans Calkers wijf over hare dochter £16," and Marechal, *Bijdrage*, pp. 81–82. We cannot know, however, if these women actively operated their exchanges, since leasing out the right to operate was probably common. The charter of 1312, edited by Marechal, gives a strong indication that in the case of the Raloos family, they may have been more interested in the income accruing to the holder of a free exchange. The charter is a result of a complaint lodged on behalf of Lijsbet by her guardian Gillis van den Scake that she had been wrongfully deprived of her fief – one of the four free exchanges in Bruges. The aldermen of the Brugse Vrije agreed and reinstated her. There is no other record of Lijsbet.

[39] The Calkere clan was significant in Bruges in the late thirteenth and early fourteenth centuries; see Marechal, *Bijdrage*, p. 49 and n. 59; the van de Walle and van Curtrike families were part of the new commercial elite whose wealth was derived from brokering and hostelling.

Women and money changing

One of the six account books left by Bruges money changers in the city archives was left in the wake of the bankruptcy of Willem Ruweel around 1370. As stated in a previous chapter, Willem Ruweel was probably not a native of Bruges. His name – Ruweel – is in fact a Flemish corruption of the French Ruyelle, and the French form was still preferred by the non-Flemish clerk of his colleague Collard de Marke. Ruweel may have been one of the many Walloons active as pawnbrokers, money changers and traders in Bruges in the fourteenth century.[40] But it was marriage that made the Ruweel exchange – in this case Willem's marriage to the *poorter*'s daughter, Margaret van Ruuslede. It was her dowry that included the comital fief allowing operation of the exchange.

Margaret's fief permitted operation of one of the "free" money exchanges, and was something of a family heirloom. The exchange had been in her family for at least two generations, reaching back to her grandfather, who held it in 1316. The exchange became part of the dowry of Griele van Ruuslede, Margaret's aunt, in her marriage to the hosteller's son Jan van der Hangele before 1325. Griele apparently died childless after 1332, leaving the operation of the exchange to her husband and later to her brother Jan, as the fief reverted to the van Ruuslede family to become in turn part of Margaret's dowry.[41] Ruweel's marriage was thus at least doubly advantageous for his business interests, to say nothing of its social benefits. First, of course, was the exchange office itself, which could provide capital for all sorts of investments. It could provide this capital, roughly 75 percent of all deposits, with only minimal requirements of space and personnel. As to business space, location was crucial, and Margaret's fief included a small "room" squarely amid the triangle of trade and finance of the Bruges market, a triangle formed by the Burg, the Old and New Cloth Halls and the Bourse square. As a side business and cash producer, a money exchange could be very useful to an investor.

The second and substantial advantage was Margaret Ruweel herself, for, as mentioned above, their marriage created in Flemish law a type of limited partnership, in which all the property was held in common under the control of the husband, while guaranteeing half of the common property as the

[40] De Roover, *Money, Banking and Credit*, p. 308; Marechal, *Bijdrage*, pp. 14–17; for a list of moneylenders from the north of France active in Bruges, see pp. 117–119.

[41] The family history of Margaret Ruweel is reconstructed largely on the basis of entries from the book of fiefs kept by the comital administration (ARA, Rekenkamer, RR 1072–1074); relevant passages are edited by Marechal, *Bijdrage*, pp. 120–132.

wife's share in case of her husband's death or business failure.[42] Strict community of property remedied in part the one great drawback of medieval exchange banking – the risk of bankruptcy from the failure of investments or failure of confidence of the bank's customers leading to wholesale withdrawal of deposits. Thus even in the event of bankruptcy, Ruweel could shelter half the family fortune from the claims of his creditors. Small wonder that a money exchange was an attractive dowry in the marriage of a burgher's daughter in fourteenth- and fifteenth-century Bruges.

For his part, Ruweel must have brought the other essential element to an exchange bank – a reputation as a businessman. Depositors would only be attracted to Ruweel's exchange rather than a competitor's by the confidence they had in him as a sound man of business. Risk of loss is always a possibility when money is entrusted to a bank, and in medieval Bruges deposits were hazarded on the personal prestige of the money changer alone. Only privileged foreigners could claim their full deposits from the city government in the event of bankruptcy. Others had to accept a fraction of the amount of their deposit. Despite the considerable role played by women in the economy of medieval Bruges, it was unlikely that a young woman could elicit this kind of trust. Margaret Ruweel's dowry was thus worth what the strength of her husband's reputation could draw by way of customers, as well as his luck and skill in managing their investments.

We know something about the staff and operation of Ruweel's exchange business through Collard de Marke's accounts, which survive for the period from April 1366 through December 1369. Most Bruges money changers had accounts with one another to facilitate book transfers for their customers. From the accounts we know that Ruweel had four Jans working for him in the period. They were his son Jan Ruweel, his wife's kinsman Jan van Ruuslede, and two varlets, Jan van Risele and Jan de Hersin. A second son, Copin (diminutive of Jacob) Ruweel, rounded out the group. Van Risele and de Hersin seem to have carried out the menial tasks involved with the exchange; de Hersin may have been the clerk of the accounts. Jan Ruweel and Jan van Ruuslede also did the menial chores, but sometimes were special assistants to Willem in some of his larger financial ventures, as might befit apprentices who were family members. But given that

42 This is an unusual aspect of Flemish property law, analyzed by E. M. Meijers, *Het Ligurische Erfrecht in de Nederlanden*, 3 vols. (Harlem, 1929–36), vol. II, pp. 54–63. David Nicholas mentions this provision as being of great importance in the economic development of Flanders, as it tended to encourage liquidity of capital and prevent large accumulations of property across generations; see "Of Poverty and Primacy," 37.

both are called by the double diminutive Hannekin – "Johnny-boy" – and were probably teenagers, their independence of action was no doubt limited.[43]

The manager of the Ruweel bank and supervisor of all its Johnnies was, judging from the evidence, Margaret Ruweel herself.[44] This is quite logical, for it would be strange if the young Margaret had not gained some experience in the part of her family's business that would become her dowry. As stressed above, there was already a considerable history of women money changers before the 1360s. As we shall see, two of Margaret's contemporaries were carrying on exchanges started by their late husbands. Ghent also had a remarkable example of an independent woman money changer, Celie Amelakens, who was active from 1352 to 1382.[45] In other words, though unusual, women money changers were far from unique.

Margaret Ruweel's independence and importance were clearly recognized by the scribe who kept Collard de Marke's accounts. At many points she is listed under a separate account from her husband's, which was a means of separating the transactions of the exchange from Willem's other investments.[46] Here are listed the daily costs and details of money changing. While the accounts were separate, Willem and Margaret could each draw from the account of the other, and Margaret's account usually makes clear her husband's ultimate authority, for she is usually referred to as "the

[43] The nature of the work of a "varlet" of the exchange is shown in the de Marke accounts. For example, Hanekin Rissele was sent to pick up twenty-four lions (gold coins) from de Marke on 14 July 1366 (SAB, de Marke 1, f. 256v); ten days later de Marke recorded a debit of sixty lions "pour se feme et pour se fil" (ibid., f. 256v). Hanekin Ruuslede appears around the same time doing the same type of delivery work: "pour Hanekin sen cousin 19 decembre [1366] 30 lions" (f. 271r). The examples could be multiplied. Margaret handled the important reconciling of accounts with de Marke, even though the account was in her husband's name; so at the start of de Marke's second ledger (2, f. 313r): "Will. Ruyelle me doit p. le reste de nos contes dou fuellet 311 contet a se femme 3 en aoust £12 1 s. 5d." Margaret could appear in her own right as an account holder synonymous with her husband, as in August, 1367: "le femme will. ruyelle me doit" (ibid., f. 315r). Such marks of independence were accorded to Hannekin Ruweel and Rissele as well: "Hankin Ruiwel me doit" (ibid.): "Hanekin le varlet Will. Ruyelle me doit"; these were all subaccounts of the exchange.

[44] The surviving account book of the Ruweels shows that it served the multiple purposes of the family's business operations, which in Margaret's case meant that the operating expenses of the exchange were recorded in her personal account. Thus, for example, in May 1370 her account was debited for the purchase of heating fuel (peat) as well as the cost of acquring gold coins; see SAB, Ruweel, f. 160r.

[45] Nicholas, *Domestic Life*, pp. 90–94.

[46] Willem, Margaret, and their son Hannekin all have separate accounts in the surviving account book, which represents different facets of their business activities. For example, Hannekin was the collection agent for the wine assize leased from the city, which resulted in deposits made to his account and large payments made to the city treasurer, Sir Jehan van Artrike. Thus on 12 November 1369, van Artrike's account was credited with £653 gro. "par Hannekin Ruwel" (Ruweel, f. 87r). Hannekin's receipts from the wine assize were listed under a separate account in the Ruweel account book (ff. 101r–v). De Roover partially edited these in "Le livre de comptes de Guillaume Ruyelle," 85–87.

wife of Willem Ruweel."[47] But her control of business was impressive, as attested by the accounts. She carried out most of the usual duties of the exchange: trading coins with other bankers and regulating accounts with them periodically in order to balance the book transfers made among their banks.[48] A close reading of Margaret Ruweel's accounts in the Ruweel account book also bears out her important business role. Charged to her account are costs for purchasing coins from other money changers, costs for acquiring gold, the price of a weighing scale, and charges for building services and materials, in all likelihood used to maintain the family's urban property.[49]

There was a second example of female-run exchange contemporary with that of the Ruweels. This was formed by Clais Rapesaert and his wife, who is referred to only as "le Demoiselle," a title of respect yet indicating her close connection with her husband in the money changing business. Clais was operating as a money changer no later than 1359, when his name appears among those contributing to a forced loan to the city. Both in that loan and the next to follow it in 1362 his contribution places him among the smaller operators among the twelve to fourteen active money exchanges.[50] Though she is not named in these records, there is no doubt that Lady Rapesaert was actively involved in the operation of the money exchange. This becomes quite clear when Clais is named, in February 1365, to a comital commission charged with supervising the Flemish coinage.[51] He bore the formal title of "Garde de la Monnaie" and his extensive duties included monitoring the quality of the coinage and changing the mint

[47] As in n. 46 above, where in de Marke's second ledger (2, f. 315r) Margaret, the younger Jan and the varlet Jan are named separately in what remained the account of Willem Ruweel.

[48] An account of 19 June to 18 July 1369 is a typical example. The account is in the name of "Medimyselle," and while there are no credits made to the account there are eighteen debits. Six of these involve losses incurred in the purchase of certain gold coins, either francs, double moutons, or écus; the rest are small sums charged against Hannekin Ruwel or for the delivery of tiles ("portage de tieules") and 6s. 6d. for the purchase of a scale, probably of the kind used by changers to weigh coin (Ruweel, f. 165r). See chapter 4 for more on the mechanics of the money-changing business.

[49] In her account on folio 165r there are various items and expenses listed. She begins with a balance of £5 gro. from which expenses are debited for house maintenance (7s. for carpentry work on 30 March). But most significant is list of losses written to her account for exchange of coins. Repeatedly she is charged for loss in exchanging for gold (f. 165r, 16s. 1d. "de perte de monoyes d'or le 19 juyn"). There were also charges for purchasing double moutons and French francs, and her husband also withdrew money from the strong box on 18 july "item 20 s.11 d. par Williaume par le tauble le 18 de juillet." Intriguing as well is the charge against her account of 4s. for transport of tiles by Jan van den Vliete.

[50] De Roover, *Money, Banking and Credit*, p. 207.

[51] Elsen, "La monnaie," 124. This was a period of reorganization of the county's coinage in the wake of a series of debasements and serious confusion in the conduct of the comital mint. Rapesaert joined a four-member commission along with two other men from Bruges, the provost of Onze-Lieve-Vrouw church and Bauduin de Vos, a prominent draper and alderman.

price, coin fineness, and seigniorage if need be. These duties must have taken him to Ghent for long periods, for this was the location of Flanders' primary mint at the time. In his absence, the exchange became known as "Le Cange de le Garde" and was run by his wife, as the accounts of de Marke clearly show.[52] Thus in 1366–1368 the account was held in her name only. In 1367–1369, Clais had a separate account in his own name, which may have dealt with business investments separate from the exchange.[53] She was assisted in running the exchange by a varlet, Jacob or Copin, the diminutive indicating that he had not yet reached majority. The business remained modest in comparison with other exchanges, judging from the statistics in de Marke's accounts.[54]

A third woman money changer shows another variation on the theme of a woman's place in the money market. This was "le Demisielle de Wite," to use the form found in the de Marke accounts, for as with the Lady Rapesaert, there is no record of her given name. The de Witte family was prominent in the world of Bruges business and politics. Her husband, Jan, was a hosteller who specialized in hosting Hanseatic merchants and was much involved in their business. He may himself have come from a Hanse city, for he was granted an exemption from the comital ban on admitting non-Flemings to the Bruges brokers' guild.[55] This may again have been an instance of a foreign merchant marrying a Bruges native, but unlike the case of the Ruweel exchange, we have no evidence of this here. As was customary, Jan represented German merchants in both business and legal affairs in Bruges, though not without complaints about some of his practices.[56] He may have been active in the diplomacy leading to the grant of a new commercial treaty to merchants of the Hanse in 1359–1360 for

[52] That is the name given in an account of Collard de Marke: De Marke 2, f. 318v and 3, f. 292r, although on 2, f. 332v the scribe crossed out "Demis[elle]" and replaced it with "Clais."

[53] Ibid., 2, ff. 318v, 322r. The distinction marked by separate accounts is confirmed in that Clais had a varlet, Gillekin, while his wife employed Copin, the "varlet dou Cange." The nature of the account entries, including payments to drapers and weavers (ibid., 4, f. 300r, to Willem van den Eke) and a payment to a rosary maker (ibid., 3, f. 292v, to Jakop Toby, paternostermaker) hint at an import/export business.

[54] For example in de Marke's first ledger, covering the period 1366–1367, Lady Rapesaert had only twenty accounts containing a mere 104 transactions encompassing the period 30 April 1366 to 16 April 1367 – scarcely more than two transactions per week.

[55] Schouteet, *Regesten*, vol. II, no. 785, p. 294. Jan may have come from Reval, given the close business relationship he maintained with a number of merchants from that Hanse city; see Dierck *et al.*, *Prosopographischer Katalog*, p. 477. For further discussion of the ban on foreigners becoming members of the Bruges brokers' guild, see chapter 5.

[56] In 1359 he apparently bought a quantity of wax on credit from two Hanse merchants, but when he took it to Sluis to sell it he incurred a loss his creditors attributed to carelessness. For the case see Gilliodts-van Severen, *Inventaire*, vol. II, pp. 37–39.

which he stood as a witness.[57] He served in the Bruges cavalry with two horses in 1357–1358, and either he, or his son by the same name, served as a *deelman* (leader) of the St. Jacob ward in 1368.[58] This was a career of steady business and political ascent.

The hostel run by the de Wittes was in operation from the 1350s as both a place of business brokerage and as a money-changing operation.[59] The exchange must have come second, since de Witte did not contribute to the forced loans raised from money changers in 1359 and 1362.[60] It apparently was operated from the hostel itself and not on St. Pieter's bridge, as Collard de Marke's accounts record a number of coin deliveries made to "her house."[61] As discussed in previous chapters, there was a natural business affinity between a hostel and exchange leading to several cases of their amalgamation. In the de Witte case, this was a joint business in which Jan and his wife's roles were interchangeable. This is proven by the fact that both Jan and "le Demisielle" are called the owners of the hostel "de Witte," though interestingly only "Lady" de Witte is mentioned in conjunction with the exchange.[62] Their bank accounts with Ruweel and de Marke were also used by them both, though again for different purposes. Jan's clearly bear the signs of business dealings, while those of his wife more frequently list details belonging to the operation of an exchange.[63] Judging from the evidence, it is probably safe to say that the running of the exchange depended almost solely on the Demoiselle de Witte.[64]

The operation of the de Witte exchange has much in common with those of its contemporaries. Their accounts with de Marke suggest that it

57 Ibid., p. 122 and *Hanserecesse*, vol. 1, 3 no. 270, p. 256.

58 A. Lowyck, "Schepenenlijsten van de stad Brugge," *Ons Heem* 17–18 (1962–1963), 213–216, 26–28, 43–48, esp. 26. For the function and importance of the *deelman* see van Houtte, *Geschiedenis*, p. 310.

59 There is a record from January 1356 of a loan to the knight Petrus de Hayschyvilla by the Elbinger merchant Hartwich Beteke, sealed in the hostel of Jan de Witte: *Preussisches Urkundenbuch*, vol. v, no. 407, p. 220.

60 De Roover, *Money, Banking and Credit*, p. 207.

61 De Marke 5, f. 376r, among debits, "par lui que je li portay en se maison, 150 mailles" (1 October 1369).

62 Ibid., 3, f. 129r: "Stevene Meye de lostel le Demisielle de Wite"; ibid., 3, f. 286v, "Biernart Lucreman a lostel Jehan de Wite, a le Demisielle de Wite"; ibid., 3, f. 102v, "pour Jak. de Rouc par le cange de le Demisielle de Wite."

63 The best example of this is in the accounts they held at the Ruweel exchange. Jan's accounts (Ruweel, ff. 7r, 12r, 19r–v, 21v, 22v, 54v) include payments made to him by the draper Jan van den Ecke, the Hanse merchants Celart Kertstop (Castorp) and Floreins Vrankonberch, and the Bruges brokers Jacob van den Eede, Gillis Honin, and Jan Huerel, as well as the merchants Lamsin de Jaghere, Jan Nodorp, and France Roukelos. His wife's accounts on the other hand record mostly the buying and selling of coins (ff. 83v, 90v) or bullion (98v, 128r).

64 This conclusion is strongly supported by the de Witte accounts held with Collard de Marke, which are without exception in the name of the Lady de Witte.

was one of the smaller operations among the active exchanges of the 1360s, with business volume similar to that of the Rapesaert exchange.[65] This suggests that it was run very much as a sideline to what must have been the more extensive business interests of Jan. It was also family run, as the Demoiselle was assisted by a son, Jakop or Copin, and a nephew, Breton.[66] As was the case with other money changers of the time, there is strong circumstantial evidence that the de Wittes were involved in the cloth trade. There are frequent payments made to Bruges drapers through the period; there is a payment to a transporter of cloth as well as a dyer.[67] Another group of payments were made to drapers from northern France, some originating from Hanse merchants.[68] This strongly suggests a brokerage business supplying Bruges cloth and the cloth of Maubeuge, St. Omer, Lille, and elsewhere to buyers from Germany.[69]

All three examples of female money changers show women at the very heart of the Bruges economy, albeit in secondary roles. Each proves that the affinity of women with money changing was solidly rooted in the customs of inheritance and the life of the household, extending to highly technical matters such as assaying coins and bullion, reconciling accounts, managing staff, and brokering trade, among other duties.[70] In all this each worked as either the managing partner or as an interchangeable partner with her husband. Each of course was also to a considerable extent tied to his fate. In the case of the Ruweel exchange, Willem's poor investment decisions, especially purchasing the tax farm on wine, brought bankruptcy and seizure

65 For example, in de Marke's first ledger (1366–1367), the de Wittes had twenty-three accounts recording 169 transactions beginning 2 May 1366 and ending 17 April 1367. As in the Rapesaert exchange, this averages out to only three transactions per week across the fifty-week period.

66 There was also a varlet, Gillekin (De Marke 2, f. 314v).

67 The names of Jan de Pinkere, Jakop Dommele, Jakop van de Kolve, and Pieter Dedeman recur with payment amounts indicating purchase of perhaps five to ten cloths at a time. For more on these men, see chapter 7. A payment of 5s. 10d. was made to Jossekin "portenier de dras" on 26 June 1367 (De Marke 2, f. 306v). On 1 June 1368 Lady de Witte posted a payment from Simon Ongeriet of £32 gro. (a considerable sum) to the account of her depositor, "le tainteniere" (the dyer). This may have been a case of finishing cloth to a buyer's specification, a frequent practice in Bruges and later in Antwerp.

68 These were Jehan le Muisit, a draper from Maubeuge (De Marke 2, f. 308v); Jehan Quarniel "le drapier," perhaps from Tournai; and there was frequent contact with Pieter van le Fine, one of Collard de Marke's partners in the cloth trade with northern France. For more on this trade via Bruges, see chapter 7.

69 In de Marke's fifth ledger (5, 372v) four transactions are recorded involving payments made via de Witte's exchange from the accounts of the German merchants Alf van de Velde, Hermant Ervesberc, Albrec van Luneberc, and Godevart Steur to the accounts of Jehan Quarniel, Will. van Drelaie, and Lambesin de St. Omer, all account holders with de Marke. The fact that all these sales occurred between 7 and 11 September 1369, involving similar amounts of money, strongly suggests cloth sales.

70 It is interesting to compare these women with many of the types discussed by Martha Howell in the context of Cologne; see Howell, *Women, Production, and Patriarchy*, pp. 124–158.

of financial assets. But it did not result in a loss of the exchange, for as part of Margaret's dowry it was safe from any claims against her husband's estate. By the 1380s, the exchange was held by Jacob Ruweel, probably in association with his younger brother. This brother, Stasin, took over the exchange after his brother's death in the late 1390s, after which it was sold, ending four generations of Ruuslede/Ruweel ownership.[71] The ladies Rapesaert and de Witte were more fortunate. Clais apparently served in his position as *Garde De La Monnaie* through one of the most active periods in the history of Flemish coinage, remaining through November 1368 and perhaps longer.[72] Nothing is known of them thereafter. And although we do not know the particular fates of Jan de Witte and his wife, the future held great success and social advancement for their descendants. They, however, would not be brokers or changers anymore.[73]

Women and the hostelling trade

In Bruges the second great institution of finance and business services was the hostel. Like the money exchange, it was really a combination of many businesses, from offering bed and board to receiving deposits, making book transfers, and investing in trading ventures. As we saw in the case of the de Witte hostel, it could even incorporate money changing into the services offered. These discreet and demanding businesses in turn were often shared between a husband and wife team. As in the case of money changing, a significant minority of Bruges inns were run by independent women. The story of Edele de Rudevorde is representative.[74]

She was a very considerable business figure in the 1350s–1370s, judging both from her accounts with the money changer de Marke, and also from the international political furore caused by her bankruptcy, which occurred sometime after 1372.[75] As was the case with the women money

71 Marechal, *Bijdrage*, p. 125. The exchange was sold to Jan de Voghel.

72 The history of the Ghent mint under Rapesaert is given in detail by Elsen, "La monnaie," 125–136. The last comital directive naming him dates from 26 November 1368, but it is followed by a lacuna in the records until May 1382, perhaps a decade after the end of Rapesaert's term of service as "Garde de la Monnaie." It is curious that Rapesaert never held an office in Bruges, not even that of treasurer, a position well suited to his skills if not his breeding. He may not long have survived his service for the count.

73 Among their illustrious descendants was Jan de Witte, bishop of Cuba 1528–1531; see van Houtte, *Geschiedenis*, pp. 364–365.

74 For a more extensive discussion of Bruges hostels, see chapter 5.

75 The bankruptcy uproar should be viewed in the context of intermittent tensions between Bruges authorities and Hanse merchants extending back to the previous embargo of 1359. In the de Rudevorde case, the Hanse seems to be unilaterally extending the surety the city guaranteed to

changers, the hostel run by Edele was a family business, whose activities were shared among the members. By the mid-1360s, when the surviving accounts begin, Edele was clearly the manager of the hostel, given that her name alone appears on most of the accounts and it was she who handled the periodic audits with de Marke.[76] Her husband, Jan, was still active in the business, for his name appeared from time to time on what was clearly the account of the hostel. In addition he had a separate account, apparently for other business purposes. He apparently died sometime in 1369.[77] A son, Jan the younger, also appears from time to time, initially as an employee of the hostel and later (1368) with his own account indicating some independent business activity. Perhaps to replace Jan the younger, Edele took on a varlet, Pieter, in 1368.[78]

The account the de Rudevordes kept with their money changer reveals a large and complex business operation. Not only did the hostel offer room and board for its customers, there were also important banking functions probably supervised by Edele.[79] These included accepting money, trade goods, and other articles on deposit, ordering and receiving coin from de Marke, and performing book transfers and other transactions for guests.[80] Above and beyond this, the de Rudevordes conducted trade on their own account, especially in furs brought by the Hanseatic merchants who often

deposits with Bruges money changers to those with hostellers. This was not explicitly granted by the treaty of 1363. On the other hand, as shown in chapters 4 and 5, Hanse merchants used their hostellers as the point of entry to the Bruges payment system organized by the money changers. Thus they may have been appealing to the spirit and not the letter of their privileges, which may explain the count's decision to grant reimbursement without establishing legal right or precedent.

[76] She possessed an extensive account with de Marke beginning at the latest in 1365 (in which year she ran a deficit of £52 gro.), and continuing through and beyond the extant account books to at least 1370. She began 1370 with a forwarded balance of £20 3s. 10d. posted to her account (de Marke 5, f. 271v). She was undoubtedly one of Collard de Marke's most important customers.

[77] Jan the elder died before April 1369, perhaps of the plague; see Schouteet, *Regesten*, vol. III, no. 546, 208. He was certainly dead by July 1369, when his wife's account with Willem Ruweel is headed "Vidua van Rudervorde" (Ruweel, f. 56r).

[78] Peter appears as "Pieter le varlet le Demisielle de Rudevorde" in that year (De Marke 3, f. 25v). Jan the younger seems to have been firmly under his mother's wing, judging from the de Marke accounts. She drew £46 from his account on 30 June 1367 (ibid., 2, f. 119r) and again in August 1368 (ibid., 3, f. 156v). His mother shifted the huge sum of £223 gro. to his account on 26 August 1368 to cover a payment made to the Bruges changer Jakop Reups (ibid., 3, f. 166v). After his father's death he seems to have gained a much greater measure of freedom, with his own varlet, and a partnership with Jehan Karlin (ibid., 4, ff. 42v, 43v). It is not clear whether it is he or his father who is the subject of a memo in de Marke's second journal mentioning a payment to be made in Paris on his behalf via a letter of exchange drawn on the Lucchese banker Biernarde Bandoute (De Marke, Journal 2, f. 3r); see also chapter 6.

[79] The de Rudevorde hostel lodged exclusively Hanse merchants. The comital letter of 1374 speaks of her "houdende herberghe en hostelrie" for merchants of Germany ("cooplieden van Aelmaengen"); for a list of her guests and other evidence, see Murray and Greve, *Hosteller Accounts*.

[80] Traces of these activities recur throughout her accounts; for examples see ibid.

lodged with them. In turn the accounts show Edele selling to two groups of customers: merchants from Hainault (Binche in particular) and French Flanders, and Forteguerra di Forteguerra, a well-known merchant/banker from Lucca.[81] The four-year totals of credits and debits in the de Rudevorde accounts show impressive amounts of money changing hands in a large number of transactions. Given the intermingling of accounts and payments, however, it is difficult to know which were performed for customers and which on Edele's own account. In reality, however, this very confusion of accounts gives a good picture of the day-to-day business managed by Mademoiselle (as the scribe called her) de Rudevorde and her very small staff.[82]

Unfortunately, there was no happy ending in this case, for in 1372 or shortly thereafter, the de Rudevorde hostel went bankrupt, leaving a large number of disgruntled Hanseatic merchants who had lost the money they had on deposit with Edele. This escalated into a bitter disagreement when the Bruges city government refused to make good the losses, as the merchants believed the city was obliged to do by treaty. Only in 1374, with an agreement worked out by the count of Flanders, was an end brought to the affair.[83] Unlike the Ruweel exchange, the de Rudevorde inn was not resurrected from bankruptcy.

Several other women operated hostels in Bruges in the 1360s, though we know considerably less about them. Trude and Pieter van Ake were clearly partners in the running of a hostel which resembled that of the de Wittes in many respects. They hosted mostly Spanish and Portuguese merchants, and although Pieter's name appears exclusively at the head of the accounts kept with Collard de Marke, their establishment is almost always referred to as "lostel Demisielle Trude."[84] Trude, like Margaret Ruweel, also possessed a money exchange, this one located in the west arcade of the Waterhalle, which she assigned to her son, also called Pieter, in 1365. She died sometime before 1384.[85]

81 For further details of this trade see chapter 5. It is clear from the accounts that de Rudevorde acted as broker for Hanseatic goods sold to northern French and Italian merchants.

82 This conforms to the pattern of hostellers' business activity as described in chapter 5.

83 The text of the agreement was published by Gilliodts-van Severen, *Cartulaire de l'ancienne estaple*, vol. 1, pp. 274–275; in it the count orders the city to make good the Hanseatics' claims but without confirming their right to reimbursement in such bankruptcy cases. This reservation probably explains why the charter was copied into one of the city's cartularies of privileges.

84 Pieter van Ake's accounts begin in June 1366 (De Marke 1, f. 14v) and continue through December 1369 (ibid., 5, f. 320r). He had a balance of 7s. posted to the 1370 account book, which does not survive.

85 Marechal, *Bijdrage*, pp. 133–134. There is no evidence that the family ever operated this exchange themselves. It may have descended from Jan van den Ackere, who paid surety for an exchange in 1347 (SAB, SR 1347–1348, f. 33v).

The other two women hostellers were apparently independent operators, perhaps as widows of members of the Bruges brokers' guild. "Demisielle" Tise or Thyze is known only by this abbreviated name and seems, like Edele de Rudevorde, to have hosted only Hanse merchants. She has only two brief account entries with de Marke, so there is not much accounting data about her.[86] We know from the account books of the Hamburg merchant Vicko von Geldersen that she acted as his banker and agent between 1375 and 1379.[87] "Le Demisielle de Rubeke" is known only by her last name. She did not hold accounts with either de Marke or Ruweel, so all that we know about her comes from the list of her guests in de Marke's accounts. From these it is clear that she specialized in hosting Spanish merchants.[88]

A remaining group of independent women is visible because they were account holders with one of the two money changers whose account books have survived. Contrary to what has been published and often repeated, banking was a very rare activity for the average person of Bruges – most of the account holders came from either resident or native merchants.[89] Of course a far larger group, including many more Brugeois, either exchanged coins or received payments at the money exchange offices; thus account holding was a mark of distinction. As was the case with both Rapesaert and de Rudevorde, many of these women were carrying on a family business in the absence of the husband. But there are other women whose accounts do not signal the shadowy presence of a male, or involvement in commerce.

Women and the cloth trades

An unusually clear demarcation of a professional group of women is given by the Ruweel and de Marke account books. As shown in chapter 7, many Bruges drapers relied on the money changers to pay for cloth purchased by them for delivery to their sales stall in the Old Cloth Hall. In most cases, the weavers simply took the money in cash, resulting in a single entry in the draper's account indicating this.[90] There were occasions, however, when either the weaver failed to go directly to the exchange for payment, or she chose to leave the money "in the exchange." In both cases an account was

86 De Marke 3, ff. 146v, 154r. The only notable detail of the four transactions is a £9 payment to the draper Jehan van Ianbeke.

87 Nirrnheim, *Handlungsbuch Vickos von Geldersen*, vol. 1, nos. 561, 667, 648; see also De Roover, *Money, Banking and Credit*, p. 248.

88 "Lopes Roys de Saint Andier" (De Marke, Journal 2, f. 63r); "Jehan de Sain Jehan, espaignart" (ibid., Journal 1, 4 January 1369).

89 See chapter 4.

90 This is indicated by the word "contet" after the stated amount in the account. For the mechanics of payment, see de Roover, *Money, Banking and Credit*, p. 269 and above chapter 5.

created and remained open until closed through withdrawal or assignment. The vast majority of the twenty-one women with accounts of this sort closed them quickly by withdrawing the money themselves.[91] A few assigned the money to someone else via a book transfer, but this was the exception.[92] Lisebette Wagenaire held an account that suggest she was building a business as a draper, which may have been the case with others of the twenty-one.[93] It is probable that a bank account was simply a temporary convenience to most of these women, not a long-term part of their business.

Another subgroup of account-holding women was identified by the title "Demisielle." They were of higher social standing than women in the textile business. This is the feminine equivalent of the male "Heer" accorded to current or former aldermen, priests, or others of important social or economic position.[94] This group, however, has no apparent connection to husbands as either partners or widows, indicating a degree of independence. Some of this may be due to ancient social position, as with "le Demisielle" Bonin, whose house was apparently in the Vlamingstraat, an important commercial street lined with hostels.[95] Her account was not very active, but did involve Bruges brokers and foreign merchants, indicating involvement in trade.[96] The account of Demisielle Marie van Ruseleghe, from

[91] These were usually amounts around £10 gro. One example that may stand for many is Kateline Andrirs, who was paid £12 5s. 5d. on 27 October 1368 by Darde Revite, possibly an Italian. The account was closed on 30 October when she picked up the entire amount – "par lui contet" as the account puts it (De Marke 3, f. 231v). Sometimes a large deposit might be withdrawn in two stages, as in the case of Marie Scoutegerne, who received a £21 gro. payment from the Bruges draper Pieter Meus on 25 October 1369. She withdrew £15 a day later and the balance on 29 October (ibid., 5, f. 248r).

[92] For example, Kateline Wautres was paid £5 gro. by the English merchant Rogier Branseby on 29 March 1369 and she transferred the entire amount two days later to Allart Darlin, an account holder with de Marke (ibid., 4, f. 142r).

[93] This is probable given that she makes payments to a number of weavers between January and September 1369 and that two of her customers were probably foreign merchants: ibid., 4, f. 5v; 5, f. 99r; 5, f. 211r. By the end of de Marke's last account, from 26 September to 4 October 1369 she had bought £42 gro. worth, of cloth from four Bruges weavers and apparently sold £38 14s. worth, leaving her with a £3 6s. overdraft.

[94] It was, in other words, a title of respect and therefore depended on its user's judgment. We know, for example, that de Marke's scribe always referred to Margaret Ruweel as "Demisielle," though her husband was never an alderman.

[95] It is possible she was related to Sir Jehan Bonin, who was an alderman as well as an important customer of de Marke's: de Roover, *Money, Banking and Credit*, p. 286 n. 39 and p. 190. Quite exceptionally she is called "Le Demisielle Bonin de la rue Flamenghe" in De Marke 3, f. 78v.

[96] There are five accounts from 5 August 1367 to 28 September 1369, with payments and receipts from Jakop van le Fine, the hosteller and cloth merchant (De Marke 2, f. 296v) and Leon Palvier from Saint Lombars, who banked with Jakop Reups (ibid); another account has the Italian merchant Lambesin Diagher receiving a payment from money received a month before by Mathis de Noien (De Marke 3, f. 78v); a last account finds a payment made to a foreign merchant, Amolant van Budric, who was a guest of hosteller Herman Minghelin (ibid., 5, f. 217v).

another important Bruges family, is tantalizingly brief but gives the strong impression that she at least dabbled in moneylending.[97] "Demisielle" Kateline Weghebrec may be descended from the Bruges money changer Boidin Wegghebed, though her account relates mostly to trade and is limited in size.[98] Of the twelve or so remaining account holders of this group only "Le Demisielle van Ausebourc" has an account suggesting trade, given that she is twice charged for "brokers' fees" in the spring of 1369 and also for the purchase of nineteen ducats.[99] Pursuit of a family business may have been the reason for this, given the occurrence of a Pieter van Ausebourc in the accounts, though he is in no way associated with "le Demieselle" as a co-holder of the account. All in all, despite the evidence of social position and economic independence, none of these women did important business with Collard de Marke.

One other subgroup is also set apart by social position conveyed in a title. These women were called "Dame" or "Vrouwe," connoting an even more exalted status than "Demisielle," though the precise gradients of prestige are difficult to measure. Curiously, "le Dame de Vos" is referred to as a furrier, so involvement in trade was not disqualifying.[100] Yet none of the seven accounts offers any evidence of business activity on the part of its holder. Only "le Dame Doudemakre" has an account of any duration, running from January to October 1369, though it contains only six transactions.[101] Quite a different account was that held by Margeritte, widow of a Master Watier le Veske, apparently a "marshal" of the court, who was from Arras

[97] This is based on a payment of £60 gro. made to her account by Bauduin le Mor, varlet of the countess of Bar, on 7 March 1367. This noblewoman and relative of the count of Flanders was a notorious spendthrift who was continously in debt. On her see de Roover, *Money, Banking and Credit*, p. 119.

[98] Boidin went bankrupt before 1315 and there is no record of any other family member as a money changer thereafter (see above, chapter 4). Kateline's account runs from 19 June 1366 until 4 December 1369 in the extant registers, and she had a balance of £4 15s. 4d forwarded to the lost account book of 1370 (De Marke 5, f. 294r). Her accounts record payments made to her by the English merchant John Goldbeter (ibid., f. 147v) and the Bruges wool broker Jakop Visch (ibid., f. 79r), and a number of payments by the unidentified merchant Willem se Provien (ibid., 3, f. 278v; 4, f. 70v; 5, f. 68v). She made payments to foreign merchants such as Ernoult and Jehan de Wile (ibid., 1, ff. 196v, 230r; 3, f. 278v,; 4, f. 70v; 5, ff. 68v, 79r, 147v, 291r), Ernout le Sauvaige (ibid., f. 148v), and the Italian Cornart Boin Adonne (ibid., 4, f. 70v).

[99] Ibid., 5, ff. 52v, 53r. The account records brokerage fees paid to the hostellers Jehan Eurle and Thideman van de Berghe, and an interesting payment to the money changer Pieter van Oudenaarde, "by command of the aldermen." The ducats were purchased by her varlet on 26 May 1369 at 30 gro. each. She was apparently an heir of the alderman and merchant Sir Simon van Artrike, from whom she received a house worth £80 gro., which de Marke purchased from her (ibid., 5, f. 52v "a le cause dune maison qui fu sire Simon dArtrike, £80 gro.")

[100] Ibid., 4, f. 150v. The single account contains only two entries, a payment made by Clais Breton on 9 April 1369 and her closing of the account by personally withdrawing the money on 14 April.

[101] Ibid., 4, f. 54r; 4, f. 66v; 5, f. 250v.

and lodged at the inn of Jehan van der Lekes. For the entire length of the preserved accounts, van der Lekes acted as her agent for payments made to chaplains who were apparently retained to say masses for the repose of her husband's soul.[102] All one can conclude is that Watier must have died while on a visit to Bruges, and his body was perhaps interred there.[103] All in all, the best way to characterize this collection of women is as casual or accidental users of the Bruges banking system.

A pair of independent women were clearly involved in trade, in contrast to the above group. Kateline van Denille probably operated a wine shop, given the large sum she paid through the exchange for the consumption tax on wine.[104] Lisebette van de Postierne seems to have been both independent and of lesser status than many of the other account holders, given the absence of the honorific "Dame" or "Demoiselle" from her accounts. From other sources we know that she traded in general merchandise – nails, spices, and paper – with England.[105] The smallness of this category in the de Marke accounts may indeed reflect the rarity of truly independent women in the Bruges business world of the time.[106]"

By far the most numerous of the women account holders were in two groups which either acted in partnership with a husband or continued the business of a deceased spouse. Here we find a much broader array of business of greater scope than was the case with the independent women. Examples run from the wife of Jakemes Wallers, a merchant involved with the cloth trade with Brittany who was probably often absent on business, resulting in a role for his wife to continue in his absence.[107] She was assisted by a

102 These were Jehan Wilay or Willars and Pieter Biese. Biese continued to receive payments through Jehan van der Lekes until August 1369 (ibid., 5, f. 1v).

103 Many "nations" of foreigners had arrangements with Bruges churches for the burial of their members. The Carmelite church, for example, allowed burial of Hanse, English, and Scottish merchants; see Rössner, *Hansische Memoria*, pp. 240–266.

104 De Marke 4, f. 56r, February 1369: "a Clais de le Bourse et Joris Wandelaire pour assise vin en Fev.[rier] £8 gro." Curiously, neither man held the farm of the wine assize at this time. Joris Wandelaire last held it for the period April–July 1366 and Clais van der Beurze farmed the beer assize in 1366–1367, but never the one for wine. The solution may be that Clais's relative, Matheuze van der Beurze, indeed held the farm from October 1368 to January 1369, and Clais and Joris acted as his agents. Both men were important hostellers at the time.

105 SAB, politieke oorkonden, 616, ff. 3r–v; 23r–24v; 11r and 26r–v and Nicholas, "English Trade," 59 n. 70.

106 This accords with findings from other medieval cities, notably Ghent and Cologne, whose urban economies offered opportunities for independent women in certain sectors while excluding them from many others. In every medieval city, however, women's work for the market in a male-headed household was the norm; on this see Howell, *Women, Production, and Patriarchy*, esp. pp. 124–158, and Nicholas, *Domestic Life*, pp. 84–106.

107 For a woman to act for an absent husband was customary among the Flemish: see Nicholas, "English Trade," 25. Wallers left one record of his travels in the de Marke accounts, recording his departure

varlet, Gilles; her account runs from 31 March 1367 to late 1369.[108] Bietris de Wintre's husband, Pieter, was a wool merchant, and her account shows a steady procession of Lucca merchants making payments to her accounts.[109] The wife of Pieter le Clerc apparently aided in a business of diversified trade. We know from other sources that he dealt in silks and fustians; yet his wife's account records payments from the Hanse merchant Tideman Rebber, the falconer Jehan van Gent, and a Portuguese merchant, Julianne de Lisebonne.[110] The wife of Clais van de Weghe held an account reflecting their interests in the cloth trade with Hainault. This was apparently part of a larger trade in cloth extending to England.[111] In common with the others, the wife of Lambesin dAlost maintained an account attesting to her husband's far-flung trading interests, ranging from Hainault to Italian merchants.[112]

Widows make up a second significant group of women account holders. In common with many other cities in northern Europe, widows in Bruges had the right to continue their husbands' businesses and guild membership.[113] Often but not invariably they are called "the widow" X or "the wife of the late Y" in the accounts, indicating in a sense the husband's continuing presence. None of these accounts approaches the importance of that held by Edele de Rudevorde; nonetheless the most active account holders, such as Kateline Provisin, had their significance as well. She had investments in property in Bruges, and though her account with de Marke extends from

for Brittany in April 1368 (de Marke 3, f. 1r). He was a close business partner of de Marke and often owed the changer money; see de Roover, *Money, Banking and Credit*, pp. 297–301.

108 De Marke 1, f. 161v; 2, f. 3v; 3, f. 3v; 5, f. 192v, c. 12 September.

109 These included Guglielmo Rapondi (ibid., 3, f. 281r); Giorgio Burlemay or Burlamacchi (5, f. 238v); and Forteguerra di Forteguerra (3, f. 106r).

110 Ibid., 1, f. 48r; 2, ff. 204v, 244v. For Rebber see chapter 5. Pieter de Clerc lost a cargo of silk kerchiefs and fustians in a pirate attack; see Nicholas, "English Trade," 58 n. 52.

111 Clais van den Weghe made a claim in 1371 for English cloth lost as a result of a raid off the coast of France: ibid., 56 n. 19. His wife's accounts record payments to known Hainault drapers like Jehan le Blanc from Valenciennes (De Marke 1, f. 121v); but also one to Lottart le Clerc, "frommegier" of Valenciennes (ibid., 1, f. 239r), indicating perhaps a more diverse trade than one simply in cloth. Other business with cheese merchants is recorded in de Marke's first journal from January 1369, with payments to Lottart Aubry and Biertrant le Frommegier (De Marke, Journal 1, 15 January 1369).

112 She received payments from the changer Jakop Reubs, the French merchants Jak. Lespesier and Gilles de Valenchiennes, and a Bruges broker from French Flanders, Raoul Coumines (ibid., 4, f. 56r, 60r, 112r, 134v). Her husband both drew on and deposited to the account (ibid., ff. 112r, 167r) with the most unusual feature being a very large payment of £160 gro to Sir Mikiel van Assenede (ibid., f. 158r) with a second subsidiary payment to the broker Joris Eurle. This was probably a sale of some sort made through Eurle.

113 For discussions of a widow's right to carry on the family business in Ghent, see Nicholas, *Domestic Life*, pp. 70–106; Daneels, *Weduwen en wezen*, pp. 344–385.

1366 to December 1369, it is difficult to get a feel for her business interests.[114] The widow of Jehan Mons clearly continued their business of cloth selling. Assisted by her son, also called Jehan, she used her account to buy and sell Bruges cloth.[115] A further ten widows left accounts too brief to track.

Conclusion: women in the market

From the assembled evidence there is every reason to believe that women were visible and involved in almost every sector of the Bruges economy. No doubt there were jobs and professions denied them, such as those of traveling merchant or fuller, where the contemporary sense of propriety or morality forbid it. This relative openness had much to do with Flemish legal traditions guaranteeing women equal rights to inheritance and equal claims to a joint estate with their husbands. In this they closely resembled the women of Cologne, Ghent, and Douai, to mention only the most intensively studied cities. On the other hand, as we saw in the case of the Ruweel bank, these guarantees could serve to shield a family's assets from creditors in a risky business like money changing. Yet while there is greater latitude of action in the Bruges context, there is no question of widespread female independence. The majority of business activity by women took place in a household headed by a man, or in the case of his death, with reference made to him, since a widow was allowed, indeed expected, to carry on the, family business. The nature of the Bruges economy, with its highly developed financial sector, resulted in several women being at the center of the business of high finance. The "wives" Rapesaert, Ruweel, de Rudevorde and a handful of others operated businesses that turned over thousands of pounds at a time when a good wage for a skilled artisan was a pound a month.

THE MARKET IN WOMEN

To medieval moralists the connection between economic development (wealth) and sexual license was clear: prostitution was simply one of the most direct results of the presence and power of money. There were other

114 Provisin was a well-known name in the Bruges elite. The only recurrent aspect of her account is payments made by the Italian merchant, Tumas Sarlande, and various other foreigners. Her accounts are De Marke 1, f. 84r; 3, ff. 37v, 131v, 212v; 4, ff. 97v, 107v, 118v, 163v; 4, ff. 110v, 162v, 190v, 252v, 259v, 305v. De Marke paid her a mortgage for a house, noted in his Journal, 1, f. 4v: "payet a Kateline Provisins pour rente dou tierme dou noel pour le maison Aulon, 9s. 1d. 2 mites."

115 De Marke 3, f. 3v is the clearest example of this. Here she buys cloth from Clare de Madre for £2 gro; her son also purchases cloth, amounting to another £14 18s. gro, and they apparently received payment for their wares in bullion ("pour plusieurs parties de billon") worth £22 18s. gro.

forms of vice that money fostered as well, including drinking and gambling. Is there evidence of such flourishing vice in Bruges at the height of its prosperity? And if so, what forms did it take and why?

By their very nature, businesses catering for vice are difficult to know much about except in those instances where the city takes up the business itself. Florence is just one particularly well-documented example of a city organizing an "official" brothel or city bureau to control private houses, sometimes describing it as choosing the lesser of two evils. In Florence there had been several periods of struggle, expulsion, and finally accommodation to the presence of prostitutes in the city. These had in succession outlawed bordellos anywhere within a half-kilometer of the city (1287); restricted the entrance of prostitutes to Mondays and Saturdays (1355); and required that distinguishing jewelry and clothing be worn by prostitutes. Similar struggles between resistance and tolerance occurred throughout Italy and southern France.[116] Common to all these southern European cities is a direct intervention of the city government in the market of sex for money. Different motives may have been at work: the desire to protect the virtue of honest women, preserve the peace of decent neighborhoods, combat sodomy, and profit from what by all accounts was a lucrative trade. Yet despite these differences, control of women and their behavior was the common denominator.

In the European north there were additional variations to the patterns of the south. The policy of German cities seems to have traveled a similar road to that taken by the French. From sometimes reluctant toleration in the thirteenth century, most German cities came to tolerate prostitution openly in the later Middle Ages. By the fifteenth century, most German cities had at least one city-owned brothel (*Frauenhaus*).[117] The purposes of this city intervention were in many cases similar to those in France and Italy, yet when a debate was held about whether or not to close Nuremberg's *Frauenhaus*, some feared that the result would be attacks on the wives and daughters of citizens by journeymen and foreign workers.[118] In English cities prostitution was officially banned but unofficially tolerated.[119] The notorious exception was the London suburb of Southwark, which was under the

[116] Leah L. Otis, *Prostitution in Medieval Society* (Chicago, 1985), explores the history of prostitution in Languedoc with excursions to northern France. Her findings are that prostitution was tolerated in the thirteenth century and institutionalized in the fourteenth and fifteenth centuries. This led to red-light districts in many French cities, and in Dijon and Toulouse, to municipally owned brothels.

[117] Merry E. Wiesner, *Working Women in Renaissance Germany* (New Brunswick, 1986), pp. 97–99.

[118] Ibid., p. 104.

[119] The usual result was assessment of fines against brothel keepers: see Ruth M. Karras, "The Regulation of Brothels in Later Medieval England," *Signs* 14/2 (1989), 399–443, esp. 407, and Karras, *Common Women: Prostitution and Sexuality in Medieval England* (New York, 1996), pp. 35–43.

jurisdiction of the bishop of Winchester. There officially sanctioned brothels appeared late in the fifteenth century after a long period of intermittent attempts to ban them. Yet here again, the intent of authorities was control of conduct. As Ruth Karras observes: "In effect the Southwark brothel regulations made the prostitute's sexuality a commodity and controlled its sale."[120]

For reasons we shall explore in a moment, Bruges and its public authorities never tried to control the prostitution trade in the manner common to the south, nor in ways comparable to other northern European cities. There were no red-light districts, no particular clothing or tell-tale items of jewelry were imposed, and above all no hint of an attempt to organize public brothels is found in any fourteenth- or fifteenth-century source. And yet there are indications, scattered in the fourteenth, clear and direct in the fifteenth century, that the vice trades flourished in Bruges as nowhere else in the Low Countries for certain, and perhaps nowhere else in northern Europe. This was true both quantitatively, given the numbers of gaming houses, brothels, bathhouses, and qualitatively, given the ribald remark of the English merchant John Pympe, making much of the reputation of the "frowys of Brvggys."[121] Why would this be so?

Two parts of the answer can be traced directly back to elements contributing to the rise of Bruges as a great commercial city. One of these, the presence of large numbers of foreign merchants resident for long periods, provided a natural customer base. We know that few of these merchants brought a wife with them, either because of the brevity of their visit or because they were apprentices or junior clerks and were unmarried.[122] Certainly there were hundreds of such men during most of the fourteenth century, and at certain times of the year, notably during the Bruges fair in the spring, their number may have swelled to a thousand or more. The

[120] Karras, "Regulation of Brothels," 426. The other English town with a history of a municipal brothel is Sandwich ibid., 411, and Karras, *Common Women*, pp. 35–36, 38.

[121] This was in a letter of 1477 written to John Paston II: "Mary, we have herd sey that the frowys of Brvggys wyth theyre hye cappys have gyven sum of yow grete clappys, and that the fete of her armys doyng is such that they smyte al at the mowthe and at the grete ende of the thyeh; but in feith we care not for yow, for we know well that ye be gode ynowh at defence. But we here sey that they be of such corage that they gyve yow moo strokys than ye do to them, and that they strike sorer than ye also." Norman Davis (ed.), *The Paston Letters and Papers of the Fifteenth Century*, 2 vols. (Oxford, 1971), vol. II, p. 414. Part of the context of this remark may have been a strong preference for Flemish women by men who had visited there. How else can one explain the popularity of Flemish and Dutch women in brothels from London to Florence? On this see Karras, *Common Women*, pp. 56–57; and Trexler, "La prostitution florentine," 985–986; Jacques Rossiaud, *Medieval Prostitution* (New York, 1988) pp. 112–113.

[122] David Herlihy noted in the case of Paris that the presence of Lombard merchants with great financial resources but no women provided "perfect customers for prostitution": *Opera Muliebria*, p. 140.

alternation of good and bad economic times may also have influenced the vice trade, as we shall see.

The second factor had to do with female migration to the city. There are no demographic data documenting this, but the incidence of single-woman heads of households, the purchase of citizenship rights by single women, the numbers of women active in business, all suggest a certain amount of immigration by single women to the city. It is likely that a considerable number of poor country women, who escape documentation, came to Bruges as well. These found employment as servants, in the crafts having to do with the cloth trade, and in other menial, low-paid jobs, which formed the recruiting grounds for prostitutes. Walter Simons has found that beguinages, admittedly of a later date, were largely filled with women of modest means who emigrated from the country to the city in search of independent employment. Ironically, the beguinage offered an institution in which a single woman could make a living, but so did the brothel. There are several examples in the records of a beguine being fined for prostitution.[123] There is also an early albeit interrupted history of a monastic establishment whose purpose was to reform prostitutes: the Filles-de-Dieu. A house was founded in Bruges in 1290, but by 1305 it had been made into a pilgrims' hostel by order of the city aldermen.[124]

We have no way of knowing for sure that there was an official policy with regard to prostitution, but there is every appearance of one in the two-century-long trail of evidence relating to the vice trades. The evidence is chiefly found in lists of fines recorded in city and comital accounts and as such poses serious problems of interpretation. The first challenge is to learn precisely what crime was being punished by the levying of the fine. The account headings are often hazy and half formulated, but there seem to have been three forms of commercial sex operations covered by the "Cuer de Mal Plait" – literally the "Law on Committed Evil," which was the short title used by some scribes who drew up the accounts.[125] The "evil"

[123] This of course was one of the great fears of critics of the beguine movement; it resulted in increasing pressure for beguines to live in convent-like surroundings known as "curtis" beguinages. On this see Ziegler, "The curtis beguinages" and; Simons, *Cities of Ladies*, pp. 118–137; for beguine prostitutes, Gilliodts-van Severen, *Inventaire*, vol. IV, pp. 154–155, from the city account of 1392–1393, "Item thuus daer Beele de beghine in woent." Additional examples: SAB, SR 1369–1370, f. 20r, "van Betten der beghinen huus 20s.," repeated ibid., 1370–1371, f. 15r.

[124] Maréchal, *Brugse Hospitaalwezen*, pp. 286–290; the movement began in the thirteenth century. Interestingly, a new house of the Filles-de-Dieu was founded in the fifteenth century ibid., p. 186 n. 19; Gilliodts-van Severen, *Inventaire*, vol. VI, p. 351.

[125] Most likely the scribes were referring to an edict, or *Hallegebod* so called because it was literally proclaimed from a balcony at the front of the Belfort. Collections of these survive only from 1490,however, though the practice considerably antedates this. These edicts were thereafter compiled

that dare not speak its name was undoubtedly prostitution, but what is striking is that the fines were levied on the places where prostitution took place and not necessarily on its practitioners. This is made clear in some accounts where separate fines are assessed against those who kept "an evil inn," which does not distinguish between the practice of renting out a house to someone who will use it for prostitution and that of operating it oneself for both gambling and prostitution.[126] In the city accounts of 1367, 1368 and 1370, this category is explicitly subdivided into those who operate "evil inns" and those who have "rented out a house for use as a bordello."[127] The vast majority of fines are assessed on "houses, rooms, and bathhouses" where "committed evil is held."[128] This again emphasizes the place of prostitution, not the person(s) committing it. There can be little doubt that prostitution was intended by such circumlocutions as "evil inn," "bordello," and "place where ribaldry and bordello of bad company" are held.[129] There is also little doubt that prostitution was openly tolerated.

and used in the thrice-yearly hearings of those charged with violations. What the scribe of the accounts recorded was the fines assessed against those violators; none of the legal records survives from the period. On the legal process, see R. C. van Caenegem, *Geschiedenis van het strafprocesrecht in Vlaanderen van de XIe tot de XIVe eeuw* (Brussels, 1956), pp. 76–113; on the Bruges *Hallegeboden*, Vandewalle, *Beknopte Inventaris*, p. 70; Dupont, *Maagdenverleidsters*, p. 51; van Houtte, *Geschiedenis*, p. 308. Jacques Toussaert, in his often flamboyantly inaccurate book on morality and religious sentiment in Flanders, claims to have found evidence that a 1491 edict against renting houses for purposes of prostitution was first issued in 1352. Consulting his citation provides no independent confirmation of the fact: Toussaert, *Le sentiment religieux en Flandre à la fin du Moyen-Age*, p. 374.

126 Separate fines for holding "quaede herberg" are relatively rare, occurring in significant numbers only in the city accounts of the 1370s. What differentiates these from those found in the common list is unclear, but most likely has something to do with activities on offer beyond mere prostitution. There are cases in which the same person was fined both for "quaede herberg" and in the ordinary list of those fined for prostitution. Beele Scerrer, for example, was fined both for renting a house and for operating a house of prostitution in 1368–1369 (SAB, SR 1368–1369, f. 19r). Renting property for use as a brothel may have indeed been a new category added to the traditional ban, since it occurs only from the 1360s. Here it involves those who did not operate a house but rented it to someone who did. For the fifteenth century, see Dupont, *Maagdenverleidsters*, pp. 50–55.

127 "Van den ghuenen die huze te bordeele verhuert hebben" is the Flemish. Subdividing offenders into the three groups is thus unusual in the accounts. The comital bailiff's accounts never itemize, although the same terminology is used. Only in the bailiff account of 1389 is someone fined more than three times the normal amount "pour che quil a lieuwe une maison lou on tient bordeel" (ARA, Rekenkamer 13676, pt. 4, 10 May to 20 September 1389, f. 12v). This seems to have been an exceptional case and overall the number of those fined for the offense was small.

128 In both French and Flemish the compound noun – "mal plait," "quaet pleit" – is used as the technical term. In most of the city accounts after mid-century the rubric simply becomes "received from houses, bathhouses and rooms that were indicted." The Flemish form had an effect on Middle English as well, for in the prologue to Chaucer's Cook's Tale the Cook repeats a Flemish proverb: "sooth pley, quaad pley." noted by Martha Carlin, *Medieval Southwark* (Rio Grande, Ohio, 1996), p. 150.

129 R. C. van Caenegem noted Flemish inventiveness with regard to names for prostitutes and houses of prostitution; see his *Geschiedenis van het strafrecht in Vlaanderen van de XIde tot de XIVde eeuw*

Officially, of course, vice crimes like gambling houses and prostitution were illegal. Bruges even levied fines on men and women living in adultery.[130] But the fact that the fines were low and repeat offenders the rule, and that the evidence shows considerable continuity both in numbers of prostitutes and the areas in the city they operated, argues strongly for an implicit policy of tolerance. For example, fines charged for operating a house of prostitution after the 1350s amounted to £3 parisis per judicial term, or at most £9 per year. This amounted to the earnings of a master mason or carpenter for about eighteen days, or thirty-six days of wages for a journeyman.[131] In contrast the fine for usury was £50 par.[132] It is unclear just how the fines were assessed. Both the city aldermen and the comital bailiff shared responsibility for levying them, dividing the spoils between them.[133] Most likely the names and locations of perpetrators were forwarded by the neighborhood *deelmannen*, who had the most intimate knowledge of the use to which houses, rooms, and bathhouses were being put. The aldermen and bailiff also had a skeleton crew of agents of their own, but these hardly sufficed to do much investigation.[134] Whether those named in the accounts actually appeared before the aldermen or bailiff is unknown. Given the routine, even monotonous, listing of the same amount under the same rubric every seventeen weeks, it seems unlikely that these fines resulted from court appearances.[135]

(Brussels, 1954), pp. 105–106. See also Dupont, *Maagdenverleidsters*, p. 55. Flemish was not alone in its ingeniousness in creating synonyms for the prostitute: see Ruth Karras, "Prostitution in Medieval Europe," in Vern L. Bullough and James Brundage (eds.), *Handbook of Medieval Sexuality* (New York, 1996). I disagree with Dupont slightly in his insistence that those fined for operating an "evil inn" were involved only in prostitution. No doubt that was one of their chief activities, but the term also allows the possibility of other forbidden pastimes like gambling.

130 The rubric was usually "van wiven die met andren mannen zaten" or "van mannen die met andren wiven zaten" (SAB, SR 1333–1334, f. 23r and elsewhere). There is seldom more than an entry or two in any given year, and many of the men seem to have been sailors or other transients. The fine was greater than that for prostitution, usually £10 par.: Dupont, *Maagdenverleidsters*, p. 56.

131 Dupont, ibid., p. 54, has these equivalences.

132 ARA, Rekenkamer, RR 1010 (1367–68), "Boeten van den guenen die leenen boven 2d. tpond de boete £50" Of course, this was both an offense against a moral injunction and a violation of a public monopoly. For more on usury and pawnbroking see chapter 4.

133 The fines seem to have little relation to the possible size or frequency of operation of the place of prostitution. Until 1350, however, there is a bit of variation in the fines, which may indicate some room for negotiation, but the range is narrow. From the 1350s the fine was fixed at 60s. parisis with 20s. for the city and 40s. for the count.

134 These were the city *schaerwetters* or the bailiff's *kolfdragers*, who functioned as a uniformed police force, but whose numbers were ridiculously small to police adequately a city of more than 40,000. See van Houtte, *Geschiedenis*, p. 323.

135 Fines covered there were three seventeen-week periods and were usually entered separately in the accounts. The missing week was probably Holy Week, in which all such places were ordered to be closed.

If the "crime" was providing a place for prostitution, it does not follow from lists of fines that all those named were actually prostitutes. Some of those named in the categories of running an evil inn or renting out property to those who did were less likely to be actual practitioners.[136] The several different buildings used for prostitutes might also determine whether the person named was a prostitute. "Houses" contained more than a single room and thus were probably capable of housing more than one practitioner.[137] Thus the name given in the list must be the renter or owner of the house, who may or may not be a prostitute. Those named as holders of "rooms," which were separate structures of one room housing a single person or household, were much more likely to be prostitutes. Bathhouses may be given under their owner/operator's name, particularly early in the century, but increasingly they are known by an institutional name.[138] Here again, we cannot know the identity or number of prostitutes in residence there. Thus the number of fines alone gives only a very rough and imprecise idea the incidence of prostitution in the city. First, recorded numbers are almost certainly underestimates given the realities of law enforcement of the time.[139] Secondly, the numbers do not capture the amateur, opportunistic nature of much prostitution in the pre-industrial city.[140] And last, but certainly not least judging from the fifteenth century, the urban enclaves controlled by the provost and canons of St. Donatian's are not included in these figures.[141] The statistics in table 8 are therefore in no way a census of

[136] Although some were, as in cases of fines assessed against houses where a particular woman lived. Given that those mentioned were never men, it is almost a certainty that the woman named was indeed a prostitute. However, these cases never amount to more than roughly 10 percent of fines.

[137] Dupont, *Maagdenverleidsters*, pp. 54–55, mentions a global average of three rooms elsewhere in Europe.

[138] Thus early in the century a bathhouse was described by either ownership or location or both as in "Belen Taisepeers stove int Ghistelhof" (from a 1305 city account in Wyffels and Vandewalle, *Rekeningen*, vol. II, pt. I, p. 662). In the accounts of 1353–1354, only three of the thirteen bathhouses fined were called by a name other than the name of their owner or location (SAB, SR 1353–1354, ff. 27v–29v). By 1375, of the seven bathhouses fined, only one was called after its location; the others– "Ter Bailge," "Ter Roder Lewe," "Te Sint Joris," "Ter Valke," "In tHol," "Ten Clenen Zwane"– all evoked a sign or symbol (ibid., 1375–1376, ff. 14v–15v).

[139] David Nicholas has pointed out that per capita there were many fewer police in a medieval city than in a modern one. See his "Crime and Punishment in Fourteenth-Century Ghent," 289–334, 1141–1176 and more generally his *The Later Medieval City*, pp. 156–160.

[140] Prostitution by streetwalkers must have been common in Bruges as elsewhere, and may have largely escaped the eye of authority. Bronislaw Geremek, *The Margins of Society in Late Medieval Paris* (Cambridge, 1987), p. 220, discusses the "semi-professional" prostitute in Paris. Sharon Farmer states also that in Paris the wages for the menial work many women performed were so low that occasional prostitution became necessary to survival: Farmer, "Down and Out," 355.

[141] We know nothing of these, at least in the fourteenth century. In the fifteenth century, and no doubt earlier, they harbored more than their share of brothels; see Dupont, *Maagdenverleidsters*, pp. 65–70. In general these urban enclaves were notorious for usury and prostitution, and as such are comparable to the bishop of Winchester's jurisdiction, Southwark outside London. On Southwark, see Karras, "The Regulation of Brothels," 411–416, and Carlin, *Medieval Southwark*, pp. 209–229.

Table 8. *Prostitution statistics*

Year	Total fines	Institutions	Brothels	"Evil inns"	Persons	Houses	Bathhouses	Rooms	# male	# female	Fines/range (in £ parisis)
ARA 1305*	52	49				13	11	3	20	25	3.0–60
SAB 1305	13	13				6	4	3	5	4	3.4–10
SAB 1306*	24	24				12	11	1	15	6	2.6–20
ARA 1306	78	61				27	23	11	23	24	10–30
ARA 1307	67	51				24	19	8	28	16	10–60
SAB 1308	39	28		2		16	7	3	6	16	2.6–15
ARA 1308*	19	19				9	3	1	6	10	10.–30
SAB 1309–1310	43	29				13	7	9	7	14	3.–15
SAB 1311–1312	42	38		4		24	4	4	14	16	2.5–11
SAB 1312–1313	42	28				14	5	1	13	13	4–18
SAB 1315–1316*	6	6				2	3	1	2	2	4–5
SAB 1316–1317*	1	1							1		6.8
ARA 1331*	26	26				2	3	2	10	15	20–40
SAB 1332	48	45				33	8	4	18	15	10–30
SAB 1333–1334	46	43				11	6	7	18	19	12–30
SAB 1334–1335*	21	17				6	4	7	12	5	6–38
SAB 1335–1336	65	54				40	6	7	27	16	10–36
SAB 1336–1337	75	73				40	6	27	39	21	8–18
SAB 1337–1338*	41	39				23	5	10	16	12	5–17
SAB 1338–1339	36	29				19	3	6	13	8	8–17
SAB 1339–1340	15	16				7	3	4	7	6	5–15

(*cont.*)

Table 8. (*cont.*)

Year	Total fines	Institutions	Brothels	"Evil inns"	Persons	Houses	Bathhouses	Rooms	# male	# female	Fines/range (in £ parisis)
SAB 1340–1341	13	13				5	3	4	5	6	12–24
SAB 1341–1342	38	35		5		19	2	7	17	15	10–20
SAB 1342–1343	42	39		1		25	3	9	16	20	9–20
SAB 1344–1345	44	42				21	2	2	11	19	8–20
SAB 1345–1346*	18	23		2		15		6	5	11	12–14
SAB 1346–1347*	42	40		2		34	3	1	18	18	14
SAB 1347–1348*	18	19				16		3	10	5	13–14
SAB 1350–1351	36	22				18	2	1	10	9	10–14
SAB 1351–1352	26	26				24	2		12	13	12–14
SAB 1352–1353	47	40				33	3	4	16	19	14–20
SAB 1353–1354	116	93		4		73	13	3	36	39	20
SAB 1354–1355	89	68		1		54	11	3	21	32	18–20
SAB 1355–1356	104	77				68	7	1	14	51	12–20
SAB 1358–1359	95	77		3		69	5		16	51	16–20
SAB 1359–1360	57	55			7	52	4		10	38	20
SAB 1360–1361	52	31			13	28	3		15	23	20
SAB 1361–1362	67	64		3		54	5	2	18	36	18–20
SAB 1362–1363	63	50	1	1		41	7		21	21	16–20
SAB 1363–1364	113	92		6		79	7		25	57	20
SAB 1366–1367	56	51	4	1		45	1		14	32	20
SAB 1367–1368	79	75	5	1		67	1	1	12	53	20
ARA 1367–1368*	32	37				34	3		9	19	40
SAB 1368–1369	99	84	5	5		72	2		24	50	20

SAB 1369–1370	148	140	21+			114	4	2	20	104	20
SAB 1370–1371	125	114	9	11		87	4	2	4	94	20
SAB 1371–1372	92	89		14		74	1		9	71	20
SAB 1372–1373	131	126		12		108	6		14	103	20
ARA 1374–1375*	43	43			1	41	1		2	38	40
ARA 1375–1376	134	114				111	3		4	102	40
SAB 1375–1376	159	127		21		96	7	3	8	97	20
ARA 1376–1377*	66	54				46	8		1	44	40
ARA 1377–1378	100	71				65	6		4	50	40
ARA 1378–1379	102	75				71	4		1	69	40
ARA 1379*	79	69				63	6		0	50	40
SAB 1379–1380	62	62				55	7		4	40	20
ARA 1380*	24	24				22	2		1	21	40
SAB 1382–1383	97										
ARA 1384*	2	2	1				1			2	40
ARA 1385–1386	22	22				19	3		0	19	40
ARA 1386*	15	15				11	4		0	11	40
ARA 1387–1388	59	51				46	5		2	42	40
ARA 1388*	24	24				21	3		0	21	40
ARA 1389*	44	38	1			35	2		2	34	40

Sources: Baillff and city accounts, 1305–1381

prostitutes in Bruges, nor are they any more than a minimum when it comes to assessing the number of places where prostitution occurred. The period covered by the table, 1305 to 1389 with a single fifteen-year gap, provides an unusually complete index of prostitution in a medieval city. It allows for a view of three distinct periods of development; the first from 1305 to 1331 the second from 1332 to 1350, and the third from 1351 to 1382. The period following the Ghent war was marked by a collapse both of regular policing and perhaps of prostitution itself. The numbers are suggestive: amid many ups and downs, the number of brothels in the first period in any given year was probably twenty-five or so (the admittedly incomplete records average out to 28.7). In the middle period however this average (again with fluctuations) increases to thirty-four. In the third period a boom begins in Bruges prostitution that sees the remarkable one-year rise in numbers of brothels from forty to ninety-three in 1352–54, where it remains more or less until reaching an absolute peak at 140 in 1369. This is more than five times the incidence of earlier in the century![142] The decline in numbers came with surprising suddenness with the outbreak of the Ghent war and the departure of most foreign merchants. The numbers of brothels in Bruges would never again approach the numbers reached in the 1360s and 1370s, even after the economy began to improve after 1390.[143]

What do the numbers mean? The post-1350 expansion is stunning and perhaps lends credence to medieval moralists' observations about the decline in public morality in the wake of the first plague outbreak.[144] Even giving the plague its due, these numbers suggest an increase in demand that could only be plausible if ever larger numbers of men visited the city. No doubt some of these came from the countryside, but many must have come as businessmen.[145] Thus their presence is an indirect indication of an expanding economy and Bruges's increasing importance in the geography

142 One must be careful here to count the total number of institutions and not the total fines. A number of brothels; were fined two or three times in the course of a year, which in the past has led historians to exaggerate their number, as did Toussaert (*Sentiment religieux*, p. 374), who mentions the number of fines (forty-two) when there were only twenty-eight brothels; Gilliodts-van Severen (*Inventaire*, vol. IV, p. 154 n. 5: "au nombre de 131 pour cette année [1352–53] . . .") not only gives the wrong year (he gives the old style date) but also fails to eliminate the duplicates. The correct number of brothels in 1353–1354 is ninety-three.

143 Dupont found a decline to sixteen by 1390, and reaching only ten to fifteen per year by the 1460s and 1470s. There were exceptional years, however, as 1394 when there were 100 fines, as there were more or less in 1397–1399; see Dupont, *Maagdenverleidsters*, appendix 2, pp. 194–195.

144 The abbot of St. Martin's abbey in nearby Tournai, Gilles li Muisit, made much of the moral decline of his time. He was also a witness to the first onslaught of the Black Death; see Toussaert, *Sentiment religieux*, pp. 372–373.

145 An example of a visitor from the vicinity of Bruges is provided by the rich countryman Simon de Rikelike, who in May 1327 visited prostitutes in Bruges on four different occasions, noting the cost

of trade. It cannot be accidental that the highpoint in the history of Bruges prostitution occurs at the same instant as merchants from the Hanse and elsewhere are present in what must have been record numbers.[146] It is by no means far-fetched to conclude that the peak of the fourteenth-century economic expansion of Bruges is at least indirectly marked by the evolution of prostitution statistics. Thus prostitution was in a sense a rough and ready indicator of the state of Bruges's urban economy.

Why was prostitution tolerated in late-medieval Bruges? Without records of the meetings of the aldermanic councils, we cannot say for sure. Certainly prostitution disrupted public order from time to time, and easily blended into or incited more serious and violent crimes. Cases of knife attacks, concealed weapons, and shouting matches occurred with unsettling regularity in those places where "evil was committed." Without detailed judicial records this disorder remains out of focus, yet a few stories survive. In 1377 Lisebette sBlonden, a "stove vrauwe" who worked at the well-known bathhouse "bachten Besemkine" near the central commercial district, was found to have a concealed knife there.[147] Perhaps the same Lysbette was fined two years later as a result of a fight with another woman. Her identity, "Lysbette, bathhouse maid, bad Johnny's girlfriend," is quite evocative.[148] Another woman bathhouse worker had a knife drawn on her by a customer in a case recorded in 1387.[149] Fights could also break out between rival prostitutes, as in 1386, when "English Bette" threw a stone goblet in the face of Bette delle Court.[150] Violence could also be visited upon prostitutes by their customers. An echo of this occurs in a bailiff's account of 1379 as a result of a rumor that reached him of an English merchant, Robert Ekelsteen, who had reportedly raped a prostitute six

of each visit in his diary. See Joseph de Smet, *Het Memoriaal van Simon de Rikelike, vrijlaat te St. Pieters-op-den-Dijk* (Brussels, 1933), pp. 54–57 and Dupont, *Maagdenverleidsters*, p. 126.

146 The 1359 commercial treaty with the German Hanse brought many more merchants to Bruges, as the lists in the city accounts show. The census statistics drawn from the de Marke accounts discussed in chapter 3 also show clearly the dimensions the foreign merchant community had achieved by the 1360s. These were all potential clients for the prostitutes.

147 ARA, Rekenkamer, RR 1018, membrane 11 (1377): "Caelengen van diversen aventuren . . . van eenen messe dat in hare stove verboren zoude zijn."

148 Ibid., 1028, membrane 12 (1379). "Ontfaen van twiste van £3 Lysbette de Mutssebredigghe contra Lisebette stove joncwyf quade Hannin vriendinne 40s."

149 ARA, Rekenkamer 13675 (1387): "Calaenges de bate de £60 Piere le Pottere qui saqua son couteel sur une fame servant en lesthuve en le Carmerstrate." He was allowed to settle for £18 par. because he was a poor man.

150 Ibid., pt. 3, f. 11v (1386): "Une fame de bordel quon apielle Inghelsche Bette pour che quelle jetta Bette delle Court dun godet de piere en sen visage quelle navra de qu elle a composse £2 de gros. Vallent £24." Neither woman appears on the list of those fined for prostitution in that year, but Bette was an extremely common name and often no last name or nickname appears on the lists.

years before. The incident was apparently concealed and the injured parties compensated.[151]

Fears about the effects of such disorder on public morality and the reputation of Bruges residents surface only in the fifteenth century, when the recommendation was made in 1477 to create a public red-light district and compel all prostitutes to live there. It came at a time of political crisis after the death of Duke Charles the Bold, when anxieties of all sorts surfaced. Yet the reason given for the proposal strikes an authentic chord that must have been far older than its first appearance in writing: "that women of notorious life be given a spot where they may live altogether so that the good women and girls of the city not be accosted."[152] The protection of honest womanhood is a common cause of government intervention to control prostitution. Protection of the commercial district was the occasion of a 1491 edict against prostitutes taking to the streets, or congregating in the Bourse or Crane squares, or in the arches of the Waterhalle.[153] In both these cases, popular concern and outrage came to nothing. Apparently the decision by those in City Hall was that the moral and criminal costs of prostitution were worth the price, so they allowed it to operate quite like any other business in the city apart from the fine/license fee extracted in each judicial session. It was just another business in service to business, in the most business-oriented city of northern Europe.

Of course prostitution was and could be no ordinary business even if left to itself, and the list of fines as well as the recorded criminal cases allow us some idea of how it operated. Whatever the official policy, by the early fourteenth century prostitution in Bruges flourished in a handful

[151] ARA, Rekenkamer, RR 1028, membrane 12 (1379). The woman was described as a "een wijf van lichtervuere," literally a woman of ill-repute. Ekelsteen's hosteller, Pieter de Scuetelare, was apparently the leading figure in keeping the affair quiet, thus showing the power money and influence could wield in the city. Nicholas refers to the case briefly in "English trade," 57 n. 38.

[152] "Item dat men den vraukins van levene beteekene [notorious life] eene plecke daer zii wonen zullen te ghadre, te dien hende dat de goede vrauwen daerbii noch de goede maechdekins vander stede nie gheblameirt en worden": SAB, politeke oorkonden, 1e reeks, 1144, f. 2r, mentioned by Gilliodts-van Severen, *Inventaire*, vol. VI, p. 131.

[153] Ibid., vol. VI, p. 354, 22 September 1491: "Dat gheene vrauwen of meysskins van wilden ende onreynen levene, by avonde achter strate te ghane, ghelike ter cranen, ter buersen, onder de halle, ter buerch oft elders binnen der stede, up den ghuenen die bevonden zullen worde den steen of de thunne te draghene, ende voort ghebannen te zyne ter discrecien van scepenen." The Waterhalle appears once on a fourteenth-century list of fines as a place of prostitution, and in the fifteenth century, according to the Spaniard Pero Tafur, it still served as a trysting place for prostitutes and their customers. See Dupont, *Maagdenverleidsters*, p. 140. SAB, SR 1355–1356, f. 29v: "Ontfangen van husen stoven ende cameren daer men quaet pleit in ghehouden heift . . van den boghe onder de niewe halle 20s." Ghent also tried to ban prostitution in and around the city's chief market places. As early as 1350 the aldermen issued a public proclamation; the text is in Napoleon de Pauw (ed.), *De voorgeboden der stad Gent in de XIVe eeuw* (Ghent, 1885), p. 44, and Stabel, "Women at the Market," 270.

of neighborhoods in several kinds of buildings. The neighborhood of the former village of St. Gillis was one place known for its prostitutes. It lay in the northwest of the city and only became legally a part of the city in 1283. By that time it had acquired its own identity and an allure of lawlessness which attracted Hanseatic businessmen and sailors from adjoining neighborhoods. In the period from 1365 to 1409 alone, a majority of the fines exacted for prostitution came from St. Gillis and its immediate surroundings making up the St. Nicholas administrative district.[154] Other neighborhoods with smaller concentrations of brothels were found near the convents of the Franciscans and Dominicans.[155] It must be stressed, however, that houses of prostitution in Bruges were in no way isolated; on the contrary they seem to have been well integrated into their largely working-class neighborhoods.

Three kinds of structures are listed in the records as sheltering brothels: "houses," multi-room dwellings where more than one woman could ply her trade; "rooms," structures common in Bruges and other Flemish cities, consisting of a single room with a hearth and sleeping porch often occupied by the poor; and bathhouses. While all three structures were employed throughout the later Middle Ages, statistics show clear differences from one period to another. For example, bathhouses seem to have been more popular early in the century, either equalling houses as a category or being outnumbered by houses by only two to one in a number of years.[156] But as prostitution expanded, bathhouses declined as the place of choice and are outnumbered five and even ten to one by houses later in the century.[157] This may have been due to the lack of flexibility and the relatively high cost of a bathhouse. They were also rarely owned by women, who, as we shall see, increasingly controlled the organization of the business after 1350.[158] "Rooms" also fell into disfavor as the century advanced. From an exceptional highpoint of twenty-seven fines in 1336–1337, they more or less

[154] See maps in chapter 2 and Dupont, *Maagdenverleidsters*, p. 142.

[155] Again the conversation manual of 1369 placed the location of Natalie's bathhouse as "behind the Franciscans' wall"; see Gessler, *Livre des Mestiers*, vol. I, pp. 14–15, 38–39.

[156] In 1306 there were eleven bathhouses to twelve ordinary houses; in 1308 the ratio was sixteen houses to seven bathhouses, and in 1309–1310, thirteen to seven; see Table 8.

[157] In 1345–1348 no bathhouses were fined at all.

[158] Only a few women were bathhouse owners in the fourteenth century: Kateline Yoiaerds was one (SAB, SR 1318, f. 45v); Beele Tayspers first rented a bathhouse in the Ghistelhof in 1305 (Wyffels and Vandewalle, *Rekeningen*, vol. II, pt. 1, p. 746) and apparently owned it or another in 1332 (ibid., 1332–1333, f. 22v, "van Beelen Tayspers stove"); Griele van Duerdrecht was fined for her bathhouse in 1333 (ibid., 1333–1334, f. 23r, she was still in the list of fines in 1339); Calle Mollins had a bathhouse in 1342 (ibid., 1342–1343, ff. 27v, 28), and in 1352, (ibid., f. 23r, "ten freren ackere"; it disappears from the fines in 1364); Griele van den Damme was fined in 1350 (ibid., 1350–1351, f. 21v); and Lisebette Sint Goos in 1351 (ibid., 1351–1352, f. 21v).

disappear from the lists of fines by the 1360s. Houses must have offered both the flexibility and the low cost sought by operators.[159]

The question of operators and control of Bruges prostitution is a thorny one, given that fines were levied against the place and not necessarily against those committing the offence. Bathhouses were the most complex site of prostitution because some – perhaps most – were legitimate businesses catering to an active desire for cleanliness among late-medieval city dwellers.[160] Yet the lists of fines in Bruges prove that a number served as fronts for prostitution, and that even the legitimate houses were located in the same neighborhoods (especially St. Gillis) where prostitution was common. A few bathhouses must have been notorious, given the frequency and duration of the fines levied against them.[161] Yet judging from the stability of the numbers of fined bathhouses and the considerable investment necessary to open and operate them, dishonest establishments were probably in the minority.[162]

There is also little reason to doubt that true to the common European pattern, the majority of Bruges bathhouses were owned by men yet operated by women.[163] The thorniest and most important question about the control of Bruges prostitution is who controlled the houses, the most popular site for brothels in the fourteenth century. The simplest answer would be their owners, but the accounts rarely give us a clear idea of who they might be. Only for the years 1366–1371 do the city accounts list those who explicitly rented out houses for use as brothels. This totals only forty-four people, and the total is almost certainly too high given that in 1369–1370 the brothel landlords are lumped together with the keepers of "evil inns." Looking at the

[159] A house offered both rooms and even an attic if need be. In at least one case, fines were assessed against both a house and its attic where a prostitute lived. See ARA, Rekenkamer, RR 1027, membrane 17 (20 September 1378 to 9 January 1379): "thuus daer Matte in woend; De zolder boven daer Calle in woend." In this case at least the prostitutes were fined individually.

[160] A good short summary history of the medieval bathhouse is by G. Jaritz in the *Lexikon des Mittelalters*, 10 vols. (Munich and Zurich, 1977–99), vol. 1, pp. 1331–1333; for the late medieval and early modern period in Germany see Wiesner, *Working Women*, pp. 159–165.

[161] Among them the bathhouse at the Potterierei, which operated from at least 1306 to 1337. But the longest-lived bathhouse-cum-bordello was that of Weiter Balx, whose establishment was fined in 1305 and in almost every year following until 1355. By 1332 it likely passed to other owners, perhaps family members, since it lost the "Weiter" and became simply "Balx Stove." The longest most other bathhouses endured was a decade or so; sources SAB, SR.

[162] To give an example of the expense involved in erecting a bathhouse: in 1318 a bathhouse was torn down to make way for the digging of a canal. Its owners, Kateline Yoiaerds and Jan vander Hanghele, were given £155 6s. 8d. par. in compensation. Apparently Kateline ran the bathhouse and owned 40 percent of it, while van der Hanghele owned the other 60 percent. The scrapped heating apparatus alone was sold for £8 par. (SAB, SR 1318, f. 45v).

[163] The case cited in footnote 162 is one example in Bruges. Merry Wiesner found that most baths were staffed largely by women. *Working Women*. pp. 95–96.

characteristics of this group, there is no clear difference between them and those who appear in the regular list of fines. They are both men and women, with women slightly outnumbering men. Most had been fined for operating a brothel before; indeed some are fined both for renting and for operating a brothel in the same year.[164] Thus there are few neophytes to prostitution among them, or individuals who may have been more interested in an investment.[165] Indeed, those fined for renting brothels in many cases seem to have done this as a natural extension of operating their own house of prostitution. This may have made them more visible to the authorities, for surely a far larger number of Bruges burghers must have rented out their property to brothel operators. This is certainly the case when fines are levied against a house described as a place where a prostitute was living. Was this a means of keeping the name of the house's owner private? There is no way of knowing.

By whatever measure, however, prostitution was big business in Bruges. If 114 different Bruges houses were used by prostitutes in 1369, that must have represented a small but still significant percentage of all the houses in the city. Though not all of these were in continuous use, judging from the accounts, a conservative estimate would place the number of brothels in operation in the peak years of expansion at between forty and sixty.[166] We know that in 1580 there were roughly 8,000 houses standing, so there could not have been many more at the end of the fourteenth century despite the greater population.[167] Very few individuals were fined for more than a single house in the lists of fines. The largest number of houses or rooms operated by a single individual was four, and that was achieved by very few. Striking as well is the volatility shown by the accounts; numbers of

164 For example, in the 1366–1367 account Lamsin den Sceere was fined not only for renting but for operating a brothel; he was also fined for keeping a brothel in the 1361–1362 account. Two of the other four fined in this year had been fined for brothel keeping in the past. In 1367–1368, Nannen van Male was a seasoned operator, not only was she fined in this year but she was fined in seven other years for brothel keeping; of the three men and two women in that year fined for renting only two had clean records. The same basic pattern holds for the other years: SAB, SR 1366–1367, 1367–1368, 1368–1369, 1369–1370, 1370–1371.

165 For a later period, Guy Dupont found evidence of a strong interest among Bruges's financial elite in renting out houses for use as brothels; see Dupont, *Maagdenverleidsters*, pp. 115–119. In a list of fines from 1390, a weaver who rented out a house for use as a bordello is mentioned (ARA, Rekenkamer 13677, pt. 2, f. 12r): "Jehan le Wol, tisseran, pour ce quil a lieuwe une maison len on a tenu bordel . . ."

166 Again, this a very conservative estimate given the absence of documentation about the enclaves controlled by the deacon and chapter of St. Donatian's church. Guy Dupont put the figure at forty-six in the 1390s, falling to twenty-seven by the 1430s – see *Maagdenverleidsters*, p. 84.

167 In 1580 the first complete survey of houses in Bruges was done resulting in a nearly complete record of property transactions from then until the end of the Ancien Régime. Its description is found in Vandewalle, *Beknopte inventaris*, pp. 75–76.

fines could vary considerably from year to year. Moreover, relatively few individuals are fined across more than a single year; many in fact are not fined across the two or three judicial terms in a single year. This strongly suggests that prostitution was an improvised and unstable profession, quick to respond to an influx of men in good economic times. But just as quickly prostitution diminished when either the economy slowed or war caused the city to empty of foreign merchants. Given the size and instability of the clientele, however, it is certain that a great many people had a financial stake in the ebb and flow of the prostitution business in the fourteenth century.

The most stunning fact about fourteenth-century prostitution in Bruges is that it became a business not only conducted by but largely controlled by women after the mid-1350s. The numbers are conclusive on this point. As table 8 shows, in most years before 1350 there is a rough parity between men and women's names in the lists of fines. This strongly supports the argument that control of the business was shared as well between the two sexes. After 1350, however, the majority swings to women, at first slightly – so that in 1351–1353 women barely outnumber men – but by the 1360s the gap is very wide indeed. By the 1370s and 1380s, men were simply not involved in the conduct of prostitution in Bruges judging from the evidence of the accounts. This remains the case for the rest of the Middle Ages, with men named about 20 percent of the time in the fifteenth century.[168]

How can this dramatic turn be explained? Part of it must be related to the relative economic freedom women enjoyed in Bruges, a freedom that extended from the hostelry and the money exchange to the brothel and bathhouse. Even though the professions of money changer and prostitute were leagues apart socially (if not morally in the eyes of the enemies of usury), their businesses were both tied to the health of the Bruges economy in general and the presence of foreign merchants in particular. The increased demand for prostitutes evidenced by the surviving lists of fines could only have been met by massive female immigration to the city. Some of these immigrants may have been prostitutes already, but a great many more were probably drawn by the availability of work of other, more respectable sorts. Some of the names hint at the heterogeneous, anonymous, and foreign origins of many of the women. There is a striking propensity to refer to women by nicknames of all sorts: "Tall," "Short," "Lame," "Beautiful," "Long," "Lap dog," "Loose," "Blue," "Green," which hint at a ribald

[168] Dupont, *Maagdenverleidsters*, pp. 194–196.

anonymity.[169] Foreign or exotic origins are also hinted at: Frisian XX, Bette the Jewess. A remarkable number of women bore a place name as their surname, which also suggests but does not prove foreign origins.[170] Sometimes there is also mention of another profession: Zoetin the apple seller, Marie the hat washer, Katherine the candle seller, and of course the occasional beguine as well.

CONCLUSION

Bruges was exceptional in its permissive, free-market approach to prostitution in the late Middle Ages. In contrast to southern European and German cities, Bruges never adopted policies designed to "institutionalize" prostitution within a district of the city or in the city-run houses. The reasons for this exceptionality lay undoubtedly in the need to cater to a large population of resident or visiting merchants. Other reasons probably have to do with a body of customary law largely untouched by Roman influence until very late in the fifteenth century. Roman law tended to view prostitution as a necessary urban phenomenon whose control and organization were a proper function of city government. Another thing not to be left out of the picture of the Bruges prostitution world is that many of the social and financial elite of the city, chiefly men, derived financial profit from renting out the houses and rooms used by prostitutes. So when all is said and done, it is Bruges's standing as a great city of commerce that had the most to do with the reality of women in the market, and the market in women. For in this commercial metropolis at least, where money was the rule and measure of most things, women were among the first to feel the extraordinary power – for good and ill – brought by unfettered capitalism.

169 Leah Otis (*Prostitution in Medieval Society*, p. 64) cites a sixteenth-century list from Toulouse of prostitutes consisting "almost entirely of nicknames, several of which indicate physical abnormalities."

170 Foreign women were frequently employed in brothels, according to historians. In Bruges, Guy Dupont found that in the fifteenth century the recruiting pattern of prostitutes mirrored the commercial network of which Bruges was a part; it is likely that the fourteenth century was similar. See Dupont, *Maagdenverleidsters*, pp. 131–136.

CHAPTER 9

Towards a Burgundian Bruges

Et erant accens[s]a omnia luminaria maiora, sicut in nativitate domini . . . et omnino campane sonabantur. Pieter van der Eeke

La ville la plus renommée par tout le monde par le fait de marchandise. Duke Philip the Good

In the year of our lord 1384, on the twenty-sixth day of April, Lord Philip, duke of Burgundy and Lady Margaret, duchess of Burgundy, entered the city of Bruges around midday. And our deacon, chapter and all the choir, clad in silk robes, went out in procession to meet and accompany them to the gate of the Burg that opens on the market square, where they [duke and duchess] entered and dismounted. Then the deacon sprinkled holy water and burned incense, and after this the singers began to sing "Honor, Virtus, etc." and they followed the procession until it reached the main altar of our church. And there, after many prayers, the deacon brought to the duke and duchess the book of privileges in which the count's oath is written, which they both swore, and then first the duke opened a Gospel book and by chance he picked the Gospel "But when the Counselor comes"; then, the said Gospel book being closed, the countess opened the book and discovered the same Gospel. After this the deacon read the prayer and collect that are traditionally read at the Joyous Advent of the count. Then the duke proceeded to the altar and offered a cloth of gold and twenty-eight pieces of gold . . . After this the duchess offered one piece of gold. And at the end of the responsory, the organist began to play a motet, and all the candelabra were lit as on Christmas day, and the choir joined in . . . and all the church bells rang.[1]

[1] The complete Latin text can be found in Murray, "The Liturgy of the Count's Advent," pp. 148–149. "Van Eyck" is the literal translation of "De Quercu," the name used by the author in his Latin writings, but he also used the variant "Van der Eeke" from time to time. See Gilliodts-van Severen, *Inventaire*, vol. III, p. 237: "Meester Pieter van der Eeke, capitel clerc van Sinte Donaes." The term "adventus iocundus" (Joyous Advent) refers to a medieval tradition of celebrating the accession of a new ruler with a ceremonial entry into his new cities and awarding him certain gifts. In France, where this tradition was most common, it became the occasion for both ceremony and taxation; in Brabant, on the other hand, the *adventus* referred also to rights and privileges of the ruler *vis-à-vis* his new subjects. For a fine discussion of these traditions, see Lawrence M. Bryant, *The King and the City in the Parisian Royal Entry Ceremony: Politics, Ritual, and Art in the Renaissance* (Geneva, 1986), esp. chap. 1.

Figure 11: Digital reconstruction of St. Donatian's church based on archeological data.

The Bruges notary and chapter secretary Peter van der Eeke wrote this account above shortly after witnessing this "Joyous Entry" of the first Valois count of Flanders. It is one of the very few chronicle entries actually penned in Bruges to survive, and the only time that any one of the chapter secretaries of St. Donatian's was so moved by history to leave such a record among the chapter *Acta*. It is as if van der Eeke caught a glimpse of the colorful and tumultuous future of these Burgundian count/dukes, which would tie the fate of his city and of all Flanders into the ambitions and adventures of the House of Burgundy. But there is an air of the antique about the passage as well, for it subconsciously echoes a much earlier notary of St. Donatian's, Galbert of Bruges, and his description of the accession of another comital dynasty after the wrenching violence of civil war.[2]

[2] The standard translation is Ross, *Murder of Charles the Good*, and a new edition of the Latin text is Rider (ed.), *Galbertus Notarius Brugensis*.

Van der Eeke was writing in a much-altered Bruges, especially in comparison with the city described by his predecessor, Galbert. Yet his account evokes timelessness: Bruges seems much the same as it was in Galbert's time, with the Burg – the site of the count's first castle and fortifications – and its church, St. Donatian's, still firmly at center stage of the greatest of urban spectacles. In reality, as we saw in chapter 2, the Burg lay at the periphery of the great commercial and building booms of the thirteenth and fourteenth centuries, as the canons and provost of the comital church struggled to hold off the tide of trade and traders on their doorstep. The counts had long since abandoned their residence in the Burg – the "Love" – which at the time van der Eeke wrote was serving as prison to dozens of rebels awaiting execution as the penalty for their support of Ghent in its revolt. But to view the spectacle of Philip the Bold's "Joyous Entry" into Bruges as an exercise in illusion or antiquarianism would be to miss the hard core of *Realpolitik* being acted out before the main altar of St. Donatian's church. For beneath the liturgical flourishes of incense, music, and holy water a political bargain was being struck between two eager, even desperate, parties. Achieving rapprochement between ruler and ruled after much bloodshed and economic disaster was the goal of that urban spectacle of 1384, but the antique and comforting forms of the advent liturgy could hardly disguise the anxiety on both sides.

Bruges, on the one hand, was a twice-conquered city with its economy in shambles and a huge war indemnity to pay. Duke Philip, on the other, was struggling to establish his authority over a war-ravaged country, whose most populous city, Ghent, still defied him.[3] The English remained allied with the Gentenars in their rebellion, despite the complete failure of the English "crusade" of 1383; but even in failure there was still much to fear from the English alliance. Philip had already seen ten years of careful political planning and patronage destroyed in this so-called Ghent war of 1379–1385, and he was determined to win back the loyalty of the richest city of Flanders – Bruges.[4]

Philip knew Bruges well. He had made lengthy visits to the city since his marriage to the heiress of Flanders, Margaret of Male, in 1369, particularly

[3] The Ghent war has never been the subject of a thorough study. Helpful are Quicke, *Les Pays-Bas*, pp. 291–367; R. De Muynck, "De Gentse Oorlog (1379–1385). Oorzaken en karakter," *Handelingen der Maatschappij voor Geschiedenis en Oudheidkunde te Gent*, n.s. 5 (1951), 305–318; J. van Herwaarden, "The War in the Low Countries," in J. J. N. Palmer (ed.), *Froissart: Historian* (Totowa, N.J., 1981), pp. 101–117, and most recently, Nicholas, *Medieval Flanders*, pp. 227–231 and Blockmans and Prevenier, *The Promised Lands*, pp. 22–24.

[4] For the relations of Bruges and Philip the Bold before 1384 see Richard Vaughan, *Philip the Bold* (Cambridge, Mass, 1962), pp. 17–19, 30.

in 1375–1376, when he was an intermediary in the English–French peace negotiations held in Bruges. By the 1370s he had come to share his father-in-law's preference for Bruges over Ghent; for even when Philip organized jousts in Ghent in conjunction with the peace negotiations, he and his company returned to Bruges for serious work at the earliest opportunity.[5] During the years of civil war, Philip had repeatedly aided both Louis of Male and Bruges through hard and dangerous times. Perhaps most crucial for the Brugeois had been Philip's role as intercessor for the Flemings with Charles VI after the crushing defeat of the Flemish militias by the French army at Westrozebeke in November 1382. At a time when nothing stood between Bruges and the pillaging hordes of French soldiers, Philip had helped negotiate a deal sparing the city in return for a large "gift" paid to the French. But if the sum was large, the terms were moderate, giving the Brugeois time to squeeze part of the money from the smaller towns and countryside of the Franc of Bruges. The French army then left West Flanders, with the most feared of their soldiers, the Bretons, muttering about the loss of such a rich prize. Philip crowned his diplomatic efforts in 1383 by forgiving the balance of the fine owed by Bruges in return for the city's support of the campaign against the English invasion led by the bishop of Norwich.[6] If Philip was indeed "sage, froid et imaginatif,"[7] as Froissart described him, his actions on behalf of Bruges amount to a conscious and careful courtship of the city whose success was crowned by the "Joyous Advent" of 1384, just three months after the death of Louis of Male.

THE GHENT WAR AND BRUGES

The conflict that erupted in 1379 caused unprecedented damage to the Bruges economy while also laying bare the social and political tensions in the city and county. The townspeople who witnessed Philip and Margaret's entry that day in April had experienced conflict, terror, dictatorship, and deliverance that must have left them uncertain and anxious about the future. As described in the first chapter, the igniting event of the civil war

[5] David Nicholas, "In the Pit of the Burgundian Theater State: Urban Traditions and Princely Ambitions in Ghent, 1360–1420," in *City and Spectacle*, pp. 270–295, esp. 271–272.

[6] The degree of panic within Bruges after the defeat at Westrozebeke can be gauged by the large numbers of burghers who fled the city on the mere rumor of the French army's approach; and by the unfortunate woman who drowned herself for fear of the approaching "Bertoenen"; see van Herwaarden, "War in the Low Countries," p. 111.

[7] Quoted in A. van Nieuwenhuysen, *Les finances du Duc de Bourgogne Philippe le Hardi, 1384–1404* (Brussels, 1984), p. 45.

was the attempt of Bruges magistrates to dig a canal connecting the city to the Leie river, the major highway to the rich grain fields of French Flanders and Picardy.[8] This directly threatened the Ghent grain staple, precisely at the moment when the crisis and uncertainty in the market for Flemish cloth had caused that city to seize even more tightly upon its control of the river passageways between the grain-rich interior and densely urbanized Flanders.

The military operations of the Ghent war saw armies and city militias criss-crossing areas of Maritime Flanders that had been long-spared the realities of war. This agriculturally rich and densely populated rural area had long served as Bruges's first provider of food and industrial raw materials, especially dyestuffs.[9] Repeated visitations of English and French armies and the Ghent militia took their toll on an area vital to Bruges's well being. Students of the effects of war on the countryside, especially Erik Thoen, point out that the damage done by armies often compounded the cumulative effects of famine and disease mortality on the rural population.[10] Thus if looted fields and burned buildings are rapidly reparable in theory, for a population already decimated by plague, recovery may be out of the question for a generation or more.[11] This indeed seems to have been the case in the area around Bruges in the aftermath of the Ghent war. We have already seen the indications of massive mortality caused by the plagues of 1349 and especially that of 1368–1369. Some hard evidence of this destruction comes from the accounts of the Bruges hospital, St. Jan's. Part of the hospital's possessions lay outside the city, including two major farms, whose rents and produce supported the work and employees of the hospital. However anecdotal and unscientific, the stark reports of no money or return of any kind from holdings in the Bruges Franc due to war damage even a decade later paint a grim picture.[12] Given that the hospital's holdings must have reflected the possessions and investments of well-to-do

8 Sortor, "The Ieperleet Affair," 1068–1100; Nicholas, *Metamorphosis*, pp. 290–293.

9 Nicholas, "Of Poverty and Primacy," 26–29.

10 Erik Thoen, "Oorlogen en platteland. Sociale en ekonomische aspekten van militaire destruktie in Vlaanderen tijdens de late middeleeuwen en de vroege moderne tijden," *Tijdschrift voor Geschiedenis* 91 (1978), 363–376.

11 Thoen, *Landbouwekonomie en bevolking*, vol. 1, p. 160, where he compares the demographic effects of the Ghent war with those of the civil war against Maximilian of Austria a century later. In both cases he finds no signs of demographic recovery in the affected countryside until nearly three decades after the hostilities ended.

12 The accounts of St. Jan are OCMW, fonds St. Jans, rekeningen sub anno. They are practically complete for most of the fourteenth and fifteenth centuries, but have never been systematically studied for what they reveal about the agrarian economy of the area around Bruges.

Brugeois, the damage of the Ghent war wiped out a significant source of urban capital.[13]

Political costs had also accrued in the decades before 1379. Many of these were the result of the tensions and conflicts between Louis of Male and Ghent, which emerged fully as Flanders' most bellicose city under his regime. As in the revolt of 1338–1345, the policies of the count and Ghent collided over both the direction of foreign policy and the balance of power within the county. In the case of the Bruges canal, Louis had renewed permission granted by his father for its construction as part of a policy to weaken Ghent's staple and control over the countryside.[14] The count was also rewarding Bruges, which had proven a much more reliable ally to the count, and seemed a promising center of potential resistance to the ambitions of rebellious Ghent. The arrest of a Ghent citizen on 5 September 1379 led in reprisal to the attack and murder of the comital bailiff, Rogier van Outrive, by a crowd of Gentenars. These, combined with repeated attacks on the canal workers by the Ghent paramilitary band known as the "White Hoods," both put a permanent end to the Leie canal and plunged Flanders into a tumult of violence. The end came only with the Treaty of Tournai in December 1385, by which time both Louis and tens of thousands of battle and riot victims were dead. By tradition, damage to lives and property from this five-year struggle was the worst in the history of a frequently ravaged land.[15]

The ferocious destructive energy released by the Ghent war allows a unique picture of the social and economic tensions at play within Bruges in this last period of our study. Division was the first result of the outbreak of hostilities: Bruges weavers and other of the cloth guilds refused to take up arms against Ghent at the command of the count.[16] This was in a sense an echo of Bruges's more revolutionary past – the glories of 1302 and the defeat of the French at Kortrijk. Bruges had changed, however. After a century

[13] For urban investment in the countryside see Nicholas, *Town and Countryside*, pp. 267–329 and Nicholas, "Structures du peuplement." The long siege by the English and their Ghent allies wreaked even greater damage on Ypres and its environs, destroying the city's suburbs and much of the countryside of southwest Flanders. To quote a letter of Philip the Bold: "Anglais et Gantois, qui ont tenu longuement siége devant la dicte ville [Ypres], [ont] ars gatés et destruit les fabours dicelle et les biens estans en iceulx et au pays denviron, par quoy leurs rentes et revenus en sont très grandement diminuées": edited in John Bartier and Andrée Van Nieuwenhuysen (eds.), *Ordonnances de Philippe le Hardi, de Marguerite de Male et de Jean sans Peur* (Brussels, 1965), pp. 7–8, no. 6.

[14] Vandermaesen *et al.*, *De Witte Kaproenen*, pp. 12–17; Nicholas, *Medieval Flanders*, pp. 227–228, 245–246.

[15] See Chapter 1, pp. 18–20 and Quicke, *Les Pays-Bas*, pp. 297–335.

[16] Vandermaesen *et al.*, *De Witte Kaproenen*, p. 15.

of development as a commercial center, business was more central to the urban economy than the textile industry. Business, as shown previously, depended on political stability without and social peace within, so it is no surprise that the goals of Bruges's magistrates meshed with the count's on foreign (i.e. outside Bruges) policy and left the task of ensuring domestic tranquility to a new social and political elite. That elite was in turn liberally laced with brokers, hostellers, bankers, and merchants whose money and interests both reshaped the urban economy and repressed the revolutionary aspirations of many urban artisans.[17] It was up to this group to keep the genie of urban revolution from escaping.

They almost succeeded. From 1380, with internal dissension put down, Bruges emerged as the count's bulwark in the war against Ghent. But even with Bruges's help, Louis could not deal a decisive blow against his enemies. Ghent was able to capture Oudenaarde, further solidifying its control over southern and eastern Flanders.[18] Further raids brought areas in northern Flanders under Ghent's control. But in 1381, the tide seemed to turn in Louis's favor with the capture and destruction of Ghent's ally, Geraardsbergen, in June, leading first to a growing isolation of Ghent and then in the winter of 1381–1382 to a true blockade of the city. The rebels faced starvation. Only the drastic action of establishing as virtual dictator Philip, the only surviving son of the legendary van Artevelde, and launching a desperate attack on Bruges on 3 May 1382, saved them. Against all odds, the Ghent army and its allies utterly defeated the Bruges militia under Louis's command, storming the city and placing it under revolutionary rule.[19]

What happened in Bruges in the aftermath of the Ghent victory throws a stark light on the bonds of social control achieved at such great cost in the course of the century. Many Bruges weavers and other clothworkers immediately joined the Gentenars in massacres and plundering raids. Chief targets were rich citizens, and in particular hostellers, brokers, butchers, fishmongers, and furriers, all known for their support of the count.[20] The money changers' stands along the St. Pieter bridge were in the path of the destruction, and it is probable that they were among the targets, although we do not know how great the loss of life and property damage

[17] See chapter 3. [18] Nicholas, "The Scheldt Trade," 189–359, esp. 196.

[19] The time was well chosen by the Gentenars to coincide with the Procession of the Holy Blood, the most important procession of the year and the occasion for general urban festivities. Many chroniclers report that Bruges soldiers were drunk when they formed up for battle. See Vandermaesen *et al.*, *Witte Kaproenen*, p. 23; Nicholas, *Medieval Flanders*, pp. 230–231.

[20] SAB, SR, 1366–1367, f. 45–46; Vandermaesen *et al.*, *Witte Kaproenen*, p. 23.

may have been.[21] We know that there were dozens, perhaps hundreds, of massacre victims whose bodies were piled into mass graves dug near the Grote Markt, where apparently much of the bloodletting took place.[22] Louis's urban residence, the Prinsenhof, was also attacked and heavily damaged. Comital and commercial Bruges certainly suffered under the blows inflicted by the politically repressed clothworkers and other guilds on that day.

Public order broke down completely in subsequent days and perhaps weeks after the Ghent victory. Eyewitness reports by several Hanse merchants confirm the picture of looting and indiscriminate violence.[23] However, one should not jump to the conclusion that urban poverty was rising up against commercial wealth, for there is evidence of widespread support for the count among the urban poor of Bruges, as well as other evidence from confiscation records that weavers and their allies were far from impoverished. Curiously, the evidence begins with a story, told by the chronicler Jean Froissart.

Night had fallen and count Louis and his men were fleeing through the streets of Bruges seeking to make their escape from the Gentenars. They were a short distance from the Grote Markt, where the Ghent militia was forming up to begin a house-to-house search for the count. Realizing time was short, Louis discarded his sword and armor, put on his servant's cloak, and set off alone through the dark streets and alleys searching for sanctuary. "Distraught and trembling," as Froissart says, Louis finally entered a poor woman's house in a desperate attempt to elude his pursuers. The woman, at first startled and afraid, recognized her lord from the many times she had received alms at his palace and agreed to hide him. Following the woman's instructions, Louis climbed to the loft of the one-room house, hid under a bed full of the woman's sleeping children and left this remarkable woman to deal with the men of Ghent. When Louis's pursuers arrived, they found the woman nursing her youngest child and in response to their charges that she had admitted a man to the house, she invited them to take a look around, for she had gone out only to empty some water in the street and had let no one enter. The men came, searched the room and looked into

[21] Van Houtte, *Geschiedenis*, pp. 121–122; Nicholas, *Van Arteveldes*, p. 73.

[22] A Ghent chronicler reported that the blood in the streets from the Bourse square to the Grote Markt reached half-way up the shoes of those who walked through: C. P. Serrure and Ph. Blommaert (eds.), *Kronyk van Vlaenderen*, 2 vols. (Ghent, 1839), vol. 1, pp. 242–245.

[23] The testimony is scattered in the correspondence of various cities of the Hanse whose merchants sought payment of damages; see *Hanserezesse*, vol. 1, pt. 2, pp. 413–417, vol. 1, pt. 3, pp. 2–4, and Assmussen, *Lübecker Flandernfahrer*, pp. 69, 325.

the loft at the miraculously still sleeping children. They left, apparently convinced of the truth of the woman's story.[24]

"Prince and Pauper Tales" were of course a literary genre rich in possibilities for a writer with a taste for colorful and moralistic stories. But in this case, there is a seemingly independent local chronicle tradition, which not only confirms Froissart but adds personal and topographical details not included by him.[25] In both these traditions there is much reason to believe that the truly poor were not to be found among the urban revolutionaries. There is no doubting Froissart's credentials as a reporter. Born and raised in a city himself, he was well acquainted with the lot of the urban poor and his description rings true. The woman's house was a "maisonette enfumée," consisting of a single room on the street and a cramped little sleeping loft reached by a ladder with seven rungs. An old soot-stained sheet divided the room and shielded the peat fire. The only sticks of furniture were two beds, a cradle, and the fireside chair in which the woman had received the "routiers" of Ghent.

The reality of the urban housing of the poor has a direct bearing on the urban revolt of 1382, for almost certainly the savior of Count Louis rented her hovel, and there is good reason to believe that her landlord was more likely to be found among the count's enemies than among any of her fellow poor. This evidence is to be found among the lists of confiscated properties drawn up in the aftermath of the recapture of Bruges in late 1382. But before analyzing what those records have to say, it is important to understand something about the background of urban housing in medieval Bruges.

As described in chapter 2, Bruges was gripped by a building boom in the thirteenth century, financed by Brugeois grown wealthy in trade and in search of suitable investments for their profits. We do not know the specifics, but it is clear that many citizens invested in land in a number of ways. The wealthiest probably acquired legal ownership of the land and built their own structures upon it, then rented out the shops and residences.[26] Others did not directly develop the property, but leased it on a long-term basis to others, who in turn built and owned the buildings but not the land on which they stood. As the cycle of cloth production and trade, immigration, building, and profit expanded throughout the century, more and more property, both urban and rural, came into the hands of

[24] *Chroniques de J. Froissart*, ed. Gaston Raynaud, 15 vols. (Paris, 1897), vol. II, pp. 230–233.

[25] J. N. Despars, *Cronijcke van den Lande ende Graefscepe van Vlaendre*, ed. J. De Jonghe, 3 vols. (Bruges, 1939), vol. III, pp. 48–49.

[26] Ryckaert, *Stedenatlas*, pp. 69–70 and chapter 2, pp. 48–52.

Brugeois, and indeed flowed into the possession of religious and charitable establishments as well.[27]

Confiscation records surviving from the uprising of 1302 give us a clear view of the importance of urban real estate to the fortunes of Bruges's wealthy class and the part that housing the poor played in that wealth. In the course of that struggle, all the goods, including real estate holdings of French sympathizers, were impounded and administered by the city. Since many Bruges francophiles were members of the wealthy elite, this gives us a good, albeit fragmentary, view of the relationship of wealth and real property.[28] Despite the shortcomings of these accounts, it is clear that many members of the urban upper class had significant investments in the housing of the poor and migrant population, in the form of what were called *cameren* (rooms) and *huurhusen* (rented houses).

From the confiscations of 1302–1305 to those made after the Ghent war, there were sweeping changes in the investments of the Bruges *poorter* (upper) class. With few exceptions, the *poorters* who suffered confiscation in 1383 owned little real estate.[29] More of their wealth was invested in business or money lending, although the scribes make no distinction between a debt incurred by a loan or by an investment.[30] *Poorters* still owned land, but it seems increasingly to have become a commodity, detached from the houses built upon it. Many *poorters* traded these ground rents among themselves, or granted them to convents or hospitals. Judging from these accounts, few *poorters* operated rental properties, because (as earlier chapters have shown) the opportunities for profit were probably greater through investment in trade. The bitter lesson taught by the confiscations of 1302–1305 may also have caused the wealthy to invest more heavily in movables. The rise of hostelling and money changing is symbolic of this change in Bruges, and there is a great deal of circumstantial evidence that the great fortunes of Bruges at the end of the fourteenth century were drawn from brokerage and trade, not real estate.

As the *poorter* class shifted its wealth away from rental property in the city, it seems two groups stepped into the breach. The first was the religious institutions in Bruges, those who received large amounts of urban

[27] See chapter 2.

[28] These records are SAB, Confiscatierekeningnen, 271. There are eleven registers in six portfolios in the archives. For a description, see Vandewalle, *Beknopte inventaris*, p. 113. A first attempt at analysis is Vandermaesen and Ryckaert, "Een miskende bron voor de sociale geschiedenis van de stad Brugge."

[29] The confiscation records of the Ghent war are ARA, Rekenkamer, RR, 2017–2020; registers 18244, 48986.

[30] See chapter 5, pp. 189–196.

land and large numbers of houses as bequests.[31] The second was the broad ranks of urban artisans, guild members who shared in the wealth brought to Bruges by foreign commerce but were apparently shut out of investments in trade, brokerage, and finance.[32] Real estate investment, particularly in housing, offered the artisan a place for his profits. Fortunately the confiscation documents of 1383–1385 identify individuals by their trade in 64 percent of the cases, and provide considerable information about the location, condition, and rental prices of artisan-owned property in the city.[33]

One hundred eighty-six artisans appear in the registers in the two years after the battle of Westrozebeke and the return of the count to power. They divide into two broad categories: workers in the textile trades (weavers, fullers, shearers, carpet and tapestry weavers), and those in trades that produced mostly for the local market – construction workers, furniture makers, shippers, teamsters, and the like. It is members of the first group, the textile artisans, the fiercest rebels and consequently most numerous battle victims, who give the clearest evidence of real estate holdings.

Textile artisans differed considerably among themselves in the value of their property holdings, indicating a great diversity of wealth within the trades. Some owned virtually nothing, subsisting in rented quarters and working for wages. But 40 percent (twenty out of forty-nine) of the clothworkers owned real estate of some sort. These twenty divide into three separate categories of owners. The first simply owned the house in which they lived and worked. Seven of the twenty fall into this category. A typical example is Pieter de Grave, who owned two small houses in which he set up looms, installed his family, and lodged his journeymen.[34] Eight other clothworkers were small real estate operators, owning at most two rental houses or a few small rooms attached to their primary dwellings. These tended to be the humblest kinds of rentals, let most often by the week to peasants or poor women. Not surprisingly, the accounts mention high turnover in tenants and frequent arrearages in rent.[35] These were transient quarters in effect. Pauwel Storin is one example. He owned and resided in a small house near the city walls with two "decrepit" (the Flemish *odelijk* is

[31] The largest mass of these is contained in the archives of St. Jan's hospital and the Godshuizen and Poor Tables, all housed in the archives of the OCMW. See Galvin, *Poor Tables of Bruges*, pp. 129–171, for an analysis of kinds and patterns of giving to these institutions.

[32] This exclusion of the artisan class from investment in trade remains true throughout the Middle Ages. Capital supplied by artisans is only tapped for the first time in sixteenth-century Antwerp. See Hunt and Murray, *History of Business*, pp. 212–225.

[33] Van Oost, "Sociale stratifikatie van de Brugse opstandigen," 830–877.

[34] ARA, RR 2019, #4.

[35] ARA, rek., f. 16v; ARA, RR 2019, #6, 12, 18.

eloquent even to an English ear) rooms attached. These rooms contained one chest and one bed as the only furniture for their residents.[36]

Five textile artisans were landlords on a larger scale, owning three or more rental units. These men went considerably beyond merely letting a few rooms to boarders, or constructing a few wooden lean-tos alongside their house. Michiel Dumen rented out a house with four rooms attached, and also ran a small farm within the city walls.[37] The weaver Willem Maes held three mortgages on various properties and owned his own house and a fourth part of another house inherited from a brother-in-law.[38] But the fuller Lamsin Smet was a clear-cut specialist in housing the urban poor. Lamsin owned exclusively *cameren* – a row of one-room dwellings, each sharing a common wall with its neighbor. These were quite similar to the "maisonette enfumée" of Froissart's story.

Smet's room must have been towards the bottom of the Bruges housing market. Even the hardened scribe of the confiscation accounts attached such labels as "extremely poor," "small," "tiny," "old." Although the five rooms are described similarly, the rents paid for them differed considerably. They ranged from 1s. 8d. a week to as little as 6d. The tenants are an interesting and perhaps typical lot. There were three single women and two men, and although no children are mentioned in the accounts, it is quite possible that children shared the cramped quarters with their mothers. Without exception the residents of this lodging were poor: "Grete Brest, a poor little woman, lives in the next room which she rents for 1s 6d the week."[39] And all are named in the diminutive – "a poor little . . ." – like a cast of characters in a Dickens novel.

The conclusion from this analysis is clear: not only artisans, particularly clothworkers, were recruits of revolution in great numbers, but many of them had invested in both industries and properties that were declining as a result of both circumstantial and political change in and around Bruges. Judging from the confiscation records, the better-off cloth workers and other artisans had invested in the most marginal properties, which they in turn rented to the newest and most impoverished of the city's residents. Peasant newcomers, the old, the poor, made up their clientele. But ironically, the plight of many of these landlords was scarcely better than that of their tenants. Many of the buildings owned by them were in extremely poor condition, as reported in the accounts. Some were without roofs; and some had deteriorated to such an extent that no value could be placed on

[36] ARA, Rekenkamer, 18244, f. 1r.
[37] ARA, RR 2019.
[38] ARA, Rekenkamer, 48986, f. 8r.
[39] Ibid., f. 16r–v.

them. Many of the owners were far behind in payment of ground rents and taxes on their properties, often as many as five years in arrears.[40] This also underlines the effects of the price inflation of the second half of the century.

All this gives a clear view of a group stretched to its limits in an unfavorable economic climate for cloth manufacture. As shown in chapter 7, the traditional cloth industry in Bruges and Flanders had been in decline for decades, leading to a decline in the numbers of clothworkers judging by the muster lists of the urban militia.[41] This decline was caused and reinforced by a reorientation of cloth production away from quantity to quality, lengthening the production process but reducing the number of workers required.[42] Real estate owners in the cloth manufacturing trades were thus damaged on two sides. Reduction in the amount of cloth produced in the city brought them lower earnings, or perhaps unemployment, as weavers and fullers, and the decrease in immigration from the countryside meant fewer tenants for their rental units. This meant a bitter fate for the wealthiest among the textile workers. They had invested in the past prosperity of Bruges, based on cloth manufacture and rural immigration. Not surprisingly, they put up the fiercest resistance to count and commerce. But the aftermath of the Ghent war was to confirm that the future belonged to trade, finance, and service to the Burgundian dukes.

REPRESSION AND RENEWAL

Historians have long recognized the delicate diplomacy required to restitch the relationship of sovereign and city in the aftermath of revolt.[43] Bruges, no matter how hesitant a rebel city, was no exception. And in effect Bruges was subjected to waves of repression before there could be any renewal. First, during the short reign of Philip van Artevelde the city's defenses had been systematically destroyed, with the razing of the "Kruis" gate, "Ghent" gate, and "Katelijne" gate as well as the filling in of defensive canals and moats.[44] Perhaps as a gesture of scorn, van Artevelde ordered the construction of a windmill on one heap of rubble.[45] Apparently, van Artevelde commanded that there be no indiscriminate looting of the city, but that did not hamper those who had scores to settle or spare certain

[40] De Smet, "De repressie te Brugge na de slag bij," esp. 13–16.
[41] De Meyer, "Sociale strukturen te Brugge," 39–40. [42] See chapter 7, pp. 277–295.
[43] The historiography of urban revolt is discussed extensively in Nicholas, *Later Medieval City*, pp. 108–179.
[44] Vandermaesen *et al.*, *Witte Kaproenen*, p. 23. [45] Nicholas, *Van Arteveldes*, p. 173.

religious institutions. We know that properties belonging to St. Donatian's church suffered considerably. The houses of both the provost and deacon were occupied by "ruffians and harlots" who were expelled with help bought from van Artevelde.[46] Other trials followed: a tax on all church property in Bruges; a canon forced on the chapter by van Artevelde and his hand-picked aldermen; and ever-deepening financial losses.[47] The extent of such losses ranged from the case of Jan Dierard, who in September 1384 informed the chapter that he could no longer afford to be buried in their church because of the losses he had suffered at the hands of the Gentenars on "that evil Saturday", to the complete absence of merchants who customarily hawked their wares in stands in front, and alongside the church rented out by the chapter.[48] The church's desperation bordered on pathos when a servant was ordered to plant banners bearing the church's insignia on church properties outside the walls in the vain hope that they would be spared destruction in the aftermath of van Artevelde's takeover.[49] Van Artevelde's clemency apparently extended no further than the city walls.

The repression of the Gentenars reached beyond the chapter of St. Donatian's. Van Artevelde's lieutenants, Francis Ackerman and Peter de Winter, took numerous hostages from among the prominent of Bruges and sent them to Ghent. Froissart reported their number at 500, but this is no doubt an exaggeration.[50] Van Artevelde continued to collect all the revenues owed the count and demanded new taxes of his own. On 2 September 1382, representatives of several Bruges churches gathered in conclave to discuss

> the subsidy that Philip van Artevelde demanded from them . . . which they had given under duress, contrary to their own will, for they only wanted to give money or subvention for expenses incurred in making peace between our venerable prince and the fatherland, his county. Otherwise it cannot be acceded to, and they may refuse to pay anything except under the threat and danger of death.[51]

Death, destruction, and taxes marked the Ghent occupation.

[46] BAB, St. Donaas, G1/12, f. 9r: "Item datum Danyel de Winter et alii famuli Philippi dArtevelde quampluros expulserunt malos garciones et meretrices tam de domo domini prepositi quam de domo domini decani, dictas domos custodien. 23 s."

[47] Nicholas, *Van Arteveldes*, pp. 173–174.

[48] BAB, St. Donaas, A48, Acta Capituli, fol. 99r; for financial losses see BAB, St. Donaas, G1/4 (accounts of the Fabric of St. Donatian's, 1381–1382), fol. 2v: "[received] de ostio occidentali ecclesie hoc anno propter paucitatem mercatorum, nichil."

[49] BAB, St. Donaas G1/4, f. 7r: "Item datum domino Jacobo de Zaemte ad procurandum vexilla pro defensione terrarum nostrarum extra villam 32s."

[50] Nicholas, *Van Arteveldes*, p. 174.

[51] BAB, St. Donaas A48, Acta Capituli, f. 99r; Nicholas, *Van Arteveldes*, p. 174.

The bodies and costs of the Ghent occupation had scarcely been buried when the great massacre at Westrozebeke occurred, where men from Bruges perished alongside those of Ghent. The news of the defeat caused panic in a city recently denuded of fortifications at van Artevelde's order. But there followed in rapid succession the fine negotiated by Philip the Bold sparing Bruges from pillage, the struggle to pay the first installment, and numerous executions and confiscations. Between January 1383 and September 1384, 224 persons were beheaded, including the former town executioner, and the possessions of 281 persons were confiscated.[52] The town jail was filled to overflowing, so that the dungeon of the ancient comital castle of Bruges was used to imprison those who could not be accommodated elsewhere.

The form and extent of these confiscations in Bruges have puzzled many historians, for they struck not only rebels but those innocents who had been sent as hostages to Ghent by van Artevelde. The leading historian of Bruges, J. A. van Houtte, claimed that Louis of Male's actions violated any modern notion of justice.[53] But it is precisely here that van Houtte and other historians have missed the point, for they mistake the "forms" of repression for the underlying reality. What was really commencing with these confiscations, and climaxed finally with the "Joyous Entry" of Philip and Margaret, was a ritual of renewal intended to purchase forgiveness and reestablish relationships. This *verzoening* therefore must be understood in terms of medieval ritual, not according to modern notions of justice.[54]

As might be expected, the confiscation records are complex and fragmentary. Only a little more than half of the known Bruges rebels are represented in the confiscation accounts at all, and that information is uneven in its fullness. For 60 percent of the rebels mentioned in the records, we know only that their goods were repurchased by someone for a particular price. Only for the remaining 40 percent do we have anything approaching a complete list of their possessions. Fortunately, these are extensive including land, money and bullion, household goods, clothing, and foodstuffs.[55]

The concept of *zoenden* or atonement was central to Flemish criminal law. Unlike in modern justice systems, however, life or loss of freedom were not the price of crime; most often money was exchanged instead. The administration of *zoenrecht* followed strict forms.[56] The atonement

[52] De Smet, "Repressie," 6–9. [53] Van Houtte, *Geschiedenis*, p. 121.

[54] Marc Boone has noted a continuum of these rituals, including the complete physical destruction of a city; see "Civitas mori potest si authoritate superioris damnetur: politieke motieven voor het bewust verwoesten van steden (14de–16de eeuw)," in *Destruction et reconstruction de villes du Moyen Age à nos jours* (Brussels, 1999), pp. 339–368.

[55] The surviving registers are described by de Smet, "Repressie," 3–4.

[56] Nicholas, "Crime and Punishment," 289–334, 1141–1176.

price (*zoengeld*) was decided upon by the comital bailiff based upon the ability of the accused to pay, the seriousness of the crime, and the quality of evidence gathered from an inquest. Often a fee was recommended by an outside authority, such as a town clerk, the receiver of Flanders, or even the count himself. When the fine was set a composition (*composicie*) was made stipulating the crime, the amount of the fine, and terms of payment. This legal form of punishment is precisely the pattern followed by the count in the confiscations in Bruges between 1383 and 1384.

Viewing the confiscations at Bruges in this light answers many questions concerning the process. The records indeed resemble tax assessments more than anything else. This is supported by what the records seek to assess. Surely the values for the goods listed are based on some rough estimate derived through the process of negotiation. They almost certainly do not reflect any kind of market value, for any such market would have collapsed given the number and extent of confiscations. We should also remember that the process of data gathering was voluntary, a function of the community and its collective memory. Rarely were documents available to supply a purchase price. And in 70 percent of the cases, no goods were sold outside of the single agreement struck with the named purchaser.

The typical pattern found in the records begins with a widow whose husband has been killed in battle. In Flemish law, half of the property was considered her share and was therefore not subject to confiscation.[57] The half that escheated to the count was nearly always repurchased by the widow for a negotiated price. The sum was usually paid in installments, and in many cases the widow was assisted by a relative in paying the debt. This was true of people from every social class. An example is the widow of Clays van den Boomgarde, whose husband had died in the battle of Westrozebeke: she was a poor woman, who was left little more than her husband's weaving implements, and a small house with a heavy mortgage. Her neighbors reported to the clerk that she was hopelessly in debt. As a result of negotiations, the price of £9 par. was demanded, which was paid in full by Willeme van den Boomgarde, Clays's brother.[58] The widow of Willem Koucke, a *poorter* in Bruges, though English born, was a wealthy woman. Her husband had been taken to Ghent as a hostage, and he had died there. The inventory of her property occupies two full pages in the register, and her fine was the enormous sum of £600 parisis. She did not pay this sum all at once, but the register notes that her debt is recorded in a charter, no doubt with provisions for its repayment.[59]

57 See chapter 8. 58 ARA, Rekenkamer, 48986, f. 5v. 59 ARA, Rekenkamer, 48986, f. 7r–v.

These two examples display the extremes of the process, but they underscore the argument that the repression was distributed throughout the Bruges community. Viewing the confiscations as simply punishment of a class of rebels is inaccurate. The count did not unleash a wave of newly destitute people into the urban community. The fines seem in most cases to fit the ability of the survivors to pay. Only the goods of those who, together with all their kin, had fled Bruges entirely were put up for sale and lost to their original owners. Moreover, the confiscations followed well-defined rules which considerably softened the blow to the community. A wife's share, as stated above, was safe and the welfare of the children (who in Flemish law had claim on their parents' property) was taken into account as well. It should also be pointed out that only a tiny minority, 1,000 at most, out of a population still probably in excess of 40,000 were affected by these repressive measures.[60]

A BURGUNDIAN BRUGES?

Philip's entry should thus be viewed in one respect as another link in this long chain of ritual of repression and renewal, a link specific to that time and place. On the other hand, cultural historians have long recognized the importance of the "Ruler's Advent," the ceremonial first entrance of a new ruler into his most important cities. For Huizinga such "Blijde Inkomsten" came third on the list of examples of "s Levens Felheid" – the violent contrasts of life – after a city's soundscape, shaped by its bells, and religious processions, which marked anxious times. He recognized that the "Entry" was in reality a simultaneous staging of many urban spectacles, "prepared with all the sensory pyrotechnics one could command."[61] Ernst Kantorowicz, influenced by Huizinga, pointed out the manifold liturgical and theological layers of the Advent ceremony. In a classic article, Kantorowicz noted the important theological message of the Advent: "Time and again it has been announced on these occasions that the comer is the Expected One and that accordingly the city . . . is another Zion. For whenever a king arrived at the gates of a city, celestial Jerusalem seemed to descend from heaven to earth." In other words, the Adventus liturgy was the symbolic

[60] The punitive measures assessed against Ghent, the most obdurate rebel, were even more moderate. See Nicholas, *Medieval Flanders*, pp. 318–322 and Nicholas, *Metamorphosis*, pp. 14–16.

[61] Johan Huizinga, *Herfsttij der Middeleeuwen* (Groningen: Wolters-Nijhoff, 1919), p. 3 (author's translation). (Published English trans., *Autumn of the Middle Ages*, tr. Rodney J. Payton and Ulrich Mammitzsch [Chicago: University of Chicago Press, 1996].)

meeting ground of the eternal city and its eternal ruler – past, present, and future.[62]

Recent scholarship has focused on the political and contextual aspects of the Entry ceremony. Hugo Soly, writing specifically about the Burgundian Low Countries, noted that *intochten* were particularly sensitive moments in the duke's relations with his cities, forcing him to "try to accomplish two nearly incompatible goals: stimulate the loyalty of the citizens and demonstrate his ducal authority." The city had its own agenda for such spectacles, wishing to win favor and confirmation of privileges from the duke, while overawing the local populace with a civic display of wealth and power.[63] For Sabine MacCormack, writing about the Adventus ceremony in late antiquity, the Adventus "remained a ceremony of persuasion, integration and consent . . .[It] acts on several levels, each capable of interpenetrating the other, thereby enhancing and extending visible and historical reality and giving it universal significance and comprehensibility . . . History makes sense because it is continuous, and one of the ways of highlighting such continuity is the use of the ceremony of adventus."[64] The Bruges Advent of 1384 shows many of the characteristics described above, but with some significant variations, which justify a more careful analysis of the setting and meaning of the event.

Why does so much of the action described by van der Eeke at the beginning of this chapter take place in the Burg square and in St. Donatian's church? One answer is that both the square and church had become ceremonial space, as the count's direct influence receded and that of the city and its administration increased. Thus the Burg, the old center of the city, became the place of execution, procession, election, and administration, with its own gates, its own church, its own ancient past.[65]

As described in chapter 2, part of St. Donatian's power lay in its role as keeper of the dynastic memory of the counts of Flanders. The church's

62 Ernst Kantorowicz, "The King's Advent and the Enigmatic Panels in the Doors of Santa Sabina," *Selected Studies* (Locust Valley, NY: J. J. Augustin, 1965), p. 42. Kantorowicz's admiration for Huizinga is shown not only in his review of Huizinga's collected essays in the *American Historical Review* 60 (1955), 853–855, but also by a project he undertook in the mid-1930s on "the history of the Dukes of Burgundy of the Valois race." I owe this reference to the kindness of Professor Robert E. Lerner.

63 Hugo Soly, "Plechtige intochten in de steden van de Zuidelijke Nederlanden tijdens de overgang van de Middeleeuwen naar Nieuwe Tijd: communicatie, propaganda, spektakel," *Tijdschrift voor Geschiedenis* 97 (1984), 341–361, esp. 343.

64 Sabine MacCormack, *Art and Ceremony in Late Antiquity* (Berkeley: University of California Press, 1981), p. 53.

65 Despite the construction of the walls of 1127 and 1297, the Burg retained both its walls and its gates until the eighteenth century: van Houtte, *Geschiedenis*, p. 262; Murray, "The Liturgy of the Count's Advent," pp. 137–152; Andrew Brown, "Civic Ritual: Bruges and the Counts of Flanders in the Later Middle Ages," *English Historical Review* 112 (1997), 277–299, esp. 279.

origins lay, according to twelfth-century legend, with the first count of Flanders, Baldwin Iron Arm, who built a chapel to house the relics of the his patron saint, the holy bishop of Reims, Donatianus. The church that later arose on the square formed by the count's castle symbolized the aspirations of the Flemish dynasty, for it was modeled on Charlemagne's chapel in Aachen, proclaiming the link to the Carolingians through Baldwin's wife, Judith. Its construction, dating from about 960, was probably the work of Count Arnulf I, who desired a grander building to house a growing collection of relics, as well as a growing dynastic reputation, with both to be tended by the twelve canons he established in the church. St. Donatian's continued to be endowed richly by Arnulf's successors, notably Robert II, who in 1089 added to his ancestors' endowments and made the church's provost the hereditary chancelor of Flanders and head of the comital administration.[66] The chapter also had St. Basil's chapel, also called the chapel of the Holy Blood, in its gift; thus canons of the church led the Holy Blood Procession, Bruges's most important procession and one of the most important in Flanders.[67] But it was the murder of the saintly count, Charles the Good, as he knelt in prayer in St. Donatian's that both gave Galbert the subject of his history and sealed the relationship of the church and the comital dynasty as the center of the cult of Charles the Good.[68] It is clear that Philip the Bold, who, as Froissart put it, "saw far where his interests were concerned," was looking both to the past and to the future as he joined in the Advent ceremony, acting a part that had been written for him. He knew that his acceptance as legitimate successor would depend in part on the essential paradox of invoking the memory of dead counts to gain the loyalty of living subjects.

The ritual of Philip's entry was clearly a many-layered and many-textured event encompassing renewal and repression, invocation of the ancient, and anxious hope for the future. But how could the ceremony described by van der Eeke serve so many purposes, from symbolizing the advent of Christ to representing a return of peace; from proclaiming the advent of a new dynasty in Flanders to helping a church chapter repair its shattered dignity and finances? Only by penetrating into the message of the rituals, their sights, smells, sounds, and offerings, and the role all parts played in the

[66] This office quickly became more honorific than of any real importance, except during the reigns of Charles the Good and Thierry of Alsace (d. 1167). On this point see Nicholas, "Of Poverty and Primacy," 20 n. 16 and Kittell, *From Ad Hoc to Routine*, p. 7.

[67] The procession took place on 3 May each year and not only was the highlight of the processional year, but also heralded the beginning of the Bruges fair; see van Houtte, *Geschiedenis*, pp. 250–51

[68] B. Janssens de Bisthoven, "Het Kapittel van Sint-Donatiaan te Brugge," in *Sint-Donaas en de voormalige Brugse Katedraal*, (Bruges, 1978), pp. 51–59.

whole, can we even approach an understanding of the political overtones of this many-voiced event.

The initial impression given us by van der Eeke is of an overwhelming sensory experience: the sight of the magnificent silk robes worn by the canons and choir; the smell of incense but above all the sounds of music and bells. Huizinga's insights come to mind here, when he wrote that bells were the most arresting element of a city's soundscape, and with the six bells of St. Donatian's ringing, accompanied by those of all the other churches of Bruges, the din must have been deafening.[69] But van der Eeke is also careful to describe the music produced by the church choir and great organ – the interior soundscape as it were. Thanks to recent research on music in Bruges, we now know that St. Donatian's was an important center for the composition and performance of polyphonic music, so the singing and playing were of an extraordinarily high order. In fact, the music was so much to Philip's taste that he hired away the church organist soon afterward. From this time on, St. Donatian's would be a rich source of musical talent and support for Burgundian court music, both as a training ground for promising talent and as a source of sinecures for Burgundian court musicians.[70]

Hardly less arresting than the soundscape was the landscape, the confined space of the Burg and its square with the oldest and holiest buildings of Bruges: St. Donatian's on one side, St. Basil's chapel housing the relic of the Holy Blood on another. The former comital castle, built in Galbert's time, stood on the east side of the square, and the Steen, perhaps the most ancient comital residence in Flanders, still stood beside Saint Basil's.[71] This was a sacred space for all the participants in Philip's entry ceremony, for – paradoxically – one and different reasons. For Philip and the chapter the association with the Flemish dynasty was clear, but the Burg was also the government square of the day, where aldermen of both the castellany around Bruges (the Franc) and the city itself held court. The *stadhuis* that still graces the south side of the Burg of Bruges was just under construction at the time of Philip's accession, and a more magnificent monument to urban pride can scarcely be imagined. The building was not completed until 1420, when its impressive façade held statues of the counts of Flanders. The painter

69 Huizinga, *Herfsttij*, pp. 2–3. St. Donatian's had six bells each of a different pitch; see Strohm, *Music in Late Medieval Bruges*, p. 104.

70 The organist hired by Philip was Jean Vise; see Strohm, *Music in Late Medieval Bruges*, pp. 18–19. Among the Burgundian court musicians who held prebends in St. Donatian's in the fifteenth century were Gilles Binchois, Guillaume Dufay, and Gilles Joye.

71 Van Houtte, *Geschiedenis*, p. 41.

Jan van Eyck would polychrome six of these statues (perhaps including that of Philip the Bold) in 1434–1435.[72] Clearly, as the original role of the Burg declined, its ceremonial role increased, symbolized by the incense and holy water with which Philip and Margaret were greeted upon entering the gate. The procession then continued the short distance to the main altar of St. Donatian's. It was there, within sight of the tomb of Charles the Good, that the ancient liturgy would take place.

It might be useful to pause a moment and consider a typology of the Adventus liturgy. Kantorowicz identified basically two liturgies, representing two concepts of advent. First was a reference to the historical entry of Christ into Jerusalem, with the biblical text "Benedictus qui venit in nomine Domini" as the antiphon. Second was the eschatological Advent, dominated by the figure of John the Baptist as the precursor of Christ with the text "Ecce mitto angelum meum, qui praeparabit viam tuam ante faciem meam." Not coincidentally, the latter text was the first lesson read on the first Sunday of Advent.[73] The biblical text employed in the Bruges Advent, however, is related only thematically and not literally to the above, for neither text appears in the liturgy. The thematic link is the shared prominence of prophecy and Christomimesis. For example, the Gospel opened by both Philip and Margaret is taken from John 15:26: "Cum venerit Paraclitus, quem ego mittam vobis a Patre, Spiritum veritatis, qui a Patre procedit, ille testimonium perhibebit de me." This is clearly a prediction of Pentecost rather than the second coming of Christ, yet it still links the new rulers to Christ, for "he (they) will bear witness to me."[74] The element of prophecy is reinforced by the "random" opening of the Gospels by both rulers, resulting in the selection of the same text.[75]

Linking the new count with Christ seems audacious at first glance, particularly given the fact that the count was neither king nor emperor, the typical rulers who invoked Christ and the prophetic tradition. But the counts of Flanders had never let the niceties of nomenclature limit dynastic ambitions, and the Burg of Bruges itself shows attempts of Flemish counts to identify with Christ. After all, the nearby chapel of St. Basil contained the relic of the Holy Blood of Christ, brought from the Holy Land, according to legend, by Count Dirk of Alsace. It became the most venerated

[72] Ibid., p. 268. [73] Kantorowicz, "The King's Advent," pp. 52–53.

[74] Thus this passage of John is strikingly similar to the "Ecce mitto angelum meum . . ." text, for it also constructs a "two-fold" role for the ruler. Either he is the one sent by God to bear witness to Christ, or, more likely, the Holy Spirit precedes and directs the ruler as the anointed of God. See Kantorowicz, "The King's Advent," pp. 52–53.

[75] Divination by opening a book was a time-honored form of fortune-telling throughout the Middle Ages and beyond. See Richard Kieckhefer, *Magic in the Middle Ages* (Cambridge, 1989), p. 88.

relic in Bruges and perhaps in all of West Flanders.[76] A second example of imitation of Christ was even closer at hand – Charles the Good, whom Galbert described as "devout and strong, Catholic, the supporter of the poor, the protector, after God, of the churches of God, the defender of the fatherland, and one in whom the residue of earthly authority assumed the form of ruling well and the substance of serving God."[77]

The sights and sounds within the church also take up the twin themes of Advent and prophecy. The music for the antiphon "Honor, Virtus" does not survive, but its text is drawn from Apocalypse 7:12, itself part of a hymn of praise to God the Father in the presence of "the lamb."[78] An explicit link with the most visionary and prophetic book of the Bible, describing a scene with striking parallels with what was taking place in St. Donatian's that day, is extremely suggestive. The sight of all the "great candelabra being lit as on Christmas Day" forms the visual link of the ceremony with the holy day that is the fulfillment of the Advent season. Thus van der Eeke makes quite explicit the juxtaposition of an earthly ruler and the Redeemer. And although van der Eeke omits the text of the motet struck up by the organist as a recessional, most likely it too was linked thematically with Advent.[79]

Unfortunately, we know nothing about the prayers or collect "traditionally read at the Joyous Advent," for the library of St. Donatian's disappeared during the French occupation of Bruges in 1793.[80] Lost as well was the *liber statutorum*, or book of privileges, containing the oath sworn by the ducal pair. It is probable that the texts quoted at length in Galbert's chronicle of 1127 were contained in this book. If that is true, Philip and Margaret swore to confirm and honor the privileges of the church, especially in the election of the provost.[81] The book must have been a beautiful object in

[76] The identification of the Holy Blood with Thierry of Alsace is certainly false, and most historians now believe that the relic was plundered from Constantinople during the Fourth Crusade and brought to Bruges in the early thirteenth century. This count did, however, rebuild his palace chapel (St. Basil's), creating four chaplaincies attached to the chapter of St. Donatian's. See van Houtte, *Geschiedenis*, pp. 247–48.

[77] Ross, *Murder of Charles the Good*, p. 81.

[78] The scene is one where all the angels stand before the divine throne and chant a hymn of praise to God: "dicentes: Amen. Benedictio, et claritas, et sapientia, et gratiarum actio, honor, et virtus, et fortitudo Deo nostro, in saecula saeculorum. Amen." This is all done "in conspectu Agni."

[79] We are also told that both the choir and the church bells joined the organ in the unnamed motet. It is thus possible that the motet was to begin with solo organ and then swell to a crescendo of choir and bells, much like a medieval "1812 Overture." See Strohm, *Music in Medieval Bruges*, p. 4, for the Netherlandish art of motet composition employing church bells.

[80] On the library of St. Donatian's Albert Derolez, "De bibliotheek van het Kapittel van Sint-Donatiaan te Brugge in de Middeleeuwen," *Koninklijke Zuidnederlandse Maatschappij voor Taal- en Letterkunde en Geschiedenis* 15 (1961), 159–174.

[81] Ross, *Murder of Charles the Good*, p. 202.

its own right, for it had recently been rebound and contained ornamented rubrics and illuminations. If the manuscript was typical of those that have survived from Bruges workshops of the time, it would have more than held its own in that opulent company.[82]

Finally, it was the turn of Philip and Margaret to make an offering to the church, and the language used to describe this maintained the tone of solemn liturgy. Philip "processed" to the main altar and did not "give" (*dare*) his gift of gold but "sacrificed" (*immolare*) it. This very biblical verb of consecration was also used to describe Margaret's gift of the single gold piece. The worth of this gift was noted down to the very type of coin given, for van der Eeke indicated that of the twenty-eight gold pieces, eight were moutons, and their total value amounted to thirty "shields" or écus.[83] This is extraordinary precision for a short chronicle entry, pointing out in effect that some of the coins were obsolete and giving their equivalent value in current coin. As a gauge of financial anxiety, such minute attention to money is eloquent.

There is one notable omission in van der Eeke's description of Philip the Bold's entry: the oath sworn by Bruges's burghers to their new count. Galbert's chronicle shows a close identification of the privileges of St. Donatian's with those of the urban *coniuratio* or commune. In fact, Galbert's account of William Clito's entry not only gives a detailed description of the privileges of the church, but also summarizes the "little charter of agreement" ("chartula conventionis") between the new count and the citizens of Bruges. This document was the foundation charter for Bruges as a commune, granting rights of self government and freedom from the toll.[84] William Clito simply swore to uphold both the liberties of the church and the newly granted privileges of the Brugeois. By 1384, a new count swore two oaths, one in St. Donatian's, the second on the Burg square in front of the *stadhuis*, facing St. Donatian's. We know from the charter of confirmation issued by Philip that he and Margaret left the church and proceeded to the square, where they both received the oath of fealty from all gathered there and took an oath themselves. Although the oath sworn by the ducal couple on that day does not survive, it was probably similar to that sworn at Ypres: "We swear that we will be good and loyal lords of Ypres and her citizens, and that the said city of Ypres and our subjects there will be kept, defended and

[82] In the church accounts of 1379 (BAB, St. Donaas, G/2, 1379, f. 24v): "item pro libro statutorum capituli religando et aliquibus scripturis ac picturis in eo factis £6."

[83] For the mouton see chapter 4; they were Flemish gold coins struck by Louis of Male from June 1356 to March 1364, but remained in circulation far longer.

[84] Ross, *Murder of Charles the Good*, p. 203.

secure in their laws, privileges, freedoms, liberty; and good customs and usages, with God's help and all the saints of paradise."[85]

We do not know what happened immediately before or after the ceremonies van der Eeke describes. If the example of later tradition holds true for 1384, then the ducal party entered the city through the Kruispoort, where it was met by delegations of aldermen and other important burghers, and the procession from St. Donatian's.[86] Townspeople no doubt thronged the streets, although relatively few could have squeezed into either the Burg or St. Donatian's church. Feasting and drinking probably followed the last oath, but it is unlikely that wine flowed from the public fountains as it would in future festivities. The church of St. Donatian's, however, presented the count and countess with wine worth £28 gro., a considerable sum, and the city government no doubt followed suit.[87]

More important than the depth of drink were the long-term implications of this Advent ceremony for the new dynasty of Burgundian counts and its relations with the Brugeois. Did it fulfill the hopes of those involved? For Philip the Bold the outcome of his Joyous Entry into Bruges was heartening. He had succeeded in replacing his late father-in-law in the affections of the Brugeois; he had furthered his policy of isolating rebel Ghent from the rest of Flanders, a policy that would finally bring Ghent to negotiate a treaty with the count; and he had established contacts within the Bruges community that would aid him in the future. For all these reasons, Bruges became a place where the Burgundian counts would often visit, sometimes dwell, and always draw upon the city's wealth of money, luxury goods, and specialized talent.

The successful if at times tempestuous marriage of Bruges and the Burgundian dynasty was in some ways predictable, given the city's social and economic patterns of the fourteenth century. One of these "patterns" was the popularity of jousts and other forms of chivalric display as part of civic-sponsored events. As Peter Arnade has argued, the meshing of civic and courtly ritual was a crucial aspect of Burgundian statecraft, and

85 Bartier and van Nieuwenhuysen, *Ordonnances de Philippe le Hardi*, pp. 21–22.

86 This was the route followed by the procession at the wedding of Charles the Bold and Margaret of York; see Alfons Dewitte, "Twee keer blijde intrede te Brugge: 1468, 3 Juli, Margareta Van York; 1515, 18 en 22 April, Karel Prince des Hespaignes," *Biekorf* 89 (1989), 250–261, esp. 260, and Peter Arnade, *Realms of Ritual: Burgundian Ceremony and Civic Life in Late Medieval Ghent* (Ithaca: Cornell University Press, 1996), p. 27.

87 BAB, St. Donaas, G/2, 1384, f. 6v. Although the Bruges city accounts do not survive for 1384, in 1385, after the peace accord with Ghent, Philip and Margaret were honored with a festive escort into the city and a gift of wine worth £5 gro. See Gilliodts-Van Severen, *Inventaire*, vol. III, p. 63. Presents of wine were frequent upon such occasions and throughout the year. They were a regular budget item in both the Ghent and Bruges city accounts. See Boone, *Geld en Macht*, pp. 92–94.

Bruges had already traveled some distance down the road to becoming, in his words, a "court" city.[88] As early as 1305, the town accounts mention "Shrove Tuesday, for jousters, burghers, and Easterlings [Germans], who jousted on the market."[89] By 1392 there was a permanent tournament society in Bruges, the "White Bear," consisting of knights and notables, who preferred to stage their tourneys on Shrove Tuesday. In 1394, a Shrove Tuesday parody of a tourney was performed at Bruges in the presence of the count himself by Jan van Hulst and his companions, who formed a brotherhood known for literary and musical activities. These men later formed the nucleus of a chamber of rhetoric, that of the Holy Ghost. So thoroughly did the chivalric ethos penetrate the upper classes of Bruges that the society of the White Bear was given a permanent meeting place in the "Poortersloge" – the house of the association of Bruges's social elite – and allowed to put their emblem on the front of the building.[90] Shooting societies, organized from the middle of the fourteenth century, also quickly evolved from their roots as adjuncts of the urban militia to gathering places for elites from both city and court.[91]

A symbol of the meshing of interests of the city and the new dynasty was the increasing importance of the annual procession of the Holy Blood as a sort of symbolic gathering place where ruler and subjects could meet. In the course of the fourteenth century the procession of the holiest of Bruges relics had become a true urban spectacle of considerable importance. Care of the relic was in the hands of the canons and provost of St. Donatian's and they organized the annual perambulation around the city's "new" walls in a common urban ritual.[92] Increased city spending on the procession points to its growing importance as a true "civic" event: a papal bull attesting to the relic's miraculous qualities was secured at city expense in 1310; city

[88] Arnade, *Realms of Ritual*, p. 13.

[89] Evelyne van den Neste, *Tournois, joutes, pas d'Armes dans les villes de Flandre à la fin du Moyen Age (1300–1486)* (Paris, 1996) p. 214.

[90] Van Houtte, *Geschiedenis*, pp. 160–161. Tournaments were not popular with townspeople in Brabant until the advent of the Burgundians; see Jan van Gerven, "War, Violence and Urban Society," in *Secretum Secretorum*, pp. 183–211, esp. pp. 200–201.

[91] Brown, "Civic Ritual," 277–299.

[92] Urban commemoration of religious feast days was common in Medieval Europe. The date of the Invention of the Cross (3 May) was also celebrated in grand style in nearby Tournai. And many English cities had similar processions on the feast of Corpus Christi. For further details see J. Dumoulin and J. Pycke, *La grande procession de Tournai* (1090–1992) (Tournai, 1992) and Miri Rubin, *Corpus Christi: The Eucharist in Late Medieval Culture* (Cambridge, 1991), pp. 164–185. Andrew Brown believes the Holy Blood procession itself dates from the completion of the walls in 1297; others have attributed it to celebrations stemming from the victory at the battle of the Golden Spurs in 1302. This may not be absolutely true, given the long residence of the relic in Bruges, but Brown is no doubt correct about the definitive form of the procession: Brown, "Civic Ritual," 281.

musicians were paid to accompany it along its route, and messengers were sent to nearby towns with invitations to attend the festivities.[93] By the middle of the century, the relic was flanked by members of the crossbow guild of St. George, who were followed by all the Bruges burgomasters, aldermen, treasurers, and employees clad in the very finest suits of clothes money could buy.[94] After 1350 the Holy Blood procession also inaugurated the fifteen days of the Bruges fair, adding numbers of visiting merchants to the throng.

Tournaments and jousts also came to be associated with this high season of civic display, which again accorded well with the tastes of the successive dukes of Burgundy.[95] The beginnings of a permanent jousting society were already apparent by the middle of the century, replacing the occasional jousts sponsored by the city and members of the foreign merchant community in the past. Bruges joined Lille as the most consistent and determined sponsor of jousts and tournaments in the Low Countries. The regularity and standardization of civic jousts becomes apparent from 1360. For two decades May jousts occurred every year, acquiring in 1376 the designation of Jousts of St. George. In 1380 they are first referred to as "feasts of the Forester," which became the name of a jousting society in Bruges.[96] From 1370 Philip the Bold attended the jousts, called l'Epinette, in Lille, and in 1375 he attended the May jousts in Bruges.[97] Philip thus established the practice of either attending or sending personal representatives to civic jousts, as well as accepting honorary membership in the tourneying societies. He was instrumental in reviving jousting in Bruges after the disruptions of the Ghent war, particularly when he joined a Bruges nobleman, John III of the Gruuthuse, in organizing a tournament pitting fifty of his men against a like number of the lord of Ghistel.[98] The efforts of the Gruuthuse family were more than matched by outlay by the city government of Bruges for the continuation of the jousting tradition.[99]

Even the commercial, financial, and manufacturing sectors of Bruges complemented the craving for chivalric display and honor so characteristic of the Burgundian dynasty and its developing state policy. As the great

[93] Ibid., 281–282; for the urban use of music and musicians, see K. Polk, "Wind Bands of Medieval Flemish Cities," *Brass and Woodwind Quarterly* 1, 2 (1966–1968), 93–113, 1–15, especially 99–100.

[94] Cloth for the procession was often named interchangeably with Easter cloth, as in SAB, SR 1335–1336, f. 51v, which records the purchase of five striped cloths purchased for the bailiff, *schouteet* and aldermen of the city for their procession garments.

[95] Brown, "Civic Ritual," 282.

[96] Van den Neste, *Tournois*, p. 253; see Brown, "Civic Ritual," 283 n. 2, for Foresters of the White Bear.

[97] Van den Neste, *Tournois*, p. 199.

[98] Brown, "Civic Ritual," 283.

[99] Brown, "Civic Ritual," 283.

entrepôt of northern Europe, Bruges offered nearly every imported luxury and its own workshops produced luxury cloth, finely made and tailored leather, furs and clothing, jewelry, the saddles, weapons, and armor necessary to the chivalric life, and of course art and music to dazzle any eye or ear.[100] With an additional group of wealthy consumers, Bruges artists and artisans developed new "products" to satisfy the demand for luxury articles. Some of these were a direct result of long-established trading contacts, such as those with the German Hanse. These resulted in the steady import of amber from the shores of the Baltic in Prussia, which provided the raw material for the manufacture of rosaries, or paternosters, in Bruges workshops.[101] Artists and copyists either came to Bruges or learned their art there, with an eye to selling to a wealthy and sophisticated clientele of Bruges burghers, Burgundian courtiers, and foreign merchants. Between 1302 and 1400 the percentage of the population involved in these luxury trades increased from about 2–3 percent to 7 percent.[102] The market in panel painting, manuscript illumination, and other objects apparently developed slowly but surely between 1380 and 1420; by the time of Philip's grandson and namesake, Philip the Good, Bruges was justly famous for the quantity and quality of its art objects.[103]

The bankers and merchants of Bruges also did their part. As discussed in chapter 4, the wars against the pagans in Prussia reached their height between 1350 and 1400: many knights from the west journeyed east to join the crusade. Bruges, as the largest Hanseatic outpost in the west, became the natural point of embarkation and financial center of the Prussian crusade. Members of the aristocracy, both lay and ecclesiastical, called in Bruges for other reasons as well. Abbots of significant West Flemish monasteries, notably that of Ter Duinen, built residences in town. Other nobles sent their purchasing agents to acquire rare goods. And we saw in chapter 4 that the quest to borrow money also brought aristocrats and their agents to Bruges.[104] Among these groups were some of the earliest and greatest collectors of Flemish art and manuscripts.[105]

100 Strohm, *Music in Bruges*, pp. 11, 18; Blockmans and Prevenier, *Burgundian Netherlands*, pp. 88–89.

101 J. A. van Houtte, "Ambernijverheid en paternostermakers te Brugge gedurende de XIVe en XVe eeuw', *ASEB* 82 (1939), 149–184, reprinted in *Essays on Medieval and Early Modern Economy and Society* (Leuven, 1977), pp. 49–79. The Hanse merchant Hildebrand Veckinhusen shipped a considerable quantity of amber rosaries to Venice in the early fifteenth century ibid., 57 and n. 48.

102 Van Houtte, *Geschiedenis*, p. 141.

103 Jean C. Wilson, *Painting in Bruges at the Close of the Middle Ages: Studies in Society and Visual Culture* (University Park, Penn., 1998), pp. 13–16.

104 See above chapter 4, pp. 140–141.

105 One of the most famous collectors of manuscripts in the fifteenth century was the abbott of Ter Duinen, Johannes Crabbe, who was not only a fervent collector but rebuilt and considerably

Philip the Bold also began the dynastic pattern of residing in Bruges, although it was Philip the Good who made Bruges a favorite residence. Already by 1396, the apartments of Louis of Male in the city had been expanded into a much grander palace, a notable departure from the neglect during Philip the Good's father-in-law's time.[106] Philip enlarged and remodeled this "Prinsenhof" in 1429 and founded the Order of the Golden Fleece there a year later. Charles the Bold completed work on the complex in preparation for his marriage to Margaret of York in 1468. All this building activity was both earlier and more extensive than was the case in most other Flemish cities, with the possible exception of Lille.[107] The large ducal compound was rivaled if not in size, in opulence by buildings of notable Bruges burghers, Burgundian courtiers, and foreign merchant communities. As a result, the fifteenth century became a great century of urban residential architecture and nearly all the surviving medieval private houses date from this time.[108]

Philip the Bold and his successors also continued Louis of Male's custom of drawing upon the financial talent of the Bruges merchant community. We have already seen his use of notable Bruges money changers, brokers, and merchants from the 1340s. The Burgundians made such recruiting commonplace as a way to fill their expanding bureaucracies.[109] Most famous were the grand men of finance who combined Italian financial acumen with long residence in Bruges. Thus Philip the Bold made much use of the skills of Dino Rapondi, the Lucchese merchant banker, and later those of Tommaso Portinari, manager of the Bruges branch of the Medici, would be similarly used.[110]

Both the city and the chapter of St. Donatian's profited from the auspicious beginning of the Burgundian dynasty. Bruges's privileges were restored nearly intact and a relatively peaceful time of cooperation with

expanded the monastery's urban retreat along the Potterierei; see Noël Geirnaert, "Brugge en het Europese geestesleven in de middeleeuwen," in *Brugge en Europa*, esp. pp. 246–248.

106 Besides damage caused during the Ghent-led conquest, the comital residence had been structurally unsound in the 1370s, requiring some extensive repair; see fragments of two accounts kept in ARA, RR 1024, September 1377–January 1378.

107 Van Houtte, *Geschiedenis*, p. 160.

108 For detailed descriptions and plans of such urban palaces as the Gruuthuus, see Devliegher, *Maisons à Bruges*; for Burgundian residences in cities see Marc Boone and Thérèse de Hemptinne, "Espace urbain et ambitions princières: les présences matérielles de l'autorité princière dans le Gand médiéval (12e siècle–1540)," in Werner Paravicini (ed.), *Zeremoniell und Raum: Symposium der Residenzen-Kommission der Akademie der Wissenschaften in Göttingen* (Sigmaringen, 1997), pp. 279–304, for Ghent and Werner Paravicini, "Die Residenzen der Herzöge von Burgund," in H. Patze and Werner Paravicini (eds.), *Fürstliche Residenzen im spätmittelalterlichen Europa* (Sigmaringen, 1991), pp. 207–249, esp. 224–226.

109 In general see Blockmans and Prevenier, *Low Countries under Burgundian Rule*, pp. 184–193.

110 De Roover, *Money, Banking and Credit*, pp. 20–21.

the Burgundians began and continued until the revolt of 1436–1438.[111] Of course the interests of the city and the counts could never be identical, particularly where relations with England were concerned; yet to an unusual extent, Philip the Bold worked to restore Bruges's damaged commerce, and the city rewarded him and his successors with financial subsidies. Canonries in St. Donatian's became a much coveted source of prebends with which the Burgundians rewarded their clerics, and in turn the chapter enjoyed the favor of the Burgundians throughout the fifteenth century, particularly as the scene of Philip the Good's funeral. The other collegiate church, Onze-Lieve-Vrouw, also enjoyed ducal favor as the burial site of Mary of Burgundy.

To a remarkable degree the hopes of 1384 were fulfilled as the Burgundian period commenced in Bruges, and, almost as a sort of musical accompaniment, the traditional ceremony as described by Peter van der Eeke was repeated at the Joyous Entry of each successive Burgundian prince.[112] The successful continuity, from Galbert's time and before down to the current count of Flanders, was always made manifest. The joining of past to present, memory to expectation, heaven to earth, all accomplished in the "Adventus Iocundus," remained crucial to both count and people. Bruges was on its way to becoming a Burgundian city.

[111] Part of the ceremony of 1384 was a confirmation of the city privileges as granted by Louis of Male in 1358; the text is printed in full by Gilliodts-van Severen, *Inventaire*, vol. III, p. 1. Philip also worked to bring back the foreign merchants who had fled Bruges during the Ghent war; see van Nieuwenhuysen, *Les finances du Duc de Bourgogne*, pp. 168–169 and in general, Nicholas, *Medieval Flanders*, pp. 320–322. On the revolt of 1436–38, see Dumolyn, *De Brugse Opstand van 1436–1438*.

[112] Soly, "Plechtige intochten," 342–360.

Select bibliography

PRIMARY SOURCES

UNPUBLISHED

Bruges, Archief van het OCMW

Dis Sint-Anna
    Charters
Dis Onze-Lieve-Vrouw
    Charters
Dis Sint-Gillis
    Charters
Dis Sint-Salvators
    Charters
Dis Sint-Walburga
    Charters
Sint-Janshospitaal
    Charters
    Accounts

Bruges, Bischoppelijk Archief

Sint-Donaas
    A251–252, Foundations
    A47–49, Acta Capituli
    D40, Testaments and foundations
    G2, G5 Accounts
Sint-Salvator
    S728–729 Charters

Bruges, Rijksarchief

Découvertes, 256
Onze-Lieve-Vrouwkerk, Charters
Ambachten, Cartulary of the fishmongers' guild
Oorkonden met Blauwe Nummers

Bruges, Stadsarchief

99. Politieke oorkonden, charters, first series
114. Wetsvernieuwingen, 1363–1374
216 Stadsrekeningen, city accounts, 1332–1390
271. Confiscatierekeningen
305. Koopmansboeken

Bruges, Stadsbibliotheek

MS 437 "Chronicke van Vlaenderen"

Brussels, Algemeen Rijksarchief/Archives Générales du Royaume

Rekenkamer/Chambre de Comptes
#1072–1074 Book of Fiefs
Rolrekeningen/Comptes en rouleaux, #999–1038
Accounts #13675–8, 48651–53
"Trésor de Flandre"
Charters

PRINTED

Bartier, John and Andrée Van Nieuwenhuysen (eds.). *Ordonnances de Philippe le Hardi, de Marguerite de Male et de Jean sans Peur*. Brussels: Recueil des Ordonnances des Pays-Bas, 1965.
Berlière, D. Ursmer. *Suppliques de Clément VI (1342–1352)*. Rome, 1906.
Suppliques d'Urbain V (1362–1370). Rome, 1914.
Caenegem, R. C. van and Ludo Milis. "Kritische uitgave van de 'Grote Keure' van Filips van de Elzas, graaf van Vlaanderen, voor Gent en Brugge (1165–1177)." *BCRH* 143 (1977), 207–257.
Campbell, Bruce A. *Encomium Emmae Reginae*. London: Royal Historical Society, 1949.
Despars, J. N. *Cronijcke van den Lande ende Graefscepe van Vlaendre*, ed. J. de Jonghe, 3 vols. Bruges and Rottedam, 1839–1842.
Espinas, Georges and Henri Pirenne. *Documents relatifs à la draperie de Valenciennes*. Paris: Société d'Histoire du Droit des Pays Flamands, 1931.
Recueil de documents relatifs à l'histoire de l'industrie drapière en Flandre, 5 vols. Brussels: Commission Royale d'Histoire, 1906–1966.
Froissart, Jean. *Chroniques*, ed. Gaston Raynaud, 15 vols. Paris: La Société de l'Histoire de France, 1897.
Galliard, J. *Inscriptions funéraires et monumentales de la Flandre occidentale, avec des données historiques et généalogiques*, 3 vols. Bruges, 1861–1866.
Oeuvres de Froissart, publiées avec les variantes des divers manuscrits, ed. Baron Kervyn de Lettenhove, 25 vols. Brussels: V. Devaux et Cie, 1867–1877, reprinted Osnabrück, 1967.

Gessler, Jean. *Het Brugsche Livre des mestiers en zijn navolgingen*, 6 vols. Bruges, 1931.

Gilliodts-van Severen, L. *Cartulaire de l'ancienne estaple de Bruges. Recueil de documents concernant le commerce interieur et maritime, les relations internationales et l'histoire economique de cette ville*. Bruges: L. de Plancke, 1904–1906.

Coutumes des pays et comté de Flandre. Coutume de la ville de Bruges. Brussels: F. Gobbaerts, 1874–1875.

"Les anciens règlements de la corporation des courtiers de Bruges." *La Flandre* 13 (1881), 145–146, 254–255.

Coutumes des Pays et Comté de Flandre: Coutume de la prévoté de Bruges, 2 vols. Brussels: F. Gobbaerts, 1887.

Inventaire des archives de la ville de Bruges, 7 vols. Bruges: E. Gailliard, 1871–1885.

Guicciardini, Lodovico. *Descrittione di tutti i Paesi Bassi, altrimenti detti Germania Inferiore*. Antwerp, 1567.

Hanham, Alison. *The Cely Letters, 1472–1488*. Oxford University Press, 1975.

Jamees, A. *Brugse poorters, opgetekend uit de stadsrekeningen*. vol. 1, 1281–1417. Handzame, Belgium: Familia et Patria, 1974.

Johnstone, Hilda. *Annales Gandenses: Annals of Ghent*. Oxford: Clarendon Press, 1985.

Limburg-Stirum, T. de. *Cartulaire de Louis de Male, comte de Flandre. Decreten van den grave Lodewyck van Vlaenderen, 1348 à 1358*. Bruges: Louis de Plancke, 1898–1901.

Luzzarreschi, Eugenio. *Libro della communità dei mercanti lucchesi in Bruges*. Milan, 1949.

Lyon, Bryce, Mary Lyon, and H. S. Lucas, *The Wardrobe book of William de Norwell: 12 July 1338 to 27 May 1340*. Brussels: Koninklijke Commissie voor Geschiedenis, 1983.

Nirrnheim, Hans. *Das Handlungsbuch Vickos von Geldersen*. Hamburg/Leipzig, 1895.

Pauw, Napoleon de. *De voorgeboden der stad Gent in de XIVe eeuw*. Ghent: C. Annoot-Braeckman, 1885.

Pegolotti, Francesco. *La pratica della mercatura*, ed. Allen Evans. Cambridge, Mass.: The Medieval Academy, 1936.

Prevenier, Walter and David Nicholas. *Gentse Stads en Baljuwsrekeningen*. Brussels: Koninklijke Commissie voor Geschiedenis, 1999.

Rider, Jeff. *Galbertus Notarius Brugensis, de Multro, Traditione, et Occisione Gloriosi Karoli Comitis Flandriarum*. Turnhout: Brepols, 1994.

Ross, J. B. *The Murder of Charles the Good*. New York: Columbia University Press, 1967.

Smet, J. J. de. *Corpus Chronicorum Flandriae*, 4 vols. Brussels: Commission Royale d'Histoire, 1837–1865.

Het Memoriaal van Simon de Rikelike, vrijlaat te St. Pieters-op-den-Dijk. Brussels: Maurice Lamertin, 1933.

Verhulst, Adriaan. "Prijzen van granen, boter en kaas te Brugge volgens de 'slag' van het Sint-Donatiaanskapittel (1348–1801)." *Dokumenten voor de Geschiedenis van prijzen en lonen in Vlaanderen en Brabant*. Edited by C. Verlinden *et al.* Bruges: De Tempel, 1965.

Warner, George. *The Libelle of Englysche Polycye*. Oxford, Clarendon Press, 1926.

Werveke, Hans van. "Bronnenmateriaal uit de Brugse stadsrekeningen betreffende de hongersnood van 1316." *BCRH* 125 (1959), 431–510.

Wyffels, Carlos and J. de Smet. *De rekeningen van de stad Brugge (1280–1319). Eerste deel (1280–1302)*. Brussels: Koninklijke Commissie voor Geschiedenis, 1965–71.

Wyffels, Carlos and André Vandewalle. *De rekeningen van de stad Brugge (1280–1319). Tweede Deel (1302–1319), eerste stuk (1302–1306)*. Brussels, Koninklijke Commissie voor Geschiedenis, 1995.

SECONDARY SOURCES

UNPUBLISHED

Auweele, Dirk van den. "Schepenbank en schepenen te Brugge (1127–1384): Bijdrage tot de studie van een gewone stedelijke rechts- en bestuursinstelling." Doctoral dissertation, University of Leuven, 1977.

Greve, Anke. "Hansen, Hosteliers und Herbergen. Studien zum Aufenthalt hansischer Kaufleute in Brügge im 14. und 15. Jahrhundert." Doctoral dissertation, University of Ghent, 1998.

PUBLISHED

Abeele, A. van den and M. Catry. *Makelaars en handelaars*. Bruges: Kamer voor Handel en Nijverheid Brugge, 1992.

Abraham-Thisse, Simone. "Les draps de Flandre en Europe du Nord: Faut-il encore parler du déclin de la draperie flamande au bas moyen-âge?" in *Drapery Production in the Late Medieval Low Countries*. Leuven and Apeldoorn: Garant, 1993, pp. 167–206.

Algemene geschiedenis der Nederlanden, 2nd edition. Haarlem: Fibula-Van Dishoeck, 1977–83.

Amman, H. "Deutschland und die Tuchindustrie Nordwesteuropas im Mittelalter." *Hansische Geschichtsblätter* 72 (1954), 1–63.

Arnade, Peter. *Realms of Ritual: Burgundian Ceremony and Civic Life in Late Medieval Ghent*. Ithaca: Cornell University Press, 1996.

Asmussen, Georg. *Die Lübecker Flandernfahrer in der zweiten Hälfte des 14. Jahrhunderts (1358–1408). Hansekaufleute in Brügge*, vol. IX. Frankfurt, New York: Peter Lang, 1999.

Auweele, Dirk van den. "De Brugse gijzelaarslijsten van 1301, 1305 en 1328: Een comparatieve analyse." *ASEB* 110 (1973), 105–167.

Bardoel, Agatha Ann. 'The Urban Uprisings at Bruges, 1280–1. Some New Findings about the Rebels and the Partisans." *RBPH* 74 (1994), 761–791.

Bartlett, Robert. *The Making of Europe: Conquest, Colonization, and Cultural Change, 950–1350*. Princeton University Press, 1993.

Bautier, R. H. "Les foires de Champagne: recherches sur une évolution historique," in *La Foire. Recueils de la Société Jean Bodin pour l'histoire comparative des institutions*, vol. v. Brussels: Editions de la Librairie Encyclopédique, 1953, pp. 133–145; republished in *Sur l'histoire économique de la France médiévale: la route, le fleuve, la foire*. Aldershot: Variorum, 1991.

Bigwood, Georges. "Gand et la circulation des grains en Flandres aux XIVe siècle." *Vierteljahrschrift für Sozial- und Wirschaftsgeschichte* 4 (1905), 397–460.

Bisthoven, B. Janssens de. "Het Kapittel van Sint-Donatiaan te Brugge," in *Sint-Donaas en de voormalige Brugse Katedraal*. Bruges: Jong Kristen Onthaal voor Toerisme, 1978, pp. 51–59.

Blanchard, Ian. "English Royal Borrowing at Antwerp, 1544–1564," in Marc Boone and Walter Prevenier (eds.), *Public and Private Finances in the Late Middle Ages*. Leuven/Apeldoorn: Garant, 1996, pp. 57–73.

Bonenfant, Paul. "L'origine des villes brabançonnes et la 'route' de Bruges à Cologne." *RBPH* 31 (1953), 399–447.

Boone, Marc. "Civitas mori potest si authoritate superioris damnetur: politieke motieven voor het bewust verwoesten van steden (14de–16de eeuw)," in *Destruction et reconstruction de villes du Moyen Age à nos jours*. Brussels: Crédit communal/Gemeentekrediet, 1999, pp. 339–368.

Geld en Macht: De Gentse stadsfinanciën èn de Bourgondische staatsvorming (1384–1453). Ghent: Verhandelingen der HMGOG, 1990.

"Geldhandel en pandbedrijf in Gent tijdens de Bourgondische periode: politieke, fiscale en sociale aspecten." *RBPH* 66 (1988), 767–791.

"L'industrie textile à Gand au bas moyen âge ou les resurrections successives d'une activité réputée moribonde," in *Drapery Production in the Late Medieval Low Countries: Markets and Strategies for Survival*. Leuven and Apeldoorn: Garant, 1993, pp. 15–58.

"Les métiers dans les villes flamandes au bas moyen âge: images normatives, réalités socio-politiques et économiques," in J.-P. Sosson and P. Lambrechts (eds.) *Les métiers au Moyen Age: Aspects économiques et sociaux*. Louvain-la-Neuve: Université Catholique de Louvain, 1994, pp. 1–21.

"Social Conflicts in the Cloth Industry of Ypres (Late 13th–Early 14th Centuries): The Cockerulle Reconsidered," in *Ypres and the Medieval Cloth Industry in Flanders*. Ypres: Instituut voor het Archeologisch Patrimonium, 1999, pp. 147–155.

"Triomferend privé-initiatief versus haperend overheidsoptreden? Over pachters van indirecte belastingen in laatmiddeleeuwse steden." *Tijdschrift voor Sociale Geschiedenis* 15 (1989), 113–138.

"Verfassungsnorm und Verwaltungswirklichkeit im spätmittelalterlichen flämischen Raum, das Beispiel Gent," in W. Ehbrecht (ed.), *Städtische Selbstverwaltungsorgane vom 14. bis 19. Jahrhundert. 21 Kolloquium des Kuratoriums für vergleichende Städtegeschichte*. Münster: Institut für vergleichende Städtegeschichte, 1990.

Boone, Marc, M. Danneel, and N. Geirnaert. "Pieter IV Adornes (1460–ca. 1496): Een Brugs Patricier in Gent." *HMGOG* new series 39 (1985), 123–145.

Boone, Marc, and Thérèse de Hemptinne. "Espace urbain et ambitions princières: les présences matérielles de l'autorité princière dans le Gand médiéval (12e siècle–1540)," in Werner Paravicini (ed.), *Zeremoniell und Raum: Symposium der Residenzen-Kommission der Akademie der Wissenschaften in Göttingen.* Sigmaringen: Akademie der Wissenschaften, 1997, pp. 279–304.

Boone, Marc, and Walter Prevenier (eds.). *Drapery Production in the Late Medieval Low Countries: Markets and Strategies for Survival (14th–16th Centuries).* Leuven and Apeldoorn: Garant, 1993.

Public and Private Finances in the Late Middle Ages. Leuven and Apeldoorn: Garant, 1996.

Blockmans, Wim and Walter Prevenier. "Poverty in Flanders and Brabant from the Fourteenth to the Mid-Sixteenth Century: Sources and Problems," in *Acta Historiae Neerlandicae* 10 (1978), 20–57.

The Promised Lands: The Low Countries under Burgundian Rule, 1369–1530. Philadelphia: University of Pennsylvania Press, 1999.

Brackett, John. "The Florentine Onestà and the Control of Prostitution, 1403–1680." *The Sixteenth Century Journal* 24 (1993), 273–300.

Brown, Andrew. "Civic Ritual: Bruges and the Counts of Flanders in the Later Middle Ages." *English Historical Review* 112 (1997), 277–299.

Brulez, Wilfred. "Brugge en Antwerpen in de 15e en 16e eeuw: een tegenstelling?" *Tijdschrift voor Geschiedenis* 83 (1970), 15–37; an abridged English version is in *Acta Historiae Neerlandicae* 6 (1973), 1–26.

Caenegem, R. C. van. *Geschiedenis van het strafprocesrecht in Vlaanderen van de XIe tot de XIVe eeuw.* Brussels, 1956.

Geschiedenis van het strafrecht in Vlaanderen van de XIde tot de XIVde eeuw. Brussels, 1954.

Childs, Wendy R. *Anglo-Castilian Trade in the later Middle Ages.* Manchester University Press, 1978.

Chorley, Patrick. "The Cloth Exports of Flanders and Northern France during the 13th Century: A Luxury Trade?" *Economic History Review* second series 40 (1987), 349–379.

Coppenolle, M. van. "Een verdwenen uitvaartgebruik: de sleutels op de put leggen." *Biekorf* 50 (1949), 3–7.

Coornaert, Emile. *Une industrie urbaine du XIVe au XVIIe siècle: L'industrie de la laine à Bergues-Saint-Winoc.* Paris: Les Presses Universitaires de France, 1930.

Coornaert, M. "Over de hydrografie van Brugge," in *Album Albert Schouteet.* Bruges: Westvlaams Verbond van Kringen voor Heemkunde, 1973, pp. 23–35.

"De middeleeuwse vestingswerken van de stad Brugge." *Het Brugs Ommeland* 31–32 (1991–1992), 177–246, 55–82.

Craeybeckx, Jan. *Un grand commerce d'importation: Les vins de France aux anciens Pays-Bas, XIIIe–XVIe siècle.* Paris: Ecole Pratique des Hautes Etudes, 1958.

Declercq, Georges. "Wanneer onstond het Sint-Donaaskapittel te Brugge?" *ASEB* 122 (1985), 245–257.

Degryse, R. "De oudste houten kranen in de Vlaamse en andere Havens (13de–16de eeuw)." *ASEB* 128 (1991), 5–46.
De Meyer, Ingrid. "De sociale strukturen te Brugge in de 14e eeuw," in W. Blockmans, I. De Meyer, J. Mertens, C. Pauwelijn, and W. Vanderpijpen (eds.), *Studiën betreffende de sociale strukturen te Brugge, Kortrijk en Gent in de 14e en 15e eeuw*. Kortrijk and Heule: Standen en Landen, 1971, pp. 7–78.
Deneweth, Heidi, and Yvette Kemel. "Een verdwenen middeleeuwse wijk tussen Koningstraat, Boomgaardstraat en Verversdijk." *Brugs Ommeland* 40 (2000), 143–168.
Derolez, Albert. "De bibliotheek van het Kapittel van Sint-Donatiaan te Brugge in de Middeleeuwen." *Koninklijke Zuidnederlandse Maatschappij voor Taal- en Letterkunde en Geschiedenis* 15 (1961), 159–174.
Derville, Alain. "Les draperies flamandes et artésiennes vers 1250–1350." *Revue du Nord* 54 (1972), 353–370.
"L'héritage des draperies médiévales." *Revue du Nord* 69 (1987), 715–724.
Des Marez, Guillaume. *La lettre de foire à Ypres au XIIIe siècle, contribution à l'étude des papiers de crédit*. Brussels: Académie Royale des Sciences, des Lettres et des Beaux-Arts de Belgique, 1901.
Despy, Guy and Adriaan Verhulst (eds.). *La fortune historiographique des thèses d'Henri Pirenne*. Brussels: Archives et Bibliothèques de Belgique, 1986.
Despy, Georges. "Bruges et les collectories pontificales de Scandinavie et de Pologne au XIVe siècle." *Bulletin de l'Institut Historique Belge de Rome* 27 (1952), 95–109.
Devliegher, Luc. *Les maisons à Bruges*. Tielt, Belgium: Lanoo, 1975.
Devliegher, Luc. *Van Waterhalle tot Provinciaal Hof*. Bruges: Marc van de Wiele, 1994.
DeVries, Kelly. *Infantry Warfare in the Early Fourteenth Century: Discipline, Tactics, and Technology*. Woodbridge, UK and Rochester, NY: Boydell, 1996.
Dewitte, Alfons. "Goud en zilversmeden in de kerkrekeningen van Sint-Donaas te Brugge, 1251–1587." *Biekorf* 76 (1975–1976), 240–241.
Dewitte, Alfons. "Twee Keer Blijde Intrede te Brugge: 1468, 3 Juli, Margareta Van York; 1515, 18 en 22 April, Karel Prince des Hespaignes." *Biekorf* 89 (1989), 250–261.
Dhondt, Jan. "De vroege topografie van Brugge." *HMGOG* new series 11 (1957), 3–30.
Dollinger, Philippe. *The German Hanse*. Stanford University Press, 1970.
Duclos, Adolphe. *Bruges, histoire et souvenirs*. Bruges, 1910, reprinted by the Vlaams Toeristenbond, 1976.
Dumolyn, Jan. "Population et structures professionnelles à Bruges aux XIVe et XVe siècles." *Revue du Nord* 31 (1999), 43–64.
Dumoulin, J. and J. Pycke. *La grande procession de Tournai (1090–1992)*. Tournai, 1992.
DuPlessis, Robert and Martha C. Howell. "Reconsidering the Early Modern Urban Economy: The Cases of Leiden and Lille." *Past and Present* 94 (1982), 49–84.
Dumon, Guy. *De oude straatnamen van Brugge. Een handleiding*. Bruges: Levend Archief, 1997.

Dupont, Guy. *Maagdenverleidsters, hoeren en speculanten: Prostitutie in Brugge tijdens de Bourgondische Periode (1385–1515)*. Bruges: Marc van de Wiele, 1996.

Eenhooghe, Dirk van. "De vroegste bakstenen huizen in Brugge." *Het Brugs Ommeland* 38 (1998), 107–128.

Espinas, Georges. "Jehan Boine Broke: Bourgeois et drapier douaisien," *Vierteljahrschrift für Sozial- und Wirtschaftsgeschichte* 2 (1904), 383–412.

Farmer, Sharon. "Down and Out and Female in Thirteenth Century Paris." *American Historical Review* 103 (1998), 345–372.

Fryde, E. B. "Anglo-Italian Commerce in the Fifteenth Century: Some Evidence about Profits and the Balance of Trade." *RBPH* 50 (1972), 346–355.

"Some Business Transactions of York Merchants." Reprinted in *Studies in Medieval Trade and Finance*. London: Hambledon Press, 1983, XI.

William de la Pole, Merchant and King's Banker. London: Hambledon Press, 1988.

Wool Accounts of William de la Pole, A Study of Some Aspects of the English Wool Trade at the Start of the Hundred Years' War. York: Borthwick Papers #25, 1964.

Fujii, Y., "Draperie urbaine et draperie rurale dans les Pays-Bas méridionaux au bas moyen âge: une mise au point des recherches après H. Pirenne." *Journal of Medieval History* 16 (1990), 77–97.

Funck-Brentano, Frantz. *Les origines de la guerre de cent ans. Philippe le Bel en Flandre*. Paris: H. Champion, 1897.

Galvin, Michael. *The Poor Tables of Bruges, 1270–1477*. Ann Arbor: University Microfilms, 1998.

Ganshof, F.-L. *Etude sur le développement des villes entre Loire et Rhin au Moyen Age*. Paris and Brussels: Presses Universitaires de France, 1943.

Geerts, Katelijne. *De spelende mens in de Boergondische Nederlanden*. Bruges: Marc van de Wiele, 1987.

Geirnaert, Noël. "Het archief van de Familie Adornes en van de Jeruzalemstichting." *De Leiegouw* 28 (1986), 289–297.

Geirnaert, Noël. *Het archief van de Familie Adornes en de Jeruzalemstichting te Brugge*, 2 vols. Bruges: Stadsarchief, 1987.

Goldschmidt, E. Ph. "Le voyage de Hieronimus Monetarius à travers la France, 17 septembre 1494–14 avril 1495." *Humanisme et Renaissance* 6 (1939), 55–75, 198–220, 324–348, 529–539.

Goris, J. A. *Les colonies marchandes méridionales à Anvers de 1488 à 1567*. Leuven: Librairie Universitaire, 1925.

Greilsammer, Myriam. *L'envers du tableau: mariage et maternité en Flandre médiévale*. Paris: A. Colin, 1990.

Greve, Anke. "Brügger Hosteliers und hansische Kaufleute: ein Netzwerk vorteilhafter Handelsbeziehungen oder programmierte Interessenkonflikte?" in *Beiträge der Internationalen Tagung in Brügge*. Frankfurt am Main: Peter Lang, 2000, pp. 151–172.

"Gast und Gastgeber: Hansekaufleute und Hosteliers in Brügge im 14. und 15. Jahrhundert," in V. Hem and A. Nedkvitne (eds.), *Norwegen und die Hanse*.

Wirtschaftliche und kulturelle Aspekte im europäischen Vergleich. Frankfurt a. M.: Peter Lang, 1994, pp. 95–107.

"Hanseatic Merchants: Banking Customs in 14th Century Bruges', in *Public and Private Finances in the Late Middle Ages*, ed. M. Boone and W. Prevenier. Leuven and Apeldoorn: Garant, 1996, pp. 3–13.

"Jacob Sconebergh and his Short Career as a Hosteller in Fourteenth-Century Bruges," in W. Blockmans, M. Boone, and Thérèse de Hemptinne (eds.), *Secretum Scriptorum: Liber Alumnorum Walter Prevenier*. Leuven and Apeldoorn: Garant, 1999, pp. 213–224.

"Vreemdelingen in de stad: Integratie of uitsluiting?" in M. Carlier, A. Greve, W. Prevenier, and P. Stabel (eds.), *Core and Periphery in Late Medieval Urban Society*. Leuven and Apeldoorn: Garant, 1997, pp. 153–163.

Gysseling, M. "Etymologie van Brugge." *Handelingen van de Koninklijke Commissie voor Toponymie en Dialectologie* 18 (1944), 69–79.

"Een nieuwe etymologie van Brugge." *Naamkunde*, 3 (1971), 1–4.

Hanawalt, Barbara A. *Women and Work in Preindustrial Europe*. Bloomington: Indiana University Press, 1986.

Hanham, Alison. *The Celys and Their World*. Cambridge University Press, 1985.

Häpke, Rudolf. *Brügges Entwicklung zum mittelalterlichen Weltmarkt*. Berlin: K. Curtius, 1908.

Herlihy, David. *Opera Muliebria: Women and Work in Medieval Europe*. New York: McGraw-Hill, 1990.

Herwaarden, J. van. "The War in the Low Countries," in J. J. N. Palmer (ed.), *Froissart: Historian*. Totowa, NJ: Boydell Press, 1981, pp. 101–117.

Higounet, Charles. "De La Rochelle à Torun: aventures de barons en Prusse et relations économiques (1363–64)." *Le Moyen Age* 69 (1963), 529–540.

Holbach, Rudolpf. "Some Remarks on the Role of 'Putting-out' in Flemish and Northwest European Cloth Production," in Marc Boone and Walter Prevenier (eds.), *Drapery Production in the Late Medieval Low Countries: Markets and Strategies for Survival (14th–16th Centuries)*. Leuven and Apeldoorn: Garant, 1993, pp. 207–250.

Holbach, Rudolf. "Brügge, die Hanse und der Handel mit Tuch," in N. Jörn, W. Paravicini, and H. Wernicke (eds.), *Hansekaufleute in Brügge, Teil 4: Beiträge der Internationalen Tagung in Brügge, April 1996*. Frankfurt am Main: Peter Lang, 2000, pp. 183–203.

Howell, Martha. "Fixing Movables: Gifts by Testament in Late Medieval Douai." *Past and Present* 150 (1996), 3–45.

The Marriage Exchange: Property, Social Place, and Gender in Cities of the Low Countries, 1300–1550. University of Chicago Press, 1998.

"Weathering Crisis, Managing Change: The Emergence of a New Socioeconomic Order in Douai at the End of the Middle Ages," in *Drapery Production in the Late Medieval Low Countries: Markets and Strategies for Survival (14th–16th Centuries)*. Leuven and Apeldoorn: Garant, 1993, pp. 85–118.

Women, Production, and Patriarchy in Late Medieval Cities. University of Chicago Press, 1986.

Houtte, J. A. van. "Ambernijverheid en paternostermakers te Brugge gedurende de XIVe en XVe eeuw." *ASEB* 82 (1939): 149–184, reprinted in *Essays on Medieval and Early Modern Economy and Society*. University of Leuven Press, 1977.

"Bruges et Anvers, marchés nationaux ou internationaux du XIVe au XVIe siècle?" *Revue du Nord* 34 (1952), 89–108.

Bruges, Essai d'histoire urbaine. Brussels: La Renaissance du Livre, 1967.

"Les courtiers au moyen âge: origine et caractéristiques d'une institution commerciale en Europe Occidentale." *Revue Historique du Droit Français et Etranger* series 4, 15 (1936), 105–114.

An Economic History of the Low Countries 800–1800. London: Weidenfeld and Nicolson, 1977.

De geschiedenis van Brugge. Tielt, Belgium: Lannoo, 1982.

"Herbergswesen und Gastlichkeit im mittelalterlichen Brügge," in H. C. Peyer (ed.), *Gastfreundschaft, Taverne und Gasthaus im Mittelalter*. Munich and Vienna, 1983, pp. 177–187.

"Makelaars en waarden te Brugge van de 13e tot de 16e eeuw." *Bijdragen voor de Geschiedenis der Nederlanden* 5 (1950), 1–30, 177–197. Reprinted in *Essays on Medieval and Early Modern Economy and Society*, pp. 19–47.

"The Rise and Decline of the Market of Bruges." *Economic History Review* 2nd series 19 (1966), 29–47.

Huizinga, Johan. *Herfsttij der Middeleeuwen*. Groningen: Wolters-Nijhoff, 1919; *Autumn of the Middle Ages*, trans. Rodney J. Payton and Ulrich Mammitzsch. Chicago: University of Chicago Press, 1996.

Hunt, Edwin S. and James M. Murray. *A History of Business in Medieval Europe, 1200–1550*. Cambridge University Press.

Jannssens, A. "Brugse bevolkingsaantal in 1477," in *Van Middeleeuwen tot heden. Bladeren door Brugse kunst en Geschiedenis*. Bruges, 1983, pp. 29–35.

Jenks, Stuart. "War die Hanse kreditfeindlich?" *Vierteljahrschrift für Sozial- und Wirtschaftsgeschichte* 69 (1982), 305–338.

Jordan, William C. *The Great Famine: Northern Europe in the Early Fourteenth Century*. Princeton University Press, 1996.

Kantorowicz, Ernst. "The King's Advent and the Enigmatic Panels in the Doors of Santa Sabina," in *Selected Studies*. Locust Valley, NY: J. J. Augustin, 1965.

Karras, Ruth M. *Common Women: Prostitution and Sexuality in Medieval England*. New York: Oxford University Press, 1996

"The Regulation of Brothels in Later Medieval England." *Signs* 14 2 (1989), 399–443.

Kermode, Jenny. *Medieval Merchants: York, Beverley and Hull in the Later Middle Ages*. Cambridge University Press, 1998.

Kittell, Ellen E. *From Ad Hoc to Routine. A Case Study in Medieval Bureaucracy*. Philadelphia: University of Pennsylvania Press, 1991.

"Guardianship over Women in Medieval Flanders: A Reappraisal," *Journal of Social History* 31 (1998), 897–930.

Koch, A. C. F. "Brugge's topografische ontwikkeling tot in de 12e eeuw." *ASEB* 99 (1962), 5–67.

Krueger, Hilmar C. "The Genoese Exportation of Northern Cloths to Mediterranean Ports, Twelfth Century." *RBPH* 65 (1987), 722–750.
Krüger, Klaus and Werner Paravicini. *Hansekaufleute in Brügge: Teil 1: Die Brügger Steuerlisten 1360–1390*. Frankfurt am Main: Peter Lang, 1992.
Laurent, Henri. *Un grand commerce d'exportation au moyen âge. La draperie des Pays-Bas en France et dans les pays méditerranéens (XIIe–XVe siècle)*. Paris, 1935.
Leloux, Herman. "Kirche und Caritas im Leben der Genossenschaft des Deutschen Kaufmanns zu Brügge." *Hansische Geschichtsblätter* 91 (1973), 34–45.
Lexikon des Mittelalters, ed. Robert Auty Munich and Zurich: Artemis-Verlag, 1977–1999.
Lloyd, T. H. *The English Wool Trade in the Middle Ages*. Cambridge University Press, 1977.
Lowyck, A. "Schepenenlijsten van de stad Brugge." *Ons Heem* 17 (1962–1963), 213–216, 26–28, 43–48.
Lucas, H. S. "Diplomatic Relations between England and Flanders from 1329 to 1336." *Speculum* 11 (1936), 59–87.
"The Great European Famine of 1315, 1316, and 1317." *Speculum* 5 (1930), 343–377.
Maréchal, Griet. *De sociale en politieke gebondenheid van het Brugse hospitaalwezen in de Middeleeuwen*. Kortrijk and Heule: Standen en Landen, 1978.
"De Zwarte Dood te Brugge (1349–1351)," *Biekorf* 80 (1980), 377–392.
Marechal, Joseph. *Bijdrage tot de geschiedenis van het bankwezen te Brugge*. Bruges: De Anjelier, 1955.
"Le départ de Bruges des marchands étrangers (xve et xvie siècles)." *ASEB* 88 (1951), 26–74.
Europese aanwezigheid te Brugge: De vreemde kolonies (XIVde–XIXde eeuw). Bruges: Genootschap voor Geschiedenis, 1985.
Geschiedenis van de Brugse Beurs. Bruges: De Anjelier, 1949.
Inventaris van het Archief der Proosdij van Sint-Donaas te Brugge. Brussels, 1960.
Masschaele, James. "Transport Costs in Medieval England." *Economic History Review* 46, 2 (1993), 266–279.
Meijers, E. M. *Het Ligurische Erfrecht in de Nederlanden*, 3 vols. Harlem: H. D. Tjeenk Willink & zoon, 1929–1936.
Mertens, Jacques. "De economische en sociale toestand van de opstandelingen uit het Brugse Vrije wier goederen na de slag bij Cassel (1328) verbeurd verklaard werden." *RBPH* 47 (1969), 1131–1153.
Mertens, Jacques. "Twee (Wevers)opstanden te Brugge." *ASEB* 110 (1973), 5–20.
Melis, Frederigo. 'La diffusione nel Mediterraneo occidentale dei panni di Wervicq e delle altre città delle Lys attorno al 1400," in *Studi in onore di Amintore Fanfani*. Milan: Dott. A. Giuffrè, 1962, pp. 234–243.
Meulepas, P. "De Predikheeren te Brugge." *Biekorf* 45 (1939), 233–234.
Mirot, Leon. 'Forteguerra Forteguerra et sa succession'. *Bibliothèque de l'Ecole des Chartes* 96 (1935), 308–309.

Munro, John H. "Bruges and the Abortive Staple in English Cloth: An Incident in the Shift of Commerce from Bruges to Antwerp in the Late Fifteenth Century." *RBPH* 44 (1966), 1137–59; reprinted in *Textiles, Towns, and Trade*.

"Cloth Manufacture and Trade," in P. Szarmach, M. T. Tavormina, and J. T. Rosenthal (eds.). *Medieval England: An Encyclopedia*. New York: Garland, 1998, pp. 194–197.

"The 'Industrial Crisis' of the English Textile Towns, c. 1290–c. 1330." *Thirteenth-Century England* 7 (1999), 133–135.

"Industrial Transformations in the North-West European Textile Trades, c. 1290–1340: Economic Progress or Economic Crisis?" in Bruce M. S. Campbell (ed.), *Before the Black Death. Studies in the 'Crisis' of the Early Fourteenth Century*. Manchester University Press, 1991, pp. 110–148.

"The Medieval Scarlet and the Economics of Sartorial Splendour," in N. B. Harte and K. G. Ponting (eds.), *Cloth and Clothing in Medieval Europe: Essays in Memory of Professor E. M. Carus-Wilson*. London: Heinemann Educational Books, Pasold Research Fund, 1983, pp. 13–70.

"The Origin of the English 'New Draperies': The Resurrection of an Old Flemish Industry, 1270–1570," in N. B. Harte (ed.), *The New Draperies in the Low Countries and England, 1300–1800*. New York: Oxford University Press, 1997, pp. 35–127.

"Textiles as Articles of Consumption in Flemish Towns, 1330–1575." *Bijdragen tot de Geschiedenis* 81 (1998), 275–288.

"Textile Technology," in Joseph Strayer (ed.), *Dictionary of the Middle Ages*, 26 vols. (New York, 1982–1989), vol. XI, pp. 693–711.

Textiles, Towns, and Trade: Essays in the Economic History of Late-Medieval England and the Low Countries. Aldershot, UK: Variorum, 1994.

Wool, Cloth and Gold: The Struggle for Bullion in Anglo-Burgundian Trade, 1340–1478. University of Toronto Press, 1972.

Murray, James M. "Cloth, Banking and Finance in Medieval Bruges," in John H. Munro and Erik Aerts (eds.), *Textiles in the Low Countries in European Economic History*. University of Leuven Press, 1990, pp. 24–31.

"The Liturgy of the Count's Advent in Bruges, from Galbert to Van Eyck," in B. Hanawalt and K. Reyerson (eds.), *City and Spectacle in Medieval Europe*. Minneapolis, 1994, pp. 137–152.

"Merchant Account Books in Fourteenth-Century Flanders," in N. Jörn, D. Kattinger, and H. Wernicke (eds.), *"Kopet Uns Werk by Tyden": Beiträge zur hansischen und preußischen Geschichte; Festschrift für Walter Stark zum 75. Geburtstag*. Schwerin: Helms Verlag, 1999, pp. 27–31.

"Moneychanging and Exchange in 14th-century Bruges," in N. Jörn, W. Paravicini, and H. Wernicke (eds.), *Hansekaufleute in Brügge, Teil 4: Beiträge der Internationalen Tagung in Brügge April 1996*, pp. 139–149.

Notarial Instruments in Flanders between 1280–1452. Brussels: Koninklijke Commissie voor Geschiedenis, 1995.

"Of Nodes and Networks: Bruges and the Infrastructure of Trade in Fourteenth-Century Europe," in P. Stabel, B. Blondé, and A. Greve (eds.), *International Trade in the Low Countries*. Leuven and Apeldoorn: Garant, 2000.

Mus, O. "Het aandeel van de Ieperlingen in de engelse wolexport, 1280–1330," in *Prisma van de Geschiedenis van Ieper*. Tielt, Belgium: Lannoo, 1974, pp. 332–355

"De Brugse Compagnie Despars." *ASEB*, 101(1964), 5–118.

Neste, Evelyne van den. *Tournois, joutes, pas d'Armes dans les villes de Flandre à la fin du Moyen Age* (1300–1486). Paris: Ecole des Chartes, 1996.

Nicholas, David. "Crime and Punishment in Fourteenth-Century Ghent." *RBPH* 48 (1970), 289–334, 1141–1176.

The Domestic Life of a Medieval City: Women, Children, and the Family in Fourteenth-Century Ghent. Lincoln and London: University of Nebraska Press, 1985.

"Economic Reorientation and Social Change in Fourteenth-Century Flanders." *Past and Present* 70 (1976), 3–29.

"The English Trade at Bruges in the Last Years of Edward III." *Journal of Medieval History* 5 (1979), 23–61.

The Growth of the Medieval City. New York and London: Longman, 1997.

The Later Medieval City. London and New York: Longman, 1997.

Medieval Flanders. London/New York: Longman, 1992.

Metamorphosis of a Medieval City: Ghent in the Age of the Arteveldes. Lincoln and London: University of Nebraska Press, 1987.

"Of Poverty and Primacy: Demand, Liquidity and the Flemish Economic Miracle, 1050–1200." *American Historical Review* 96 (1991), 17–41.

"The Scheldt Trade and the "Ghent War" of 1379–1385." *BCRH* 154 (1978), 189–359.

"Structures du peuplement, fonctions urbaines et formation du capital dans la Flandre médiévale," *Annales*. E.S.C. 33 (1978), 501–527.

Town and Countryside: Social, Economic and Political Tensions in Fourteenth-Century Flanders. Bruges: De Tempel, 1971.

Trade, Urbanisation and the Family: Studies in the History of Medieval Flanders. Ashgate: Variorum, 1996.

The Van Arteveldes of Ghent. Ithaca: Cornell University Press, 1988.

Nightingale, Pamela. *A Medieval Mercantile Community: The Grocers' Company and the Politics and Trade of London, 1000–1485*. New Haven: Yale University Press, 1995.

Nightingale, Pamela. "Capitalists, Crafts and Constitutional Change in Late Fourteenth-Century London." *Past and Present* 124 (1989), 3–35.

Nowé, Henri. *Les baillis comtaux de Flandre, des origines à la fin du XIVe siècle*. Brussels: Académie Royale de Belgique, 1929.

Oost, A. van. "Sociale stratifikatie van de Brugse opstandigen en van de opstandige ingezeten van de kleinere kasselrijsteden en van de kasselrijdorpen in Vlaanderen van 1379–1385." *RBPH* 56 (1978), 830–877.

Otis, Leah L. *Prostitution in Medieval Society*. University of Chicago Press, 1985.
Paravicini, Werner. "Brugge en Duitsland," in Valentin Vermeersch (ed.), *Brugge en Europa*. Antwerp: Mercator, 1992, pp. 99–127.
"Edelleute, Hanse, Brügger Bürger: Die Finanzierung der Westeuropäischen Preussenreisen im 14. Jahrhundert." *Hansische Geschichtsblätter* 104 (1986), 5–19
"Lübeck und Brügge. Bedeutung und erste Ergebnisse eines Kieler Forschungsprojekts," in H. Menke (ed.), *Die Niederlande und der europäische Nordosten: ein Jahrtausend weiträumiger Beziehungen (700–1700)*. Neumünster: Karl Wachholtz Verlag, 1992, pp. 91–166.
"Die Preußenreisen des europäischen Adels." *Historische Zeitschrift* 232 (1981), 25–38.
Die Preußenreisen des europäischen Adels. Sigmaringen: J. Thorbecke, 1989, 1995.
"Die Residenzen der Herzöge von Burgund," in H. Patze and Werner Paravicini (eds.), *Fürstliche Residenzen im spätmittelalterlichen Europa*. Sigmaringen: J. Thorbecke, 1991, pp. 207–249.
Paravicini, Werner and Horst Wernicke (eds.). *Hansekaufleute in Brügge, Teil 4: Beiträge der Internationalen Tagung in Brügge April 1996*. Frankfurt am Main: Peter Lang, 2000.
Paviot, Jacques. *Bruges, 1300–1500*. Paris: Editions autrement, 2002.
Peeters, J. P. "Bouwstoffen voor de geschiedenis der laatmiddeleeuwse stadsdraperie in een klein Brabants produktiecentrum: Vilvoorde (1357–1578)." *Handelingen van de koninklijke Commissie voor Geschiedenis* 151 (1985), 1–48.
Pirenne, Henri. *Histoire de Belgique*, 6 vols. Brussels: M. Lamertin, 1909–1926.
Poerck, Guy de. *La draperie médiévale en Flandre et en Artois. Technique et terminologie*. Bruges: De Tempel, 1951.
Prevenier, Walter. "Bevolkingscijfers en professionele strukturen der bevolking van Gent en Brugge in de 14de eeuw," in *Album Charles Verlinden*. Ghent, 1975, pp. 269–303.
"Het Brugse Vrije en de Leden van Vlaanderen." *ASEB* 96 (1959), 5–63.
"La démographie des villes du comté de Flandre aux XIVe et XVe siècles. Etat de question. Essai d'interprétation." *Revue du Nord* 65 (1983), 255–275, 256.
"Henri Pirenne et les villes des anciens Pays-Bas au bas moyen âge." *Archives et Bibliothèques de Belgique* extra number, 28 (1986), 27–50.
"Inzicht van kritische tijdgenoten in de sociale facetten der fiscaliteit en in sociaal-politiek onrecht in Vlaanderen (13de–15de eeuw)," in *Arbeid in veelvoud. Een huldeboek voor Jan Craeybeckx en Etienne Scholliers*. Brussels: Vrije Universiteit, 1988, pp. 51–60.
"Motieven voor Leliaardsgezindheid in Vlaanderen in de periode 1297–1305." *De Leiegouw* 19 (1977), 273–288.
"Les perturbations dans les relations commerciales anglo-flamandes entre 1379 et 1407. Causes de désaccord et raisons d'une réconciliation," in *Economies et sociétés du Moyen Age. Mélanges Edouard Perroy*. Paris: Publications de la Sorbonne, 1973, pp. 477–497.

"Réalité et histoire: le Quatrième Membre de Flandre." *Revue du Nord* 43 (1961), 5–14.

Prevenier, Walter and Wim Blockmans, *The Burgundian Netherlands*. Cambridge University Press, 1986.

Prevenier, Walter and M. Boone, "De steden in de Zuidelike Nederlanden in de late middeleeuwen: stedelijke identiteit en corporatieve solidariteiten." *Het Tijdschrift van het Gemeentekrediet* 183 (1993), 25–42.

Quicke, Fritz. *Les Pays-Bas à la veille de la période bourguignonne (1356–1384)*. Brussels: Presses de Belgique, 1947.

Renouard, Yves. *Les relations des papes d'Avignon et des compagnies commerciales et bancaires de 1316 à 1378*. Paris: E. de Boccard, 1941.

Reyerson, Katherine. *The Art of the Deal: Intermediaries of Trade in Medieval Montpellier*. Leiden: Brill, 2002.

"Medieval Hospitality: Innkeepers and the Infrastructure of Trade in Montpellier during the Middle Ages." *Proceedings of the Western Society for French History: Selected Papers of the Annual Meeting* 24 (1997), 38–51.

"Women in Business in Medieval Montpellier," in *Women and Work in PreIndustrial Europe*, pp. 117–144.

Reynolds, R. L. "The market for Northern Textiles in Genoa, 1179–1200." *RBPH* 8 (1929), 831–850.

Rider, Jeff. *God's Scribe. The Historiographical Art of Galbert of Bruges*. Washington, DC: Catholic University Press, 2001.

Rogghé, Paul. "De Zwarte Dood in de Zuidelijke Nederlanden." *RBPH* 30 (1952), 834–837.

Roover, Raymond de. "La balance commerciale entre les Pays-Bas et l'Italie au quinzième siècle." *RBPH* 37 (1959), 374–386.

The Bruges Money Market around 1400 with a Statistical Supplement. Brussels: Vlaamse Academie voor Wetenschappen, 1968.

"La communauté de Lucquois." *ASEB* 86 (1949), 23–89.

"Les comptes communaux et la comptabilité communale à Bruges au XIVe siècle," in *Finances et comptabilité urbaines du XIIe au XVIe siècle*. Brussels: Gemeentekrediet/Crédit communal, 1962.

"Le livre de comptes de Guillaume Ruyelle, changeur à Bruges (1369)." *ASEB* 72 (1934), 15–95.

Money, Banking and Credit in Mediaeval Bruges. Cambridge, Mass.: Medieval Academy, 1948.

"Quelques considérations sur les livres des comptes de Collard de Marke (1366–1369)." *Bulletin d'Etudes et d'Informations de l'Ecole Supérieure de Commerce St. Ignace* 4 (1930), 445–475.

"Renseignements complémentaires sur le marché monétaire à Bruges au XIVe et au XVe siècle." *ASEB* 109 (1972), 51–91.

Rossiaud, Jacques. *Medieval Prostitution*. New York: Blackwell, 1988.

Ryckaert, Marc. "Brandbestrijding en overheidsmaatregelen tegen brandgevaar tijdens het Ancien Régime," in *Het Openbaar Initiatief van de Gemeenten in België*. Brussels: Gemeentekrediet, 1982, pp. 252–255.

"Brügge und die flandrischen Häfen vom 12. bis 18. Jahrhundert," in H. Stoob (ed.), *See- und Flußhäfen vom Hochmittelalter bis zur Industralisierung.* Cologne, 1986, pp. 129–139.
"De Brugse havens in de Middeleeuwen." *ASEB* 109 (1972), 5–27.
"Geographie eines Weltmarktes: Handel und Stadttopographie im mittelalterlichen und frühneuzeitlichen Brügge," in K. Friedland (ed.), *Brügge-Colloquium des hansischen Geschichtsvereins.* Cologne and Vienna, 1990, pp. 3–12.
Historische Stedenatlas van België, Brugge. Brussels: Gemeentekrediet, 1991.
"De Oudeburg te Brugge," in *Album Albert Schouteet.* Bruges, 1973, pp. 155–168.
Ryckaert, Marc. and W. P. De Zutter. "Brandgevaar en Bouwvoorschriften in de Middeleeuwen. Een vroeg Vlaams Voorbeeld: Aardenburg 1232." *Archief uitgegeven door het Koninklijk Zeeuwsch Genootschap der Wetenschappen.* Middelburg: Zeeuws Genootschap, 1976, pp. 14–38.
Ryckaert, Marc and André Vandewalle. *Brugge: De geschiedenis van een Europese stad.* Tielt, Belgium: Lannoo, 1999.
Sabbe, Jacques. *Vlaanderen in opstand, 1323–1328.* Bruges: Genootschap voor Geschiedenis, 1992.
Samsonowicz, Henryk. "Die wirtschaftlichen und politischen Beziehungen zwischen Flandern, Polen und Preußen," in *Hansekaufleute in Brügge, Teil 4: Beiträge*, pp. 309–318.
Schouteet, Albert. *Regesten op de Oorkonden*, 4 vols. Bruges: Genootschap voor Geschiedenis, 1978.
Simons, Walter. "The Beguine Movement in the Southern Low Countries: A Reassessment." *Bulletin de l'Institut Historique Belge de Rome* 59 (1989), 63–105.
Cities of Ladies: Beguine Communities in the Medieval Low Countries, 1200–1565. Philadelphia: University of Pennsylvania Press, 2001.
"Mendicant Collaboration in the Fourteenth Century: the Bruges Pact of 1370', in P. Chandler and K. J. Egan (eds.), *The Land of Carmel: Essays in Honor of Joachim Smet, O. Carm.* Rome, 1991, pp. 171–187.
Stad en apostolaat: de vestiging van de bedelorden in het graafschap Vlaanderen (ca.1225–ca.1350). Brussels: Koninklijke Academie voor Wetenschappen, 1987.
Bedelordekloosters in het Graafschap Vlaanderen. Chronologie en topografie van de bedelordenverspreiding vóór 1350. Steenbrugge, Belgium: Stichting Jan Cobbaut, 1987.
Smet, A. de. "L'origine des ports du Zwin, Damme, Mude, Monnikerede, Hoeke et Sluis," in *Etudes d'histoire dediées à la mémoire de Henri Pirenne, par ses anciens élèves.* Brussels: Nouvelle Société d'Editions, 1937, pp. 125–141.
"Het waterwegennet ten noordoosten van Brugge in de XIIIe eeuw." *RBPH* 12–13 (1933–1934), 1023–1059, 83–121.
"De werken bij de Reie tusschen Brugge en Damme in de XIVe eeuw." *RBPH* 14 (1935), 859–863.
"Smet, Joseph de. Monnikerede. Een verdwenen zeestad van het Zwin." *Biekorf* 45 (1939), 1–8.

"De oude hydrografie van de stad Brugge." *ASEB* 86 (1949), 5–22.
"De repressie te Brugge na de slag bij Westrozebeke." *ASEB* 84 (1947), 71–118.
Soly, Hugo. "Plechtige intochten in de steden van de Zuidelijke Nederlanden tijdens de overgang van de Middeleeuwen naar Nieuwe Tijd: communicatie, propaganda, spektakel." *Tijdschrift voor Geschiedenis* 97 (1984), 341–361.
Sortor, Marci. "The Ieperleet Affair: The Struggle for Market Position in Late-Medieval Flanders." *Speculum* 73 (1998), 1068–1100.
Sosson, J.-P. "Finances communales et dette publique. Le cas de Bruges à la fin du XIIIe siècle," in *Peasants and Townsmen in Medieval Europe. Studia in Honorem Adriaan Verhulst.* Ghent: Snoeck-Ducaju & Zoon, 1995, pp. 239–257.
"Les petites villes du Zwin (XIVe–XVe siècles): des espaces urbains inviables?' in P. Contamine, T. Dutour and B. Schnerb (eds.), *Commerce, Finances et Société* (XIe–XVIe siècles). *Recueil de travaux d'histoire médiévale offert à M. le Professeur Henri Dubois.* Paris, 1993, pp. 171–184.
"La structure sociale de la corporation médiévale. L'exemple des tonneliers de Bruges de 1350 à 1500." *RBPH* 44 (1966), 457–478.
Les travaux publics de la ville de Bruges, XIVe–XVe siècles. Brussels: Crédit Communal, 1977.
Spicciani, Amleto. *Capitale e interesse tra mercatura e povertà nei teologi e canonisti dei secoli XIII–XV.* Rome: Jouvance, 1990.
Stabel, Peter. *Dwarfs among Giants: The Flemish Urban Network in the Late Middle Ages.* Leuven/Apeldoorn: Garant, 1997.
De kleine stad in Vlaanderen. Bevolkingsdynamiek en economische functies van de kleine en secundaire stedelijke centra in het Gentse kwartier (14de–16de eeuw). Brussels: Koninklijke Academie voor Wetenschappen, 1995.
"Women at the Market. Gender and Retail in the Towns of Late Medieval Flanders," in Wim Blockmans, Marc Boone, and Thérèse de Hemptinne (eds.), *Secretum Secretorum: Liber Alumnorum Walter Prevenier.* Leuven and Apeldoorn: Garant, 1999, pp. 259–276.
Spufford, Peter. *Money and Its Use in Medieval Europe.* Cambridge University Press, 1988.
Stein, H. "Les conséquences de la bataille de Cassel pour la ville de Bruges et la mort de Guillaume de Deken son ancien bourgmestre (1328)." *BCRH* 68 (1899), 647–664.
Strohm, Reinhard. *Music in Late Medieval Bruges.* Oxford University Press, 1985.
Strubbe, E. I. "De parochies te Brugge voor de XIIe eeuw," in *Album Michiel English: Studies over de kerkelijke en kunstgeschiedenis van West-Vlaanderea.* Bruges, 1952, pp. 355–380.
"Van de eerste naar de tweede omwalling van Brugge." *ASEB* 100 (1963), 271–300.
TeBrake, William H. *Plague of Insurrection: Popular Politics and Peasant Revolt in Flanders, 1323–1328.* Philadelphia: University of Pennsylvania Press, 1993.
Thoen, Erik. *Landbouw, ekonomie en bevolking in Vlaanderen gedurende de late Middeleeuwen en het begin van de Moderne Tijden*, 2 vols. Ghent: Belgisch Centrum voor Landelijke Geschiedenis, 1988.

"Oorlogen en platteland. Sociale en ekonomische aspekten van militaire destruktie in Vlaanderen tijdens de late middeleeuwen en de vroege moderne tijden." *Tijdschrift voor Geschiedenis* 91(1978), 363–376.

"Verhuizen naar Brugge in de Late Middeleeuwen," in Hugo Soly and René Vermeir (eds.), *Beleid en bestuur in de Oude Nederlanden. Liber amicorum Prof. Dr. M. Baelde*. Ghent: Vakgroep Nieuwe Geschiedenis, 1993, pp. 329–349.

Thoen, Hans. *De Belgische kustvlakte in de Romeinse tijd. Bijdrage tot de studie van de landelijke bewoningsgeschiedenis*. Brussels, 1978.

Tits-Dieuaide, M.-J. "Les campagnes flamandes du XIIe au XVIIIe siècle, ou les succès d'une agriculture traditionnelle." *Annales E.S.C.* 39 (1984), 590–610.

Toussaert, Jacques. *Le sentiment religieux en Flandre à la fin du Moyen-Age*. Paris: Plon, 1963.

Trexler, Richard. "La prostitution florentine au XVe siècle: patronages et clientèles." *Annales E.S.C.* 36 (1981), 983–1015.

Trio, Paul. "Armenzorg te Gent. Een onderzoek naar de steunverlening aan armen bij de broederschappen in de late middeleeuwen," in *Feestbundel Achiel de Vos*. Evergem, Belgium, 1988, pp. 181–187.

Unger, Richard W. *The Ship in the Medieval Economy*. London and Montreal: Croom Helm, 1980.

Uytven, Raymond van. "Plutokratie in de 'oude demokratieën der Nederlanden,." *Handelingen Koninklijke Zuidnederlandse Maatschappij voor Taal- Letterkunde en Geschiedenis* 16 (1962), 373–409.

Production and Consumption in the Low Countries, 13th–16th Centuries. Aldershot, UK: Variorum, 2001.

"Stages of Economic Decline," in J.-M. Duvosquel and E. Thoen (eds.), *Peasants and Townsmen in Medieval Europe: Studia in Honorem Adriaan Verhulst*. Ghent: Snoeck-Ducaju & Zoon, 1995, pp. 259–269.

Stadsfinanciën en stadsekonomie te Leuven van de XIIe tot het einde der XVIe eeuw. Brussels: Koninklijke Vlaamse Academie voor Wetenschappen, 1961.

Vandermaesen, Maurice. "De rekening der Brugse Gijzelaars 1328–9/1338–41." *ASEB* 115 (1978), 1–16.

Vandermaesen, Maurice and M. Ryckaert. "Een miskende bron voor de sociale geschiedenis van de Stad Brugge bij het begin van de 14de eeuw. De registers van 'forfaiture et sequestre' 1302–1304." *Het Brugs Ommeland* 17 (1977), 143–151.

Vandermaesen, Maurice, Marc Ryckaert, and Maurits Coornaert. *De Witte Kaproenen: De Gentse Opstand (1379–1385) en de Geschiedenis van de Brugse Leie*. Ghent, 1979.

Vandewalle, André. *Beknopte inventaris van het Stadsarchief van Brugge* Bruges: Gemeentebestuur, 1979.

Vanhoutryve, André. *De Vishandel en het visambacht te Brugge tot op het einde van het oud regiem*. Bruges: Heemkundige Kring Maurits van Coppenolle, 1975.

Vaughan, Richard. *Philip the Bold*. Cambridge, Mass.: Harvard University Press, 1962.

Verbruggen, J. F. *Het Gemeenteleger van Brugge van 1338 tot 1340 en de namen van de weerbare mannen*. Brussels: Koninklijke Commissie voor Geschiedenis, 1962.
"De Getalsterkte van de ambachten in het Brugse Gemeenteleger (1297–1340)." *Belgisch Tijdschrift voor Militaire Geschiedenis* 25 (1984), 461–480.
"De Goede Vrijdag van Brugge, 18 mei 1302." *Het Brugs Ommeland* 17 (1977), 115–131.
"De historiografie van de guldensporenslag." *De Leiegouw* 19 (1977), 245–272.
Verdam, E. and E. Verwijs, *Middelnederlansch woordenboek*, 12 vols. The Hague: M. Nijhoff, 1885–1919.
Verhulst, Adriaan. "Initiative comtale et développement économique en Flandre au XIIe siècle: Le rôle de Thierry et de Philippe d'Alsace (1128–1191)," in *Miscellanea Mediaevalia in Memoriam J. F. Niermeyer*. Groningen: J. B. Wolters, 1967, pp. 227–240.
"La laine indigène dans les anciens Pays-Bas entre le XIIe et le XVIIe siècle." *Revue Historique* 96 (1972), 281–322.
"Les origines urbaines dans le Nord-Ouest de l'Europe: essai de synthèse." *Francia* 14 (1987), 57–81.
"Les origines et l'histoire ancienne de la ville de Bruges (IXe–XIIe siècle)." *Le Moyen Age* 66 (1960), 37–63.
"The Origins of Towns in the Low Countries and the Pirenne Thesis." *Past and Present* 122 (1989), 1–35.
Verlinden, Charles "Draps des Pays-Bas et du nord-ouest de l'Europe au Portugal au XVe siècle." *Anuario de Estudios Medievales* 2 (1966), 235–261.
"Draps des Pays-Bas et du nord de la France en Espagne au XIVe siècle," *Le Moyen Age* 47 (1937), 21–36.
Vermaseren, B. "De Carmel van Brugge en de buitenlandse kooplieden." *Carmel* 3 (1950), 19–31.
Warlop, Ernest. *De Vlaamse Adel voor 1300*, 3 vols. Handzame: Familia et Patria, 1968.
Warnkoenig, L. "Sur la ville de Damme au moyen âge." *Messager des Sciences et des Arts de la Belgique* 3 (1886), 457–474.
Wee, Herman van der. *The Growth of the Antwerp Market and the European Economy (Fourteenth–Sixteenth centuries)*, 3 vols. The Hague: Nijhoff, 1963.
Wee, Herman van der. "Un modèle de croissance interséculaire du commerce mondial (XIIe–XVIIIe siècles)." *Annales E.S.C.* 25 (1970), 100–126.
Wensky, M. *Die Stellung der Frau in der stadtkölnischen Wirtschaft in Spätmittelalter*. Cologne and Vienna, 1980.
Werveke, Hans van. *Bruges et Anvers; Huit siècles de commerce flamand*. Brussels: Editions de la Librairie Encyclopédique, 1944.
Burgus, versterking of nederzetting? Brussel, 1965.
"Les charges financières issues du traité d'Athis (1305)." *Revue du Nord* 32 (1950), 81–93, reprinted in *Miscellanea Medievalia: Verspreide Opstellen over Economische en Sociale Geschiedenis van de Middeleeuwen*. Ghent: Story-Scientia, 1968.
"La famine de l'an 1316 en Flandre et dans les régions voisines." *Revue du Nord* 41 (1959), 5–14, reprinted in *Miscellanea Mediaevalia*, pp. 326–338.

De gentsche stadsfinanciën in de Middeleeuwen. Brussels: Académie Royale de Belgique, 1934.
De koopman-ondernemer en de ondernemer in de Vlaamsche lakennijverheid van de Middeleeuwen. Antwerp and Utrecht, 1946.
"De opbloei van Handel en Nijverheid," in *Algemene geschiedenis der Nederlanden.* Utrecht, 1950, vol. II, pp. 417–419.
"Die Stellung des hansischen Kaufmanns dem flandrische Tuchproduzenten gegenüber," in *Beiträge zur Wirtschafts- und Stadtgeschichte. Festschrift für Hektor Ammann.* Wiesbaden: F. Steiner, 1965, pp. 296–304.
De Zwarte Dood in de Zuidelijke Nederlanden Mededelingen Konink. Vlaamse Ak., Kl. Letteren, 12 no. 3, Brussels, 1950.
Wiesner, Merry E. *Working Women in Renaissance Germany.* New Brunswick, NJ: Rutgers University Press, 1986.
Wilson, Jean C. *Painting in Bruges at the Close of the Middle Ages: Studies in Society and Visual Culture.* University Park, PA: Penn State University Press, 1998.
Witte, Alfons de. "De werken bij de reie tusschen Brugge en Damme in de XIVe eeuw." *RBPH* 14 (1935), 859–863.
Wolff, Philippe. *Automne du Moyen Age ou Printemps des Temps Nouveaux? L'économie européenne aux XIVe et XVe siècles.* Paris: Aubier, 1986.
Wyffels, Carlos. *Analyses de reconnaissances de dettes passées devant les échevins d'Ypres, 1249–1291.* Brussels: Koninklijke Commissie voor Geschiedenis, 1991.
"Kanttekening bij de Brugse 'Moerlemaye' 1280–1281," in *Album Albert Schouteet.* Bruges, 1973, pp. 253–258.
"Nieuwe gegevens betreffende een XIIIde eeuwse 'democratische' stedelije opstand: de Brugse 'Moerlemaye' (1280–81)." *BCRH* 132 (1966), 37–142
De oorsprong der ambachten in Vlaanderen/Brabant. Brussels: Koninklijke Vlaamse Academie voor Wetenschapen, 1951.
"De vlaamse hanze van Londen op het einde van de XIIIe eeuw." *ASEB* 97 (1960), 5–30.
"De Vlaamse Hanzen opnieuw belicht," in *Academiae Analecta. Mededelingen van de Koninklike Academie voor Wetenschappen, Letteren en Schone Kunsten van België, Klasse der Letteren* 53 (1991), pp. 8–13.
Yamada, M. "Le mouvement des foires en Flandre avant 1200," in *Mélanges Georges Despy.* Liège, 1991, pp. 773–789.
Ziegler, Joanna E. "The *curtis beguinages* in the Southern Low Countries and Art Patronage: Interpretation and Historiography." *Bulletin de l'Institut Historique Belge de Rome* 57 (1987), 31–40.

Index